THUD!
BOILK!
BOOM
BLAM
SPLUTCH!
CRASH
AAARGH!
MACK!
BIFF!
CRACK!

THE HISTORY OF The Beano

2 CWT
2 CWT
CHOCOLATES
PROGRAMMES SPECIAL EDITIO

THE HISTORY OF

THE BEANO

2D

THE STORY SO FAR

D. C. Thomson & Co. Ltd.

WAVERLEY BOOKS

The History Of The Beano – The Story So Far

First published 2008
by D. C. Thomson & Co. Ltd., Dundee, Scotland DD1 9QJ,
and Waverley Books Ltd., New Lanark, Scotland ML11 9DJ.

In preparing this book the publishers wish to thank the following people who made this book possible
Contributors: Daniel Adams; Bill Graham; Morris Heggie; Iain McLaughlin; Bill McLoughlin; Michael Stirling; Gareth Whelan

For advice and for sharing information with the contributors:
Leo Baxendale; Stuart Cameron; George Cobb; Alan Digby; David Donaldson; Dave Eastbury; Walter Fearn; Alison Gardiner; Peter Hansen; J Euan Kerr; Pauline Mackie; David Marshall; Carol Moonie; Ray Moore; Frances O'Brien; Jim Petrie; Bill Ritchie; Bill Stirton; Dave Sutherland; David Torrie; Roddie Watt
Editor-in-chief: Christopher Riches
Cover design: Gary Aitchison and Mark Mechan

The publishers wish to acknowledge their thanks to the following for permission to reproduce illustrations on the pages listed:
page 105: The Mary Evans Picture Library (photographer: Roger Mayne); page 159: courtesy of Decca (from the sleeve of 'Blues Breakers' album, John Mayall with Eric Clapton); page 201: from the D. C. Thomson archive with thanks to HRH The Princess Royal; page 225: PA Photos (photographer: John Stillwell); page 251: Cumbrian Newspapers Ltd.; page 279: Alamy (photographer: Roger Cracknell)

ISBN 978-1-902407-73-9

Pre-press, page make-up and graphic restoration by Tegra Premedia, Hyderabad, India
Additional pre-press by Davidson Pre-Press Graphics, Glasgow, Scotland

Printed and bound in Scotland
by D. C. Thomson & Co. Ltd.,
West Ward Works, Dundee, Scotland

Dear People,

I was asked by the Editor to do the fourword for this book 'cos I'm famous. I thought no problem doing a fourword for a book and I wrote back sayin', here is my fourword.... *The Beano* is great! But the nice Editor said it was foreword, not fourword! So I said, I may be a child, but I can count and *The Beano* is great is four words!!!! Then he said foreword was an introduction to a book!! DUH! Why didn't he say that in the first place.

So, I read this book and it is really great. I never knew half the things in the book, specially the bits about before I was born, y'know history an' that. I also spoke to the people who wrote this book. And there were lots. I was going to list them all and do them in age order. There are actually two blokes who did stuff for the book who are so old...I didn't know people could get that old and still stand up. Anyway I couldn't remember all their names so thanks for the book anyway.

AN INTRODUCTORY NOTE

The Beano is a national institution and we should all salute this uniquely British comic as it celebrates its 70th birthday. While there is no record as to why a slang name for a party – or 'jollification' as the Chambers Dictionary has it – was chosen for the comic, mention *The Beano* to anyone today, and recollections of childhood come streaming back. For a comic that prides itself on making fun of grown-ups and those in authority to be in such vibrant health after 70 years says much about the nature of British humour and the innate tolerance of British society. Some, however, might draw the line at the classification of *The Beano* annuals as 'non-fiction' in the bestseller charts!

Over all these years *The Beano* has reflected and laughed at the society of the world around it. During the Second World War it fought with laughter when it turned Hitler, Goering and Mussolini into comic characters that wily British children could push around (quite literally in the case of Pansy Potter). It was immensely creative in the 1950s – 'Dennis the Menace', 'Roger the Dodger', 'Minnie the Minx' and 'The Bash Street Kids' all appeared within a three-year period – and it has never lost that knack of responding to what children find funny, rather than what we think they should laugh at. It has always been a child of its time, however, and as one looks over 70 years of *Beanos*, there is some content that would no longer be thought acceptable. When *The Beano* was first published in 1938, the drawing of 'Peanut' appeared on the front cover, something that would never even be contemplated today. To place *The Beano* in the context of the time, we keep the image of Peanut in this history but we certainly do not wish to cause any offense by so doing. In that first issue there is also a cartoon strip called 'Big Fat Joe' with the subtitle '1 Ton of Fun' which would not pass muster today, but then what would have been the response in 1938 to such popular current strips as 'Robbie Rebel – Nobody Tells Him What To Do'?

This book tells the story of *The Beano*, primarily through the pages of the comic itself. Its compilation has depended upon the great support of all at D. C. Thomson in Dundee, coordinated by the immensely knowledgeable Morris Heggie, who brought together the writers of the text and marshalled the amazing selection of illustrations that will be found in this book. The Publishers would like to thank all the contributors to the book and the many people who provided assistance with this project. Outwith D. C. Thomson we are extremely grateful to Ray Moore for permission to reproduce much information from *The Beano Diaries*, his wonderful reference resource that details, year by year, the history of the comic and provides information on all the strips and stories that appeared since 1938. The final selection of material for this history has been mine, and it has been wonderful to relive childhood memories of laughing at 'Dennis' and 'Bash Street' and of going on adventures with 'General Jumbo' and 'Red Rory of the Eagles' in the process.

Christopher Riches
Editor
July 2008

CONTENTS

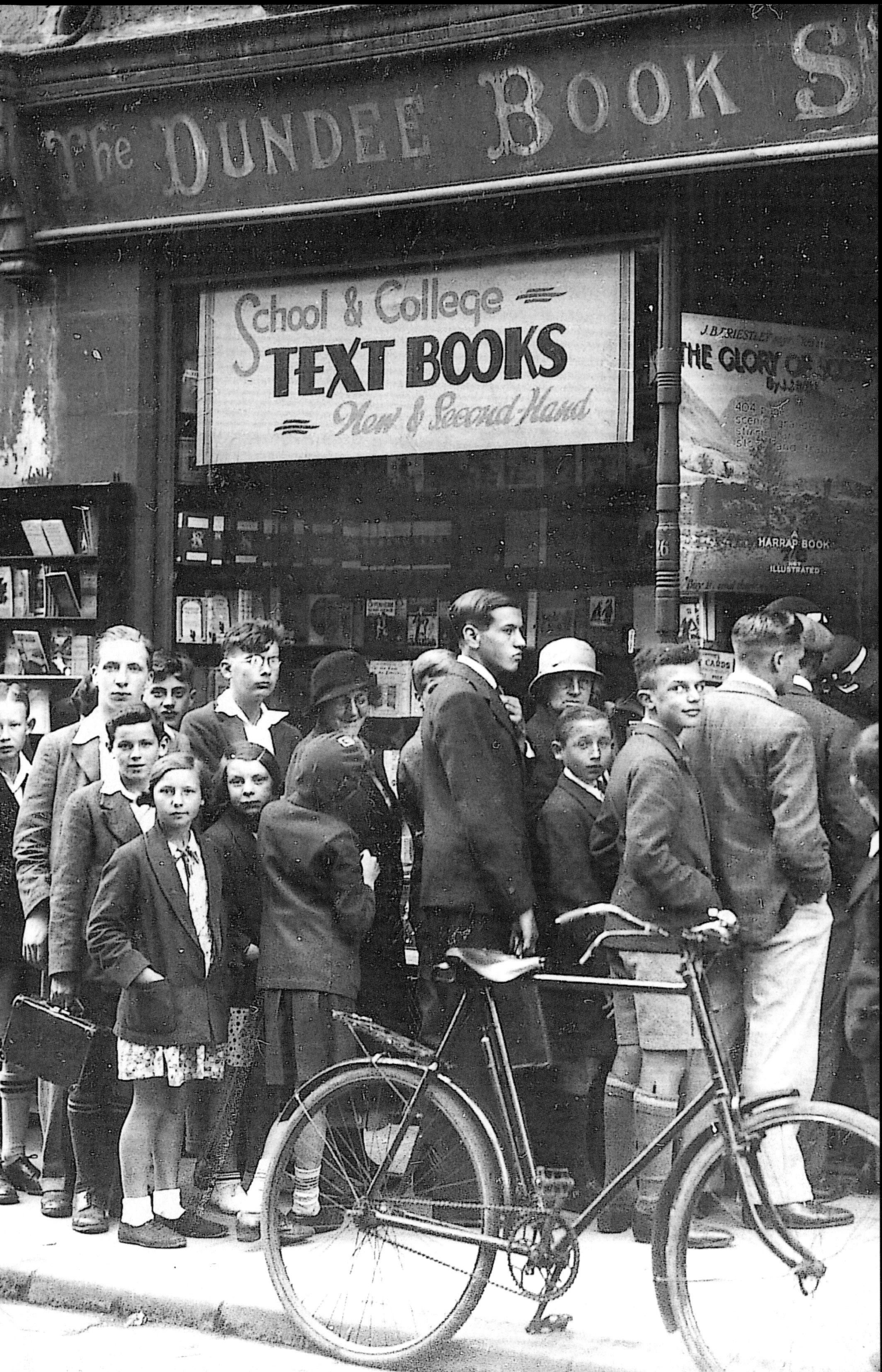
The DUNDEE BOOK
School & College
TEXT BOOKS
New & Second-Hand
HARRAP BOOK
ILLUSTRATED

PART 1

THE BIRTH OF *THE BEANO*

1930–1939

BEFORE THE BEANO

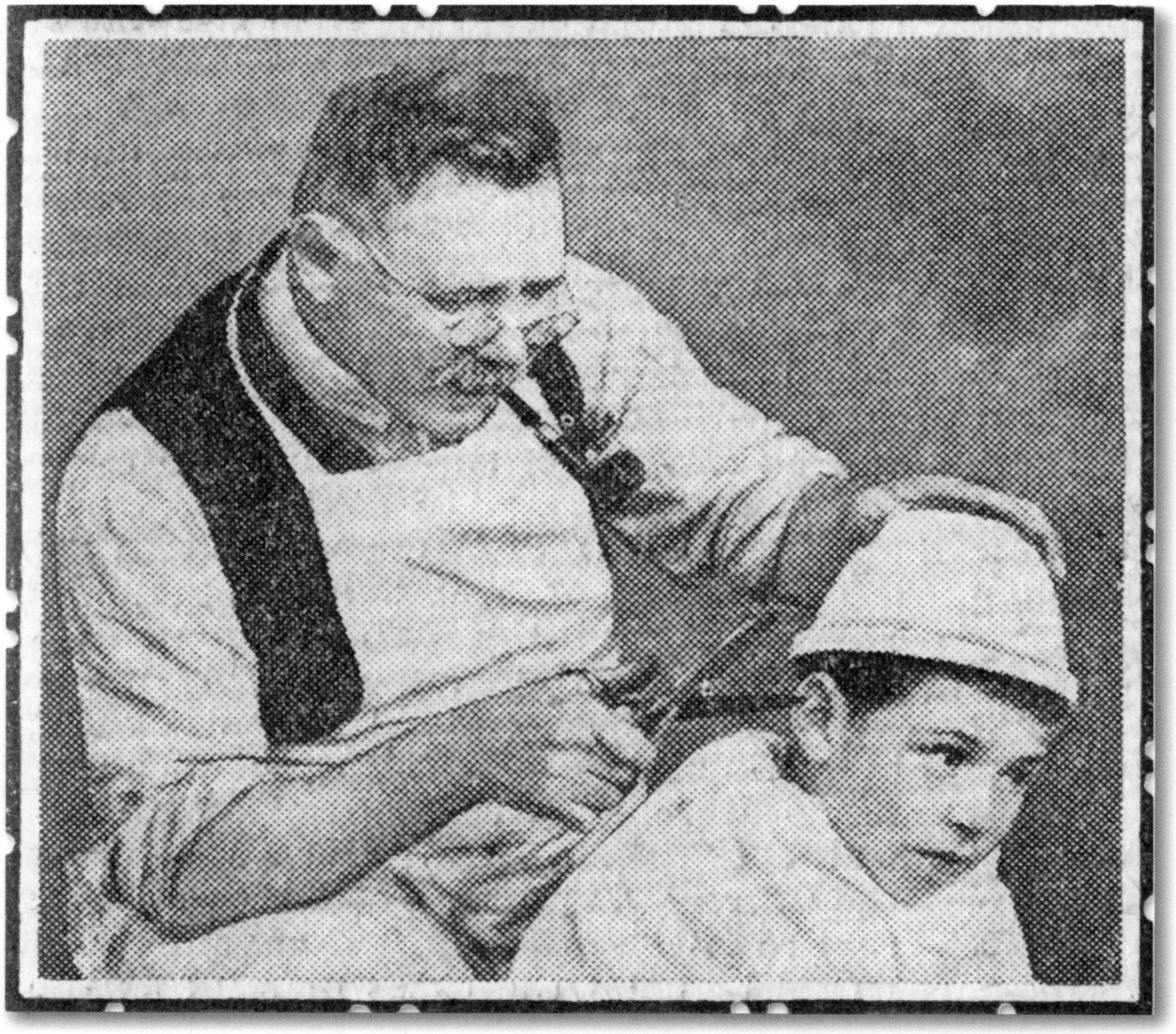

The world of entertainment was turned upside down in the late 1920s with the arrival of talking films. ***The Jazz Singer*** in 1928 is generally considered the first feature-length talking movie, but there had been shorter talkies before. The Depression took its miserable grasp on the world in the 1930s and people turned in their millions to the cinema. The studio system with production-line films was in full swing, and this created the environment for the animated cartoon film. The rise of both Warner Brothers and Disney opened up a whole new world for children. On Saturday mornings, cinemas were regularly packed out with hordes of excited children waiting to see the next episode of their favourite, whether it be Cowboys and Indians or the many cartoons that flooded in from Hollywood. A parallel development was the adventure comic, which offered some sort of escapism to children. Comics, such as ***The Dandy*** and ***The Beano,*** were a natural progression, transferring the style of the cinematic cartoon to the printed page of a comic.

CINEMATIC MILESTONES

1928	*Steamboat Willie*, the first 'Mickey Mouse' cartoon with a soundtrack
1932	*Tarzan the Ape Man*, featuring Johnny Weissmuller. Between 1918 and 1999 it is estimated that 88 Tarzan movies were made.
1933	*Betty Boop*, *Popeye*
1937	*Snow White*, the first feature length animated film *The Wizard of Oz*
1939	*Gone With the Wind*, which also led to the first doll being made of a movie character, Scarlett O'Hara, no less.

A scene from Wishbone Wuzzy – The Merry Magician, a 1938 strip in The Skipper.

Seventeen years before the first guffaws were heard from the pages of *The Beano*, the D. C. Thomson empire had moved into the world of rip-roaring yarns and quirky humour with its series of comics aimed at boys. Starting with ***Adventure*** in 1921, ***The Rover*** and ***The Wizard*** followed in 1922, ***The Vanguard*** in 1923, ***The Skipper*** in 1930 and the last, but not least, ***The Hotspur*** in 1933. All these magazines had strands of humour that reflected the mirth of the time. While ***The Vanguard*** ceased in 1926, the other titles were so successful that they were referred to as the Big Five.

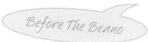

OUR ART GALLERY OF LAUGHS
CAMPING DEPT.
Assistant (in big store)—" It's raining, so I didn't want to go home for lunch."
" You'd better be careful, Pa, or a gust of wind may blow you over !"
Small Boy—" Dad there's some water in the bottom of the boat. Shall I pull up the cork and let it run out ?"
DUST.
Tramp (ex-sword-swallower) — " Can you spare a hungry man a couple of razor blades, guv'nor ?"
Airman—" Gosh, Tommy's gone camping with my parachute !"
A Fakir takes up cycling.
" You'd better go over and apologise, Bill."
Bather—" Now which rock did I leave my clothes behind ?"
Footpad—" Hands up! And don't raise a racket !"

FLIP and FLOP THE S REET ACROBATS
GET OVER QUICK
TENNIS CHAMPION-SHIPS TO-DAY AT 3
TENNIS CHAMPION-SHIPS TO-DAY AT 3
THE COP'S GOT MY LEG!
I'LL SHIFT HIM
OWF!
TENNIS CHAMPION-SHIPS TO-DAY AT 3
WE'RE NOT SAFE THERE
I'VE AN IDEA! LET'S HAVE A GAME OF TENNIS WITH THESE RIDDLES
ROAD UP
I'LL SMACK HIM ON THE BEAN
BONK!

A page of cartoons (above) from the mini-comic given away with The Rover *in 1938. Dudley Watkins drew 'Flip and Flop' (left) for the same mini-comic. This comic also contained a page of jokes and a page of suggestions for 'That Camp-Fire Sing-Song'. The 'Crazy Camping Hints' give a flavour of the humour: 'The best way to get your tent down quickly is to pitch it in the same field as a bull', 'You need never be short of firewood as long as you have the tent-pole', 'If you're feeling hungry and the camp larder is empty, just take a roll in the grass'. One suggested song was 'Pack Up The Doings' to be sung to the tune of 'Pack Up Your Troubles':*

Pack up the doings in your old kit-bag, and hike, boys, hike.
We have a terribly long way to go, and no one's got a bike.
What's the use of grumbling? It won't do any good.
So pack all the doings in the old kit-bag, and hike, boys, hike.

The Big Five of D. C. Thomson: *Adventure, The Hotspur, The Rover, The Skipper* and *The Wizard* pioneered the comic strip format. As the 1930s came to a close there was more and more humour in all the comics, and along with the action illustrations, the artists began to turn their hands to humour.. The examples on these two pages are from *The Wizard* of 1936 and *The Rover* of 1935. Some of these strips were published in D. C. Thomson newspapers in the 1950s.

Softie Simpkins
I'LL HELP WITH THE HOUSE-WORK TO-DAY!
WHACK!
SORRY SIR!
ALLOW ME TO BRUSH YOU DOWN!
KICK ME
KICK ME
SOMEONE'S BEEN PLAYING PRANKS SIR!
KICK ME
LEAVE THIS TO ME CONSTABLE! I KNOW WHO DID IT!
KICK ME
NOW I'LL WASH THE STEP!
BRUSH ME DOWN EH?
KICK ME
NERO AND ZERO THE ROLLICKING ROMANS
A PRESENT FROM ME O NOBLE ONES!
TA! O MIGHTY CAESAR!
WE CAN'T BOTH SIT IN IT AT ONCE!
BRAIN WAVE
?
?
BRING THE CHAIR OUT HERE!
AH!
THUMBS UP! O NERO!
HOW'S THAT O ZERO?
A SMART GUY TURNS PINK WHEN HE'S GIVEN A DRINK.
IT'S LUCKY I MET HIM!
CARRY ON! I'M SMOKING WITH MY HEAD UNDER WATER!
CRASH!
NEVER MIND! THIS'LL MAKE QUITE A FUNNY PICTURE!

A page from The Wizard *in 1936. 'Nero and Zero' was drawn by Allan Morley, a prolific artist who went on to draw for The Beano.*

THE DANDY COMIC
No1 DEC. 4 1937
EVERY FRIDAY
2d
KORKY THE CAT
IDEA!
No1 EXPRESS WHISTLER FREE INSIDE

The artists who had drawn the tales of derring-do in the boys' comics turned their hand to humour, and, on December 4, 1937, ***The Dandy*** was launched. It was the first of what was planned to be another series of five comics, this time with humour rather than adventure as the overall theme. ***The Dandy*** was an immediate success. 'Korky the Cat' was chosen over a black rabbit, the other contender for cover treatment. Korky was drawn by the D. C. Thomson staff artist James Crighton. He drew Korky for nearly 25 years, and he also drew for ***The Beano***.

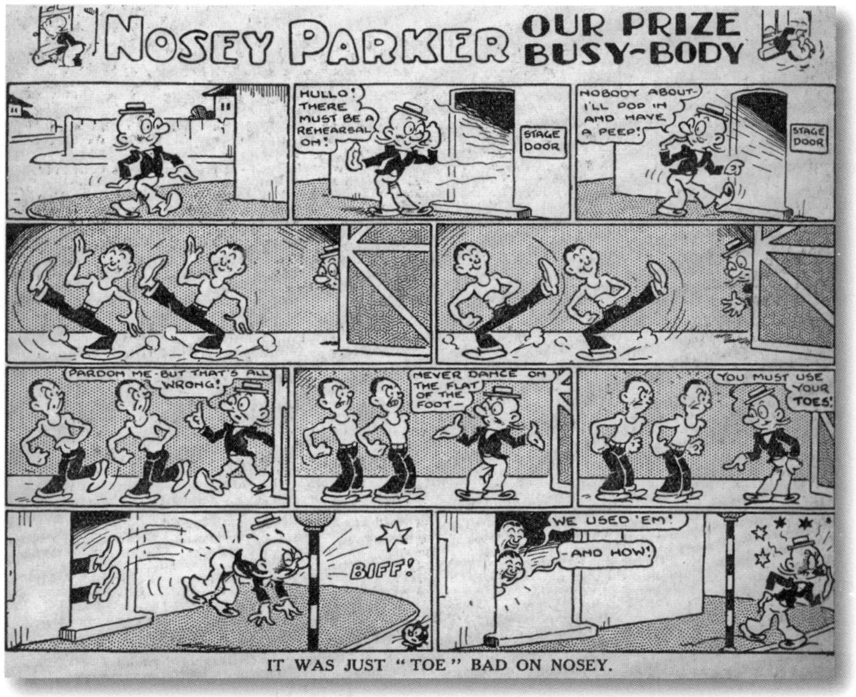
NOSEY PARKER OUR PRIZE BUSY-BODY
HULLO! THERE MUST BE A REHEARSAL ON!
STAGE DOOR
NOBODY ABOUT- I'LL POP IN AND HAVE A PEEP!
STAGE DOOR
PARDON ME-BUT THAT'S ALL WRONG!
NEVER DANCE ON THE FLAT OF THE FOOT-
YOU MUST USE YOUR TOES!
BIFF!
WE USED 'EM!
-AND HOW!
IT WAS JUST "TOE" BAD ON NOSEY.

Allan Morley also drew 'Nosey Parker', this time for The Rover *in 1935.*

PAGE SIX
HERE COMES PING THE ELASTIC MAN
HOOKY'S MAGIC BOWLER HAT
GET READY FOR FUN WITH THE BEANO'S FREE WHOOPEE MASKS!
PAGE THREE
SEVEN BIG STORIES IN "THE BEANO"
THE ADVENTURES OF TOM THUMB
"THE APE'S SECRET"
"THE SHIPWRECKED KIDDS"
"BLACK FLASH THE BEAVER," "MY DOG SANDY," "THE WISHING TREE," are other splendid tales.
THE WANGLES OF GRANNY GREEN
GREAT "BEANO" STORIES TO READ ON TUESDAY, JULY 26.
Please hand this Comic to the youngsters.
PAGE TWO
THE STRONGEST MAN IN THE WORLD
MORGYN THE MIGHTY
BLACK ISLAND
BIG EGGO FOR BIG LAUGHS ON THE SPLENDID COLOURED COVER OF THE BEANO
PAGE SEVEN
GREAT PALS to LOOK AT and LAUGH AT
Meet them all in No. 1 of "The Beano."
LORD SNOOTY AND HIS PALS
WHOOPEE HANK
HAIRY DAN
UNCLE WINDBAG
BIG FAT JOE
CRACKER JACK THE WONDER WHIP-MAN
WILD BOY OF THE WOODS
NOTE THE DATE "THE BEANO" IS ON SALE—TUESDAY, JULY 26TH
Please hand this Comic to the youngsters.

A contrast in advertising. The handout (above) came from The Wizard, along with the instructions to 'Please hand this Comic to the youngsters', and gives a real flavour of the contents of the first Beano. The advert in The Dandy (right) is distinctly understated, though it should be noted that both The Beano and The Dandy offered a free gift with their first issue, clearly a long-lasting promotional idea for comics.

A few short months later, on July 30, 1938, *The Beano* slipped out of the stocks and sailed into the public gaze for the first time. With a different type of humour from that of *The Dandy*, it too struck a chord and soon became a major success. Adverts were carried in a number of other D. C. Thomson publications to announce the imminent arrival of *The Beano. The Wizard* carried a do-it-yourself pull-out sample of *Beano* pages, as did *Adventure.* Contrast this approach with the rather reluctant offering from *The Dandy.*

2
BIG COMICS EVERY WEEK
FROM NOW ON!
"The Dandy's" new companion paper is coming!
OUT ON
Tuesday, July 26
GREAT NEW FUN PAPER
The BEANO
COMIC
Price 2d.
FREE with every copy
WHOOPEE MASK
These TWO great companion papers will give double fun every week for every boy and girl.
TUESDAY— The BEANO
FRIDAY— The DANDY
The Shrinking Chimney

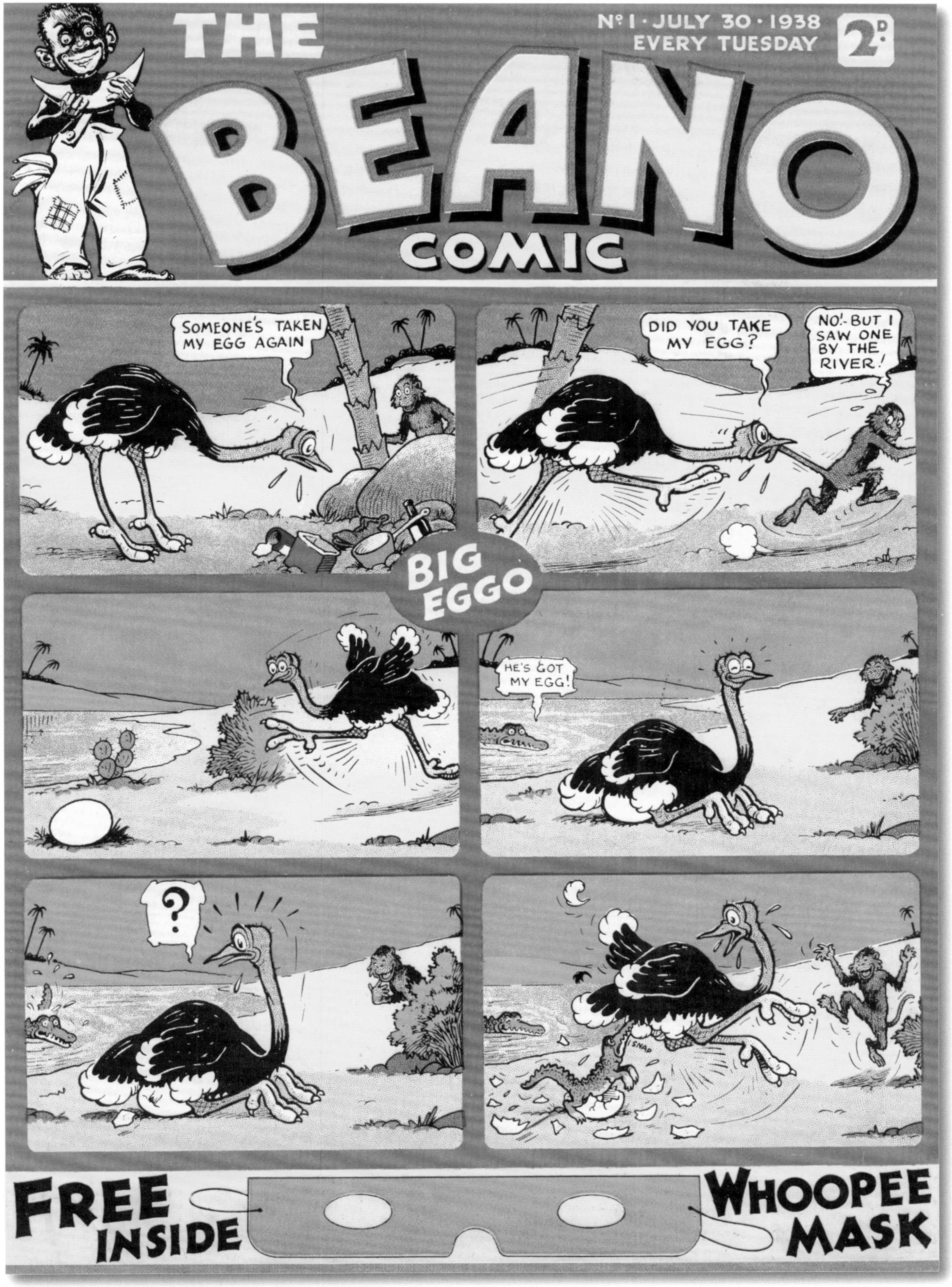
THE
BEANO
COMIC
Nº1 · JULY 30 · 1938
EVERY TUESDAY
2D.
SOMEONE'S TAKEN MY EGG AGAIN
DID YOU TAKE MY EGG?
NO!- BUT I SAW ONE BY THE RIVER!
BIG EGGO
HE'S GOT MY EGG!
?
SNAP
FREE INSIDE
WHOOPEE MASK

The first issue of ***The Beano*** was dated July 30, 1938, but was actually issued on July 26. Arriving six months after ***The Dandy***, it was also a great success, with nearly 443,000 copies sold. The 'Big Eggo' story was drawn by Reg Carter (see page 53). The original idea for Eggo came from R. D. Low, who had first named the strip 'Oswald the Ostrich'. The bottom of the cover highlights the special free gift of a 'Whoopee Mask'. 'Big Eggo' remained the cover story until January 1948.

This opening set of comic strips was very much influenced by the look of American newspaper 'funnies'. Ping was a new character illustrated by Hugh McNeill. Initially the strip was titled 'Indy the Rubber Man', which was changed first to 'Here Comes Ping the Elastic Man', later shortened to 'Ping the Elastic Man'. The title change would have been decided on when the finished dummy copy was passed around the various departments for comment. The Board of Directors were very pro-active in the discussions about new publications and final decisions would ultimately lie with them.

'Brave Captain Kipper' has a pronounced international look, due in no short measure to the fact that it was produced by the Torelli Brothers in Milan. This Italian art agency produced finished strips and syndicated them to various comics worldwide, but they did not work this way with *The Beano*. Strip ideas were created in Dundee and only the artwork was done by the agency. The finished rhyme for the story was written by the Thomson subs.

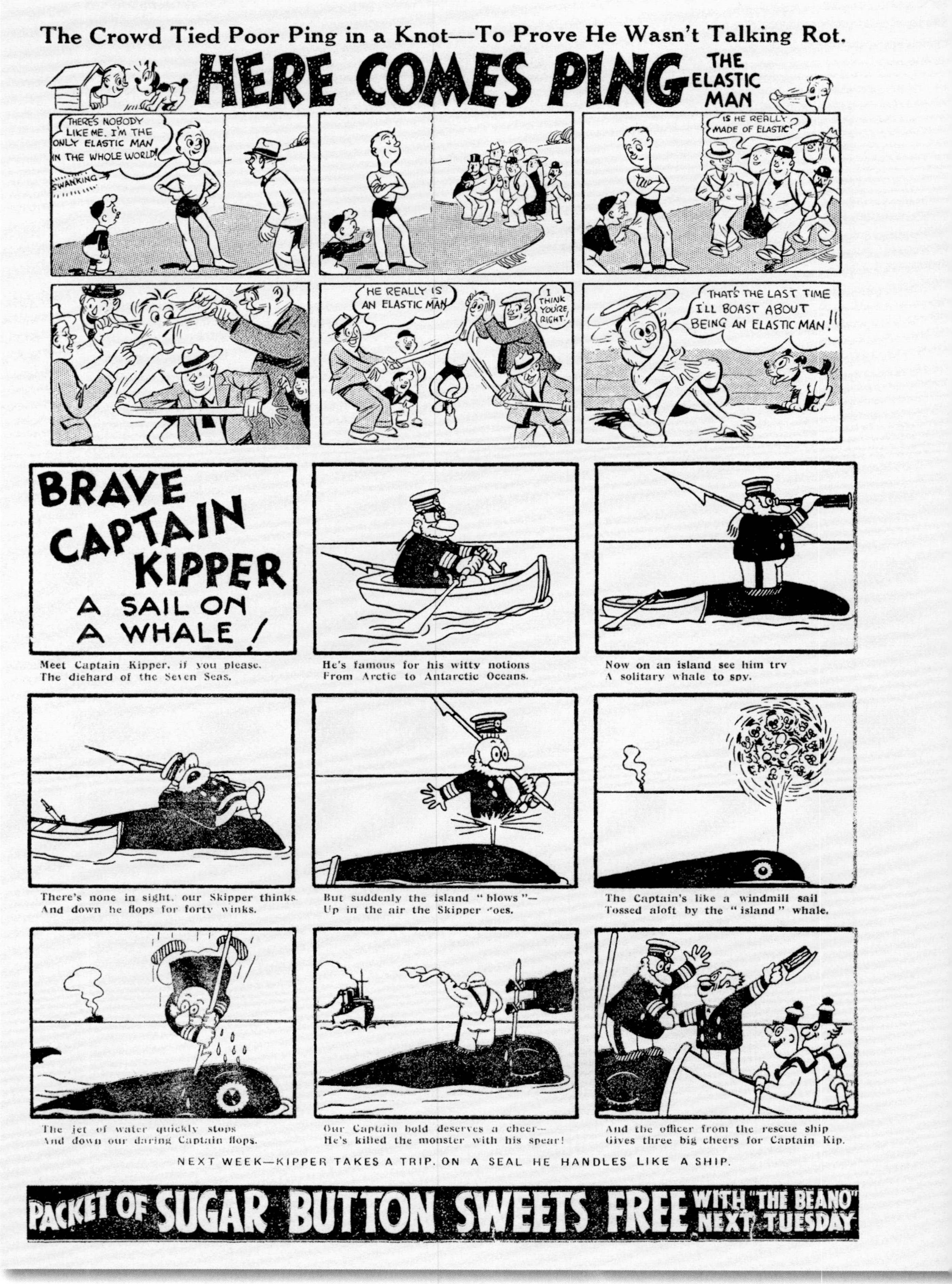
The Crowd Tied Poor Ping in a Knot—To Prove He Wasn't Talking Rot.
HERE COMES PING THE ELASTIC MAN
THERE'S NOBODY LIKE ME. I'M THE ONLY ELASTIC MAN IN THE WHOLE WORLD!
SWANKING
IS HE REALLY MADE OF ELASTIC?
HE REALLY IS AN ELASTIC MAN
I THINK YOU'RE RIGHT!
THAT'S THE LAST TIME I'LL BOAST ABOUT BEING AN ELASTIC MAN!!
BRAVE CAPTAIN KIPPER
A SAIL ON A WHALE!
Meet Captain Kipper, if you please, The diehard of the Seven Seas.
He's famous for his witty notions From Arctic to Antarctic Oceans.
Now on an island see him try A solitary whale to spy.
There's none in sight, our Skipper thinks And down he flops for forty winks.
But suddenly the island "blows"— Up in the air the Skipper goes.
The Captain's like a windmill sail Tossed aloft by the "island" whale.
The jet of water quickly stops And down our daring Captain flops.
Our Captain bold deserves a cheer— He's killed the monster with his spear!
And the officer from the rescue ship Gives three big cheers for Captain Kip.
NEXT WEEK—KIPPER TAKES A TRIP. ON A SEAL HE HANDLES LIKE A SHIP.
PACKET OF SUGAR BUTTON SWEETS FREE WITH "THE BEANO" NEXT TUESDAY

Son of a Duke But Always Pally—
With the Beezer Kids of Ash-Can Alley.
LORD SNOOTY AND HIS PALS
LORD MARMADUKE— "SNOOTY" TO YOU!
ROSIE.
HAIRPIN HUGGINS.
SKINNY LIZZIE.
SCRAPPER SMITH.
"HAPPY" HUTTON.
GERTIE THE GOAT
MANY HAPPY RETURNS OF THE DAY, YOUR LORDSHIP!
GOOD MORNING, AUNT!
GOOD MORNING, MARMADUKE LOOK AT ALL THE NICE BIRTHDAY GIFTS YOUR FRIENDS HAVE SENT YOU!
MECCANO
WHAT'S MORE, ALGERNON, PERCIVAL AND VERNON TOOTLE ARE ON THEIR WAY HERE NOW WITH A PRESENT OF A DOG-CART FOR YOU!
H-M!
NOW, GO UPSTAIRS AND WASH. YOU MUST BE VERY NICE TO THE LITTLE BOYS WHEN THEY COME!
HUH! THOSE THREE TOOTLE GUYS GIVE ME A PAIN IN THE NECK! I'LL DODGE 'EM BY SNEAKING DOWN THE DRAIN-PIPE!
I'LL CHANGE INTO MY DISGUISE AND GO TO MEET MY REAL PALS DOWN IN ASH-CAN ALLEY!
GEE! I'M GOING TO SPEND A REAL HAPPY BIRTHDAY WITH MY PALS!
HI! FELLERS!
HAPPY BIRTHDAY, SNOOTY! LOOK WHAT WE'VE GOT FOR YOUR BIRTHDAY PRESENT!
GEE! THIS IS THE BEST BIRTHDAY PRESENT I'VE EVER HAD!
AW SHUCKS!
ALGY PERCY VERNON
CORKS! IT'S ALGY, PERCY AND VERNON!
WOOF
GASP
THEY DIDN'T KNOW ME IN THESE OLD CLOTHES! GOSH! WHAT A LARK IT'LL BE WHEN THEY BRING HOME THAT DOG-CART FOR ME!
CHEERIO, GANG! I'M GOING BACK TO CHANGE INTO MY ETON SUIT—KEEP THE CART FOR ME!
S'LONG SNOOTY!
GOOD MORNING, YOUR LORDSHIP.—WE HAVE—ER—A BIRTHDAY GIFT FOR YOU OUTSIDE, THOUGH WE HAVE HAD AN ACCIDENT ON THE WAY HERE!
THOUGHT. GEE! IF THEY ONLY KNEW IT WAS ME WHO SMASHED IT UP!
WHAT! YOU CALL THAT A BIRTHDAY PRESENT? HOW DARE YOU INSULT THE EARL OF BUNKERTON WITH A WRECK LIKE THAT! TAKE THAT AWFUL THING AWAY!!
EVERY TUESDAY LOOK FOR FUN—"THE BEANO'S" ON SALE FOR EVERYONE.

The all-important page 3 (the first strip to hit your eyes as you open the comic) belonged to 'Lord Snooty'. Illustrator Dudley Watkins was *The Beano*'s lead artist. In these early days the storylines were along the lines of the 'Prince and the Pauper'. Snooty's full title was Marmaduke, Earl of Bunkerton, and, the first strip informs us, he attended Eton public school. However, the young lord would sneak away from the grandeur of Bunkerton Castle to play with his true pals, the fun-loving honest urchins from Ash-Can Alley. The mass of *Beano* readers would identify themselves with these playful working class kids and fully understand why Snooty liked them. Life at the castle would be seen as a life of discipline that lacked freedom and fun. Watkins caught this idea beautifully; everyone connected with life at the castle wore an expression of severe aloofness, whereas the gang playing in the Ash-Can Alley had happy animated faces full of energetic fun.

This strongman story would have been very topical at launch time of *The Beano* as the Johnny Weissmuller *Tarzan* films were attracting huge audiences and were very much at their peak. Playgrounds would have been full of budding Tarzans. Though castaway on his Black Island, Morgyn had become the strongest man in the world – not even Tarzan claimed that! His world was shared by monster-sized beasts and birds that seemed always ready to attack. The story lines were very simple, relying on the drama of the battle and the size and ferocity of Morgyn's seemingly impossible opponents.

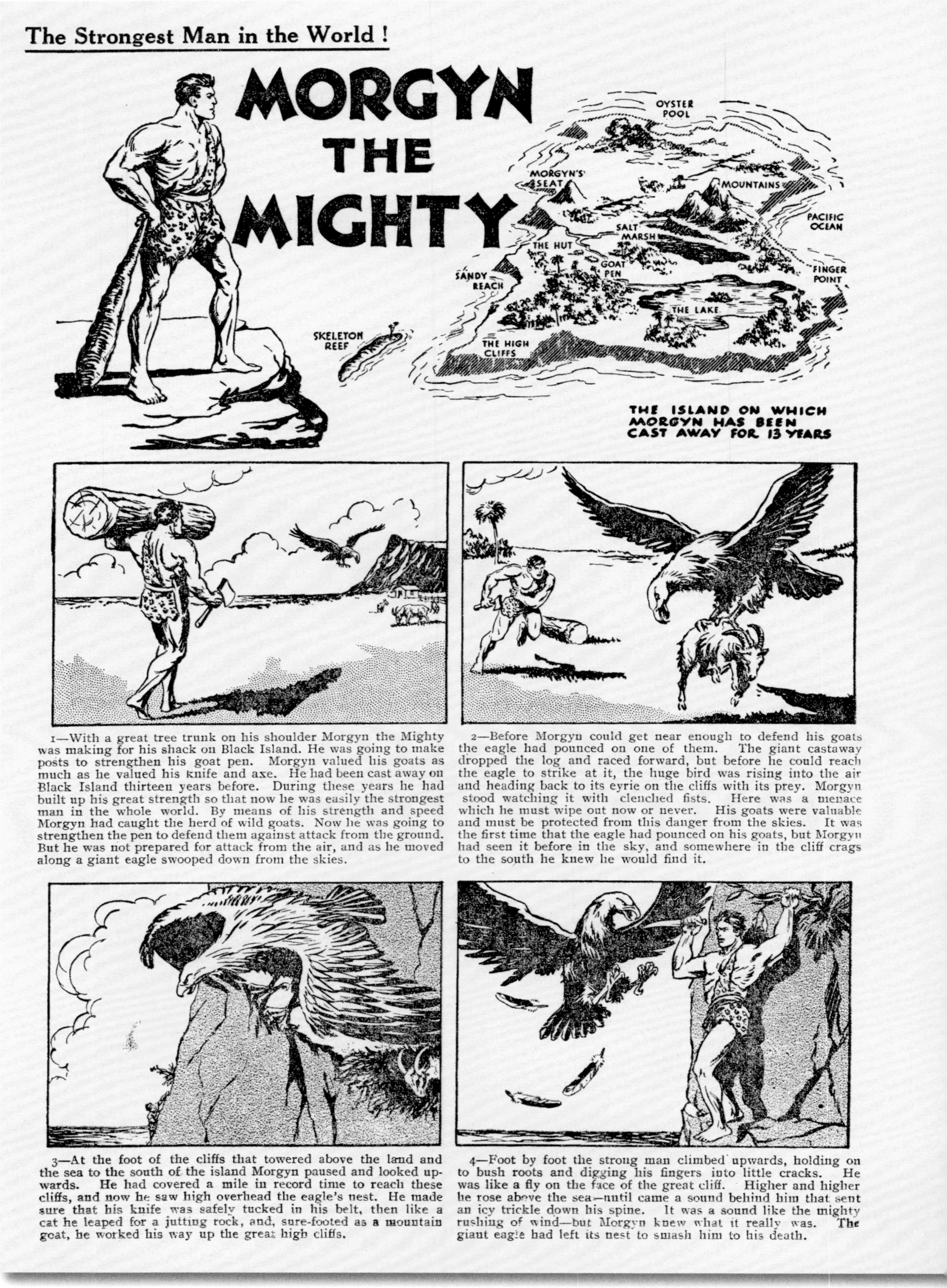
The Strongest Man in the World!
MORGYN THE MIGHTY
OYSTER POOL
MORGYN'S SEAT
MOUNTAINS
PACIFIC OCEAN
SALT MARSH
THE HUT
GOAT PEN
SANDY REACH
FINGER POINT
THE LAKE
SKELETON REEF
THE HIGH CLIFFS
THE ISLAND ON WHICH MORGYN HAS BEEN CAST AWAY FOR 13 YEARS
1—With a great tree trunk on his shoulder Morgyn the Mighty was making for his shack on Black Island. He was going to make posts to strengthen his goat pen. Morgyn valued his goats as much as he valued his knife and axe. He had been cast away on Black Island thirteen years before. During these years he had built up his great strength so that now he was easily the strongest man in the whole world. By means of his strength and speed Morgyn had caught the herd of wild goats. Now he was going to strengthen the pen to defend them against attack from the ground. But he was not prepared for attack from the air, and as he moved along a giant eagle swooped down from the skies.
2—Before Morgyn could get near enough to defend his goats the eagle had pounced on one of them. The giant castaway dropped the log and raced forward, but before he could reach the eagle to strike at it, the huge bird was rising into the air and heading back to its eyrie on the cliffs with its prey. Morgyn stood watching it with clenched fists. Here was a menace which he must wipe out now or never. His goats were valuable and must be protected from this danger from the skies. It was the first time that the eagle had pounced on his goats, but Morgyn had seen it before in the sky, and somewhere in the cliff crags to the south he knew he would find it.
3—At the foot of the cliffs that towered above the land and the sea to the south of the island Morgyn paused and looked upwards. He had covered a mile in record time to reach these cliffs, and now he saw high overhead the eagle's nest. He made sure that his knife was safely tucked in his belt, then like a cat he leaped for a jutting rock, and, sure-footed as a mountain goat, he worked his way up the great high cliffs.
4—Foot by foot the strong man climbed upwards, holding on to bush roots and digging his fingers into little cracks. He was like a fly on the face of the great cliff. Higher and higher he rose above the sea—until came a sound behind him that sent an icy trickle down his spine. It was a sound like the mighty rushing of wind—but Morgyn knew what it really was. The giant eagle had left its nest to smash him to his death.

Next Tuesday—" The Beano " treats every boy to Button Sweets !
3
5—The mighty wings and the sharp talons missed Morgyn by a hair's breadth as the eagle swept past. The great gust of air that followed it nearly tore Morgyn from his perch. He waited. Again the eagle swept in. Morgyn's knife flashed and the blade bit deep into the eagle's breast. The power behind the thrust sent the bird backwards, but the sudden jerk tore the bush root from the cliff, and Morgyn lost his balance on the ledge.
6—Morgyn snatched at the only chance he had of escaping a fall to his death on the rocks far below. As the eagle wheeled from the cliff, he clutched at its legs and hung on. The blood from the bird's wound splashed in his face, and as it flapped its way seawards the giant castaway knew that the great bird was making its last flight. Below him, he could see the jagged rocks that skirted the foot of the cliff.
7—But the mighty bird was driving out to sea with the last of its strength. All the time it was screaming harshly, and trying to slash at Morgyn with its cruel beak. The big castaway hung on. Now they were clear of the great jagged reef below. Gradually the eagle's wing beats lost their power and Morgyn waited for the end. Without warning the great wings crumpled up, and the eagle and Morgyn plunged into the sea.
8—With a mighty splash Morgyn hit the water and disappeared into the depths. Down he dropped until he felt his lungs would burst. And then as he began to rise a black shape swirled through the water towards him. It was a tiger shark—a fifteen-foot man-eater of the deep, and Morgyn was glad that he had not dropped his knife, for it was all he had to defend himself against the huge shark. He gripped the knife grimly as the shark attacked.
9—Down in the green depths a grim battle began. Only by a desperate effort did Morgyn slip past the shark, and then he shot to the surface for air. The shark swam after him. One swift breath was all that Morgyn could take before the tiger shark was on him. A swift roll sideways and the shark swept past. Then next moment the great brute was in the grip of the world's strongest man, his knife ready to strike. On the surface, beneath the surface, the battle raged until the waters were stained crimson with the shark's blood.
10—Then the threshing waters calmed down again, and at last Morgyn struck out for the shore with the body of the tiger shark in tow. The strong man had won battles in the air and in the sea—and he could make good use of the skin and flesh of the tiger shark. He dragged it ashore and then walked off to his shack to begin the work of strengthening his goat pen. Morgyn the Mighty could always find plenty of work to do on Black Island—and he could usually find thrills and excitement in plenty, too!
MORGYN, THE MAN WITH THE STRENGTH OF TEN, APPEARS IN " THE BEANO " EACH WEEK.

The 'Morgyn' artist was George 'Dod' Anderson, a staff illustrator with D. C. Thomson. Anderson cleverly posed Morgyn in most action frames to show off the fantastic physique he had designed. This debut series appeared as a double page for a 14-week run. 'Morgyn' had been appearing in ***The Rover*** since 1928 in text stories, and, subsequently, this illustrated series was reprinted in ***The Rover*** in 1954, when the famous boys' paper started to use picture stories.

Text stories with pen and ink heading pictures was the tried and tested way the Big Five presented their ripping yarns to their readers. 'Tom Thumb' was a character well known to children from the famous fairytale about the 6-inch-tall woodcutter's son, and new tales of the little boy were well received. Most of the text stories were written by freelance authors, working to a staff-produced synopsis. This heading block was drawn by Dudley Watkins who would go on to draw 'Tom Thumb' picture story adventures for many years. When D. C. Thomson produced the nursery title *Bimbo* in 1961, it led with a version of 'Tom Thumb', drawn by Dudley Watkins.

The Boy Who is Only Six Inches High !

THE ADVENTURES OF TOM THUMB

The Wood-cutter's Son

WAT, the wood-cutter, propped his big axe in the corner of the room, and sat down in the chair at the end of the table. His day's work was done, and it was good to be home again in his cottage in the clearing.

The wood-cutter was always thirsty when he came home from work, and his wife had already poured out for him a tankard of goat's milk.

Wat took a long drink, put down the tankard, and smiled.

"Where's Tom ?" he asked suddenly. "What's happened to the boy ? He's usually the first at the table for a meal."

His wife looked about the room, then went to the window and opened it wide.

"Tom !" she called. "Tom, come in for your supper. There is goat's milk and wheat-cakes."

Minutes passed, but there was no reply. Wat leaned forward rather anxiously.

"Tom, you little rascal, where are you ?" he shouted.

Splash ! A spot of milk jumped out of his tankard and dropped on the back of his hand. A tiny arrow had whizzed through the air and splashed into the tankard. The wood-cutter cried aloud in surprise, and there was a little peal of laughter from almost under his nose.

That peal of laughter came from Tom Thumb, Wat the wood-cutter's tiny son. He popped up from inside the bowl that held the wheat-cakes, his eyes gleaming with mischief. There was a cheery grin on his tiny face, and in his right hand was a very small bow. It was from this bow he had shot a tiny arrow which had splashed into his father's milk.

"You young rascal !" roared the wood-cutter, trying to look angry, and he reached out and picked his son up between forefinger and thumb. "Always up to mischief, aren't you ? If you were only a bit bigger I'd spank you."

Tom Thumb did not seem to mind the scolding at all. He laughed and wriggled in his father's grasp, an amazing little chap no more than six inches high.

Except for his size, however, Tom was just like an ordinary boy. His tiny body was perfectly shaped. He had sturdy little arms and legs, and he looked a proper little dandy in his bright-coloured doublet.

At Tom's side dangled a tiny leather scabbard which his father had made for him. In it he carried his sword, which was really a darning needle. He needed that mighty weapon sometimes to keep off the rats or cats which tried to snatch him up.

"I thought I'd make you jump, father !" he chuckled. "Did you see how I landed the arrow right in the middle of the milk ? I never miss. Please give it back to me The thorns I use for arrows are hard to get the right shape and length."

His father set him down on the table edge, and fished in his cup with a horn spoon until he had found the thorn which Tom called an arrow. It was no more than an inch long, and as sharp as a needle.

"Here you are, you little rascal !" growled Wat. "Now eat your food."

Tom's mother put a tiny thimble on the table and filled it with milk. Tom Thumb squatted there drinking his milk and eating a slice of bread and butter no bigger than a postage stamp.

To-night, Wat and his wife were in good spirits, for Wat had caught a rabbit during his day in the woods, and that meant there would be a fine stew the next day.

Suddenly the wood-cutter stopped talking and held up his hand The sound of a hunting horn came from the distance. Tom's mother turned pale, and Wat thumped the table with his fist.

"They are hunting again ! I vow it will be Jasper, the son of the Black Baron."

The horn sounded again, louder than before, and Tom jumped up with a yell of excitement. Before his mother or father could stop him, he had climbed on top of the loaf, from where he could see out of the window.

"I see a wild boar passing !" he squeaked. "It has just come through the hole in our fence and gone out of the gateway. It is running for its life."

A grunt of anger came from Tom's father as he rose to his feet.

"That means it has come over our land, and the hunters will ride across my corn patch and ruin my vegetables. They always do that to poor, simple folks like us. Then next week the Baron will come and demand the rent for the cottage. How can I pay when my crops are ruined and I have no money ?"

Both he and his wife went to the window to watch for the hunters. Tom Thumb was left on top of the loaf, but he did not stay there long. Here was a chance for him to show his mother and father what a brave fellow he was ! He would stop those wild huntsmen from riding over their ground and trampling the crops into the earth.

Down from the loaf jumped Tom. Then he ran to the edge of the table, slid down the table leg, and slipped out through a hole in the bottom of the door.

On the step of the cottage slept Peterkins, the big black cat which was the pet of the house. Without pausing, Tom Thumb leapt astride its back, and roused it with a kick of his tiny heels.

The Tiny Warrior

"UP, Peterkins, and away !" shouted Tom, sitting on the cat as though it was a horse. "Gallop to where the hunters are blowing their horns."

Peterkins leapt up and bounded down the garden path. The big cat enjoyed the fun when his tiny master was on his back.

Clinging tightly to the long fur of the cat, Tom Thumb hung on as Peterkins cleared the fence and headed for the forest. Peterkins was a great jumper, but Tom was a clever rider and he stuck fast on his mount's back.

Suddenly the cat stopped. The chief huntsman had ridden into sight on a great brown horse that seemed bigger than a house to Tom Thumb.

Just then the main party of huntsmen

Mary's lamb, nicknamed " Button," rushes motor—Button's mutton. 7

arrived. Leading them was Jasper, the son of the Black Baron.

Tom Thumb raised his bow. He meant to prick the horse so that it would toss Jasper into the dust. He fired an arrow dart, but as he did so Jasper's horse moved, and the dart pricked the leg of the rider instead of finding its mark in his mount.

" Ow !" cried Jasper. " What was that ?" And he rubbed his leg, groaning at the pain, until suddenly his eyes opened wide in startled amazement.

He had just seen the black cat with the tiny figure on its back. He stared, then blinked as though he could not believe his eyes.

Tom Thumb wanted to fit another arrow and shoot it, but Peterkins was afraid the horses would tread on him, and the cat darted away.

" Hey, come back ! Hi !" roared the Black Baron's son. " Did you see that funny little fellow on a cat, men ?"

However, the cat did not stop. It was going like the wind, straight for the house. Peterkins saw that trouble was coming, and wanted to hide in the wood cellar.

The cat leapt the garden fence so fast that Tom Thumb was thrown off, and rolled under a cabbage.

He picked himself up angrily, hearing the huntsmen approaching at full gallop. They had seen which way he had gone, and they had stopped chasing the wild boar to chase Tom Thumb.

There were so many huntsmen that Tom Thumb grew scared. Up to the cottage door he rushed. In the bottom corner of this big door Wat the wood-cutter had fitted another tiny door. Lifting the little latch, Tom opened this and scampered inside. His mother and father were still looking from the window, wondering what was happening.

They did not see Tom Thumb climb inside one of the boots his father had taken off. Tom hid in the toe, and lay there panting.

The Baron's son and his men came galloping up the garden path. They bellowed out orders for the wood-cutter to come and open his door, and poor Wat could not disobey.

" What can I do for you, young master ?" he asked, bowing to the burly Jasper.

" I saw a little midget running this way—a boy no more than six inches high !" roared Jasper.

" That will be my son, Tom Thumb. He must have been out to see your hunting party," replied Wat.

" I want him," cried the Baron's son. " He must return with me to the castle. He'll amuse us there on rainy days. Where is he ? Fetch him out !"

" Honoured, sir, you cannot have Tom Thumb," replied the wood-cutter boldly. " He is very small, but he is all we have got. He is our only son."

" Never mind about that ! You fetch him out," commanded the Black Baron's son. " If you don't, I'll burn your cottage around your ears."

Wat's wife began to cry loudly, and that was more than Tom Thumb could stand. His head popped out of the boot.

" Don't hurt my mother and father ! Here I am !" he cried. " What is it you want with me ?"

Tom Thumb climbed out of the boot and drew his darning needle. Then he stood there waving it, and that looked very funny, for he did not stand as high as the top of Jasper's boot.

The huntsmen roared with laughter, and one of them standing behind Tom reached down and picked him up. Tom Thumb squealed with rage, and jabbed at the man's hand with the needle, but the huntsman wore a gauntlet and was not hurt.

" This Tom Thumb is a real little spitfire, my lord," he said to the Baron's son. " Shall we take him back with us ?"

" Yes, that is what I want ! Come !" cried Jasper.

Without a word to poor Wat and his wife, the cruel men turned and headed for their horses. The huntsman took away Tom's " sword " and put the lad in his pouch for safety, buttoning it from the outside.

However, before he was popped into the pocket, Tom just had time to cry—

" Don't worry, mother ! I'll look after myself. I'll be back again soon."

Then the hunters mounted their horses and rode back towards the great castle where the Black Baron lived. They laughed and joked all the way back, because they thought that they had made a fine capture.

On the journey poor Tom Thumb was bumped and jolted till he was all sore and aching. He sighed with relief when at last they reached the Black Castle. The huntsman then took the youngster from his pocket and gave him to the Baron's son.

Tom found that struggling did him no good. The great hand of Jasper nearly crushed him. But his darning needle was given back to him, and he proudly returned it to its scabbard. Tom had heard he was to be shown to the Baron, and he wanted to look his best.

Tom Thumb's Revenge

THE Black Castle was a fearsome place. It was filled with the Baron's men, and there were awful dungeons where he kept the poor people who could not pay him the taxes he demanded.

The place was so big that it took Tom's breath away to look up at the ceiling of the great hall into which he was carried after he had been given his sword back.

The Baron was seated at a long table, drinking from a great horn.

" Well, did you bring back a good boar or a deer ?" he croaked, without looking at his son.

" No father, but we have caught something else, something much better than a boar or a deer," grinned Jasper, and he signed for one of the servants to bring forward a tray.

He popped Tom Thumb on to the tray, and made the servant carry him across to the Baron. The Black Baron was a huge, fierce man with a bushy beard. And now his eyes bulged when he saw the little figure on the tray.

" What's this—a doll ? Where did you get it, son ? It's most life-like. It——" the Baron broke off to give a sharp cry of pain.

He had reached forward to touch the supposed doll, and Tom had whipped out his darning needle and jabbed him in the hand. The Baron yelled, and his son roared with laughter.

" It's Tom Thumb, the son of the wood-cutter," he explained. " He'll make fine sport for us. He'll make a lot of fun for us here in the castle, father !"

The Baron grunted, licked his pricked finger, and made a sudden grab for Tom.

" If he is to remain here, he'll have to learn manners !" roared the Baron.

He turned Tom upside down and pretended to drop him into his big horn of ale. Tom yelled and fought furiously. Then the Baron made him push dishes full of food across the table. The Baron kept playing with Tom and teasing him for a long time, and then set him down on the floor.

" Tell the Chamberlain to catch some fierce rats," he growled. " To-morrow I'll watch this little man fighting them in a cage."

Tom was furious at the way he had been treated. He must show them he could look after himself.

Nearby, in front of a huge log fire, there slept a fat old wolf-hound. It had not moved even when Tom was put down. All the men were crowding round the Baron, who was giving them orders about something or other.

There was a piece of cord tied to the wolf-hound's collar. Tom's eyes gleamed. He picked up the end of this cord, and tied it to the leg of the Baron's chair. Then he waited until the Baron, who had got to his feet, might sit down again.

A few minutes later the Baron bent to sit down. With a grin of delight, Tom Thumb raised his sword. He gave the fat wolf-hound a quick jab, and the startled dog leapt to its feet and dashed away.

Crash ! The dog had dragged the chair after it, and the Baron had sat down heavily on the floor.

" Oo-oh, I've broken my back ! Oo-oh !" he roared. " Help me up. I've broken my back."

Half a dozen frightened men lifted him to his feet and got him to bed, while Tom Thumb sat on the cross-piece under one of the benches and laughed until he was sore.

The Black Baron and his son would soon learn that Tom Thumb could always get his own back !

Next Tuesday—Tom Thumb in a fight with a great big rat!

Not every artist could handle the scale differences between a 6-inch-tall character and the normal-sized adults in the stories. Dudley Watkins would often bring Tom into action in the foreground and, though the background characters were much bigger, they did not totally dominate. When he was defending himself from, say, a fierce dog, by brandishing his tiny sword, the scene would be drawn from behind Tom's shoulder.

Stories from the wilds of Canada were popular with British children, and they conjured up scenes of the pioneering days of discovery in the wilderness parts of the Empire. A good amount of natural history information was included in these stories which the author would write as one long tale and which *The Beano* sub-editors would revise into weekly episodes. The 'Black Flash' title block was drawn by staff artist Richard 'Toby' Baines.

The Wonder Animal of the Forest.

BLACK FLASH THE BEAVER

Danger at the Dam

BLACK FLASH, the young beaver, was having the time of his life.

Old Broadtail, his father, had made a slide down the steep bank of the creek, and had plastered it with wet clay. Black Flash had only to lie on the slide and he would go shooting down head first into the cool, deep waters of the beaver dam. Time and time again he did this, squealing with delight as he sped downwards.

All around, the older grey beavers were working hard. Grey Ear, the wise old leader of the colony, had ordered that the dam should be strengthened. Some beavers were cutting down trees with their sharp chisel teeth.

Others were making chutes down which these felled logs could be pushed to the water.

Old Broadtail was one of the beavers felling trees, and he did his work with such amazing speed and care that they always fell in just the place he wanted them. Then Broadtail would strip the branches from the trunk, leaving a smooth log.

Sometimes he glanced up from his work to where his son, Black Flash, was enjoying himself on the slide. Seeing that the little black beaver was happy and out of mischief, Broadtail did not disturb him.

Then suddenly Broadtail sniffed the air. A look of fear seemed to come to his eyes for a moment, and he stared and listened with his nose pointed into the woods.

Then his flat tail struck the hard ground with a noise like a pistol shot. Smack!

It was the signal that danger was near. The beavers understood it, and before you could blink, they had dived silently into the pool, making scarcely a ripple.

In ten seconds the great colony of beavers that had been busily working around the creek were safe and sound in their lodges, those marvellous houses of theirs built on the creek bed and made of clay and twigs.

Within those lodges the beaver colony waited for the danger to pass. There was no panic, for the beavers knew well enough that their lodges were strong enough to withstand any attack. Even a wolverine, the steel-clawed demon of the backwoods, had failed to tear an opening in the solid walls of their house.

Meanwhile, outside in the woods, a big Indian crept along heading for the beaver dam. The sun glinted on the rifle he carried in his hand, and it was evident he was up to no good, for an ugly scowl twisted his face as he glared down on the dam.

There was not a beaver to be seen except one, and that was Black Flash The little black beaver had been too busy on his slide to notice the danger signal. Perhaps he was too young to know the meaning of danger.

Just as he was getting ready to slide down into the water once more, little Black Flash heard the footsteps of the Indian in the woods. To see what was approaching, he waddled back into the woods a bit, smelling the air with his blunt little nose.

He moved forward again, and then something did happen that scared the wits out of him. A shot rang out, then another. They gave the little black beaver such a fright that he couldn't move.

Running Coyote, the beaver poacher, had shot at Broadtail, who had come up from under the water to look for his son.

The bullets had missed Broadtail. Now, as the Indian moved forward towards the dam, he saw little Black Flash.

" I will get you!" he grunted, and he darted forward to cut off the black beaver's retreat to the dam. Instead of scuttling back to the water, Black Flash waddled further into the forest.

" I find him!" grunted the big Indian excitedly. " That little beaver, he worth much money. He has a black skin, not grey one like ordinary beavers."

He began to beat around the bushes and, thoroughly frightened, Black Flash was driven deeper and deeper into the forest, but he managed to keep out of the hands of the Indian. Finally, Running Coyote gave up the search, and started back towards the Indian village. He was afraid that Pat Casey, the Game Warden, might have heard the shots.

The Outcast of Elbow Creek

BLACK FLASH had escaped, but he was lost. He kept going, hoping to find the dam where his father and mother lived, but he was really heading away from it.

Then as he trotted along he met a queer beast that looked something like a small-beaver, but it was all covered with long sharp quills.

At sight of Black Flash, the porcupine curled up into a ball. Scared by the deadly looking array of quills, Blach Flash made a dive past the porcupine and ran for his life.

He was pretty tired when finally he smelled water. Then he saw it—a little creek. Black Flash was too scared to venture into the water, but he followed the creek downstream, and after a while he saw a great stretch of water bigger than the stretch where he had always lived.

He knew that it was a beaver dam. Happy to be among his own kind again, he waddled around the edge of the great pond, until he came to a mud slide, just like the one he had been playing on when Running Coyote, the Indian, fired the shots.

Half a dozen baby beavers were playing on the wet slide, and Black Flash waddled in among them. The result was not very pleasant for the lonely little black beaver. They were all grey beavers, and they had never seen a black beaver before. So Black Flash's colour scared the little beavers of Elbow Creek for a while. But soon they got curious, and, finally, sure that this little black beaver was harmless, they closed in on him.

It was clear to Black Flash that he wasn't wanted, and he got ready to fight for his life as the biggest of the baby beavers made a slap at him with his tail. The little fellow fought back the best way he could, but he was getting the worst of it when a big grown-up beaver scattered the fighters and came face to face with Black Flash.

The big beaver stared at little Black Flash, for he had never seen a black beaver before, and he knew that Black Flash did not belong to Elbow Creek. It was his duty, he thought, to drive this little stranger away, and he got busy doing that, using his tail to slap Black Flash.

Whimpering, Black Flash retreated before the blows, and was thinking of scuttling back into the forest, when another big beaver appeared on the scene. It was the wife of the Old Man Beaver who was trying to drive Black Flash away.

The little black beaver scuttled towards her, whimpering, and crouched between her fore-legs. The male beaver tried to get at him, and slapped at him savagely, while Black Flash tried to dodge the blows.

Wham! The beaver Black Flash was cowering against lashed out with her broad tail, and Old Man Beaver went smack head over heels. Before he could recover, Old Man Beaver was cuffed and scratched so badly by his wife that he turned tail, took a header down the mud-slide, and swam back to his lodge.

The mother beaver turned to little Black Flash and began to nuzzle him tenderly. At the same time, she talked to the other baby beavers, and they began to crowd around the little black stranger. Then one of them coaxed him to the mud-slide, and down went Black Flash into the water, with a joyous splash.

He had been adopted by the pair of beavers who ruled the big colony on Elbow Creek, and a new life of adventure lay ahead for the little black beaver.

Next Tuesday—The baby beaver faces an angry rattlesnake.

Star on His Shirt—Slugs in His Gun,
Laugh at the Sheriff—He's Chock-Full of Fun.
WHOOPEE HANK
THE SLAP-DASH SHERIFF
SAY, STRANGER — LIKE TO WIN A BET?
Tough guy in big city street
Thinks Whoopee Hank is easy meat.
BET YOU AREN'T STRONG ENOUGH TO HOLD THIS DOOR SHUT!
"You got no muscle!" jeers the tough.
"Yeah?" snorts Hank. "Watch my stuff!"
NOW TO JUMP INTO MY CAR
BET I CAN!
Whoopee heaves with all his might,
While tough guy vanishes from sight.
HI, LET US OUT YOU MUTT! THIS IS A BANK AND WE'VE JUST BEEN ROBBED!
What a shock for Whoopee Hank!
He finds he's helped to rob a bank!
O.K., BOYS, I WAS FOOLED BUT I'LL GET THE CROOK WITH THESE THINGS I'VE GOT. HE MUST USE THE NORTH ROAD AND I'VE GOT A SWELL IDEA!
BANK
NAILS
GUN POWDER
Whoopee runs to fetch his moke.
Thinks this is beyond a joke.
TO THE OLD CANNON
Slap-Dash Sheriff on the trail.
Big-Shot Smith he means to nail.
OLD CANNON RELIC OF THE CIVIL WAR
Jumping snakes! Look out for fun!
Whoopee's going to use that gun!
I'VE PUT IN THE GUNPOWDER NOW FOR THE NAILS — AND THEN TO AIM AT THE NORTH ROAD!
NAILS
Slap-Dash loads the cannon full,
Vows that he will score a bull.
Mighty roar and flash of flame.
What is Whoopee's little game?
Slap-Dash Sheriff sure can shoot.
See his scheme? It's pretty cute.
CURSES! MY TYRES ARE ALL BUSTED!
BANG
BANG
POP
POP!
BANG
Pop! Bang! Boom! and Whizz! Bang! Slap!
Big-Shot's caught in Whoopee's trap.
O.K., BIG SHOT, I NAILED YOU THAT TIME!
Whoopee Hank don't never fail.
Big-Shot Smith is booked for jail.
YOU'LL LAUGH UNTIL YOU SCARCE CAN SPEAK—AT WHOOPEE ON THIS PAGE EACH WEEK.

Whoopee Hank had a look that was evocative of newspaper comic strips – not surprising as its artist, Roland Davies, was the man behind the popular ***Sunday Express*** strip 'Come On Steve'.

Compared to ***The Dandy, The Beano*** had more strips where the lead character was an adult, like 'Whoopee Hank'. It was small points like this that forged their separate identities. The two comics shared most artists but not Roland Davies, who only worked on ***The Beano***. Hank, the slap-dash sheriff, wore the star on his chest for exactly one year before riding off into a ***Beano*** sunset.

Cracker Jack Silver was a modern-day celebrity cowboy who tackled gangsters in motor cars one week and Apaches on the warpath the next. *The Dandy* was running a very popular cowboy strip called 'The Daring Deeds of Buck Wilson' which was illustrated by Jack Glass, and *The Beano* recruited him for this strip. Scots-born Jack Glass produced the action pictures to go with the text. His distinctive, heavily inked style became a building block in both the developing *Beano* and *Dandy*, though in later years, when more colour was coming in to the comics, his crafted line work proved very difficult to add colour to.

The Fighting Cowboy with the 30-Foot Lash.
CRACKER JACK
THE WONDER WHIP-MAN
RODEO
1—Cracker Jack Silver stood alone in the arena at Sunset City Rodeo ground. Ten thousand people were watching him—and cheering him as loud as they possibly could. It was the biggest cheer of the day. There had been many exciting things to watch at the Rodeo—but Cracker Jack was getting the biggest cheer of all. There was nobody watching who had not heard of the Wonder Whip-Man—Cracker Jack Silver. His name was famous in the West, and the vast crowd was looking forward to seeing him do marvellous feats with his whip—the wonder whip that had a mighty thirty-foot thong.
2—Crack! Crack! Crack! Sounds like pistol shots rang out, and as if these had been a signal, the cheering died away. Crack! It was the long lash of the great whip which was making the noise as Cracker Jack sent it flicking in all directions. The 30-foot raw-hide lash was like a living thing. It seemed to flicker in and out like the tongue of a striking rattlesnake. At a sign from Cracker Jack, a cowboy ran towards the Whipman, his hands in the air. The Whipman's arm flashed twice and the lash plucked the revolvers from the cowboy's holsters and brought them spinning to the Whipman's feet.
RODEO
3—"Gosh! That was a great trick!" breathed a little Texas lad on the stand. "What's he doing with that apple, Dad?" he asked. But his father was too busy watching the Whipman to reply. Then a roar of cheering went up from the crowd, for from a distance of thirty feet Cracker Jack had just split an apple which was sitting on a cowboy's head. Cracker Jack had certainly earned the title of the Wonder Whipman, and he kept the great crowd on tip-toe with his tricks.
4—He snuffed out candles with the end of his lash, burst floating balloons, tripped up a runaway steer, tore holes in the bull's-eye of a target. And when his amazing display was over ten thousand spectators went wild with enthusiasm. "Sure, an' I ain't seen nothin' like it for fifty years," wheezed an old-timer, and that old-timer had seen many amazing things in his time! But it was all part of a day's work to the Wonder Whipman. Coiling his whip, he strode from the arena.
RODEO
5—As Cracker Jack rode away from the Rodeo Ground on Nugget, his black horse, the great crowd cheered him to the echo. Young lads wanted autograph books signed, men wanted to shake his hand—and hot and bothered, the modest Whipman urged Nugget down a side street to escape the fuss. Meanwhile, several streets away in Sunset City's Central Bank, a daring robbery was being carried out by masked bandits.
6—Across the counter of the bank a scared cashier was pushing the big sum of money which had been collected at the Rodeo Ground. Under the guns of the killers who threatened him, he could not refuse. "One squeak out of you and it'll be your last!" snarled one of the gangsters as they backed to the door with the money. Outside, with engine running, was a big open car. Everything was set for a getaway.

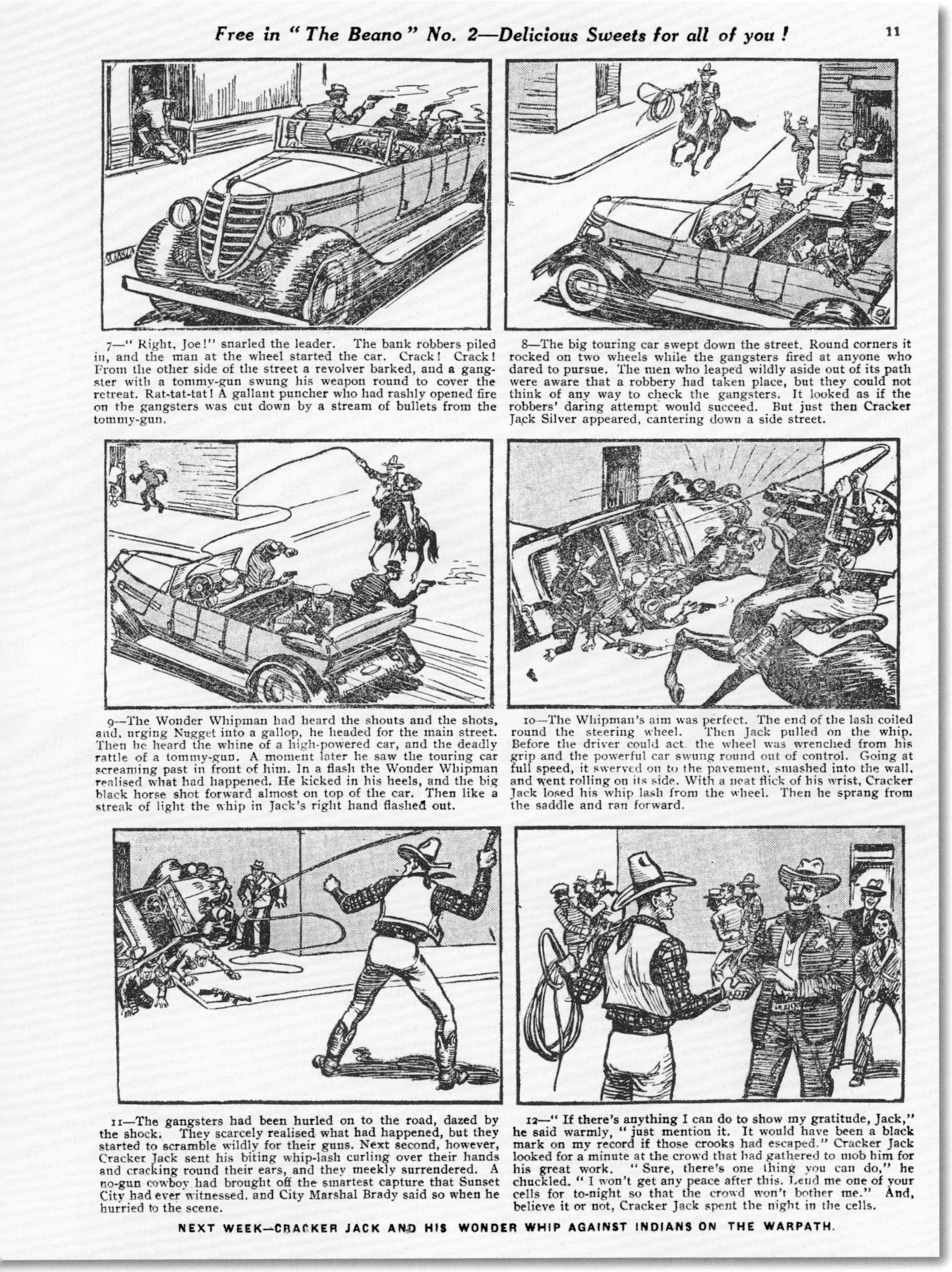

Free in "The Beano" No. 2—Delicious Sweets for all of you! 11

7—"Right, Joe!" snarled the leader. The bank robbers piled in, and the man at the wheel started the car. Crack! Crack! From the other side of the street a revolver barked, and a gangster with a tommy-gun swung his weapon round to cover the retreat. Rat-tat-tat! A gallant puncher who had rashly opened fire on the gangsters was cut down by a stream of bullets from the tommy-gun.

8—The big touring car swept down the street. Round corners it rocked on two wheels while the gangsters fired at anyone who dared to pursue. The men who leaped wildly aside out of its path were aware that a robbery had taken place, but they could not think of any way to check the gangsters. It looked as if the robbers' daring attempt would succeed. But just then Cracker Jack Silver appeared, cantering down a side street.

9—The Wonder Whipman had heard the shouts and the shots, and, urging Nugget into a gallop, he headed for the main street. Then he heard the whine of a high-powered car, and the deadly rattle of a tommy-gun. A moment later he saw the touring car screaming past in front of him. In a flash the Wonder Whipman realised what had happened. He kicked in his heels, and the big black horse shot forward almost on top of the car. Then like a streak of light the whip in Jack's right hand flashed out.

10—The Whipman's aim was perfect. The end of the lash coiled round the steering wheel. Then Jack pulled on the whip. Before the driver could act. the wheel was wrenched from his grip and the powerful car swung round out of control. Going at full speed, it swerved on to the pavement, smashed into the wall, and went rolling on its side. With a neat flick of his wrist, Cracker Jack losed his whip lash from the wheel. Then he sprang from the saddle and ran forward.

11—The gangsters had been hurled on to the road, dazed by the shock. They scarcely realised what had happened, but they started to scramble wildly for their guns. Next second, however, Cracker Jack sent his biting whip-lash curling over their hands and cracking round their ears, and they meekly surrendered. A no-gun cowboy had brought off the smartest capture that Sunset City had ever witnessed. and City Marshal Brady said so when he hurried to the scene.

12—"If there's anything I can do to show my gratitude, Jack," he said warmly, "just mention it. It would have been a black mark on my record if those crooks had escaped." Cracker Jack looked for a minute at the crowd that had gathered to mob him for his great work. "Sure, there's one thing you can do," he chuckled. "I won't get any peace after this. Lend me one of your cells for to-night so that the crowd won't bother me." And, believe it or not, Cracker Jack spent the night in the cells.

NEXT WEEK—CRACKER JACK AND HIS WONDER WHIP AGAINST INDIANS ON THE WARPATH.

After reading this story I wonder just how many boys would run around their streets and gardens attempting to crack huge whips made from sticks and lengths of the family washing line? The ending of the story is hardly one a present-day celebrity would seek. Asked by the City Marshal if there was anything he could do, Cracker Jack responds, 'Sure, there's one thing you can do. I won't get any peace after this. Lend me one of your cells for to-night so that the crowd won't bother me.'

All things magical appealed to the readers of the comics. Various stories involving genies who could grant wishes appeared regularly. For *Beano* readers a genie in a bowler hat was a funky variation, guaranteed to bring a laugh. Years later this same scenario would be used in a strip that would become a *Beano* classic called 'Jimmy and His Magic Patch'.

Characters who had magical powers were popular with the office-based comic scriptwriters. If you were stuck on part of your story, a magical happening would often be the way out of an implausible situation. In this first story it enables Hooky to escape a charging bull when the genie gives him a coat of spiky armour! Charles 'Chic' Gordon, from the D. C. Thomson art department, was the illustrator.

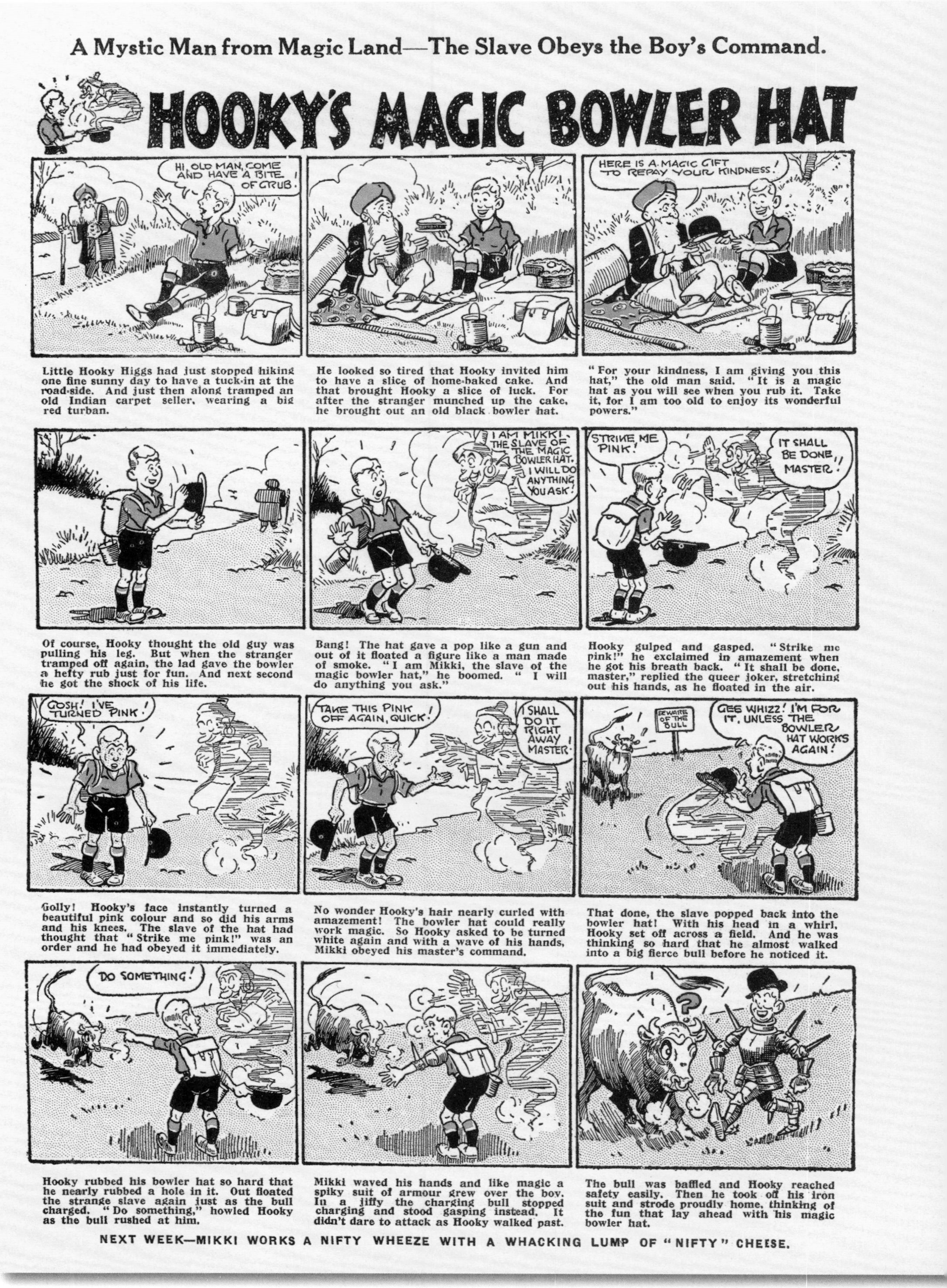
A Mystic Man from Magic Land—The Slave Obeys the Boy's Command.
HOOKY'S MAGIC BOWLER HAT
HI, OLD MAN, COME AND HAVE A BITE OF GRUB!
Little Hooky Higgs had just stopped hiking one fine sunny day to have a tuck-in at the road-side. And just then along tramped an old Indian carpet seller, wearing a big red turban.
He looked so tired that Hooky invited him to have a slice of home-baked cake. And that brought Hooky a slice of luck. For after the stranger munched up the cake, he brought out an old black bowler hat.
HERE IS A MAGIC GIFT TO REPAY YOUR KINDNESS!
"For your kindness, I am giving you this hat," the old man said. "It is a magic hat as you will see when you rub it. Take it, for I am too old to enjoy its wonderful powers."
Of course, Hooky thought the old guy was pulling his leg. But when the stranger tramped off again, the lad gave the bowler a hefty rub just for fun. And next second he got the shock of his life.
I AM MIKKI, THE SLAVE OF THE MAGIC BOWLER HAT. I WILL DO ANYTHING YOU ASK!
Bang! The hat gave a pop like a gun and out of it floated a figure like a man made of smoke. "I am Mikki, the slave of the magic bowler hat," he boomed. "I will do anything you ask."
STRIKE ME PINK!
IT SHALL BE DONE, MASTER!
Hooky gulped and gasped. "Strike me pink!" he exclaimed in amazement when he got his breath back. "It shall be done, master," replied the queer joker, stretching out his hands, as he floated in the air.
GOSH! I'VE TURNED PINK!
Golly! Hooky's face instantly turned a beautiful pink colour and so did his arms and his knees. The slave of the hat had thought that "Strike me pink!" was an order and he had obeyed it immediately.
TAKE THIS PINK OFF AGAIN, QUICK!
I SHALL DO IT RIGHT AWAY MASTER.
No wonder Hooky's hair nearly curled with amazement! The bowler hat could really work magic. So Hooky asked to be turned white again and with a wave of his hands, Mikki obeyed his master's command.
BEWARE OF THE BULL
GEE WHIZZ! I'M FOR IT, UNLESS THE BOWLER HAT WORKS AGAIN!
That done, the slave popped back into the bowler hat! With his head in a whirl, Hooky set off across a field. And he was thinking so hard that he almost walked into a big fierce bull before he noticed it.
DO SOMETHING!
Hooky rubbed his bowler hat so hard that he nearly rubbed a hole in it. Out floated the strange slave again just as the bull charged. "Do something," howled Hooky as the bull rushed at him.
Mikki waved his hands and like magic a spiky suit of armour grew over the boy. In a jiffy the charging bull stopped charging and stood gasping instead. It didn't dare to attack as Hooky walked past.
The bull was baffled and Hooky reached safety easily. Then he took off his iron suit and strode proudly home, thinking of the fun that lay ahead with his magic bowler hat.
NEXT WEEK—MIKKI WORKS A NIFTY WHEEZE WITH A WHACKING LUMP OF "NIFTY" CHEESE.

Tell Your Mum, Tell Your Pa—Jimmy Green's His Own Grandma!

THE WANGLES OF GRANNY GREEN

The Three Sneaks

JIMMY GREEN peeped cautiously through the attic window of his cottage. Down below in the lane he could see three boys tip-toeing about.

"There they go again," growled Jimmy. "Sneaking about spying on me. Then they'll go home to tell their mothers just what I'm doing. I don't want their mothers to look after me! They're interfering busybodies. Can't they leave me alone?"

Though only eleven years old, Jimmy lived by himself in Ash Cottage on the outskirts of Middleton. His mother was dead and his father was an engineer whose job took him away for long periods. Mr Green had gone away on another job only ten days before. He couldn't take Jimmy with him, because Jimmy had to attend school.

Things were all right until some of the mothers in the town got it into their heads that it wasn't proper for a schoolboy to be living alone. And they were terribly keen to act the part of parents to Jimmy and look after him.

The boys out in the lane were Sneaky Thorpe, Reg Clinton and Ginger Nutting—and their mothers were among those who pestered Jimmy most.

"It's time the sneaks were getting home," growled Jimmy, drawing his catapult from his pocket. Fitting a pebble into the sling, Jimmy took careful aim.

Wham! Sneaky Thorpe jumped a clear three feet into the air with a howl.

"I'll tell my mother you're just a ruffian, Green!" he bellowed.

"Oh, yeah!" Jimmy leaned out as far as he could, and jeered at Sneaky and his pals. "Run home, you dirty spies, and tell your mothers that my Granny is coming to look after me. She'll be arriving by the two o'clock train from London to-day."

"That's just bluff, Green," Sneaky replied. "We'll be at the station, just to see if your Granny does arrive."

When they turned the corner into Main Street, Jimmy withdrew his head.

"Well, I've done it now," he muttered. "To-day, I'll know whether or not my idea is going to work. If it works—then I'll have the funniest grandmother in the world."

It was a strange remark for Jimmy to make, because he didn't have a grandmother! But what he did mean was that he was going to invent a grandmother. He was going to disguise himself as one!

For a whole week Jimmy had thought about this brilliant idea of his.

It was the clothes in the old tin trunk in the attic that had given him the idea.

Now he pulled the big, dusty trunk over to the window and got the lid open. It was full to the top with clothes.

"Just what the doctor ordered!" he chuckled, as he pulled some of them out. He scrambled into the heavy black skirt that swirled around his ankles, then draped a flowing cape around his shoulders and pulled on an old-fashioned poke bonnet. There was also a grey wig and a pair of steel-rimmed spectacles.

Jimmy ran to the bedroom—almost tripping headlong as his feet caught in the skirt—and then had another look at himself in the mirror. There was grease-paint lying handy. He used it to sketch a few wrinkles on his face. In less than a minute he wasn't a schoolboy any longer. He was Granny Green!

After a time, Jimmy, dressed as Granny Green, slipped round to the railway station a minute or two before the train from London was due in. He hid in the waiting room until the train pulled in, then left the station by the main door.

Just outside, Sneaky and his pals were standing, watching the people leaving the train. Jimmy hesitated a moment, made sure that his disguise was in perfect order, then went over to the boys.

Granny's First Wangle

"DO any of you boys know my grandson, Jimmy Green?" he asked, in a squeaky, wheezing voice, gripping tight the umbrella and basket in his hand. "I expected him to be meeting me here."

Sneaky winked at his pals.

"You'll be Granny Green," he said. "Jimmy told us about you. We're his pals. We'll take you to where he lives."

So Jimmy, hobbling slowly and stiffly, went down the road with Sneaky and his friends. When Sneaky turned into a little-used lane that led to Ash Cottage by a long, roundabout way, Jimmy guessed it was Sneaky's idea to get Granny Green in a quiet place, then begin to torment her.

They came to a bridge, which crossed the canal. Pretending to be tired, Jimmy leaned over the wall.

"Look down there!" he pointed a gloved hand at the water. "There's a fish!"

The boys beside him leaned over, too, craning their necks. They couldn't see any fish, but continued to peer down into the depths of the water.

Jimmy stepped back a pace, lifted his skirt a trifle, raised his foot, and gave Sneaky Thorpe a kick on the seat of his pants. Sneaky gave a howl and turned quickly, but not quickly enough to spot Jimmy's move. Granny Green was already leaning over the wall again.

Sneaky wheeled on Ginger Nutting, who stood next to him. He gave Ginger a hefty kick, and Ginger was about to hit him back when Granny took a hand.

"Now, now, boys, you mustn't fight!" Granny Green wagged a finger at them, and they contented themselves with glaring at each other.

"I'll go on to Ash Cottage myself," said Jimmy, a minute or two later. "Just tell me how to get there."

"We'll take you there," growled Sneaky. "We're passing the very door."

"All right," Jimmy squeaked. "You're being very kind to an old woman Here is a pear for each of you."

Luckily, there was a bag of pears in the basket, rather over-ripe ones that Jimmy had felt would come in useful as ammunition for his catapult. He gave the boys one each, and they took them greedily.

Then, just a few hundred yards further along, Jimmy saw a well-known and heartily disliked figure come striding down the road. It was Captain Moffat, a surly bully, who lived at the other end of Green Lane. The Captain's bulldog trotted along at his heels.

Sneaky and his pals contentedly munched their pears. Under his cape, Jimmy had another pear in his hand. He slowed down so that he was slightly behind the three boys, and waited until Captain Moffat had passed.

Then Jimmy turned. He threw the pear full at the Captain's head. It landed on his red neck and seemed to burst like a bomb.

With a roar that might have come from a man-eating lion, Captain Moffat turned. He had seen the boys eating pears, and naturally he was sure that one of them had thrown the pear at him. Waving his stick and shouting threats, he rushed towards Sneaky and his companions.

"You young rips!" he stormed. "I'll teach you! I'll break this stick over your backs!"

Sneaky and the two others didn't wait to argue. They got off the mark like crack sprinters. The Captain did not dash after them, but sent his dog. Soon, the boys and the pursuing dog were lost in a cloud of dust.

"Bah! Don't know what boys are coming to!" Captain Moffat remarked to Granny Green, wiping his neck and collar.

In his squeaky voice, Jimmy muttered some sort of a reply. Then he went on his way. He had got his own back on an old enemy—and also got rid of Sneaky Thorpe and his pals! Which wasn't bad going, thought Jimmy, grinning to himself. Granny Green was certainly a useful sort of person to have around!

Granny Green hits a policeman with a ripe tomato next week.

A young person who could dress up and impersonate his own granny to thwart authority was another scenario that comics used again and again. I last saw it used in 'Beryl the Peril' in *The Dandy* sometime around 2004. In this comic text version, Granny Green, a.k.a. 11-year-old Jimmy Green, manages to stay independent and outwit his sneaky pals with the help of some old clothes and grease paint. Jimmy, being master in his own house and putting one over on sneaks and authority, would be an inspirational bedtime read. The little illustration is by Chic Gordon.

This double page of six separate strips copies the modern-looking layout that *The Dandy* had introduced several months before. The mix of different artists gives the spread a busy look, almost a cartoon section within the comic. The strips were drawn in black and white, then, with a colour pencil, a colourist would mark on the page where the red or black stipple effects should be placed by the print department. For a more colourful look, the blacks would be printed in blue, known in Thomson's as bronze blue.

WEE PEEM
HE'S A PROPER SCREAM
"THROW AWAY THAT CIGAR AT ONCE, SIR!"
"DISGRACEFUL! A BOY OF YOUR AGE SMOKING —"
BANG
"GIVE ME THAT BOX!"
"CONSTABLE! SEE IF HE HAS ANY MORE OF THOSE CIGARS."
LITTLE DEAD-EYE DICK
HE'S A FUN-MAN AND A GUN-MAN
HAIRY DAN
HOW DAN WON THE RACE WITH HIS HAIRY FACE
I GUESS I'LL ENTER FOR THAT
GRAND SAILING BOAT RACE
TOMORROW
BIG PRIZES
THE NEXT DAY
START
READY — STEADY — GO!
GUST
SNAP
?
WOW
PHEW! THAT WAS SOME GUST — EVERYBODY'S LOST THEIR SAILS. I KNOW — I'LL TIE MY BEARD TO THE OLD MAST AND THIS OAR!
!
WHOOPEE! MY BEARD MAKES A FINE SAIL
FINISH
HURRAH!
ALL YOURS FOR A GRAND WIN

YOU CAN'T PLAY A JOKE ON MARY THE MOKE
CONTRARY MARY
COME BACK HERE!
OH DEAR! I DONT KNOW WHAT TO DO. THE REGIMENT'S MASCOT HAS RUN AWAY, AND THERE'S AN INSPECTION THIS AFTERNOON
IDEA
TO THE BARRACKS
WAIT TILL THE GENERAL MISSES THE MASCOT
MY GOODNESS! OUR MASCOT'S GROWING. GOOD WORK CORPORAL. TAKE A DAY OFF!
A CLEVER WHEEZE FOR CATCHING BEES
SMILER THE SWEEPER
LOOK OUT SMILER, RUN FOR YOUR LIFE!
BUZZ-Z
BUZZ-Z
WOW! A SWARM OF BEES!
SWOOSH-H
I'LL SUCK THE BEES INTO MY VACUUM CLEANER
FLIES?
BEE FARM
HONK-K!
BUZZ-Z-Z
BUZZ-Z
FIVE BOB!
JUST TOO BAD FOR HENRY'S DAD
HELPFUL HENRY
HELLO, DAD. MAKING A CRAZY PAVING PATH?
YES, HENRY. I ONLY WANT A FEW MORE LARGE STONES TO BREAK UP TO FINISH IT
LET ME BORROW THE WHEELBARROW DAD, AND I'LL GET YOU SOME
HERE'S ONE LOT. I'LL SLIP BACK AND GET SOME MORE.
THERE YOU ARE, HENRY. THE PATH'S FINISHED. YOU WERE A GREAT HELP GETTING THOSE STONES FOR ME.
OI! YOU COME ALONG TO THE POLICE STATION WITH ME!
STEAL THE PAVING STONES WOULD YOU!
SO THAT'S WHERE HENRY GOT THE STONES FROM!

All the comic scripts were written by the young staff writers, and six artists were used. 'Wee Peem' was drawn by James Jewell; 'Little Dead-Eye Dick' by Charles Holt; 'Hairy Dan' by Basil Blackaller; 'Contrary Mary' by Roland Davies; 'Smiler the Sweeper' by Steve Perkins; and 'Helpful Henry' by Eric Roberts.

Of the six strips, 'Hairy Dan' would run continuously for the longest time, until 1946. 'Little Dead-Eye Dick' initially lasted only 20 weeks but he reappeared in 1949 for two more short series, taking him into the 1950s.

Another short story in which magic and the granting of wishes once again holds the key. Jack Glass drew the illustration at the top of the page. 'The Wishing Tree' was popular as there was a sequel immediately after this first series ended in 1939. It was titled 'Acorns From the Wishing Tree'. Wishes would be granted if you came into possession of an acorn from the tree, giving much greater scope for the script writer, who no longer had to work with a tree that remained rooted in one place. The heading illustration on the sequel would be the first time *Beano* readers saw the artwork of Jack Prout, a young staff artist who would become very well known as the pen behind ***The Dandy*** classic, 'Black Bob'. Also of note was the way the sequel ended in October 1939. Wartime paper shortages meant that, with very little notice, ***The Beano*** had to cut its page count, so without any warning 'Acorns From the Wishing Tree' vanished before the story was completed.

Reprinted stories from this first series appeared in the weekly *Beano* in 1946 and also in the 1959 *Beano Book*.

Make a Wish at the Wishing Tree—And Lo! Your Wish Will Answered Be!

THE WISHING TREE

The Two Wishes

THE Wishing Tree grew on the moor not far from the town. It was an old, old oak tree with twisted branches, and patches of moss grew on the gnarled trunk. To many people who passed that way the trunk of the tree looked like the face of a very old man.

Johnny Gray didn't know anything about the tree when he came to visit his grandmother, who lived just outside the small town that had sprung up beside the moor. Johnny's home was in the town of Swinbourne on the other side of the moor.

As they were walking along the lane towards her cottage on the outskirts of the town, the old lady pointed out the tree.

"That's the Wishing Tree," she said mysteriously. "Very few people know about it. They say that if you touch the tree and wish, whatever you wish for will be granted."

"You don't expect me to believe that, Grandma," said Johnny, whose father was a police sergeant. "That's silly."

The bright little eyes of the old lady twinkled.

"Well, believe it or not," she said wisely, "but be careful what you wish near that tree, Johnny!"

They reached the cottage and Mrs Gray went in to prepare tea, leaving Johnny to play with his marbles on the smooth garden path. Somehow Johnny could not get the Wishing Tree out of his mind.

Finally, he slipped away from the cottage and trotted up to the corner of the moor where the old tree stood.

"What will I wish for?" he wondered.

He thought of asking for a new bicycle, or a cricket bat, but he felt he was being too greedy, and in any case the whole thing seemed silly. Then he had an idea, for he remembered that just before he had left home his father had told him he was hunting for a burglar who had robbed some big houses nearby.

He put his hand on the rough bark of the tree and closed his eyes. Then he whispered, "I wish that Dad could capture the thief who did the burglary last night."

It might have been a trick of the wind, but as Johnny finished his wish—the branches of the tree dipped and swayed and he backed away in alarm.

Then his heart gave a jump as a heavy hand clamped on his shoulder and he turned quickly to see a man rising from the clump of bushes behind him.

"What's your game?" he growled suspiciously.

"N-Nothing!" stuttered Johnny.

"You were doing something," growled the man, as he grabbed the boy by the arm and twisted it. "Come on, now," he went on. "What were you doing to that tree?"

"I was just making a wish, mister. It's a Wishing Tree. You touch it, make a wish, and then it's granted. Let go my arm, you're hurting me, you big brute."

The stranger cuffed Johnny's ear and gave him a push that almost sent him sprawling on his face.

"Beat it!" he snarled, and then as Johnny moved off the stranger looked at the tree doubtfully.

"Bloomin' childish nonsense," he grunted. "But I'll try it. I've got to do something."

His hand touched the tree.

"I wish that I had—— " He hesitated and glanced at the wild stretch of moor again. "I wish I had a horse to get off this bloomin' place! I don't want a car, because I'd have to drive it on the roads, and the roads— Lummy!"

The big fellow jumped like a startled rabbit as the spreading branches above his head swayed in mysterious fashion.

"What was that?" he whispered. "I'm gettin' the wind up. This place gives me the creeps."

Then suddenly over the rise cantered a horse. It was a fine, glossy animal and there was a saddle on its back and a bit in its mouth. It shied at the sight of the man and then came to a dead stop.

Caught by a Horse

THE man gaped, shut his eyes, and looked again, but the horse was still there. He blinked as he walked away from the tree, looking at it in awed fashion over his shoulder. Then he gingerly stepped forward and put his hand on the horse.

"It's real!" he muttered. "That Wishing Tree really works."

He put one foot in the stirrup and vaulted into the saddle. Then he gathered up the reins. His thin lips twisted into a grin as he gave the horse a slap with his hand, but the grin faded as the animal went forward with a violent bound.

Across the moor it thundered, with the big fellow hanging on for dear life, scared to jump off.

The horse cleared a low hedge and the rider's feet were jerked out of the stirrups. The man clung on like grim death and screamed threats, which didn't have any effect. Then he tried to get hold of the reins and pull the animal round, but it had the bit between its teeth and there was no stopping it.

Finally the horse jumped down a bank into the lane and tore off in the direction of the main road and the town of Swinbourne. It had crossed the moor. The speed was so great that the man could only hang on, his eyes wide with fear.

Past the little houses outside the town they went at full speed. People turned in the streets to stare, but nobody tried to stop the runaway. The galloping animal turned a corner and kicked up its heels like a racehorse on the final stretch.

At the end of the street was a building with official-looking notices stuck up in the windows. Above the door were the words "County Police," and it was here that the horse finally decided to stop.

It stopped so suddenly that the unfortunate rider went straight over its head and floundered on his face at the feet of a large police sergeant, who was just leaving the station.

The sergeant looked at the horse and recognised it immediately.

"Constable Roberts' horse!" he exclaimed.

Then he bent down to pick up the groaning man on the ground.

"How did you get hold of this police horse?" he demanded.

Then he gave a gasp and looked closer at the man.

"Why, you're the fellow we want!" roared the sergeant. "You're the crook who broke into the big house last night!"

"Lemme go!" yelled the man. "It's all a mistake. It ain't true!"

"What about this, my lad?" demanded the sergeant, and he pulled a string of pearls from the fellow's pocket. "In you get!" he said, as he ran him into the station.

* * * * * * *

When Johnny Gray came back from his visit to his grandmother the next day, he found his father, Sergeant Gray, looking very pleased.

"We caught the burglar, sonny!" chuckled the sergeant. "And you would never believe how it happened. The crook fell off a horse right at my feet. It was Constable Roberts' horse. The horse threw Roberts on the moor and it must have been wandering about on its own when the burglar grabbed hold of it, thinking he could make a getaway."

"You captured the burglar, Dad?" Johnny gasped. "Then—then, it's true! The tree does grant wishes!"

"What tree?" demanded Sergeant Gray. He listened to the tale and laughed.

"Rubbish!" he said. "It was just a lucky chance. Your Grandma shouldn't fill your head with such tales."

But Johnny thinks to this day that the Wishing Tree caught the crook. What do you think?

Next week, two bad boys go to the Wishing Tree—and their wishes come true in a way they don't expect!

He Hasn't Been Weighed Since the Age of Three
—The Weighing-Machine Always Broke, You See.
BIG FAT JOE
1 TON OF FUN
COME ON IN JOE!
OK! I'LL GET MY BATHING COSTUME!
OPEN AIR SWIMMING POOL
HAW! HAW! WHAT FUN!!
HEE! HEE!
OPEN AIR SWIMMING POOL
HE WON'T LET US SWIM - THE NASTY BULLY!
OH!
GREAT SCOT! LOOK AT THE BABY ELEPHANT!
SWOOSH!
OPEN AIR SWIMMING POOL
GROO!!
OPEN AIR SWIMMING POOL
O.K! NOW BOYS!
NEXT WEEK—JOE SITS DOWN ON A WOODEN SEAT. A FUNNIER SIGHT IT'S HARD TO BEAT.

For the first *Beano* this is a more traditional set, both in layout and content, drawn by the Scarborough-based artist Allan Morley, who was anchorman for all D. C. Thomson's cartoon ventures at that time. R. D. Low described Morley as a 'fun factory', as he was so reliable and prolific, and wondered what would become of the comics without him. Later, Allan would be allowed to sign his work, albeit with just his initials, a mark of recognition allowed to very few Thomson artists. The character 'Big Fat Joe' would last for no more than nine months, but he reappeared as one of the gang of pals who lived with Lord Snooty in Bunkerton Castle when the 'Snooty' strip was refreshed in 1950.

derring-do with four plucky castaways, adrift on the sea – two spoilt children, Cyril and Ethel Kidd, Mickey, assistant to the ship's cook, and Big Bill Thomson 'who knew all there was to know about sailing'. This story was a lesson on how to produce maximum excitement for kids in 2,000 words or so. The drama and danger deepened from paragraph to paragraph. It was the type of story the young readers were used to seeing at the matinee cinema shows.

Four Castaways Lost in a Strange Land!

THE SHIPWRECKED KIDDS

The Terrible Storm

IN the dining-saloon on board the splendid steam yacht, "Swallow," a boy of about ten was sitting at a table with a girl who was slightly younger. They were Cyril Kidd and his sister, Ethel, the children of the yacht's wealthy owner. Both kids were looking very peevish, and presently Cyril jabbed his finger against the electric bell push. Then with a nasty grin, he kept the bell ringing.

"I'll make those blooming servants jump to it when we're ready for our dinner," he snorted.

Ethel nodded her head, laughing as she heard the distant buzzing of the bell, which was meant to call Mickey Swift, the young assistant to the ship's cook.

At that minute, Mickey was in the kitchen on the yacht, dishing up soup. The cook had gone ashore, like most of the people on the yacht, and Mickey had been left to get dinner for Cyril and Ethel.

At last he went trotting along with his tray to the saloon. When he went in, the two children glared at him.

"Why didn't you come quicker?" demanded Cyril. "I'll tell dad about you when he comes on board."

Mr Kidd, the millionaire owner of the Swallow, had gone ashore with his guests and most of the crew. There were only four people on board the yacht at the moment—Cyril, Ethel, Mickey and Big Bill Thomson, a sailor, who knew all there was to know about sailing.

"If I'd been any quicker, I wouldn't have been able to bring your soup," said Mickey. "You see, it wouldn't have been ready."

"Don't answer back!" snapped Cyril, who, like Ethel, had been spoilt by his father. Anything they wanted, they were allowed to have, and they expected their orders to be obeyed instantly.

"Oosh!" gurgled Ethel, who had burnt her tongue with the soup. "What did you make it so hot for?"

"Why did you make it at all?" demanded Cyril. "I believe it is the water you washed the dishes in—that's what it tastes like."

In spite of their grumbling, the two children lapped up the soup quickly. When it was finished, Mickey picked up the empty plates and darted off.

On the way to the kitchen Mickey met a big, bronzed sailor. It was Big Bill Thomson who had come below to talk to him.

"I'm fed up with these two kids," said the boy

"They certainly think a lot of themselves," remarked Bill. "That's because they get too much of their own way. I guess they aren't bad kids at heart, but Mr Kidd treats them like a duke and duchess, so what do you expect?"

"Gosh!" snorted Mickey as a buzzing sound began. "They've started ringing that bell again. I'm off, Bill. Just grab your own grub."

In the kitchen the big sailor helped himself to some food. Then he returned on deck, and gazed towards the low-lying shore. He had been below only a few minutes, but during that short time the weather had changed almost as if by magic.

A mighty gust of wind hit the yacht, which was moored to a wooden quay, making her heel over. In a few seconds, the blue sky had become overcast with great black banks of clouds. Gust after gust of terrific wind lashed the sea into great foaming breakers. Then Bill Thomson's eyes filled with horror. Out of the distance a strange funnel-shaped cloud was rushing towards the yacht with the speed of a bullet.

"Hurricane!" yelled the big sailor, leaping into action.

Before the storm hit the Swallow, Big Bill jumped to the hatchways and slammed some of them down. Then next minute the yacht seemed to be picked up by a huge hand and hurled forward. Big Bill was flung to the deck, and down in the kitchen Mickey Swift found himself on the floor in a heap of broken crockery.

As Bill climbed to his feet and battled his way against the howling wind, he saw that the storm's first mighty blast had snapped the Swallow's mooring ropes like pieces of thread. Now the yacht was sweeping out to sea at terrific speed.

Setting his teeth, Bill ran along the lurching deck. From the dining-saloon, he could hear the frightened screams of Ethel and Cyril, who were being tossed about wildly.

But Bill paid no attention to their calls for help. Instead, he climbed to the bridge and grabbed the swinging wheel.

Breaker after breaker swept over the Swallow, roaring along her deck, smashing her boats, carrying away all loose tackle, flinging her about as if she was a cork. Big Bill clung to the wheel, but he knew it was hopeless. The steering gear was smashed, and it was only his great strength which kept him from being swept over into the sea.

Like great hammers the mighty waves dealt the yacht blow after blow, and she was driven on and on hour after hour.

Down in the saloon Big Bill found Mickey Swift with Ethel and Cyril. All three were badly bruised and they were hanging on to a pillar while broken furniture slid all over the place.

Adrift on a Raft

ON through the darkness of the night the ship was hurled by the mighty seas, until towards dawn the storm died down a little. Then Big Bill left the saloon. Very soon he came back, but his face was grave and set for he was bringing bad news.

"There's a leak in the hold. Water is coming in fast!" he said. "She'll sink. But we've still got a chance, though."

When daylight broke, the sea was still raging. And Bill and Mickey worked with all their might making a raft of petrol drums and spars.

At last the great waves died down, and the wind stopped whistling and screaming, but by now the Swallow was so low in the water that her deck was almost level [illegible] sea.

[illegible] launching the raft, Bill and Mickey and [illegible] and a small tank of water on it.

Then with the help of Cyril and Ethel, they searched for anything that would be useful and heaped the stuff on the raft, too.

At last the Swallow gave a dangerous lurch. Quickly Bill ordered the youngsters aboard, pushed the raft off with an oar, and began to row with all his might.

Just in time the raft got clear. They were no more than fifty yards from the Swallow when, with a great sucking roar, the yacht vanished under the surface. Cyril and Ethel stared moodily at where the vessel had been, and then the boy screwed up his face.

"You two are going to get in a row for that, when dad catches you," he said, gazing at Big Bill and Mickey. "I'm hungry—get me something to eat!"

"Feed them, Mickey!" said Bill, and the lad opened a tin of beef.

While the two children were eating, Mickey and Bill lay down, and were fast asleep in a moment. Ethel stared at them in angry amazement.

"Well, I never!" she exclaimed. "They didn't wait to see if we wanted anything more to eat or drink. What impudence!"

The spoilt children did not realise the danger they were in even now. They kept on grumbling while they ate. After the meal, they became drowsy and they slept, too. When they awoke later in the day, they found they were in the middle of a smooth and empty sea.

Mickey was making a meal, and Big Bill since he had nothing to do, was amusing himself by slinging a knife at a target he had rigged up.

When at length he spoke, it was to Mickey, who had managed to prepare a tasty feed.

"You're a marvel, son," said Bill. "We're mighty grateful to you. Aren't we?" he added, glancing at the children.

"What for?" snapped Cyril. "It's his job."

"How much longer are you going to keep us out here on this silly thing?" demanded Ethel presently, turning up her nose as she stared round the raft.

Big Bill did not speak. He turned away, and got busy making a mast and sail out of a spar and a bit of canvas.

In silence Big Bill finished his task, which he had done so well that the raft was driven along briskly by the fresh breeze. He set the sail, and then began his knife-throwing again. The boy and girl watched him, and saw the queer tattooing on his bare arms. Then all at once, both Ethel and Cyril got the strange feeling that Big Bill Thomson was no ordinary sailor.

Just why they thought so, they would have found it hard to explain. But it was probably because in the last twenty-four hours everything had changed so much. No longer was Big Bill just one of the crew—now he was the man on whom everything depended.

Big Bill and Mickey found plenty to say to each other. But neither said much to Cyril or Ethel, who sat together, with sulky looks on their faces. Suddenly Mickey saw Bill stare at the sea, then at the sky, and then at the sail.

"By gosh!" exclaimed the sailor. "We're not going with the wind, Mickey! Look!"

Sure enough, the wind was coming from the west, but the raft was travelling south. Faster and faster, she sped in the grip of a powerful current. Nothing could be done to alter the raft's course, and Bill lowered the useless sail. Then hour after hour the raft was swept along at great speed.

"Land!" shouted Bill suddenly, pointing to a dim line that stretched away on the horizon ahead. The current was carrying them towards this and Bill told them that they were being taken towards the mainland. At last they saw looming before them a wall of high, rocky cliffs dropping sheer to the sea.

On and on rushed the raft towards the cliffs. Then Big Bill gasped in amazement. He had just spotted a great black hole in the rock into which the powerful current streamed.

"Gosh," he cried. "We're going to be swept into that cave. And we can't raise a finger to stop the raft."

The Lake of Doom

BIG BILL was right. They could do nothing. Had they jumped off the raft into the sea, the current would have swept them along in its grip just the same.

They just sat still, staring wide-eyed, until the racing current carried them up to the dark, tunnel-like opening in the cliffs. Then, with a mad rush, the raft was swept inside, under the curving rock roof and into the gloom.

"Hang on!" shouted Bill, who feared that the raft would be dashed against the walls of the mysterious tunnel, and would overturn. But the force of the current kept the bobbing raft in midstream, and it was swept on through pitch darkness.

For a space that seemed like hours they were whizzed along by the surging water. Then all of a sudden, they saw a pin-point of light ahead, and a shout of relief broke from all four of them. Bigger and bigger grew the light. It was the end of the tunnel and the raft was swept out into a stretch of queer dark water.

The castaways found themselves on a gloomy lake. All round it there grew thick, green jungle except on the side where a great rock wall towered—the rock wall under which they had just sailed.

"Now where have you brought us?" wailed Ethel, as if Bill and Mickey were to blame.

Neither answered, for they were too busy staring round the strange lake. Then suddenly a wild shout broke from Bill's lips, as he pointed ahead. There they saw a strange dip in the water which was spinning round in foaming circles.

"Whirlpool!" roared Bill, grabbing the oar.

Already the raft had been gripped by the swing of the water on the outer edge of the whirlpool, and it went spinning round in a wide sweep. Big Bill dug the oar deep into the water.

"Grab a plank and row, Mickey!" he yelled. "Quick, or we'll be sucked into the centre of the pool and drowned."

Using every ounce of his strength, Big Bill dug his oar deeper, and a gasp of relief left his lips.

"We're out!" he panted, sinking back and wiping the sweat off his face as the raft was driven into quiet water.

Then he blinked with astonishment. He had just seen that Ethel and Cyril had been using planks to drive the raft out of danger. If it hadn't been for their help, all four might have been sucked into the whirlpool and drowned.

"So they've got something in them, after all," Big Bill said to himself with a quiet grin.

Then suddenly a whirring noise was heard, like the rushing of a great wind, and the four castaways stared up at the sky, to see a startling sight.

From the top of the line of cliffs a great flock of seagulls came swooping towards the raft. At least, they looked like sea-gulls, but they were immense birds, almost as big as eagles.

They opened their sharp beaks as they dived, and a dreadful screaming broke the stillness. Mickey and Big Bill got ready to defend the raft with chunks of wood. As the giant birds swooped, Big Bill spotted the top of a petrol drum, which he knew to be half empty. It was tied to the raft, and as fast as he could Bill wrenched off the lid.

"Down," he howled, striking a match. "Get down!" And as Mickey and the two children dropped flat on their faces, Bill tossed the lighted match into the petrol drum and hurled himself flat, too.

Just as the terrible birds, with their gaping beaks and cruel talons, were within a few feet of the raft, the petrol caught fire. In a split second there was a thunderous explosion, and a great spout of flame was flung skywards.

Many of the flying brutes were killed by the searing flame and many were so badly scorched that they dropped into the water to be snatched below by strange fish. Screaming in terror, what was left of the flock wheeled and flew back to the cliffs.

However, splashes of blazing petrol had dropped on the raft and the wood began to burn. Bill jumped to put out the flames, but Cyril got there before him. Dipping a lump of canvas in the water, the boy swiftly dropped it over the flames and smothered them.

A grin of pleasure lit Big Bill's face.

"Yes, he's surely got something in him," he said, under his breath. "Maybe I'll be able to make a man out of him!"

Then his gaze shifted to the dark jungle, towards which the raft was drifting, and he wondered what unknown perils were hidden in its gloomy depths.

A fight with the monster of lost lake, next week.

The Dandy had a castaway story in their first edition too, 'Lost on the Mountain of Fear', only their family were not shipwrecked but were in a plane wreck instead. Again we see *The Beano* content influenced by what had proved popular in *The Dandy*.

In the 1960s Editor George Moonie used this title again when he edited the girls' paper ***Judy.*** The heading illustration is again by Jack Glass.

Rip Van Wink not only slept for 700 years, but he also appeared in the comic for a very long time too. This first series ran for 10 years until mid-1948. Londoner Eric Roberts produced the artwork for the first few years continuously and then staff artist James Crighton took over. A further 10 years on and a second series of 'Rip' appeared, this time a mix of Eric Roberts reprints and sets from a new artist called Gordon Bell, a good way to evaluate a new talent.

'Rip Van Wink' had a traditional layout with speech bubbles and captions in rhyme. The writers agonised over this type of story, as often the gags would be compromised because of the need to get words to rhyme. Even the plug for the next week's story is in rhyme at the bottom of the page.

Poor Rip Van Wink is All at Sea, There's Something Wrong, He Fears.
He Doesn't Know He's Been Asleep for Seven Hundred Years!
RIP VAN WINK
ZZZZZZZ
Y-Y-YAWN!
GADZOOKS! I HAVE A MIGHTY HUNGER!
In a little cave, on a slab of rock,
Sleeps Rip Van Wink, and he'll get a shock
When he finds that instead of a simple nap
He's dozed for centuries—poor chap!
Suddenly Rip Van's body shakes—
He rubs his eyes and then awakes.
Will he find out the secret deep
That all those years he's been asleep?
Van Wink feels hungry, and so would you
If you had slept for centuries, too!
So he seizes his bow that's made of yew
And goes out in search of venison stew.
OUCH!!
SORRY, SIRE, I THOUGHT YOU WERE A DEER AND I'M HUNGRY – I MUST HAVE SLEPT RATHER LONG LAST NIGHT
Away in the distance Rip spots a deer
With its spreading antlers—a target clear.
An arrow to his bow Rip fits,
The deer is doomed—Rip always hits.
The deer a hiker proves to be,
And Rip has hit him, you can see.
Perhaps he'll knock Van Wink to bits,
For Rip has plugged him where he sits.
"My lord, your pardon I must crave,"
Poor Rip Van Wink begins to rave.
"I thought you were a fine big deer."
"Oho!" the hiker thought. "That's queer."
YOU LOOK AS THOUGH YOU'VE BEEN ASLEEP FOR YEARS! WHEN DID YOU GO TO BED?
ER-LET ME SEE I REMEMBER THE DATE. IT WAS ON THE 24TH OF JULY IN THE YEAR 1238!
BLIMEY! – NO WONDER YOU'RE HUNGRY! THIS IS THE YEAR 1938! HERE TAKE THIS BEEF AND A COUPLE OF, BANANAS
BEEF
QUEER HARD BEEF HE GAVE ME! MAYBE IF I COOK IT. IT'LL BE ALL RIGHT
BEEF
"I'm glad you only use a bow,"
The hiker said. "Because, you know,
If you had fired a gun at me,
I would be dead as dead can be."
The queer word "gun" to Rip meant nix.
He said, "For food I'm in a fix."
So the hiker, murmuring, "O K. chief!"
Produced two bananas and a can of beef.
The hiker went away at last,
And Rip began to break his fast.
The meat to him seemed rather tough,
So he lit a fire to cook the stuff.
UGH! THAT VARLET CALLED THESE THINGS BANANAS. THEY HAVE A MIGHTY BAD TASTE.
BANG!
Then Wink did something never seen
Before in all that forest green—
Cooking roast beef with the tin on
And eating banana with the skin on.
Meanwhile the fire was waxing hot,
The roast beef wasn't in a pot,
But in its tin, which swelled and burst,
And hurled Van Wink sky-high, head first.
When Rip Van Wink came back to earth
He gave the fire a real wide berth,
Then ran as if his life to save,
And vanished once more in his cave.
NEXT WEEK RIP MAKES MISTAKES IN PLENTY. LOOK OUT FOR HIM UPON PAGE TWENTY.

The Great Story of a Clever Sheepdog.

MY DOG SANDY

The Bad Master

SANDY was a pure-bred Border Collie, and as clever at handling sheep as any dog. In fact, he was too clever and willing for big Sam Watkins, his rough and loud-mouthed master. Watkins had a small-sized sheep farm but he was also a dealer. He was excitable and liked things done in a hurry, and when they didn't go to suit him his brutal temper usually got the better of him.

Watkins was driving a flock of sheep through a little county town with Sandy helping him, when bad luck overtook him. Behind him, round the corner of the street, a bell began to clang loudly, and Sam Watkins began to yell like blue murder.

The more the big shepherd shouted, the more puzzled Sandy became, and he paused for clearer directions. Next thing he knew, a big red fire-engine, with clanging bell, was thundering down the narrow street straight for the flock.

True to his training, Sandy raced in front of the sheep and kept them from galloping ahead of the fire-engine. That seemed to the dog to be the right thing to do, and it was the right thing to do.

The driver of the fire-engine was excited, however, and so were the sheep. They scattered all over the narrow street and Sam Watkins' wild shouting only made them more frightened. Two sheep were hit and killed instantly before the fire-engine got past the flock.

Had it not been for Sandy, the Border Collie, more sheep would have been run down. But all he got for doing his duty was a thrashing.

"You stupid brute!" roared big Sam Watkins, in one of his wild rages. "I'll teach you!"

He caught Sandy, and kicked the dog savagely until several good-hearted people interfered, and caused him to let go the dog.

"I'll kill the brute, if ever I get my hands on it again!" yelled the dealer, shaking his fiist at Sandy, as the little sheep dog slipped away down the street.

"I can believe that!" remarked one of the men who had stopped his cruelty, "I hope you never do get your hands on the dog again, Watkins!"

Cruelly beaten and aching all over, Sandy decided that he would rather die in a ditch than go back to his cruel master. Paying no attention to the shouts and whistles of the dealer, who now wanted the willing little dog back, Sandy raced up a side street.

He kept on going until the fear of his former master began to leave him.

For the rest of that day, poor Sandy hung around the outskirts of the town. One or two men spoke to him, but he always dodged away from them. Night came, and, hungry and tired, he crept into a big yard and slept behind some barrels.

Early in the morning, he set out again. He was very hungry, and when he saw pails of rubbish sitting in the street, waiting to be carted away, he was glad to pick bones and crusts out of some of them. That was all the food he got that day.

Sandy Finds a Friend

SANDY spent the next night—and a miserable one it was—in a lane. Morning came, and with it a cold rain. The wandering dog was soon soaked, but he kept prowling around the little town, looking for something to eat.

A group of boys, on the way to school, spied him, and one of them gave a yell.

"That's the stray dog!" he shouted.

Picking up stones, the boys started to chase Sandy. A stone hit the poor dog. He gave a yelp of pain. More stones were thrown at him. To escape the crowd of howling boys, Sandy bolted up a lane, but found it had a blind end. Trapped, he did his best to dodge the stones hurled by the senseless boys, who were now grouped around the opening of the lane.

Suddenly Sandy heard the bleating of sheep, and a moment or two later a flock went past the open end of the lane.

A tall shepherd from the hills was driving this flock along, and when he came opposite the boys who were throwing the stones at Sandy, he halted.

The shepherd took one look at the miserable dog, saw that it was a well-marked Border Collie, then turned to the boys.

"You ought to be ashamed of yourselves, boys," he said, and sheepishly the boys dropped their stones and sneaked away.

The shepherd—John Murray—took a step into the lane and spoke to Sandy in a kind voice.

"What's the matter, old fellow?" he asked. "Come on out!"

Sandy had never heard such a voice before. It sounded like music, and it had to be obeyed. He trusted the tall man from the hills. With a wag of his drooping tail, he came out of the lane, and just as he reached the street a bell began to clang loudly.

As soon as he heard that bell, Sandy was off down the street like an arrow from a bow. He caught up with the flock and raced around them, forcing the sheep towards a side street.

Amazed by the dog's sudden and strange action, the shepherd ran forward, but before he had taken ten steps he halted.

A fire-engine, its great brass bell clanging a warning, was coming straight for his sheep at terrific speed.

Would it crash in among them? It looked as if it would, for the driver could not stop, but Sandy, by a frantic effort, managed to get the last few sheep into the side street just as the fire-engine thundered past harmlessly.

John Murray, the shepherd, ran forward to find Sandy waiting for him, with wagging tail and eager eyes. It was quite plain to the shepherd, who had handled clever collies all his life, that the stray dog had driven the sheep up the side-street, to get them out of the path of the clanging fire-engine.

His eyes were shining as he bent down to pat the little sheepdog's head.

"And you're a stray dog, eh?" he asked, his big hand tenderly stroking Sandy's head.

Sandy wagged his tail, and his brown eyes seemed to plead with the tall man he had served so well.

"I'd take you home with me if it wasn't for the fact that your owner will be looking for you," said the shepherd. And he was standing there, making up his mind what to do, when a man in uniform came up.

"I'm the dog-catcher," he announced. "This is the second time this stray dog has chased sheep out of the street. He won't do it again, though. Sam Watkins, his owner, told us to destroy Sandy if we could lay our hands on him."

"You must be crazy!" said the shepherd, and he called an order to the dog.

Like a shot, Sandy was away up the side street after the sheep.

"He's no longer a stray dog—if he'll have me as his master," said the shepherd to the dog-catcher.

"You'll—you'll take him?" exclaimed the dog-catcher.

"I'll do that!" replied John Murray. "I know a clever dog when I see one."

The shepherd turned, and he gave a whistle that carried to the waiting sheep-dog.

"Bring them out, Sandy!" he called. "Out here."

He waved his arm in the direction of the main street. Like a shot Sandy was on the move, driving the flock of ewes back to their master, while John Murray watched him with shining eyes.

"Yes, you're my dog from now on!" murmured the big shepherd. "My dog Sandy!"

Next Tuesday—Sandy's great battle with a jealous sheepdog.

Animal interest is provided in this tale of man's best friend in trouble. The exploits of a brave border collie, Sandy, and his cruel master, generate a tear in the eye of the comic's reader and lead on to a feel-good ending – a story that was intended to appeal to girls. Jack Glass also drew this heading.

The Ape's Secret provides drama in the sawdust ring, under the big top. If any of the young readers planned to run away to join the circus, then this was the story for them – at 10 years of age, Jimmy Samson runs his own. This type of storyline was a *Beano* anchor and variations on this theme would appear at regular intervals.

This whole story was basically rerun in picture form in the late 1950s under the title 'The Kangaroo Kid'. The D. C. Thomson staff artist Richard 'Toby' Baines produced the heading drawing.

The Story of a Boy, a Clown, a Cunning Ape, and a Circus.

GRAND CIRCUS

THE APE'S SECRET

Spring-Heel Jimmy

It was early evening on the fair-ground just outside Gateshead, in Durham. People were pouring through the gates in large numbers, for the big attraction was Samson's Road Circus.

All the children were keen on seeing Samson's Circus. Happy, laughing voices could be heard everywhere.

But inside the yellow and red caravan at the back of the circus tent there was no laughter.

Old Jed Samson, owner of the circus, was very ill. The doctors had said that he could not live much longer. He had been a grand old man, admired and liked by everyone, but now he was dying. Old Jed knew that his time had come, but he was facing death bravely.

At his bedside stood little Jimmy Samson, his nephew. Although he was only ten years of age, Jimmy had been a star in the circus ring since his own father had died six years ago.

"Jimmy, I've something to tell you," said the dying man. "You've been a good boy to me—a very good boy. You've been like a son to me, and I'm not forgetting it."

He reached under his pillow and drew out an envelope. It was a strong, yellow envelope sealed with red wax.

"See here, Jimmy, when I die look after this envelope," said his uncle, waving it feebly. "This is my will, and I've made sure that that brother of mine will never run this show. I've left everything to you, Jimmy. When I'm gone, the fair-ground and circus will be yours. You deserve it."

Somewhere out on the fairground a band struck up, and Uncle Jed knew what it meant. The evening show was about to begin. He gripped Jimmy's hand.

"Now get back to the ring and forget all about me," he said with a smile. "Go and give them your best. Let the crowd see what Spring-heel Jimmy can do. Go to it, Jimmy! And always remember—the show must go on!"

He gave the boy a gentle push, and Jimmy backed to the door of the van. One last look he gave his dying uncle, then he brushed the tears from his eyes and sprang down the steps to the ground outside.

Uncle Jed was right. The show must go on. All his life Jimmy had heard this. It had become the one rule he could never forget, the rule that all circus people obeyed.

So Spring-heel Jimmy ran across the clearing to the dressing tent at the back of the huge tent known as the big top where the circus ring was placed. Outside there was a brightly-coloured bill on which his name was printed.

As he ducked under the flap of the tent, someone struck him a stinging slap in the face. At the same time a harsh voice snarled—

"Late again! I thought you were never coming. Get dressed at once."

Jimmy's eyes glowed with rage as he looked up at the burly man who had hit him. But he closed his mouth tightly.

It was no use talking to Jules Samson, Uncle Jed's brother. He was the circus manager and like everybody else in the circus, Jimmy hated him for his sly, nasty ways. Now Jules stalked out, growling and twirling his greasy moustache.

The boy choked down his rage and ran to his locker. A few moments later he slipped into his crimson tights and put on his special spring-boots.

A great gust of laughter from the crowd told Jimmy that Tumbler, the old clown, had just put in an appearance. That meant that it was almost time for Jimmy to enter.

In the ring with Tumbler was Algy, the Intelligent Chimp. The clown and the ape were larking about together, and a roll of drums told Jimmy that it was his turn to enter the ring.

He ran forward a few paces down the passageway, jumped down hard on the ground and the springs on his boots bounced him high into the air. A gasp of delight came from the crowd as Jimmy flashed into the ring.

Clank! Down he came in full view of everyone then bounced in the air once more. But at the end of this bounce he came down with his legs astride old Tumbler's shoulders.

At that Tumbler fell flat on his face and a mighty roar of laughter shook the tent. The children yelled with delight, and their parents had to hold them to their seats when Algy, the chimpanzee, tried to catch Jimmy.

Then, just when Algy seemed about to grab Jimmy, the boy bounced so hard on his springs that he shot right up in the air and caught hold of the flying trapeze.

The crowd roared with laughter, the band thundered out the final tune, and the three partners bowed together in the middle of the ring. It was easily the best turn of the evening, and Spring-heel Jimmy's cheeks were flushed with pleasure as he hurried out amidst loud applause.

Algy the Thief

But Jimmy Samson did not feel happy very long. He had just got his boots off when Jules Samson came over.

"You'll have to pull yourself together after this, my lad," he said in a nasty voice. "No more running to your Uncle Jed with tales."

"Why not?" asked the boy.

"Because he's dead, that's why!" was the brutal answer. "He died while you were in the ring. And now the circus belongs to me! You'll have to do as I say."

Jimmy bent his head and wept, while Jules Samson turned away with a grunt. It was Tumbler, the clown, who put his arm around the boy's shaking shoulders and said—

"There, there, lad, don't fret! Your uncle Jed had a good life of it and he died happy. But I only hope that bawling brother of his doesn't throw us all out of the circus."

"He won't!" rapped Jimmy, suddenly looking up. "He won't have the circus. I forgot to tell you, Tumbler. My uncle told me he had left the show to me. His will is in an envelope. It's in his caravan."

"What's that? What nonsense is that you're talking?" cut in the harsh voice of Jules Samson, and the circus manager pushed his head through the tent door.

Little boy, on a bike—hit stone, had to hike. 23

"It's true. Uncle Jed said he didn't want you to have it. He's said so in his will," the lad cried.

"Oh, he did, did he? We'll see about that!" growled the man, and he turned sharply on his heel.

Jimmy did not worry about the will, for he was too sorry about his uncle's death. He hid himself in a quiet corner and wept on a pile of hay.

But the next day Jimmy saw that everyone expected him to keep the show going. All these men and women depended on the circus for their living.

Jules Samson had gone away some place, but he came back just after lunch with two grave-looking men. They were Uncle Jed's lawyers, and they had come to read the will. Someone had told them about the sealed envelope being in the van, and they were going to open it before witnesses.

It was just before the afternoon show was due to begin, and Jimmy already had on his spring-boots.

The lawyers and Jules Samson went inside the caravan. Jimmy stood at the top of the steps. There were a lot of circus folk waiting outside.

"Yes, here is the envelope," said one of the lawyers, holding it up. "The boy was right, after all. I'll read it when I get my glasses on. Dear me, where are they?"

He put the envelope down near the window while he searched for his glasses. The next moment the voice of Tumbler the clown was heard at the entrance to the big top. "Look out, there, Algy's loose," he was crying.

The clown had been preparing Algy for the ring when the ape had broken free from its rope and escaped. Now the ape scampered across the circus ground, to old Jed Samson's caravan.

The red sealing-wax on the envelope containing the will caught Algy's eye. With one leap he reached the window, his long arm darted inside, and he snatched the will up right under the lawyer's nose.

With another leap, he sprang to the roof of the next van. Then off he darted across the circus ground at great speed.

"After him! He's got the will!" bellowed everyone at once, and the crowd broke up and started to run.

Quicker than anyone was Spring-heel Jimmy. He jumped straight for the top of the van steps, and his springs sent him flying right over the heads of the running men. As he landed in front of the rushing mob, he sent himself bouncing along after the runaway chimp.

Round behind the animal cages went Algy, screeching all the time. He darted beneath the lions' cage as quick as a flash.

There was a lot of hay piled up under that cage, as well as many boxes and crates belonging to the circus. Algy disappeared among the boxes and the hay. And although Jimmy looked everywhere, he could not find the chimp.

"There he goes!" someone shouted. Sure enough when Jimmy looked round, Algy was dancing on top of the roundabouts on the other side of the circus ground.

Away went everyone, but Jimmy again forged to the front. Nobody could move as quickly as he could on his spring-boots. He jumped right up to the top of the roundabout, chased Algy round and round, and at last managed to catch him.

"Now give me the envelope!" ordered Jimmy, but suddenly he noticed that it was no longer in Algy's hand.

The boy shouted down the news to those below, and Jules Samson grinned with satisfaction, but he had to order everyone to search the grounds. A hundred men began the hunt for the yellow envelope with the red sealing-wax, but by the time the show began they had not found it.

Jimmy Leaves the Circus

JIMMY had to go into the ring and give his usual turn with Algy and Tumbler, but his mind was not on his work. He was thinking of that will, and of what would happen if it was not found.

"You did me a bad turn when you lost that will, Algy," he said sadly to the ape, as they came out of the ring.

The circus people had been searching for the will all the time Jimmy had been in the ring, but it had not been found yet. As soon as Jimmy had changed his clothes, the lawyers sent for him again.

Jules Samson was with them, and he was smiling as he tugged at his greasy moustache.

"Well, my lad, the will can't be found," he sneered. "I don't suppose it matters very much. The circus would have been mine just the same."

Jimmy looked at the elder of the lawyers, who cleared his throat and spoke.

"Well, according to the law, my boy, the circus belongs to the nearest relative of your dead uncle. That is Jules Samson, and I have no doubt he will give you a share in your uncle's property."

Then they took up their gloves and their bags and went away, leaving Jimmy so astonished that he did not even move.

The circus now belonged to Jules Samson! That was just the thing his Uncle Jed had not wanted to happen. It was all wrong! That will had to be found!

The youngster turned to start the search for it all over again, and found his way barred by Jules Samson. The man was grinning as he drew a shilling from his pocket and held it out.

"Here you are, my boy. The lawyers said I would give you a share. Here it is! You're leaving the circus. I've had enough of your whining and sneaking around the place. Get out!"

The bully grabbed Jimmy by the scruff of the neck and threw him down the van steps. The boy fell in a heap, and just then old Tumbler, the clown, popped up. He had been passing at the time and had heard the rough talk.

"You brute, Samson!" he shouted. "You ought to be ashamed of yourself, you hulking bully. The boy belongs here with us. The circus ought to be his, and as soon as that will is found we'll all know the truth."

"Really?" drawled Jules Samson, coming slowly down the steps. "Well, you won't be here to see it, because you are going out as well. You're too old for my show, and you are no use to me."

Without a word Tumbler turned and caught Jimmy by the arm. His old, wrinkled face was grave, but his words were cheerful enough.

"Well, we go together, Jimmy," he cried. "We'll look after each other. We'll see this through side by side."

Sadly the boy turned away and went to his tent. Leaving the circus was like the end of the world to him.

He was packing his spring-heel boots when a hand touched his arm, and he turned to find Little Judy, the bareback rider, looking at him anxiously.

"What has happened, Jimmy?" the girl gasped. "You aren't leaving us?"

She was a frail little girl, not as big as Jimmy. And they were great pals, for they had grown up together in the circus.

"Yes, I'm afraid so," replied the lad. "Jules Samson owns the circus now that the will can't be found. He kicked me out!"

To his surprise, Judy burst into tears.

"I can't bear to be here without you and old Tumbler," she sobbed. "I hate Jules Samson. I'm frightened of him. Please take me along as well, Jimmy."

The boy thought hard, then decided that that would be impossible. But a good idea had come to him.

"No, Judy, we can't do that. Besides, you might be useful to me. You stay here with the circus and we won't be far away. I'm going to find the will that Algy hid. It's somewhere in the circus. I know it is. Algy didn't have time to take it outside. I've got to find it before Jules Samson, or he'll tear it up. Will you look for it whenever you have the chance?"

"Yes, of course I will, Jimmy," said the girl. "And you—you won't be too far away?"

"I'm not going away at all," said the boy, promptly. "Jules has thrown me out, and he won't pay my wages any more. But I'm going to stick to the circus just the same. Uncle Jed wanted me to. He said the show must go on."

"But if you have been kicked out, Jimmy, how can you stick to the show?" asked the little girl in wonder.

"Don't you worry. I'll find a way. You watch out to-night, when the show is on. The people will expect Tumbler and Algy and me to give our usual show—and we will! We'll slip in somehow, even if it's right under Jules Samson's nose. I promise you that, Judy. Now I must run and tell Tumbler my idea. Good-bye for the present!"

The little girl waved as Spring-heel Jimmy ran off into the growing darkness. She hoped he would keep his promise, but she did not see how he could

Sure enough Springheel Jimmy gets back to the circus, next week How does he manage?

At the top of pages on which there is no title header, there is a joke, an amusing comment or an advertisement for *The Beano*. Those used in this first issue make a surprising mixture – pheasant pie (on page 33) would not have been familiar to most *Beano* readers!

A classic tale of a lonely, resourceful boy, brought up in the way of the woods by a mystery hermit. The office staff questioned the choice of the name 'Derek' for a wild boy of the woods, but in 1938 the word of *The Beano*'s Editor was final.

Beano readers must have enjoyed the 'Wild Boy' stories for they ran in an unbroken series for four years. After a break of five years, a second series ran for another two years. An unusual three-week-long third mini-series appeared in 1949, where the Wild Boy was in Africa attempting to capture some rare birds for a circus, a storyline a little out of character for Derek.

Here is a Picture-Story of a Young Tarzan.

WILD BOY OF THE WOODS

1—The brown-faced boy in the strange clothes made of rabbit skin came down the glade in the wood. The deer, the badgers, and the birds were not afraid of him, for this young boy was their friend and they often received tit-bits of food from him. He had been fishing, and carried three big fat trout. Before a withered oak tree at the foot of the cliff the boy paused and looked about him carefully. Then he did a curious thing. He reached for a knot in the trunk of the oak tree and pushed.

2—Immediately a strange thing happened. The knot controlled a hidden spring, and part of the trunk swung outwards on hinges. It was a secret door! The oak tree was hollow, and no one looking at the tree would have guessed its secret. It was a secret that this young boy of the woods was keen to keep, for again he looked about him carefully. Then he slipped quickly through the door, and a second later it closed silently behind him.

3—Once inside the trunk, Derek, as the wild boy was called, entered a sloping tunnel. The old oak hid the mouth of this tunnel which ran upwards through the cliff. All the way up were iron holds for hands and feet, and nimbly as a squirrel the young boy climbed upwards, towards a circle of light above him.

4—As he thrust his head through the narrow opening at the top end of the tunnel, the boy gave a cheery shout. "Good morning, Grandad!" he cried. Then he emerged into a roomy cave, furnished just like a house. This was the wild boy's home where he lived with the fine old man he knew as his grandfather.

5—Soon, in this cave in the cliffs, the strange pair were sitting down to breakfast and the wild boy was telling the old hermit how he had caught the trout down at the river in the woods. The old hermit listened, his eyes fixed on the young lad's eager face. Then he spoke slowly: "I've got a special job for you this morning, Derek," he said when the meal was over and the dishes were washed. "I want you to cut my hair and my beard." Derek readily fetched a bowl and scissors. He had often cut the old hermit's hair before, and he made a neat job of it. "I'm going away, Derek," said the old man quietly when the job was done. "I'm leaving to-night for the city on a mission which concerns you." "Going away, Grandad? Why?" exclaimed the boy.

6—There and then the old hermit told his story. He told Derek how, six years before, he had found the little lad wandering in the forest and how he had carried him back to the secret cave and brought him up. "I do not know who you are, Derek," he said. "But I must find out before I die. I cannot bear the thought of losing you, but I must find out who you are, for your own sake." No amount of pleading could change the old hermit's mind, and on the outskirts of the wood as darkness fell, the old hermit, in his city clothes, turned to say goodbye. "Take good care of yourself, Derek," he said huskily. "You will have enemies to guard against. And watch the oak tree for any message I may be able to send. Some day I will return."

Every boy and girl should know of this big, bright new paper, "The Beano." 25

7—With a gulp, the wild boy turned back into the woods. He knew that the old man was right in leaving, but he would be lonely in the cave without him. But there were always the books the old man had left behind, for the hermit had taught the wild boy as much as he could. Then there were always the animals and the birds—and as the wild boy moved along thinking of these things he began to feel lighter at heart—until suddenly a harsh voice rang out. "There he is, men, the dratted young poacher!" The wild boy turned round to see three husky gamekeepers running to catch him. Then he fled for his life.

8—The gamekeepers chased after the wild boy through the trees, but it was no easy matter catching him, for the wild boy could run like a deer. Without looking where the wild boy was going, the gamekeepers pounded on his heels, and then, before they could draw back, they went floundering up to their waists in thick black slime. Derek had just crossed a marsh, but he had taken the secret path across it, and the gamekeepers had been bluffed into following him. Now Derek turned on the other side of the marsh and laughed merrily at what he saw. "Just wait," roared Harkins, the head gamekeeper. "We'll get you for this."

9—Two days passed, and the wild boy had spent them in the cave. He had enough food in the cave to keep him for that time—and he had passed the hours reading the books the old man had left behind, and feeding the birds which came to the cave mouth for tit-bits. He felt, however, that he would have to make another trip to the river for fish. At nightfall he would risk it, he decided. Little did he know that in the woods the gamekeepers had set a trap which they thought the wild boy could not escape.

10—The wild boy was heading for the river when through the trees rang the deep-throated bay of a bloodhound. A chill ran down the wild boy's spine as he heard the noise of dogs, and he looked all round for a hiding place. He knew that the dogs were hunting for him, and he did not want to lead them back to the secret cave. So he turned and headed for the nearest marsh. As he did so a bloodhound burst from the trees and headed him off. The chase was on, and the wild boy ran for his life, but he could not escape the dogs, and he was driven down a rocky gully.

11—Once through the gully he knew of a swamp that he could cross in safety—but he never reached the end of the gully. He felt something rise from the ground and smother him, and next instant he was swinging in the air. He had run right into the net that had been laid for him!

12—The wild boy clawed and kicked to get free of the net, but he failed, and as the gamekeepers gathered round him and pulled him free he fought like a wild-cat. "Well, we've got you, my lad," growled Jed Harkins, as he gripped the wild boy and hustled him forward. "You've been poaching long enough."

NEXT WEEK—DEREK IN AN ADVENTURE WITH ANGRY GAMEKEEPERS AND A WILD BULL.

All these 'Wild Boy' strips were drawn by staff artist Richard 'Toby' Baines. He drew some of the most memorable wartime propaganda material in his 'Wild Boy' strips of 1940 (shown in detail later in this history, on pages 93–95).

In 1958 the 'Wild Boy' was modernised by young artist Andy Hutton and the story was set in suburbia, where Derek had been living in a deserted house. It appeared for a final 11-week run.

A clever piece of editorial work made this page look good, blending two quite different strips. 'Uncle Windbag' was traditional in that it had captions under the drawings. However, the artwork by Charles Holt was very modern looking.

Below this was 'Monkey Tricks' which used the then modern layout of speech bubbles only, combined with the very traditional artwork of Reg Carter. 'Monkey Tricks', which R. D. Low and Reg Carter worked out between them, was originally titled 'Gus the Gorilla' and was the front runner for getting *The Beano* cover slot. Until, that is, they designed 'Oswald the Ostrich' who made it to the cover as 'Big Eggo'.

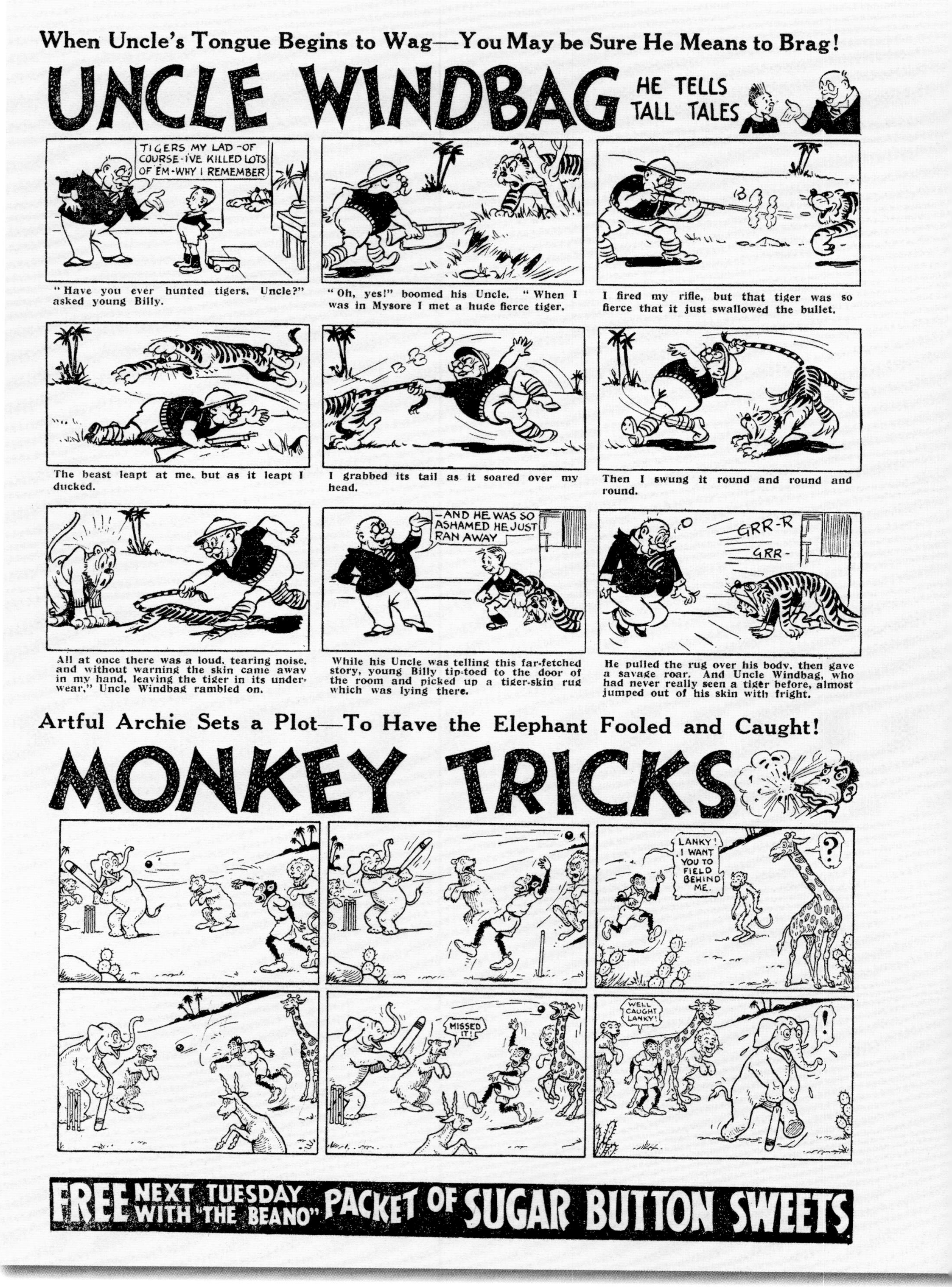
When Uncle's Tongue Begins to Wag—You May be Sure He Means to Brag!
UNCLE WINDBAG
HE TELLS TALL TALES
TIGERS MY LAD -OF COURSE-I'VE KILLED LOTS OF EM-WHY I REMEMBER
"Have you ever hunted tigers, Uncle?" asked young Billy.
"Oh, yes!" boomed his Uncle. "When I was in Mysore I met a huge fierce tiger.
I fired my rifle, but that tiger was so fierce that it just swallowed the bullet.
The beast leapt at me, but as it leapt I ducked.
I grabbed its tail as it soared over my head.
Then I swung it round and round and round.
All at once there was a loud, tearing noise, and without warning the skin came away in my hand, leaving the tiger in its underwear," Uncle Windbag rambled on.
-AND HE WAS SO ASHAMED HE JUST RAN AWAY
While his Uncle was telling this far-fetched story, young Billy tip-toed to the door of the room and picked up a tiger-skin rug which was lying there.
GRR-R
GRR-
He pulled the rug over his body, then gave a savage roar. And Uncle Windbag, who had never really seen a tiger before, almost jumped out of his skin with fright.
Artful Archie Sets a Plot—To Have the Elephant Fooled and Caught!
MONKEY TRICKS
LANKY! I WANT YOU TO FIELD BEHIND ME.
?
MISSED IT!
WELL CAUGHT LANKY!
!
FREE NEXT TUESDAY WITH "THE BEANO" PACKET OF SUGAR BUTTON SWEETS

LITTLE PEANUT'S PAGE OF FUN

JOLLY JOKES

PEANUT'S LETTER TO HIS PALS.

Shake hands, all you "Beano" readers. It sure is a great pleasure to meet you—and I want you to meet me. My name is Peanut, and the Editor says it is my job to make you laugh each week. So I've done my best.

Here is a page of jokes and riddles, which I hope will tickle all of you week by week.

Have a good time with the Whoopee Mask you got FREE with this copy of "The Beano"—and I don't mind telling you "The Beano" No. 2 is packed from cover to cover with big laughs and plenty of excitement.

Tell everybody about "The Beano"—and tell everybody about the packet of Sugar Button Sweets which are FREE with No. 2.

The Sugar Buttons are great sweets. I know. I've tasted them.

Cheerio,

Peanut

Mother—"What are you playing with, Jimmy?"
Jimmy—"A caterpillar and two little kitten-pillars."

Mother (angrily)—"I'll teach you to tie a kettle on a cat's tail."
Chick—"I wish you would, Ma. Every time I try it the string slips off."

What is the best thing out?—An aching tooth.

Tramp—"In my job it's impossible to get a day's work."
Old Lady—"Poor chap! Here is a sixpence. What are you?"
Tramp—"A night watchman."

Sergeant—"Come out of that. You can't go in there. That's the General's tent."
Private Jones—"That's funny. They've got 'Private' above the door."

Lady—"What are you digging for, sonny?"
Little boy—"We're looking for father. We've forgotten where we buried him."

John—"How is your pony getting on? Is it tame?"
Ron—"Well, it's tame in front, but awfully wild behind."

Sammy—"Why are you riding your bike with the tyres flat, Pat?"
Pat—"Well, the seat was too high, so I let the tyres down to lower it."

What is always behind time?—The back of a clock.

Uncle—"Jimmy, I'm going to give you a bright new penny."
Sandy—"I'd rather have a dirty old sixpence."

Motorist—"Is the water very deep here, sonny?"
Peter—"No, sir, look! It only comes up to the middle of that duck."

Simple Sammy—"If you can guess how many apples I have behind my back, I'll give you both of them."

Johnny—"I'm not going to play with Percy any more. He hit me on the nose when my back was turned."

Get ready, boys, and wait with glee
For "The Beano" No. 2;
A Packet of Sugar Buttons FREE
For every one of you!

FREE NEXT WEEK
SUGAR BUTTON SWEETS
Sugar Buttons Black as Jet Best You've Ever Tasted Yet
WITH The BEANO COMIC No2

THEY'RE SCRUMPTIOUS SWEETS IN EVERY WAY
SO BOOK YOUR "BEANO" NEXT TUESDAY!

Angry Gent—"When I bought this dog, you said he was splendid for rats. But he's afraid to touch them."
Dog-Dealer—"Well, that's splendid for rats, isn't it?"

Teacher (giving lesson on trees)—"Now what pine has the largest and sharpest needles?"
Tommy—"Please, sir, the porcupine."

Why is a piece of toffee like a lazy horse?—Because the more you lick it, the faster it goes.

Teacher—"You're late, Jones. What's your excuse?"
Billy Jones—"Please, sir, I fell downstairs."
Teacher—"Well, that oughtn't to have taken you long."

School Inspector—"Where is Ben Nevis?"
Boy—"I don't know. He ain't in our class!"

Old lady—"What's the idea of fitting that muzzle on your little brother?"
Johnny—"Safety first. You see, Tom here buys "The Beano" for me—and this is one way to make sure he brings back the packet of sweets free with the next copy."

Jockey—"That horse you sold me dropped dead this morning."
Dealer—"That's strange. He never did that before."

Bill—"Do you know Billy Jones?"
Fred—"Yes. He sleeps behind me in the English class at school."

Why is an angry man like 59 minutes past 12?—Because he is ready to strike one.

Teacher—"How many seasons are there in a year."
Willie — "Four. Cricket, marbles, conkers, and football."

On a visit to the doctor's, Dick was asked to put out his tongue. 'No blinking fear," said the youngster. "I did that to teacher yesterday, and got a licking for it."

Teacher—"Who was the father of the Black Prince?"
Billy—"Please, sir, Old King Cole."

Cute little Peanut was the front-cover mascot and spokesman for the comic. He brought news of forthcoming events and free gifts, adding his own personal thoughts to whatever was being mentioned, so on this page he says, 'Tell everybody about "*The Beano*" – and tell everybody about the packet of Sugar Button Sweets which are FREE with No. 2. The Sugar Buttons are great sweets. I know. I've tasted them.'

It would be the job of the junior sub-editor, Stan Stamper, to produce this page crammed full of gags and cartoons. Eventually *The Beano* would encourage readers to send Peanut their own cartoons and jokes, and the junior sub would then have a massive daily mailbag to contend with.

The first issue contained a free 'Whoopee mask', possibly named after Whoopee Hank (see page 23). It is thought that the original mask was produced in a number of colours, but only one is known to have survived.

Tin-Can Tommy, with the looks of a newspaper strip, fills the back page. The strip was the brainchild of *The Beano* staff but produced by the Torelli Brothers in Milan, and it does somehow feel continental. The Professor's anguished caption under the second frame has caused laughs over many years. Wartime put a premature end to the Torelli Brothers working for *The Beano*. They normally syndicated strips Europe wide, but for *The Beano* they acted as an art agency, producing pages to office scripts.

When all contact between Italy and Britain ceased with the outbreak of war, *The Beano* then used staff artists Sam Fair, George Drysdale and Chic Gordon to keep the strip going until early 1947.

28 * THE BEANO Comic July 30, 1938
TIN-CAN TOMMY
THE CLOCKWORK BOY
Professor Lee is deep in gloom, While sounds of sobbing fill the room, For it had been a bitter blow When his son had died a year ago.
The Professor's wife, with tear-filled eyes, Looks startled when her husband cries : " We're sad because we've lost our son, But I'll try to make another one."
WORK-ROOM
Still shedding tears, poor Mrs Lee Sees her husband grab his work-room key.
Professor Lee is a clever man, And very soon he draws a plan.
He shouts—" Ah, yes! It can be done!" And starts to build a clockwork son.
Some springs, some tin and a screw or two, A splash of paint, and the job is through.
Now see the Professor show his wife Their clockwork son chock-full of life.
And Mr Lee jumps as he thinks of the fun He'll have with Tommy, his tin-can son.
PRINTED AND PUBLISHED IN GREAT BRITAIN BY D. C. THOMSON & CO., LTD., 12 FETTER LANE, FLEET STREET, LONDON, E.C.4.

R. D. LOW

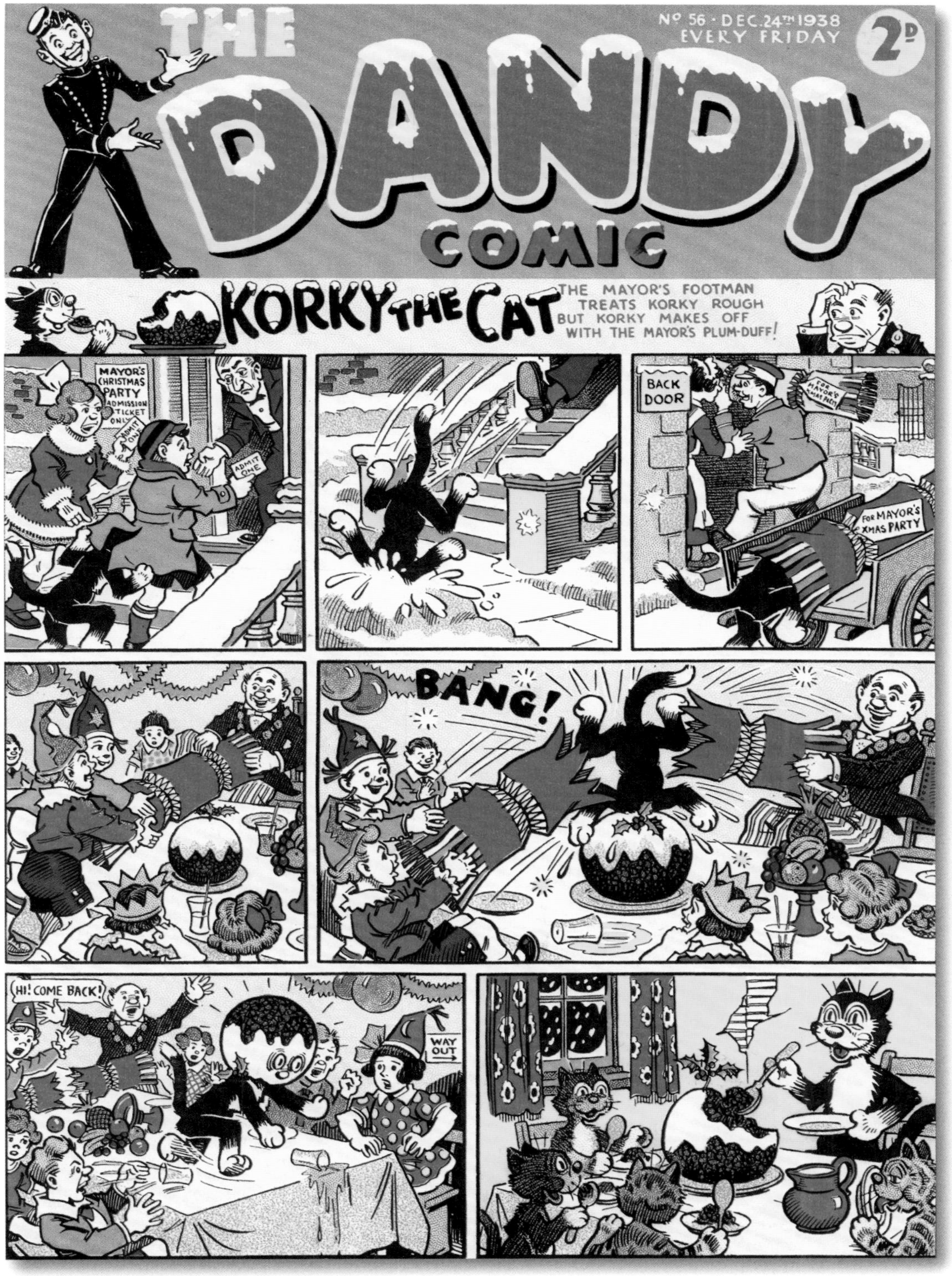
THE DANDY COMIC
No 56 · DEC. 24TH 1938
EVERY FRIDAY
2D
KORKY THE CAT
THE MAYOR'S FOOTMAN TREATS KORKY ROUGH BUT KORKY MAKES OFF WITH THE MAYOR'S PLUM-DUFF!
MAYOR'S CHRISTMAS PARTY ADMISSION TICKET ONLY
ADMIT ONE
BACK DOOR
FOR MAYOR'S XMAS PARTY
BANG!
HI! COME BACK!
WAY OUT

The cover of the Christmas 1938 Dandy. The two caricatures of R. D. Low were drawn by Dudley Watkins.

The creative force behind the Big Five and all the juvenile publications was the head of the children's publications department for D. C. Thomson, a shrewd Scot, Robert Low, more usually known as R. D. Low or just R. D. In 1937 he set about building a second Big Five, starting with *The Dandy* in 1937, *The Beano* in 1938 and *The Magic* in 1939. Only the start of the Second World War stopped further expansion.

Each of the new titles was built to the same formula. Whereas the Big Five were adventure papers that included some humour strips, the New Three were humour papers that included some adventure strips, a major change of emphasis. They brought in a type of humour that was powerful in visual slapstick, and scorned officials and authority in the shape of parents, policemen and, especially, teachers. This had been done before but the new vigorous trio pushed its gags and situations further, which built their appeal to children all the more strongly.

The sales ledger figures show how close and how large the immediate sales were of both *The Dandy* and *The Beano*. The first *Dandy* amassed sales of 481,895 copies and the first *Beano* 442,963 copies. The circulation of *The Wizard,* the most popular of the Big Five, was only around 350,000 per week at this time so it is no exaggeration to say the comics were an immediate success.

245 — 1937 — DANDY

SPECIAL SUBJECT OR SUPPLEMENT	Issue Dated	Aberdeen City	Aberdeen-shire	North	Forfar	Perth	Stirling	Fife	Glasgow and We[st]
Supp. Express Whistler	Dec 4	3970	1601	1915	1618	1923	1054	4059	4206
" Jumping Frogs	11	3930	2040	2130	2141	2436	1268	5166	4653

COMIC — 245

Edinburgh	Dundee	Irish	Old English	Yorks	Lancs.	Birming-ham	Wales	London	Total Scotch	Total English	Total Circulation
11460	4552	13684	25389	47274	70343	64668	17979	168237	87905	393990	4,81,895
12794	5983	12823	22638	38532	61014	51532	16445	152262	97245	342423	439,668

256 — 1938 — THE BEANO

SPECIAL SUBJECT OR SUPPLEMENT	Issue Dated	Aberdeen City	Aberdeen-shire	North	Forfar	Perth	Stirling	Fife	Glasgow and We[st]
Supp – Whoopee Mask	July 30	5706	3459	3925	3882	3377	2405	8929	6226
" Packet of Sugar Button Sweets	Aug 6	5576	3735	3906	4168	3462	2508	9400	6374

256

Edinburgh	Dundee	Irish	Old English	Yorks	Lancs.	Birming-ham	Wales	London	Total Scotch	Total English	Total Circulation
19764	5120	18033	28899	38298	61113	50817	17073	109902	136861	306102	442,963
[illegible]	5362	14145	29510	38077	62793	49743	16545	108680	138577	305348	443,925

The hand-written sales ledgers for the first issues of The Dandy *(top two rows) and* The Beano.

FREE INSIDE – SUGAR BULLETS TO EAT
THE MAGIC COMIC
No 1 22nd JULY 1939 EVERY THURSDAY
2d
KOKO THE PUP
FULL OF TRICKS AND FULL OF FUN. KOKO'S A PAL FOR EVERYONE!

The first issue of The Magic *was published on July 22, 1939.* The Magic, *which sold in excess of 300,000 copies a week, became a victim of wartime shortages and ceased publication on January 25, 1941 after 80 issues. The comic was similar in size, content and price to* The Dandy *and* The Beano, *though aimed at a slightly younger age group. Harry Banger drew 'Koko the Pup' on the cover. Dudley Watkins provided the lead character in 'Peter Piper', a boy who brought objects to life with his pan pipes and (as the sub-title said) 'picked people out of pickles'.*

THE BEANO STAFF

R. D. Low selected 24-year-old George Moonie to be Editor of ***The Beano***. George had joined D. C. Thomson from school, eight years earlier, starting out as junior sub-editor on ***The Rover.*** He became a sub editor on ***The Wizard*** and then, the year before ***The Beano*** launched, chief sub-editor on ***The Hotspur.*** Rapid promotion indeed – in comic terms, young George Moonie was a whiz kid!

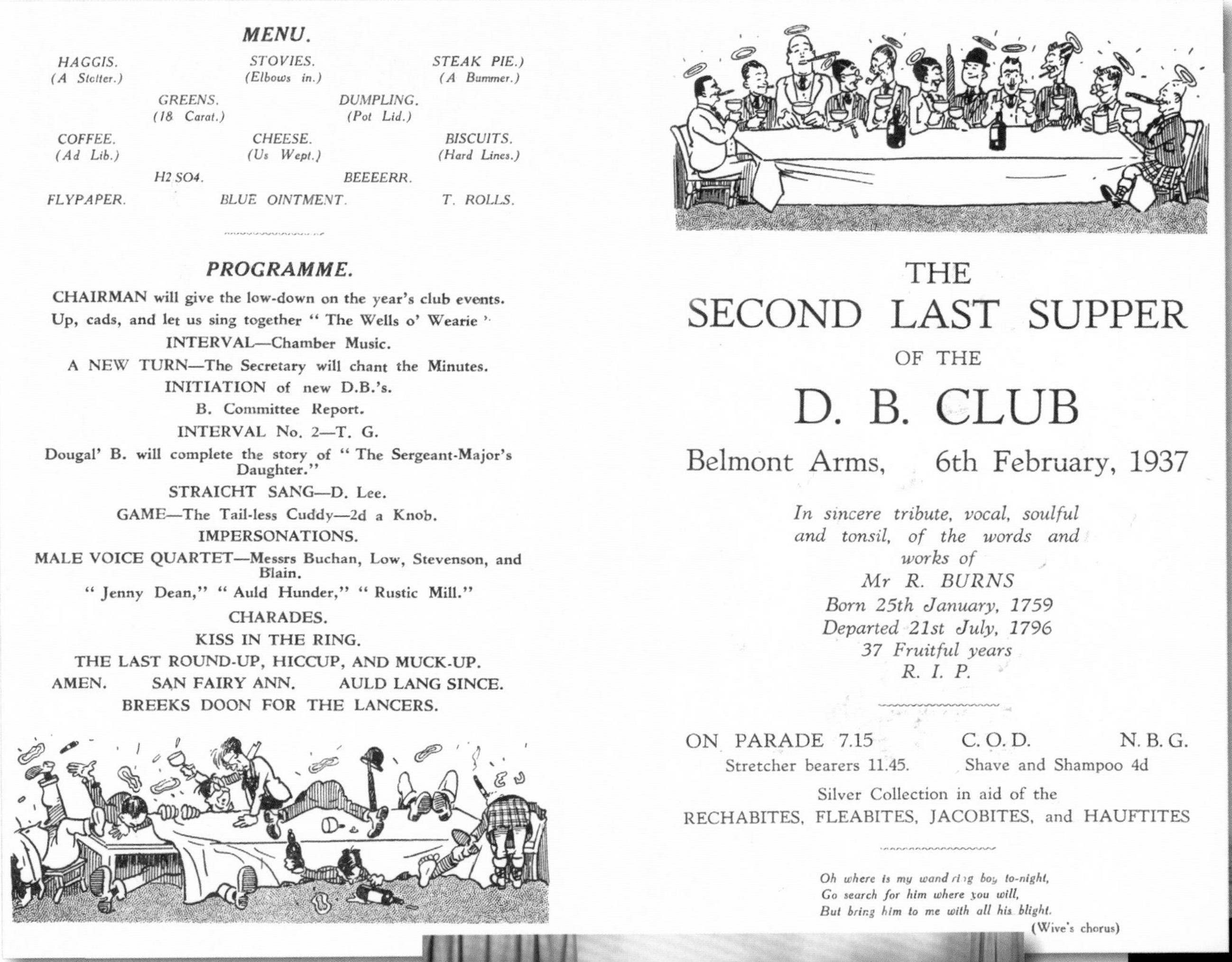

MENU.

HAGGIS. (A Stoiter.) — STOVIES. (Elbows in.) — STEAK PIE.) (A Bummer.)

GREENS. (18 Carat.) — DUMPLING. (Pot Lid.)

COFFEE. (Ad Lib.) — CHEESE. (Us Wept.) — BISCUITS. (Hard Lines.)

H2 SO4. — BEEEERR.

FLYPAPER. — BLUE OINTMENT. — T. ROLLS.

PROGRAMME.

CHAIRMAN will give the low-down on the year's club events.
Up, cads, and let us sing together " The Wells o' Wearie "
INTERVAL—Chamber Music.
A NEW TURN—The Secretary will chant the Minutes.
INITIATION of new D.B.'s.
B. Committee Report.
INTERVAL No. 2—T. G.
Dougal' B. will complete the story of " The Sergeant-Major's Daughter."
STRAICHT SANG—D. Lee.
GAME—The Tail-less Cuddy—2d a Knob.
IMPERSONATIONS.
MALE VOICE QUARTET—Messrs Buchan, Low, Stevenson, and Blain.
" Jenny Dean," " Auld Hunder," " Rustic Mill."
CHARADES.
KISS IN THE RING.
THE LAST ROUND-UP, HICCUP, AND MUCK-UP.
AMEN. SAN FAIRY ANN. AULD LANG SINCE.
BREEKS DOON FOR THE LANCERS.

THE
SECOND LAST SUPPER
OF THE
D. B. CLUB
Belmont Arms, 6th February, 1937

In sincere tribute, vocal, soulful and tonsil, of the words and works of
Mr R. BURNS
Born 25th January, 1759
Departed 21st July, 1796
37 Fruitful years
R. I. P.

ON PARADE 7.15 — C. O. D. — N. B. G.
Stretcher bearers 11.45. — Shave and Shampoo 4d

Silver Collection in aid of the
RECHABITES, FLEABITES, JACOBITES, and HAUFTITES

Oh where is my wand'ring boy to-night,
Go search for him where you will,
But bring him to me with all his blight.
(Wive's chorus)

The Burns Night dinner programme of the D.B. Club (above) illustrated by Dudley Watkins. R. D. Low was chairman of this club. George Moonie at his desk (far right) and as captain of his local football team, Harris Academy FP (right).

Making up George Moonie's team on ***The Beano*** were chief sub-editor Ron Fraser, sub-editors Ian Chisholm and Fred Simpson and junior sub-editor Stan Stamper. Ron Fraser looked after the adventure stories and Ian Chisholm was the energy behind the funnies. The nucleus of the early ***Beano*** artists and writers were staff men, so George had a good knowledge of their strengths and weaknesses from his work on the Big Five. The freelance artists had been selected by R. D. Low, and most of them were already working on ***The Dandy.*** R. D. travelled the length of the country and beyond seeking out new talent, holding numerous interviews in the D. C. Thomson London offices in Fleet Street.

Early Beano *staff (left to right) Ron Fraser, Fred Simpson, Ian Chisholm, Ken Walmsley, with George Moonie seated.*

THE D. B. F. C.—Season 1936-37.

C. E. W. CHECKLEY.—Height, 17 hands. Original model of the "Stalk o' Doo's Mulk." Too young for war, where he would have been a useful pull-through. Since made up for it by blowing instead of pulling. Clever contortionist at entertaining lady friends in a three-wheeler. Fond of mutton and nuts.

SANDY CUTHBERT.—What a man. Sired in Fife and damned ever since. Twister by nature. Bookie's runner. Thinks he is a great motorist Diseases—Several, including D.T.s and B.O. Hobbies—Dug breeding. Used to lead the pack, but now snuffs along at the rear

BASIL H. GIBSONE.—Middle name (Some) Hope. Public House boy. Served apprenticeship as a navvy, but failed to graduate. Height, 6 ft., but higher when he goes highbrow. Hobby—Hiking when he can get a lift. Claims to have slept on Embankment (name of partner unknown: either Lousy Liz or Mrs S——n). Motto—A "Woman's Way" is "The Way of All Flesh"

D. R. (SMILER) LEE.—The etchers little ray of sunshine. Never happy unless he's bloody miserable. Well known long-distance melodeon playing champion. Only hobby—Secret drinking in public lavatories. Religion—Dark blue. Place of worship—Dens Park. Used to hate all editorial folk like poison, but was converted January 25, 1936.

DOUGAL (HALF-PINT) BUCHAN.—The light-weight of the team, Birthplace unknown. Supposed found under the rhubarb. M.P. during War. Also V.C. (Cologne). Breeds maggots. Hunts nippies, lyons and fishes with fly. Three-colour man—Yellow Label, White Horse and Black Bull.

GEORGE SMITH.—Transferred from Hearts to Dundee, but now going to a Glasgow club. Belongs Edinburry, but couldn't help it. Knows all the women's periodicals. Touts poetry written by commercial travellers. Off form recently with a bair selly or pain in the guts. (That's his story.) Plays a grand game at Open-handed Abdominal Castigation. Once heard a lecture on "Bees," and is now a B—— expert. President, secretary and treasurer of the as yet unformed D.B.B. Club. Present holder club dart championship (1936)

R. I. (P.) STEVENSON.—Suckled by a beer-barrel, and is now in second childhood. Magician. Can turn ½ pint beer into 1 pint water. Regrets leaving army, as it was easier performing this trick in kilt. Talks in high-pitched voice, but this is misleading. Introduced new word to Paris—"Zig Zag." Hobbies—Going upstairs, and escorting home his inebriated friends. Fond of walking tours, and has discovered many unknown pubs and cathedrals.

J. M. CAMERON.—Ball boy. Bit of a dark horse. Says he was educated in France. Noted man of letters. Also wears rubber collars. Affects Robert Donat whiskers and overcoats. Down at heel, but up Helly-a. Hobby—Street-walking and going hiking

FRED (HAIRY) TAIT.—Belted Galloway (his old-man supplied the belting). Height—and a wee hauf. Two "star" man, but prefers three. St... a bald-headed infant. H... Hobbies—Pontoon for ... Never looks a woman betw... Goes straight to the po... bought four tyres and got a... thrown in. Travelled ... Known in Cologne as "G... in Brussels and Han as ... Man."

STEWART D. GILCHRIS... and front. Born in a... backland, but has sinc... morally. Went to ... School, and now frequ... House. Tried the sea instead of... work. Travelled extensively... Sister Street (Cairo). Gran... cutta), Cannebiere (Marseille... gives the benefit of his exper... possible. Member of the S... throw his dinner further th... Very neighbourly. Practicall... teetaller. Favourite song, "I... Comin' Up Than Goin' Doon." ... admirer of Duke of Windsor, Dunure Footprint and Barney's Bull. Invented "Treacle Belly Flap Back."

R. D. (RED-DEVIL) LOW.—Skipper of the team. The mitey atom, the * * * * ! ! ! Born in a telephone booth. Height—two under fours. Known as Bert and various other names beginning with B. Also Jimmy Bruce and Jimmy Paterson. Elder of the church. Hobbies—Alibi inventing; exploring side-roads; answering lawyers' letters. Favourite holiday resort—Friockheim. Author of "Drawing-Room Tales."

W. BLAIN (OOR WULLIE).—Known as the "Goalie's Nightmare," same applies to artists, typists, R. G. T. and Mrs W. B. Came from Glesca, but won't go back. Raising his own team. Has goalie and two backs, but is inscrutable regarding halves and forward-line. Visited Paris, but found "Folies Bergeres" very provincial. Visited Louvre, but not impressed by sanitary arangements. Hobbies—Conjuring, telephoning, bottle parties, author baiting and bottle parties.

HANDY ANDY HUNTER.—The shy and ... bridegroom. Known in Edzell as ...some." Explored Ostende, Paris ...manergau, then came home and ...ffers from cold feet, and has ...ut on his socks. Swell ... cutlery and towels, all ... and has one wife. ...rrier. For further ...arnardo's Home,

... most of the best ... people. Can tell ... the other. Social ... of Ceremonies. ... traffic and can ...nber of females ... Hobbies—Gin, ...nd the Ardenne

...Y.—Ex-choir-boy, ...tura. Expert on ... tipples. Sports—...rn, digging in sand, ...e Caley. Good all-

MISS PSORIASIS

A large part of the Editor's week was spent ensuring that all the elements were pulled together in time to get the comic to press. Stories and artwork were sent in from all over the country and the vagaries of the parcel and postal service could work against you. For that reason ***The Beano*** had a long lead time, the copies being produced six weeks ahead of the sale date.

R. D. Low was an energetic, hands on leader, and office life was lively. New storylines were talked about constantly and artists to illustrate them selected. Subsequent pencil rough sketches arrived at the office daily for editorial approval. Subbed text stories were cut or increased to fit page designs. Letters of encouragement or words of caution were sent to typists for despatch to contributors. Freelance artists and writers were paid weekly, so methodical book-keeping was required to keep the accounts department happy. Print schedules were revised to match the increasing sales. Readers' letters, be they of praise or complaint, were opened and answered faithfully. Office junior Stan Stamper faced a mammoth mail delivery every day, which reached nightmare proportions on a Monday morning.

This said, the fun the staff had producing the weekly ***Beano,*** falls out of the pages of the comic. The happy feeling ***The Beano*** projected came from the crew who put it to bed every Thursday.

R. D. Low was chairman of the D. B. Club, a gang of editorial chums who would meet on Burns Night every year to celebrate Scotland's national bard in the traditional high spirited style. Dudley Watkins did the drawings for a printed programme that was edited by Low and lampooned fellow editors and departmental chiefs. When you were working with cartoonists you often suffered at their talented hands!

MAKING THE BEANO

All the work preparing ***The Beano*** for printing (including the making of the printing plates) was done in Dundee. The printing was split between D. C. Thomson's Glasgow and Manchester print works, Glasgow catering for Scotland and Ireland with Manchester producing for England and Wales. Here is a glimpse of what was involved.

The Dundee headquarters of D. C. Thomson in 1937. It was the home of ***The Beano*** and is known as The Courier Building, after the daily Dundee newspaper published by D. C. Thomson.

The paper store in Dundee. Each roll (the trade term is 'reel') contained around 5 miles of paper. At the time of ***The Beano's*** launch, D. C. Thomson's presses were using about 380,000 miles of paper in a year for its newspapers, magazines and comics.

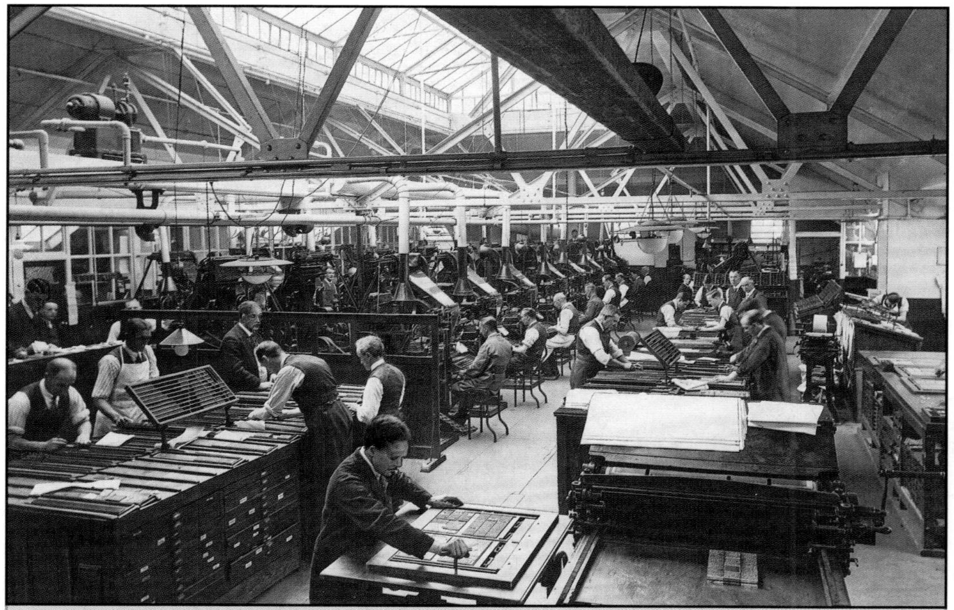

The Composing Room at Dundee, where all the text stories and advertising copy was set. In the foreground the pages of text are being assembled. In the background are the Linotype machines where the text was typed in and lines of metal type produced.

The Camera Room, Dundee. The original artwork drawn for ***The Beano*** was photographed by these huge cameras, which converted the image into a very large number of dots. The resulting film was used to make zinc plates. Light was then shone through the negative film on to a coated zinc plate. Where light shone through the negative, it hardened the surface of the zinc.

The Etchers' Shop, Dundee. The zinc plates were put in acid baths. The acid bit into the zinc that had not been hardened by light. The solids in the picture are left standing out in relief. This processed zinc plate is called a block.

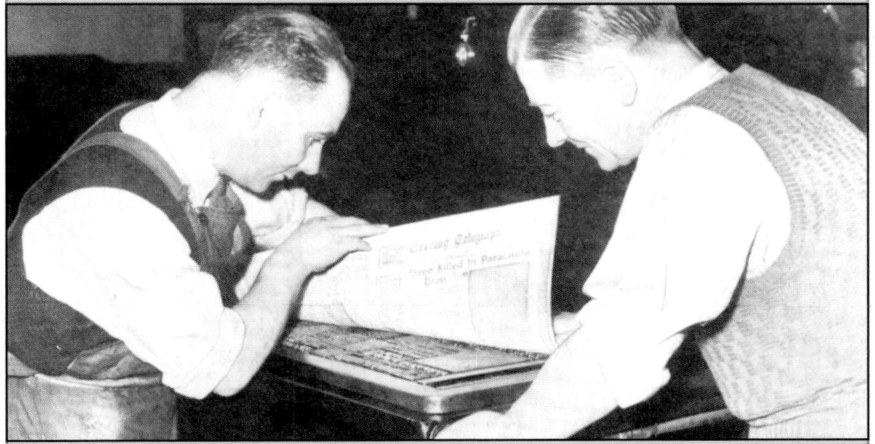

The Stereotyping Department, Dundee. The blocks were locked into steel frames and an imprint of the page (called a mat) was made using flexible papier-mâché.

The Stereo Foundry, Dundee. The mat was placed in a semi-circular casting box and molten metal was poured in. When the metal solidified, it formed a single curved cast which was locked to the cylinder of a printing press.

The Glasgow print works, showing a five-deck rotary printing press, seen from the end where printed and folded papers have been completed.

The Manchester printing works, showing the printing presses from the paper reel end. The paper flowed continuously into the printing press and was cut after printing.

'TOBY' BAINES

Richard 'Toby' Baines was born in 1896 in South Shields and was a student at Sunderland School of Art. During the First World War he served with the 17th Lancers, the Dublin Fusiliers. He joined D. C. Thomson in 1921 as a staff artist and worked on headings for *The Rover*, *Adventure* and *The Hotspur*. He became a specialist in animal illustrations, and was especially recognised for his drawings of dogs. In the first *Beano* Toby drew heading blocks for various text adventure stories and he was given the weekly picture adventure strip 'Wild Boy of the Woods' to illustrate. His distinctive style used process white to correct and build up drawings, giving a low-relief look to the original boards. This was very effective in reproduction.

Toby had a long career with D. C. Thomson, retiring in 1965, after 44 years of service.

WILD BOY OF THE WOODS

£50 REWARD FOR THE CAPTURE OF THE WILD BOY WHO HAS BEEN SEEN IN BARCHESTER RECENTLY — APPLY LORD NORTH

1—From his hiding-place inside a dust-bin, Derek, the wild boy of the woods, read the notice which had just been pasted up by a bill-poster. What he saw came as a shock to him. The notice said that there was a reward of fifty pounds offered for his capture. The reward was offered by Lord North, whose game-keepers had accused Derek of being a poacher. "I'll have to get out of this town!" muttered Derek. "Everybody will be

2—The wild boy scrambled out of the dust-bin, after makin sure that there was no one about. It was still early mornin He ran swiftly across the street and climbed up a big drain-pip The wild boy was taking to the roofs, where he was safe from tl Barchester Police. Derek raced across the roofs. Then he sl down another pipe and hurried across a yard towards a high wa He climbed the wall and looked down the street, as if watchin

How the Spring-Heel Boy Was Trapped by Treacle!

THE APE'S SECRET

The Flying Rescue

In a fair-ground at Darlington, Little Judy, the girl trick-rider of Samson's Road Circus, stood on the steps of her caravan and stared out into the darkness.

Then suddenly a voice shouted a warning—a voice which she recognised as that

that he was wearing spring-boots. He sped across to the roof of the roundabouts, more than thirty feet away. As he dropped on it, he clutched one of the decorated poles to steady himself.

What a shock he got. Algy the Ape had already taken shelter there. The ape screeched and screamed at the boy

his act was popular, and that it would harm the show if he did not appear.

They had managed to get to Darlington with the circus. That night they had crept into the grounds to try and get Algy to show them where the will was hidden.

Then Algy had spotted the escaped

The Cage That Trapped Twelve Beavers at Elbow Creek.

BLACK FLASH THE BEAVER

The Professor's Beaver Trap

Pat Casey, the Game Warden up at Elbow Creek, was clearing away his breakfast dishes when a knock sounded on the door of his cabin. He crossed to

and I will pay you well," said the Professor. "I intend to build a wooden cage, which I will lower into the dam. It will not fail, I am certain of that, but I will need your help to carry it to the dam,

loose. I've been kinda looking af it."

"Let the black beaver loose!" exclaim Professor Meeker. "Certainly not, dear fellow. That little black bea will cause a great deal of interest Chicago."

"Oh, all right," growled Pat.

He helped the excited Professor move the trap and trapped beavers fr the dam to his cabin, and watched l gloating over it and making notes.

Night came. The trapped beavers w too scared to move, all except Bl Flash. He had been out of the c before, and visited the Game Ward cabin. He had not been scared by

BASIL BLACKALLER

On his quest for artists R. D. Low met Basil Blackaller in London in January 1938. R. D. Low was impressed, as his notes from the meeting show. Young Basil did work for *The Beano*, but his mother was not keen on him moving to Dundee for a staff job.

R. D. Low reported that: 'I am very sorry to say that there is no likelihood of Blackaller coming in. The position is still the same only it is clear from what he said that his mother is dead against coming North. She seems to be rather nervous and possibly a hysterical type of person and he tells me that she would not shift on any account and he does not feel that it would be fair of him to walk out on her.' Some weeks later he got a job with an art agency in Bournemouth and was clever enough to get them to agree to his continuing to do freelance work for D. C. Thomson.

'Hairy Dan' was his first job and it was a very professional, polished set for a 16 year old. Two years later he produced the wonderful 'Cinderella and the Ugly Sisters' for *The Beano*. This work is so lively in composition and effect that it can be mistaken for early Dudley Watkins, a great compliment in *Beano* terms. Basil Blackaller took over 'Pansy Potter' from Hugh McNeill, and he brought to the strip a look that was taken from early cartoon movies.

In the 1950s Blackaller produced the science-fiction newspaper strip 'Ace O'Hara' which had a large, loyal following.

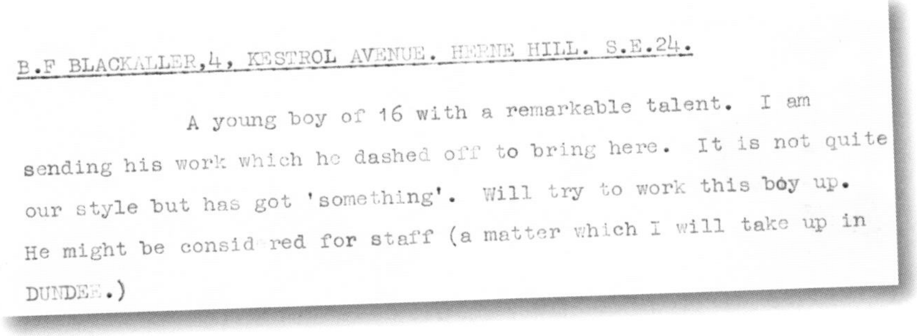

B.F BLACKALLER,4, KESTROL AVENUE. HERNE HILL. S.E.24.

A young boy of 16 with a remarkable talent. I am sending his work which he dashed off to bring here. It is not quite our style but has got 'something'. Will try to work this boy up. He might be considred for staff (a matter which I will take up in DUNDEE.)

WE'LL GO BUT YOU'VE GOT NOTHING TO WEAR!
SMAK
HA! HA! – WE'LL TELL LORD AND LADY GOOGLESBY YOU'VE GOT A COLD—!
TA,TA!
NOW'S YOUR CHANCE TO MAKE MY SISTERS SQUIRM, GOBLIN!
COO! LOOK AT THE FLASH CAR THEY'VE SENT TO FETCH US IN!
IDEA
WE'RE ALMOST THERE – THIS IS WHAT I CALL STYLE!
TOO BAD CINDERS HAS A COLD – HAR! HAR!
I'LL TURN LORD GOOGLESBY'S CAR INTO AN OLD CROCK AND MAKE THE SISTERS LOOK LIKE TRAMPS!
1904
HA! HA! NOW CHANGE THE CAR BACK AGAIN GOBLIN!
JUST WAIT TILL I CATCH YOU— I'LL TEACH YOU TO CHANGE MY CAR INTO AN OLD CROCK— YOU WITCHES!

HAIRY DAN—A Kid Makes Hairy Very Wild—But Dan's Beard Silences That There Child !
WILL YOU LOOK AFTER MY DEAR LITTLE WILLIE – WHILE I GO SHOPPING, DAN? HE'S SUCH A TENDER CHILD!
WITH PLEASURE, MRS FAGGOT!
GUSH GUSH
OUCH!
SPLOSH
COME ON, HAIRY— LET'S PLAY MUDBALLS!
SO YOU WANT TO PLAY MUDBALLS DO YOU? G-R-R-R!
HA! HA!
SPLOSH
I'VE AN IDEA, WILLIE – LET'S PLAY COWBOYS AND INDIANS – I'LL TIE YOU UP WITH MY BEARD FIRST— THEN YOU TIE ME UP!
O.K. DAN
HA-HA-HA! NOW PERHAPS I CAN GET SOME PEACE TILL YOUR MA COMES HOME!
SILENCE!

REG CARTER

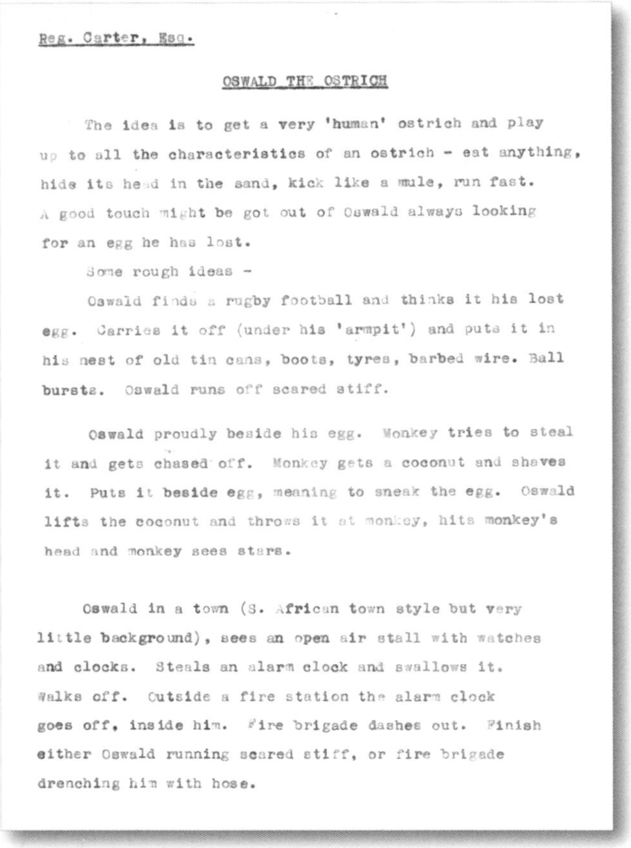
Reg. Carter, Esq.

OSWALD THE OSTRICH

The idea is to get a very 'human' ostrich and play up to all the characteristics of an ostrich - eat anything, hide its head in the sand, kick like a mule, run fast. A good touch might be got out of Oswald always looking for an egg he has lost.

Some rough ideas -

Oswald finds a rugby football and thinks it his lost egg. Carries it off (under his 'armpit') and puts it in his nest of old tin cans, boots, tyres, barbed wire. Ball bursts. Oswald runs off scared stiff.

Oswald proudly beside his egg. Monkey tries to steal it and gets chased off. Monkey gets a coconut and shaves it. Puts it beside egg, meaning to sneak the egg. Oswald lifts the coconut and throws it at monkey, hits monkey's head and monkey sees stars.

Oswald in a town (S. African town style but very little background), sees an open air stall with watches and clocks. Steals an alarm clock and swallows it. Walks off. Outside a fire station the alarm clock goes off, inside him. Fire brigade dashes out. Finish either Oswald running scared stiff, or fire brigade drenching him with hose.

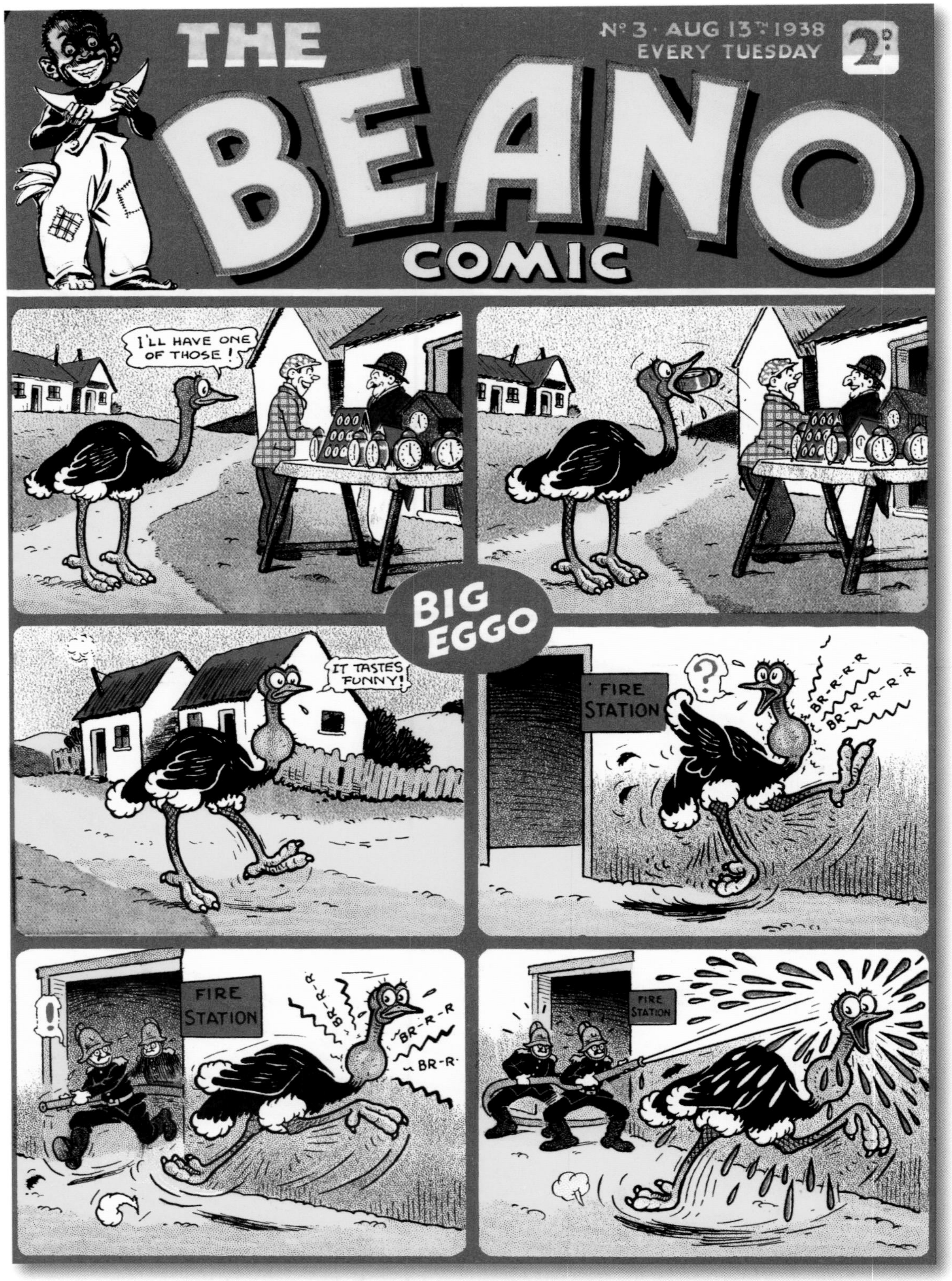
THE
BEANO
COMIC
Nº 3 · AUG 13TH 1938
EVERY TUESDAY
2D
I'LL HAVE ONE OF THOSE!
BIG EGGO
IT TASTES FUNNY!
FIRE STATION
?
BR-R-R-R
BR-R-R-R-R
FIRE STATION
BR-R-R
BR-R-R
BR-R-
FIRE STATION

In January 1938, a month after the launch of *The Dandy*, R. D. Low started looking for artists for his new project – *The Beano*. Reg Carter replied to an advert that R. D. had placed in the *Daily Telegraph* and the pair met up in London that same month. Reg Carter's work was well known to R. D. as he was drawing for Amalgamated Press and Fleetway titles plus the *Mickey Mouse Weekly*, (see his elephant, far right).

Reg Carter drew 'Eggo' on the front cover of The Beano *until 1948. The letter (above left) gives R. D. Low's original ideas for 'Oswald the Ostrich'.*

MAN WANTED
TO MAKE A
MILLION
POUNDS
APPLY HERE

As the correspondence shows, the pair started working on ideas immediately. R. D. sent down notions and Reg would work them into pencil sketch roughs (see sketches for 'Big Eggo' and 'Monkey Tricks' below). Many hours went into getting the characters to take on the signature *Beano* look that R. D. was so definite about. The 'Oswald the Ostrich' strip would become 'Big Eggo' and be the cover character. 'Gus Gorilla' sets were worked to become the 'Monkey Tricks' strip. ***The Beano*** was due to hit the streets in six months, so time was tight for getting things right.

Apart from comic work Reg Carter was a prolific illustrator of humorous postcards for the tourist market. Reg Carter produced various other strips for ***The Beano***, 'Peter Penguin' and 'Freddie Flipperfeet' among the best known. 'Eggo' continued on the cover until 1948 and into 1949 as a strip inside, but Reg Carter was not keeping in good health by this time and died in April 1949.

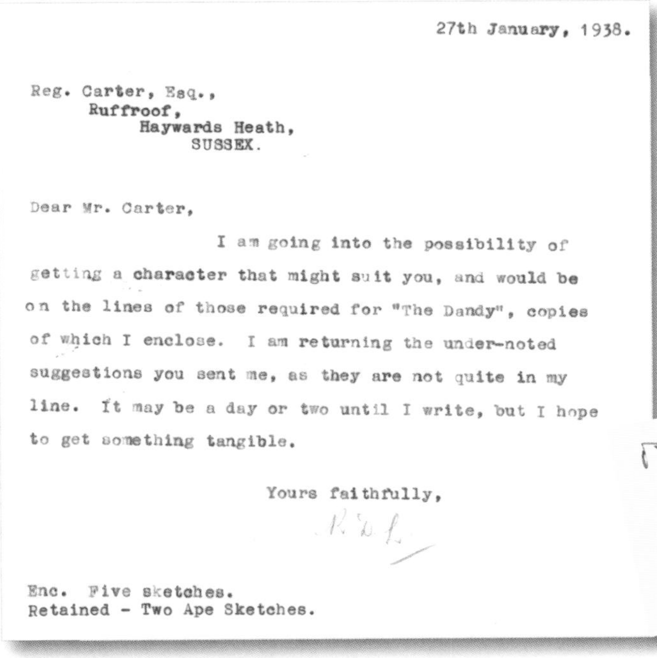

27th January, 1938.

Reg. Carter, Esq.,
Ruffroof,
Haywards Heath,
SUSSEX.

Dear Mr. Carter,

I am going into the possibility of getting a character that might suit you, and would be on the lines of those required for "The Dandy", copies of which I enclose. I am returning the under-noted suggestions you sent me, as they are not quite in my line. It may be a day or two until I write, but I hope to get something tangible.

Yours faithfully,

R.D.L.

Enc. Five sketches.
Retained - Two Ape Sketches.

REG CARTER

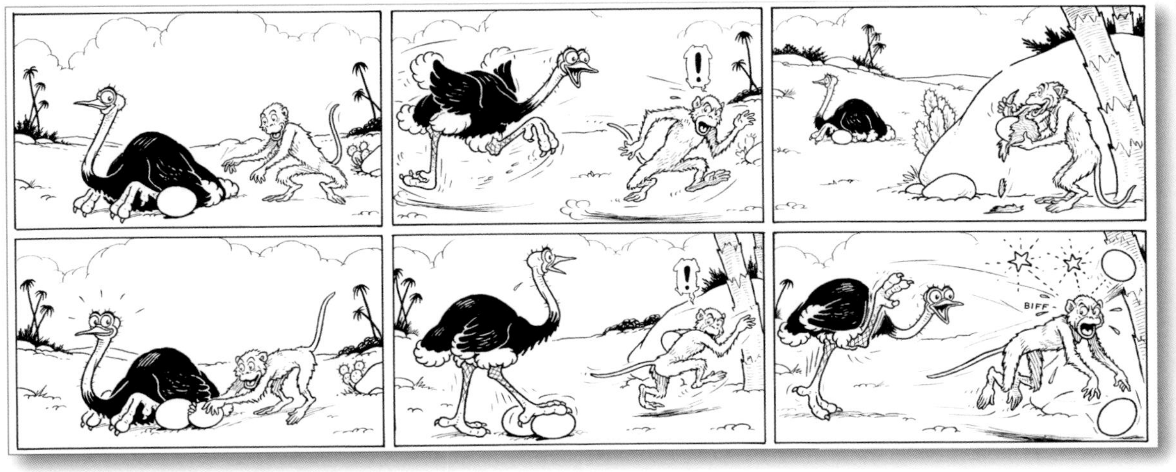
!
!
BIFF

COO! I'M OFF!
GASP
BIFF
!

ROLAND DAVIES

Roland Davies was famous for his 'Come on, Steve!' newspaper strip cartoon that ran in the ***Sunday Express*** then the ***Sunday Dispatch***, about a lovable but occasionally stupid carthorse. To get such a talent to illustrate 'Contrary Mary', ***The Beano's*** smart mule, was quite a coup. He also drew 'Whoopee Hank (The Slap-Dash Sheriff)' for a 12-month period in 1938–39. Hank was an action-packed strip with some great western characters in it. Davies' clear style told the stories beautifully and they would have been enjoyable without any speech bubbles or captions. 'Boney the Brave (He Lives in a Cave)' ran for 10 issues in 1939 and often ran almost without text.

COME ON! YOU'VE GOT TO PULL THIS CART FOR ME!
NOW THEN, LET'S GET THE HARNESS ON!
IDEA
STEEP HILL

BAKERY.
TRY TO PINCH ONE OF MY LOAVES, WOULD YOU? TAKE THAT!
HUNGER.
IDEA!
I'LL GET SOME WATER AND CLEAN THE WINDOWS!
EAT OGLE'S OATS
EAT OGLE'S OATS
MUNCH! MUNCH!

WHOOPEE HANK
THE SLAP-DASH SHERIFF

THIS IS HARD WORK CLIMBING THESE STAIRS
IDEA
THIS INVENTION OF MINE WILL SAVE A LOT OF HARD WORK!
MOVING STAIRCASE TO THE CAVES
MY LATEST INVENTION. NO MORE WALKING.
MOVING STAIRCASE TO HE CAVES
BUZZ ZZ-Z
HELP
TAKE THIS
GET HIM!
HELP

CHARLES HOLT

Uncle Has a Crazy Scheme—At the North Pole He Sells Ice-Cream !
UNCLE WINDBAG
HE TELLS TALL TALES
FISH AND POULTRY
AH, ICE! NOW I CAN TELL YOU A YARN ABOUT ICE!
ICE DEAL
1.—Uncle Windbag was strolling through the town one hot afternoon when he saw a boy unloading an ice-waggon. Windy just couldn't miss the chance of boasting. " You know, every time I see ice I think of the time when it saved my life," he said.
BUY MY HOT ICE CREAM
2.—" I was up in Alaska on a shooting trip when I hit on a grand scheme. Why not sell ice-cream to the Eskimos at the North Pole? You see, away up in the frozen North, the air is so cold that an ice-cream cone is as warm as a plate of hot soup.
HOT ICE-CREAM SOLD HERE
3.—" So off I went to the North Pole with a team of penguins pulling my ice-cream barrow. Oh boy! What a roaring trade I did with the Eskimos. Such a heat came off my ice-cream that they warmed their hands at my barrow as if it was a stove.
HOT ICE CREAM
4.—" I was soon sold out, and the Eskimos who hadn't been served were so disappointed that I at once decided to rush back to Alaska as quickly as possible and get more ice-cream. I set off with my penguin team.
MUSH
HOT ICE CREAM
5.—" I was whizzing along at a good speed when I heard a blood-curdling howl behind me. I looked back and saw a huge pack of wolves tearing after me. I didn't stop to deal with them, as I was in a hurry.
FASTER!
MUSH
6.—" Although my team kept going for four days and four nights, the wolves drew closer and closer. I was about to shoot at them when I noticed that the words I yelled at my penguin team froze solid as I spoke!
MUSH
7.—" When I saw this, a great idea struck me and I saw how to fool these starving wolves. I drove my team through a narrow gully and stopped at the other end. Then I stopped and began to shout as quickly as I could, and, believe me, the frost was so cold that each word froze in mid-air as it left my lips and then fell to the ground.
MUSH
8.—" I kept shouting, and soon there was a pile of frozen words right across the gully. By this time the howling wolves were rushing through the gully. But they had to stop when they reached the barrier of frozen words, for the spiky icicles kept them from climbing over. They howled with rage as I sped with my team across the snow.
HAVE A SLIDER SIR?
ICE
9.—" So I was able to get my ice-cream in Alaska and go back to the North Pole. Within three months I made 10 trips to the North Pole and I made £5000 selling that ice-cream." Windy puffed out his chest as he said this, and he didn't see the lump of ice the boy had dropped—so he went on his neck as he deserved.

IN THE CLUTCH OF THE RED MAN
TODAY
REGAL CINEMA
PICTURE
IN THE CLUTCH OF THE RED MAN

The Beano picked up former D. C. Thomson staffman, Charles Holt, to do 'Little Dead-Eye Dick' and 'Uncle Windbag' for issue No. 1. The first series was popular and ran for five months. The original artwork for two 'Little Dead-Eye Dick' strips are shown at the bottom of this page. Charles Holt then continued freelance work away from *The Beano*, and the second series of 'Little Dead-Eye Dick' was not done until 1949.

HUGH MCNEILL

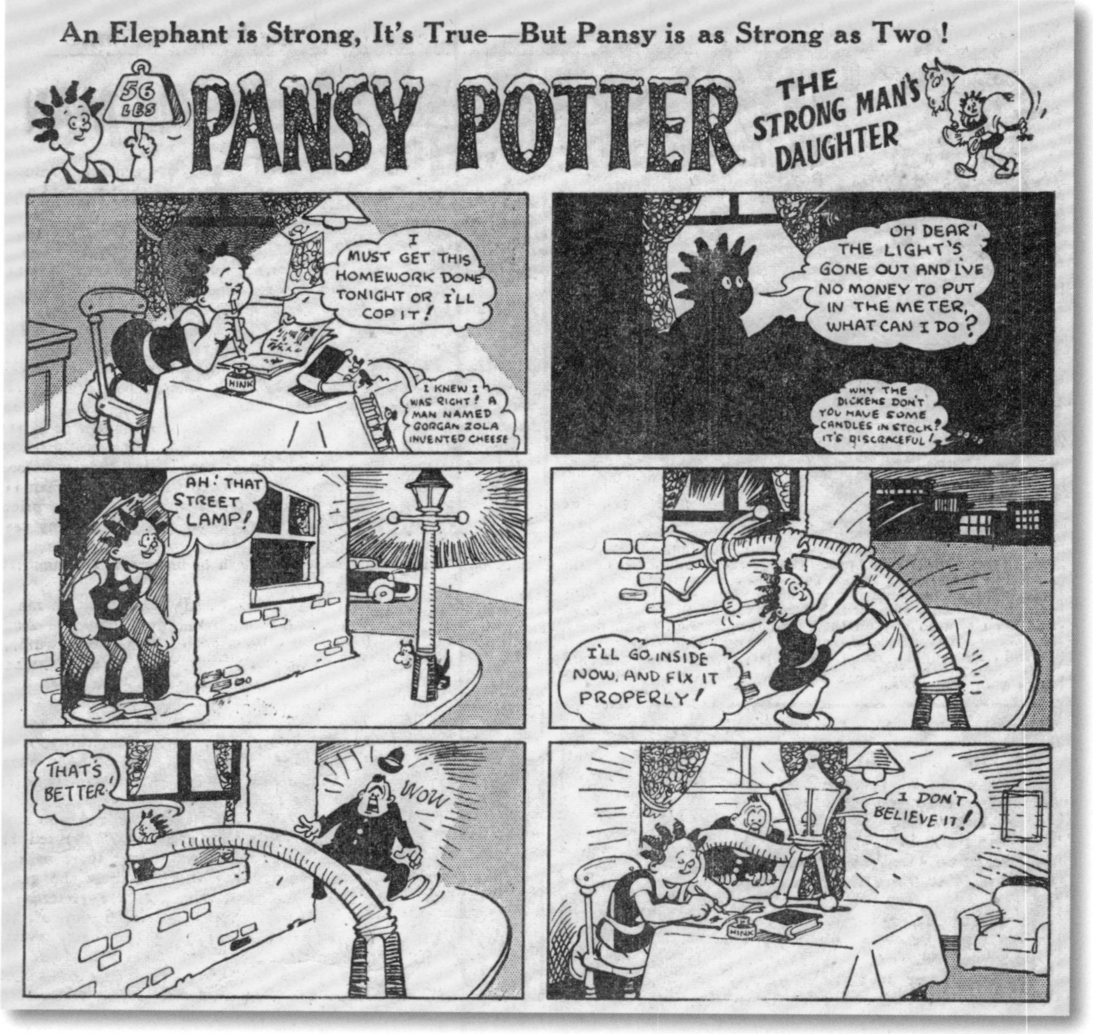
An Elephant is Strong, It's True—But Pansy is as Strong as Two !
56 LBS
PANSY POTTER
THE STRONG MAN'S DAUGHTER
I MUST GET THIS HOMEWORK DONE TONIGHT OR I'LL COP IT!
I KNEW I WAS RIGHT! A MAN NAMED GORGAN ZOLA INVENTED CHEESE
OH DEAR! THE LIGHT'S GONE OUT AND I'VE NO MONEY TO PUT IN THE METER, WHAT CAN I DO?
WHY THE DICKENS DON'T YOU HAVE SOME CANDLES IN STOCK? IT'S DISGRACEFUL!
AH! THAT STREET LAMP!
I'LL GO INSIDE NOW, AND FIX IT PROPERLY!
THAT'S BETTER
WOW
I DON'T BELIEVE IT!

In 1938 Hugh McNeill replied to a D. C. Thomson advertisement seeking new artists. Manchester born and bred, McNeill was then working with Kayebon Press, an advertising agency. He sent off sample work to R. D. Low, who recognised McNeill's potential immediately. Story lines were worked on and in *The Beano* No. 1, Hugh McNeill was illustrating 'Ping the Elastic Man'. Original artwork for the two versions are shown at the bottom of the page. Initially it was entitled 'Indy the Rubber Man'. A few weeks later, in *The Beano* No. 21, he started off a character that would last long after McNeill had stopped working with *The Beano* – 'Pansy Potter the Strong Man's Daughter'. He was one of the artists that, according to Editor George Moonie, gave the infant *Beano* character.

"INDY" The RUBBER MAN
DEAR ME I'VE BROKEN THE FENCE AGAIN HA! HA!
KEEP OFF THE FENCE
CRACK
CRACK
THAT'S THE THIRD TIME HE'S DONE IT!
OH, IS IT! WELL I'LL SETTLE HIM FOR YOU!
I'LL STRETCH MY ARM ACROSS HERE, AND WE'LL SEE WHAT HAPPENS.
STRETCH
I'LL BREAK THE TOP BAR, HA! HA!
W-WHAT'S HAPPENED?
I'M GETTING OUT OF HERE!
GLUG

PING THE ELASTIC MAN
CRASH!
DRAUGHT
GOAL!

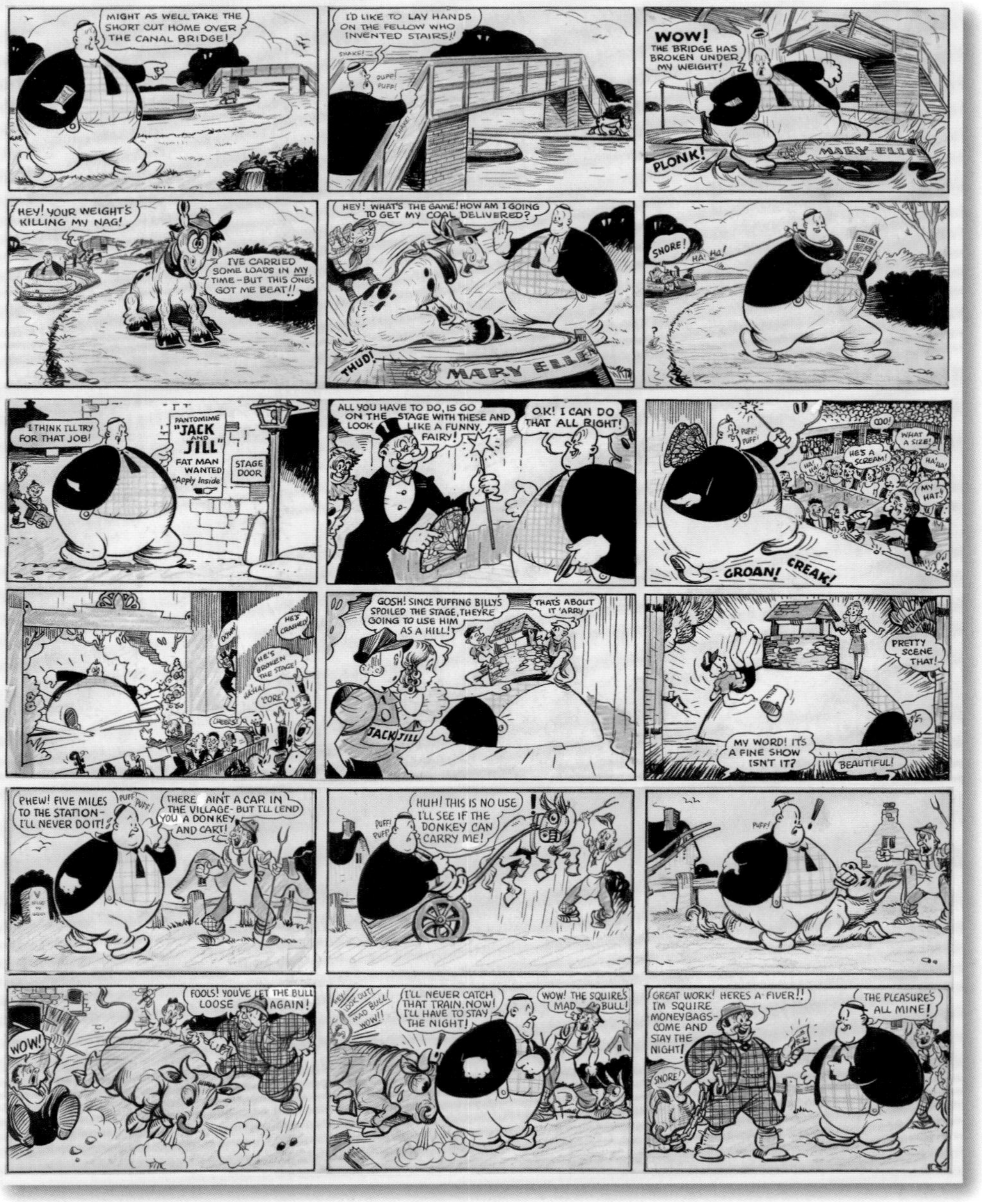
MIGHT AS WELL TAKE THE SHORT CUT HOME OVER THE CANAL BRIDGE!
I'D LIKE TO LAY HANDS ON THE FELLOW WHO INVENTED STAIRS!!
SHAKE!
PUFF! PUFF!
WOW! THE BRIDGE HAS BROKEN UNDER MY WEIGHT!
PLONK!
MARY ELLEN
HEY! YOUR WEIGHT'S KILLING MY NAG!
I'VE CARRIED SOME LOADS IN MY TIME – BUT THIS ONE'S GOT ME BEAT!!
HEY! WHAT'S THE GAME! HOW AM I GOING TO GET MY COAL DELIVERED?
THUD!
MARY ELLEN
SNORE!
HA! HA!
I THINK I'LL TRY FOR THAT JOB!
PANTOMIME "JACK AND JILL" FAT MAN WANTED –Apply Inside
STAGE DOOR
ALL YOU HAVE TO DO, IS GO ON THE STAGE WITH THESE AND LOOK LIKE A FUNNY FAIRY!
O.K! I CAN DO THAT ALL RIGHT!
PUFF! PUFF!
OOO!
WHAT A SIZE!
HE'S A SCREAM!
HA! HA!
MY HAT!
GROAN!
CREAK!
DOWN!
HE'S CRASHED!
HE'S BROKEN THE STAGE!
HA! HA!
'CORE!
GOSH! SINCE PUFFING BILLYS SPOILED THE STAGE, THEYRE GOING TO USE HIM AS A HILL!
THAT'S ABOUT IT 'ARRY
JACK JILL
PRETTY SCENE THAT!
MY WORD! IT'S A FINE SHOW ISN'T IT?
BEAUTIFUL!
PHEW! FIVE MILES TO THE STATION – I'LL NEVER DO IT!
PUFF! PUFF!
THERE AIN'T A CAR IN THE VILLAGE – BUT I'LL LEND YOU A DONKEY AND CART!
HUH! THIS IS NO USE I'LL SEE IF THE DONKEY CAN CARRY ME!
PUFF! PUFF!
PUFF!
FOOLS! YOU'VE LET THE BULL LOOSE AGAIN!
WOW!
I'LL NEVER CATCH THAT TRAIN, NOW! I'LL HAVE TO STAY THE NIGHT!
WOW! THE SQUIRE'S MAD BULL!
GREAT WORK! HERES A FIVER!! I'M SQUIRE MONEYBAGS – COME AND STAY THE NIGHT!
THE PLEASURE'S ALL MINE!
SNORE!

Three original two-row strips (left) for 'Puffing Billy', which ran from April 1939 until February 1940. 'Good Deed Danny' (below) was drawn as a trial strip for The Beano, *but it never actually appeared in the comic.*

GOOD DEED DANNY AND HIS DOG PESKY
WE'LL CRACK THE CRIB AT TEN TO-NIGHT
YOU SAY THE NUMBER'S 88
THAT'S WHAT I CALL A NASTY PLOT
WE'LL PUT THE BLIGHTERS "ON THE SPOT"
WANTED
PINCHING PETE
DIRTY DICK
£50 REWARD FOR THEIR CAPTURE
HERE'S A JOB FOR YOU AND ME – THEY'LL SOON BE UNDER LOCK AND KEY
88
NOW WE'LL SET OUR LITTLE TRAP
I MUST SAY – YOU'RE A BRAINY CHAP!
TACKS
AND THEN THE WATCHING PAIR ESPIED – THE BURGLARS LEAVE THEIR SHOES OUTSIDE
OUCH!!
HELP!!
TACKS IN SOCKS GAVE 'EM SHOCKS
ROUND AND ROUND MY TRUSTY PUP WE'LL TIE THE DIRTY WORKERS UP
THERE THEY ARE – I'VE DONE THE TRICK ON PINCHING PETE AND DIRTY DICK
THIS CAPTURE WAS A MARVELLOUS FEAT – NOW GO AND GIVE YOURSELVES A TREAT!
CASH

He also praised his professionalism in never being late with a job, even under difficult wartime circumstances. Hugh McNeill worked with ***The Beano*** on 'Good Deed Danny', but it never got off the starting blocks. Later, for ***Knockabout*** comic, McNeill would draw 'Deed-a-Day Danny', a strip about a keen boy scout. 'Puffing Billy' made a start in April 1939 and ran until McNeill was called up for active service in the Second World War. During the war he drew maps, at one time travelling with Montgomery. He also created 'Our Ernie', a character who was a typical British serviceman. The cartoons were published in the British press. McNeill would go on to become a major influence in British comics. He drew many notable characters and such was his ability that he could draw beautifully in several, very different styles. From the standard 'funnies' to adventure strips and nursery titles, all was effortless to him.

ALLAN MORLEY

The cartoonist Allan Morley was well known to R. D. Low. He had worked on various strips in the Big Five. His distinctive style formed a large part of 'The Fun Section' in D. C. Thomson's ***Sunday Post*** newspaper and he had three famous strips running in the new *Dandy* – 'Keyhole Kate', 'Hungry Horace' and 'Freddy the Fearless Fly'. Allan Morley was so prolific that R. D. was on record as saying that if anything happened to the Morley fun factory then the comics might close. 'Big Fat Joe' ran for a few months, until March 1939. On the right is the original artwork for the strip that appeared in the first *Beano* (see page 31 for the effect after colour was added). He reappeared in 1950 as one of Lord Snooty's gang of new pals. 'Cocky Dick (He's Smart and Slick)' started in *The Beano* in November 1939, while 'The Magic Lollipops (Suck 'Em and See)' first appeared in *The Beano* in 1941. Below is original artwork for 'The Magic Lollipops' (left and right) and 'Cocky Dick' (centre).

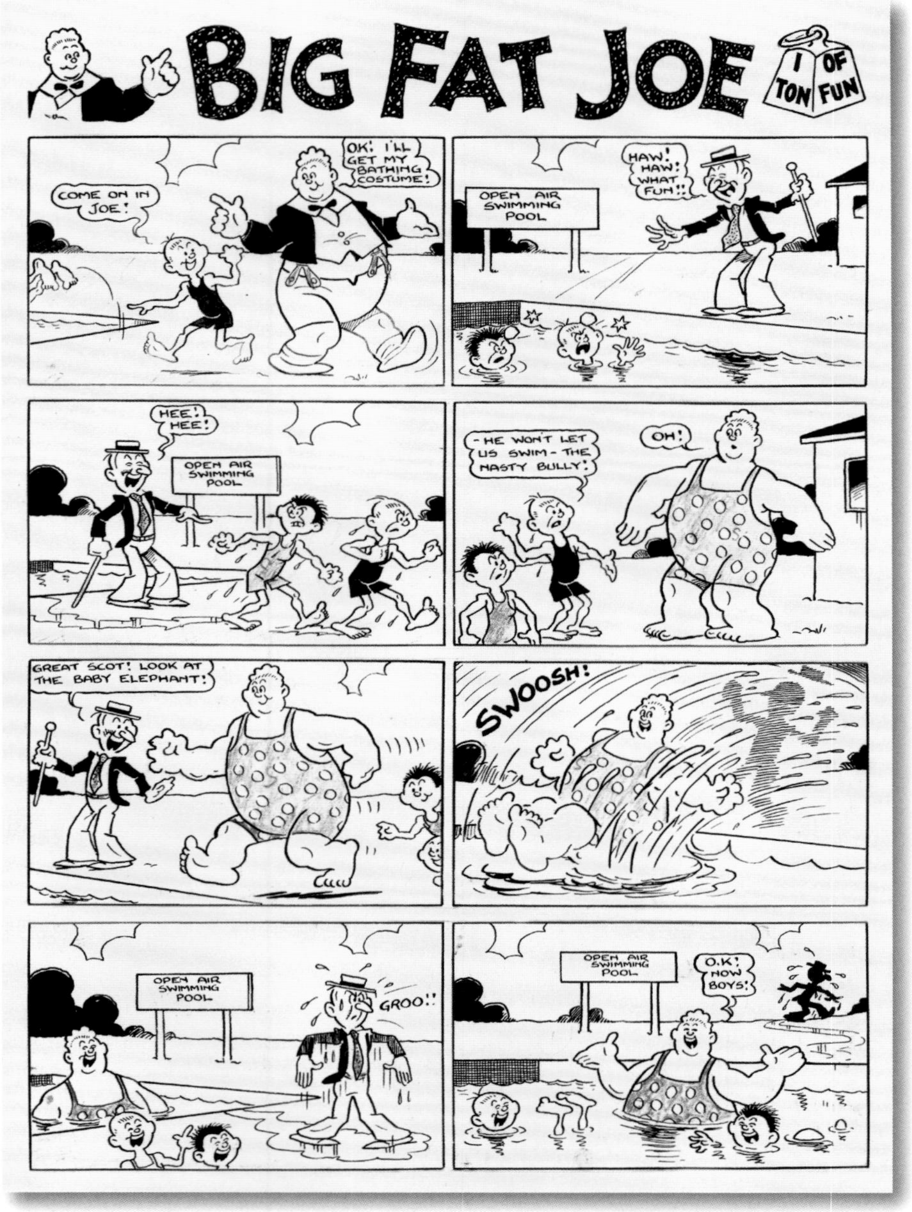
BIG FAT JOE
1 TON OF FUN
COME ON IN JOE!
OK! I'LL GET MY BATHING COSTUME!
OPEN AIR SWIMMING POOL
HAW! HAW! WHAT FUN!!
HEE! HEE!
OPEN AIR SWIMMING POOL
HE WON'T LET US SWIM - THE NASTY BULLY!
OH!
GREAT SCOT! LOOK AT THE BABY ELEPHANT!
SWOOSH!
OPEN AIR SWIMMING POOL
GROO!!
OPEN AIR SWIMMING POOL
O.K! NOW BOYS!

?
OW! WOW! HELP!

CALL 'EM OFF!
HA! HA! THOSE WASPS MUST HAVE BEEN AT MY MAGIC LOLLIPOPS!

GR-R! I'LL STOP THOSE KIDS SWINGING ON THE ROYAL TREES!
GET OFF!
SWINGING ON ROYAL TREES STRICTLY FORBIDDEN Signed King Coke
TO COKEVILLE MARKET SQUARE
THIS IS BETTER THAN SWINGING FROM A TREE!
GOOD KING COKE

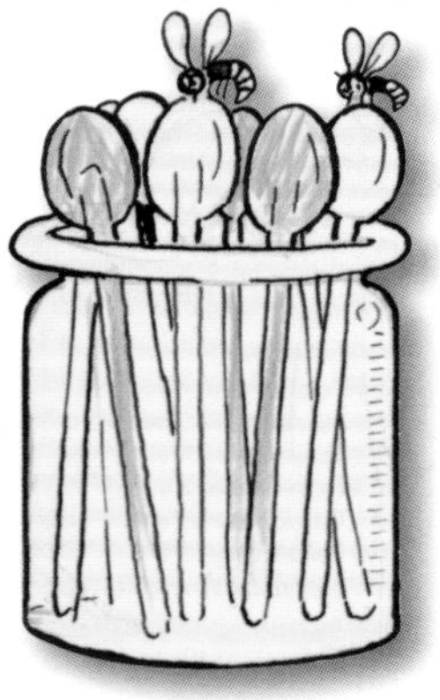

ERIC ROBERTS

BOO HOO! WE'VE LOST OUR AUNT! SNIFF! SNIFF!
HUSH, HUSH, MY LITTLE MEN. DON'T CRY — I'LL SOON REPLACE YOUR LOSS. JUST WAIT HERE FOR ME
I'LL JUST POP A FEW OF THESE INTO A BOX FOR THOSE LITTLE BOYS
DO NOT TOUCH
MOORTOWN NATURAL HISTORY MUSEU
MODEL ANTS' COLONY
ANTS AT WORK
PUFF! PUFF! I'M BACK, BOYS. NOW CLOSE YOUR EYES AND HOLD OUT YOUR HANDS
THOUGHT
I EXPECT THE KIND GENTLEMAN HAS BOUGHT US SOME SWEETS
SHAKE!
SHAKE!
HELP!
WOW! WHAT'S BITING ME?
BAH! YOU UNGRATEFUL MONKEYS. I THOUGHT YOU WOULD BE PLEASED TO SEE YOUR ANTS
WHACK!
HURT MY DEAR LITTLE NEPHEWS, WOULD YOU? TAKE THAT, AND THAT!
GIVE HIM WHAT FOR, AUNTIE
HUH! AND I WILL!
DRY CLEANERS
THE MOORTOWN DRY CLEANERS
PANTS WANTED BRING THEM IN NOW!
2/6
PANT!
YELP!
YOICKS! TALLY HO! THIS WAY TO THE SHOP THAT WANTS PANTS
PANT!
PANT! PANT!
PANT! PANT!

GET OFF!
SWINGING ON ROYAL TREES STRICTLY FORBIDDEN Signed King Coke
THIS IS BETTER THAN SWINGING FROM A TREE!
GOOD KING COKE

Original artwork for 'Rip Van Wink' (top) and 'Good King Coke (He's Stony Broke)' (bottom). 'Rip Van Wink' featured in the first Beano. 'Good King Coke' appeared first in December 1939.

Eric Roberts was working with *The Dandy*, illustrating the 'Podge' strip when *The Beano* chose him to work on 'Rip Van Wink'. His art style, using certain character types that would often look similar, was very popular. 'Good King Coke (He's Stony Broke)' was introduced in *The Beano* No. 21 as a two-line short. With a second series, the strip lasted up to 1946.

Eric Roberts was always more of a *Dandy* comic artist. He drew many stories for them including 'Winker Watson', who became a mainstay of that comic for decades. *The Dandy* editorial claimed that if Roberts was your artist, then even a fairly weak storyline would be well received.
For a time around 1950 he also drew 'Billy Bunter' for Amalgamated Press.

TORELLI BROTHERS

The Torelli Brothers art agency, based in Milan, produced two strips for the first *Beano* - 'Brave Captain Kipper' and 'Tin Can Tommy (the Clockwork boy)'. *The Beano* editorial team put the story in 'Tin-Can Tommy' (originally entitled 'The Adventures of Robert Robot') into rhyme – as they also did with 'Brave Captain Kipper'. The strips looked different; the thinking then was that they brought a cinematic cartoon quality to the comic. Within nine months the Italian brothers had two more strips in *The Beano*, 'Hicky the Hare' and 'Tricky Dicky Ant'. At a time when artists were at a premium and D. C. Thomson was expanding its comic division, having an agency produce so much usable material was a bonus. Unfortunately, world events were about to overtake the blossoming partnership.

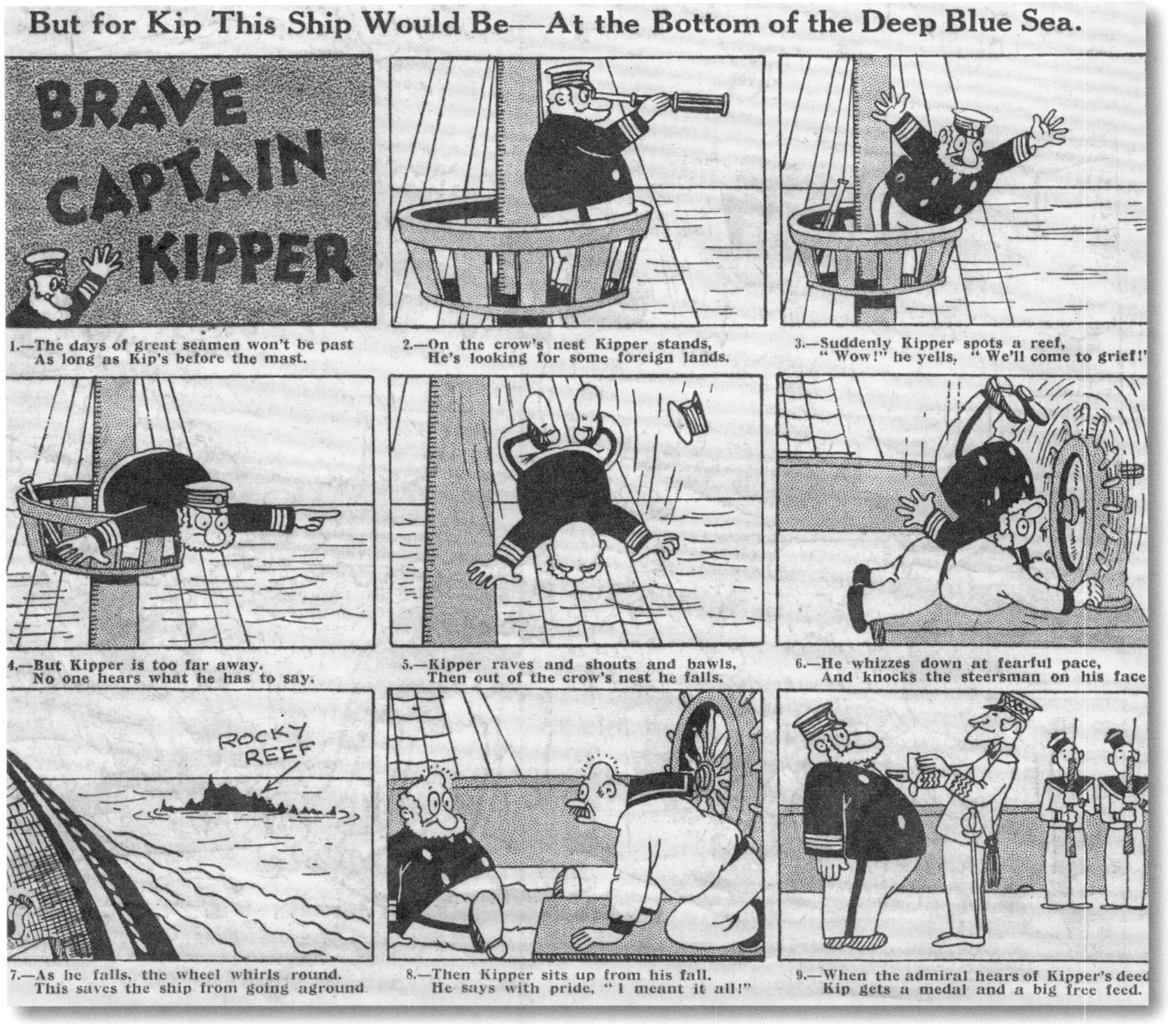
But for Kip This Ship Would Be—At the Bottom of the Deep Blue Sea.
BRAVE CAPTAIN KIPPER
1.—The days of great seamen won't be past As long as Kip's before the mast.
2.—On the crow's nest Kipper stands, He's looking for some foreign lands.
3.—Suddenly Kipper spots a reef, "Wow!" he yells, "We'll come to grief!"
4.—But Kipper is too far away. No one hears what he has to say.
5.—Kipper raves and shouts and bawls, Then out of the crow's nest he falls.
6.—He whizzes down at fearful pace, And knocks the steersman on his face
ROCKY REEF
7.—As he falls, the wheel whirls round. This saves the ship from going aground
8.—Then Kipper sits up from his fall. He says with pride, "I meant it all!"
9.—When the admiral hears of Kipper's deed Kip gets a medal and a big free feed.

THE ADVENTURES OF ROBERT ROBOT

NOW I'LL DRIVE MY CAR OVER THE BRIDGE

Original drawings for 'Hicky the Hare', 'Tricky Dicky Ant' and 'Tin-Can Tommy'. The coloured version of this strip is on page 42.

JAMES 'PEEM' WALKER

The Terrible Guardian of the Fifth Ruby of Runa.
The PRINCE ON THE FLYING HORSE

A D. C. Thomson staff man who, on his retiral in 1973, had spent 47 years as an artist with the company. He had studied at Gray's School of Art in Aberdeen after leaving school. In 1939 he drew two very popular stories for ***The Beano***. One was an early science fiction tale called 'The Prince on the Flying Horse', for which he drew the heading scene. The other was a full picture story called 'In the Land of the Silver Dwarves'. Early readers' letters all mention liking this story.

He is well known to generations of girls, as he drew the long running 'The Four Marys' story for ***The Bunty***. Apart from his full-time commercial artwork, Peem Walker was a gifted water-colourist and his paintings were exhibited at the Royal Scottish Academy.

The top illustration shows the header for 'The Prince on the Flying Horse' while all the other drawings are from the picture story 'In the Land of the Silver Dwarves.'

DUDLEY WATKINS

Dudley Dexter Watkins was born in Nottingham on February 27, 1907, the oldest of three children. He showed his artistic abilities at a very early age and, aged only 11, had a display of his work at an annual art competition in Nottingham. He attended evening classes at Nottingham School of Art and in the 1920s was employed in the window display department of Boots the Chemist, whose headquarters were in Nottingham. Before joining D. C. Thomson, and even subsequently, he exhibited at the annual art exhibition in Nottingham.

After gaining a scholarship, Dudley studied art on a full-time basis before being spotted by a representative of D. C. Thomson, probably R. D. Low, and was offered a job on the spot. Aged 18, he moved to D. C. Thomson's base in Dundee, where he was a staff artist, drawing anything that was given to him. Initially on a six-month trial period, Dudley soon showed his enormous talent and worked on the boys' adventure papers, supplementing his income by teaching life drawing at Dundee Art School.

I'M GOING ASHORE TO DO A BIT OF SHOPPING FOR YOU BOYS! — I'VE SOMETHING SPECIAL TO BUY TODAY!
I'LL BE BACK SOON—UNLESS I GET LOST!
THIS COMPASS AND CHART WILL HELP YOU, SIR! -- WE DON'T WANT YOU TO GET LOST!
DAVY GOT LOST THREE TIMES LAST WEEK, BUT HE SHOULD BE O.K. TODAY.
I WONDER IF HE'LL BRING BACK CHOCOLATES AND ICE CREAM!
H'M-THIS IS THE RIGHT DIRECTION!
CHEMIST
AHOY, MY LADS — I'M BACK AND I'VE BROUGHT YOU A WHACKING BIG BOTTLE OF CASTOR OIL!
UGH!-WHOSE IDEA WAS IT GIVING HIM THOSE MAPS AND A COMPASS? -- WE SHOULD HAVE LET HIM GET LOST!

LATER
FIRE!

PERCY VERE
AND HIS TRYING TRICKS
MAGIC
I'LL SHOW YOU A TRICK WITH THAT BUCKET OF WATER!
I CAN TURN IT UPSIDE-DOWN WITHOUT THE WATER COMING OUT!
THAT'S AN OLD DODGE!
WATCH ME!
PUSH OUT THIS LADDER!
I CAN KEEP THIS UP FOR HOURS HA-HA!

'Percy Vere' appeared in The Wizard, *'Monty Mug' (centre) in* The Wizard *and 'Wavy Davy' (top and bottom) in* The Beano.

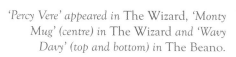

MORE FUN INSIDE WITH SPADGER AND THE BROONS
THE SUNDAY POST
FUN SECTION
'OOR WULLIE'
SUPPLEMENT TO THE SUNDAY POST, SEPTEMBER 20, 1936.
I'M ON THE LOOK OUT FOR HIM WULLIE
MAN WANTED
£50 REWARD FOR CAPTURE
I'D LIKE TAE HAE A SHOTTIE AT GETTING THAT REWARD.
DO NOT PARK CARS HERE WET CEMENT
CEMENT
WHAT ARE YE LOOKIN' AT?
YOU'RE NO' HIM!
THERE HE IS!
GARAGE
SIX GALLONS!
IS THERE A CAR PARK NEAR HERE?
YES SIR, JUST ROOND THE CORNER
I'VE GOT IT!
DO NOT
PARK CARS HERE WET CEMENT
HAH! THIS MUST BE THE PARKING PLACE
PARK CARS HERE
NOW I'VE GOT HIM
HOTEL
I'VE GOT THAT WANTED MAN
HOW'D YE MANAGE IT?
HIS CAR'S STUCK IN CEMENT
HA-HA!
QUICK! HE'S GOT MEN TAE BRAK AWA THE CEMENT
THATS NO' HIM—THATS THE CHIEF CONSTABLE!

It is difficult to identify some of his earlier work because he was required to draw in the style of some of the more senior artists of the time, but by the 1930s he had developed his own distinctive style. His first comic strip venture was as an inker for Chic Gordon in 1933.

R. D. Low had an idea to produce a different style of comic that focused on humour rather than adventure. In 1936 *The Sunday Post* gave away a free comic supplement featuring some of Dudley's work. R. D. noticed that Dudley had the rare ability to combine the comic with reality and 'Oor Wullie' and 'The Broons' were born.

WHEN I GROW UP I'LL HAE MUSCLES LIKE DESPERATE DAN!
AYE! IT'S COMIN' ON.

Poor Paw! There's Nae Peace But Or Ben.
He Takes The Lobby For His "Den."
SNORE
BURN
THIS IS GRAND! NAEBODY AT HAME! I'LL HAE A NICE SMOKE BY THE FIRE, LISTEN IN, AN READ MA "WEEKLY NEWS"
COME ON IN A MINUTE, MAK YERSELS AT HAME
AS I WIS SAYIN' MRS BROON—
YE CAN A' PLAY IN OOR HOOSE TH' NICHT!
SO I SAYS TAE HER, I SAYS, MRS SMITH—
O' COURSE ITS NAE GUID SAYIN' THAT TAE ME ABOOT THE CELTIC
WELL, LAST TIME I SAW 'EM PLAY AGAINST RANGERS—
DINNA TELL ONYBODY BUT YON WOMAN UP THE STREET IS—
I THINK CLARK GABLE'S WONDERFUL!
I LIKE GARY COOPER BEST
YE'LL HAE A CUP O' TEA WONT YE?
AS I WIS SAYIN', WHEN I WIS AT THE BATTLE O' WATERLOO, OLIVER CROMWELL SAYS TAE ME "BROON, MA BOY, YE LOOK A GEY SICHT BETTER IN THAT GAS MASK!"
MRS JOHNSTON—
BEAT CELTIC—
—AT THE BATTLE
O' WATERLOO—
PLAYING AT GANGSTERS—
—WITH BENNY LYNCH—
AND THE WOMAN NEXT DOOR
CLARK GABLE
I CANNA HEAR YE. I'VE LOST MA GLASSES
I SAID IT WIS A SAIR FECHT.
SAIR FEET? AYE, MINE'S ARE HURTIN' ME TAE!

LOOK AT OUR BEEZER NEW AEROPLANE GRAN'PAW!
AH, BUT IT'S NAE LIKE THE AULD GAMES WE USED TAE PLAY NAEBODY PLAYS THEM NOO!
AYE! WE'D RARE FUN IN THE DARK NICHTS. D'YE MIND CHICKEY MELLY AN' SNOUTS AN' ROBBERS?
AYE, AN' BEEZY, AN' BROKEN FLOO'ER POTS!—MAN, I'D LIKE TAE PLAY THEM AGAIN! HERE, THAT'S AN IDEA, WHIT ABOOT IT?
WE USED TAE TURN OOR JECKITS INSIDE OOT AS DISGUISES, AN' WEAR EACH OTHER'S BONNETS! COME ON OOT FOR A BIT FUN AT CHICKEY MELLY!
JINGS! WHIT A SICHT YOU LOOK IN MY BOWLER JOE!
GIE'S A SHOTTIE, GRAN'PAW!
GIGGLE
CHICKEY CHICK
JINGS! IT'S YOU BROON! PLAYIN' CHICKEY MELLY—AT YOUR AGE!—MAN, I HAVENA PLAYED THAT GAME FOR 35 YEARS!
ER-ER,—HULLO JOCK—ER, WE'RE JUIST HAVIN' A WEE BIT FUN LIKE AULD TIMES!
LOOK OUT!—HERE'S THE WIFIE!!

'The Broons', drawn by Dudley Watkins, who started drawing the strip in 1936. The strip still continues today.

Following the instant success of these two strips, R. D. Low moved to produce a comic that was to hit the streets in December 1937, ***The Dandy***. Following ***The Dandy***, in July of the next year ***The Beano*** arrived, perhaps the stage for some of Dudley's greatest work. His 'Biffo the Bear' appeared on every front page from January 1948 until his death in 1969.

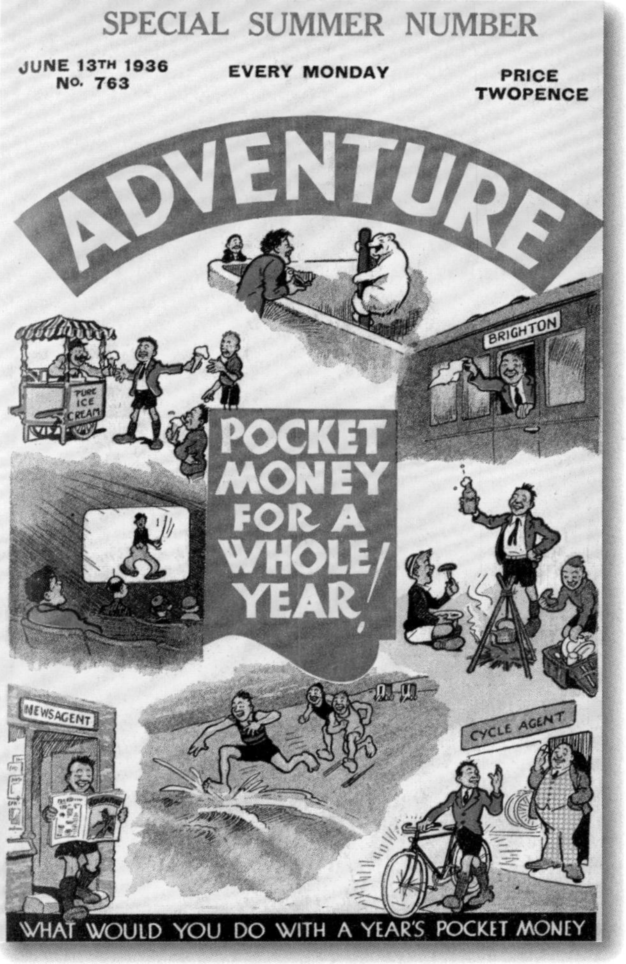
SPECIAL SUMMER NUMBER
JUNE 13TH 1936 No. 763
EVERY MONDAY
PRICE TWOPENCE
ADVENTURE
BRIGHTON
POCKET MONEY FOR A WHOLE YEAR!
NEWSAGENT
CYCLE AGENT
WHAT WOULD YOU DO WITH A YEAR'S POCKET MONEY

A cover for Adventure and a 'Desperate Dan' strip, both by Dudley Watkins.

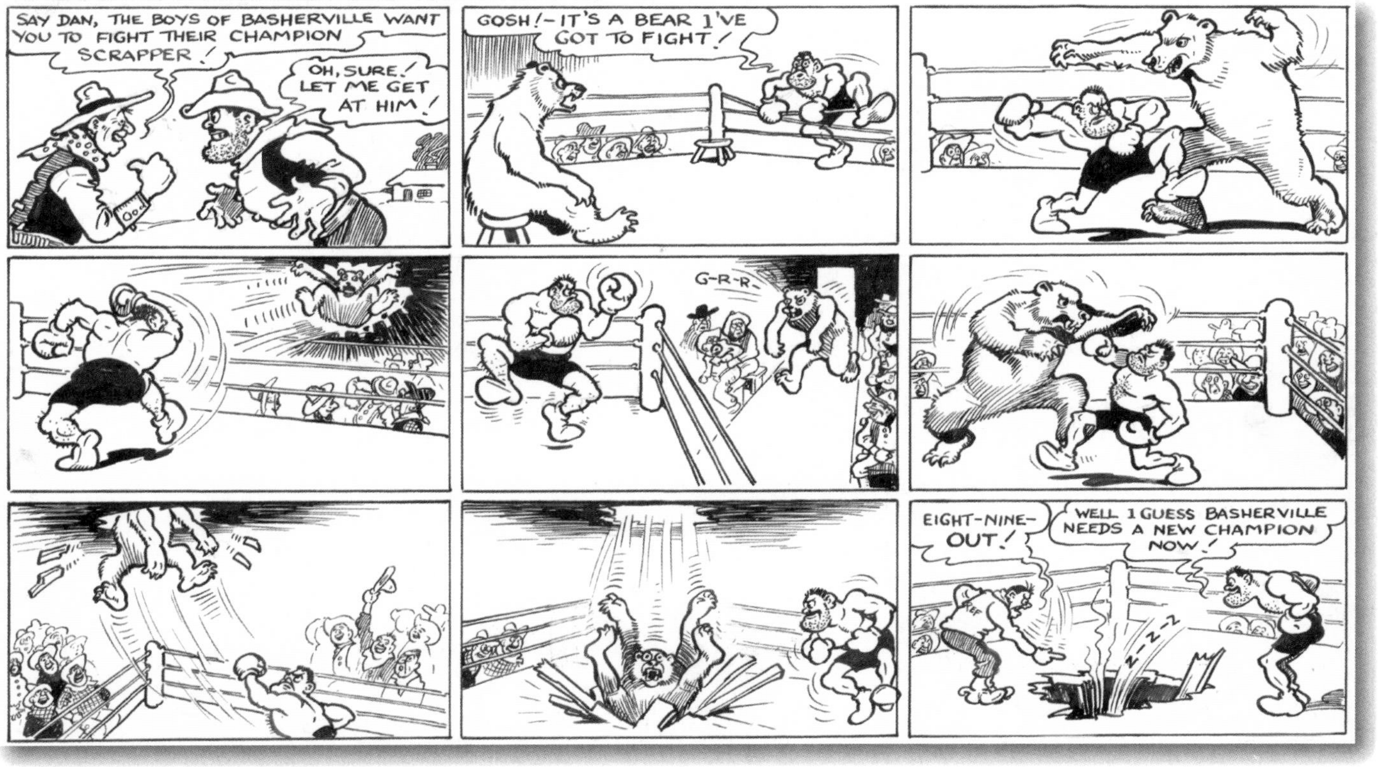
SAY DAN, THE BOYS OF BASHERVILLE WANT YOU TO FIGHT THEIR CHAMPION SCRAPPER!
OH, SURE! LET ME GET AT HIM!
GOSH! - IT'S A BEAR I'VE GOT TO FIGHT!
G-R-R-
EIGHT-NINE-OUT!
WELL I GUESS BASHERVILLE NEEDS A NEW CHAMPION NOW!

STARTING NOW— THIS GREAT NEW STORY OF A POLICEMAN WITH AN AWFUL SECRET! HE CAN TURN HIMSELF INTO A MOUSE ANY TIME HE CARES!
THE WHITE MOUSE WILL GET YOU—
IF YOU DON'T WATCH OUT!

Will Humbert Overcome His Greed—In Time to Save a Friend in Need?
THE KING'S GOT A TAIL!

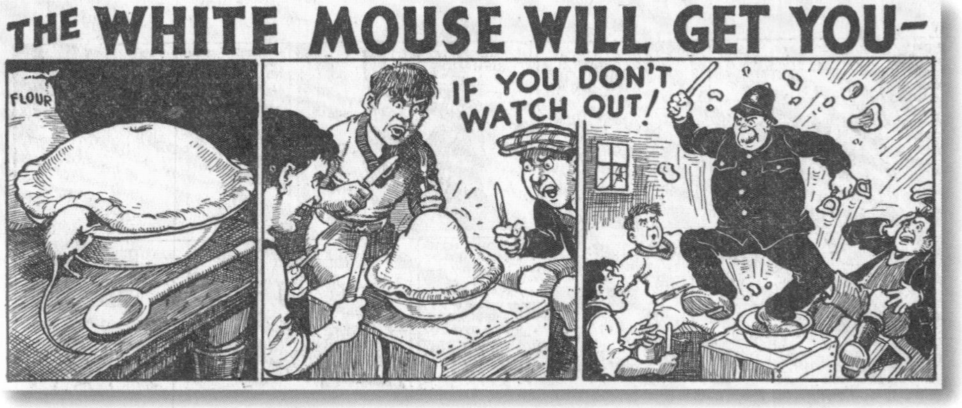
THE WHITE MOUSE WILL GET YOU—
FLOUR
IF YOU DON'T WATCH OUT!

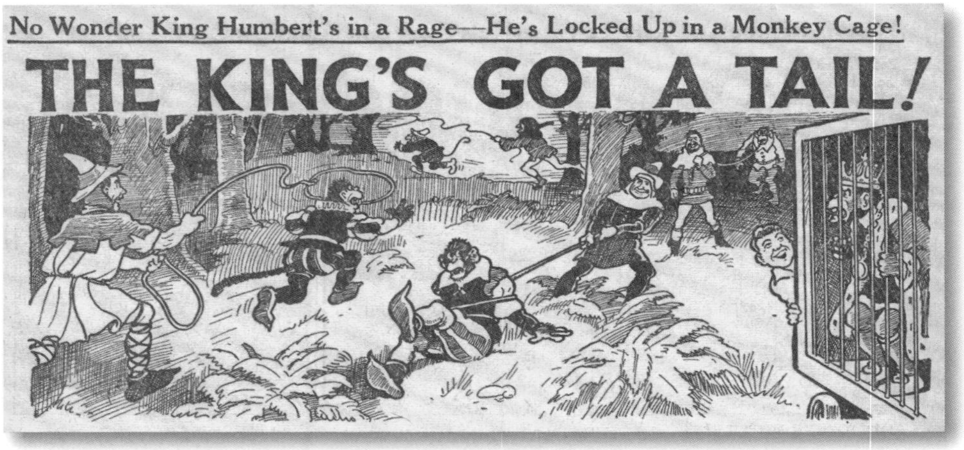
No Wonder King Humbert's in a Rage—He's Locked Up in a Monkey Cage!
THE KING'S GOT A TAIL!

His output was incredible and the stories he drew ranged from adventure tales such as 'Tom Thumb' (some illustrations are shown on the far right) to the inimitable 'Lord Snooty'. 'The White Mouse Will Get You (If You Don't Watch Out)' and 'The King's Got a Tail', for which he drew the title illustrations. A true genius who had the rare ability to take the written word and turn it into a comic masterpiece.

LORD SNOOTY AND HIS PALS
LORD MARMADUKE- "SNOOTY" TO YOU!
ROSIE.
HAIRPIN HUGGINS.
SKINNY LIZZIE.
SCRAPPER SMITH.
"HAPPY" HUTTON.
GERTIE THE GOAT
AND HERE, DUCHESS, IS A PORTRAIT OF SIR AUGUSTUS, LORD MARMADUKE'S GREAT-GREAT GRANDFATHER!
I'M FED UP WITH AUNTY YAPPING ABOUT THOSE OLD FAMILY PICTURES! THIS IS WHERE I BEAT IT!
I'LL CHANGE INTO MY DISGUISE AND BUZZ OFF TO ASH-CAN ALLEY!
HULLO GANG! HOW ARE YOU DOIN'?
WE'RE GLAD TO SEE YOU, SNOOTY!
MOVE ON THERE, YOU LAZY SCOUNDREL! IT'S AGAINST THE LAW TO BLOCK THE PAVEMENT WITH THOSE PICTURES!
THERE'S SCROGGS THE COP, GRUMPING AGAIN!
WAIT HERE A QUARTER OF AN HOUR, MISTER. WE'LL HELP YOU!
AUNTY'S OUT JUST NOW, LADS. HURRY UP AND GET THOSE PICTURES OFF THE WALL!
NOW WE'RE ALL SET TO HELP THAT POOR OLD STREET ARTIST!
IS THAT THE INSPECTOR OF POLICE? THIS IS THE EARL OF BUNKERTON TALKING. PLEASE PARADE YOUR MEN. I WILL BE DOWN TO INSPECT THE TOWN POLICE FORCE IN TEN MINUTES!
THIS OFFICER'S A DISGRACE! HIS FACE IS DIRTY, AND HIS BUTTONS DONT SHINE! KEEP HIM OFF THE STREET IN FUTURE!
VERY GOOD, SIR, I WILL GIVE HIM A JOB IN THE OFFICE!
THIS IS GRAND! I HAVEN'T SEEN A COP FOR HOURS, AND THOSE SWELL PICTURES ARE FAIRLY DRAWING THE CROWD!
GOODNESS GRACIOUS! THESE LOOK LIKE THE PICTURES FROM THE CASTLE GALLERY! I MUST HURRY HOME AND MAKE SURE!
CORKS! IT'S SNOOTY'S AUNT!
I'LL RUSH DOWN TO THE POLICE STATION AND WARN SNOOTY!
HEY, SNOOTY! GET YOUR PICTURES, QUICK! YOUR AUNT'S SEEN THEM!
POLICE STATION
WE'VE GOT TO PUT THESE PICTURES BACK BEFORE AUNT GETS HOME!
I MUST HAVE MADE SOME MISTAKE! HERE ARE ALL THE PICTURES SAFE AND SOUND!
EAT AS MANY FISH SUPPERS AS YOU LIKE, GANG! I'VE TONS OF MONEY!
I BET OLD SCROGGS THE COP WON'T BOTHER YOU AGAIN!

WITC

THE EARLY BEANO BOOKS

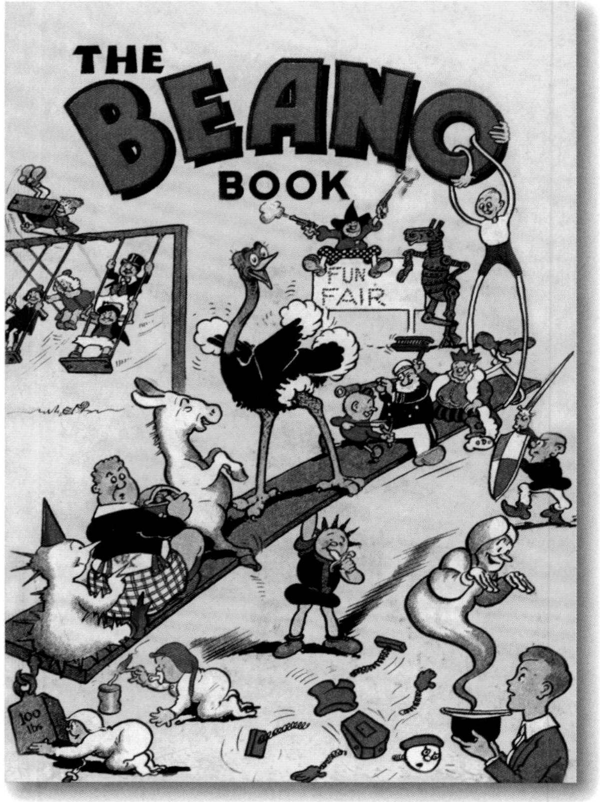
THE
BEANO
BOOK
FUN FAIR

THE
MAGIC-BEANO
BOOK

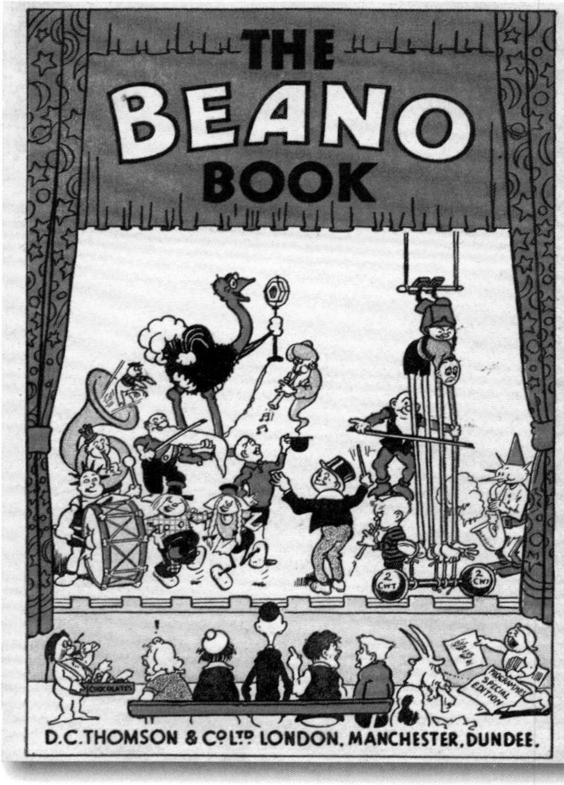
THE
BEANO
BOOK
D.C.THOMSON & Co LTD LONDON, MANCHESTER, DUNDEE.

MARMADUKE MEAN
THE MISER
I'LL GO TO THE GOLF LINKS AND SEE IF I CAN FIND ANY LOST BALLS!
WHO? ME? NO!!
HAVE YOU SEEN MY BALL?
NOW I'LL SELL IT TO HIM!
YOW!
DOCTOR!!
AH! THERE'S MY BALL!
A-MUSE-ING!
Said a ragged old beggar called Muse,
" My presence you'll have to excuse.
My best Sunday coat
Is in rags, and you'll note
That both soles are quite off my shoes."
THE TIGER WAS TICKLED
There was a bad boy of Pekin
Who tickled a lean tiger's chin.
The tiger's now fat.
Can you wonder at that ?
But where is that boy of Pekin ?

The immediate success of *The Beano* in 1938 created a demand for an annual. The launch of *The Beano* in July meant that it was too late to produce an annual for the 1938 Christmas market, but it was all hands to the pumps to create 128 pages of fun and laughter for the following year. By the time *The Beano Book* reached the shops, war had broken out. This first annual, although released in 1939, is generally catalogued as the 1940 edition. The book contained strips that appeared in *The Magic* and even one that appeared in *The Dandy. The Beano Book* became *The Magic–Beano Book* in 1943. This eclectic mix continued until *The Beano Book* reappeared in 1951 and it has remained under that flag ever since. Some of the stories did not appear in the weekly comic, and some only lasted for one issue of the annual, such as 'Marmaduke Mean the Miser', 'Dingo the Doggie' and 'Boss and Bert'.

CINDERELLA
AND THE UGLY SISTERS
AND WHERE DO YOU THINK YOU'RE GOING CINDERELLA?
I'M GOING TO THE PICTURES YOU TOLD ME I COULD!
OH YEAH --- WELL YOU'RE NOT -- YOU GET BUSY AND MAKE SOME MINCE MEAT!
SLAP
O, GOBLIN OF THE SLIPPER -- PLEASE HELP ME PUNISH MY SISTERS FOR KEEPING ME FROM GOING TO THE PICTURES!
HA-HA! I HAVE A BONNY WHEEZE I'LL MAKE YOUR SISTERS WEE AS FLEAS!
NOW PICK THEM UP AND PUT THEM IN THE MINCING MACHINE!
GOSH! THEY ARE TINY!
HAVE MERCY!
IN YOU GO IN THE MINCING MACHINE!
PLOP
HO-HO! THIS IS BETTER THAN THE REAL PICTURES NOW THAT GOBLIN HAS TURNED THE MINCER INTO A PROJECTOR!
The slipper-goblin never sticks. Here's Cinderella's private flicks.

TOOTSY McTURK
THIS IS TERRIBLE! I DON'T HAVE ENOUGH COUPONS FOR A NEW SUIT!
CLOTHIER
Tootsy's rags from head to foot.
He requires a brand new suit.
HELLO, WHAT'S THIS? SAY, I CAN MANAGE THREE COUPONS!
SOCKS TO SUIT ALL FEET 3 COUPONS
HOSIER
Though his coupons are so few,
Pair of socks will maybe do.
YOUR NOTICE SAID "TO SUIT ALL FEET," MISTER!
I KNOW, BUT THIS, WILL RUIN ME. IT WILL TAKE MILES OF WOOL!
Hosier measures Tootsy's feet.
They are very far from neat.
NOW, IF I UNRAVEL THESE SOCKS I SHOULD GET A LOT OF BALLS OF WOOL
SOCKS
Our old Tootsy is no fool.
See him winding balls of wool.
I'LL TAKE FOUR BALLS, TOOTSY
I'LL TAKE SOME, TOOTSY!
2 BALLS OF WOOL FOR ONE COUPON
Wool is selling with a swing.
Lots of coupons people bring.
WELL, I'VE GOT A NEW SUIT AT LAST! THANKS!
THANK YOU FOR THE COUPONS!
With the coupons thus acquired
Tootsy gets the suit desired.

THE FREEZY WHEEZE MAN
FROSTY McNAB
I'VE JUST GOT TO FIX THE STICKS IN THE TOFFEE APPLES, THEN THEY ARE READY.
"Now the sticks
I will fix."
WOW! FROSTY'S KNOCKED THE STICKS INTO THE MUD!
See them frown!
Sticks knocked down.
WE WANT OUR TOFFEE APPLES.
Youngsters cry.
Frosty, fie!
THAT WATER-CART GIVES ME A GOOD IDEA
I'LL FREEZE THE WATER WITH MY ICY BREATH
WATER CART
Icy wheezes—
Water freezes.
NOW I'LL BREAK OFF THE ICICLES.
WATER CART
Pointed ice
Very nice.
THESE ICICLES SURE MAKE GOOD STICKS FOR THE TOFFEE-APPLES, FROSTY. I'LL FORGIVE YOU FOR KNOCKING OVER MY CART.
Pleased as punch
Are the bunch!
TEACHER-TEASERS
TEACHER:—What is a goldfish?
HENRY:—A sardine that has got very rich.
TEACHER:—What a zebra?
CUTHBERT:—A donkey wearing a football jersey.

While the weekly, and subsequently, fortnightly *Beano* contained some hilarious propaganda stories, as will be seen in the next chapter, the books continued on an altogether more genteel path, with little or no mention of the war. However, the back cover of the 1943 book did contain a message, for Tootsy McTurk's feet are displaying the V for Victory sign, while below the illustration are three dots and a dash, which is V in Morse code. The first few bars of Beethoven's Fifth Symphony, which spell out in music the V in Morse code, were used to introduce the BBC radio broadcasts during the war.

PART 2

The Beano's War

1939-1949

LAUGHING IN THE FACE OF DANGER

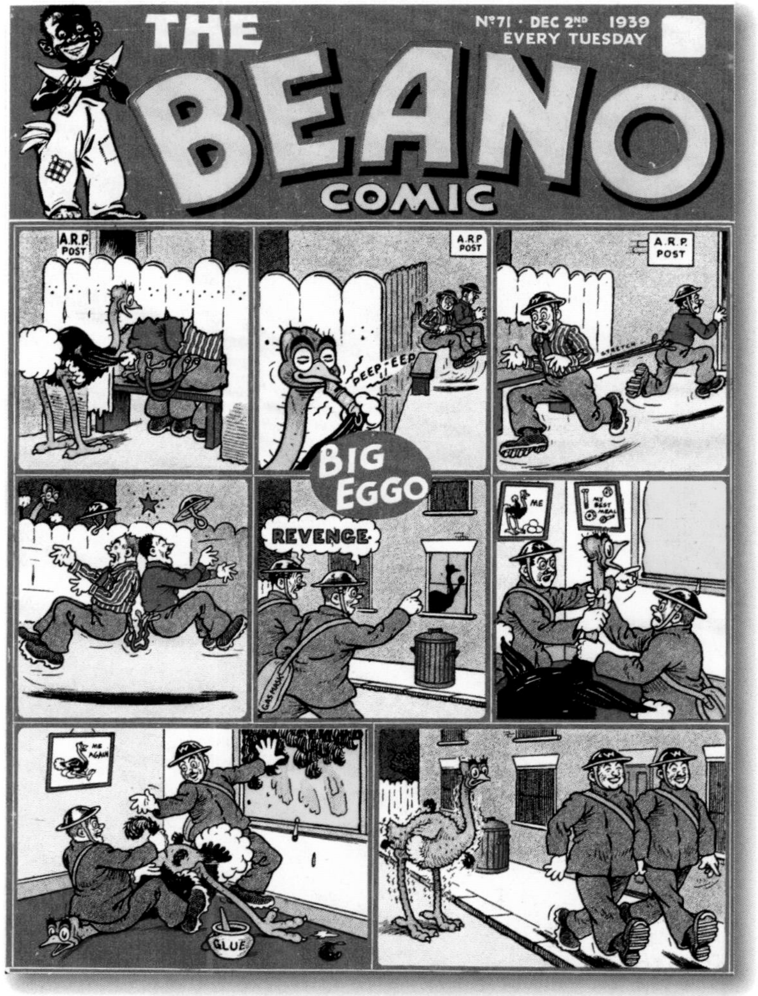
THE BEANO COMIC
Nº71 · DEC 2ND 1939
EVERY TUESDAY
A.R.P. POST
PEEP, PEEP
BIG EGGO
REVENGE
GLUE

BIG EGGO
KENNELS
ALL BREEDS OF DOGS

BIG EGGO
TOY BALLOONS

Wartime 'Big Eggo' front covers, drawn by Reg Carter, the story on the right reinforcing the message of the importance of obeying the blackout.

For British children during the 1940s, the advent of war presented a bizarre conundrum. It was the best of times and the worst of times; bitter, yet also sweet. This was a generation raised on a media diet of good triumphing over evil, whatever the odds, in movies and comics. When war was declared, children puffed their chests out and faced their fate with confidence.

As the harsh reality of evacuations, air raids, rationing and losing friends, relatives and fathers unfolded, attitudes were tested. In some ways, wartime added tangible adventure to children's lives. Gas masks, the blackout, air raid shelters, warnings of spies, brave soldiers and school being closed all represented new and exciting times. Sweets may have been rationed, but imagination wasn't and the scope for exercising this was wider than ever. Every stranger was a possible spy, every child was a potential soldier and every day was another adventure. ***The Beano*** took advantage of this.

THE
BEANO
COMIC
No 72 · DEC 9TH · 1939
EVERY TUESDAY
2d
YOU CAN HELP THE ARMY BY KNITTING SOCKS SEND THEM TO
BIG EGGO
BATHING PARADE
WANTED GIRLS TO KNIT BABY CLOTHES PAY WILL BE ONE LOLLIPOP AN
NEXT DAY
DRILL HALL

HE'S ASLEEP AT LAST!
BIG EGGO
LET ME HAVE THOSE
ARMY BARRACKS
DREAM
JUMP TO IT YOU LAZY LOAFERS. BLOW THE COOK-HOUSE CALL!

DON'T TICKLE!
PAINT
BIG EGGO
IDEA
IF ONLY THESE DUCKS KNEW THAT THIS IS ONLY A BARRAGE BALLOON WITH A FACE PAINTED ON IT!

Certain children's magazines ceased publication during the war years but ***The Beano*** completed its National Service with distinction. It quite literally had children laughing in the face of danger, and promised readers that, as long as they did their bit, everything would work out just fine.

LAUGHING IN THE FACE OF THE ENEMY

The Beano didn't simply amuse children by taking their minds off the danger they faced; it had a duty to become involved in the propaganda battle too. British propaganda was unique amongst the war nations in that it was based around humour. This type of indoctrination won hearts as well as minds. Propaganda works best when the enemy is diminished and portrayed as a manageable entity, certain to be defeated. The contrast with the war's other protagonists was stark. Much of the German propaganda was sinister, especially in the portrayal of Jewish citizens. It showed them as people to be feared and issued dire warnings of the disasters Germany would face should Jews prosper.

Who could be afraid of enemies like these?

LORD SNOOTY AND HIS PALS
LORD MARMADUKE,— "SNOOTY" TO YOU!
ROSIE
HAIRPIN HUGGINS
SKINNY LIZZIE
SCRAPPER SMITH
"HAPPY" HUTTON.
SNITCHY AND SNATCHY
GERTIE THE GOAT
SNIVELLING SNITZELS! I HAF SLEPT IN! THAT DUMB-CLUCK OF A SERVANT OF MINE HAS FORGOTTEN TO WAKEN ME! AND BAKE MY BOOTS, MINE TEA, TOO, IS COLD! OOH! SOME-VUN FOR THIS SHALL SUFFER!
COLD
ATTENTION, YOU LOAFING LOUNGER! WHY HAF YOU LET YOUR FUHRER SLEEP IN? WHY ISS MY TEA COLD? I WILL HAF YOU SHOT FOR THIS
AW, PIPE DOWN, ADDY! I DO NO MORE WORK FOR YOU. I'M FED UP WITH DIS LIFE. NO CINEMAS, NO FOOD, NO FUN!
VOT IS DER MEANING OF DIS, HERMAN? HAF YOU GONE DER NUTS?
ACH! IF ONLY WE HAD DER "BEANO" COMICS LIKE DER BRITISH KIDS, WE'D BE AS HAPPY AS DER LARKS!
OH, DEAR, ADOLF, SAVE ME PLEASE FROM DER SOLDIERS. DEY ARE SO FED UP DEY WON'T WORK.
GET A MOVE ON YOU BURSTING BUTTER BARREL! FOR ONE PIN I'D BLOW YOU INTO TINY-BITS—JA!
THAT'S VOT I THINK OF YOU, MINE FUHRER! VOT A PITY IT ISS ONLY DER STATUE!
HERR HITLER THE FURIOUS FUHRER

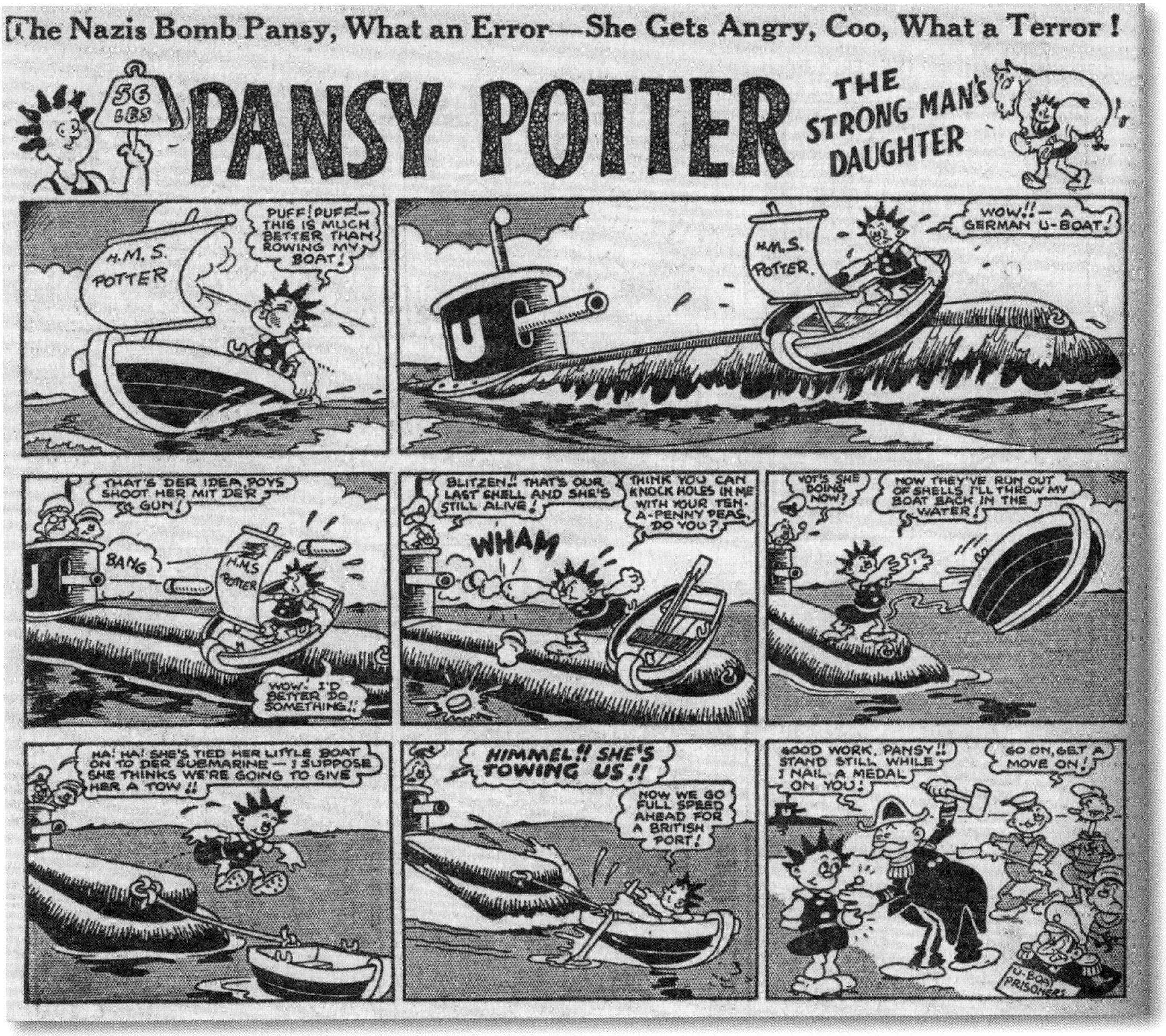
The Nazis Bomb Pansy, What an Error—She Gets Angry, Coo, What a Terror !
56 LBS
PANSY POTTER
THE STRONG MAN'S DAUGHTER
H.M.S. POTTER
PUFF! PUFF!— THIS IS MUCH BETTER THAN ROWING MY BOAT!
WOW!!— A GERMAN U-BOAT!
H.M.S. POTTER.
THAT'S DER IDEA, POYS SHOOT HER MIT DER GUN!
BANG
H.M.S. POTTER
WOW! I'D BETTER DO SOMETHING!!
BLITZEN!! THAT'S OUR LAST SHELL AND SHE'S STILL ALIVE!
THINK YOU CAN KNOCK HOLES IN ME WITH YOUR TEN-A-PENNY PEAS, DO YOU?
WHAM
VOT'S SHE DOING NOW?
NOW THEY'VE RUN OUT OF SHELLS I'LL THROW MY BOAT BACK IN THE WATER!
HA! HA! SHE'S TIED HER LITTLE BOAT ON TO DER SUBMARINE — I SUPPOSE SHE THINKS WE'RE GOING TO GIVE HER A TOW!!
HIMMEL!! SHE'S TOWING US!!
NOW WE GO FULL SPEED AHEAD FOR A BRITISH PORT!
GOOD WORK, PANSY!! STAND STILL WHILE I NAIL A MEDAL ON YOU!
GO ON, GET A MOVE ON!
U-BOAT PRISONERS

American propaganda for children was cautionary. The Disney short 'Der Fuhrer's Face' portrayed none other than Donald Duck as a Nazi stormtrooper. In it, he suffers an ignominious existence in this role before waking to realise it was all a bad dream! Although this sounds like a comical scenario, the actual portrayal was very dark and represented another chilling vision of what might come to pass.

The Beano's treatment of the conflict was, perhaps unintentionally, relatively subtle and almost always hilarious. It guaranteed that no child reading was unduly scared by the enemy; how could they be? The Axis powers were portrayed as abject idiots and complete buffoons.

A constant *Beano* editorial prerequisite has been that the righteous should prevail and that those in the wrong – whether errant schoolchildren, bullies, robbers or even wartime leaders – should never succeed in their nefarious intentions.

The first propaganda strip to appear in *The Beano* was 'Pansy Potter (the Strong Man's Daughter)' on November 18, 1939. In it, she single-handedly captures a German U-boat and tows it ashore with her rowing boat.

CHUCKLING AT HAW-HAW!

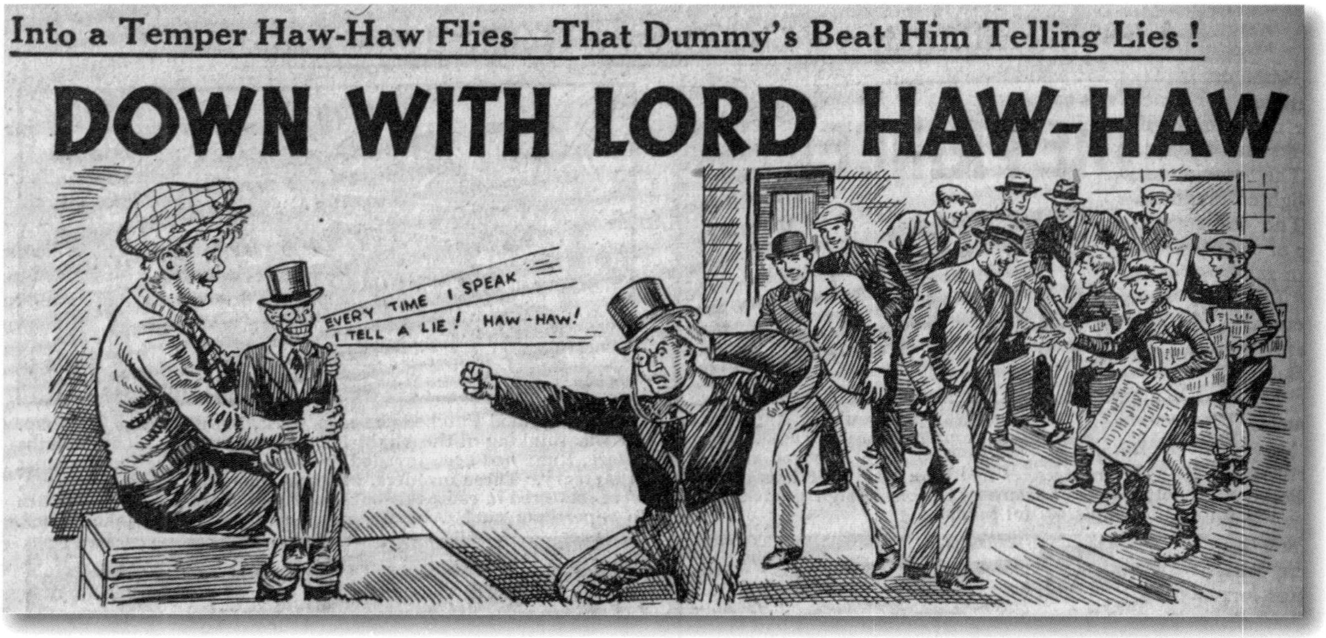
Into a Temper Haw-Haw Flies—That Dummy's Beat Him Telling Lies!
DOWN WITH LORD HAW-HAW
EVERY TIME I SPEAK I TELL A LIE! HAW-HAW!

The majority of propaganda stories centred around the enemy in general, although most tended to feature the Nazis, or the 'Nasties' as ***The Beano*** liked to call them. As the war progressed, individuals of notoriety began to emerge from the Axis nations. ***The Beano*** did its best to eliminate them as credible foes as quickly as possible with a variety of humorous character assassinations. The Nazi propagandist popularly known as Lord Haw-Haw was the first target. June 1940 (No. 101) saw the start of a text-based story, 'Down With Lord Haw-Haw', illustrated by Jack Glass, which ran for four issues and described the battle between the heroic children from Northtown and the dastardly Honourable Augustus Snobley. Snobley was nicknamed Lord Haw-Haw due to his tendency to lie, like the infamous Nazi propagandist who was notorious for broadcasting deliberately false dispatches from behind enemy lines.

It was important that the enemy's morale-busting tactics were exposed quickly and effectively and this rubbishing of Haw-Haw (for example in the story on the right from 'Hooky's Magic Bowler Hat'), was a speedy way of getting the message through to Britain's children that this broadcaster was full of mince! This was the first of many occasions where ***The Beano*** rubbished Haw-Haw, but he was a comparatively minor player in the conflict overall, and it wasn't long before ***The Beano*** moved on to bigger – or perhaps 'fatter' – targets.

GOOD FORTUNE! LORD HAW-HAW I SEE
I'LL MAKE HIM WHAT HE REALLY SHOULD BE!
THIS IS STATION BREMEN BROADCASTING IN ENGLISH. HAW! HAW! WE HAF KILLED BEN NEVIS, DER CHAMPION OF SCOTLAND AND SUNK DER CARGO OF CANDY APPLES, HAW! HAW!

BOG DOGGLED SAUSAGES! DER LORD HAW-HAW ISS A DONKEY!
HAW! HAW!

BASHING BENITO

December 1940 saw the debut of a strip dedicated to lampooning the Italian leader, Il Duce, Benito Mussolini – or 'Musso' as he was henceforth known in ***The Beano***! Artist Sam Fair's stated intention was to portray Britain's enemies as bumbling idiots. Mussolini, himself a journalist and keen student of media before he became the Italian dictator, was an easy target. As well as Musso, Il Duce was also portrayed as a figure of fun in several other strips. Most often he was presented as a fat, arrogant buffoon, with his pride typically coming shortly before an embarrassing fall!

HEY! YOU CAN'T BOMB ME- I'M HITLER'S PAL!
THAT'S WHAT YOU THINK!
MUSSOLINI

MUSSO THE
HE'S A BIG-A-DA FLOP
AH! I HAVE-A-DA BRAIN-A-WAVE!
PET TORTOISES — DA CHEAP
PET STORES
GIVE DA GREAT MUSSO DA DOZEN TORTOISES!
TRY OUR CANARY BIRD-A-SEED
AND NOW I JUST PAINT DA LETTERS ON DA TORTOISES, SO-
MUSSO DA GREAT
-AND HOW'SA THAT?
AW GEE! - I'M FED UP WITH THIS LARK - I'M GETTING OUT OF HERE!
YOU'RE RIGHT BUDDY- SO AM I!
LATER
DA YIPPEE! NOW TO TAKE ANOTHER LOOK AT-A-MY CLEVER TORTOISE IDEA!
MUSSO DA RAT
DA BIGGA DA SWOON

In 1941, *Beano* readers demonstrated their feelings for the Italian dictator in a storyline which saw them send a package of remedies for a bout of insomnia he was enduring. These 'treats' included a massive mallet to knock himself out with, rat poison and 'a sock to stuff into his big mouth'! Imagine the suggestion that a child should attempt to handle poison nowadays?

Fascists were ambivalent about the presence of comics in Italian society. They recognised the medium was a potentially powerful propaganda tool, particularly in targeting the young. However, they also believed modern comic strips – particularly the ballooned speech bubbles typical of *The Beano* – were an anathema to the conservative Italian cultural tradition. This uncertainty was reflected by the way Mussolini reportedly procrastinated over a ban on imported Disney comic art due to his own children's fondness for Mickey Mouse!

Despite this, after the war began, all foreign comics were outlawed in Italy. Native Italian comics were also banned from using speech balloons and obliged to use only lengthy text picture captions. With his war on comics in *The Beano* style it's unsurprising Mussolini became a favourite target of the acerbic wit of *The Beano* team.

AH! DA CAMERA!
HEY-A-YOU! JUST WAIT-A-HERE WHILE I GO AND BRING MY PAL HITLER – I WANT TO HAVE DA PHOTOGRAPH TAKEN OF DA TWO OF US!
BUT-MUSSO-
JUST SHUT-A-YOUR MOUTH UP AND DO AS YOU ARE-A-TOLD!
NOW-A-THEN- TAKE DA SNAPPY PHOTO OF DA GREAT MUSSO AND DA GREAT HITLER!
DER WOW!
SOCK!
THAT'S WHAT I TRIED TO TELLA YOU, MUSSO-
PRESS
DA WOW!
-THIS IS DA TRICK CAMERA!!
PLAY DER TRICKS ON DER GREAT ADOLF!-EH?-
DA HELP! SAVE-A-ME FROM MY BEST-A-FRIEND!!

V FOR VICTORY FOR DA BRITISH
TAKE-A-THAT,-AND DON'T LET ME CATCH YOU MAKING DA V SIGN AGAIN!
OUCH!
V FOR VICTORY FOR DA BRITISH
KICK
DA NOTICE
ANY-A-ONE FOUND MAKING DA V SIGN WILL BE PUT IN DA STOCKS FOR AN HOUR
I'LL GET MY REVENGE BY JUST CUTTING OUT DA V SIGN ON DA WHEELS OF MUSSO'S MOTOR BIKE!
MUSSO
WHO PUT DA V SIGNS ON DA ROAD?
YOU DID, MUSSO!
DA BIGGA DA WOW!
STALE

THE FOOLHARDY FUHRER

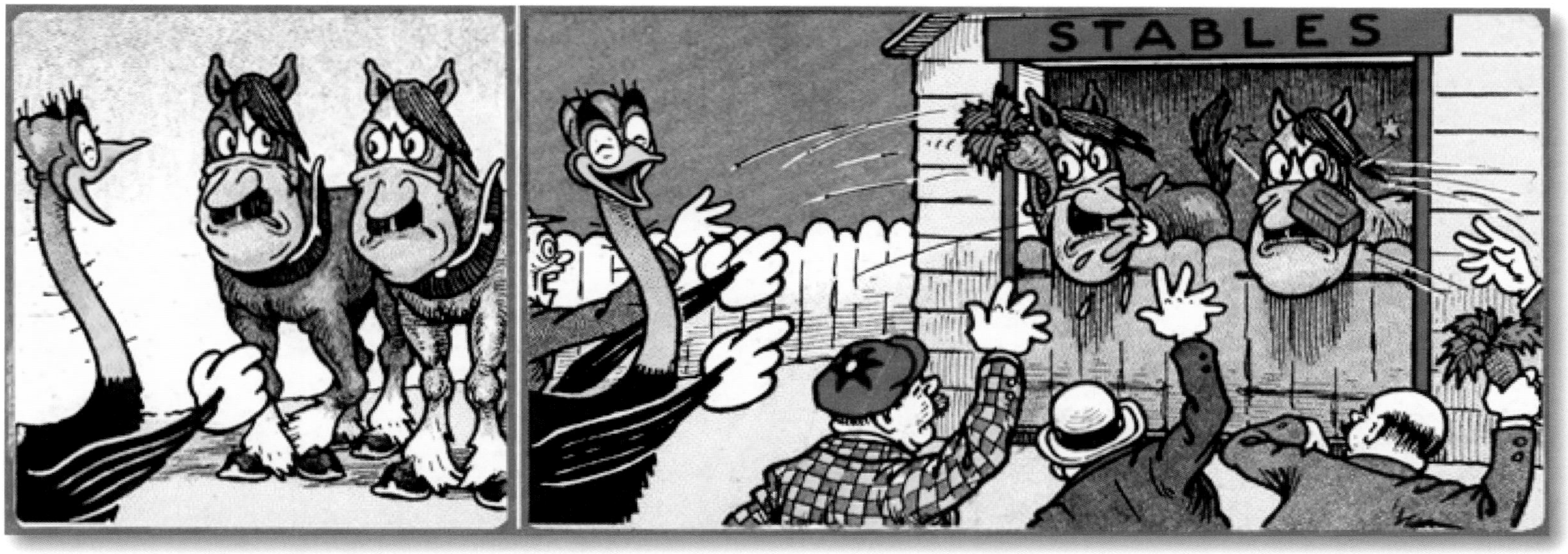
STABLES

THAT HITLER GUY GIVES ME THE PIP
SO I THINK I'LL TAKE A TRIP BACK TO BRITAIN, THERE TO LOOKY FOR MY MASTER, LITTLE HOOKY!

DER MAGIC HAT HAS BEEN PINCHED! GO AND CHASE DER SMOKY GUY WITH DER AEROPLANES AND GET IT BACK!
YES, YES, HERR HITLER!

Der Fuhrer himself was not spared humiliation. Hitler was portrayed in a variety of deprecating comic styles by a range of artists. It has been observed that Hitler and Mussolini were both vainglorious individuals, so it's reasonable to assume that their pride was stung by this incessant mockery. This suggestion is backed up by intercepted wartime records of a planned German invasion which stated that a list of prominent newspaper editors and publishers were to be captured and made answerable to Hitler for the crime of 'gross disrespect'.

This list included the Editor of *The Beano* as well as the prodigious artist Dudley Watkins, who was held back from active military service due to the irreplaceable positive impact he was deemed to be making on the nation's morale. Had the Nazis successfully invaded, it's conceivable that not only would *The Beano* have been closed immediately, but that the Editor and his staff would have faced the ultimate sanction. The courage they displayed in refusing to moderate their output, particularly when wartime superiority was in the balance prior to 1943, is to their eternal credit.

HECKLING HERMANN

While barbed observations about Mussolini's personality were the main drivers of his mocking character assassination, physical characteristics were the source of the humour directed at Herman Goering. As Hitler's designated successor and Commander of the Luftwaffe, he was another easy target due to his heavy appearance. Even in Germany, commentators, somewhat affectionately, would refer to him as 'fat'. ***The Beano*** didn't refrain from exploiting this.

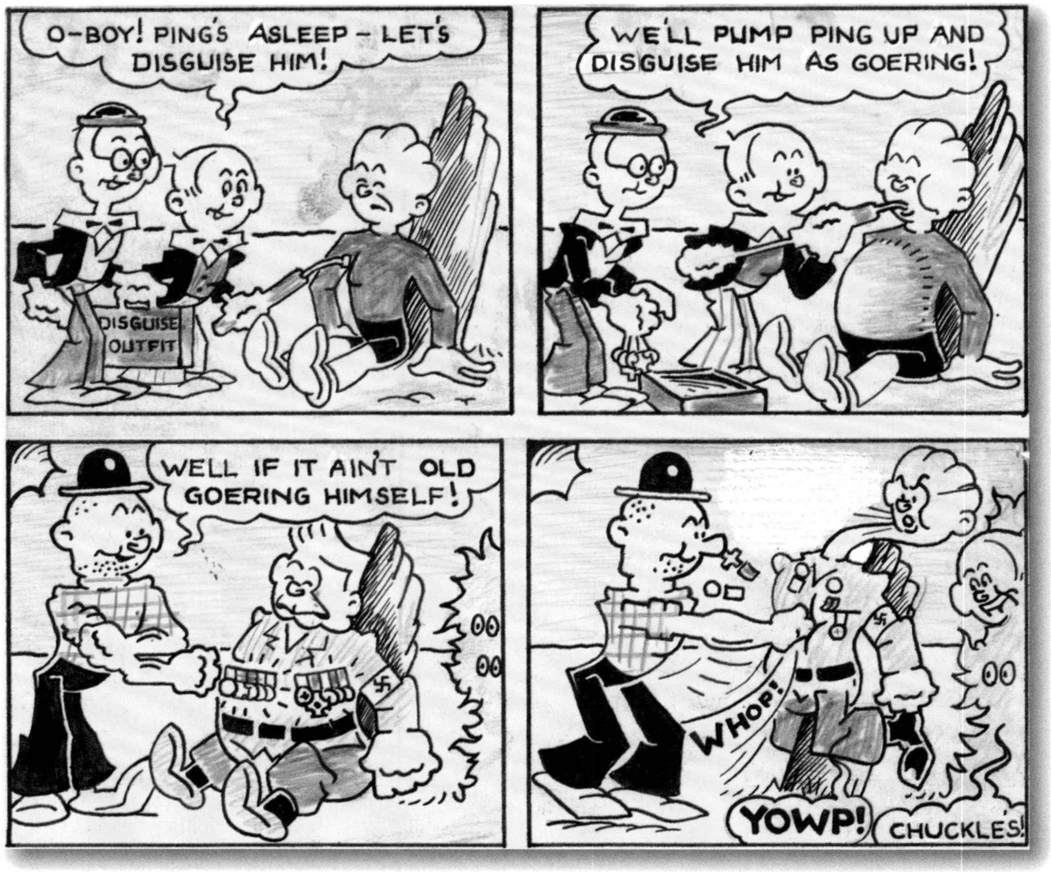
O-BOY! PING'S ASLEEP - LET'S DISGUISE HIM!
DISGUISE OUTFIT
WE'LL PUMP PING UP AND DISGUISE HIM AS GOERING!
WELL IF IT AIN'T OLD GOERING HIMSELF!
WHOP!
YOWP!
CHUCKLES!

O MEDALS MAKE FAT GOERING A CLOWN - GROW IN SIZE AND WEIGH HIM DOWN.
GOSH! HITLER AND GOERING.

Goering features in many strips. Examples here come from "Ping the Elastic Man', 'Hooky's Magic Bowler Hat', 'Pansy Potter' and 'Lord Snooty'.

HIMMEL—!!! IT'S A DIRTY BRITISH SUBMARINE!
PULL OUT DER PLUGS - WE MUST SINK OURSELVES!
SCUTTLE LIKE BRAVE MEN!
BOOM
WE SHALL SINK OR SWIM TOGETHER HERMANN!
I WOULD SWIM WITH YOU, MINE LEADER BUT MY MEDALS ARE MADE OF LEAD!

SWASTIKA, COME DOWN FROM THE WALL-KICK FAT GOERING, MAKE HIM BAWL!
HIMMEL, STOP! I CAN'T STAND UP STRAIGHT!
BUMFOOZLED BROWNSHIRTS! VOT ISS DER MATTER? VOT ISS IT YOU, LOOK FOR? PENNIES ON DER FLOOR?
OOF! VOT? ISS.
BONK!
IT CAN'T BE TRUE!

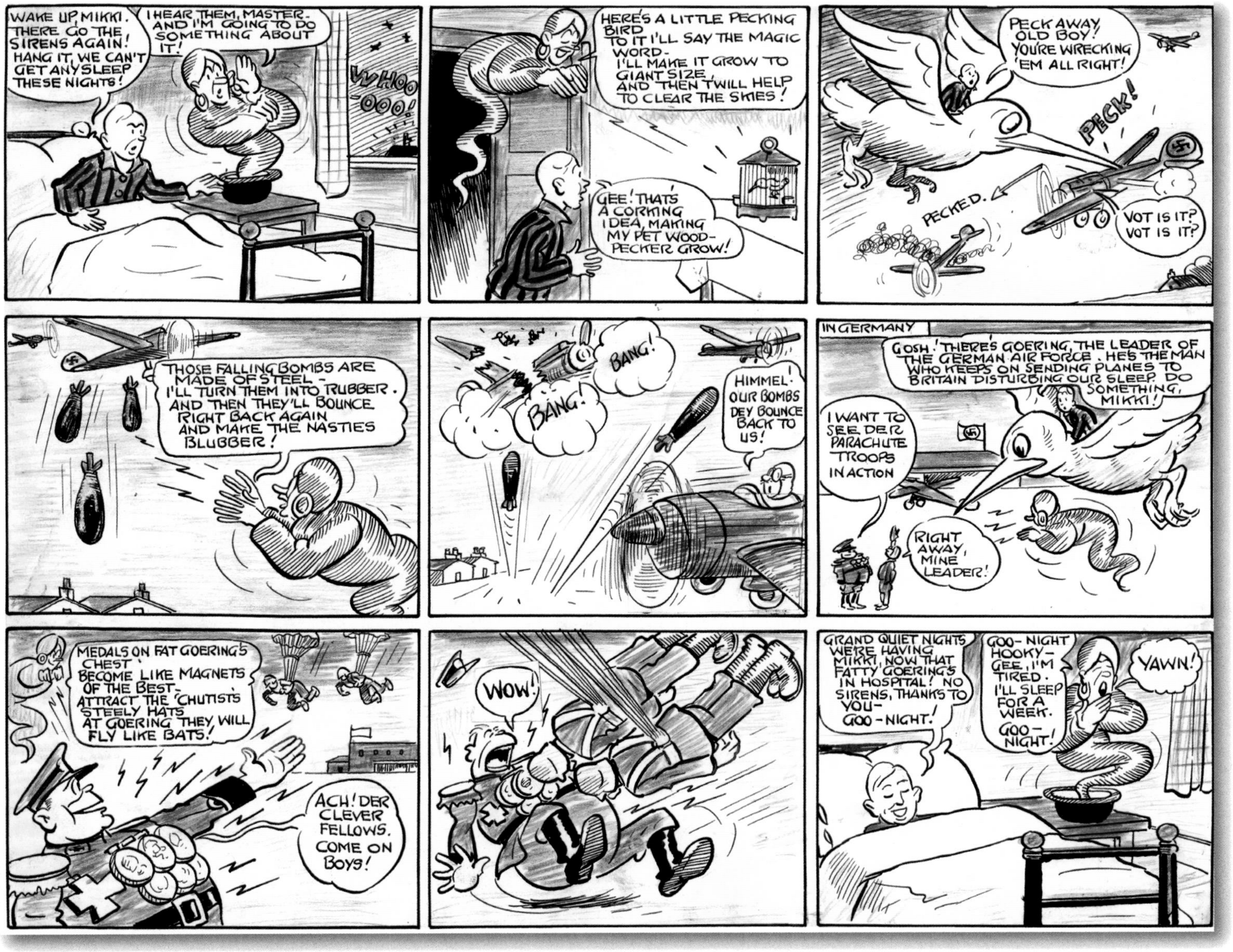
WAKE UP, MIKKI. THERE GO THE SIRENS AGAIN! HANG IT, WE CAN'T GET ANY SLEEP THESE NIGHTS!
I HEAR THEM, MASTER - AND I'M GOING TO DO SOMETHING ABOUT IT!
WHOO-OOO!
HERE'S A LITTLE PECKING BIRD TO IT I'LL SAY THE MAGIC WORD - I'LL MAKE IT GROW TO GIANT SIZE, AND THEN 'TWILL HELP TO CLEAR THE SKIES!
GEE! THAT'S A CORKING IDEA, MAKING MY PET WOOD-PECKER GROW!
PECK AWAY OLD BOY! YOU'RE WRECKING 'EM ALL RIGHT!
PECK!
PECKED.
VOT IS IT? VOT IS IT?
THOSE FALLING BOMBS ARE MADE OF STEEL - I'LL TURN THEM INTO RUBBER. AND THEN THEY'LL BOUNCE RIGHT BACK AGAIN AND MAKE THE NASTIES BLUBBER!
BANG!
BANG!
HIMMEL! OUR BOMBS DEY BOUNCE BACK TO US!
IN GERMANY
GOSH! THERE'S GOERING, THE LEADER OF THE GERMAN AIR FORCE. HE'S THE MAN WHO KEEPS ON SENDING PLANES TO BRITAIN DISTURBING OUR SLEEP. DO SOMETHING, MIKKI!
I WANT TO SEE DER PARACHUTE TROOPS IN ACTION
RIGHT AWAY, MINE LEADER!
MEDALS ON FAT GOERING'S CHEST BECOME LIKE MAGNETS OF THE BEST - ATTRACT THE 'CHUTISTS STEELY HATS AT GOERING THEY WILL FLY LIKE BATS!
ACH! DER CLEVER FELLOWS. COME ON BOYS!
WOW!
GRAND QUIET NIGHTS WE'RE HAVING MIKKI, NOW THAT FATTY GOERING'S IN HOSPITAL! NO SIRENS, THANKS TO YOU - GOO-NIGHT!
GOO-NIGHT HOOKY - GEE, I'M TIRED. I'LL SLEEP FOR A WEEK. GOO-NIGHT!
YAWN!

The original drawings from a 'Hooky's Magic Bowler Hat' strip, drawn by Chic Gordon.

Apart from Goering's girth, ***The Beano*** also mocked his military worth. Highly decorated as a First World War fighter pilot, Goering was rarely photographed without an impressive collection of medals pinned to his chest. ***The Beano*** mocked Goering's medals to the point that any child reading would have recognised them as only sham baubles. So, instead of an opponent to be feared, Goering was portrayed as enemy worthy of ridicule, as he's regularly outwitted by a collection of children, old people and animals.

THE BEANO'S WAR HEROES

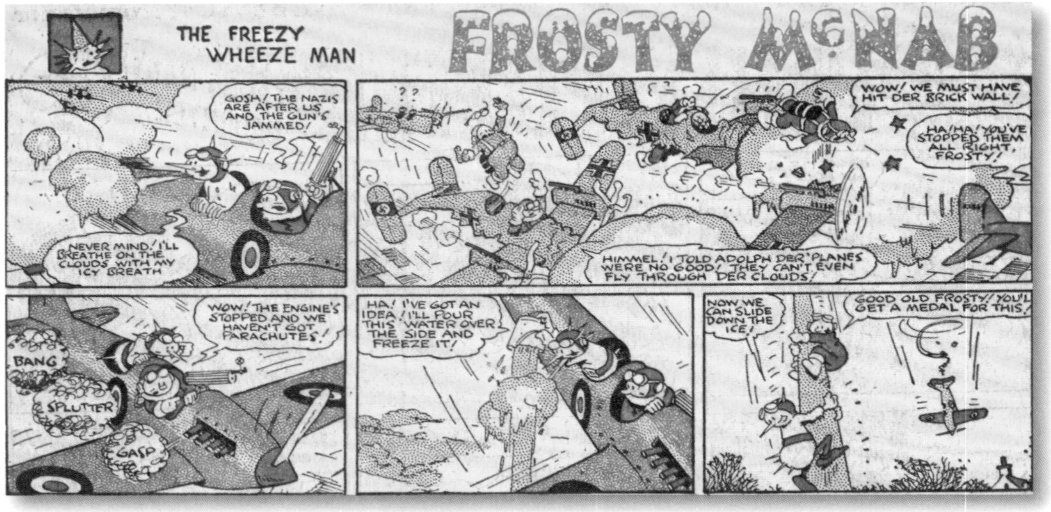
THE FREEZY WHEEZE MAN
FROSTY McNAB
GOSH! THE NAZIS ARE AFTER US AND THE GUN'S JAMMED!
NEVER MIND! I'LL BREATHE ON THE CLOUDS WITH MY ICY BREATH
WOW! WE MUST HAVE HIT DER BRICK WALL!
HA! HA! YOU'VE STOPPED THEM ALL RIGHT, FROSTY!
HIMMEL! I TOLD ADOLPH DER 'PLANES WERE NO GOOD! THEY CAN'T EVEN FLY THROUGH DER CLOUDS!
WOW! THE ENGINE'S STOPPED AND WE HAVEN'T GOT PARACHUTES!
BANG
SPLUTTER
GASP
HA! I'VE GOT AN IDEA! I'LL POUR THIS WATER OVER THE SIDE AND FREEZE IT!
NOW WE CAN SLIDE DOWN THE ICE!
GOOD OLD FROSTY! YOU'LL GET A MEDAL FOR THIS!

ONE TON OF FUN
PUFFING BILLY
GEE WHIZZ, PAL, AREN'T THOSE KIDS HAVING A SWELL TIME? I WISH I WASN'T SO HEAVY, AND I'D JOIN 'EM!
HIPPEE!
I'LL FIX YOU UP, BILLY, AND YOU CAN HAVE AS MUCH FUN AS YOU LIKE!—COME ON!
SAY THE WORD, BILLY!
LET HER GO, CHUM!
ZOOOM!
OH BOY! THIS IS GREAT!
WHIRRR!!
SNAP!
WOW! MY WEIGHT HAS CAST ME ADRIFT!
ACH! DER NEW BRITISH DOUBLE-TORPEDO! YES! WE ARE LOZT!!
THIS'LL SHIFT THOSE PESKY SUBS!
U-BOAT
THAT'S ONE LESS U-BOAT CAPTAIN!
GOOD OLD BILLY!

DOUBTING THOMAS
OH, TOMMY, COULD YOU SCARE THE BIRDS OFF MY GROUND WITH THIS GUN FOR ME?
I DOUBT IT, BUT I'LL TRY!
AH! THERE'S ONE BIRD!
BANG!
CRASH!
GOSH! WHAT KIND OF BIRD WAS THAT?
HEIL DIDDLER!
WHOOPEE! I'VE BAGGED A GERMAN BOMBER!

The Beano mobilised a battalion of heroes to inspire British children in their wartime endeavours. The mantra was that every character should do their bit. Everyone and everything rallied against the Nazis in *The Beano*.

From 'Frosty McNab' (The Freezy Wheeze Man) to 'Puffing Billy' (One Ton of Fun), all were conscripted to mock the enemy. One such unconventional hero was 'Doubting Thomas', a youngster bravely facing the enemy. Thomas appeared in *The Beano* from 1940 to 1942 and returned as a member of Lord Snooty's new gang in 1950. The contribution of Britain's Home Guard was referenced by strips featuring 'Hairy Dan', who proved, with considerable

HAIRY DAN
HIS WHISKERS NEAT REACH TO HIS FEET
I'VE JOINED THE "PARASHOTS" THIS WEEK READERS — JUST LET A GERMAN PARACHUTIST LAND NEAR ME!
YES SIR! I'D LIKE TO SEE A GERMAN PARACHUTIST RIGHT NOW—!
OH, YOU WOULD, WOULD YOU?
WOW A REAL GERMAN!
HIMMEL!! — AND I THOUGHT DER ENGLISH WERE SLOW!!
CRASH
TWANG
AND I JUST GAVE HIM A SOCK ON THE NOSE AND DOWN HE WENT — AHEM!
COO!

KEEP ON GOOSE-STEPPING MY BEAUTIES OR I'LL LET YOU HAVE IT!
GRRR — IF WE COULD GET DER "BEANO" IN GERMANY WE SHOULD HAVE KNOWN ABOUT DER PANSY POTTER!
JA! YOU'VE SAID IT, AND HOW!
STOP KICKING ME IN DER PANTS HERR DOCHENHEIMER

THE LITTLE DUTCH KIDS WINKEN AND BLINKEN
COME HERE, YOU LITTLE DUTCH BRATS, DER TYRE IS PUNCTURED AND YOU WILL COME IN HANDY!
PUSH US TO DER NEAREST GARAGE, AND MAKE IT DER SNAPPY!
I WILL UNSCREW DER SIDE-CAR WHILE DER NASTIES ARE IN DER GARAGE!
PUNCTURE OUTFITS
TYRE
SPARE
NOW DER TYRE IS FIXED, I WILL SHOW YOU SOME SPEED, I AM DER FASTEST DRIVER IN DER GERMAN ARMY!
HA! HA!
HIMMEL! I AM SCUTTLED IN DER DUCK POND!
SO YOU ARE DER FASTEST DRIVER, EH? WELL I AM DER HARDEST HITTER — TAKE THAT!
WOW!
HA! HA! NOW WE HAVE GOT OUR OWN BACK ON BOTH DIRTY ROTTERS AT ONCE!

aplomb, that age was no barrier to Nazi-bashing, while 'Winken and Blinken' became heroes of the Dutch resistance. Heroines were present too, as we have seen with 'Pansy Potter' using her very own strong-arm tactics against the Axis powers.

It wasn't just the nation's children who were inspired by Pansy's treatment of the enemy. One visitor to a munitions factory saw that a 'strip depicting Pansy Potter bringing down Jerries with giant flypapers attached between barrage balloons', had been framed and displayed as an inspiration to encourage staff to develop new techniques to hinder the enemy.

IDEA

Lord Snooty

Following Pansy, the first major character to sign up for *The Beano* war effort was Lord Snooty. On January 6, 1940 the first 'Lord Snooty' strip with a war propaganda theme was published.

The 'Lord Snooty and his Pals' strips during the war years were largely dedicated to storylines inspired by the conflict. In fact, it was almost as if Dudley Watkins was living out his National Service vicariously through his comic creations. Watkins' attention to detail and desire to include as many topical references as possible made the government's decision to prevent him swapping his drawing board for military service seem entirely justified.

COME ON IN, FELLOWS, AND I'LL SHOW YOU THE NEW WIRELESS SET I GOT FROM AUNTIE. IT CAN SEND OUT MESSAGES AS WELL AS RECEIVE THEM!
GOLLY! WHAT A WHOPPER!
LISTEN! ALL DER BRITISH PIGS! DER MIGHTY COMMANDER OF DER GREAT GERMAN SUBMARINE U1 IS SPEAKING. I AM COMING TO SHELL TO DER THOUSAND BITS DER CASTLE OF DER LORD SNOOTY FOR CALLING DER GREAT HITLER UN SKINNY BABOON, HEIL!
LET HIM COME!
SHURRUP, YOU FOOL, IF HE HEARS YOU HE'LL SHELL ASH-CAN ALLEY TOO!
COME ON, GANG! WE'VE GOT TO WARN THE COPS ABOUT THAT U-BOAT!
COP SHOP
GO AWAY, YOU KIDS! CAN'T YOU SEE I'M BUSY WITH MY KNITTING? YOU CAN'T PULL OUR LEGS WITH YOUR STORIES ABOUT U-BOATS!
COUNT TEN Every time You Drop A Stitch. BY ORDER.
BUT IT'S TRUE MR POLICEMAN!
BEANO
COP SHOP
CLEAR OUT, AND IF YOU BOTHER US AGAIN WE'LL GET THE SERGEANT TO YOU!
HEIL! DIS IS DER GREAT GERMAN LEADER, ADOLF HITLER, CALLING DER BRAVE COMMANDER OF DER SUBMARINE U1. DO NOT SHELL DER CASTLE OF DER LORD SNOOTY. DER BRITISH PIGS HAVE SURRENDERED, AND ME AND DER GOERING ARE AT DER CASTLE OF DER SNOOTY. COME THERE MINE FRIEND AND MEET DER MIGHTY ME — HITLER!!
O.K., DER MIGHTY ADOLF!
GEE, I HOPE SNOOTY CAN FOOL THAT GUY
DISGUISE YOURSELVES AS GERMANS, LADS. I'LL BE HITLER. I'VE KIDDED THAT U-BOAT COMMANDER THAT GERMANY'S WON THE WAR. WHEN HE COMES HERE TO-NIGHT WE'VE GOT TO NAB HIM AND HIS MEN!
HOW'M AH DOIN' AS FAT OLD HERMAN GOERING?
HEIL, SNOOTY!
THAT NIGHT
COME ASHORE, MINE FRIENDS!
HEIL, DER GREAT COMMANDER! THIS IS DER MIGHTY HITLER WHO CONQUERED ALL BRITAIN!
HEIL! DER HITLER IS BOSS OF BRITAIN, NOW!
AH! DER GOERING SPEAKS AND ROCKS DER SUBMARINE!
GEE! WHAT A LIFE! IT'S WORSE THAN THE BLACK OUT!
U1
SLIP
BRITISH TROOP CAMP.
O.K, BOYS! GRAB THESE GERMANS! THEY THINK WE'RE HITLER AND GOERING!
WINK
FOLLOW DER GREAT HITLER, MEN!
HURRAY! DER HITLER'S WON DER WAR! DER BRITISH ARE NO MORE WE'LL TRAMP ON THEIR FACES WE'LL STEAL THEIR BRACES 'COS HITLER'S WON DER WAR!
O.K. JUST WATCH US!
SO HITLER'S WON THE WAR, 'AS 'E? AND CONQUERED BRITAIN, TOO? WE'LL SOON SHOW YOU YER MISTAKE, WON'T WE BOYS?
ACH! HELP! WE HAF BEEN TRICKED! DER HITLER IS UN DIRTY DOG — NO, DER TWO DIRTY DOGS, HE IS!
HA! HA!
SURE WE WILL, SERGE!
NICE WORK, LORD SNOOTY! THOSE GERMAN SAILORS ARE SAFE WHERE THEY CAN DO NO HARM. AND NOW I PRESENT YOU WITH THIS MEDAL!
MODESTY
HEIL, LORD SNOOTY!
SHURRUP! WE AIN'T PLAYING GERMANS, NOW. BESIDES I WANT A MEDAL, TOO!
KICK ME HARD, SERGEANT, WHAT FOOLS WE WERE!!
JEALOUSY
TAKE THAT, YOU SILLY BLIGHTER! —OW!!

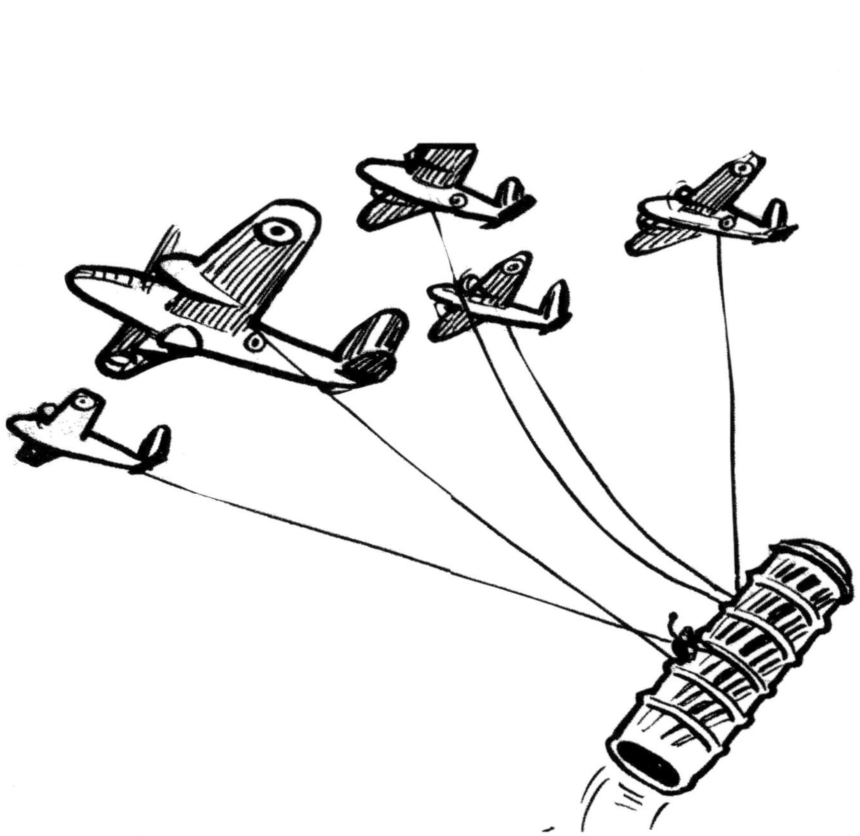

A MESSAGE FROM OUR SPY IN ENGLAND, FUEHRER!
SNIFF, SNIFF! THIS IS DER TERRIBLE! NOBODY IN BRITAIN HAS EVER HEARD OF ME, DER GREAT ADOLF HITLER — SNIFF! WHERE IS LORD HAW-HAW? WHY HAS HE NOT TOLD DER BRITISH PIG-DOGS ABOUT ME? SNIFF—SNIFF!
WHAT IS IT, ADDIE? DON'T CRY!
TEARS OF RAGE
DER DIRTY BRITISH PIG-DOGS MUST BE TOLD ALL ABOUT ME. I AM DER GREATEST MAN IN DER WORLD — SO SET OFF AT ONCE IN YOUR BOMBERS WITH ALL THOSE LEAFLETS TELLING THE BRITISH WHO I AM!
HEIL HITLER! THREE TIMES!
LEAFLETS

EVERY MAN, WOMAN AND CHILD IN STALINGRAD FOUGHT TO SAVE THE CITY! THAT'S WHY THE KING PRESENTED STALINGRAD WITH A SWORD OF HONOUR!
LET'S GET SOME TOGGLE ROPES AND DO SOME TOWN FIGHTING! WE CAN USE THE BOMBED AREA IN THE TOWN!
WE'LL SHOW 'EM!
FISH & CHIPS
AND WE WOULD BE AT THE TAIL END OF THE QUEUE TOO!
DUDLEY D. WATKINS

This sophistication is demonstrated by examples such as the reference to the Second World War's epic turning-point, the Battle of Stalingrad, in the strip which appeared in January 1944. In fact, the bravery of the Russian defenders was even presented as inspiration for Britain's youngsters (see below left).

The year 1946 was notable for it being the first time Dudley Watkins actually signed his work – a hitherto unheard of practice in the comic – with 'Lord Snooty' in the issue dated September 7 (see left). Watkins was the first artist afforded this privilege and it was perhaps an indication of the power his natural talent had started to bestow upon him. It's unclear whether this initiative was the brainchild of George Moonie, who had resumed his position as Editor around this time, following his return from Military Service.

EVACUEES

A text story which must have resonated with children at this time was 'Jimmy's Mother Wouldn't Run Away'. In it, a 12-year-old British lad named Jimmy Allen and his mum are evacuated to America. They soon discover the small town where they've relocated is under the control of a widowed gangster's moll! What makes a bad situation even worse is that she takes an instant dislike to the evacuees and vows to make their lives a misery.

STARTS BELOW!
A Grand New Yarn of How the Allens Fought a Town of Gangsters!
JIMMY'S MOTHER WOULDN'T RUN AWAY
HOTEL

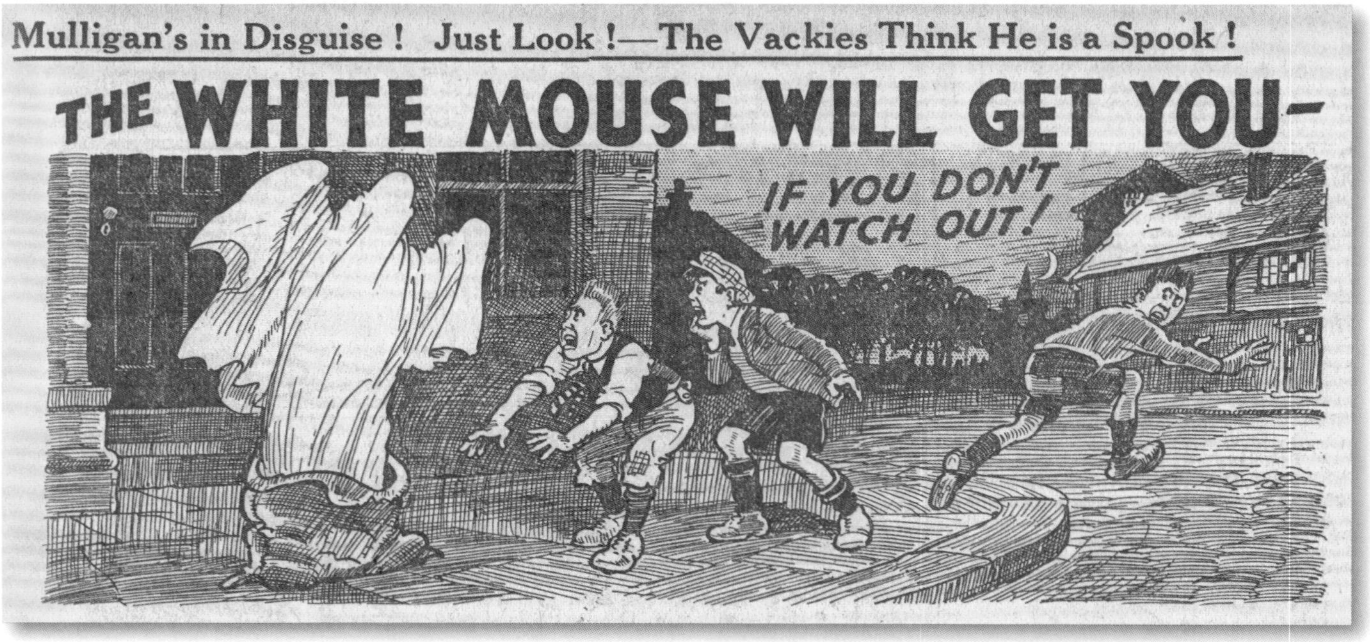
Mulligan's in Disguise! Just Look!—The Vackies Think He is a Spook!
THE WHITE MOUSE WILL GET YOU-
IF YOU DON'T WATCH OUT!

Nearly two million British children were evacuated from their homes at the start of the Second World War. They were relocated to the countryside to escape the bombing. Few knew where they were going, or if they would be split from the brothers and sisters who accompanied them. They were frightened about being away from their families and had to adjust to new schools and make new friends. As the heading on the right (drawn by Dudley Watkins) shows, the 'Vackies' were not always at home in the countryside.

THE WILD BOY OF THE WOODS

One ***Beano*** character who had no problems making new friends – of any species – was Derek, the Wild Boy of the Woods. Described as the 'Nazis' greatest enemy', 'The Wild Boy of the Woods' was based on the legend of Tarzan. However, instead of apes, he was raised by a mysterious hermit, who imbued him with the ability to communicate with wild animals. On several occasions these creatures were enlisted to help the allied war effort, including whales; snakes and gorillas wielding machine guns; and a team of kestrels who swoop to rescue a stricken fighter plane! During one episode, the story ends with a portrayal of true terror as the Nazi diver realises that Derek has tried to trick him and brandishes a deadly weapon. Perhaps the Editor worried that things were going too far at this point, as the weapon turns out to be an underwater flame thrower (see original sketches above right, drawn by Toby Baines).

A darker side to 'The Wild Boy of the Woods' storyline became apparent when the threat of chemical warfare was touched upon. A bomb containing bizarre metal-munching worms – bred by German scientist in a bid to disarm British artillery – became the latest challenge for the Wild Boy. However, German ineptitude was again apparent when Derek discovered that, while the creatures could happily munch through metal, they were stumped by wood!

'It was a typical German trick,' ***The Beano*** observed, when Derek encountered an army of flesh-eating insects during his next adventure. Analysis of German war strategy was also included, by way of explanation for the motivation for this nefarious tactic: 'Hitler and the Nazi bullies had planned that the more food that was destroyed, the less there would be for the people of Britain to eat – and the starvation of the British Isles is Hitler's main hope of victory in the present war.' Such a message, whilst true, must have been frightening for a war child so ***The Beano*** was quick to follow it with an explanation of just how easily the Nazis could be vanquished, by dint of British ingenuity; a pot of homemade raspberry jam was all it took to thwart Hitler's evil scheme on this occasion.

Perhaps Derek's most extravagant adventure – and that's saying something given a typical 'day' in his life – was the one where he used a 30-foot tall Hitler to invade a Nazi camp, in the style of a Trojan horse. The same episode witnessed Derek using – of all

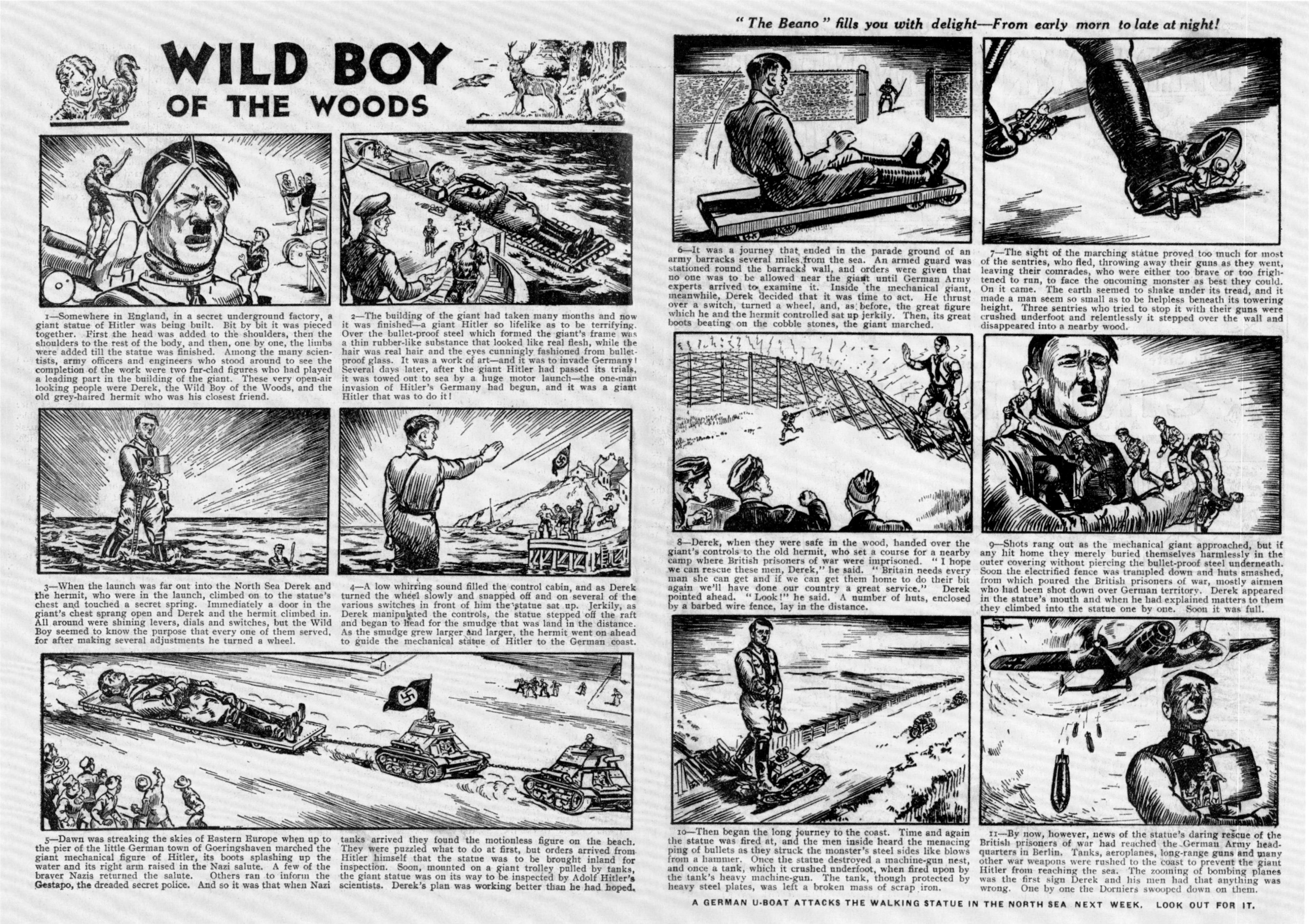
"The Beano" fills you with delight—From early morn to late at night!
WILD BOY OF THE WOODS
1—Somewhere in England, in a secret underground factory, a giant statue of Hitler was being built. Bit by bit it was pieced together. First the head was added to the shoulders, then the shoulders to the rest of the body, and then, one by one, the limbs were added till the statue was finished. Among the many scientists, army officers and engineers who stood around to see the completion of the work were two fur-clad figures who had played a leading part in the building of the giant. These very open-air looking people were Derek, the Wild Boy of the Woods, and the old grey-haired hermit who was his closest friend.
2—The building of the giant had taken many months and now it was finished—a giant Hitler so lifelike as to be terrifying. Over the bullet-proof steel which formed the giant's frame was a thin rubber-like substance that looked like real flesh, while the hair was real hair and the eyes cunningly fashioned from bullet-proof glass. It was a work of art—and it was to invade Germany! Several days later, after the giant Hitler had passed its trials, it was towed out to sea by a huge motor launch—the one-man invasion of Hitler's Germany had begun, and it was a giant Hitler that was to do it!
3—When the launch was far out into the North Sea Derek and the hermit, who were in the launch, climbed on to the statue's chest and touched a secret spring. Immediately a door in the giant's chest sprang open and Derek and the hermit climbed in. All around were shining levers, dials and switches, but the Wild Boy seemed to know the purpose that every one of them served, for after making several adjustments he turned a wheel.
4—A low whirring sound filled the control cabin, and as Derek turned the wheel slowly and snapped off and on several of the various switches in front of him the statue sat up. Jerkily, as Derek manipulated the controls, the statue stepped off the raft and began to head for the smudge that was land in the distance. As the smudge grew larger and larger, the hermit went on ahead to guide the mechanical statue of Hitler to the German coast.
5—Dawn was streaking the skies of Eastern Europe when up to the pier of the little German town of Goeringshaven marched the giant mechanical figure of Hitler, its boots splashing up the water and its right arm raised in the Nazi salute. A few of the braver Nazis returned the salute. Others ran to inform the Gestapo, the dreaded secret police. And so it was that when Nazi tanks arrived they found the motionless figure on the beach. They were puzzled what to do at first, but orders arrived from Hitler himself that the statue was to be brought inland for inspection. Soon, mounted on a giant trolley pulled by tanks, the giant statue was on its way to be inspected by Adolf Hitler's scientists. Derek's plan was working better than he had hoped.
6—It was a journey that ended in the parade ground of an army barracks several miles from the sea. An armed guard was stationed round the barracks wall, and orders were given that no one was to be allowed near the giant until German Army experts arrived to examine it. Inside the mechanical giant, meanwhile, Derek decided that it was time to act. He thrust over a switch, turned a wheel, and, as before, the great figure which he and the hermit controlled sat up jerkily. Then, its great boots beating on the cobble stones, the giant marched.
7—The sight of the marching statue proved too much for most of the sentries, who fled, throwing away their guns as they went, leaving their comrades, who were either too brave or too frightened to run, to face the oncoming monster as best they could. On it came. The earth seemed to shake under its tread, and it made a man seem so small as to be helpless beneath its towering height. Three sentries who tried to stop it with their guns were crushed underfoot and relentlessly it stepped over the wall and disappeared into a nearby wood.
8—Derek, when they were safe in the wood, handed over the giant's controls to the old hermit, who set a course for a nearby camp where British prisoners of war were imprisoned. "I hope we can rescue these men, Derek," he said. "Britain needs every man she can get and if we can get them home to do their bit again we'll have done our country a great service." Derek pointed ahead. "Look!" he said. A number of huts, enclosed by a barbed wire fence, lay in the distance.
9—Shots rang out as the mechanical giant approached, but if any hit home they merely buried themselves harmlessly in the outer covering without piercing the bullet-proof steel underneath. Soon the electrified fence was trampled down and huts smashed, from which poured the British prisoners of war, mostly airmen who had been shot down over German territory. Derek appeared in the statue's mouth and when he had explained matters to them they climbed into the statue one by one. Soon it was full.
10—Then began the long journey to the coast. Time and again the statue was fired at, and the men inside heard the menacing ping of bullets as they struck the monster's steel sides like blows from a hammer. Once the statue destroyed a machine-gun nest, and once a tank, which it crushed underfoot, when fired upon by the tank's heavy machine-gun. The tank, though protected by heavy steel plates, was left a broken mass of scrap iron.
11—By now, however, news of the statue's daring rescue of the British prisoners of war had reached the German Army headquarters in Berlin. Tanks, aeroplanes, long-range guns and many other war weapons were rushed to the coast to prevent the giant Hitler from reaching the sea. The zooming of bombing planes was the first sign Derek and his men had that anything was wrong. One by one the Dorniers swooped down on them.
A GERMAN U-BOAT ATTACKS THE WALKING STATUE IN THE NORTH SEA NEXT WEEK. LOOK OUT FOR IT.

things – pan pipes to control eagles into dropping dynamite onto a German battleship. The story concluded with the giant Hitler destroyed on a bonfire, with readers assured that 'so, one day, will perish the Nazi Germany of Adolf Hitler'.

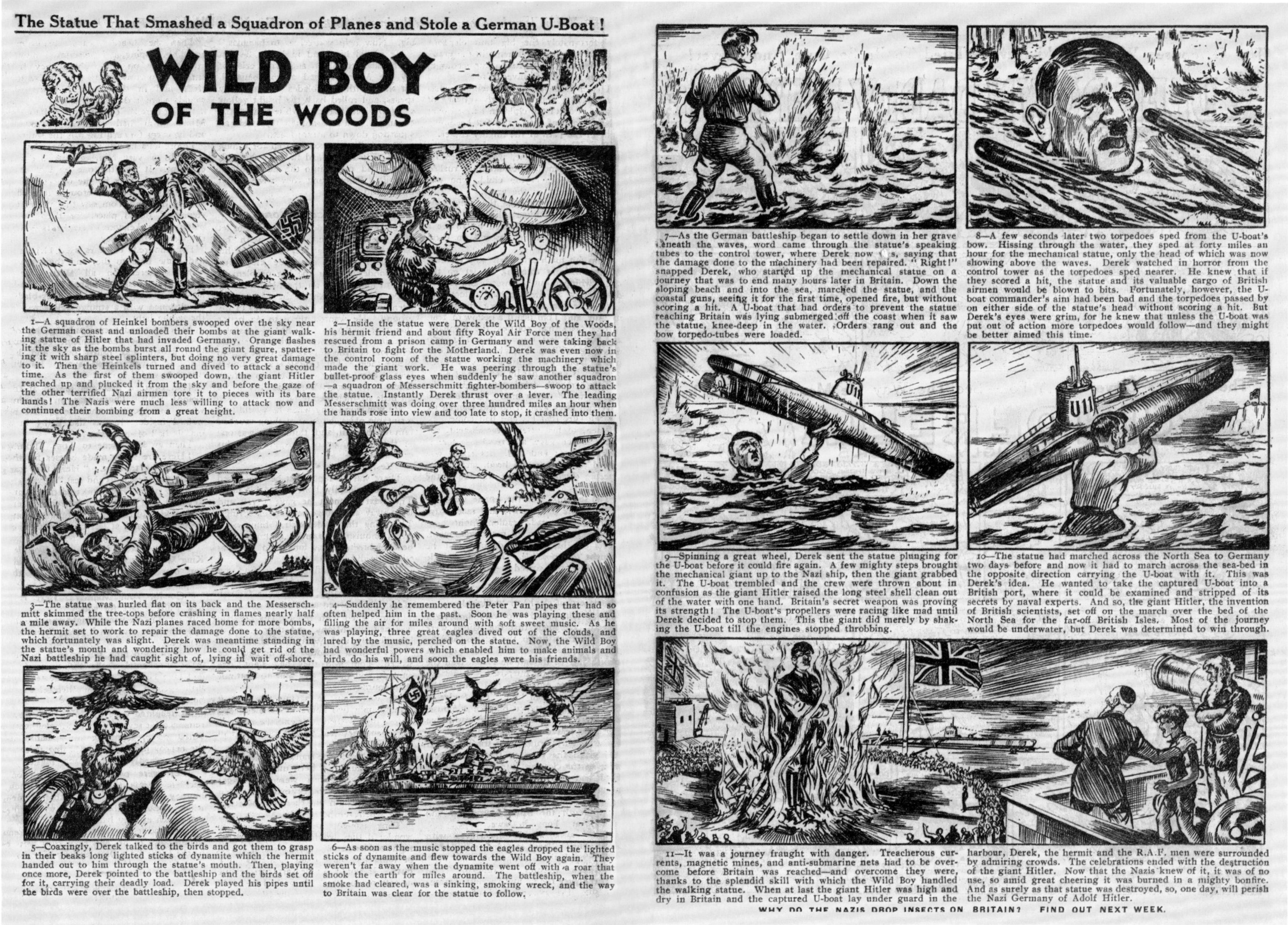
The Statue That Smashed a Squadron of Planes and Stole a German U-Boat !
WILD BOY
OF THE WOODS
1—A squadron of Heinkel bombers swooped over the sky near the German coast and unloaded their bombs at the giant walking statue of Hitler that had invaded Germany. Orange flashes lit the sky as the bombs burst all round the giant figure, spattering it with sharp steel splinters, but doing no very great damage to it. Then the Heinkels turned and dived to attack a second time. As the first of them swooped down, the giant Hitler reached up and plucked it from the sky and before the gaze of the other terrified Nazi airmen tore it to pieces with its bare hands! The Nazis were much less willing to attack now and continued their bombing from a great height.
2—Inside the statue were Derek the Wild Boy of the Woods, his hermit friend and about fifty Royal Air Force men they had rescued from a prison camp in Germany and were taking back to Britain to fight for the Motherland. Derek was even now in the control room of the statue working the machinery which made the giant work. He was peering through the statue's bullet-proof glass eyes when suddenly he saw another squadron —a squadron of Messerschmitt fighter-bombers—swoop to attack the statue. Instantly Derek thrust over a lever. The leading Messerschmitt was doing over three hundred miles an hour when the hands rose into view and too late to stop, it crashed into them.
3—The statue was hurled flat on its back and the Messerschmitt skimmed the tree-tops before crashing in flames nearly half a mile away. While the Nazi planes raced home for more bombs, the hermit set to work to repair the damage done to the statue, which fortunately was slight. Derek was meantime standing in the statue's mouth and wondering how he could get rid of the Nazi battleship he had caught sight of, lying in wait off-shore.
4—Suddenly he remembered the Peter Pan pipes that had so often helped him in the past. Soon he was playing these and filling the air for miles around with soft sweet music. As he was playing, three great eagles dived out of the clouds, and lured by the music, perched on the statue. Now, the Wild Boy had wonderful powers which enabled him to make animals and birds do his will, and soon the eagles were his friends.
5—Coaxingly, Derek talked to the birds and got them to grasp in their beaks long lighted sticks of dynamite which the hermit handed out to him through the statue's mouth. Then, playing once more, Derek pointed to the battleship and the birds set off for it, carrying their deadly load. Derek played his pipes until the birds were over the battleship, then stopped.
6—As soon as the music stopped the eagles dropped the lighted sticks of dynamite and flew towards the Wild Boy again. They weren't far away when the dynamite went off with a roar that shook the earth for miles around. The battleship, when the smoke had cleared, was a sinking, smoking wreck, and the way to Britain was clear for the statue to follow.
7—As the German battleship began to settle down in her grave beneath the waves, word came through the statue's speaking tubes to the control tower, where Derek now [illegible]s, saying that the damage done to the machinery had been repaired. "Right!" snapped Derek, who started up the mechanical statue on a journey that was to end many hours later in Britain. Down the sloping beach and into the sea, marched the statue, and the coastal guns, seeing it for the first time, opened fire, but without scoring a hit. A U-boat that had orders to prevent the statue reaching Britain was lying submerged off the coast when it saw the statue, knee-deep in the water. Orders rang out and the bow torpedo-tubes were loaded.
8—A few seconds later two torpedoes sped from the U-boat's bow. Hissing through the water, they sped at forty miles an hour for the mechanical statue, only the head of which was now showing above the waves. Derek watched in horror from the control tower as the torpedoes sped nearer. He knew that if they scored a hit, the statue and its valuable cargo of British airmen would be blown to bits. Fortunately, however, the U-boat commander's aim had been bad and the torpedoes passed by on either side of the statue's head without scoring a hit. But Derek's eyes were grim, for he knew that unless the U-boat was put out of action more torpedoes would follow—and they might be better aimed this time.
U11
U11
9—Spinning a great wheel, Derek sent the statue plunging for the U-boat before it could fire again. A few mighty steps brought the mechanical giant up to the Nazi ship, then the giant grabbed it. The U-boat trembled and the crew were thrown about in confusion as the giant Hitler raised the long steel shell clean out of the water with one hand. Britain's secret weapon was proving its strength! The U-boat's propellers were racing like mad until Derek decided to stop them. This the giant did merely by shaking the U-boat till the engines stopped throbbing.
10—The statue had marched across the North Sea to Germany two days before and now it had to march across the sea-bed in the opposite direction carrying the U-boat with it. This was Derek's idea. He wanted to take the captured U-boat into a British port, where it could be examined and stripped of its secrets by naval experts. And so, the giant Hitler, the invention of British scientists, set off on the march over the bed of the North Sea for the far-off British Isles. Most of the journey would be underwater, but Derek was determined to win through.
11—It was a journey fraught with danger. Treacherous currents, magnetic mines, and anti-submarine nets had to be overcome before Britain was reached—and overcome they were, thanks to the splendid skill with which the Wild Boy handled the walking statue. When at last the giant Hitler was high and dry in Britain and the captured U-boat lay under guard in the harbour, Derek, the hermit and the R.A.F. men were surrounded by admiring crowds. The celebrations ended with the destruction of the giant Hitler. Now that the Nazis knew of it, it was of no use, so amid great cheering it was burned in a mighty bonfire. And as surely as that statue was destroyed, so, one day, will perish the Nazi Germany of Adolf Hitler.
WHY DO THE NAZIS DROP INSECTS ON BRITAIN? FIND OUT NEXT WEEK.

MAGICAL ESCAPISM

The Wild Boy of the Woods ran until 1942, by which time a certain change in editorial direction started to become apparent. As the war ground on, stories began to move towards more fantastical themes. The feeling of adventure which surrounded the outbreak had been replaced by war weariness and magical escapism now became the order of the day.

THE SHIPWRECKED CIRCUS
TAR

THE SHIPWRECKED CIRCUS

1943 welcomed the first appearance of the classic *Beano* adventure strip 'The Shipwrecked Circus'. The first 12 episodes were illustrated by Watkins before being passed on to Jack Prout to complete the series. The story saw Samson the Strongman's travelling circus shipwrecked in the South Seas on Crusoe Island. Gloopy the clown, Trixie the acrobat and Horace the chimp made the best of their predicament, encouraging the nation's children to adopt a similar outlook. In the first frame, Horace is sawing through the pole he is sitting on and duly fell to the ground to everyone's amusement. He complained 'They've got no sympathy for me at all. Dashed if I should work my paws to the bone for them!'

1653

The Shipwreaked Circus were marooned in an environment perhaps inspired by Kong Island.

JIMMY AND HIS MAGIC PATCH
TELL ALL YOU KNOW ABOUT SIR FRANCIS DRAKE AND THE SPANISH ARMADA

JIMMY AND HIS MAGIC PATCH

1944 saw the arrival of another classic *Beano* adventure, with the imaginative tale of schoolboy Jimmy Watson, who saves a mysterious traveller's cat from the jaws of a vicious bull terrier, ripping his trousers in the process. The grateful pet owner performs an impromptu repair with a scrap of cloth cut from his magic carpet, providing the story with its memorable title; 'Jimmy and His Magic Patch'.

The remarkable quality of the newly repaired trousers is that they give Jimmy the power to travel back in time by merely thinking about it. The illustration on the left shows the heading and six of the 12 illustrations by Dudley Watkins that accompanied the original story. The text accompanying the final two frames describes the magical effects of the patch: *'Swoosh! Jimmy felt himself lifted from the paving stones of the square. It seemed as if a great gale was blowing him away. Jimmy held on to his cap as he whizzed though the air. What was going to happen to him? Jimmy soon found out, for, suddenly, he landed with a thump on the ground. One minute he was walking across the square thinking about the Spanish Armada. The next minute he had landed in the middle of Sir Francis Drake and his men playing bowls!'*

HELPING ON THE HOME FRONT

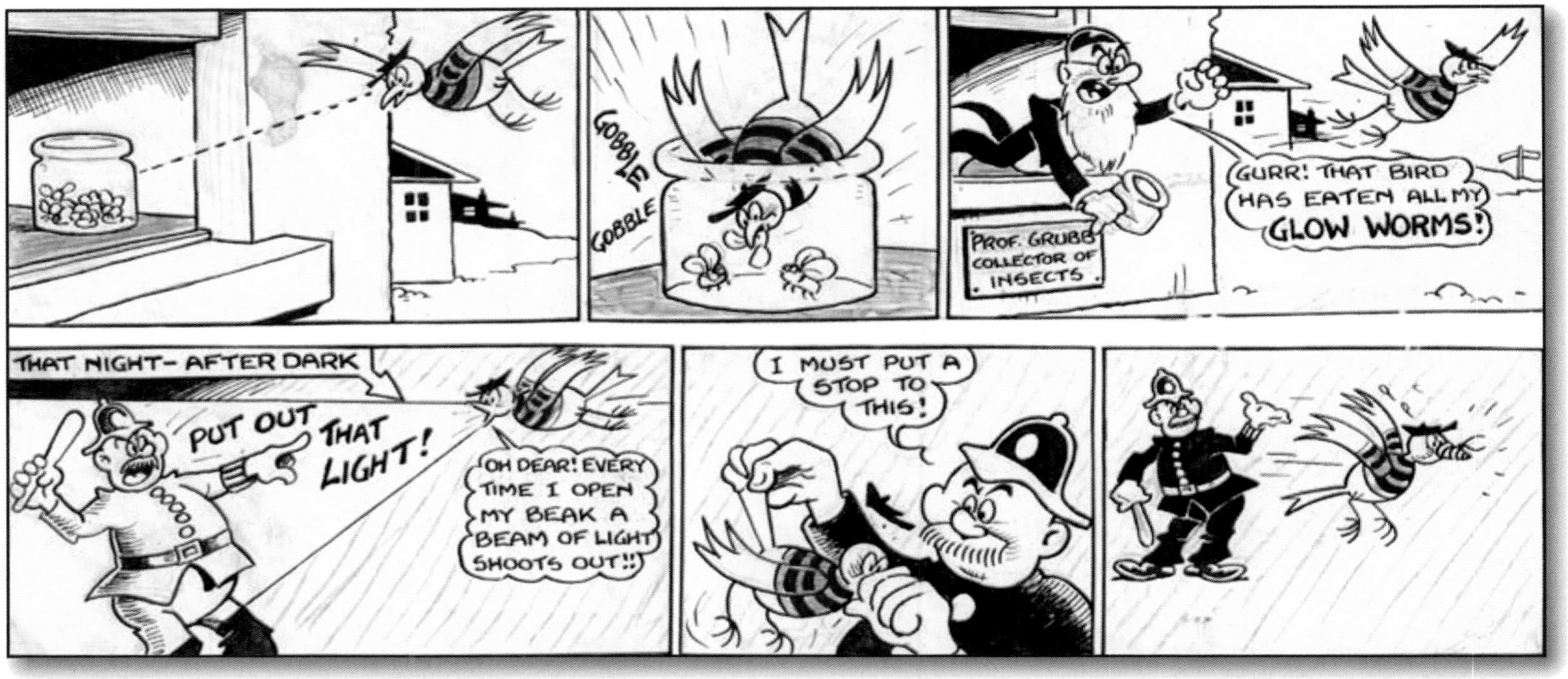
GOBBLE
GOBBLE
PROF. GRUBB COLLECTOR OF INSECTS
GURR! THAT BIRD HAS EATEN ALL MY GLOW WORMS!
THAT NIGHT– AFTER DARK
PUT OUT THAT LIGHT!
OH DEAR! EVERY TIME I OPEN MY BEAK A BEAM OF LIGHT SHOOTS OUT!!
I MUST PUT A STOP TO THIS!

The Beano conscientiously reminded those left on the home front that they were bound to do their duty for King and country in every conceivable way. Whether by collecting old comics to recycle, supporting the Home Guard, bearing privation, or simply maintaining prudent war etiquette, everyone had to play their part. Primarily, *The Beano* concentrated on encouraging children. Every aspect of a war child's life, and indeed their potential contribution to the war effort, was covered. Here, with the original artwork of Hugh McNeill, 'Ping the Elastic Man' is seen doing his duty when a 'Nasty' parachutist lands, capturing him and taking him to the 'Cop Shop'.

WOW! A NASTY!!
RAT! TAT! RAT!-A-TAT!
BOUNCE!
ILL HIDE IN THIS OLD ARMOUR!
RUBBISH DUMP
HA! HA! ILL SQUEEZE MY HEAD IN AN' HE'LL THINK HE'S SHOT IT OFF!!
RAT-A-TAT!
HA! HA! HE THINKS I'M A GHOST— IDEA! I'LL CAPTURE HIM WITH MY ARM AS A LASSO!
HIMMEL! DER GHOST!
D-DER WOW! I-ITS G-GOT M-M-ME!
WOOOO!! YOUR DOOM IS SEALED!
JERK!
GO ON! KEEP GOOSE-STEPPING TILL YOU GET TO THE COP SHOP! HA! HA!
DER GRRR!
COP SHOP

COCKY DICK

The crucial campaign to maintain blackout conditions – to avoid inadvertently providing target beacons fort German bombers – was supported with several editorial reminders and even by subtle allegory in this episode of Cocky Dick. The original artwork, by Allan Morley, shows Cocky Dick being chastised by a policeman because he inadvertently emits a revelatory light after guzzling a jar of glowworms!

TEE HEE! YOU GO AND SOUND THE AIR RAID SIREN, AND WHEN COKE DIVES INTO THIS SHELTER —!
HA! HA! O.K.!
WHOO-OO-OO-OO-OO-OO
WHOO-OO-OO--OO-OO-OO-
SAFE AT LAST!
B-B-BUT!
HA! HA!
HA! HA! OUR JAPE WORKED!
WORKED MY FOOT! I WAS ABOUT TO TELL YOU—
BOOM!
HE WHO LAUGHS LAST—
GROAN!
I DIDN'T SOUND THE SIRENS! IT WAS A REAL WARNING!

WOW! LOOK AT THAT NAZI PLANE DROPPING INCENDIARY BOMBS!
HELP! IT'S SET MY GOWN ON FIRE!
COO! IF ONLY I COULD AFFORD STIRRUP PUMPS. AH! THESE WATER PISTOLS GIVE ME AN IDEA!
NOTICE
ALL BOYS WITH WATER PISTOLS MUST REPORT TO COKE'S PALACE IMMEDIATELY! SIGNED KING COKE
GO TO IT BOYS! DO YOUR STUFF!
THREE CHEERS FOR KING COKE! HE KNOWS HOW TO DAMP THE NAZIS' SPIRITS!
GOOD OLD COKE!
I'VE PUT MY BOMB OUT!
HISS-S-S-S
FIZZ!

GOOD KING COKE

'Good King Coke' strips often reminded children of their responsibilities. The first of the two strips on this page, drawn by Eric Roberts, is a reminder about the dangers of a false alarm. It shows Coke's air raid shelter being sabotaged and warns mischievous children of the folly of such actions. Practical jokes during wartime were safer on paper than in real life. It was easy for Coke to 'enlist' these erstwhile hooligans (in the other strip) to disarm incendiary devices . . . with their water pistols!

WARTIME WORKING

BOOM

COURIER PLACE
ALBERT SQUARE
COURIER PLACE
SOVIET
TROOPS
POLAND

The Courier Building in Dundee protected by sandbags

The curse of any comic editor is the prospect of freelance artists failing to deliver their artwork in time. Over the decades a multitude of creative excuses have been proffered. However, few trump those of Allan Morley, who wrote to apologise for a delay in submitting completed artwork in May, 1942. Morley, who drew 'The Magic Lollipops' as well as 'Cocky Dick', reported that he'd fallen behind due to having been called out on impromptu air raid fire duty every night during the preceding week in his hometown of Scarborough!

Things seemed slightly safer in Dundee where D. C. Thomson made their city centre base in the Courier Building resemble a fortress by stacking thousands of sandbags around the perimeter.

This reassured the artist Reg Carter, who wrote to ***The Beano*** stating: 'I hope Hitler doesn't start his Battle of Britain before I arrive. I'm anxious to go into battle with a claymore in one hand and a bottle of whiskey in t'other. The last stand can be made at Fort Courier.'

The Beano also inspired a more tangible element in warfare, becoming the inspiration behind the eponymous Beano Hand Grenade, introduced to allied forces in September 1943. The same size and weight as a cricket ball, with an impact-detonating mechanism, this was no laughing matter.

WHOO
GOLLY! IT'S THE SIRENS!
POLICE BOX
WOW! BOMBS!
MADE IN GERMANY
GAS MASK
Hugh McNeill

I'VE GOT TO COLLECT SAVINGS FOR THE LOCAL WAR SAVINGS GROUP THIS WEEK!
KILL HIM with WAR SAVINGS
PUT YOUR MONEY INTO WAR SAVINGS
HUH!— DOING ME OUT OF BUSINESS, EH?—I'LL SOON PUT A STOP TO THAT!
PUT YOUR MONEY INTO WAR SAVINGS
Harry Hargreaves

I'M OFF TO DO A BIT OF DEEP-SEA FISHING TODAY READERS!
HAR!-HAR! WE'LL FIRE DER TORPEDO AT DER PIG-DOG BRITISH BRAT!
H'M, NOT A BITE YET!— I WAS HOPING FOR SOME EXCITEMENT
Basil Blackaller

WELL, I NEVER! IT'S PANSY POTTER!
I WOULD LIKE TO HELP YOU. WHAT ABOUT ALL OF US GETTING ON MY BIKE?
THE TUMBLER FAMILY ACROBATS
THE TUMBLER FAMILY ACROBATS
Unknown Staff artist

Some *Beano* staff joined the war effort directly on the frontline. Editor George Moonie enlisted with the Royal Marines and his duties passed over to *Adventure* Editor, Stuart Gilchrist. Moonie referred to his wartime service in typically self-deprecating fashion in correspondence with the film director Sir David Puttnam in 1976. In it, he claimed that 1941 was a good year for the armed forces because it saw him sign up. However, he also admitted that 'Lord Snooty did more to save the country than I ever did.'

'Pansy Potter' was a good example of where a number of different artists had to work on the same character due to the war. Four different artists (from top to bottom, Hugh McNeill, Harry Hargreaves, Basil Blackaller, and an unknown staff artist) left their mark on her during the war years, with differences that are easy to spot.

SAVING PAPER

COME ON, GANG, IT'S TUESDAY MORNING! "THE BEANO'S" OUT AGAIN!
HERE YOU ARE, BOYS. THERE'S ONE FOR EACH OF YOU, SINCE YOU ORDERED THEM IN ADVANCE!
BEANO
GIVE ME MINE FIRST, MR NEWSAGENT, AND I'LL GIVE YOU A LICK OF MY TOFFEE-APPLE!

The air raid shelter was familiar to *Beano* readers and has been credited with creating a new army of fans. During the long blackout nights, children would often amuse themselves by reading comics and doing puzzles. Long hours and shortages of supply meant any available reading material was thoroughly circulated.

Paper shortages made comics a particularly valuable commodity. They became an unofficial currency amongst children who would trade their collections with each other. Copies would be swapped in the playground and re-read before eventually being recycled to support the war effort. This was thanks, in no small part, to the presence of continual nagging reminders to readers throughout the 1940s to present wastepaper to the authorities.

If you keep waste paper saving going with a swing
maybe you'll soon see Hitler swing!

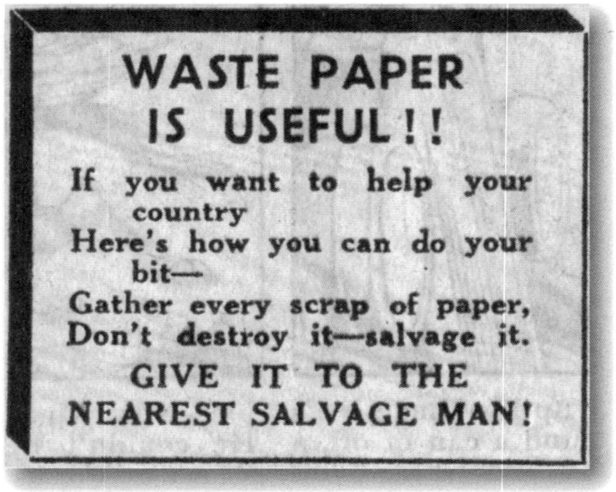
WASTE PAPER IS USEFUL!!

If you want to help your country
Here's how you can do your bit—
Gather every scrap of paper,
Don't destroy it—salvage it.
GIVE IT TO THE NEAREST SALVAGE MAN!

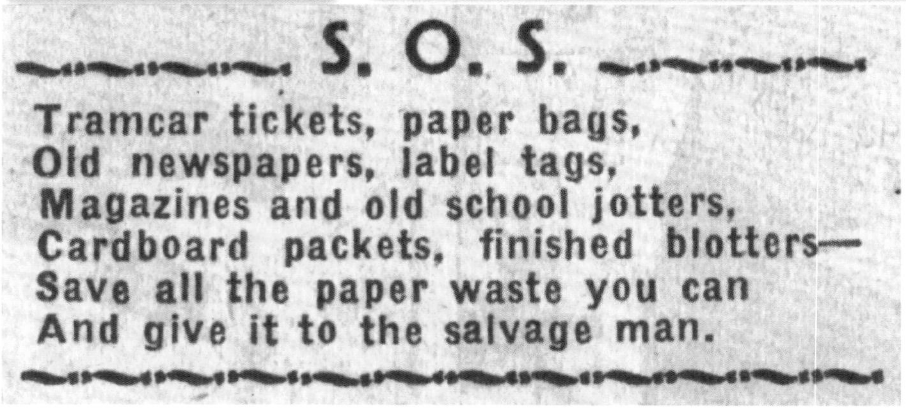
S. O. S.

Tramcar tickets, paper bags,
Old newspapers, label tags,
Magazines and old school jotters,
Cardboard packets, finished blotters—
Save all the paper waste you can
And give it to the salvage man.

WE'RE GOING TO FLY OVER MOORTOWN THIS AFTERNOON AND PRETEND IT'S BERLIN AND DROP LEAFLETS ALL OVER THE TOWN!
THOUGHT
I WAS LUCKY TO GET THIS JOB OF KEEPING THE STREETS CLEAN!
RIGHT, BILL, WE'RE FLYING OVER MOORTOWN. DROP THE LEAFLETS!
OK, THERE'S THOUSANDS OF 'EM, THERE THEY GO!
THAT AFTERNOON
GRR! IF I CATCH THE KNAVE WHO'S THROWING ALL THIS PAPER ABOUT I'LL STAB HIM WITH ONE OF MY SPEAR-STICKS!
STRANGE! I CAN'T SEE ANY OF THE LEAFLETS THAT OUR PLANE WAS SUPPOSED TO HAVE DROPPED ALL OVER THE TOWN!
WOW! LOOK!
HEY! THOSE ARE OUR LEAFLETS!
OH, ARE THEY? WELL, IF YOU THROW ANY MORE PAPER ABOUT, I'LL TELL THE WAR OFFICE, SO THERE!
GO OVER TO THAT TENT AND REPORT TO FLIGHT-LIEUTENANT PHIPPS AS BATMAN!
OUCH! YESSIR!
FOR SPOILING THE LEAFLET RAID RIP IS SET TO WORK AT THE AERODROME
PUFF! HOORAY! IT'S STILL OPEN!
CRICKET BA
The SPORTS SHOP
WE STOCK CRICKET BATS PING PONG BATS BASEBALL BATS TENNIS AND BADMINTON RACQUETS

Look at the youngsters saving waste paper. Snitchy and Snatchy know that it's worth the bother and that they are doing great work
YOU can help them!
JUST SAVE WASTE PAPER!

The paper drive became a recurring theme throughout the war years with a variety of appeals being made by popular characters. These reminders took the form of entire strips (as with 'Rip Van Wink', above, drawn by Eric Roberts, who also worked for the RAF producing propaganda leaflets), adverts, text boxes or even just a rhyming couplet. Some of the encouragement tended toward the macabre – like the example opposite, with Hitler in a noose, or in this little reminder:

'It's up to you – speed old Hitler to his grave
With all the paper you can save'
'Waste Litter – paste Hitler'

'Big Eggo' was still being used as a role model in 1948 when he was shown encouraging children to dispatch their old comics into the neighbourhood salvage bin. The danger of the war itself was receding so it was an art of persuasion to encourage children to part with their comics. Considering their unofficial currency status and remembering the fact that comics could be swapped for scarce confectionery rations, this was quite an undertaking. It seems, however, that these messages were readily observed, resulting in a shortage of *Beano* comics on the collector's market – 1940s issues are now extremely expensive collectables, exchanging hands for around £150 per copy.

RATIONING PAGES

The first material effect of the war on *The Beano* occurred less than a month after war was formally declared, when a page reduction, from 28 to 24, was introduced. Paper shortages were an obvious problem and became a constant theme in *The Beano* throughout the war years. Whether it was repeating the mantra for children to gather old copies and return them to boost the war effort, or through surreal comic strips which involved a giant wasp chewing trees into paper pulp outside the Dundee printworks. This entire 'Lord Snooty' strip suggested a most ingenious way of solving the paper crisis and terrifying the Nazis at the same time!

A specific victim of the shortage was the text story 'Acorns From The Wishing Tree'. The final episode of the story was unceremoniously dropped, never to be concluded, when pagination was reduced.

SNIVELLING SNITZELS! I HAF SLEPT IN! THAT DUMB-CLUCK OF A SERVANT OF MINE HAS FORGOTTEN TO WAKEN ME! AND BAKE MY BOOTS, MINE TEA, TOO, IS COLD! OOH! SOME-VUN FOR THIS SHALL SUFFER!
COLD
ATTENTION, YOU LOAFING LOUNGER! WHY HAF YOU LET YOUR FUHRER SLEEP IN? WHY ISS MY TEA COLD? I WILL HAF YOU SHOT FOR THIS!
AW, PIPE DOWN, ADDY! I DO NO MORE WORK FOR YOU. I'M FED UP WITH DIS LIFE. NO CINEMAS, NO FOOD, NO FUN!
VOT IS DER MEANING OF DIS, HERMAN? HAF YOU GONE DER NUTS?
ACH! IF ONLY WE HAD DER "BEANO" COMICS LIKE DER BRITISH KIDS, WE'D BE AS HAPPY AS DER LARKS!
OH, DEAR, ADOLF, SAVE ME PLEASE FROM DER SOLDIERS. DEY ARE SO FED UP DEY WON'T WORK.
GET A MOVE ON, YOU BURSTING BUTTER BARREL! FOR ONE PIN I'D BLOW YOU INTO TINY-BITS—JA!
THAT'S VOT I THINK OF YOU, MINE FUHRER! VOT A PITY IT ISS ONLY DER STATUE!
HERR HITLER THE FURIOUS FUHRER
YOU HAF YOUR ORDERS, HERR FRIED FACE. YOU FLY OVER TO DER BRITAIN UND PINCH DER "BEANOS" MIT DER SPECIAL PLANE. WE NEED THE "BEANOS" TO CHEER MINE TROOPS!
AND MAKE IT DER SNAPPY!
JA—GROOCH, JA—MINE FUHRER!
LATER
"THE BEANO" OFFICE
HEY! LEAVE THAT ALONE, YOU BLIGHTERS. YOU CAN'T READ ENGLISH!
WELL, HERE'S THE "BEANOS" FOR THIS WEEK ALL TIED UP, GANG! CORKS! WHAT'S HAPPENING?
GOSH! THE NAZI PLANE'S PINCHIN' ALL THE "BEANOS" WITH ITS TELESCOPIC CLAW!
BEANO
WELL, THANKS TO THE NAZIS YOU WON'T GET ANY "BEANOS" THIS WEEK. I'VE USED UP ALL MY PAPER RATION!
DON'T WORRY, MR EDITOR. WE'LL ASK OUR PROFESSOR PAL TO HELP US!
YEAH, HE'S SURE TO THINK UP SOMETHING!
HA! HA! HA!!
GOSH! JUST LISTEN TO THE LAUGHS COMING FROM GERMANY. THE NAZIS ARE LAUGHING AT THE JOKES IN "THE BEANO"
NEVER MIND! HERE'S THE PROFESSOR'S HOUSE. WE'LL SOON FIX THOSE ROTTERS!
PROFESSOR
SURE, I CAN HELP YOU, SNOOTY! YOU WANT SOME PAPER, EH? WELL, THIS NATURE STUDY BOOK SAYS THAT WASPS MAKE PAPER TO BUILD THEIR NESTS WITH—AND I HAVE A SWARM HERE!
I HOPE THESE OVERGROWN FLIES IN FOOTBALL JERSEYS KNOW WE'RE THEIR PALS!
NOW I'LL POUR SOME MAGIC LIQUID ON THIS WASP TO MAKE IT GROW—AND GROW!
HEY! LAY OFF! MY BATH NIGHT'S SATURDAY—NOT TO-DAY!
THERE YOU ARE, BOYS! IT'S GROWN ALL RIGHT, HASN'T IT? JUMP ON AND HE'LL FLY US TO THE "BEANO" OFFICE.
OH BOY, AM I A BEAUTY? HOTCHA!
LET'S STICK A PIN IN HIM!
YES, I WAS STUNG BY A WASP LAST YEAR!
HERE WE ARE, MR EDITOR, WITH OUR PATENT PAPER MACHINE.
"THE BEANO" OFFICE
HOORAY! THE GIANT WASP'S TURNING OUT ROLLS OF PAPER FOR US AND NOW WE CAN PRINT THE "BEANOS" AFTER ALL!
SAY WHEN, BOYS, THERE'S LOTS MORE WHERE THIS CAME FROM!
FULL STEAM AHEAD, BOYS! THANKS A MILLION, SNOOTY!
THE BEANO PRINTING MACHINE
"BEANOS"
I KNOW, I GOT CAUGHT IN THE MACHINE!
ROLL UP FOR YOUR "BEANOS", FOLKS! BUY THE BEST COMIC IN THE WORLD HERE!
NO PUSHING, PLEASE—THANK YOU, MADAM—ER—WHAT ARE YOU DOING TONIGHT?
YEAH! PRINTED ON SPECIAL WASP PAPER! I MADE IT MYSELF!
NOW WE'LL FIX THE WASP UP IN A CRATE—AND SEND IT OVER TO GERMANY. THINK YOU CAN MANAGE THAT, MR POSTMAN?
OUT OF THE WAY, HAIRPIN! LET A MAN SHOW YOU HOW TO DO THAT!
DON'T MAKE SUCH A DIN, PLEASE—I WANNA SLEEP!
G.P.O.
NEXT DAY
AMAZING PICTURES FROM GERMANY! HITLER AND GOERING CHASED BY MONSTER WASP!
10,000 JERRY SOLDIERS IN HOSPITAL—STUNG BY BRITAIN'S NEW SECRET WEAPON
HA! HA! WILLY THE WASP'S CUT UP ROUGH IN GERMANY. HO! HO! TEN THOUSAND JERRY SOLDIERS IN HOSPITAL—THAT'LL TEACH 'EM TO PINCH OUR "BEANOS."

1939

In October, after less than a month of hostilities, the pagination of the comic was reduced for the first time, from 28 pages to 24. In issue No. 69, dated November 1939, readers were given the final free gift before rationing was introduced – a liquorice pipe.

1940

During June, paper shortages necessitated another cut in the page count, with *The Beano* dropping to 22 pages for two issues then down to 20 pages by the end of the month. This was followed by another reduction in November, down to 18. Despite the dwindling number of pages, issue No. 90 (April 13, 1940) saw the bonus of an unexpected, and no doubt gratefully received, free gift of two liquorice 'Black Eyes', the last free gift to be given away for over 20 years!

1941

The beginning of 1941 saw the page count reduced yet again, to 16. While this was bad news for *Beano* readers, they were grateful when they compared this misfortune to the absolute demise of *The Magic Comic* which was withdrawn after just 80 issues. Another D. C. Thomson stable mate, *The Skipper,* was also withdrawn in February. The end of these papers perhaps put the decision to reduce publication of *The Beano* to a fortnightly frequency during August a less bitter pill to swallow.

1942

The almost customary page reduction again occurred at the beginning of 1942, with a drop to 14 pages of fun. A further drop occurred in April leaving readers with only 12 pages to pore over.

1943

This was the first year since the beginning of the war without a cut in pagination.

1947

In April the final cut in pagination occurred, with the comic being reduced to just 10 pages. This followed production difficulties the preceding month when there was an unprecedented gap of four weeks between the issue dates of Nos. 305 and 306. This didn't represent the final act of wartime austerity – that occurred the following year when the actual size of the comic was reduced from 216 mm x 305 mm to 178 mm x 298 mm.

1948

A boost to readers occurred in October when the pagination was actually increased back to 12, albeit only on alternate issues.

1949

In July, weekly publication resumed with every issue now going on sale on Fridays, instead of Tuesday as had previously been the case.

HERR
HITLER
THE
PURIOUS
FUHRER

AFTER THE WAR

JACK FLASH COMICS
BIG 32 PAGE COMIC
JACK FLASH THE FLYING BOY OF "THE BEANO" IN "THE WHIZZ BANG WIZARD"
A FAWCETT PRODUCTION
ENGLISH EDITION BY
L. MILLER & SON LTD.
LONDON

Although the war ended in 1945, the continuation of rationing until 1954 and the process of picking up the pieces after the initial elation of victory had receded meant that heroes were gratefully received by readers until the end of the decade.

JACK FLASH

The final year of the decade was perhaps most notable for the emergence of 'Jack Flash – The Flying Boy' on February 19. This was the final new adventure story from Dudley Watkins, who drew the first 11 episodes, before passing on the baton to fellow staffer, Freddie Sturrock. The header and first two pictures in the first strip are shown below, illustrating Jack Flash's arrival on Earth. This style of story signalled an acknowledgement of the popularity of the American comic strip.

JACK FLASH
THE FLYING BOY

This Thrilling Fight Appears Inside
READ
"DEEP-SEA DANNY'S IRON FISH"
THE
BEANO
2d
EVERY FRIDAY. No. 368. AUG. 6th. 1949.
COMIC

'Jack Flash' was based in Cornwall, although the eponymous hero did in fact originate from the planet Mercury! Part of the novelty of the story was that this particular flying boy sported tiny wings on his ankles. The success of *Jack Flash* is perhaps best demonstrated by the fact that the D. C. Thomson archive holds a mock-up cover (shown opposite) of a bespoke *Jack Flash* comic, based upon an imported edition of the *Captain Marvel* comic.

Perhaps only the ongoing paper shortage prevented Jack Flash from having his own title. His enduring popularity at D. C. Thomson was confirmed in a more unexpected fashion when the company's girl's title *Mandy* ran a story called *Jackie Flash* during 1973!

Deep-Sea Danny's Iron Fish

August 1949 saw the arrival of another action adventure thriller in the shape of 'Deep-Sea Danny's Iron Fish'. This told the story of Professor Jim Gray who built a mechanical swordfish for his 12-year-old son Danny (see left, as drawn by Jack Glass).

Combined with 'Jack Flash', it meant *Beano* readers were once again spoiled for a choice of glamorous heroes.

WE'LL MEET AGAIN?

Though *The Beano* survived the Second World War, certain stalwart characters did not make it to the end of the 1940s.

December 1947 witnessed the last appearance of title mascot Peanut, the forerunner of the first major change to *The Beano* cover the following month, when 1948 was greeted with the last ever 'Big Eggo' cover story shown here. 'Big Eggo', drawn by Reg Carter, was on the very first *Beano* cover. He stayed there for 10 years, until January 24, 1948, when he was ousted by newcomer 'Biffo the Bear' drawn by Dudley Watkins until 1969. 'Biffo' would remain there until 1974.

'Big Eggo' was relocated inside the comic, in a black and white strip, until his final appearance on April 2, 1949. Even after this, Eggo still appeared on the front cover, standing next to *The Beano* title, as can be seen on the first 'Biffo' cover (shown opposite).

George Moonie made the decision to replace Eggo when feedback from readers suggested that they would identify more readily with a character sporting four limbs, like themselves. Some futile attempts were made to introduce arms and hands to the ostrich. However, it soon became clear that editorial had their heads in the sand with this reliance on their original talisman.

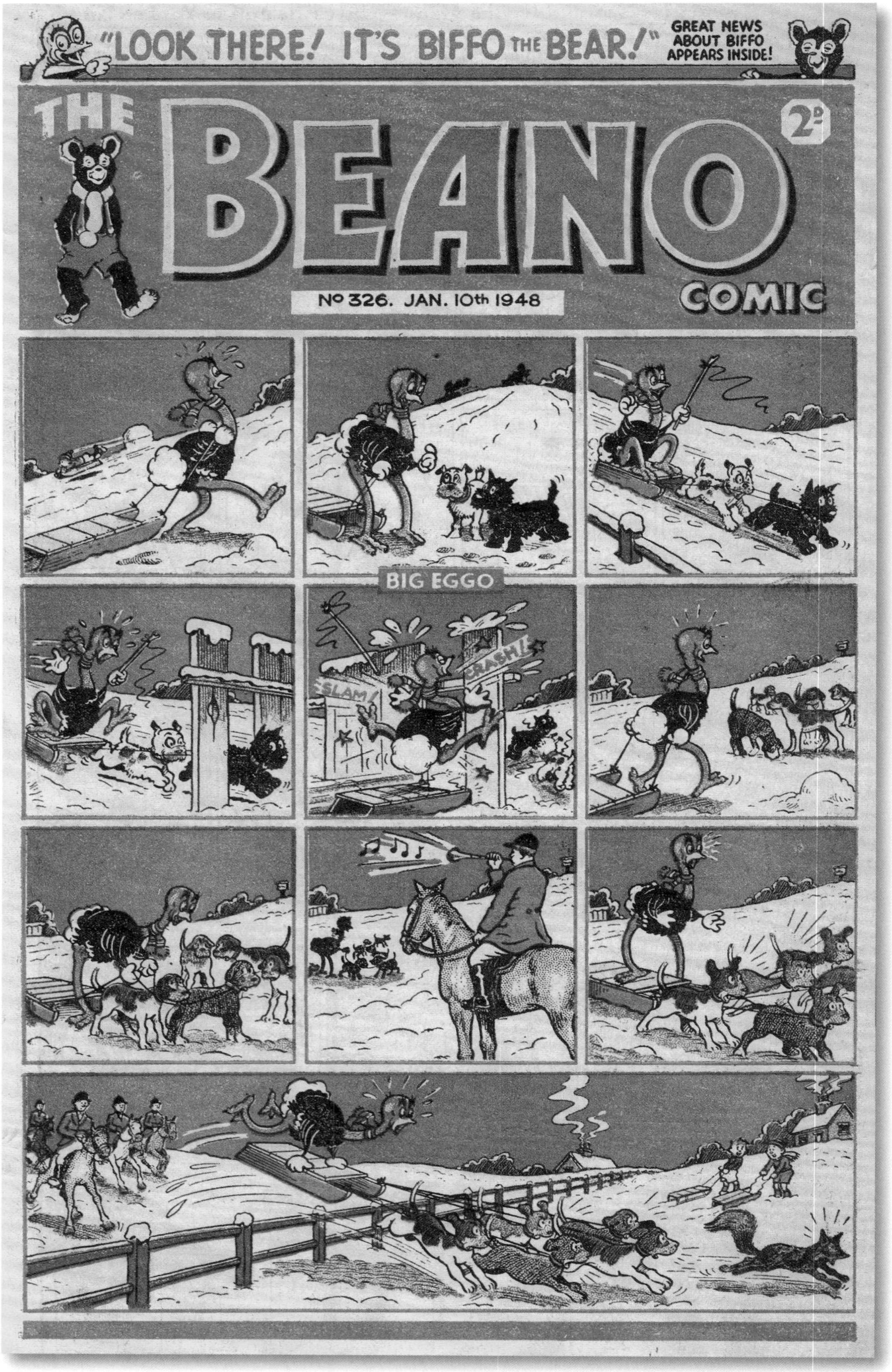
"LOOK THERE! IT'S BIFFO THE BEAR!"
GREAT NEWS ABOUT BIFFO APPEARS INSIDE!
THE BEANO COMIC
2d
No 326. JAN. 10th 1948
BIG EGGO
SLAM!
CRASH!

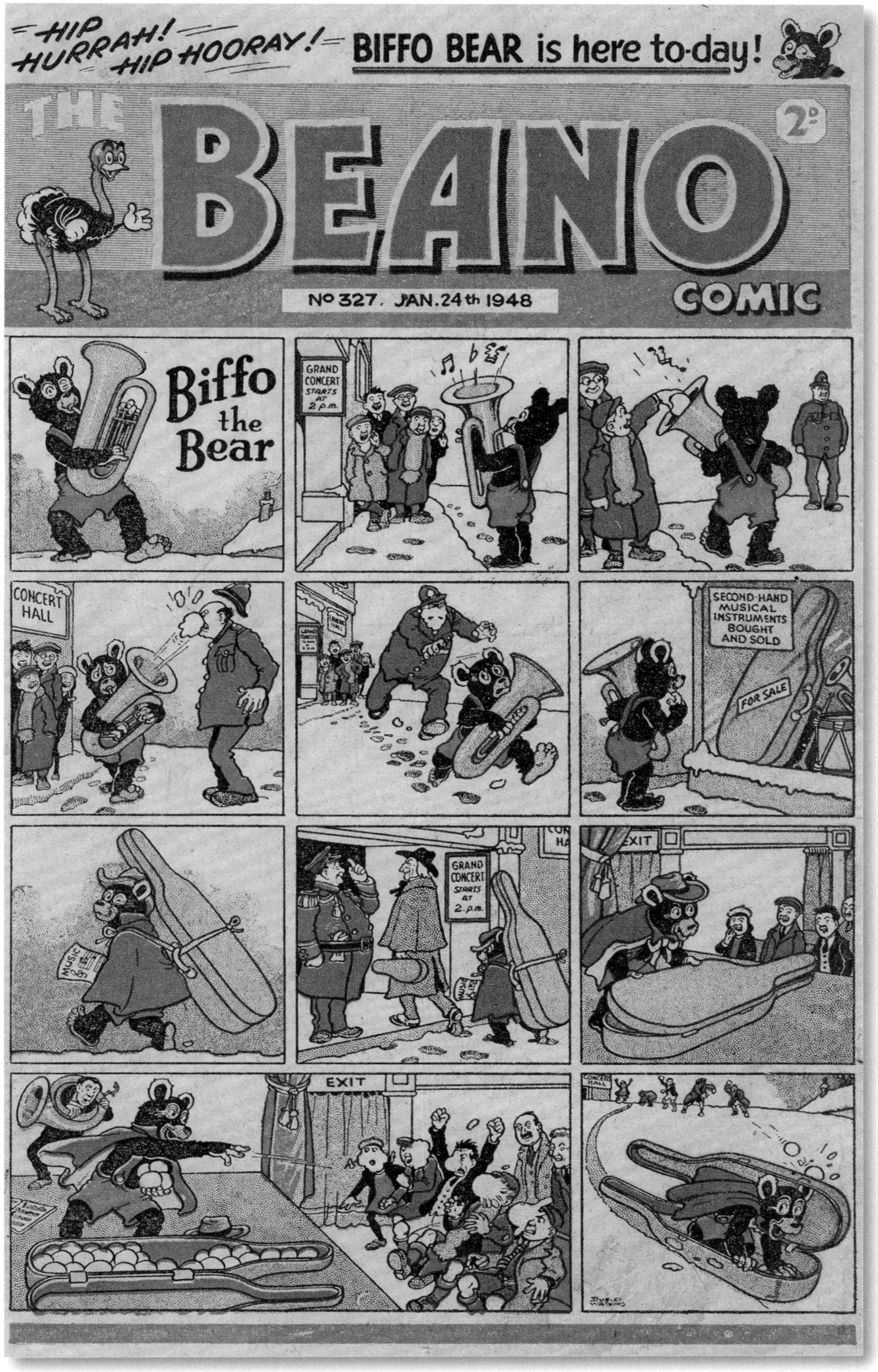
HIP HURRAH! HIP HOORAY!
BIFFO BEAR is here to-day!
THE BEANO
2D
No 327. JAN. 24th 1948
COMIC
Biffo the Bear
GRAND CONCERT STARTS AT 2 p.m.
CONCERT HALL
SECOND-HAND MUSICAL INSTRUMENTS BOUGHT AND SOLD
FOR SALE
EXIT
EXIT

The week prior to Eggo's demise, readers were introduced to 'Biffo the Bear', who, while not strictly human, certainly sported characteristics and a lifestyle which readers could more readily identify with.

Issue No. 367, which went on sale on July 30, 1949, exactly 11 years after the first issue, saw the first run of 'Lord Snooty and His Pals' draw to a conclusion. This *Beano* was the first which did not include at least one character who had featured in Issue No.1. Despite the sadness some readers may have felt at their passing, *The Beano* was about to step confidently into its golden era. The ultimate comic icon was yet to be born, but fans didn't have long to wait for the world's wildest boy.

"BIFFO BEAR" is simply great!
It's lucky he can roller skate.
You may be sure he won't be late—
He's hurrying to keep his date—
ON THE FRONT PAGE OF THE NEXT "BEANO"

BEANO

PART 3

THE GOLDEN AGE

1950-1959

As the 1950s dawned, *The Beano* didn't look all that different from the first issue published back in 1938. But all that was about to change. *The Beano* was about to enter its Golden Age, the decade that would give birth to some of the greatest – and funniest – characters in British comics and in which the circulation was to reach almost two million copies every week.

This Golden Age didn't come about by accident. Apart from the time he spent in the armed forces during the Second World War, George Moonie had been the Editor since the comic was launched in 1938. But, by 1950, George and his editorial team had decided that *The Beano* needed to be up-dated with fresh, more dynamic characters to whom the young readers would relate.

The Beano Book *published for Christmas 1950.*

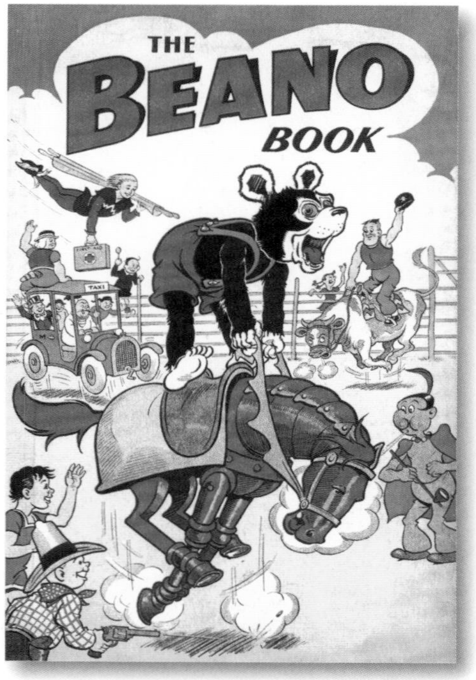
THE
BEANO
BOOK

SINBAD THE SAILOR FIGHTS THE RED EAGLE!
THRILLING PICTURES INSIDE
THE BEANO
2D
EVERY THURSDAY. No. 413. JUNE 17th, 1950.
Biffo the Bear
ZOO
RIDE ROUND THE ZOO ON ANY ANIMAL YOU FANCY FOR 3D
CHINK
RIDE ROUND THE ZOO ON ANY ANIMAL YOU FANCY FOR 3D
ZOO
TAILOR
COLLARS MADE TO MEASURE ANY SIZE 6D PER COLLAR
ZOO
COLLARS MADE TO MEASURE ANY SIZE 6D PER COLLAR
D. WATKINS

THE COMIC FOR LAUGHS
THE BEANO
2d
EVERY THURSDAY. No. 405. APRIL 22nd, 1950.
COMIC
Biffo the Bear
FROGS AS PETS
BREAKING THIS PAVEMENT IS A TOUGH JOB.
CRACK
THANKS, BIFFO!
ALL THE FUN O' THE FAIR
CLANG
TRY YOUR STRENGTH! RING THE BELL AND WIN A COCONUT
D.D.W.

No 'Dennis the Menace', no 'Bash Street Kids' and no 'Minnie the Minx', yet the issue for April 22, 1950, will go down in history. It was the highest selling *Beano* of all time with 1.9 million copies sold. In fact, records show that an even higher sale could have been achieved but the presses just could not print any more!

So, what makes a record-selling comic? For a start it was called *The Beano Comic.* The word 'comic' wouldn't be dropped from the title until June that year, as seen on the cover opposite.

On the front cover was 'Biffo the Bear', drawn by Dudley Watkins. This was a rather bizarre strip for this long-running character. Biffo wants to catch a frog as a pet but inexplicably halfway through the strip he switches from using a net to a sledgehammer! Look at the deranged expression on his face in frames 7 to 9. Then he ends by feeding the frog with a piece of coconut!

Pages 2 and 3 of The Beano *for April 22, 1950.*

This school has Belle guessin'—There's trouble in each lesson !
Ding-Dong Belle
THERE'S SOMETHING FISHY ABOUT THIS NEW SCHOOL.
SCHOOL FOR YOUNG COW-BOYS — HEADMASTER — K.C. JONES, BA-ND-IT, Etc.
BEG PARDON, MA'AM. WOULD YOU LIKE TO SEE WHAT I TAUGHT THE CLASS THIS MORNING?
I SURE WOULD!
HEY! STOPPIT! LEMME GO!
VERY GOOD, BOYS. YOU CERTAINLY LEARNED YOUR LESSON ON HOW TO LASSO SHERIFFS.
IT MUST BE A SCHOOL FOR YOUNG BANDITS. I'LL LOOK INTO THIS.
HERE'S THAT NOSEY SHERIFF. WHERE'S MY DUSTER? I'LL FIX HER!
LESSON 1. RUSTLING.
CATTLE PEN
CATTLE
YOU
SHERIFF
HM!
JOHN'S NOT AT THE TOP OF THE CLASS FOR NOTHING.
LESSON 2. GETTING RID OF STRANGERS
JOHN SLICK IN BACK ROW WILL FIRE AT THE SASH CORD IN THE WINDOW.
HE MEANS ME—I'LL GET FULL MARKS IF I BRING THE WINDOW DOWN.
JOHN'S BULLETS
ZING
BUZZ
OW!
BELLE GOES UPSTAIRS INTO ANOTHER CLASSROOM
TAKE COVER, BOYS! THE FUSE IS LIT.
LESSON 4. DEMONSTRATION ON HOW TO OPEN SAFES, STRONG-ROOMS, MONEY-BOXES, JAIL DOORS, ETC. ETC. ETC.
SAFE
BOOM!
LATER
DON'T FORGET TO DO YOUR HOMEWORK WHILE WE'RE AWAY, BOYS.
I'LL PUT YOU IN JAIL OUT OF MISCHIEF!
THIS SCHOOL CLOSED BY LAW.
THERE YOU ARE. YOU CAN USE YOUR SPARE TIME STUDYING TO TEACH A PROPER SCHOOL!
A.B.C.
WHAT'S GOING ON OUT HERE? WOW! SO THIS IS THE HOMEWORK THOSE KIDS ARE DOING— RUSTLING!
BANG
BANG
CRACK
BANK
I'LL ROUND UP THE LITTLE RASCALS—I'LL HEAD FOR THE HILLS. THEY'LL BE UP THERE SOMEWHERE.
BELLE'S MOBILE SWEET SHOP
HEY, FELLAS! HERE COMES A TRAVELLING SWEET SHOP.
OH, BOY! OH, BOY! LOOK AT THEM—BIG BARS OF TOFFEE THAT HAVE FALLEN OFF THE SHOP!
HO! HO! IT WORKED! I MADE THEM FROM EXTRA SPECIAL STICKY STUFF. AND NOW I'VE GOT THEM!
WE'RE STUCK!
YOU'VE LOST A LOT OF SCHOOLING, BUT YOU'LL MAKE IT UP PRONTO OR MY NAME'S NOT DING DONG BELLE!
HOMEWORK
GEOGRAPHY
HISTORY
ARITHMETIC
ENGLISH
Three Hours Each

There's always good cheer—when the Gang's all here !
HAVE-A-GO JOE
Look out, below—Here comes Joe!
STAND BY FOLKS, FOR MY HIGH DIVE!
WATCH JOE DIVE 300 FEET INTO A TANK OF WATER
WOW! HE'S MISSED THE TANK AND GONE THROUGH THE CONCRETE!
SORRY I MISSED IT, FOLKS. I'M O.K.
HE'S NOT EVEN SCRATCHED!
IT TAKES MORE THAN THAT TO KNOCK ME OUT!
WHOOPS!
LOOK OUT, JOE! IT'S A BANANA SKIN!
SLIP
QUICK! BRING A STRETCHER! JOE'S OUT FOR THE COUNT!
MAXY'S TAXI
The taxi's quite—a shining light!
TAXI!
TO THE CLIFF LIGHTHOUSE—QUICK! THE LIGHT'S BROKEN.
WAIT THERE, MAXY!
THE REPAIR WILL TAKE HOURS. WE WANT YOUR TAXI!
HEAVE AWAY!
GREAT STUFF, MAXY!
THE MAGIC LOLLIPOPS
SUCK 'EM AND SEE.
LOOK! I'VE LOST MY KITE!
CHEER UP—ONE LICK AND—
—I CAN FLOAT UP AND GET IT FOR YOU!
HE'S GONE—AND SO HAS MY OTHER MAGIC LOLLIPOP!
I'LL STOP HIM LICKING IT!
BOO-HOO! HE'S BROKEN MY KITE AND TAKEN MY LOLLIPOP AWAY, DAD!
SMACK
THERE! NOW HE'S GOT IT BACK AGAIN!
LICK!
OW! HE'S LOST HIS HEAD!
THAT WAS A MAGIC LOLLIPOP, MISTER!
NOW YOU'LL HAVE TO WAIT UNTIL THE MAGIC EFFECTS WEAR OFF BEFORE HIS HEAD APPEARS AGAIN!
A.M.
THE BIGGEST LAUGHS YOU'VE HAD FOR AGES—YOU'LL FIND THEM PACKED INTO THESE PAGES!

Pages 4 and 5 of The Beano *for April 22, 1950.*

How Edric won a dragon's tooth—to save the Magic Sword!

THE BOY WITH THE WONDER HORSE

The Talking Sword.

ACROSS a windswept plain in Morania rode a boy on a jet black horse.

The horse's hoofs hardly seemed to touch the ground as it galloped madly towards a mountain in the centre of the plain. The horse was Vulcan, the Wonder Horse. He was shod with Magic Horseshoes and could run like the wind.

Mounted on the Wonder Horse was Edric, the blacksmith's boy from the city of Karlsburg. His hair streamed in the wind and his teeth were chattering in the intense cold, but he clung on grimly.

Ahead of him he could see the glittering mountain which had been bewitched and turned into glass by Merla, an evil wizard who had sworn to place the country of Morania at the mercy of its enemies.

The air for miles around the mountain was icy-cold, but Edric had no thought for that. His eyes were fixed on the Magic Sword of Morania, which Merla had imprisoned deep in the centre of the Glass Mountain.

The blade of the Magic Sword gleamed as if afire, but Edric's heart was heavy. The Sword could not help King Ivor to protect the country against its many enemies now. Unless Edric could free it from the Glass Mountain, the Sword, which could cut through stone and steel, was useless.

Vulcan was racing along as if he would never tire, and soon they were at the foot of the mountain. Edric brought the Wonder Horse to a standstill and looked thoughtfully at the glassy surface of the mountain.

"If only we could find a way in, Vulcan!" he muttered, and he rode the Wonder Horse slowly round the foot of the mountain to look for a gap in the glass.

But there was none big enough to allow Edric to reach the Sword.

"We'll have to break a way in!" cried Edric. "Up, Vulcan."

At the order from his master Vulcan reared on his hindlegs and brought his forehoofs crashing downwards. The mountain shuddered under the impact of the Magic Horseshoes, but even the wonderful metal of Vulcan's shoes could not shatter the glass.

Again and again Vulcan reared and brought his hoofs flashing downwards, but the surface of the mountain remained unbroken and the Sword still stayed in its glass prison.

Edric clenched his teeth. He had to free the Sword somehow. Then as the boy glared angrily at the Glass Mountain he saw that the Sword was swinging to and fro.

The force of Vulcan's hoofs had shaken the mountain and now the Sword was vibrating. As it vibrated Edric heard a low, humming note like the note of a harp. As Edric listened, his face grew thoughtful. There was even more wonderful magic than he had ever dreamed of in the blade of the Magic Sword.

"Quiet, Vulcan!" hissed Edric, and he kept the Wonder Horse perfectly still as he listened.

The singing note grew louder and louder, till at last it formed words. The Sword was speaking.

"Listen, blacksmith's boy," said the Magic Sword. "I will tell you how to split the mountain and return me to my master, King Ivor. Ride forth to Sangor Forest, many miles away. There you will find a Golden Apple Tree. Drop the seed from a Golden Apple in the crack you will find in the top of the Glass Mountain. As the seed grows it will burst the Glass Mountain asunder."

Edric crouched on Vulcan's back listening in amazement.

"You will face many dangers," went on the Sword. "But if Vulcan stamps on the ground I will speak to you through the Magic Horseshoes and help you."

All at once the Sword stopped vibrating and the voice died away.

But Edric had not been the only one listening to the Sword. Hidden behind a pile of boulders a short distance away was Merla the magician, and, at the sound of the Sword's voice, he flew into a rage, spread his black cloak, and flapped the ends in the breeze with a noise like thunder.

Instantly there was a flash of lightning high above the mountain, clouds came racing together to shut out the sky, and within a few seconds lashing rain began to fall.

Edric and Vulcan were exposed to the full force of the storm. There was no shelter. The rain poured down the slopes of the Glass Mountain forming rushing torrents which almost swept Vulcan away.

Frantically Edric urged Vulcan into a gallop. Soon Vulcan was well away from the falling rain. The blacksmith's boy laughed aloud. Merla had driven them away from the Glass Mountain but now Edric knew how to free the Sword.

One little seed from a Golden Apple would do it. Although nothing could break the Glass Mountain from the outside, the sprouting of a tree from within would shatter it in a thousand pieces.

"We have the voice of the Sword to guide us now, Vulcan!" gasped Edric, as they headed westwards. "There is hope at last. No wonder Merla was in a rage! Even he did not know the Sword could talk!"

The Dragon's Tooth.

SOON it was dark, but Vulcan's hoof-beats broke the stillness of the night as Edric headed his Wonder Horse westwards. The Sangor Forest lay in that direction, deep in the heart of a mysterious country from which few travellers had ever returned. Edric had heard about it from Hugo. He knew he was taking his life in his hands if he travelled too far to the west.

But he also knew that Merla would spread the news far and wide that King Ivor had lost his Magic Sword. Soon the enemies of Morania would be massing on the borders to attack the little country.

The thought of that kept Edric riding far into the night. Vulcan did not seem to tire, but Edric was beginning to nod and he was in danger of falling from Vulcan's back. At last he halted a few hours before dawn far beyond the borders of Morania.

Tired as he was, Edric knew his journey was only beginning. He slipped from Vulcan's back and fell fast asleep behind some rocks while Vulcan stood guard.

But an hour later Edric was up again. He took a flying leap on to Vulcan's back, and off they raced again. The sun was slowly rising above the mountains as they went on their way, following a hard, beaten track.

Vulcan's hoofs beat out a merry tune on the rocky ground. Edric was still sleepy, and his eyes were half-shut but all at once his eyes opened wide. In his ears he could once more hear the voice of the Magic Sword.

It was faint, so faint that Edric had to listen very hard to catch the words coming through Vulcan's horseshoes as they beat on the ground.

"A dragon's tooth is what you need to help you win the magic seed," said the voice, and it repeated the same words over and over again.

"I see now what the Magic Sword meant!" cried Edric. "When Vulcan stamps with his Magic Horseshoes on hard ground, the vibration is felt as far away as the Glass Mountain, and the Sword can speak."

Edric was delighted with the discovery, but could not understand the words that kept reaching his ears—

"A dragon's tooth is what you need to help you win the magic seed."

"What on earth do I want with a dragon's tooth?" thought the blacksmith's boy. "What could I do with it if I had one?"

A giant guards the bridge which Edric must cross!

They were passing beneath a rocky cliff, when, suddenly, a ferocious bellow made Vulcan shiver with fear. Snorting and roaring, a huge dragon lumbered out of a cave in the cliffs. It had been wakened by the thud of Vulcan's shoes on the rocky ground. Edric pulled Vulcan to a halt. With its gaping jaws open the dragon was right in their path.

Shocked as he was, Edric remembered the words of the Magic Sword. Whipping a horseshoe from his belt he hurled it straight at the ugly jaws of the dragon.

There was a loud clang as the whirling horseshoe hit the dragon's teeth, and Edric saw a tooth fly out on to the grass at the side of the road.

With a cry of triumph he brought Vulcan about and kicked in his heels. With the dragon in pursuit Vulcan raced back the way they had come.

They led the dragon a pretty dance. They led it so far that finally the monster could go no further. Mad with rage as it was, it could not keep up with the pace set by the Wonder Horse.

Smiling, Edric ordered Vulcan to slacken speed. They circled the breathless dragon, and cantered slowly back to the dragon's cave. There, gleaming in the grass, lay the dragon's tooth.

It was about six inches long. Edric picked it up and examined it carefully. Then he put it away in a wallet slung beneath his tunic.

"I can't imagine what the Sword meant by telling me to get a dragon's tooth," he said. "But I shall keep it and see."

On they went on their way to the west. Vulcan had had a good feed of grass while they had rested, but Edric was very hungry. He had eaten nothing since the day before. His face lit up when he saw a tall building in the distance.

"Perhaps we'll get a meal here, Vulcan," he cried, overjoyed at seeing a sign of life.

Vulcan trotted faster, and as they drew nearer they saw that the building was on the edge of a mighty gorge. The gorge was so deep that it was impossible to see the bottom, but a narrow bridge ran across it. The tall building was at the near end of the bridge.

When he got even nearer Edric felt a chill of horror as he saw that the door to the house was twenty feet high, and the windows were four times the usual size.

"A giant must live here," whispered Edric, and at that moment the door swung open and the biggest man Edric had ever seen dashed out.

He was twenty feet high as broad as a hayrick, and he carried a huge sword.

"Halt!" he cried, and towered over them in the middle of the road, raising his sword.

The Giant's Price.

EDRIC gripped one of the horseshoes in his belt. He knew he had to keep going westwards to save the Magic Sword, and he was determined to ride on even if he had to fight the giant.

"What do you want here?" thundered the giant.

"I want to cross the bridge!" answered Edric, trying to keep his voice steady.

"Oho, so you want to cross the bridge, do you?" roared the giant, catching hold of Vulcan's bridle and almost lifting the horse off his feet. "Let me tell you that I own that bridge. Nobody crosses that bridge unless they pay a toll. And I hurl anyone who cannot pay into the gorge."

"But I have no money——" began Edric, getting a firmer grip on the horseshoe, ready to hurl it at the giant's head.

What do you like best about "The Beano"?

Drop the Editor a postcard and tell him your favourite characters.

"Money!" bellowed the giant. "Who said anything about money? I've no use for money. The only thing in the world I want is something that nobody ever has. My fee for allowing anyone to cross the bridge is one dragon's tooth! I wager that is something you have never even seen. Nobody has ever been able to pay my toll, so they've all gone into the gorge."

He started to drag Edric and the horse towards the edge of the yawning chasm.

"Wait a minute!" cried Edric, when he had recovered his breath. "I'll give you a dragon's tooth!"

"Eh?" gasped the giant, releasing his hold, and staring as though he did not believe his ears. "What did you say? You have a dragon's tooth?"

"Of course!" said Edric, feeling in the wallet below his tunic.

He placed the huge tooth in the mighty hand that was held out towards him, and almost laughed at the wonder in the giant's face.

At last the giant found his voice.

"Wonderful!" he boomed. "You are the first person who has ever paid me my fee. All my life I've wanted a dragon's tooth!"

He slapped Edric on the back so hard that the blacksmith's boy felt Vulcan's legs buckle under him. Then the giant gently lifted Edric from the saddle.

"I'm sorry I was rough," he said. "You've given me the one thing I want in life. You are welcome to cross the bridge as many times as you like, but is there any other way I can help you? Ask anything, and if I have it, it shall be yours!"

Edric steadied himself on his feet.

"I'm hungry!" he said boldly. "I would like a good meal."

"Excellent!" roared the giant. "I have plenty of food—and oats for your horse, too. Come with me!"

He led them towards his house, and he emptied a whole sack of oats on the ground before Vulcan.

Then it was Edric's turn. The giant practically carried him into the house. The table was far over Edric's head. The chairs were six feet from the ground, but the giant lifted the boy on to one of these, and ran to his larder.

A few minutes later he was back with plates that must have been a yard across. On them he had piled roast chickens, legs of mutton, huge hams, beef, and about forty pounds of baked potatoes.

"Eat!" he roared. "Eat all you want. There is plenty more in the larder."

The food was piled higher than Edric. The boy tried to explain that he could not eat a quarter of what was there, but the giant fetched a long knife and began to carve the meat.

"Eat, and you may grow as big as me!" he thundered.

Edric ate until he nearly burst. He was very hungry, and it was marvellous how much he got through, but he was nearly done for when the giant brought in a monster apple-pie.

The blacksmith's boy did his best, and between mouthfuls he told the giant of his quest.

The twenty-foot toll-keeper stroked his chin.

"Hm! If I didn't have to keep watch on this bridge, I would come with you," he said. "There is dangerous country ahead of you. I know the way well. I'll show you."

With the pointed end of the dragon's tooth he drew a map on the table-cloth, and showed Edric the way that he must take. Edric studied the map well.

"There is one thing I would like to know!" he said, when he had finished his meal. "Has Merla the Magician any friends in these parts?"

The giant shook his head.

"Merla has no friends. Everyone hates him. He is a bad enemy. But he will do his utmost to stop you getting to the Sangor Forest."

Edric climbed down from the lofty chair.

"I know that, but I'm going on just the same," he said grimly. "The Sword must be recovered before Morania is invaded."

The giant held out his hand, which dwarfed Edric's.

"Good luck," he said. "If I can help you any time, let me know."

He followed Edric out to where Vulcan stood dozing in the sun, and lifted the boy on to the horse's back. Edric rode slowly over the bridge to the other side of the gorge, then paused to look at the twenty-foot toll-keeper, who stood waving the dragon's tooth.

"Well!" exclaimed Edric, as he turned Vulcan's head towards the west. "If it had not been for the warning from the Magic Sword we would both be at the bottom of the gorge by now. Now, westward, Vulcan, to fetch the Golden Apple!"

Next Thursday—Merla bars Edric's way —with a regiment of living scarecrows!

Little Dead-Eye Dick

That's no snake—It's Dick's mistake!

THERE HASN'T BEEN A BULL IN THIS FIELD FOR AGES — AND I'M NOT AFRAID OF BULLS ANYHOW.
BEWARE OF THE BULL
GOSH! A SNAKE CRAWLING UP THE TREE... I'LL SOON SETTLE IT!
BANG!
GOSH! THAT WAS NO SNAKE. IT WAS A BULL'S TAIL!
HELP!
SNORT

Pages 6 and 7 of The Beano *for April 22, 1950.*

SAILORS' HOME

The Strange Behaviour of the Man with the Lost Memory !

THE RUNAWAY ROBINSONS

1—At seven o'clock in the morning, Jim and Judy Robinson left Ginger Jones's house, where they had spent the night unknown to Ginger's parents. Shivering in the chilly early air, they made their way down to the docks and quietly took up positions at a convenient corner where they could watch the door of the Sailors' Home. They were waiting for their father, who had lost his memory in an accident at sea. At last, Skipper Robinson walked down the steps.

2—Skipper Robinson had acted strangely ever since his accident and did not know his own children! Once before he had stolen the box which Jim was carrying and which contained his own savings! As the Skipper crossed the narrow street, Jim and Judy began to move off, their intention being to watch their father from another hiding-place down the road. But the twins were too slow off the mark. The Skipper had seen their shadows on the pavement. He raced forward.

3—Scarcely heeding the traffic speeding by, Jim and Judy took to their heels across the street. Skipper Robinson, in his hazy, sick mind, knew that the boy and girl ahead of him had been following him around for days—and he knew that the box contained hundreds of pounds. His head was throbbing with the pain of the blow he had received at the time of his accident.

4—Just as the Skipper darted across the road, the throbbing pain in his head became unbearable. Suddenly, everything went dark and misty. He stopped dead in his tracks and failed to see the heavy lorry approaching a few yards away. The runaway twins heard a screaming of brakes and looked back in alarm just in time to see their father fall heavily on his head in the road.

5—A crowd gathered in a flash and Jim and Judy kept well to the back of it while an ambulance raced up and two stretcher-bearers hoisted the unconscious Skipper into the back. Poor Jim and Judy longed to go with their father, but they dared not make themselves conspicuous. Weeks before, Jim had been wrongfully accused of being a thief and he was wanted by the police!

6—Jim's eyes lit up as he saw Ginger Jones and his Gang on the other side of the crowd. Jim waved, and in a minute the youngsters were round the twins. They had their bicycles with them and two of them gladly loaned theirs to the little Runaways. As the ambulance flashed off down the road towards the hospital, Jim and Judy and the Gang went speeding after it.

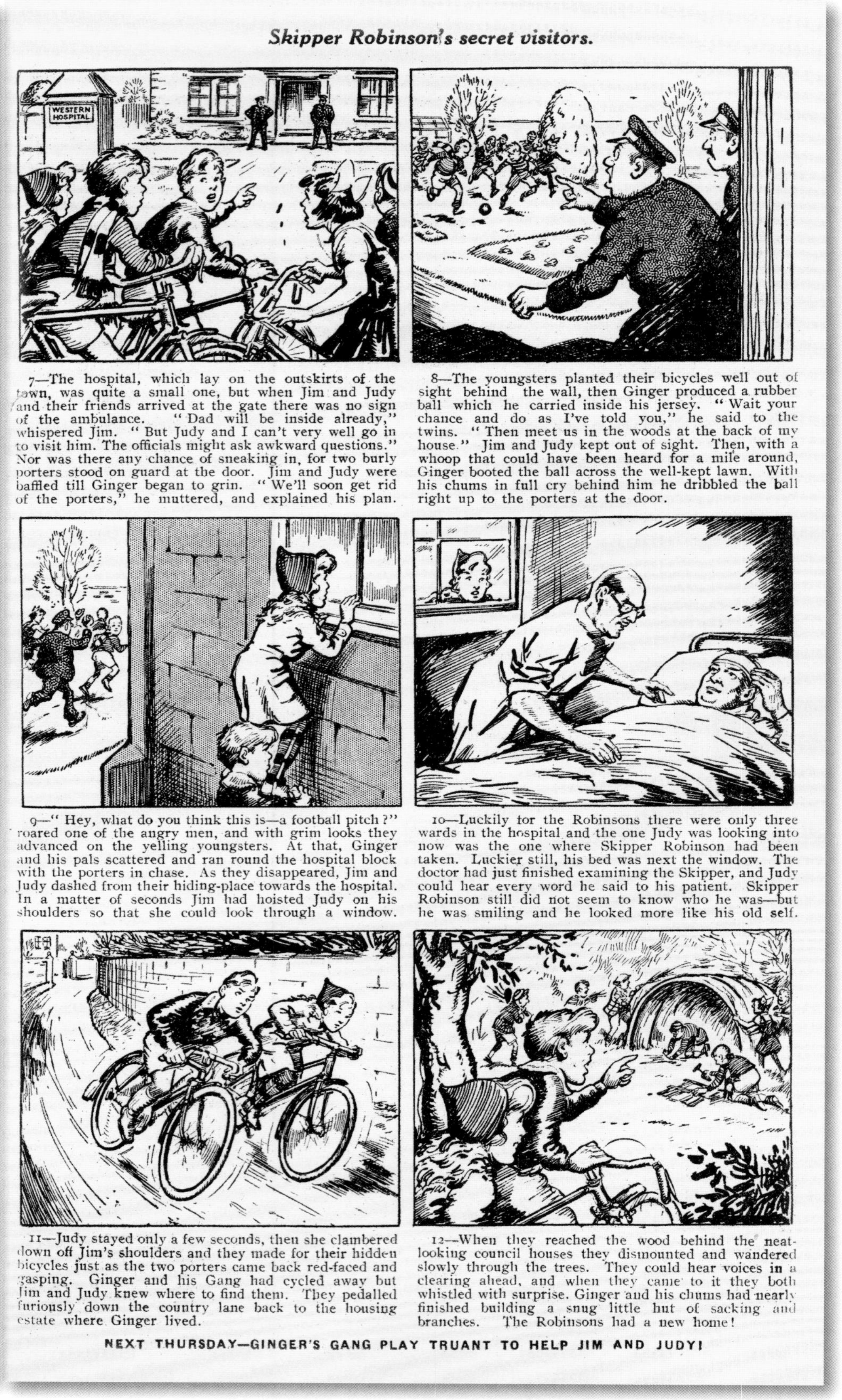
WESTERN HOSPITAL

Skipper Robinson's secret visitors.

7—The hospital, which lay on the outskirts of the town, was quite a small one, but when Jim and Judy and their friends arrived at the gate there was no sign of the ambulance. "Dad will be inside already," whispered Jim. "But Judy and I can't very well go in to visit him. The officials might ask awkward questions." Nor was there any chance of sneaking in, for two burly porters stood on guard at the door. Jim and Judy were baffled till Ginger began to grin. "We'll soon get rid of the porters," he muttered, and explained his plan.

8—The youngsters planted their bicycles well out of sight behind the wall, then Ginger produced a rubber ball which he carried inside his jersey. "Wait your chance and do as I've told you," he said to the twins. "Then meet us in the woods at the back of my house." Jim and Judy kept out of sight. Then, with a whoop that could have been heard for a mile around, Ginger booted the ball across the well-kept lawn. With his chums in full cry behind him he dribbled the ball right up to the porters at the door.

9—"Hey, what do you think this is—a football pitch?" roared one of the angry men, and with grim looks they advanced on the yelling youngsters. At that, Ginger and his pals scattered and ran round the hospital block with the porters in chase. As they disappeared, Jim and Judy dashed from their hiding-place towards the hospital. In a matter of seconds Jim had hoisted Judy on his shoulders so that she could look through a window.

10—Luckily for the Robinsons there were only three wards in the hospital and the one Judy was looking into now was the one where Skipper Robinson had been taken. Luckier still, his bed was next the window. The doctor had just finished examining the Skipper, and Judy could hear every word he said to his patient. Skipper Robinson still did not seem to know who he was—but he was smiling and he looked more like his old self.

11—Judy stayed only a few seconds, then she clambered down off Jim's shoulders and they made for their hidden bicycles just as the two porters came back red-faced and gasping. Ginger and his Gang had cycled away but Jim and Judy knew where to find them. They pedalled furiously down the country lane back to the housing estate where Ginger lived.

12—When they reached the wood behind the neat-looking council houses they dismounted and wandered slowly through the trees. They could hear voices in a clearing ahead, and when they came to it they both whistled with surprise. Ginger and his chums had nearly finished building a snug little hut of sacking and branches. The Robinsons had a new home!

NEXT THURSDAY—GINGER'S GANG PLAY TRUANT TO HELP JIM AND JUDY!

Pages 8 and 9 of The Beano *for April 22, 1950.*

The man who did not believe there was a monster in Loch Linn !

DEEP-SEA DANNY'S IRON FISH

The Trapped Monster.

YOUNG Danny Gray raced like a deer down the rocky slope towards the sea loch where his Iron Fish lay at the water's edge. He was racing to save the Ross farmhouse which was built on the slopes above him.

The farm was in danger. The stout walls were shaking as if in an earthquake and crockery and pictures were being smashed to pieces. There was a threat of the roof collapsing.

The farmhouse was built on a cliff and beneath the cliff was a vast, unexplored cavern. Danny believed that the Monster of Loch Linn had found its way into the cavern and was causing the tremors. Now the boy was determined to find out what was happening in the cavern.

The Iron Fish lay moored beside the bank of the loch.

Danny settled down swiftly in the tiny cockpit of the Iron Fish and closed the transparent hatch cover over his head.

He started the motor and the mechanical tail began to thresh the water like the tail of a real fish. Like a silver torpedo, the Fish glided forward and Danny headed for the tall cliffs below the Ross farm. A hundred yards from the cliff, he put the Fish into a steep dive.

The light grew dim and Danny switched on the headlights in the "eyes" of the Iron Fish. Then, helped by the light, he began to pick his way between the thick masses of water-weed. Down, down, down he went until the powerful beams lit the entrance to the underwater cave in the cliffs.

The entrance was dark and mysterious. What lay beyond it, Danny could only guess.

For a moment Danny hesitated. He knew the risk he was taking. Then his jaw set grimly and with steady hand he sent the Fish gliding into the darkness of the underwater tunnel. He took care to keep in the middle of the passage, for he did not want to damage the mechanical tail against the rugged walls of rock.

Still there was no sign of the great sea monster which had been haunting the loch these past few months, killing livestock and damaging crops. Already the creature had scared many people from the district, and it was slowly ruining Donald Ross, the farmer who had befriended Danny. Danny had vowed to do all he could to rid the loch of the monster.

Any day now the boy expected the arrival of his father's yacht. Professor Gray was a scientist and he was eager to help. But his private yacht, the Tarpon, was having engine trouble about ten miles down the Scottish coast.

The underwater tunnel was dark and sinister and even the powerful headlights of the Iron Fish pierced only a little way through the gloom. As he cruised along, Danny noticed that the width of the tunnel was increasing. Soon he could no longer see the walls of the tunnel and he had a feeling that he was inside the cavern beneath the farm. Carefully, Danny nosed the Fish upwards.

All at once the Fish broke the surface.

Quickly, Danny stopped the Fish. The twin beams of the headlights played on the dripping wall of the cavern. Slowly Danny turned the Fish to examine the whole of the huge cavern. It was about two hundred feet long and half that in width.

Glittering stalactites, great stone spikes, hung from the roof, and in several places touched the water.

Then, as the Iron Fish drifted round, the headlight shone into the far corner of the cavern, and Danny saw the monster.

The brute was half-submerged and tearing at the roof overhead with its powerful claws. Rocks and earth were pouring down from the hole they had made. Then the monster stopped its frenzied clawing and turned to glare at the dazzling light. Danny shuddered as the huge eyes turned on him.

He could guess what had happened. Only that morning Danny had lured the monster into eating the carcase of a sheep coated with poison. The monster, dazed by the poison, had entered the tunnel and reached the cavern. It had failed to find the way out again, and was trying to dig its way out.

Directly overhead was the Ross farmhouse. The monster's frenzied digging was the cause of the tremors.

The Chase In The Tunnel.

SUDDENLY the monster gave a bellow of rage and its great tail lashed at the water, churning up large waves which made the Fish rock madly. Danny's mouth dried as he stared across the cave.

Then he remembered that he was the only person who could deal with the monster. If he left it there it would destroy the foundations of the house and bring the building crashing to the ground. He must find a way of getting the monster out of the cave.

Hurriedly, Danny started the motor, and steered the Fish slowly over the surface of the water towards the monster.

The great brute had given up digging to watch the approach of the Fish, and Danny eyed the lashing tail. One blow from that tail would smash the Iron Fish to pieces.

Danny brought the Fish to a halt about fifty feet away from the monster. Then he focussed the headlights on the monster's eyes and began to switch the powerful beams off and on.

For a few seconds the brute blinked in the fierce glare then it gave another hideous bellow and lunged towards the Iron Fish.

Danny spun the Iron Fish about, and sped across the cave, zig-zagging between the stalactites. After him came the monster, churning along on the surface. But for Danny's skilful handling of the Fish, the monster would surely have caught the little craft.

Then, when the Fish drew near to the flooded tunnel, Danny closed the hatch with a click, and sent the Iron Fish diving down into the dark water.

Still the monster followed. Danny could feel the Fish lurch as the brute set up fierce currents in the water.

Into the tunnel shot the Iron Fish. Then began the dangerous journey through the dark passage.

Several times Danny felt the Fish scrape along the rocky walls, but he dared not slow down. The monster was close behind, its huge bulk almost filling the tunnel. One snap from those powerful jaws, and the thin metal structure of the Iron Fish would be crushed to pieces.

Then, after what seemed like hours, Danny saw the cave entrance ahead. A minute later the Fish darted out of the opening.

Up and up went the Fish, travelling at such speed that it shot clear of the surface and soared through the air for nearly fifty feet. Water fowl rose screaming into the air as the great silvery craft glided into their midst. Danny looked back.

In a cloud of foam, the head of the monster broke the surface. Dazzled by the sunlight, it did not see the Iron Fish on the surface several hundred yards away.

Danny held his breath. Would the monster see him or would it head for the island in the centre of the loch?

It was on that island that Jasper Manton lived. Manton, known as the Man With The Crooked Back, was hated by the local people, and Danny had found out that he had some mysterious control over the monster. It was Manton who sent the brute to raid the surrounding farms.

What's Navvy Len done now?—My, my! He's drained a big canal quite dry!

The monster moved along the surface towards the eastern end of Donald Ross's land. Danny followed at a safe distance.

He saw the monster moving slowly in towards the shore, trying to decide where to land, and Danny feared that the cattle in the field behind the Ross farm had attracted the brute, for it must have been ravenous. He watched it splash into the shallows and crawl into the wide, marshy patch at the mouth of a river which entered the loch. There the brute wallowed in the mud and tore up the reeds with its huge teeth.

Danny went as close as he dared, watching the monster as it roamed up and down. Nearby was the road which ran along the lochside.

Danny kept looking anxiously at the road.

"I hope no one comes along the road until the monster goes back into the loch," he muttered anxiously.

The Smashed Bicycle.

FOR half an hour the boy waited in the loch. Then his eye caught a movement on the road which travelled round the head of the loch. A cyclist was approaching! The man was making for the bridge which spanned the river, and would have to pass within twenty yards of the brute, which was concealed in the thick rushes of the marsh.

As the cyclist drew nearer, Danny saw that he was a police constable.

"Sandy More!" muttered the boy.

Donald Ross had sent the constable a message asking him to come and make inquiries about the Man With the Crooked Back. The local postman had told the farmer that his message had got through, but the constable was not expected until the next day. Yet there he was, blindly pedalling into danger.

Danny put the Iron Fish at full speed, and flashed along the surface to where the road came very close to the water's edge. The Fish reached the point at the same time as the burly, fair-haired policeman.

"Hi, Constable More, stop!" shouted Danny, waving frantically from the cockpit of the Iron Fish.

The policeman blinked in amazement at the Iron Fish, but he recognised the note of urgency in Danny's voice.

"What's the matter, lad?" he asked.

"Are you going up to the Ross farm?" inquired Danny.

"I am," came the stern reply.

"Then don't cross the bridge!" said Danny quickly. "The monster will see you. It's down there in the marsh!"

P.C. More rubbed his chin with the back of his hand. There was a look of disbelief on his face.

"You're seeing things, lad," he said. It was obvious that he did not believe Danny or realise the danger.

"No, it's true. Don't go any farther," said Danny. "The monster is down by the bridge."

"Then I'll see it for myself!" snorted the constable, and pedalled off briskly. At that point the road swung inland away from the lochside, and Danny lost sight of the constable.

Swiftly, Danny sent the Iron Fish skimming towards the mouth of the river. Here he could see the road and the bridge. It was not a very large bridge, just a single stone span carrying the narrow road, and it was no more than a dozen feet above the water.

The boy waited, listening to the squelching noises made by the monster in the swamps nearby. Then he saw the constable appear round a bend and cycle briskly towards the bridge.

Look for News
of

JACK FLASH

THE FLYING BOY

in "THE BEANO" soon.

The boy touched a lever and the Fish moved up the river towards the bridge. As Constable More cycled on to the bridge, Danny opened the throttle. The powerful motor inside the Fish hummed like a colony of bees. The tail threshed the water to foam, and then suddenly the Iron Fish lifted into the air in a wonderful leap.

The Fish soared over the head of the constable on the bicycle and a shower of water from the Fish descended on the policeman, drenching him to the skin. Before the constable could open his mouth to shout the Iron Fish had landed with a plop! in the river on the upstream side of the bridge.

The bicycle wobbled as the constable jammed on his brakes. With a roar of anger, the constable rushed to the parapet and glared at the river. The Iron Fish broke the surface fifty yards upstream. With his face red with rage, Sandy More propped his bicycle against the parapet of the bridge and raced in pursuit of the Iron Fish.

Danny kept to the centre of the river and drove the Fish along until there was danger of it grounding in the shallow water. He nosed his way inshore and leapt out of the cockpit. He gave a gasp of relief as Sandy More came stumbling through the long grass on the river bank.

The constable's heavy hand fell on Danny's shoulder.

"Now, you young imp!" he panted. "What's your name? You've got yourself into trouble with your nonsense. Come on. Let's have it."

Danny did not flinch.

"I told you the Monster of the Loch was down in the marshes," he said quietly. "You didn't believe me, but now that you're here I can tell you more about it."

The constable listened as Danny began to tell the strange story of the monster and the Man With The Crooked Back. The constable was convinced. With Danny leading the way, the pair carefully made their way back to the bridge. Great puddles of water had been formed, and in the middle of one of these lay the bicycle, the strong metal frame twisted and smashed.

Danny merely pointed.

"Look at your bicycle! The monster did that," said Danny. "Look at those footprints in the mud."

"D'ye mean to say there's a creature wi' a foot as big as that?" said Sandy More, his mouth open wide in amazement.

"Yes, and a mouth large enough to swallow a sheep. The brute was over there in the swamps, but it's gone now," said Danny.

"You saved my life, laddie, an' I'm grateful," said Sandy More. "I thought this talk of a monster was an old wives' tale. Where do you think it's gone now?"

Danny pointed across the loch to the tiny island with the ruined castle. The figure of a man could be seen getting down from the top of the highest wall. It was too far to see clearly without field-glasses, but the boy felt sure it was Jasper Manton, the Man With The Crooked Back. He may have been watching the bridge through his powerful glasses.

"I think the brute's gone back to the island. That's what Donald Ross wants to talk to you about. We believe that the man who owns that island has control over the monster and is using it to terrorise the farmers. Folks are being driven away from this area, farms are being abandoned, and children are terrified to go to school."

Satisfied that the Iron Fish was safely moored and in no danger, Danny set off with Sandy More to the Ross farmhouse. Several times More halted to look back across the loch to that grim castle which stood on the little island.

Over the water came the faint sound of a bell.

"Listen!" said Danny, urgently. "That's the bell which summons the monster. The Man With The Crooked Back is calling the monster to the island. Can't we do something to get rid of this brute, constable?"

"We'll have a try, laddie," said Sandy More.

Next Thursday—Danny's desperate bid to escape from the monster—over the thundering falls of a mountain stream.

DANGER! LEN AT WORK
HEY, LEN—AS FAST AS I PUMP WATER OUT OF THIS HOLE, IT FILLS UP AGAIN.
LET ME HAVE A TRY.
2 HOURS LATER
I'LL GET THIS HOLE PUMPED DRY IF I HAVE TO PUMP TILL CHRISTMAS.
LATER STILL
THE WATER'S GOING DOWN. ANOTHER TEN MINUTES, AND I CAN PUT THE PUMP AWAY!
PHEW! AT LAST!
THERE! I'VE FINISHED NOW. WHAT'S ALL THAT SHOUTING FROM OVER THE FENCE?
HOI! HELP! POLICE!
GULP!
I GO INTO MY CABIN FOR A SHORT NAP, AND SOMEBODY PINCHES ALL THE WATER OUT OF THE CANAL!
I'VE BEEN PUMPING THE WATER OUT OF THE CANAL!

Pages 10 and 11 of The Beano *for April 22, 1950.*

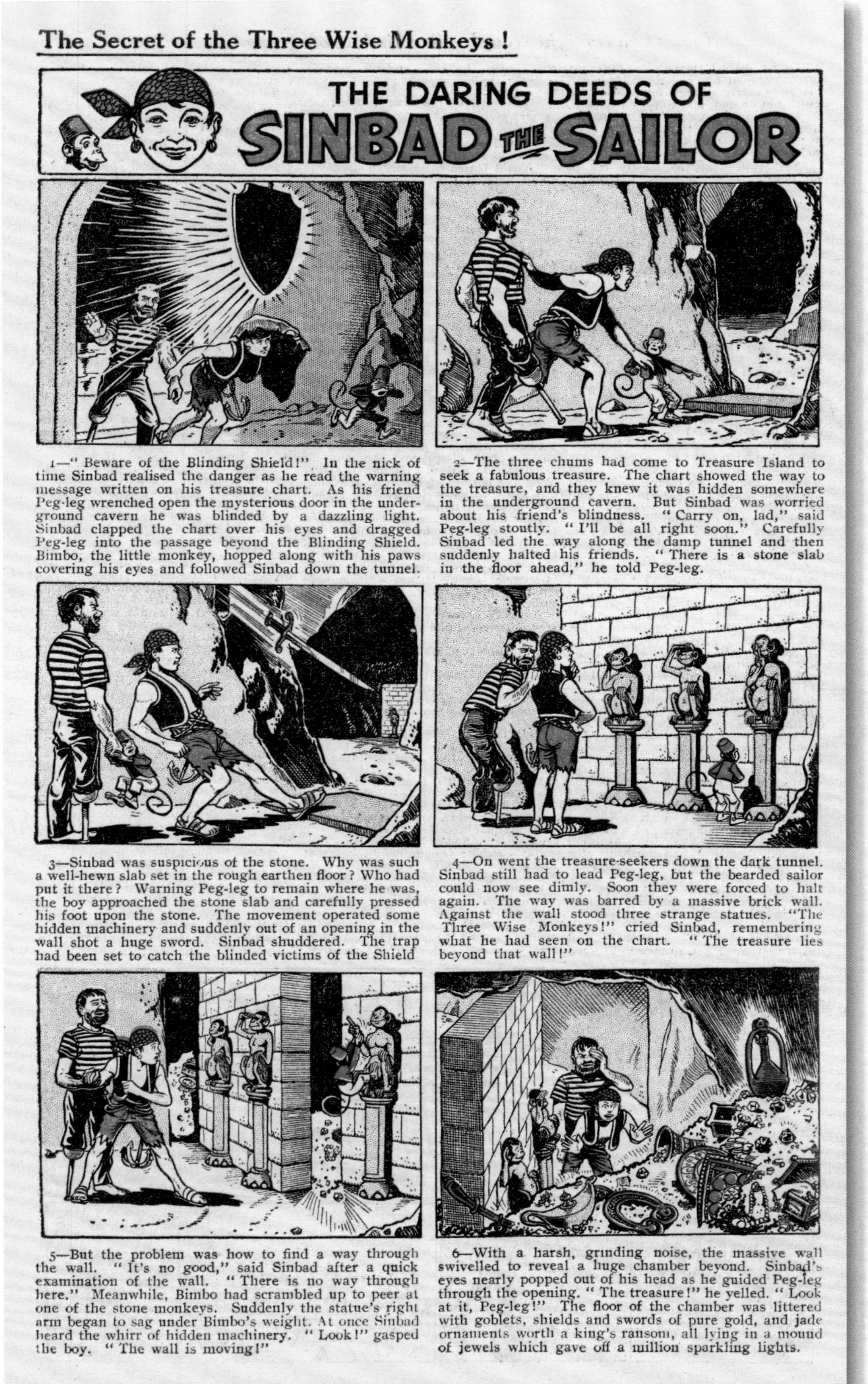

The Secret of the Three Wise Monkeys !

THE DARING DEEDS OF SINBAD THE SAILOR

1—" Beware of the Blinding Shield!" In the nick of time Sinbad realised the danger as he read the warning message written on his treasure chart. As his friend Peg-leg wrenched open the mysterious door in the underground cavern he was blinded by a dazzling light. Sinbad clapped the chart over his eyes and dragged Peg-leg into the passage beyond the Blinding Shield. Bimbo, the little monkey, hopped along with his paws covering his eyes and followed Sinbad down the tunnel.

2—The three chums had come to Treasure Island to seek a fabulous treasure. The chart showed the way to the treasure, and they knew it was hidden somewhere in the underground cavern. But Sinbad was worried about his friend's blindness. " Carry on, lad," said Peg-leg stoutly. " I'll be all right soon." Carefully Sinbad led the way along the damp tunnel and then suddenly halted his friends. " There is a stone slab in the floor ahead," he told Peg-leg.

3—Sinbad was suspicious of the stone. Why was such a well-hewn slab set in the rough earthen floor? Who had put it there? Warning Peg-leg to remain where he was, the boy approached the stone slab and carefully pressed his foot upon the stone. The movement operated some hidden machinery and suddenly out of an opening in the wall shot a huge sword. Sinbad shuddered. The trap had been set to catch the blinded victims of the Shield

4—On went the treasure-seekers down the dark tunnel. Sinbad still had to lead Peg-leg, but the bearded sailor could now see dimly. Soon they were forced to halt again. The way was barred by a massive brick wall. Against the wall stood three strange statues. "The Three Wise Monkeys!" cried Sinbad, remembering what he had seen on the chart. " The treasure lies beyond that wall!"

5—But the problem was how to find a way through the wall. " It's no good," said Sinbad after a quick examination of the wall. " There is no way through here." Meanwhile, Bimbo had scrambled up to peer at one of the stone monkeys. Suddenly the statue's right arm began to sag under Bimbo's weight. At once Sinbad heard the whirr of hidden machinery. " Look!" gasped the boy. " The wall is moving!"

6—With a harsh, grinding noise, the massive wall swivelled to reveal a huge chamber beyond. Sinbad's eyes nearly popped out of his head as he guided Peg-leg through the opening. " The treasure!" he yelled. " Look at it, Peg-leg!" The floor of the chamber was littered with goblets, shields and swords of pure gold, and jade ornaments worth a king's ransom, all lying in a mound of jewels which gave off a million sparkling lights.

The Genie from the Bottle!

7—In a fever of excitement the friends began to examine the treasure. Slowly but surely Peg-leg's sight was returning. He stumbled forward to peer closely at the glittering jewels while Sinbad scrambled over a heap of rubies and diamonds to reach an ornamental bottle which had attracted his attention. The bottle was securely stoppered.

8—For a moment Sinbad examined the bottle and then tugged hard at the stopper. " I wonder what's inside?" he muttered. With a loud pop the stopper came out of the neck of the bottle, and a strange wispy smoke came streaming out of the opening. As the chums watched, the smoke suddenly formed itself into the head and shoulders of a man. " It's a genie!" gasped Sinbad.

9—The genie floated in the air above Sinbad. Then suddenly he gave a deafening bellow of laughter and jabbed a fore-finger at Sinbad. " Foolish boy!" cackled the genie. " You'll be sorry you freed me from my prison bottle. Ho-ho-ho-ho!" And with that the genie made swift movements with his hands. The next moment Sinbad, Peg-leg and Bimbo found themselves whirling round and round in the air. The genie had worked a magic spell!

10—Several of the golden ornaments, too, were whizzing through the air and more than once Sinbad winced as a heavy goblet crashed into him. Then suddenly the genie waved his hands again. The mad whirling stopped and the chums toppled back on the heap of treasure. Sinbad, half-buried in jewels, looked round for the genie. He was hovering nearby, fairly rocking with laughter. " Ho! Ho! Ho!" he roared. " The funniest thing I've seen for years! Ho! Ho! Ho!"

11—Sinbad was beginning to recover from his fright. His hand closed on a huge ruby and he was preparing to throw it at the genie when the genie gave another bellow of laughter. " Ho! Ho!" he roared. " Here is another trick of mine. Watch this!" As the genie made more mysterious passes with his hands, Sinbad suddenly felt a movement at his waist round which was coiled a rope attached to a grapnel. Then the grapnel began to rise swiftly into the air!

12—Sinbad was rolled over and over as the rope uncoiled. Then all at once the rope jammed around Sinbad's waist. And, as Sinbad made a wild grab at the genie's bottle, he was suddenly whisked into the air by the enchanted rope. Across the treasure chamber flew Sinbad, and once again the genie roared with mirth. " Ho! Ho! Ho! The fun is only starting, my friend! I was a prisoner in that bottle for a hundred years—and now that you've let me out, I'll make you suffer for it."

NEXT WEEK—SINBAD TAMES THE GENIE—WITH A SPRINKLING OF SALT!

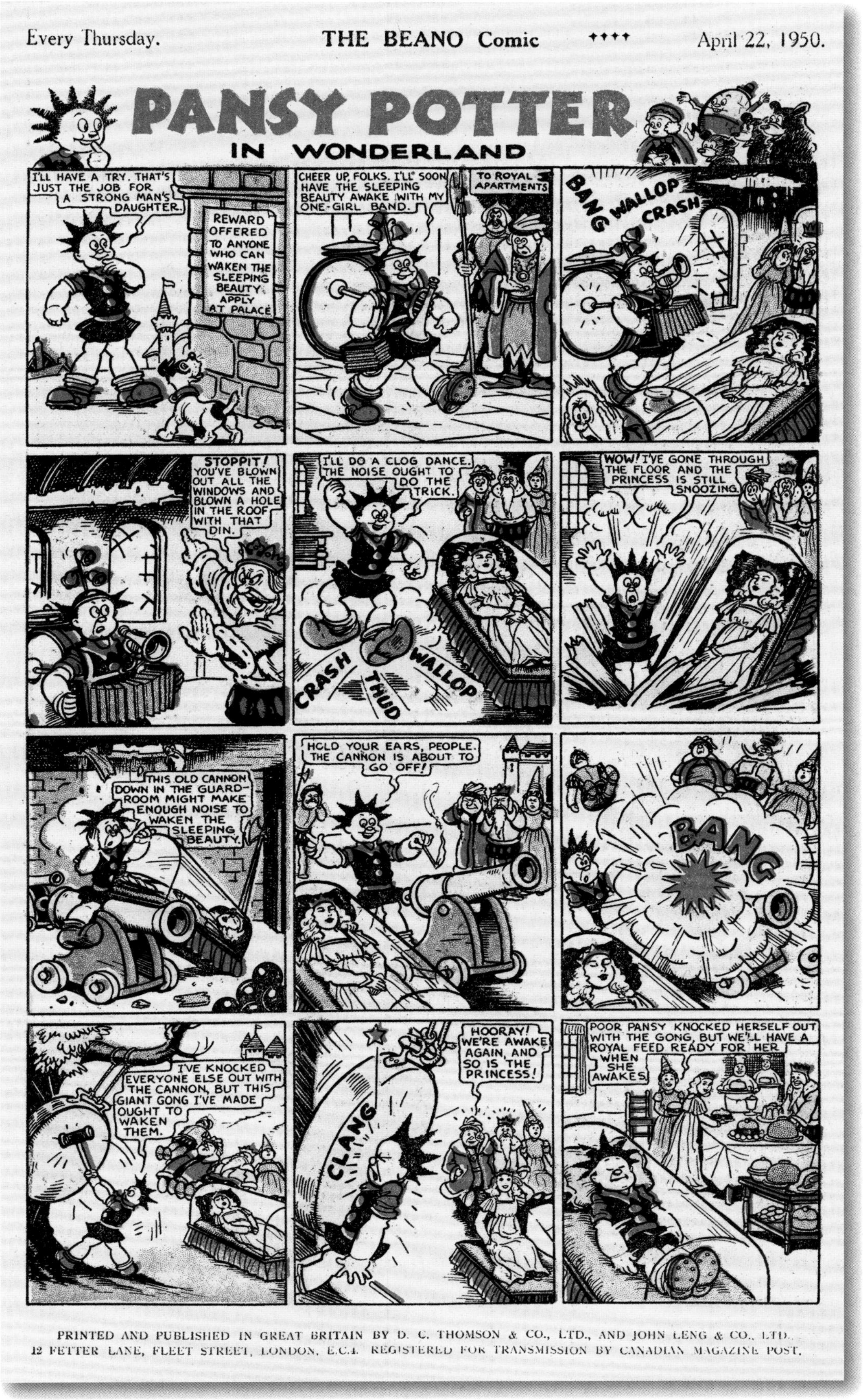
Every Thursday.
THE BEANO Comic
April 22, 1950.
PANSY POTTER
IN WONDERLAND
I'LL HAVE A TRY. THAT'S JUST THE JOB FOR A STRONG MAN'S DAUGHTER.
REWARD OFFERED TO ANYONE WHO CAN WAKEN THE SLEEPING BEAUTY. APPLY AT PALACE
CHEER UP, FOLKS. I'LL SOON HAVE THE SLEEPING BEAUTY AWAKE WITH MY ONE-GIRL BAND.
TO ROYAL APARTMENTS
BANG
WALLOP
CRASH
STOPPIT! YOU'VE BLOWN OUT ALL THE WINDOWS AND BLOWN A HOLE IN THE ROOF WITH THAT DIN.
I'LL DO A CLOG DANCE. THE NOISE OUGHT TO DO THE TRICK.
CRASH
THUD
WALLOP
WOW! I'VE GONE THROUGH THE FLOOR AND THE PRINCESS IS STILL SNOOZING.
THIS OLD CANNON DOWN IN THE GUARD-ROOM MIGHT MAKE ENOUGH NOISE TO WAKEN THE SLEEPING BEAUTY.
HOLD YOUR EARS, PEOPLE. THE CANNON IS ABOUT TO GO OFF!
BANG
I'VE KNOCKED EVERYONE ELSE OUT WITH THE CANNON, BUT THIS GIANT GONG I'VE MADE OUGHT TO WAKEN THEM.
CLANG
HOORAY! WE'RE AWAKE AGAIN, AND SO IS THE PRINCESS!
POOR PANSY KNOCKED HERSELF OUT WITH THE GONG, BUT WE'LL HAVE A ROYAL FEED READY FOR HER WHEN SHE AWAKES.
PRINTED AND PUBLISHED IN GREAT BRITAIN BY D. C. THOMSON & CO., LTD., AND JOHN LENG & CO., LTD.
12 FETTER LANE, FLEET STREET, LONDON, E.C.4. REGISTERED FOR TRANSMISSION BY CANADIAN MAGAZINE POST.

There was certainly plenty for the kids to read with two prose stories – 'The Boy With the Wonder Horse' and 'Deep-Sea Danny's Iron Fish' – plus two adventure strips – 'The Runaway Robinsons' and 'The Daring Deeds of Sinbad the Sailor' (they didn't exactly go in for short snappy titles in these days). Both of the latter were really illustrated prose stories with huge captions beneath the panels.

But the editorial team still managed to pack in seven more comic strips, from 'Little Dead-Eye Dick' with four frames to 'Ding-Dong Belle' with 18 pictures on a single page. So the readers got a lot for their 2d – about 0.8 pence in today's money.

THE GOLDEN AGE

George Moonie could look around from his Editor's chair and see a unique group of very talented individuals – chief sub-editor Ron Fraser and sub-editors Harold Cramond, Ian 'Chiz' Chisholm, Ken Walmsley and Doug Johnstone. Joining them in 1950 was the office junior, Walter Fearn. They would provide the ideas for the new characters and write the scripts. What was needed now was a group of artists to match the creative talent of the editorial team – who would bring the new characters to life on the pages of the comic. Four artists in particular defined the new look of *The Beano*. Two were already on the staff of D. C. Thomson. Dudley Watkins, who had now worked for more than 20 years with the company, had already played a key part in developing *The Beano*. Davey Law was also a staff artist. In the next few years they would be joined by two freelance artists – Leo Baxendale and Ken Reid. Four artists with totally different styles but with one thing in common. They could all take the scripts provided by George and his team and turn them into picture strips which had children the length and breadth of Britain chuckling and chortling.

ONCE IN A LIFETIME A GUY LIKE JONAH TURNS UP. HE MEANS WELL—BUT HE'S SO FULL OF BAD LUCK THAT WHEN PEOPLE SEE HIM COMING THEY GO ROUND THE WORLD THE OTHER WAY JUST TO AVOID HIM.
LOOK AT ALL THOSE SHIPS! I'LL FIND A JOB ON ONE FOR SURE!

Working in *The Beano* office in the 1950s was different. As the working day drew to a close, George Moonie and his staff would rise to their feet and push back their chairs and desks to form a clear space. The ritual of the 'Keepie Up' was about to start. The object was to keep a ball in the air for as long as possible without letting it touch the ground. The 'ball' was a piece of cloth stuffed with paper – old comic scripts, so rumour has it. The players were allowed to use every part of the body – except their hands.

Then one day the door opened and there stood the diminutive, but imposing, figure of Managing Editor R. D. Low. The room fell silent and R. D. looked at an apprehensive George Moonie, 'Carry on, lads. I'll come back when you're not so busy.' With that he turned and left. He recognised that normal office rules could not be applied to the young men whose job was to chronicle the adventures of some of Britain's greatest comic creations and he knew that this noisy maelstrom of flailing arms and legs was actually a vital part of the creative process in *The Beano* office of that time. In this jovial atmosphere, someone would think of a script idea. Others would join in and many a hilarious script was created in this fashion.

When D. C. Thomson decided to expand their stable of comics it was inevitable that they would turn to the talented *Beano* team. In 1953 Ron Fraser left to become editor of the newly launched *The Topper*, followed by Ian Chisholm who became the first editor of *The Beezer* two years later.

DENNIS AND DAVEY

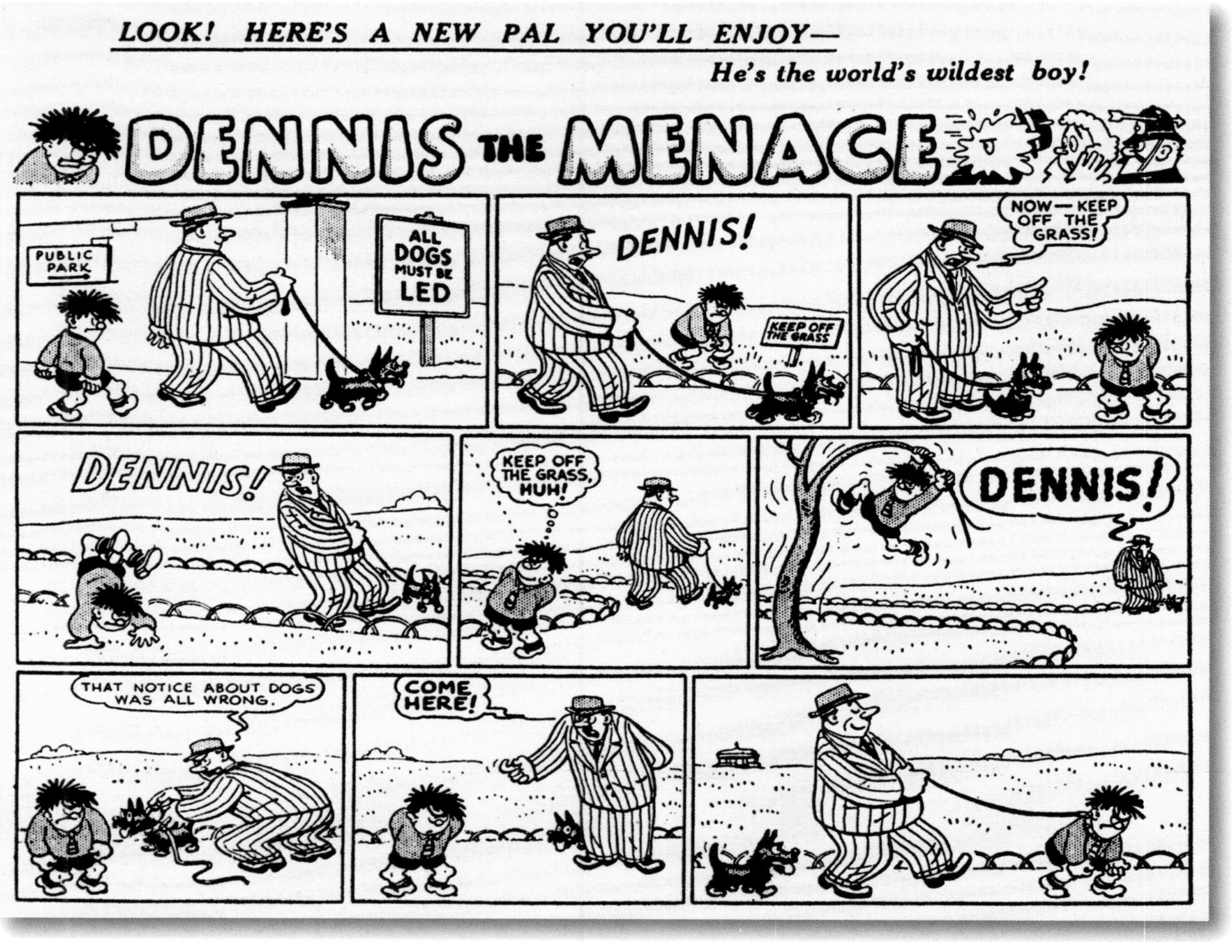
LOOK! HERE'S A NEW PAL YOU'LL ENJOY—
He's the world's wildest boy!
DENNIS THE MENACE
PUBLIC PARK
ALL DOGS MUST BE LED
DENNIS!
KEEP OFF THE GRASS
NOW—KEEP OFF THE GRASS!
DENNIS!
KEEP OFF THE GRASS, HUH!
DENNIS!
THAT NOTICE ABOUT DOGS WAS ALL WRONG.
COME HERE!

No one can remember just who came up with the original idea for the boy in the red-and-black-striped jersey who became a comics legend. What is known is that he was brought to life by the inspired pairing of Chiz Chisholm and Davey Law.

David Law was born and raised in Edinburgh, and gained a diploma at the city's College of Art. His career as an illustrator started at Odhams Press, but in the early 1930s he joined the staff of D. C. Thomson in Dundee. Originally he drew cartoons for local newspapers such as the ***Evening Telegraph*** but he had never worked for ***The Beano***. Although he was on the staff, Davey worked from home and one day George asked him to come into the office. They had a new character and they thought that Davey might be just the man to draw him.

The usual creative process was for the artist to sit down with the editorial team, who would describe how they saw the new character. The artist would make pencil sketches until the editorial team was satisfied. But this time, it was not working. After several attempts, Davey was struggling to translate the verbal description into a drawn image. Then Chiz, who fancied himself as a bit of an artist, picked up a pencil and cigarette packet and quickly doodled on it. There, in rough form, was the familiar hairstyle, knobbly knees and mischievous grin. Davey did some more sketches and George and Chiz grinned at each other. There he was on Davey's sketch pad – Dennis the Menace.

Wild wee Dennis chokes. He's wishin'—he hadn't swallowed his ammunition!
DENNIS THE MENACE
WHAT'S WRONG WITH THAT CAT?
SQUAWK!
YEOW!
SOMETHING'S STINGING IT!
I THOUGHT SO!
PEAS
BAH! MA'S LOCKED UP THE PEAS, AND PA'S TAKEN MY PEA-SHOOTER.
LOCK-PICKING MADE EASY
"TAKE A HAIRPIN OR SIMILAR OBJECT"---
LARDER
LATER
P-SS-SS-SST
SURE YOU WANT THE WHOLE HALF-POUND?
UGH... GULP...
YES! ...ULP.
SOAP
WHERE'S THAT CAT?
BUMP
GULP!
PEAS, DENNIS?
NO THANKS!

PAH! KIDS' STUFF---- BLOWING BUBBLES.
SORRY, KIDS— NO MORE CLAY PIPES.
IDEA!
CLAY PIPES 2d.
DAD WON'T BE HOME YET!
ANYWAY HE'S GOT SO MANY— HE'LL NEVER NOTICE.
AH, TO BE YOUNG,—AND BLOW SOAP BUBBLES.
?
MY MEERSCHAUM!
MY FAVOURITE BRIAR!
A LITTLE BOY----
----WITH LONG HAIR----
COME ON!
---THIS WAY---
SO!
PIPES FOR BUBBLES ALL SHIPS AND SIZES 6d.
TILL
I'LL NEED A NEW PAIR OF SLIPPERS— PUF!— DENNIS IS WEARING THEM OUT!

At the top a Dennis strip (with a striped jumper) from May 5, 1951. Below is Davey Law's original artwork for the June 23, 1951 strip.

IDEA!

Dennis began his reign of terror on March 17, 1951, as a half page strip in black and white insert (shown opposite), and there was no sign of the iconic red-and-black-striped jersey. That was to come later.

Ian Chisholm was the main writer on Dennis and his inventive, action-packed scripts brought out the best in Davey's artwork. Davey kept his backgrounds to a minimum and his use of filmic-style low horizons could make Dennis look very menacing indeed!

Chiz and Davey were very much admired by their colleagues. Davey was a perfectionist and he would often redraw entire frames if he wasn't satisfied with his first attempt. The editorial team became used to receiving pages from Davey covered in patches. But, on examining what was under the patch, the editorial team would find that both versions were perfect!

ROGER AND KEN

Ken Reid was born in Manchester and, according to his mother, started drawing almost as soon as he could walk. By the age of 14, he had won a scholarship to Salford Art School. Just before he was due to graduate, Ken was caught by the school principal in a café when he should have been in class.

Here comes Roger! Always scheming! You will never catch him dreaming!
ROGER THE DODGER
HISTORY. III
I'M GOING OUT BEFORE DAD MAKES ME DO MY HOMEWORK!
OOPS!
TRIP
I WAS READY FOR YOU, ROGER.
DON'T FORGET YOUR HOMEWORK
SO—
CHEMISTRY TONIGHT, DAD!
CHEMISTRY SET
STICK IN, ROGER!
FIZZ
CHEMISTRY SET
ONE MINUTE LATER
CHEMISTRY SET
AS I THOUGHT! INSIDE!
I'VE A LOT OF HOMEWORK TONIGHT, DAD.
YOU MUST BE BUSY THERE, ROGER. FOR THE THIRD TIME— HAVE A SWEET!
NO ANSWER
LATER
I MIGHT HAVE KNOWN HE WAS GONE. HE LOVES SWEETS!
GONE
YOU'RE ORDERED OFF!
DAD!
HOMEWORK!
YOU'LL STAY THERE WHERE I CAN SEE YOU, TILL YOUR HOMEWORK'S DONE!
DOWN AT THE FOOTBALL FIELD

The first Roger strip from April 18, 1953 (above) and a trailer for Roger from the week before. Other early strips are shown on these pages.

Roger dodges the barber's chair—But just the same he'll lose h's hair!
ROGER THE DODGER
NAG—NAG—NAG— MUM SAID IT WAS TIME YOU HAD A HAIRCUT, AND I'M GOING TO SEE YOU GET ONE
NATTER—NATTER—NATTER— YOU'RE A DISGRACE TO THE FAMILY, THE NEIGHBOURHOOD, THE SCHOOL, THE—
DODGE
WHERE IS HE?
GONE
SO!
KEEP OUT OF MY COAL-CELLAR, BOY!
IN YOU GO— AND DON'T TRY ANY DODGES.
BARBER
PUSH
H'M! JUST AS I EXPECTED. WHOA BACK!
PUSH
INSIDE AT LAST!
WE WANT IT CUT NICE AND SHORT.
GONE
WHERE IS HE?
LATER.
AH! THERE HE IS, PLAYING COWBOYS AND INDIANS WITH HIS PALS.
BANG!
THAT'S THE ONE— THE ONE WITH THE MOP OF HAIR.
BUT YOU SCALP FOLKS WITH TOMAHAWKS—NOT SCISSORS!
MA! COME AND SEE ROGER. HE'S HAD HIS HAIR CUT!

GREAT NEWS! ROGER THE DODGER IS COMING!
I'M GOING OUT BEFORE DAD MAKES ME DO MY HOMEWORK!
OOPS!
TRIP
I WAS READY FOR YOU, ROGER.
DON'T FORGET YOUR HOMEWORK
Is Roger really a dodger? You think his dad has really caught him dodging his homework, don't you? JUST YOU WAIT! ROGER ISN'T FINISHED YET! HE HAS OTHER DODGES UP HIS SLEEVE. These pictures are only part of a funny story told in pictures next week in "The Beano"—and the story tells you why Roger is the world's craftiest dodger. He is trickier than a cageful of monkeys.
FOLLOW ROGER'S WILY ADVENTURES EACH WEEK IN "THE BEANO."
STARTING NEXT THURSDAY

ROGER
THE
DODGER

WERE OFF TO THE PICTURES, ROGER. GET BUSY WASHING DISHES— AND NO DODGING!
BUT ROGER IS DODGING.
HELLO! IS THAT THE MAKERS OF THE 'NIFTY' DISHWASHING MACHINE? I'D LIKE TO ARRANGE FOR A DEMONSTRATION THIS EVENING.
SO—
SO YOU'RE THINKING OF BUYING A 'NIFTY' FOR YOUR MUM'S BIRTHDAY? WELL, I'LL SHOW YOU HOW IT WORKS.
THANKS FOR THE DEMONSTRATION. I'LL—ER—THINK IT OVER. THIS WAY OUT.
CLEAN
SLAM
THAT'S THE DISHES WASHED. NOW I CAN USE THAT DODGE ANOTHER WAY. WATCH THIS!
HELLO! IS THAT THE 'DUSTFREE' VACUUM CLEANER COMPANY?
ROGER GOT THE FLOOR VACUUMED.
WONDERFUL, ISN'T IT ?
THE BLANKETS WASHED.
IF YOU'RE STILL INTERESTED, YOUNG MAN, I HAVE NOW REACHED THE RINSING PROCESS.
YES! YOUR MACHINE'S MARVELLOUS.
AND THE FURNITURE POLISHED.
YOU MIGHT WATCH ANYWAY. YOU ASKED FOR A DEMONSTRATION.
Z-Z-Z
GLOSSO FURNITURE POLISH
LATER—MA RETURNS.
MY! I AM PLEASED, ROGER, BECAUSE—
SHINE
SPOTLESS
—AUNT BESSIE'S ILL AND I WAS GOING TO KEEP HOUSE FOR HER. BUT AS YOU'RE SO GOOD AT HOUSEWORK, YOU CAN GO INSTEAD.
AT AUNT BESSIE'S.
ROGER, DEAR! IT'S TIME FOR MY MEDICINE AND WHEN YOU COME UP BRING THAT BOOK I ASKED FOR AN HOUR AGO.

Roger's dodge works out O.K.—But it's poor Dad who has to pay!
ROGER THE DODGER
YOU'RE NOT GOING FISHING UNTIL YOU'VE MENDED THIS CHAIR.
AND DO THE JOB PROPERLY. I'LL WANT TO SEE THE CHAIR WHEN I GET BACK.
GLUE
FANCY FALLING FOR A JOB LIKE THAT, DAD!
NOW, IF YOU WERE TO GIVE ME THE MONEY FOR THAT NEW CRICKET BAT, I COULD PUT YOU UP TO A GOOD DODGE.
VERY WELL! IT'S A DEAL. WHAT'S THE DODGE?
YOU JUST PUSH THE BROKEN CHAIR BEHIND THE TABLE—
—AND LEAVE THIS GOOD ONE IN ITS PLACE. THEN YOU CAN GO FISHING.
NOW, WHY DIDN'T I THINK OF THAT MYSELF?
LATER
GOOD! THAT HASN'T TAKEN DAD LONG.
GONE FISHING
STILL LATER
NOT A BITE— AND THE RAIN POURED DOWN ALL AFTERNOON.
SQUELCH
I'M SO HUNGRY I COULD EAT A HORSE. I CAN'T WAIT ANOTHER MINUTE.
GOSH! THE BROKEN CHAIR
CRASH
WHOOSH
DAD'S GONE RIGHT THROUGH THE WINDOW!
YOU'D BETTER TAKE YOUR MONEY BACK, DAD. YOU'VE PAID ENOUGH FOR THAT DODGE.

When asked to sign a letter of apology, Ken refused and was expelled. Undaunted, Ken started work as a freelance artist. Over the next 15 years he drew strips for the *Manchester Evening News*. By 1952, Ken was looking to move into comics and he finally secured work with Amalgamated Press, drawing his own creation 'Foxy' and ghosting another strip called 'Super Sam' in *Comic Cuts*. But, not long after he started working for them, Ken received a letter telling him that *Comic Cuts* was about to fold.

Then came the turning point in Ken's career. His brother-in-law, Bill Holroyd (see page 148), was an artist who worked for D. C. Thomson and he recommended Ken to R. D. Low. Low travelled down from Dundee to Manchester to discuss a new character for *The Beano* – a boy who was always concocting bizarre schemes to dodge out of things. Following Low's description, Ken pencilled several versions of the character and Low chose the one he preferred . . . and 'Roger the Dodger' was born.

JONAH

Every Thursday
THE BEANO
March 15, 1958.
JONAH
ONCE IN A LIFETIME A GUY LIKE JONAH TURNS UP. HE MEANS WELL—BUT HE'S SO FULL OF BAD LUCK THAT WHEN PEOPLE SEE HIM COMING THEY GO ROUND THE WORLD THE OTHER WAY JUST TO AVOID HIM.
LOOK AT ALL THOSE SHIPS! I'LL FIND A JOB ON ONE FOR SURE!
WHICH ONE WILL IT BE? EENY-MEENIE-MINIE-MO—OOPS! THE WIND'S BLOWN OFF MY NEW HAT!
LOWER AWAY!
IRON
WHOOSH!
SHIVER ME TIMBERS! IT'S BLOWN INTO THE CABIN OF THAT CRANE!
'SCUSE ME, MATEY, WHILE I GET ME HAT!
MIND THAT LEVER!
RELEASE
CLANK!
POING!
CAST IRON
ABANDON THE PERISHIN' SHIP!
CLEAN THROUGH THE BOTTOM OF THE HOLD!
OH, DEAR!
THERE'S YOUR PESKY HAT—IN THE DRINK.
NO!
GLUG! GLUG!
QUICK! LEND ME YOUR FACE-PIECE, DIVER!
EH?
THAT HAT COST ME FIVE BOB!
ZIP!
A SUBMARINE! HARD TO STARBOARD—SHARPISH!
AYE, AYE, SIR!—OH, NO!
STAND BY TO PICK UP SURVIVORS!
ABANDON SHIPS! MAKE FOR THE "SAUCY JANE"!
SAUCY JANE
BUT THE "SAUCY JANE" GETS SO OVERCROWDED, THAT—
ABANDON SHIP! SHE'S GOIN' DOWN.
MAKE FOR THE SHORE! IT'S THE ONLY UNSINKABLE PLACE!
LATER
GOT IT—!! OOH—!!!? WHAT'S HAPPENED?
'NOTHIN' COMPARED TO WHAT'S GONNA HAPPEN NOW!
THANK GOODNESS THERE WAS ONE BOAT LEFT AFLOAT! IT'S ME FOR THE OPEN SEA!
GR-R-R!
GLUG! GLUG!
WAIT TILL YOU SEE WHAT JONAH SINKS NEXT WEEK!
PRINTED AND PUBLISHED IN GREAT BRITAIN BY D. C. THOMSON & CO., LTD., AND JOHN LENG & CO., LTD., 12 FETTER LANE, FLEET STREET, LONDON, E.C.4. REGISTERED FOR TRANSMISSION BY CANADIAN MAGAZINE POST.

Ken went on to draw several popular characters for Thomson's comics but his greatest triumph made his debut in *The Beano* on March 15, 1958. This was 'Jonah', the sailor who managed to sink – in a thousand different ways – every vessel he ever stepped aboard. Scripted by Walter Fearn, 'Jonah' was Ken's personal favourite and, in the opinion of many, it was the best thing he ever drew. Walter's original scripts usually ran to around twelve frames but it wasn't unusual for Ken to stretch them out to more than 30! Ken once explained that the way the script described an incident would often set him off on a train of thought that had him creating additional panels. Ken admitted, 'I sometimes just got carried away!' The results were some of the funniest artwork ever to be seen in a British comic.

'Jonah' also featured in The Beano Books. *On this page and the next is the original artwork for a complete story from the 1961* Beano Book.

JONAH
IN THIS HUMBLE COTTAGE, IN THE VILLAGE OF WORMWOOD-ON-WOLD, WAS BORN SIR HORATIO CRUMPINGTON—HERO OF THE BATTLE OF TRIFLEJAR!
IN THAT GREAT NAVAL BATTLE, HE AND HIS SHIP THE "AVENGER," WON FAME AND GLORY. NOW THE VILLAGERS ARE PLANNING TO COMMEMORATE THE BATTLE WITH A PAGEANT.
NOW, THE MAIN EVENT, GENTLEMEN, WILL BE THE STAGING OF THE "AVENGER'S" VICTORY AT TRIFLEJAR—AND WE'RE GOING TO USE A REPLICA OF THAT NOBLE SHIP!
AR-R!
NATURALLY, I, YOUR SQUIRE AND A DIRECT DESCENDANT OF SIR HORATIO, WILL PLAY THE PART OF THAT DISTINGUISHED GENT—A-HR-R-RM!
SO—ON THE GREAT DAY
MAN THE "AVENGER," GENTLEMEN! WE ARE DUE ON THE RIVER IN HALF AN HOUR.
AYE-AYE, SQUOIRE!
MEANWHILE—UP-RIVER.....
GOSH, I WISH I COULD HAVE HAD A PART IN THAT PAGEANT.
QUARRY
GRAND PAGEANT TODAY AT WORMWOOD-ON-WOLD
BEING ON EVEN A REPLICA OF A SHIP'S BETTER THAN NOTHIN'!
I CAN JUST IMAGINE MYSELF AS OLD HORATIO—KEEPIN' THOSE FRENCHIES AT BAY WITH MY TRUSTY SWORD—
OOPS!
SNAP!
SWISH-H-H-H!
GREAT GRAPPLING IRONS! THOSE BARRELS BELONG TO THE QUARRY—AND THEY'RE CHOCK-FULL OF DYNAMITE FOR BLASTING!
GRAND PAGEANT TODAY AT WORMWOOD-ON-WOLD
SPLASH!
RUMBLE!
COO! THEY'LL DRIFT DOWN TO WORMWOOD-ON-WOLD AND GET TANGLED UP WITH THE RIVER PAGEANT! WHAT'LL I DO?
AH! I'LL GRAB THAT BOAT AND BEAT THE BARRELS TO THE PAGEANT. IF I CAN WARN 'EM OF THE DANGER IN TIME, THEY MIGHT GIVE ME A PART AFTER ALL!
WORMWOOD-ON-WOLD—HERE I COME——AGH-H! THIS MUD'S FOUR FEET DEEP!
WHOOSH!
SPLUTCH!
WHILE JONAH IS STRUGGLING OUT OF THE MUD-BANK, LET US JOIN THE PAGEANT HALF A MILE DOWNSTREAM—
RIGHT! RUN UP THIS MESSAGE, HARDY—"THIS DAY, WORMWOOD-ON-WOLD EXPECTS EVERY MAN TO DO HIS DUTY!"
AR-R! SHE BE A FAIR LIKENESS TO THE OLD "AVENGER," FRED! I HEAR THE SQUOIRE'S EVEN GOT BAGS O' SELF-RAISIN' FLOUR ABOARD TO GIVE THE EFFECT OF SMOKE AN' GUN-FIRE!
IT'S A PITY SIR HORATIO MET HIS END AT THE HEIGHT O' VICTORY, THOUGH! THEY RECKON HE WAS WARNED OF IT JUST BEFORE THE BATTLE OPENED UP, Y'KNOW.
AR-R!
UPSTREAM—
ONE—OUT! TWO—OUT! THREE—OUT!—GASP!—I'M BEATING THE BARRELS!—I'M BEATING 'EM!
MADE IT!
Pageant
Avenger
NOW TO WARN 'EM!

AYE, FRED. THEY RECKON THAT JUST BEFORE THE BATTLE BEGAN, THE STRANGE FIGURE OF A MARINER, ALL DRIPPING, ROSE ABOVE THE POOP DECK, AND IN A HOLLOW VOICE, SAID TO SIR HORATIO—
YOU'D BETTER CALL THIS LOT OFF, MATE, AN' PULL IN TO THE SIDE, OTHERWISE YOU'LL GET BLOWN SKY-HIGH!
!
HAW-HAW! JOLLY GOOD! THE PAGEANT COMMITTEE HAVE EVEN USED THE LEGEND OF THE BLACK MARINER! EXCELLENT PERFORMANCE, OLD BOY. NOW, HOPPIT—YOU'RE SUPPOSED TO DISAPPEAR!
B-BUT—!
HOPPIT! YOU'RE STEALING ALL THE LIMELIGHT FROM ME!
B-BUT— ERK!
Avenger
SQUOIRE! THERE BE SOMETHING FAMILIAR ABOUT THAT LAD. I'VE SEEN HIS FACE BEFORE!
LET ME SEE NOW—WHERE WAS IT?
FORGET HIM, HARDY. 'TIS TIME FOR ACTION!
SIR HORATIO GAVE THE SIGNAL TO ATTACK BY FIRING A FLINT-LOCK PISTOL OVER THE SIDE—LIKE THIS!
BANG!
PTCHWEE-E-E-E!
PHUT!

AGH-H-H!
BOOM
WHOOSH
BANG
BY JINGO, FRED! LOOKS JUST LIKE A REAL EXPLOSION—AND ALL DONE WITH SELF-RAISIN' FLOUR!
AYE, BUT I THOUGHT THE "AVENGER" SAILED BACK HOME VICTORIOUS, HENRY. SHE WASN'T SUNK!
AR-R! YOU BE RIGHT, FRED! SOMETHING'S GONE WRONG!
WHAT HAPPENED?
BLEWP!
WELL—I WARNED THEM, DIDN'T I!
ASHORE—
SQUOIRE! I'VE JUST REMEMBERED WHERE I SAW THAT LAD BEFORE! 'T WERE AT SLUSHTON-ON-SLOPP, WHEN HE SANK THE PIER! HIS NAME'S JONAH!
OH, NO!
WELL! WHAT HAVE YOU GOT TO SAY TO THAT, SQUOIRE?
!
KICK ME, HARDY!

LEO BAXENDALE

CHARLIE CHOO
Always Has A Clue
DETECTIVE AGENCY
ALL MYSTERIES SOLVED
SEND FOR CHARLIE CHOO. HE KNOWS WHAT TO DO.
AH CHOO
CHOO CHOO
HONOURABLE BANK MANAGER ON PHONE SAY~ BANK MONEY MISSING. WANT HONOURABLE CHARLIE TO INVESTIGATE.
OUCH! MISERABLE JOKER HAS NAILED PIGTAIL TO WALL.
UNCLE
TUG
TEE-HEE!
MEMBERS OF FAMILY PLEASE LINE UP WHILE HONOURABLE SELF EXAMINES THEM WITH MAGNIFYING GLASS.
INNOCENCE
SO! I FIND HAIR OFF HONOURABLE SELF'S PIGTAIL ON CLOTHES OF CHOO CHOO!
NOW HONOURABLE SELF NEEDS MUCH BIGGER MAGNIFYING GLASS!
CHINESE PROVERB SAY~ HE WHO PULLS LEGS SHOULD USE OWN LEGS TO MAKE SELF SCARCE!
HOWL
LATER
COME, BOYS~ BRING MYSTERY BOXES No.1 AND No.2 TO BANK.
BANK
No. 1 BOX
No. 2 BOX
VELLY GLAD TO MEET FAMOUS MISTER CHARLIE CHOO~SOME THIEF WITH KEY IS OPENING HONOURABLE SAFE AT NIGHTS.
THIEF MUST BE ONE OF BANK WORKERS. BOYS, PLEASE GIVE ME HONOURABLE No.1 BOX.
HONOURABLE SELF HAS PUT No.1 BOX IN SAFE TO CATCH THIEF.
SAFE
No. 1 BOX
NEXT MORNING
SAFE HAS BEEN BROKEN INTO AGAIN. BANK STAFF LINE UP SO THAT HONOURABLE SELF CAN POINT OUT CULPRIT. MAN WEARING HAT PLEASE REMOVE SAME.
2 BOX
SEE! No.1 BOX WAS FULL OF VELLY GOOD BANANAS. THIEF EATS BANANAS AND THEN SLIPS ON BANANA SKIN IN DARKNESS. THIS CAUSES BUMP ON HEAD! VELLY GOOD!
EMPTY
No 1 BOX
I MAKE HONOURABLE SELF SCARCE, VELLY QUICK.
CHOO-CHOO, PLEASE TAKE THE LID OFF No. 2 BOX.
No. 2 BOX
YOWP!
HONOURABLE BLOODHOUND JUMP FROM No. 2 BOX AND CATCHEE THIEF.
GRRR
LATER
VELLY GOOD SUPER FEED!
CRIME SOLVED. CHINESE PROVERB SAY~ HE WHO EATEE BANANA FRUIT WATCHEE WHERE HE PUTEE FOOT!
BIRDS-NEST SOUP
CHOP-SUEY

Baxendale was destined to become one of the biggest names in British comics and many of the top comic artists cite him as having had a major influence on their work. But, at one time, it looked as if Leo would never have a future in comic art.

From an early age, Leo had been convinced that he would make his living as a professional artist, but, by the age of 22, it seemed like his prospects were bleak. Leo was drawing cartoons for his local newspaper, the *Lancashire Evening Post.* By his own admission, 'they were pretty terrible', and the work was not very well paid. Then one evening late in 1952, Leo happened to glance through a copy of his younger brother's *Beano*. There on the page in front of him was 'Dennis the Menace'. Leo was inspired and quickly sent off examples of his newspaper work to the editor of *The Beano*. Soon he was meeting R. D. Low and George Moonie at D. C. Thomson's offices in Manchester.

Leo managed to make a big enough impression on the men from D. C. Thomson to persuade them to commission several picture strips, like the long-forgotten 'Oscar Krank, The Mad Inventor' and 'Charlie Choo Always Has a Clue'. But these strips were a throwback to the early days of *The Beano*. Leo wanted to draw in the new, vibrant style, exemplified by Davey Law's 'Dennis'.

LITTLE PLUM

Just as it looked like Leo's career as a comic artist was over before it had begun, he dreamed up a new character, a cross between Hiawatha, the legendary Native American, and Dennis the Menace, and sent it to George Moonie. As Baxendale recalls, 'This was my last try. Happily, George accepted the new character immediately, and gave him a working title of "Booster", though when he appeared in *The Beano*, George had settled on the title "Little Plum, Your Redskin Chum" – a rhyming couplet.' The first strip, from October 10, 1953, was in two rows and is shown below. Artists always drew their strips at a larger scale than they appear in the comic. The 'Little Plum' drawings opposite are taken from the original artwork.

LITTLE PLUM
~ YOUR ~
REDSKIN CHUM
HO-HO! LITTLE PLUM FANCIES HE IS HEAP-BIG BEAR HUNTER.
ME CATCHUM PLENTY BEAR!
BUT IN THE WILDS—
ST-T-AND ST-T-ILL WH-WHILE I SH-SHOOT YOU!
H'M! LITTLE HUNTER SHAKE TOO MUCH TO SHOOT ME!
MISSED!
SAVED!
PLUNK
NOW THAT WE'RE PALS YOU CAN DO ME A FAVOUR!
SHAKE
LATER IN PLUM'S WIGWAM
ENVY!
SEE! HEAP-BIG BEARSKIN!
PSSST! THEY'VE GONE NOW~ YOU CAN CLIMB OUT.
5 MINUTES LATER
DRINK UP! WE FOOLED 'EM!
HOME MADE POP

IT'S NO USE SCROUNGING ROUND HERE, VULTURE – I'VE ONLY GOT ONE UM SAUSAGE, SO THERE ISN'T ANY TO SPARE FOR YOU!
SIZZLE
UM SAUSAGE IS COOKED. NOW I'LL JUST SPLOSH UM DOLLOP OF SAUCE OVER IT!
GONE! UM SOSSY'S GONE!
GULP
SO!
MISSED 'IM!
HOP
CLANG
DYNAMITE STORE
I'LL FIX THAT VULTURE!
DYNAMITE
SO – LATER
YOO-HOO! LOOK AT UM NICE PERCH I'VE MADE FOR YOU!
THINKS – IT'S A TRICK. HE MUST HAVE A HATCHET BEHIND HIS BACK – HE'LL CLOBBER ME WITH IT AS SOON AS I FLY DOWN THERE!
IT'S UM ALL RIGHT! LOOK! I'M UNARMED!
DYNAMITE
NICE WEATHER WE'RE HAVING!
SQUAWK!
STRIKE
GOING TO HAVE A BIT OF THUNDER SOON THOUGH, I THINK!
SSSS
I'VE GOT TO GO NOW. BYE-BYE!
WAVE
COO! LOOK AT THIS NICE PERCH! – GET OUT OF IT, VULTURE!
BOP
ANY SECOND NOW!
THERE! IT MAKES A SMASHING PERCH FOR MY PET TALKING PARROT!
THREE-TWO-ONE-ZERO-
VERY COMFY!
SULK
BLAM

MINNIE THE MINX

Soon, George Moonie was visiting Leo at his home in Preston and suggesting he draw a female version of 'Dennis the Menace'. Leo agreed and 'Minnie the Minx' was born. She made her debut in the comic in December, 1953. The first Minnie was six panels in black and white (see below). She quickly moved to a full page in two colours as these other strips show.

MINNIE THE MINX
THIS IS WHERE MINNIE THE MINX LIVES.
BEWARE OF THE MINX!
THIS IS MINNIE! SHE'S WILD AS WILD CAN BE.
SCRAP BOOK
FIGHTING AGAIN, MINNIE? STOPPIT! GO AND PLAY WITH THIS!
YES, MA, DEAR!
OO-WOO-WOO! I'M ON THE WARPATH! TAKE THAT, CHARLIE!
CLONK!
OUCH!
TUMMY IN, FATTY!
SCRAP BOOK
HIYA, TWINS! THIS IS FOR MAKING FACES AT ME LAST TUESDAY!
BASH!
LATER
GOLLY, MUM, THAT SCRAP-BOOK'S SUPER! I WON NINE SCRAPS WITH IT!
SCRAP BOOK

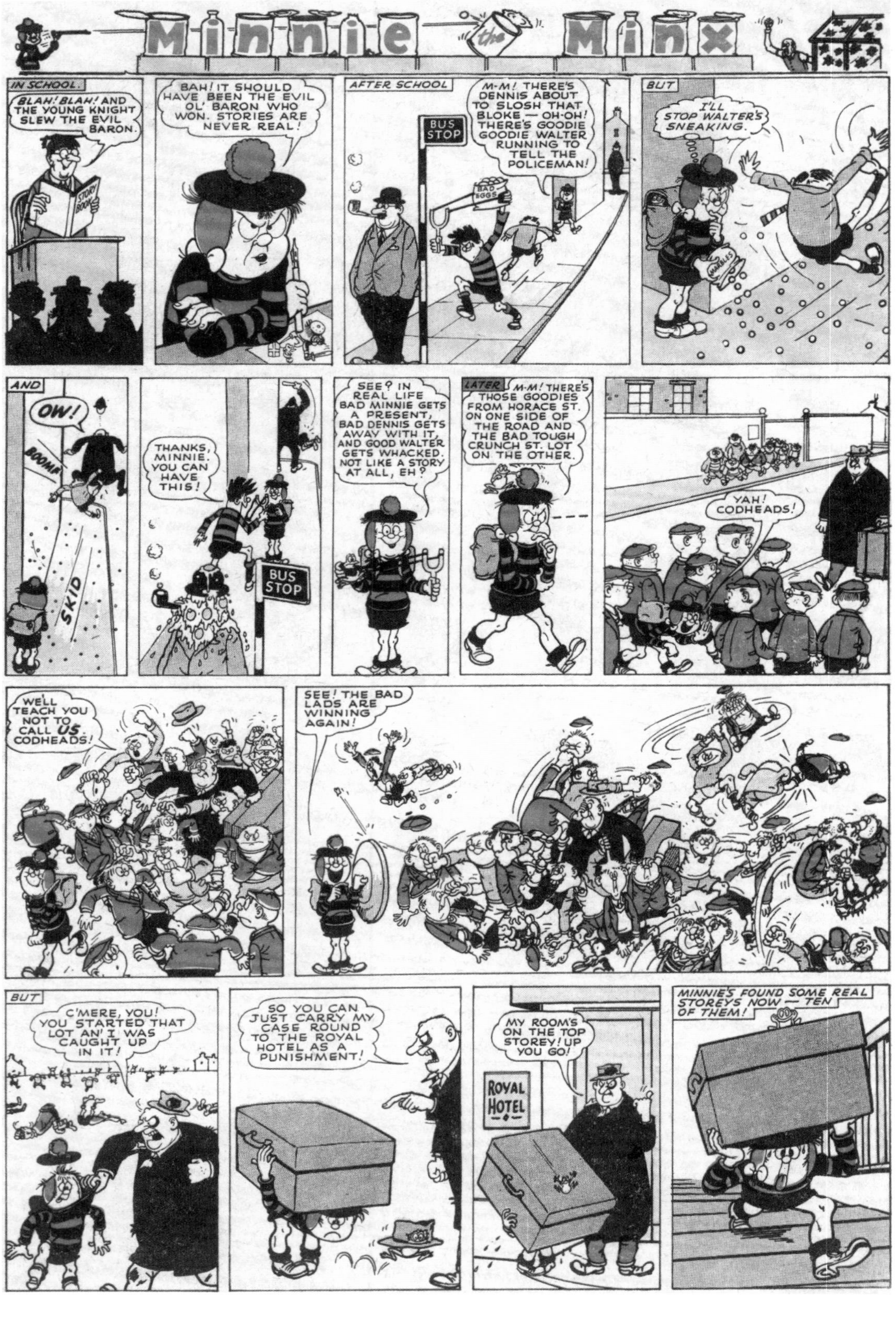
Minnie the Minx
IN SCHOOL.
BLAH! BLAH! AND THE YOUNG KNIGHT SLEW THE EVIL BARON.
BAH! IT SHOULD HAVE BEEN THE EVIL OL' BARON WHO WON. STORIES ARE NEVER REAL!
AFTER SCHOOL
M-M! THERE'S DENNIS ABOUT TO SLOSH THAT BLOKE — OH-OH! THERE'S GOODIE GOODIE WALTER RUNNING TO TELL THE POLICEMAN!
BUS STOP
BUT
I'LL STOP WALTER'S SNEAKING.
AND
OW!
BOOMP
SKID
THANKS, MINNIE. YOU CAN HAVE THIS!
BUS STOP
SEE? IN REAL LIFE BAD MINNIE GETS A PRESENT, BAD DENNIS GETS AWAY WITH IT, AND GOOD WALTER GETS WHACKED. NOT LIKE A STORY AT ALL, EH?
LATER
M-M! THERE'S THOSE GOODIES FROM HORACE ST. ON ONE SIDE OF THE ROAD AND THE BAD TOUGH CRUNCH ST. LOT ON THE OTHER.
YAH! CODHEADS!
WE'LL TEACH YOU NOT TO CALL US CODHEADS!
SEE! THE BAD LADS ARE WINNING AGAIN!
BUT
C'MERE, YOU! YOU STARTED THAT LOT AN' I WAS CAUGHT UP IN IT!
SO YOU CAN JUST CARRY MY CASE ROUND TO THE ROYAL HOTEL AS A PUNISHMENT!
MY ROOM'S ON THE TOP STOREY! UP YOU GO!
ROYAL HOTEL
MINNIE'S FOUND SOME REAL STOREYS NOW — TEN OF THEM!

Minnie the Minx
IN TOWN
AH! JUST THE PERSON I WANT TO SEE! DELIVER THIS TO YOUR FATHER, MINNIE.
RIGHT, MR. JONES!
OL' FATTY CONFISCATED MY BALL LAST WEEK. THIS'LL PAY 'IM BACK!
BOOMERANG
HE'S SO STIFF HE'LL NEVER CATCH ME.
W. FEARN SWEEP
I'LL USE THE SWEEP'S BRUSH TO VAULT OVER THIS PATCH OF STINGING NETTLES.
NOW I'LL NIP ACROSS THE DISUSED CANAL.
WOBBLE
BUT
WELL, I'VE LOST FATTY— OOOH— I'VE LOST DAD'S LETTER, TOO! AN' I BET IT WAS IMPORTANT!
SNIGGER
MAYBE I DROPPED THE LETTER IN THE SMELLY OL' CANAL.
PHOO
PONG
SNIGGER
MAYBE—OW— I DROPPED THE LETTER—OW—IN THIS PATCH OF—OW—NETTLES!
STING
STING
STING
MAYBE I DROPPED THE LETTER AS I WAS PASSING THIS HEAP OF SOOT.
W. FEARN SWEEP
SNIGGER!
HAVE YOU BEEN LOOKING FOR THIS? YOU DROPPED IT ON THE PAVEMENT AFTER YOU KNOCKED MY HELMET OFF.
ROTTEN OL' BLUEBOTTLE! WHY DIDN'T YOU TELL ME BEFORE?
AT HOME
THIS IS FOR YOU, DAD!
BAH! IT'S AN INVITATION TO TEA FROM THAT HARRY JONES! I CAN'T STAND HIM! CONCEITED ASS!! WHY COULDN'T YOU HAVE LOST THIS OR SOMETHING?
FREE
SOUVENIR BOOK OF THE FAMOUS BUNTY PICTURE STORY.
"Girl of The Islands"
YOU'LL LOVE THE MOVING STORY OF MARINA, THE GIRL FROM THE SEA.
THIS SPLENDID PICTURE STORY BOOK IS GIVEN FREE IN
BUNTY
The PICTURE STORY PAPER FOR GIRLS.
ON SALE NEXT TUESDAY

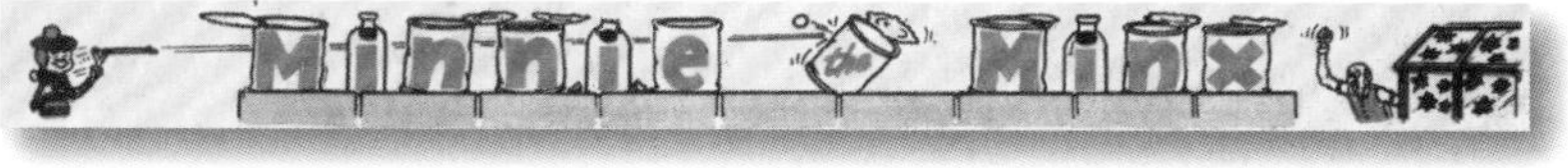
Minnie the Minx

MINNIE the MINX

Minnie the Minx

Minnie the Minx
THIS HOUSE IS SO QUIET, I COULD SCREAM. EVERYBODY'S DOWN IN THE DUMPS. I'LL HAVE TO SEE IF I CAN CHEER THEM UP!
SO—
I KNOW WHY GRANDPA'S IN THE DUMPS! HE'S SO RHEUMATICKY, HE CAN'T GET AROUND AS MUCH AS HE'D LIKE TO— BUT I'LL SOON FIX THAT!
AH! THAT'S IT!
?
SCRATCH!
EE-OW!
SCRATCH
OOOH! ME RHEUMATICS! IT'S AGONY!
DEARIE ME! IT'S MADE GRANDPA WORSE!
GERROUTOFIT!
LATER—
MA'S DOWN IN THE DUMPS BECAUSE SHE HAS TOO MUCH HOUSEWORK TO DO. I'LL FILL THE COAL SCUTTLE FOR HER!
MINNIE USES HER CATAPULT TO SAVE HERSELF CARRYING IN A SCUTTLE-FULL OF COAL FROM THE CELLAR.
G-GOLLY! I'M NOT SUCH A GOOD SHOT AS I THOUGHT I WAS!
CRASH!
OH, NO! MY LOVELY NEW WALLPAPER!
GULP!
LATER—
DAD'S IN THE DUMPS BECAUSE HE'S MISLAID HIS FALSE TEETH AN' HE CAN'T EAT NUTS— HE'S VERY PARTIAL TO NUTS!
I'LL MASH 'EM UP SMALL WITH THIS HAMMER OUT OF MY WOODWORK SET, THEN DAD'LL BE ABLE TO EAT 'EM!
YIPE!
CRUNCH!
THIS IS THE SAFEST PLACE FOR THESE!
I WAS ONLY TRYIN' TO HELP!
MA, DAD AND GRANDPA ARE CHEERY NOW— BUT MINNIE'S DOWN IN THE DUMPS!
RUBBISH DUMP
MY PRECIOUS WEAPONS— LOST FOREVER!
High-Flying Thrills With—
Parachute NURSE
Exciting Picture Story in
BUNTY
EVERY TUESDAY – PRICE 4d
THE PICTURE PAPER FOR EVERY BRIGHT GIRL

THE BASH STREET KIDS

But the best was still to come. . . . With *The Beano*'s anti-authoritarian streak, a school seemed an ideal setting for a new strip. As Baxendale explains, 'Bash Street was a figment of my imagination, a surreal school unlike any school that existed in real life.' The first strip, shown below, was headed 'With a roar out they pour, every afternoon at four. When school is done, the kids of Bash Street School have fun' – so much fun that the police appear 'to put a stop to this'.

WHEN THE BELL RINGS!
HI SLEEPY! OPEN THE DOOR! IT'S FOUR!
SCHOOL
WAKEY, WAKEY!
D-DING D-D-DING
CREAK
GROAN
DON'T FORGET—SKATING ON THE OLD MILL POND TONIGHT!
WE'LL BE THERE!
GIVE A MAN A CHANCE TO OPEN THE DOOR, CAN'T YOU!
SQUAD—HALT! WE'LL HAVE TO PUT A STOP TO THIS!
COME ON AN' SKATE, GRANDAD, DON'T BE SHY!
BASH
THESE CUSHIONS WILL PROTECT ME WHEN I HIT THE WALL!
DANGER
DRY YOUR CLOTHES 2D A TIME
WHO SAID I COULDN'T JUMP THREE BARRELS?
TRIP
CRACK
REFEREE
HOCKEY MATCH KEEP OFF PITCH
SPLASH!
HOLE DONE BY BLOWLAMP!
BUY TOOTS' ICE LOLLIES MILL POND FLAVOUR! ONLY 1D
DAZE
AMBULANCE
HUH!
GROOGH!
DING DONG PING PONG
COME ON, HUSKY! MUSH!

THE BASH STREET KIDS
THE ALARM GOES OFF IN TEACHER'S HOUSE AT 7 A.M.
HORRORS! IT'S TUESDAY!
I'LL HAVE TO BE REALLY FIT TODAY!
8 O'CLOCK
9 O'CLOCK
NOW TEACHER FEELS READY TO TEACH THE BASH ST. KIDS THAT FEARFUL SUBJECT—ARITHMETIC!
THE LESSON BEGINS
NOW WE'LL TRY A SIMPLE TAKE-AWAY SUM. FATTY HAS TEN SWEETS AND DANNY TAKES AWAY FIVE. HOW MANY SWEETS HAS FATTY LEFT?
!!?!!
IT'S A SWINDLE! FATTY HASN'T ANY SWEETS IN HIS POCKET!
WE'LL TRY AGAIN. THERE ARE FIFTEEN DESKS IN THE ROOM. IF YOU TAKE AWAY FOURTEEN HOW MANY ARE LEFT? THINK THAT ONE OVER WHILE I ATTEND TO SOME IMPORTANT BUSINESS!
TEACHER'S IMPORTANT BUSINESS!
TEACHER'S ROOM
BANG! CLUMP! CRASH! BANG!
BACK IN CLASS!
WE GOT THE ANSWER!
ONE DESK, SIR!
THIS IS HOW THE KIDS WORKED OUT THAT SUM!
ALL RIGHT! I'M NOT GOING TO BE ANGRY WITH YOU— BUT LET'S GET ONE SIMPLE TAKE-AWAY SUM DONE CORRECTLY WITHOUT ANY BOTHER. NOW, I HAVE FIFTEEN CHAIRS AND YOU TAKE AWAY ONE—
TOUGH LUCK ON TEACHER! HE HAD TO BE TAKEN AWAY AT THE FINISH!
BEANO BOOK
THE BEANO

The first 'When the Bell Rings' strip, drawn by Leo Baxendale for the February 13, 1954 issue.

THE BASH ST. KIDS
GIANT'S CASTLE
GIANT
SO YOU'RE A GOOD FAIRY—WELL I'M A BAD ONE. HERE'S A FLY-PAPER TO READ!
BAD FAIRY
COTTON WOOL CLOUDS
SWAY!
SPLAT!
BAD SPELLS
GOOD SPELLS
SHOVE!
JACK
PUFF! GRUNT! CREAK! GROAN!
AH, TEACHER! I'M GLAD TO SEE YOU'RE REHEARSING THE CHRISTMAS PANTO NICE AND EARLY.
HERE I COME—CINDERELLA'S FAIRY-GODMOTHER WITH MY MAGIC WAND—YOW!
I'LL SAY WE'RE EARLY! IT TAKES THESE NITS SO LONG TO LEARN THEIR LINES, WE'RE REHEARSING THE PANTO FOR CHRISTMAS 1961!
BEAN POD
BASH ST. SCHOOL HALL
WE'RE THE BABES IN THE WOOD AN' WE'RE COVERED WITH LEAVES!
LEAVES FROM THE SCHOOL BOOKS!
YOW!
CREAK!
BEAN STALK
BONK!
GOLDEN EGG
GIANT'S CLUB
CRUMP!
I DREAM OF GENIE WITH THE LIGHT BRO-OWN HAIR...
JAB!
CINDERS
CREAK!
PANTO SCRIPT
PUT YOUR SHIRT ON AT ONCE, JONES MINOR!
THERE'S GONNA BE A BIG CRASH!
JACK AND THE BEANSTALK SCRIPT
PREFECT
BUT IT SAYS HERE THAT DICK TURPIN RODE BARE-BACK TO LITTLE WOLLOP!
DICK TURPIN
ALADDIN'S LAMP
TEACHER MUST HAVE BEEN CRACKERS TO PICK FATTY TO CLIMB THE POOR OL' BEANSTALK!
ROBINSON CRUSOE
I'LL MAKE A FIRE WITH THIS BIT OF DRIFT-WOOD THAT'S FLOATED UP TO THE ISLAND!
THERE'S THE SLEEPING BEAUTY, HANDSOME PRINCE!
SPLAT!
HANDSOME PRINCE
PANTO RAT
PUSS IN BOOTS
WE'VE ONLY ONE PAIR OF WELLINGTON BOOTS SO WE HAD TO SHARE 'EM BETWEEN PUSS IN BOOTS AND THE GIANT!
HOP
HOP
7-LEAGUE BOOT
SLEEPING BEAUTY
WHAT? I'M NOT PLAYIN' THE HANDSOME PRINCE IF HE'S THE SLEEPING BEAUTY! LEMME GO!
JACK THE GIANT KILLER
POLARIS
HOP

Leo Baxendale had a mischievous sense of humour and he would add to the scripts with asides and hilarious facial expressions on the kids. George Moonie, on the other hand, was able to draw never-ending inspiration from just outside his office window. The view of the pupils cavorting in the neighbouring High School of Dundee playground was invaluable to this extremely talented Editor and script writer. 'When The Bell Rings' first appeared in ***The Beano*** on February 13, 1954. Eventually, this mass mayhem became focused on one class and one teacher, and on November 11, 1956, the title was changed to 'The Bash Street Kids'. The detail in the examples on this page (preparing for a pantomime) and the next (how to cheat at an exam while Teacher remains oblivious to all that is going on around him) are inspired classics.

MIRROR
GREAT FIRE OF LONDON 1666
READERS – HALF CLOSE YOUR EYES AND LOOK AT THE FLIES ON THIS FLY-PAPER
SPANISH ARMADA 1588
PET SPIDER
BATTLE OF TRAFALGAR 1805
The BASH STREET KIDS
STEPHENSON INVENTED "ROCKET" 1829
FLIES
FLY-PAPER
HADRIAN'S WALL BUILT 121. A.D.
JULIUS CAESAR LANDED IN BRITAIN 55. B.C.
BANNOCK-BURN 1314
HENRY VIII 1509-1547. A.D.
I'M GOING TO WATCH YOU LOT LIKE A HAWK WHILE YOU'RE DOING THIS EXAM AND IF I CATCH ANYBODY CHEATING YOU'LL GET GOOD MARKS ALL RIGHT—
—ON THE SEATS OF YOUR TROUSERS.
AGINCOURT 1415
WORLD'S LONGEST RIVERS
AFRICA - RIVER NILE 4,000 MLS
S. AMERICA - RIVER AMAZON 4,000 MLS
ASIA - YANGTZE. 3,500 MLS
EUROPE - VOLGA. 2,300 MLS
BRITISH ISLES. SHANNON. 230 MILES.
BASH ST. RIVER PUDDLE 1½ MLS
OUR DADS PROMISED US EXPENSIVE PRESENTS IF WE GET GOOD MARKS IN OUR SCHOOL EXAM! SO WE'RE MAKING SURE WE GET GOOD MARKS!
LOOKING AT THE CEILING FOR INSPIRATION!
THE KIDS HAVE BEEN FEEDING THIS ROBIN WITH BREADCRUMBS
TOOT'S CAT
NINE SEVENS ARE SIXTY-THREE NINE EIGHTS ARE SEVENTY-TWO NINE NINES ARE..
PET TALKING PARROT
WATERLOO 1815
WASTE BASKET
HIGHEST MOUNTAIN MT. EVEREST 29,002 FT
MIRROR
BLACK DEATH 1348
PENCIL CASE
SMIFFY WROTE A DATE ON HIS NOSE!
1837 1901
GLASS DESK LID!
THIS PEN DON'T RITE GOOD
KINGS OF ENGLAND HENRY VII CHARLES II JAMES I EDWARD I
TEACHER CAN'T SEE ME CRIBBING IF I DO MY EXAM INSIDE MY DESK!
FALSE NOSE
THE CAPITALL OF SCOTTLAND IS CALLED HAGGIS
1066
12×7=84
THE CAPPITAL CITY OF ENGLAND IS CALLED LONDONEGAN
BATTLE OF HASTINGS 1066
SWEETS
FATTY'S GOT THE ANSWERS WRITTEN ON HIS TOFFEE PAPERS!
HISTORY
BUT TEACHER SOON DISCOVERED THAT HE HAD A CLASS OF CHEATS — AND HE KEPT HIS PROMISE ABOUT GIVING 'EM GOOD MARKS!

The characters 'Little Plum', 'Minnie the Minx', 'The Bash Street Kids' – all classic comic creations and all drawn by Leo Baxendale. But what is perhaps not quite so well known is that he also 'ghosted' other ***Beano*** greats such as 'Dennis the Menace', 'Lord Snooty' and 'Biffo the Bear'.

Leo Baxendale – one of the greatest comic artists this country ever produced.

A BIG DRAW! - Well over a hundred funny pictures!
ALL FOR TWOPENCE!
THE BEANO
2D
EVERY THURSDAY
No. 601. JAN. 23rd, 1954.
Biffo the BEAR
GOSH! WHAT A SUPER JUGGLER!
I CAN USE THESE EGGS!
SO CAN I!
H'M! VERY CLEVER! BUT WHAT IF HE DROPS THEM?
WHOO-OO!
AH! THE ONE O'CLOCK HOOTER! TIME FOR LUNCH!
AFTER LUNCH
HI! PAY FOR MY EGGS, YOU BULLY!
GO AND CHASE YOURSELF!
SPARE A COPPER
I'LL THROW THIS CLOCKWORK MOUSE AMONG THE BALLS!
SPARE A COPPER
THE CAT'S AFTER THE MOUSE~
SPARE A COPPER
YOU BRUTE! MY PUSSY CAT!
MY PUPPY DOG!
-AND THE DOG'S AFTER THE CAT!
SPARE A COPPER
AFTER HIM!
COME BACK AND BE LICKED!
HE CAN SPARE A FEW COPPERS TO PAY FOR MY EGGS!
SPARE A COPP
D. WATKINS

On the outside the issue of *The Beano* for January 23, 1954, did not look all that different from the record-selling comic from 1950, apart from a wider page size. 'Biffo the Bear' was still the front cover character while 'Pansy Potter' remained on the back page. But there were major changes inside.

There was now only one prose story and two adventure picture-strips. More significantly, the classic characters 'Dennis the Menace', 'Minnie the Minx', 'Roger the Dodger' and 'Little Plum' were all now firmly established. In fact, 'Minnie' is featured twice – in her own strip and making a guest appearance in 'Dennis'.

Pages 2 and 3 of The Beano *for January 23, 1954, showing the contrasting styles of Dudley Watkins, with Lord Snooty, and Davey Law with Dennis (note that Minnie the Minx is also included in the story). There are 18 frames on the 'Dennis' page, twice as many as a modern day 'Dennis' strip. Yet, thanks to the genius of artist Davey Law, the page never looks cluttered and the pictures do not seem crowded.*

According to Beano office legend, in those days the picture description for the final frame of every 'Dennis' script contained only one word, 'Slipper'.

LORD SNOOTY
AND HIS PALS
BIG FAT JOE
SCRAPPER
DOUBTING THOMAS
SNITCH and SNATCH
PONGO
POLLY
ROSIE
I'M GOING AWAY FOR A WEEK, SO I'VE ADVERTISED FOR A HOUSEKEEPER—YOU CAN TAKE YOUR PICK.
WE'LL TEST THEM BY MAKING AN AWFUL DIN AND SEE HOW THEY REACT!
CLANG!
BELLOW!
SCREECH!
CLASH!
BLARE!
CRUNCH
THUD!
THUMP!
SH-SH! BE QUIET!
SH-SH! STOP THAT NOISE!
SH-SH! QUIET THERE!
SHE SHUSHED, SO SHE DOESN'T GET THE JOB!
SO DID SHE!
GOOD DAY TO YOU, MADAM. YOU'VE HAD IT, TOO!
NOW FOR THE NEXT TEST! WE'LL BLACKEN OUR FACES WHILE YOU GIRLS PLACE THE SOAP AND WATER IN FRONT OF THE LADIES.
HO! HO! THIS WILL REALLY TEST THEM.
TUT-TUT! WHAT DIRTY FACES!
DISGUSTING!
NOW TO SEE WHAT THEY DO!
OH! LET THEM BE DIRTY! THEY'RE HAPPY THAT WAY!
I CAN'T BE BOTHERED TO WASH THEM.
THESE LADIES HAVE PASSED THIS TEST!
THESE TWO LADIES HAVE FAILED! THEY WOULD ALWAYS BE WASHING US!
ANOTHER TEST
WILL YOU STEP INTO THIS ROOM, PLEASE?
I WONDER WHAT'S IN HERE?
OHO! I WONDER WHAT THEY KEEP IN THIS BOX?
NOW WATCH!
I'LL OPEN IT AND SEE!
GOODBYE! YOU'RE TOO NOSEY!
SHE'S FAILED!
ONLY THREE LEFT. TRY THEM WITH A SAD STORY, SNOOTY!
HERE'S A SAD STORY ABOUT BIG FAT JOE OUT ON A PICNIC. HE TOOK WITH HIM A LARGE PIE, SIX BARS OF CHOCOLATE, FIVE CREAM BUNS, TEN ROCK CAKES AND A DOZEN SAUSAGE ROLLS—BUT HE DROPPED ONE OF HIS CREAM BUNS IN SOME MUD, AND SO HE COULDN'T EAT IT! WASN'T IT A SHAME?
HA-HA!
SOB!
HE-HE!
YOU TWO LADIES ARE DISQUALIFIED! YOU LAUGHED AT THAT SAD STORY. THIS LADY GETS THE JOB BECAUSE SHE CRIED. SHE'S JUST THE LADY WE'RE LOOKING FOR. SHE'S SYMPATHETIC AND SHE'S PASSED ALL THE OTHER TESTS.
SNOOTY HAS CHOSEN YOU AS A HOUSEKEEPER, SO NOW I'LL GO AND LEAVE YOU IN CHARGE.
SHE'S A SCOTS LADY, TOO!
THAT NIGHT
YOWL
WAIL
WHEEZE!
WHAT'S ALL THE NOISE ABOUT? WE CAN'T SLEEP A WINK!
HOUSE-KEEPER
BAH! AFTER ALL OUR TROUBLE! WE HAD TO PICK A HOUSEKEEPER WHO PLAYS THE BAGPIPES!

DENNIS the MENACE
AHA! OHO!
BAH! A DOLL'S PRAM'S NO GOOD TO ME! I'M MINNIE THE MINX!
I'LL LEND YOU MY SUPER CATAPULT FOR A LOAN OF YOUR DOLL'S PRAM!
SUITS ME!
H'M! THAT'S NOT LIKE DENNIS!
WHERE ARE YOU GOING TO, MY PRETTY MAID?
CISSY!
BONK!
WERE YOU SAYING SOMETHING?
BONK!
NOW I'VE GOT A DOLL AND A PRAM I'LL NEVER BE STUCK FOR A SCRAP!
CAREFUL!
HOI!
OH, I BEG YOUR PARDON!
HE'S DOING IT DELIBERATELY!
I'M CRIPPLED!
HO, HO, HO!
SWEEP
A LITTLE SOOT ON THE WHEELS NOW—
MY CLEAN STEPS!
MINE, TOO!
SUCH FUN!
TIME DOLLY HAD A SWIM!
SHE'S DROWNING—HELP!
I'LL SAVE HER!
POOR LITTLE GIRL!
OH, THANK YOU! YOU'VE SAVED MY LITTLE DOLLY!
I'VE HAD FUN! NOW I'LL RIDE DOWNHILL AND HAND THIS BACK!
I HAD FUN, DENNIS! THANKS!
I HAD FUN, TOO—AND DAD WILL NEVER BELIEVE PEOPLE IF THEY COMPLAIN ABOUT ME AND A DOLL'S PRAM!
MINNIE'S HAD FUN ALL RIGHT! AN' PEOPLE WILL THINK IT WAS ME!
GO-BREAKING WINDOWS!
DAD!
BUT, DAD, I WAS PLAYIN' WITH A DOLL'S PRAM!
NO LIES, DENNIS!

Pages 4 and 5 of The Beano *for January 23, 1954, a double page adventure strip, with drawings from the D. C. Thomson staff artist, James 'Peem' Walker.*

Slaves of the killer of Thunder Island.
"GET RID OF THE RUNAWAY TWINS!"
1—The castaway Kidds of Thunder Island were in deadly danger. Tom and Trixie, the orphan twins, had gone to sleep in a clearing on the lonely South Seas island. A few hours before, the cargo liner on which they were travelling to Australia had struck a floating mine. Just before the ship sank, the twins discovered the mate, Karl Jason, robbing the Captain's safe of a valuable collection of jewels. Realising that the twins were the only witnesses of his crime, Jason tried to kill them. But the twins escaped in a raft, taking Blackie, the ship's cat, with them. Unseen, the evil mate had arrived on the island, and Tom and Trixie awoke with a start as his hoarse voice snarled, "Get up, you brats! Get on your feet—quick!"
2—Eyes wide with horror, the two children looked up at the burly figure outlined by the light of the tropical moon. Karl Jason had a rifle gripped firmly in his big hands, and at the sight of it, the twins scrambled to obey his order. Blackie the cat slunk fearfully out of sight into the jungle. Tom and Trixie fully expected to be shot down at any moment, but Karl Jason had other ideas. "Make for your raft on the beach," he rapped, "an' be quick about it!" Dawn was breaking as Jason and his prisoners arrived at the raft. Nearby was the little boat which the mate had used. "I'm getting rid of you kids!" snarled the mate. "But before I do, you'll work, and work hard. Get busy unloadin' the stores from my boat."
3—The Kidds toiled away at their task under the ugly eye of Karl Jason. Heavy crates had to be unloaded. As the sun became hotter, the perspiration began to stream down their faces. But Jason allowed the Kidds no rest. He sat on a crate watching the twins. He was firmly gripping a canvas satchel and several times Jason opened it, chuckling to himself as he ran his fingers through the stolen jewels inside.
4—Soon the twins had nearly finished their task. They were hot and weary, and Tom was hoping that Karl Jason would allow them to rest. But his hopes were soon dashed. The burly mate suddenly delved into a crate and took out a fishing-line, which he flung at Tom. "I've another job for you, kid," he rapped. "Get out there on the reef an' catch some fish for my breakfast. An' no tricks!" Jason lifted his rifle meaningly.
5—Tom bit his lip and, with the fishing-line in his hand, set out along the beach and began to probe for sandworms to use for bait. "Get a move on, you!" bellowed Jason. When he had sufficient bait, the boy made his way out along a strip of coral that jutted into the sea and began to swing his line.
6—A stiff wind was blowing across the ocean and often the seas broke over the reef with a thunderous roar. Tom stuck to his task and soon two fat fish lay on the reef at his feet. The boy baited his line and was making another cast when a big wave thundered against the reef and swept him into the sea.

Tom casts his fishing line—and catches a killer's rifle.
7—On the beach, Trixie gave a cry of horror. There was a big shark in the sea near Tom, and Trixie made as if to run towards the reef. But with a hoarse laugh, Karl Jason reached out a hand and roughly held her back. "Stay here!" he growled. "If the shark gets the boy it'll save me the trouble." Trixie watched helplessly as her brother swam desperately for the reef.
8—Tom was in a desperate plight. Gasping for breath, he reached the reef and looked quickly round. The shark was almost on him. He would be attacked before he had time to scramble on to the coral. Then he saw the two fish he had caught lying on a ledge within reach. In a desperate effort, Tom grabbed a fish and hurled it towards the approaching shark.
9—The fish splashed into the water near the shark and the great brute swerved to pounce on the tasty morsel. That swerve saved Tom's life. It gave the plucky boy time to climb up on to the reef. He stood there for a moment to recover his breath. Then he picked up the remaining fish and his line and made his way back to the beach. Jason, seated on one of the crates, watched his approach with eyes aglitter with hate. "Give the fish to the girl," he snarled. "Hurry up, I'm hungry!" Tom bit his lip and quickly handed over the fish.
10—"Cook the fish, girl!" growled Jason. "An' do it nice an' tender or I'll thrash the life out o' ye." Trixie took the fish and quickly cleaned it. Then she went to the camp fire which Jason had forced her to kindle. Using utensils from the sea-chest, she soon had the fish done to a turn. Suddenly a gleam came into Tom's eyes. Jason had propped his rifle against the crate while Trixie brought him his meal. The mate was greedily eyeing the fish, too occupied to see Tom swinging the fishing-line. Then with a cunning throw the boy made a cast at the rifle.
11—With a faint scraping noise the hook caught on the trigger guard of the rifle. Jason swung round. "What's up?" he snarled, springing to his feet and upsetting the plate of fried fish. At the same instant Tom pulled on the line and the rifle was jerked from the crate right into the heart of the blazing camp-fire, sending sparks showering into the air.
12—Tom leaped into action instantly. "Get the jewels, Trixie!" he yelled, and even before the words were out of his mouth the girl had snatched up the precious satchel. Then the two Kidds raced for the jungle. Livid with rage, Jason sprang to the camp-fire to grope frantically amongst the flames for the rifle that would put an end to the daring runaways.
NEXT WEEK—Karl Jason sets a cunning trap for the runaway twins!

Pages 6 and 7 of The Beano *for January 23, 1954, with a text story for most of the spread (with a header drawn by George Drysdale) and then an early 'Minnie the Minx' strip, already with colour, by way of contrast. 'Minnie' fares no better than 'Dennis' at the end of the strip – political correctness was unheard of then.*

"You son-of-a-gun!" hear Hawkeye wail—"I asked for a tiddler—not a WHALE!"

Smarty Smokey

THE GENIE IN THE SIX-GUN

This is a MAGIC genie here. YOU can make him disappear!
Get a piece of clear red glass, transparent red plastic, or red celluloid. Then look at the picture of Smarty through it. HEY PRESTO! He will vanish!

The Frightened Mayor.

IN his office in the tough little Wild West town of Rattler Gulch, old Hawkeye Hankey, the Sheriff, pulled out his new six-shooter.

It was just like any other gun to look at. Only the Sheriff knew its strange secret.

He sat in his chair with his feet on his desk, and pointed the gun at a row of bottles on a shelf. Then he pulled the trigger.

No bullet flew from the gun. But all the bottles on the shelf tumbled off, one after the other, and crashed on the floor.

Then a puff of smoke swirled before the Sheriff. Out of it appeared the dusky, beaming face of a young Genie.

"Did I perform my task well, O master?" he inquired hopefully.

"You sure did, partner," declared Hawkeye, delighted. "I never saw a finer bit of gunplay in all my life. I sure liked the way you knocked the bottles off the shelf, young Smokey."

Smokey, the young Genie, beamed proudly. He was pleased to get a word of praise on his first job. Having finished his training as a Genie under Mysto, the great Eastern magician, Smokey had been sent as Slave to a Magic Lamp in America. But that same day, the Lamp had been melted down as scrap, and made into a six-gun.

Smokey refused to give up, however. The magic gun had come into the hands of Hawkeye Hankey, a short-sighted sheriff, and now, as Slave to the six-gun, Smokey was helping the Sheriff to uphold law and order in Rattler Gulch.

It was a lucky day for the Sheriff, for although he called himself Hawkeye, he was so short-sighted he couldn't hit a barn door at two yards' range. That was why Rattler Gulch was over-run with rustlers and outlaws.

But the Sheriff didn't have to worry about hitting the target now. All he had to do was pull the trigger. Then, keeping invisible, Smokey would pop out and attack the target for him, whether it was an empty bottle or a bloodthirsty bandit.

"Reckon it's about time I got to work," decided Hawkeye and just at that moment he heard a step outside the door. "Scram, Smokey!" he hissed, waving his hand frantically at the fluttering Genie. He didn't want anybody else in Rattler Gulch to know he had a Genie to help him in his job.

As Smokey vanished, a bony man strode into the office. It was Mr Caleb Cuttle, the Mayor of Rattler Gulch.

"Sheriff," gasped Mr Cuttle, who was shaking with fright, "you've got to take care of this for me. It's the town funds. My life has been threatened by an outlaw, and I want this money kept in a safe place."

The Mayor dumped a tin box on the desk. It was crammed with dollar bills. Then he glared at Hawkeye.

"You ought to be out arresting the outlaw, not sitting here twiddling your thumbs!"

"Doggone it, there ain't a tougher lawman in the whole West than me," said Hawkeye warmly. "You just tell me the name of this guy who's been threatenin' you, Mayor, and I'll round him up."

"It's Leatherneck Morgan," said the Mayor grimly.

Hawkeye blinked uneasily. Leatherneck was one of the toughest outlaws in the district. He was so fast on the draw that nobody dared argue with him.

"He's over in the Silver Dollar Saloon," added the Mayor. "He's boasting that he's going to fill me with lead. and steal the town funds."

Hawkeye heaved himself to his feet trying to look as fierce as his cheery face would allow.

"I'll get him!" he snorted.

With the Mayor nervously following, Hawkeye strode to the Silver Dollar Saloon.

Pushing the swing doors open, the Sheriff ambled in.

Immediately there was a rattle of shots. Old Hawkeye came tumbling out faster than he had ever moved in his life. Leatherneck hadn't waited to ask his business. At the sight of the Sheriff's badge, the outlaw had whipped out his guns and blazed away.

"Jeepers," gurgled Hawkeye, taking off his hat to peer at the bullet holes in it.

Then he jammed his hat back on his head and pulled out his six-gun.

"You're not going in again, Sheriff?" gasped Mr Cuttle, quaking at the knees.

"Guess not," said Hawkeye loudly. "I'll plug him from here." And he pulled the trigger of the magic six-gun.

A puff of smoke came from his gun. It swirled under the door. Next moment there was a thud inside the saloon.

The Mayor nervously pushed open the door an inch and peered in. His jaw dropped in amazement. Leatherneck was sprawled on his back in the middle of the floor.

Smokey had stunned him with a bottle. But the Mayor didn't know that. He gaped at Hawkeye in awe.

"My goodness!" he stuttered. "How—how did you do it, Sheriff?"

"Aw, that big palooka ain't so tough," said Hawkeye modestly. "Not when he comes up against a guy like me. I'll clap him in jail."

He did so. But Mr Cuttle remained behind, peering in wonder at the door. He was trying to find the bullet hole!

Smokey Opens The Jail.

AFTER dinner, the Sheriff ambled along to the river for a spot of fishing. Having captured Leatherneck, he felt he had earned an afternoon off. He locked the town funds in his safe, made sure the jail door was properly bolted, and then closed his office for the day.

It was very pleasant sitting on the river bank in the sun, dangling a line over the water. There was only one snag. Hawkeye couldn't catch any fish!

He pulled out his gun and jerked the trigger. Smokey swirled before him.

"Say, Smokey, can't you do anything about this?" grumbled Hawkeye. "I want a bite."

Smokey blinked at the Sheriff in astonishment.

"That is a strange desire, O master! However, it shall be obeyed."

He vanished.

A moment later Hawkeye let out a wild shriek and leapt to his feet as if a bomb had exploded under him.

"Jumpin' coyotes!" he howled. "Something bit me!"

Smokey swirled before him, beaming.

"But is not that what you wished, O master?" he asked.

"I didn't mean that kind of bite," hooted the Sheriff. "I meant I wanted a fish."

Smokey vanished again. Then the Sheriff felt a sudden jerk on his line. He was nearly pulled into the river. He was amazed to see a huge head, spurting water, rise to the surface.

"A pesky whale!" gurgled Hawkeye, stunned.

He fired his gun wildly as he was dragged along the bank by the whale pulling on his line. Once more Smokey swirled before him.

"What is it now, O master?" asked the Genie, looking anxious. "Is not the fish big enough?"

"It's too big," spluttered Hawkeye. "Get it out of here!"

A moment later the whale had vanished. The Sheriff sat on the bank, mopping his brow as Smokey fluttered before him.

"Listen, son, you and I gotta have a talk," gulped the Sheriff. "When I ask for a fish, I don't mean a pesky whale—I just mean a kind of medium-sized tiddler."

Minnie has a super time—She's the BAD fairy in a pantomime!

Smokey beamed understandingly. He vanished. Shortly afterwards the river was swarming with small fish and for the rest of the afternoon Sheriff Hankey sat dangling his line happily.

Then he looked at his watch and sighed.

"It sure is a hard life being a Sheriff, pardner," he said gloomily to Smokey, who still fluttered around him. "Especially with a prisoner in jail. The trouble with prisoners is they gotta be fed—that's the law. I'll have to pack up fishin' and go make his tea."

Smokey waggled his ears in sympathy. He was anxious to do everything he could to help Hawkeye. Suddenly he vanished.

Hawkeye was just rolling up his line when Smokey came back.

"All is well, worthy master," beamed Smokey happily. "I have fixed everything."

"How?" asked Hawkeye, surprised.

"I opened the jail door," said Smokey. "The man has gone. You do not need to worry about his tea now."

Hawkeye nearly swooned. With a startled screech he tore off back to town. He clattered along the street and into his office at breakneck speed. But he was too late.

Not only was the jail door open, but so was the door of the safe. The prisoner had gone—and so had the town funds!

"Doggone my hide," croaked Hawkeye, clutching his forehead in horror. "And the Mayor will be along presently! He'll want to see the prisoner and he'll want me to hand over the funds. What am I gonna do?"

A Shock For Leatherneck.

IN desperation Hawkeye drew his gun and pulled the trigger. Smokey rose before him.

"Listen, you son of a gun, you got me into this jam, so it's up to you to get me out," gasped the Sheriff. "I could get fired for this. To start with, I gotta have a prisoner in my jail."

"Your wish shall be obeyed, master," said Smokey, and he vanished.

The Genie swirled out into the street. He picked on the first person he saw, and bounced a small kerb-stone on the man's head.

A couple of minutes later Smokey was swirling happily in front of Hawkeye again.

"Your command has been carried out, O master. There is a prisoner in your jail."

Hawkeye galloped to the cell door and peered in through the bars. His eyes bulged in horror. There was a prisoner there all right—sitting dazedly on the floor with a huge bump on his head, wondering what had hit him.

But Smokey had made a very unfortunate choice. The prisoner was Mr Caleb Cuttle, the Mayor!

"Jeepers!" gurgled Hawkeye.

"I'll have to try and find out where that crook went to," "I gotta have some explanation ready before I can let the Mayor out."

He started along the street, but he hadn't gone more than five yards when he felt the hard end of a gun muzzle in his back.

"Stick 'em up!" snarled a voice.

Hawkeye's hair stood on end when he heard that voice. There was no mistaking it. It belonged to Leatherneck Morgan.

Hawkeye's hand had dropped to the six-shooter at his hip. But he was too late. Leatherneck's fist shot out and snatched it.

"I'm warnin' you, don't try any tricks, Hankey," snapped the outlaw. "I'm leaving town at sundown, but not without gettin' even with you first!"

Leatherneck Morgan, digging his gun in Hawkeye's back, marched the Sheriff along to an old shack at the end of the town. Inside, on the table, was the cashbox containing the town funds.

"I'm sure gonna enjoy spending that," cackled Leatherneck.

Hawkeye was racking his brains, trying to think of a way of fetching Smokey to the scene. Suddenly a grin came over his face.

"You won't get away with this, Leatherneck," he said warningly. "I've got this place surrounded."

And he yelled through the window. "Come on out from behind that water-barrel, Shorty! Rush the place!"

Leatherneck flew to the window, whipping out his gun. He fired rapidly. Bang-bang!

"You were kidding," he snarled, as nothing moved. "There ain't anybody here at all."

"That's what you think," said Hawkeye. "How about those three over the fence?"

Leatherneck whirled round again. He blazed away at the fence. Bang-bang-bang!

"There's nobody there," he roared.

"I know," said Hawkeye. "They were too quick for you. They're right outside the door."

Leatherneck jerked up his gun. There was only one bang this time. He had fired his last bullet. Hawkeye knew because he had been counting them.

"All right, boys," he yelled. "You can rush the place now. His gun's empty."

"You ain't so smart as you think, Hankey," rapped the outlaw. "Mebbe MY gun's empty, but I've still got yours."

He raised the Sheriff's six-shooter and leaned out of the window and fired, which was exactly what Hawkeye wanted him to do.

Leatherneck had the shock of his life when Smokey appeared from the gun.

"Yes, O master?"

"Punch that guy, pardner," gasped Hawkeye.

Leatherneck never knew what happened after that, until he was sprawling in jail with a huge bump on his head.

In the meantime, having recovered the cashbox, Hawkeye freed the Mayor.

"I had to lock you up for your own safety, Mayor," he explained cheerfully. "That guy Leatherneck broke out of jail and was out to get you."

"You needn't have been quite so rough," snorted the Mayor. However, as Leatherneck was back in jail and the funds were safe, he was really quite happy.

In fact, Hawkeye was congratulated by the citizens for recapturing Leatherneck, although they couldn't quite make out how he had managed it. The bad men of the town were beginning to feel very worried indeed!

Next week—A Rodeo in town means thrills and fun—especially when Smokey comes out of the gun.

MINNIE THE MINX
YAH! MINNIE'S THE FAIRY IN THE SCHOOL PANTO!
YES, I'M A FAIRY—A BAD FAIRY!
BASH
THUD
SCHOOL
BOOMF
BONK
HURRY, MINNIE! DON'T DAWDLE!
LATER
OUT OF THE WAY, FAIRY-FACE!
CHIEF GNOME
NOW I'LL WAVE MY MAGIC WAND—UNDER FATTY'S FEET!
TRIP
HARK! IS THAT THE TWINKLING FEET OF MY DAINTY GNOMES I HEAR?
IN A HURRY, AREN'T YOU?
HAVE A SEAT, FATTY!
DAZE
OHO! SEE HIM JUMP!
OW!
GRAB THAT FAIRY!
BASH
FAIRIES CAN FLY—ONE—TWO—THREE—
EENY
MEENY
MINY
MO
GRR-RR
-GO!
R-R-RIP
I CAN'T SEE ANY WIRES HOLDING THAT FAIRY UP—CAN YOU?
FANCY BUMPIN' INTO YOU, DAD!
STOP WIPING YOUR FEET ON MY NOSE!
BONK!
BACK AT HOME—
I'LL USE THE MAGIC WAND TO SPANK MINNIE. MAYBE IT'LL TURN HER INTO A GOOD LITTLE GIRL.
SWISH
HERE WE GO AGAIN!

Pages 8 and 9 of The Beano *for January 23, 1954, with a comic adventure strip, drawn by Bill Holroyd, about a policeman who can, unknowingly, make his dreams come true.*

There's one more tiger in the zoo—We know who it is! DO YOU?

NOBBY THE ENCHANTED BOBBY
ZOO
PAY HERE
ZOO

1—"WHO? ME?" snorted P.C. Nobby Clark of the Mudbury Police. "I don't pay to come into the Zoo when I'm on patrol. Not likely!" Business was slack at the Zoo, and the worried man in the pay-box was trying to charge Nobby Clark. He needn't have bothered!

2—Nobby wasn't in a very good mood these days. He'd been promoted to Sergeant, then to Inspector—then—BANG! CRASH!—down he had come to being a constable again—all because of a Magic Spell! WHOOSH! SPLOSH! Suddenly a jet of water hit Nobby on the helmet!

3—Thump! Nobby's helmet landed on the ground, while another jet of water hit Nobby on the chin. The Zoo elephant had opened fire on Nobby with its trunk! Nobby raged and roared. But neither the keeper nor the elephant listened. In fact, the keeper was whispering in Jumbo's ear!

4—Jeb Jolson, the keeper, liked his little joke! At Jeb's command, the hefty tusker lifted its size twenty-five hoof and brought it down on our angry bobby's right toe. "Ow, mind my foot!" bawled Nobby. "That hurt me!"

5—Nobby couldn't say any more. HE DIDN'T HAVE TIME! There were metal toecaps on his boots, and the metal came from a Magic Lamp. The elephant had touched the magic metal. Flash! Kerwhizzle! The magic began.

6—"Whatizzit I've turned into now?" gasped Nobby. At least, that's what he tried to say. All that came from his lips was a growl. He was a tiger! The elephant backed away so quickly it sat down on the keeper, nearly flattening him.

7—"Hoi! Gerroff! I'm not an easy chair!" howled Jeb. Then he saw the tiger. "What's that doin' out of a cage?" he muttered. Spoiling for a fight, Nobby moved forward, growling—as if to say, "Try and put me in a cage, then!" The keeper didn't stay to argue.

8—SPLASH! That was Jeb landing in the seal-pond. He didn't think the tiger would follow there. But the seals must have thought Jeb wanted a game of foot-ball—they began to bounce him about on their heads. "Ho, ho!" purred Nobby. "I've paid him back, all right!"

9—Nobby was having fun—but he knew when to stop. If he stayed in the Zoo he would be locked up, and he didn't fancy pacing backwards and forwards in an iron cage. With a tremendous leap Nobby cleared the Zoo wall—only to land slap-bang into more trouble!

10—A squad of soldiers was marching past the Zoo. "An escaped tiger!" gulped the officer in charge. "It looks dangerous! Shoot first, men, and ask questions afterwards." In two ticks Nobby found himself before a firing squad.

11—"Somebody's going to have a tiger-skin rug if I don't do something!" thought Nobby. He looked pleadingly at the armed soldiers, but it didn't help. Then Nobby had a plan. He pointed urgently into the air with one paw.

12—It was an old trick, but it saved Nobby's bacon! Curiously, all the soldiers looked up. That was Nobby's chance. With a tremendous leap he soared high over the soldiers' heads. "Thank goodness I'm a smart tiger!" thought Nobby.

Of all the funny hiding-places!—Two thieves hide in mummy cases!

MUSEUM
JUNGLE GROUP
INDIAN JEWELLERY
INDIAN JEWELLERY
GARAGE
WANTED
WANTED

13—Before the soldiers could take aim at the Enchanted Bobby he was round a corner. "Double up, men!" roared the officer. "Follow that tiger!" But the window of the local museum was open. Nobby bounded in like a striped bullet!

14—"I'll bet I'm the first live tiger they've had here!" Nobby was thinking. "But there ought to be plenty of stuffed animals. People will think I'm one of them. Ah, there they are!" He joined a nearby group of stuffed tigers.

15—Nobby was quite prepared to stay with his stuffed pals until the hunt for him had died down. But he didn't get the chance. Two crooks had come quietly into the museum. In a flash they attacked the keeper, and gagged and bound him.

16—The keeper was lying on the floor when Nobby padded up to him and began to chew the keeper's bonds. That was a relief to the keeper. He thought Nobby was going to chew him up! Once free, he raced away to fetch the police.

17—Nobby decided to have the crooks all ready for collection when the police arrived. He gave a tigerish smile when he saw the crooks going into a room where Indian jewellery was displayed, and slunk in after them to deal with them.

18—The crooks were gloating over the jewellery. "Look at it, Mike!" said one. "All ours! Load up the case and we'll beat it!" He propped the attache case up behind him to fill it. Silly crook—he'd put the case on Nobby's back!

19—"This has gone on long enough!" thought Nobby. "I'd better let them know I'm here!" He did, too. He suddenly bounced the case into the air. Jewellery went flying in all directions. And the crooks saw Nobby at last.

20—"HELP! I'm off!" howled Mike. The crooks bolted. They hadn't the heart to face a tiger for all the jewellery in the world. They bolted towards two empty mummy cases and flung themselves inside, to get away from Nobby.

21—Then—zoom-fizzle-flash!—the tiger vanished. The magic spell was off! The crooks didn't know—they had slammed the lids of the mummy cases behind them. But P.C. Nobby Clark was quite himself again and ready to do his duty.

22—There was a handcart in the yard, and Nobby loaded the crooked "mummies" on to it. He was pushing the barrow along the road when policemen came charging up. The museum keeper had fetched them. "Everything's under control," chuckled Nobby.

23—Nobby opened the cases in the police station, and transferred the crooks to the cells. "Where's that tiger?" muttered Mike fearfully. "Now, now!" answered Nobby. "Don't you worry about tigers. We'll see you're kept where tigers can't touch you for a long time."

24—"Tell us how you did it, Clark!" pleaded the Chief Constable when he got over the shock. But Nobby kept mum. He couldn't spill the beans, could he? Still, the Chief Constable was so pleased he made Nobby a Sergeant—again! For a little while, anyway!

NEXT THURSDAY—*The latest spell is simply great. It gives our pal eight arms—yes, EIGHT!*

Pages 10 and 11 of The Beano *for January 23, 1954, a full spread – in addition to 'Roger the Dodger' and 'Little Plum', it features 'Kat and Kanary', drawn by Charlie Grigg and 'Matt Hatter', drawn by George Drysdale.*

ROGER THE DODGER
I'M OFF TO BUY PAINT! WHAT'S MORE—YOU WILL DO THE PAINTING!
I'VE GOT TO THINK FAST!
SLAM
WAIT, DAD! I'LL CARRY THE PAINT.
HE'S DODGING, I'LL BET!
IN THE PAINT SHOP
I'VE BROUGHT MY SON ALONG TO CARRY THE PAINT. BUT FIRST, I WANT YOU TO—WHISPER—WHISPER—
I SEE, SIR.
WATCH ME CARRY IT! HO, HO!
I'VE TRIPPED AND SPILLED THE PAINT. HO, HO!
FOOLED AGAIN, ROGER! THOSE CANS WERE FILLED WITH WATER. CLEAN UP THE MESS. I'VE GOT THE REAL PAINT!
AT HOME
YOUR FIRST JOB IS TO PAINT THE FLOOR OF THE KITCHENETTE—GET CRACKING!
BUT ROGER TRIES ANOTHER DODGE
DAD! DAD! I'M MAROONED IN A CORNER. NO MORE PAINTING FOR ME TODAY UNTIL THE FLOOR DRIES! SORRY, DAD!
BUT DAD FETCHES A BOATHOOK
OUT OF THERE, YOU! I'LL TEACH YOU DISCIPLINE!
DISTEMPER BEDROOM WALLS BY NUMBERS—COMMENCING AT WALL NUMBER ONE—
BE-E-E-GIN!
—AND AFTER THE BEDROOM
ON THE WORD OF COMMAND, YOU WILL BEND DOWN SMARTLY, PICK UP THE BRUSH, AND COMMENCE PAINTING THE GARDEN FENCE.
HEY, THERE, BOY! BACK ME INTO YOUR DRIVE, WILL YOU? I'VE A LOAD OF GRAVEL HERE FOR THE NEW PATHWAY.
HERE'S WHERE I GET RID OF THE FENCE. NO FENCE—NO PAINTING!
CRUNCH! CRASH! GRATE
OK, DRIVER! BACK YOU COME. THAT'S THE WAY. A LITTLE MORE TO THE RIGHT. HA, HA! THERE GOES THE FENCE!
5 MINUTES LATER
GOODNESS! THERE'S THE RAIN ON. NOW WHAT'S ROGER UP TO?
SMART BOY, ROGER! CLEVER OF YOU TAKING THE FENCE DOWN WHEN IT STARTED TO RAIN. YOU CAN PAINT IT INDOORS AND PUT IT UP WHEN IT STOPS RAINING.
LITTLE PLUM
—YOUR REDSKIN CHUM
JEALOUSY!
CHIEF MOOSE HUNTER
ME GET UM MOOSE, WITH ONE SHOT!
LATER
MOOSE CALL
LATER, IN LITTLE PLUM'S TROPHY HUT!
SEE? NOTHING TO IT!
ME GOT UM ALL FOUR. MOOSES WITH ONE SHOT. Little Plum
NOW WE HAVE CELEBRATION MEAL—OOPS! ME KNOCK UM PEPPER OFF TABLE.
AH-CHOO!
CHOO!
FAKE! CHEAT! YOU GOT UM MOOSES TO STICK UM HEADS THROUGH HOLES IN WALL!

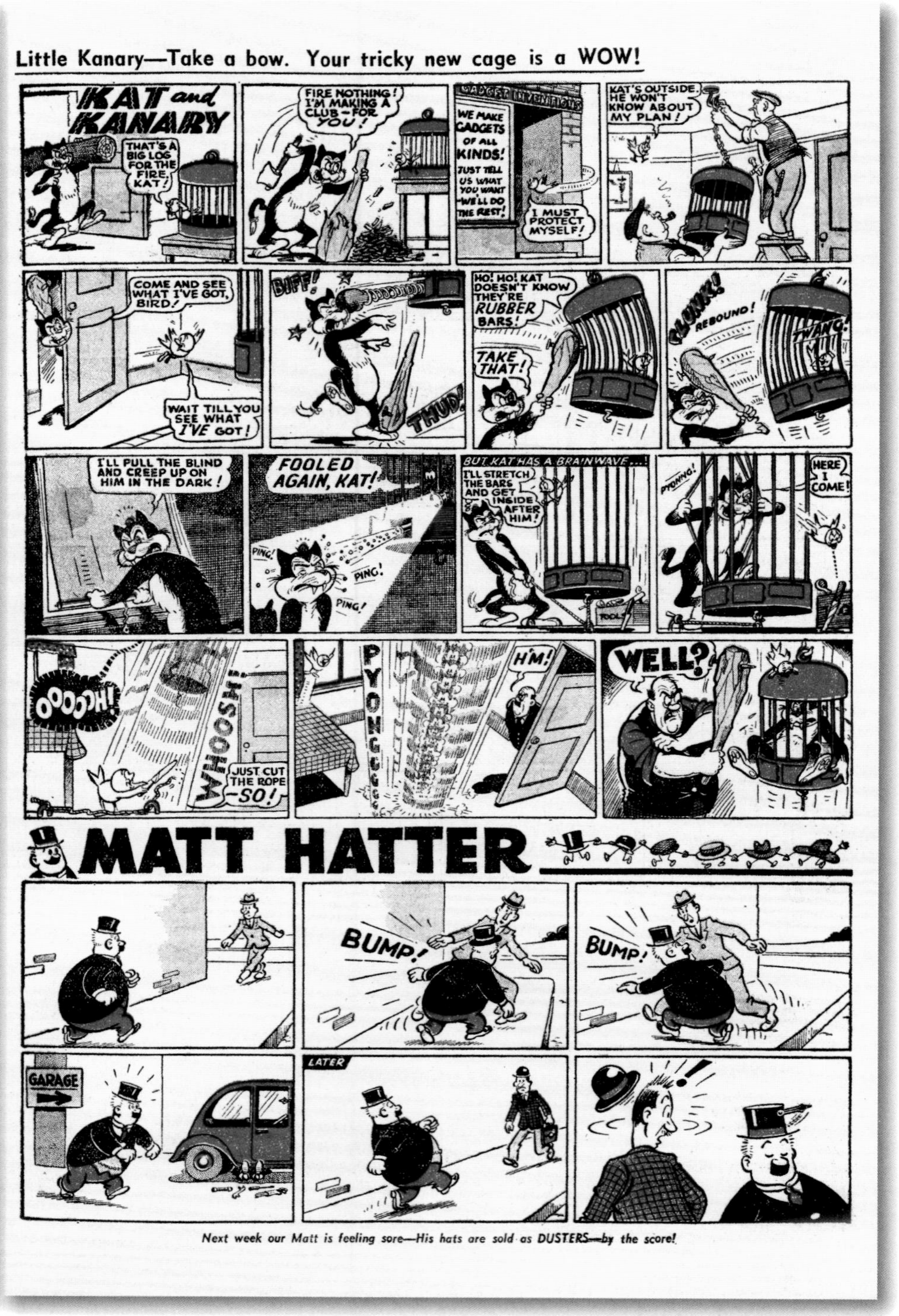
Little Kanary—Take a bow. Your tricky new cage is a WOW!
KAT and KANARY
THAT'S A BIG LOG FOR THE FIRE, KAT!
FIRE NOTHING! I'M MAKING A CLUB—FOR YOU!
WE MAKE GADGETS OF ALL KINDS! JUST TELL US WHAT YOU WANT—WE'LL DO THE REST!
I MUST PROTECT MYSELF!
KAT'S OUTSIDE. HE WON'T KNOW ABOUT MY PLAN!
COME AND SEE WHAT I'VE GOT, BIRD!
WAIT TILL YOU SEE WHAT I'VE GOT!
BIFF!
THUD!
HO! HO! KAT DOESN'T KNOW THEY'RE RUBBER BARS!
TAKE THAT!
REBOUND!
I'LL PULL THE BLIND AND CREEP UP ON HIM IN THE DARK!
FOOLED AGAIN, KAT!
PING!
PING!
PING!
BUT KAT HAS A BRAINWAVE...
I'LL STRETCH THE BARS AND GET INSIDE AFTER HIM!
HERE I COME!
OOOOH!
WHOOSH!
HM!
JUST CUT THE ROPE—SO!
WELL?
MATT HATTER
BUMP!
BUMP!
GARAGE
LATER
Next week our Matt is feeling sore—His hats are sold as DUSTERS—by the score!

Every Thursday
THE BEANO
January 23, 1954.
PANSY POTTER
THE STRONG-MAN'S DAUGHTER
GOSH! IT DOESN'T SOUND AS IF THE BOYS AND GIRLS ARE HAVING MUCH FUN SKATING.
HELP!
SCRAM!
SMACK!
SKATING
CLEAR OFF!
OUT OF THE WAY, SMALL FRY.
MY STRENGTH WILL HELP TO FIX THESE BULLIES.
YIPPEE! WE'RE THE BOYS! LET'S SHOW THESE KIDS SOME SPEED SKATING.
GOOD OLD PANSY!
HI! STOP PUSHING!
YOU'RE GOING FOR A TRIP!
WHOOSH
HURRAH!
THEY'LL HAVE A LONG WALK BACK HERE. HO, HO, HO!
BUT LATER
THERE SHE IS! WE'LL TEACH HER NOT TO PLAY TRICKS ON US!
THAT'S WHAT YOU THINK!
GRAB HER!
I'LL SKATE EXTRA FAST.
HO, HO, HO! I WENT SO FAST THE SUCTION MADE THEM HIT EACH OTHER.
UGH!
OUCH!
SUCK!
AH, A BROOM! I CAN USE THIS.
I'LL SWEEP AWAY THE RUBBISH.
WE'LL BE BACK WITH OUR BIG BROTHERS!
H'M! WE'LL NOT GET MUCH PEACE TO SKATE HERE.
I'LL DO A QUICK SPIN!
CRACK
HOI! PANSY! WHAT ARE YOU DOING?
FOLLOW ME!
SCHOOL
DANGER
THE BULLIES WILL NEVER LOOK FOR US IN THE SCHOOL GYM-SHED!
PRINTED AND PUBLISHED IN GREAT BRITAIN BY D. C. THOMSON & CO., LTD., AND JOHN LENG & CO., LTD, 12 FETTER LANE, FLEET STREET, LONDON, E.C.4. REGISTERED FOR TRANSMISSION BY CANADIAN MAGAZINE POST.

Page 12 of The Beano *for January 12, 1954, with 'Pansy Potter' still holding on to her position on the back cover.*

PADDY BRENNAN

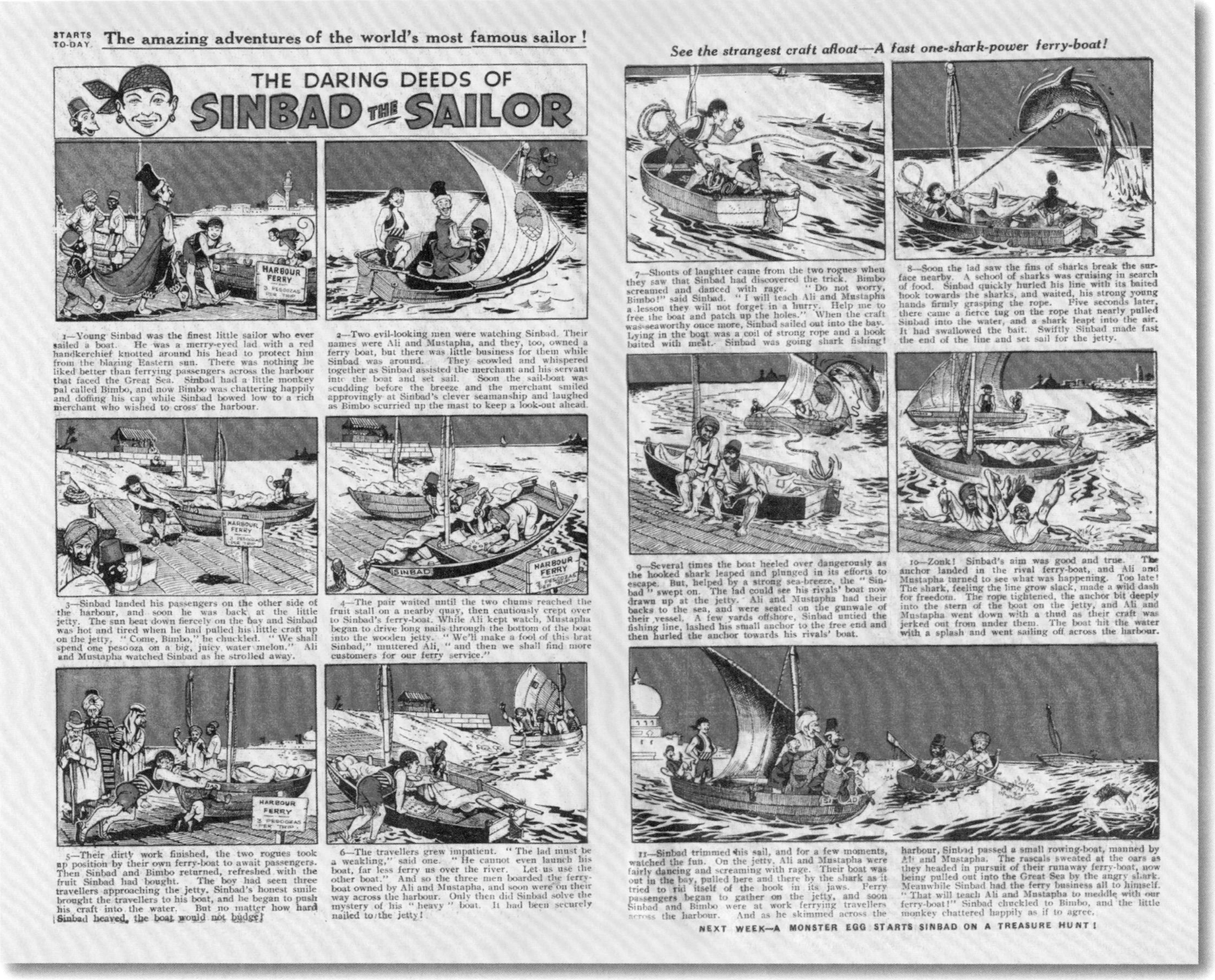
STARTS TO-DAY
The amazing adventures of the world's most famous sailor!
THE DARING DEEDS OF SINBAD THE SAILOR
HARBOUR FERRY 3 PESOOZAS PER TRIP
1—Young Sinbad was the finest little sailor who ever sailed a boat. He was a merry-eyed lad with a red handkerchief knotted around his head to protect him from the blazing Eastern sun. There was nothing he liked better than ferrying passengers across the harbour that faced the Great Sea. Sinbad had a little monkey pal called Bimbo, and now Bimbo was chattering happily and doffing his cap while Sinbad bowed low to a rich merchant who wished to cross the harbour.
2—Two evil-looking men were watching Sinbad. Their names were Ali and Mustapha, and they, too, owned a ferry boat, but there was little business for them while Sinbad was around. They scowled and whispered together as Sinbad assisted the merchant and his servant into the boat and set sail. Soon the sail-boat was scudding before the breeze and the merchant smiled approvingly at Sinbad's clever seamanship and laughed as Bimbo scurried up the mast to keep a look-out ahead.
HARBOUR FERRY
3—Sinbad landed his passengers on the other side of the harbour, and soon he was back at the little jetty. The sun beat down fiercely on the bay and Sinbad was hot and tired when he had pulled his little craft up on the jetty. "Come, Bimbo," he chuckled. "We shall spend one pesooza on a big, juicy water melon." Ali and Mustapha watched Sinbad as he strolled away.
SINBAD
HARBOUR FERRY 3 PESOOZAS PER TRIP
4—The pair waited until the two chums reached the fruit stall on a nearby quay, then cautiously crept over to Sinbad's ferry-boat. While Ali kept watch, Mustapha began to drive long nails through the bottom of the boat into the wooden jetty. "We'll make a fool of this brat Sinbad," muttered Ali, "and then we shall find more customers for our ferry service."
HARBOUR FERRY 3 PESOOZAS PER TRIP
5—Their dirty work finished, the two rogues took up position by their own ferry-boat to await passengers. Then Sinbad and Bimbo returned, refreshed with the fruit Sinbad had bought. The boy had seen three travellers approaching the jetty. Sinbad's honest smile brought the travellers to his boat, and he began to push his craft into the water. But no matter how hard Sinbad heaved, the boat would not budge!
6—The travellers grew impatient. "The lad must be a weakling," said one. "He cannot even launch his boat, far less ferry us over the river. Let us use the other boat." And so the three men boarded the ferry-boat owned by Ali and Mustapha, and soon were on their way across the harbour. Only then did Sinbad solve the mystery of his "heavy" boat. It had been securely nailed to the jetty!
See the strangest craft afloat—A fast one-shark-power ferry-boat!
7—Shouts of laughter came from the two rogues when they saw that Sinbad had discovered the trick. Bimbo screamed and danced with rage. "Do not worry, Bimbo!" said Sinbad. "I will teach Ali and Mustapha a lesson they will not forget in a hurry. Help me to free the boat and patch up the holes." When the craft was seaworthy once more, Sinbad sailed out into the bay. Lying in the boat was a coil of strong rope and a hook baited with meat. Sinbad was going shark fishing!
8—Soon the lad saw the fins of sharks break the surface nearby. A school of sharks was cruising in search of food. Sinbad quickly hurled his line with its baited hook towards the sharks, and waited, his strong young hands firmly grasping the rope. Five seconds later, there came a fierce tug on the rope that nearly pulled Sinbad into the water, and a shark leapt into the air. It had swallowed the bait. Swiftly Sinbad made fast the end of the line and set sail for the jetty.
9—Several times the boat heeled over dangerously as the hooked shark leaped and plunged in its efforts to escape. But, helped by a strong sea-breeze, the "Sinbad" swept on. The lad could see his rivals' boat now drawn up at the jetty. Ali and Mustapha had their backs to the sea, and were seated on the gunwale of their vessel. A few yards offshore, Sinbad untied the fishing line, lashed his small anchor to the free end and then hurled the anchor towards his rivals' boat.
10—Zonk! Sinbad's aim was good and true. The anchor landed in the rival ferry-boat, and Ali and Mustapha turned to see what was happening. Too late! The shark, feeling the line grow slack, made a wild dash for freedom. The rope tightened, the anchor bit deeply into the stern of the boat on the jetty, and Ali and Mustapha went down with a thud as their craft was jerked out from under them. The boat hit the water with a splash and went sailing off across the harbour.
11—Sinbad trimmed his sail, and for a few moments, watched the fun. On the jetty, Ali and Mustapha were fairly dancing and screaming with rage. Their boat was out in the bay, pulled here and there by the shark as it tried to rid itself of the hook in its jaws. Ferry passengers began to gather on the jetty, and soon Sinbad and Bimbo were at work ferrying travellers across the harbour. And as he skimmed across the harbour, Sinbad passed a small rowing-boat, manned by Ali and Mustapha. The rascals sweated at the oars as they headed in pursuit of their runaway ferry-boat, now being pulled out into the Great Sea by the angry shark. Meanwhile Sinbad had the ferry business all to himself. "That will teach Ali and Mustapha to meddle with our ferry-boat!" Sinbad chuckled to Bimbo, and the little monkey chattered happily as if to agree.
NEXT WEEK—A MONSTER EGG STARTS SINBAD ON A TREASURE HUNT!

Adventure picture-strips had been an integral part of *The Beano* from its launch. Readers had been enthralled by such stories as 'Deep-Sea Danny's Iron Fish' and 'The Shipwrecked Circus', drawn by a team of talented artists of whom Dudley Watkins is the best known. But, in the opinion of many, the finest of all the artists who drew these adventure stories was Paddy Brennan. Paddy was born in Ireland and had his first work published while still in his teens. He worked for several minor publishers before joining D. C. Thomson in 1949. Paddy's first work for *The Beano* was 'Sinbad the Sailor', which started in March 1950. Even then he showed he was a master of detail and composition.

'General Jumbo' came to life in September 1953 with Paddy providing the drawings. The first story is reproduced in full below, telling how young Alfie Johnson became General Jumbo, with his radio-controlled army. The story appeared regularly until 1975, by then the last adventure strip in *The Beano*.

Meet the world's youngest Commander-in-Chief!
GENERAL JUMBO
PRIVATE KEEP OUT
KEEP OUT PRIVATE
1—"Pass the ball, Jumbo! Don't keep it to yourself!" Three young schoolboys were playing football in a quiet street on the outskirts of Dinchester. From the noise the lads were making you'd have thought that the Cup Final was being played. Alfie Johnson and his two pals, Jim Blake and Fred Peters, were putting in some practice for the football season. Alfie was twelve years old, a cheery, likeable lad and because of his plump, hefty figure, his chums called him Jumbo. Biff! Jumbo's sturdy right leg suddenly sent the battered old ball soaring. Then his big grin gave way to a groan. The ball had sailed over a high wall.
2—"Crumbs!" moaned Jim. "More crumbs!" wailed Fred. "That's the last we've seen of the old ball. Look at these notices!" Along the wall were fixed several boards labelled "Private," "Keep Out," "No Admittance." The boys knew that beyond the wall stood a big grey house in which a certain Professor Carter lived. The boys had never seen the Professor, for he rarely left the grounds. In fact, Professor Carter was a bit of a mystery. Jumbo hitched up his trousers. "I'm going to get that ball," he told his pals. "Give me a leg up, you two." Jim and Fred helped their chum to the top of the wall.
3—Immediately Jumbo spotted the ball on a lawn where it had come to rest. "This is too easy!" he called to his pals, then dropped to the ground. Swiftly Jumbo ran to the ball and bent to pick it up. Then an amazing thing happened. A jet-plane, its engines whining, came swooping towards him. Maybe there's nothing very amazing about a jet-plane—but this one was no bigger than a crow, and perfect in every detail.
4—Jumbo heard the noise and looked skywards, expecting to see an R.A.F. machine looping the loop. Instead, it was Jumbo who looped the loop. The little plane swooped between his legs, the wings striking him a glancing blow. Jumbo fell back with a thud that shook the lawn. Then he got a bigger shock than ever. A squad of soldiers, each about a foot high, were charging towards him! Poor Jumbo could scarcely believe his eyes.
5—"I'm dreaming!" gasped the startled boy. "Either that or I'm a giant." The soldiers were still advancing towards him with jerky movements. What's more, tiny army tanks were rumbling from a small doorway in a nearby building. "Ow!" Jumbo gave a yell as one of the soldiers pointed his tiny gun and fired a volley of peas at Jumbo's nose. The boy was too alarmed to see a face watching him from a window in the building.
6—That face belonged to Professor Carter and he chuckled as he stepped outside. Strapped to his wrist was a mysterious gadget with a small aerial fixed to it. "You are a prisoner of war!" he boomed at Jumbo, but there was a merry twinkle in his eye. Jumbo's mouth gaped open. He was just about to stutter something when the jet-plane, which had been circling overhead, suddenly zoomed over the high garden wall.
The march-past of Jumbo's midget army!
KEEP OUT
SUCK'EMS
7—"Goodness gracious!" gasped the Professor. "It's out of control!" He forgot all about Jumbo surrounded by tiny soldiers and ran to a door in the wall and raced outside. Jumbo looked at the soldiers. Now that the Prof. was away, they seemed to have gone lifeless. Jumbo gingerly stepped over them and ran to the door. The Prof. was in the middle of the street picking up his plane, heedless of the approach of a big double-decker bus!
8—The bus was coming round a corner of the street and as the driver saw the Professor he jammed on his brakes. But Jumbo knew the vehicle would never stop in time. "Look out, sir!" he yelled and fairly threw himself forward. With a dive that would have made a star goalkeeper green with envy, Jumbo hurled the Professor out of the way of the bus. The Prof. rolled on the grass verge, and as Jumbo sprawled on the street the bus skidded past!
9—The bus drew to a halt and the driver came running over. "Everything all right?" he gasped. "Close shave, that was. Couldn't stop in time. You're a plucky young fellow, son." After making sure no harm was done, the driver set off again. The Professor was sitting on the verge staring up at Jumbo. "It was stupid of me not to see that bus," he said shakily. "You did a very brave thing, my boy. I want to shake your hand."
10—"It was nothing, sir——" began Jumbo, but the Professor was not listening. A very thoughtful look had come into his face. "I am going to reward you, Jumbo," he said after asking the boy's name. "Come with me." Jumbo followed the Professor through the garden and into the building. It was a kind of workshop. Jumbo gasped. On shelves and in boxes all around the workshop were lines of soldiers, tanks, lorries, ships and planes!
11—Jumbo stared in astonishment as the Professor pressed some buttons on the strange gadget strapped to his wrist. Immediately the soldiers began to march, the tanks began to move, and the planes took off. "Gosh!" gurgled Jumbo. "I will let you into my secret," chuckled the Professor. "I made all these things. They are models, of course, and I can control them by radio with this control panel on my wrist. It has taken me many years of work. But now I am ready to put all my models through their paces. Would you like to be my assistant, Jumbo?" "WOULD I?" yelled Jumbo, and gave a jump of joy. Soon the Professor was teaching Jumbo how to use the amazing control panel and after a few lessons he was nearly an expert. And the first thing the Prof. made him do was have a march-past of all the soldiers and a fly-past of all the aircraft. "It was the greatest day in Jumbo's life. He was a General now, in charge of an army, a navy, and an air force as well. A great new adventure had begun!
NEXT THURSDAY—Jumbo traps a crook when he sends his navy out to sea.

Caught in the thick of a desert sand-storm!
LONGLEGS
THE DESERT WILD BOY

His figure work was exceptional and he flourished throughout the 1950s, producing hundreds of pages of top quality artwork for stories such as 'General Jumbo', 'Longlegs the Desert Wild Boy' and 'Red Rory of the Eagles'.

Strangely, for all his brilliance, Paddy lacked belief in his own abilities. Correspondence between Paddy and R. D. Low showed the latter doing his best to bolster Paddy's confidence. This at a time in the mid 1950s when Paddy was probably at his peak. Paddy remained a freelance artist and divided his time between Dublin and London. Described as urbane and cosmopolitan, Paddy was a lover of the theatre.

'Red Rory of the Eagles' started as an adventure story in 1951 with just an illustrated header (provided by Jack Glass). Rory's adventures in the Highlands of Scotland with his two eagles, Flame and Fury, caught the imagination of readers, and in 1952 'Red Rory' became an adventure strip, illustrated by Paddy Brennan. His first strip, from June 7, 1952 is shown below.

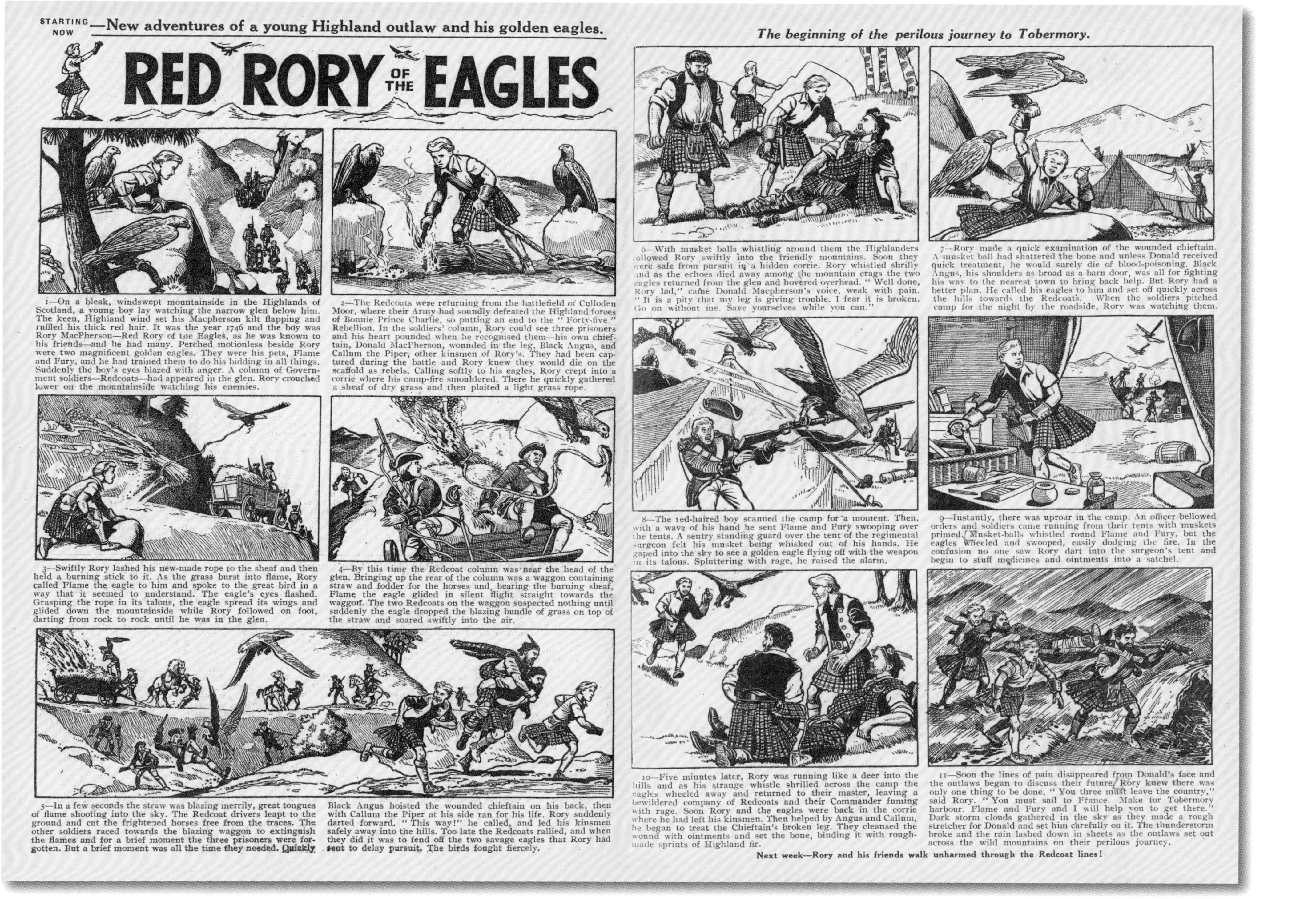
STARTING NOW —New adventures of a young Highland outlaw and his golden eagles.
RED RORY OF THE EAGLES
The beginning of the perilous journey to Tobermory.
1—On a bleak, windswept mountainside in the Highlands of Scotland, a young boy lay watching the narrow glen below him. The keen, Highland wind set his Macpherson kilt flapping and ruffled his thick red hair. It was the year 1746 and the boy was Rory MacPherson—Red Rory of the Eagles, as he was known to his friends—and he had many. Perched motionless beside Rory were two magnificent golden eagles. They were his pets, Flame and Fury, and he had trained them to do his bidding in all things. Suddenly the boy's eyes blazed with anger. A column of Government soldiers—Redcoats—had appeared in the glen. Rory crouched lower on the mountainside watching his enemies.
2—The Redcoats were returning from the battlefield of Culloden Moor, where their Army had soundly defeated the Highland forces of Bonnie Prince Charlie, so putting an end to the "Forty-five" Rebellion. In the soldiers' column, Rory could see three prisoners and his heart pounded when he recognised them—his own chieftain, Donald MacPherson, wounded in the leg, Black Angus, and Callum the Piper, other kinsmen of Rory's. They had been captured during the battle and Rory knew they would die on the scaffold as rebels. Calling softly to his eagles, Rory crept into a corrie where his camp-fire smouldered. There he quickly gathered a sheaf of dry grass and then plaited a light grass rope.
3—Swiftly Rory lashed his new-made rope to the sheaf and then held a burning stick to it. As the grass burst into flame, Rory called Flame the eagle to him and spoke to the great bird in a way that it seemed to understand. The eagle's eyes flashed. Grasping the rope in its talons, the eagle spread its wings and glided down the mountainside while Rory followed on foot, darting from rock to rock until he was in the glen.
4—By this time the Redcoat column was near the head of the glen. Bringing up the rear of the column was a waggon containing straw and fodder for the horses and, bearing the burning sheaf, Flame the eagle glided in silent flight straight towards the waggon. The two Redcoats on the waggon suspected nothing until suddenly the eagle dropped the blazing bundle of grass on top of the straw and soared swiftly into the air.
5—In a few seconds the straw was blazing merrily, great tongues of flame shooting into the sky. The Redcoat drivers leapt to the ground and cut the frightened horses free from the traces. The other soldiers raced towards the blazing waggon to extinguish the flames and for a brief moment the three prisoners were forgotten. But a brief moment was all the time they needed. Quickly Black Angus hoisted the wounded chieftain on his back, then with Callum the Piper at his side ran for his life. Rory suddenly darted forward. "This way!" he called, and led his kinsmen safely away into the hills. Too late the Redcoats rallied, and when they did it was to fend off the two savage eagles that Rory had sent to delay pursuit. The birds fought fiercely.
6—With musket balls whistling around them the Highlanders followed Rory swiftly into the friendly mountains. Soon they were safe from pursuit in a hidden corrie. Rory whistled shrilly and as the echoes died away among the mountain crags the two eagles returned from the glen and hovered overhead. "Well done, Rory lad," came Donald Macpherson's voice, weak with pain. "It is a pity that my leg is giving trouble. I fear it is broken. Go on without me. Save yourselves while you can."
7—Rory made a quick examination of the wounded chieftain. A musket ball had shattered the bone and unless Donald received quick treatment, he would surely die of blood-poisoning. Black Angus, his shoulders as broad as a barn door, was all for fighting his way to the nearest town to bring back help. But Rory had a better plan. He called his eagles to him and set off quickly across the hills towards the Redcoats. When the soldiers pitched camp for the night by the roadside, Rory was watching them.
8—The red-haired boy scanned the camp for a moment. Then, with a wave of his hand he sent Flame and Fury swooping over the tents. A sentry standing guard over the tent of the regimental surgeon felt his musket being whisked out of his hands. He gaped into the sky to see a golden eagle flying off with the weapon in its talons. Spluttering with rage, he raised the alarm.
9—Instantly, there was uproar in the camp. An officer bellowed orders and soldiers came running from their tents with muskets primed. Musket-balls whistled round Flame and Fury, but the eagles wheeled and swooped, easily dodging the fire. In the confusion no one saw Rory dart into the surgeon's tent and begin to stuff medicines and ointments into a satchel.
10—Five minutes later, Rory was running like a deer into the hills and as his strange whistle shrilled across the camp the eagles wheeled away and returned to their master, leaving a bewildered company of Redcoats and their Commander fuming with rage. Soon Rory and the eagles were back in the corrie where he had left his kinsmen. Then helped by Angus and Callum, he began to treat the Chieftain's broken leg. They cleansed the wound with ointments and set the bone, binding it with rough-made sprints of Highland fir.
11—Soon the lines of pain disappeared from Donald's face and the outlaws began to discuss their future. Rory knew there was only one thing to be done. "You three must leave the country," said Rory. "You must sail to France. Make for Tobermory harbour. Flame and Fury and I will help you to get there." Dark storm clouds gathered in the sky as they made a rough stretcher for Donald and set him carefully on it. The thunderstorm broke and the rain lashed down in sheets as the outlaws set out across the wild mountains on their perilous journey.
Next week—Rory and his friends walk unharmed through the Redcoat lines!

BEANO BOOK 1956

Christmas was approaching and in hundreds of thousands of homes up and down the country *Beano* readers were eagerly anticipating their annual treat – *The Beano Book.* There was no better example of this than the book which went on sale for Christmas 1955. It was a magical mixture of comic strips, picture stories and prose stories featuring nearly all of the characters that made *The Beano* great. Here is the original artwork for some of those classic pages.

ME UM PAINTER!
PAINT
UM WAR-PAINTIN' IS HEAP FUNNY!
SPLUP
UM NET FOR STOPPING ENEMIES FROM RUNNING BETWEEN UM LEGS
NOW BRAVES GO ON WARPATH!
THANKS, PLUM! —WAHOO!
YIPPEE! WE GO BEAT UP UM PUTTYFOOT TRIBE!
YAHOO!
PAINT
NOW ME PAINT UM FENCE!
?
LATER
BOO-HOO! I WANT UM MOTHER —THEY HIT ME!
OOH! HERE COME UM BRAVES WITH UM PUTTYFOOT BRAVES CHASIN' UM!
HELP!
UM HELP!
PAINT
PLEASE, PLUM—YOU HEAP CRAFTY—THINK UP UM CRAFTY TRICK TO SAVE US—QUICK!
ME HIDE BEHIND YOU, LITTLE RUNNIN' MOOSE!
PAINT
?
PLOP
GURR! WE GET STUCK TO WET PAINT ON UM FENCE!
UM MISSED!
SULK
THEY RUN OUT OF UM TOMAHAWKS—NOW ME FIT UM WHEELS ON UM FENCE!
TOOL KIT
GOOD OL' PLUM!
NOW ME PUSH 'EM HOME!

Roger the Dodger
2 MILES
DAD'S TAKING ROGER FOR A TWO-MILE HIKE
THAT'S WHAT DAD THINKS!
GLUE
NAILS
HEY! TAKE IT EASY, ROGER. WE'VE TWO MILES TO GO YET!
I'LL PUSH ON AHEAD, DAD.
ROUND THE BEND
THIS WOOD AND CARDBOARD MILESTONE WILL MAKE DAD THINK WE'VE WALKED A MILE.
PUFF
1 MILE
SO THIS IS WHAT ROGER WAS MAKING!
GASP
HERE HE COMES.
SURELY WE HAVEN'T WALKED A MILE ALREADY!
THERE'S THE PROOF, DAD!
1 MILE
HO! HO! IT WORKED. NOW TO RACE ROUND THE NEXT BEND, AND REPEAT THE DODGE!
FUNNY! IT ONLY SEEMED LIKE A FEW YARDS TO ME.
ROUND THE NEXT BEND
ALL I DO IS CHALK "2 MILES" ON THE DUMMY MILESTONE AND —!! GOSH! A REAL ONE!
PUFF
1 MILE
BETTER PULL THIS UP, AND THROW IT IN THE BUSHES BEFORE DAD SEES IT— PHEW— IT'S SOME WEIGHT!
PUFF
1 MILE
(THE DUMMY)
GOSH! HE'S HERE ALREADY! I'LL HAVE TO HIDE THE REAL MILESTONE IN MY RUCKSACK AND SET UP THE DUMMY ONE, QUICK.
TEE-TUM TI-TA
1 MILE
(DUMMY)
GOODNESS! WE'VE WALKED ANOTHER MILE, ROGER. WE OUGHT TO GO HOME NOW!
(GASP) Y-Y-YES, DAD.
2 MILES
HALF AN HOUR LATER—
PUFF—NOW I'M STUCK WITH THE REAL MILESTONE FOR THE REST OF THE HIKE!
I'M ENJOYING THIS!
HOME AT LAST, ROGER. NOW FOR A —!! GOSH! —HEY! MUM!
WHOOSH
CRASH
AH! NO WONDER HE COLLAPSED. LOOK AT THIS BIG, HEAVY MILESTONE HE'S BEEN CARRYING!
?
WHAT DID YOU SAY IT WAS, DOCTOR—DODGERITIS?
HE'LL BE ALL RIGHT AGAIN IN A MINUTE.

LITTLE PLUM
YOUR REDSKIN CHUM
ME MAKE YOU TRIBAL PEACEMAKER WHILE ME AWAY~ IF THERE'S ONE BLACK EYE IN UM TRIBE WHEN I GET BACK~ME GIVE YOU UM BIG ROW!
CHIEF
BETTER STOP THIS BEFORE THEY START FIGHTIN'.
GNASH
NATTER! NATTER! NATTER!
GURR!
ME NIP ROUND HEAP QUICK~GIVE EVERYBODY UM BIG BAR OF TOFFEE!
TOFFEE!
MUNCH
MUNCH
SPEECHLESS!
UM TOFFEE STUCK UM TEETH TOGETHER~NOW THEY CAN'T ARGUE!
BUT LATER–
UM BRAVES HAVE UM TOOTHACHE NOW WITH UM TOFFEE, AND WANT UM BIG FIGHT AGAIN. ME BETTER CARVE UM PEACE PIPE WITH UMPTEEN SPOUTS!
GURR!
PUFF-PUFF
PUFF-PUFF
THEY ALL FRIENDLY NOW~ LITTLE PLUM VERY SMART!
OOH! SMOKE'S GETTING HEAP THICK!
THUD!
BANG!
CRASH!
OUCH!
WALLOP!
WHAT'S GOING ON IN THERE?
HONEST, CHIEF, THEY ALL BUMPED INTO TOTEM POLES IN UM FOG AN' GOT UM BLACK EYES!
NO LIES! THERE HASN'T BEEN ANY FOG! YOU'VE BEEN LETTING 'EM FIGHT!
CHIEF

GO STICK UM NOTICE ON TOP OF UM DANGEROUS CLIFF~UM BRAVES HAVE BEEN FALLING OVER!
WHAT UM LIFE! UM CHIEF KEEPS LITTLE PLUM BUSY!
DANGEROUS CLIFF
SOME DAY LITTLE PLUM'S GONNA GIVE UM CHIEF UM BIG DROP!
ME ON UM ISLAND IN UM MID-AIR!
CATCH
THEN UM BEAR FELL OVER, TOO!
GRAB
AHA! I'LL GRAB THIS YOUNG TREE STICKING OUT.
SNAP
UM BEAR'S WEIGHT MADE UM BRANCH SNAP
WHEN WE REACH THE GROUND, I'M GONNA HAVE PLUM FOR DINNER!
BEAR CAUGHT ON UM OTHER TREE!
DANGEROUS CLIFF
THUD
BOOMF!
DAZE
PLUM PUT UM NOTICE IN WRONG PLACE. ME PUT UM IN PROPER PLACE!
BUT LOOK WHAT HAPPENED!
ME GOT FUNNY SINKING FEELING!
RUMBLE
WE WON'T NEED UM NOTICE NOW~UM CHIEF FELL OVER AND REMOVED UM DANGEROUS CLIFF!
DONG
PLUM'S HIDEY HOLE

For those who liked their ribs tickled there were 'Biffo', 'Lord Snooty', 'Dennis', 'Minnie', 'Little Plum', 'Roger' and that irrepressible bunch from Bash Street, all showcasing the brilliance of Davey Law, Leo Baxendale, Dudley Watkins and Ken Reid. There were also contributions from James Clark and Charles Grigg. The cover was drawn by James Crighton, who illustrated every *Beano Book* from 1942 to 1960 with the exception of 1951.

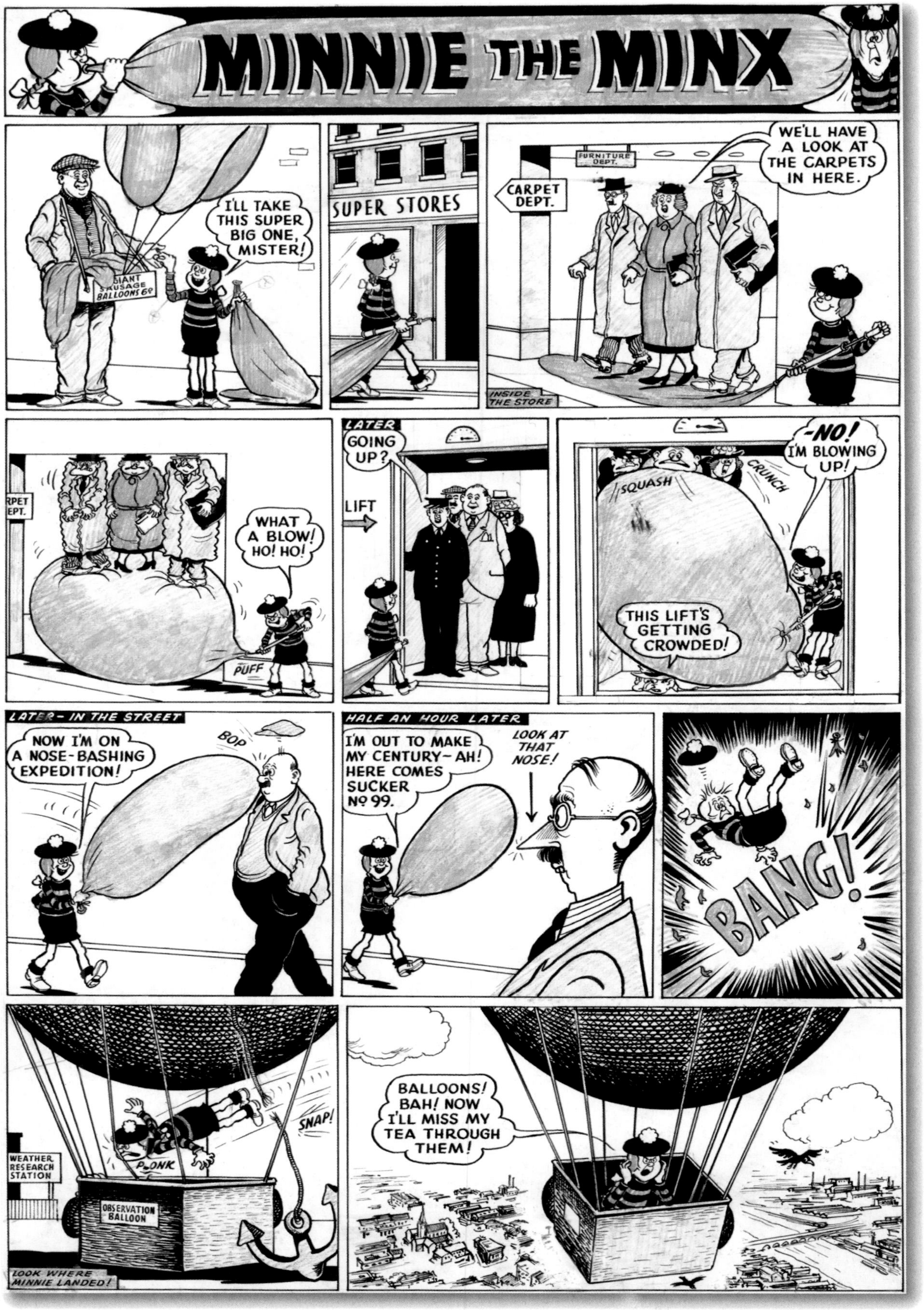
MINNIE THE MINX
I'LL TAKE THIS SUPER BIG ONE, MISTER!
GIANT SAUSAGE BALLOONS 6d
SUPER STORES
FURNITURE DEPT.
CARPET DEPT.
WE'LL HAVE A LOOK AT THE CARPETS IN HERE.
INSIDE THE STORE
WHAT A BLOW! HO! HO!
PUFF
LATER
GOING UP?
LIFT
-NO! I'M BLOWING UP!
SQUASH
CRUNCH
THIS LIFT'S GETTING CROWDED!
LATER – IN THE STREET
NOW I'M ON A NOSE-BASHING EXPEDITION!
BOP
HALF AN HOUR LATER
I'M OUT TO MAKE MY CENTURY – AH! HERE COMES SUCKER Nº 99.
LOOK AT THAT NOSE!
BANG!
WEATHER RESEARCH STATION
PLONK
SNAP!
OBSERVATION BALLOON
LOOK WHERE MINNIE LANDED!
BALLOONS! BAH! NOW I'LL MISS MY TEA THROUGH THEM!

Lovers of adventure stories could thrill to the exploits of 'Red Rory', 'General Jumbo', 'The Iron Fish', 'The Shipwrecked Circus' and 'The Clockwork Horse', superbly illustrated by Paddy Brennan, Bill Holroyd, Ken Hunter, Jack Glass and James Walker. Ken Reid and Leo Baxendale were better known as comic strip artists but here they provided the illustrations for several of the prose stories, including the intriguingly named 'The Daring Deeds of a Cabbage Muncher' about a fearless rabbit who sets out to rescue his sister.

The price of this collection of comic delights? A mere six shillings. Only 30p in today's money.

MINNIE the MINX
CRACK
DEAR ME! MISSED!
CRASH
DID YOU BREAK THAT WINDOW, LITTLE GIRL?
WHO? ME?
THEN WHAT ARE THOSE STONES DOING IN YOUR HAND?
HOW STRANGE! I WONDER HOW THEY GOT THERE?
I'LL TAKE DOWN YOUR NAME AND ADDRESS – SHE'S GONE!
GONE
JAS. SMITH MARKET GARDENER
BETTER THROW THESE STONES AWAY – GOSH, I'VE BROKEN MORE PANES!
ZOOOOM
CRASH
SNORE
BAH – I'M LOCKED OUT AN' I CAN HEAR DAD HAVIN' A NAP IN THE BEDROOM – I'LL THROW THIS GRAVEL AT THE WINDOW TO WAKEN HIM!
MINNIE!
CRASH
LATER
IN YOU GO FOR YOUR SINGING LESSON – THAT'LL STOP YOU BREAKING WINDOWS FOR HALF AN HOUR!
MUTTER MUTTER
BUT AT THE SINGING LESSON –
STOPPIT! THAT HIGH NOTE'S CRACKING ALL MY WINDOWS!
SPLINTER
ON THE WAY BACK HOME
CRACK
CRASH
TINKLE
CRASH
CRACK
SNOOSH
DAIRY
ALL MY MILK BOTTLES HAVE CRACKED!
CRASH
BAH! – NOW SHE'S CRYING ON THAT HIGH NOTE – AND STILL BREAKING WINDOWS!
WHACK

START
DENNIS the MENACE
FINISH
SCHOOL SPORT
I'VE ENTERED FOR THE 100 YARDS RACE, AND I'M GONNA WIN IT~ WALKIN'!
R-RIP!
ALL I HAVE TO DO IS TIE THIS ELASTIC ROPE BETWEEN THE WINNIN' POSTS!
THE 100 YDS R
THEY'RE OFF! - THE MUGS!
WHAT'S ALL THE HURRY, FELLAS?
TAKE YOUR TIME, DENNIS LAD. YOU'LL PASS THOSE MUGS ON THEIR WAY BACK!
PUFF!
GASP!
DENNIS IS 50 YDS BEHIND ~ STILL WALKING!
BUT
WHERE ARE YOU GOIN', BOYS? THIS AIN'T THE HIGH JUMP!
PYONNG!
SNIP!
THE ONE WHO BREAKS THE TAPE IS THE WINNER. I WIN!
HERE'S YOUR PRIZE, DENNIS!
TA VERY MUCH! I DESERVE IT - AFTER WALKIN' ALL THAT DISTANCE!
A STRAP! I CAN'T DO ANYTHING WITH THIS!
NO, BUT I CAN, DENNIS. HOLD OUT YOUR HAND. THIS IS FOR WINNING THE RACE THE WRONG WAY!
WELL, IT'S A CHANGE FROM DAD'S SLIPPER!

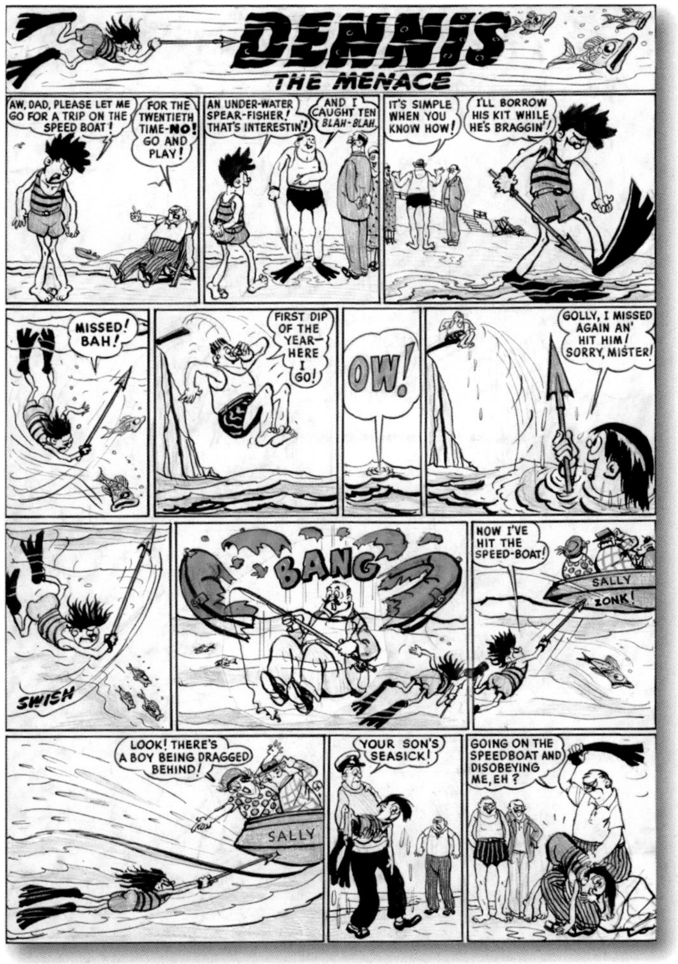
DENNIS THE MENACE
AW, DAD, PLEASE LET ME GO FOR A TRIP ON THE SPEED BOAT!
FOR THE TWENTIETH TIME-NO! GO AND PLAY!
AN UNDER-WATER SPEAR-FISHER! THAT'S INTERESTIN'!
AND I CAUGHT TEN BLAH-BLAH.
IT'S SIMPLE WHEN YOU KNOW HOW!
I'LL BORROW HIS KIT WHILE HE'S BRAGGIN'!
MISSED! BAH!
FIRST DIP OF THE YEAR- HERE I GO!
OW!
GOLLY, I MISSED AGAIN AN' HIT HIM! SORRY, MISTER!
SWISH
BANG
NOW I'VE HIT THE SPEED-BOAT!
SALLY
ZONK!
LOOK! THERE'S A BOY BEING DRAGGED BEHIND!
SALLY
YOUR SON'S SEASICK!
GOING ON THE SPEEDBOAT AND DISOBEYING ME, EH?

HE! HE! HE! I'VE GOT ALL THE DOOR KEYS- INCLUDING DAD'S!
ONE HOUR LATER
DENNIS!
LOOK AT 'EM! THE STAMPEDE OF ANGRY FATHERS!

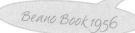

KEN HUNTER

During the early fifties Yorkshire artist Ken Hunter contributed in no small way to *The Beano*, both the weekly and the annual. He started illustrating the Wee Davie series in 1952 with 'Wee Davie and the Great Big Giant'. A second series followed in 1953, 'Wee Davie – the Great Big Game Hunter'.

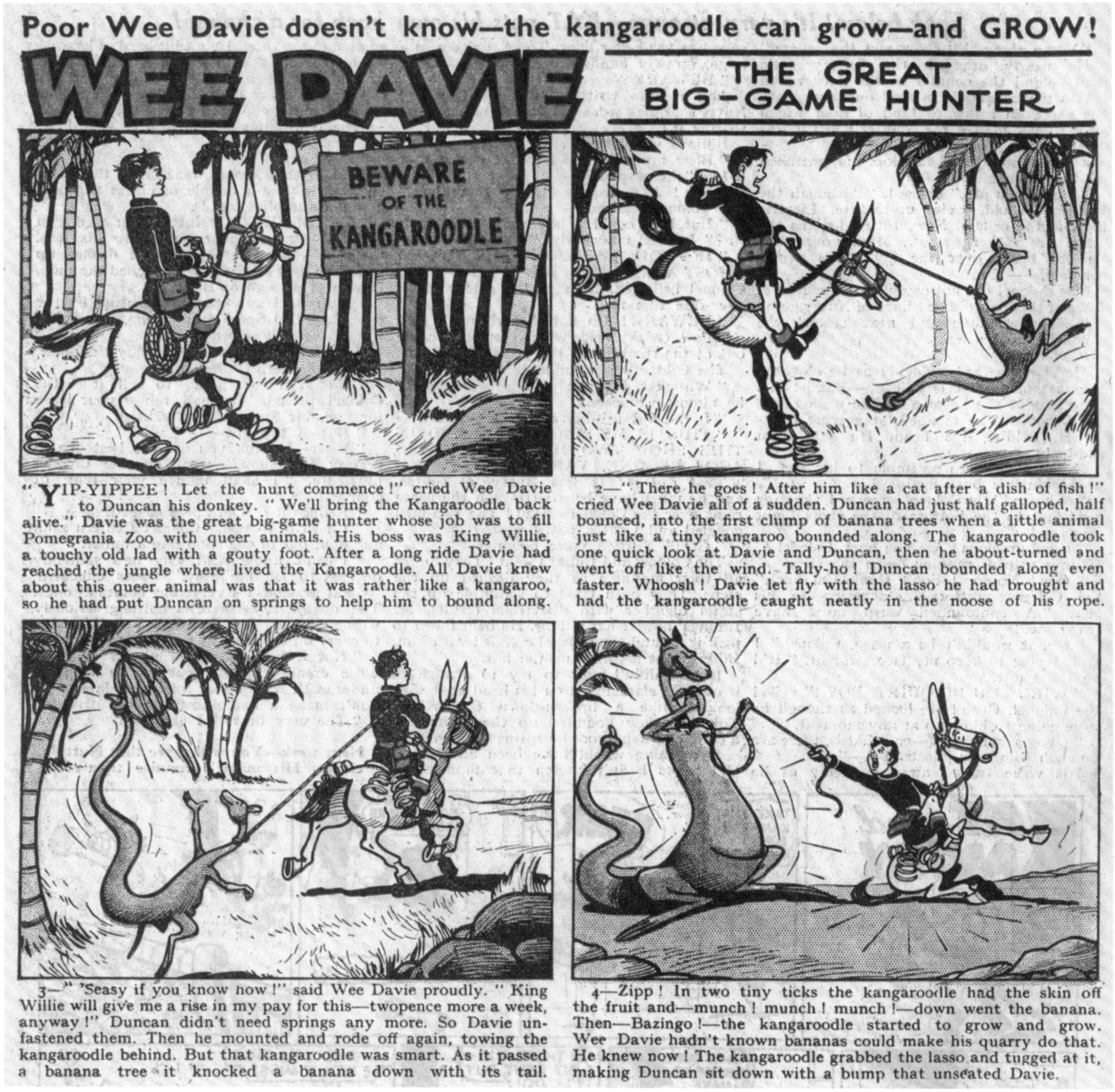
Poor Wee Davie doesn't know—the kangaroodle can grow—and GROW!
WEE DAVIE
THE GREAT BIG-GAME HUNTER
BEWARE OF THE KANGAROODLE
"YIP-YIPPEE! Let the hunt commence!" cried Wee Davie to Duncan his donkey. "We'll bring the Kangaroodle back alive." Davie was the great big-game hunter whose job was to fill Pomegrania Zoo with queer animals. His boss was King Willie, a touchy old lad with a gouty foot. After a long ride Davie had reached the jungle where lived the Kangaroodle. All Davie knew about this queer animal was that it was rather like a kangaroo, so he had put Duncan on springs to help him to bound along.
2—"There he goes! After him like a cat after a dish of fish!" cried Wee Davie all of a sudden. Duncan had just half galloped, half bounced, into the first clump of banana trees when a little animal just like a tiny kangaroo bounded along. The kangaroodle took one quick look at Davie and Duncan, then he about-turned and went off like the wind. Tally-ho! Duncan bounded along even faster. Whoosh! Davie let fly with the lasso he had brought and had the kangaroodle caught neatly in the noose of his rope.
3—"'Seasy if you know how!" said Wee Davie proudly. "King Willie will give me a rise in my pay for this—twopence more a week, anyway!" Duncan didn't need springs any more. So Davie unfastened them. Then he mounted and rode off again, towing the kangaroodle behind. But that kangaroodle was smart. As it passed a banana tree it knocked a banana down with its tail.
4—Zipp! In two tiny ticks the kangaroodle had the skin off the fruit and—munch! munch! munch!—down went the banana. Then—Bazingo!—the kangaroodle started to grow and grow. Wee Davie hadn't known bananas could make his quarry do that. He knew now! The kangaroodle grabbed the lasso and tugged at it, making Duncan sit down with a bump that unseated Davie.

The Dandy
The Beano
The Topper

Adventure
The Rover
The Wizard
The Hotspur

The Sunday Post
The Weekly News
The People's Journal

Red Letter
Weekly Welcome
Red Star Weekly
Family Star

My Weekly
Secrets
People's Friend
Scots Magazine

PRIZE DRAWING COMPETITION

£750 IN PRIZES

For Drawings

BOYS' PAPERS : HOME PAPERS
COMIC PAPERS : NEWS PAPERS

HAVE you a gift for drawing?

Can you draw people, outdoor scenes, fast-moving aeroplanes, cars — all in a realistic manner? . . . Are you expert in the drawing of engineering subjects presented in an interesting popular style? . . . Can you tell a "story" in pictures, or depict a bit of rousing action or drama with realistic characterisation?

Perhaps you have a natural ability for funny drawing? Can you create a comic character and draw his adventures in comic strip style?

If, then, you have some talent for drawing, this competition offers you the chance to win a big cash prize, and, later, the possibility of earning good money.

£750 IN CASH PRIZES

PICTURE STORIES - - - - - - £330
COMIC STRIPS - - - - - - - £210
PICTORIAL FEATURES - - - £210
For the Best Work Submitted

THE competition is open to all—to the amateur as well as the professional artist.

The accompanying pages represent the style and the standard of drawing required. You should not copy the work in these pages. Send original work on subjects of your own choice.

There is no bar of any kind to the subjects or setting in any of the three sections. Obviously it is best to exploit your speciality and to stick to subjects in which you are happiest.

See back page for Conditions

Ken was freelancing in London, doing work for *Radio Times* and *Picture Post* and teaching art at the Press Art School when he heard D. C. Thomson were looking for artists. He entered a competition the firm was running which offered cash prizes and commissioned work for the winners. The outcome was favourable – Ken shared first prize and was invited to start work with *The Beano*. In fact, he was soon picking up so much work that he moved up to Dundee to be closer to the office, though Ken always stayed freelance.

During that time Ken also illustrated 'Ali Ha Ha and the Potty Thieves', 'The Horse that Jack Built', 'Daniel the Spaniel' and 'Thunderflash the Rocky Mountain Ram'. Over his long career, Ken would do classy illustrations for all the D. C. Thomson comic titles and was drawing sets for the *Comic Libraries* when well into his eighties.

STARTING NOW —Fast-moving adventures of the four-legged King of the Rocky Mountains!
THUNDERFLASH
"STEADY, there, Thunderflash! Steady!" Jeff Bradley, chief circus hand of Carter's Circus, warily emptied a pail of raw turnips into one of the boxcars of the circus train that had halted at a station on the lower slopes of the Rocky Mountains. Inside the gloomy car, two angry eyes flashed at Jeff and he backed away as the animal tried to reach him with curling horns, thick as a man's arm. The animal was a huge Rocky Mountain ram, known to all the trappers and gold prospectors in the district as Thunderflash, the King of the Rockies.
2—For years Thunderflash had roamed the heights, leading his wild flock of mountain sheep. Now, expert hunters employed by Carter's Circus had trapped him and brought him down from the mountains. Such was the power behind those great horns that Jeff Bradley was thankful that Thunderflash had been chained to a staple in the wall of the car. That chain was driving the ram to a fury, and as Jeff slid the door shut Thunderflash tugged furiously until the foam flecked his mouth. Then came the tearing of wood as the staple was jerked from the wall.
3—Thunderflash stood panting in the centre of the car, the heavy chain dangling from the thick collar round his neck. Then a jolt made him stagger. The train was moving, heading down into the plains. Thunderflash, who loved to leap among the rugged mountaintops, free as the air, glared at the enclosing walls, and, with a fierce snort, he charged at the door. Crash! Splinters of wood flew under the impact of the massive horns.
4—Crash! Thunderflash charged again and such was the force of his charge that the thick wood cracked. Crash! The car trembled under the impact of another charge and a great chunk of wood flew off to drop on the side of the track. For the fourth time, the ram backed away from the door and charged, and this time the door did not stop him. It burst open with a splintering crack, and Thunderflash hurtled out into space.
5—At the moment of that last great charge, the circus train was passing over the high bridge which spanned the swift Thompson River. Thunderflash dropped like a stone into the river to be swept away by the surging waters. Meanwhile, a fisherman was quietly plying a rod and line further downstream. He was a rancher called Tom Collins and two fat salmon lay on the bank nearby. Suddenly his hand flew to the reel as his hook caught in something below the surface of the swift water.
6—Carefully Tom Collins took the strain on the line. "Must be a big 'un!" he muttered. Then he nearly fell over backwards as his catch rose to the surface and he could see a sleek head with huge spiral horns. It was Thunderflash. The force of the current had kept him below the surface. By good fortune, the fisherman's hook had caught in a horn and brought him up. Tom Collins quickly realised that Thunderflash was in trouble, though he wondered why the huge ram came to be in the river.
Thunderflash returns to his flock.
7—Tom tugged on his line and it took the strain, dragging Thunderflash out of the grip of the current. Soon the ram was standing on the bank, shaking the water from his woolly coat. Then he bounded away up the slopes, the chain rattling and swinging. Tom Collins stared, perplexed, at the chain. "Now, how did that get there?" he muttered, too busy with his thoughts to see a huge grizzly bear shambling up behind him.
8—But Thunderflash had scented the bear. He had stopped on the shoulder of the hill, his dark, flashing eyes following the huge shaggy creature, for bears were his natural enemies. Tom Collins was calmly cutting open one of his salmon when he heard a savage grunt behind him. Round he whirled and saw the huge creature towering above him, its great mouth open and the big, white fangs gleaming in the sunlight.
9—Tom Collins hurled himself back as the long claws tried to seize him, but caught only in his shirt and ripped it. The bear ambled forward again, snarling. Then Thunderflash went into action. His instinct told him that this man needed help and like a thunderbolt he charged the bear. THUD! With terrific force, the lowered horns crashed into the bear's body and hurled the brute into the river. SPLASH! Spray drenched the ram's coat.
10—For a moment, Thunderflash stood on the bank glaring at the bear as the strong current swept it downstream. Then he turned and raced away up the hillside. Tom Collins, his face pale from the close escape from death, watched the magnificent ram that had saved him. "Thanks, pal!" he muttered. "I reckon you've paid your debt to me for pulling you out of the river, though how you got there sure beats me!"
11—Thunderflash went steadily up the mountainside, never faltering in his stride, never missing a foothold on treacherous rocky slopes. He was eager to rejoin his flock, which he knew roamed high on the mountains above him. Soon he scented them and his pace increased. Then they came in sight—a small group of young rams, ewes and a few lambs. But something was wrong. Thunderflash sensed an atmosphere of terror in the flock. Then he almost stumbled across the body of a dead ram.
12—The fallen ram was not long dead for the blood was still gushing from several big wounds in the body—wounds made by the savage claws of some animal. Thunderflash sniffed the air and suddenly he caught the scent of the killer—the dread scent of a wolverine, a savage animal that kills for the sake of killing. The scent was strong. The wolverine was somewhere close by. Then came a spitting snarl as a black and white fury leaped from a rock straight down on Thunderflash.
Next week—How Thunderflash gets rid of the savage wolverine.

BILL HOLROYD

Salford-born artist Bill Holroyd started drawing for *The Beano* in 1948 – the little comic strip 'Alf Wit the Ancient Brit' being his first published *Beano* work. Bill served with the Royal Artillery in the Second World War and had found time to send sample illustrations to D. C. Thomson, but then *The Beano* was on war rations with few pages and appearing fortnightly and so was not taking on new artists. Bill was a born cartoonist, a completely natural artist with a great sense of humour – he enjoyed a laugh with the office staff and was a great favourite at *Beano* headquarters.

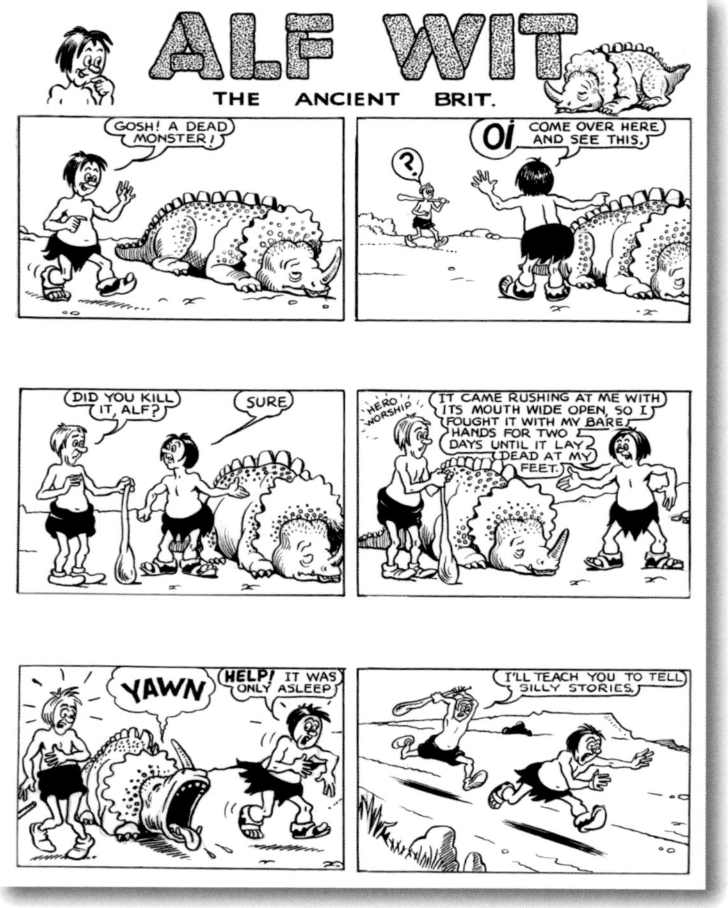
ALF WIT
THE ANCIENT BRIT.
GOSH! A DEAD MONSTER!
OI
COME OVER HERE AND SEE THIS.
DID YOU KILL IT, ALF?
SURE
HERO WORSHIP
IT CAME RUSHING AT ME WITH ITS MOUTH WIDE OPEN, SO I FOUGHT IT WITH MY BARE HANDS FOR TWO DAYS UNTIL IT LAY DEAD AT MY FEET.
YAWN
HELP! IT WAS ONLY ASLEEP
I'LL TEACH YOU TO TELL SILLY STORIES.

Two crafty crooks are up to tricks. See how they fool Big Hugh –
The Adventures of
BIG HUGH
YOU'RE IN THEM, TOO!
HELLO HUGH!
COMING FOR A WALK, READER? IT'S A FINE DAY!
IT IS THAT. SAM BUT DON'T SPEAK TO THESE TWO CHAPS. THEY LOOK LIKE CROOKS TO ME.
WE'LL MAKE SOME MONEY OUT OF THIS COUNTRY BLOKE.
GOOD!
HELLO, BIG LAD! YOU LOOK CLEVER. HOW MUCH MONEY HAVE YOU GOT?
OH – ER – FIVE BOB!
THAT'S GOOD! SHORTY CAN DO A FINE TRICK WITH FIVE BOB!
DON'T GIVE THEM THE MONEY, SAM. THEY'LL TWIST YOU!
MIND YOUR OWN BUSINESS, READER!
SHUCKS READER. THESE ARE HONEST CHAPS!
OF COURSE WE ARE. WE ONLY WANT TO GIVE YOU A LAUGH. BUZZ OFF, YOU!
PUT YOUR FIVE BOB IN MY HAT AND I'LL MAKE IT APPEAR AGAIN IN THAT HOLE IN THE WALL OVER THERE
THAT SOUNDS GOOD! HO HO!
TWISTERS! CHEATS!
DON'T DO IT, HUGH!
YOU'LL LOSE YOUR MONEY!
NOW I PUT MY HANKIE OVER THE HAT SO – EVER SO CAREFULLY –
– AND MUTTER A FEW MAGIC WORDS – OGGLESWIGGLE-PIGGLE-POGGLE!
HEY PRESTO – IT'S GONE!
SO IT HAS!
AND YOU'LL FIND IT IN THE HOLE IN THE WALL ALONG WITH A TWO-BOB PIECE FOR LUCK.
DON'T BELIEVE IT, HUGH. YOUR MONEY IS IN THE HANKIE. TAKE IT FROM HIM.
HO-HO! – THAT'S A CLEVER TRICK – I'LL GO AND GET THE MONEY.
HE'S FALLEN FOR IT, SHORTY. LET'S RUN FOR IT WITH HIS FIVE BOB!
COME BACK, HUGH!

BUCKTOOTH
THE BOY WHO LIVES IN A BARREL
OH, MY! DOES THAT SMELL NICE!
SWEET FACTORY
I'LL PAY A VISIT INSIDE. IT WON'T DO ANY HARM IF I GO IN AND LOOK AROUND.
OW!
I CAN'T HOLD ON MUCH LONGER. I'LL TRY TO GET ON TO THE LEDGE
GOLLY! THAT TOUGH HAS JUST ROBBED THE FACTORY SAFE. I'LL WATCH FOR HIM COMING OUT.
STOP, THIEF!
HOORAY! I'VE FALLEN ON TOP OF THE THIEF.
YOU SAVED US A LOT OF MONEY BY LAYING OUT THAT CROOK. WE'LL HAVE TO REWARD YOU.
YOU HAVE A DATE WITH THE SHERIFF, MISTER!
FILL UP HIS BARREL WITH SWEETS, MEN.
STORE
CANDY
CANDY
I'VE HAD ENOUGH SWEETS FOR NOW — IN FACT, I RECKON I'VE HAD TOO MANY.
THAT OUGHTA KEEP FOLKS OUTA MY SWEETIE STORE WHILE I HAVE A HUNDRED AND FORTY WINKS.
DANGER DYNAMITE
I'VE HAD A SNOOZE NOW I'LL HAVE A SWEET.
THEY'VE MELTED!
IDEA
I'LL STICK THIS POLE IN THE MELTED TOFFEE.
NOW FOR THE RIVER.
WE'LL SEE IF MY PLAN HAS WORKED IN HALF A TICK!
OUT YOU COME! YESSIR! IT'S WORKED! I'VE MADE THE MELTED TOFFEE HARDEN INTO A GIANT LOLLIPOP.
THIS LOOKS INTERESTING!
D. WORMWOOD'S AUCTION ROOMS
SALE TODAY OF WORLD'S BIGGEST LOLLIPOP
D. WORMWOOD'S AUCTION ROOMS
TEN CENTS!
ONE HUNDRED DOLLARS!
TWO HUNDRED DOLLARS!
TWO HUNDRED HERE — ANY ADVANCE ON TWO? GOING, GOING —
SALE TODAY
THE WORLD'S BIGGEST LOLLIPOP
LOT 1
I WAS ABLE TO BUY MORE SWEETS WITH WHAT I GOT FOR THE LOLLIPOP. AM I SMART!

In the 1950s he drew over 20 different characters for *The Beano*. 'Ding-Dong Belle', the tough lady sheriff, was one of the rather unusual ones, for adult female cartoon characters had been unheard of in *The Beano* (see page 108 for a 'Ding-Dong Belle' strip). 'Big Hugh' was another strip with a difference – reader participation. Country hick, Hugh, talked to the readers all through the story.

The story of 'Nutty the Coal Imp', in which a coal wizard imprisoned Nutty in a lump of coal for stealing spells, amused Bill, and he produced some hilarious scenes for the tale. It was a similar story with 'Bucktooth the Boy Who Lives in a Barrel', a zany situation dreamed up by editor George Moonie.

NUTTY
THE COAL IMP

THE IRON FISH

Bill was probably most famous for his classy series of 'The Iron Fish' and 'Red Rory of the Eagles'. The pencil drawing for 'The Iron Fish' shows the original idea, but Bill was not pleased with the dynamics of the scene, so he completely remodelled it to give a much more powerful effect in the final drawing.

Bill Holroyd continued his marvellous work with D. C. Thomson until he retired in 1986. Apart from his *Beano* works, he had drawn for nearly all the comics. 'Brassneck' and 'Screwy Driver' come to mind for *The Dandy* and the immaculate illustrations for 'Coral Island' in *The Hotspur.*

Bill's brother Albert also drew for the D. C. Thomson stable. On 'Hookey's Bust 'Em Book' Albert took over the illustration from his brother. It was one of the many strips he had running alongside those from his brother. A further *Beano* family connection was that Bill and Albert's sister was married to cartoonist Ken Reid.

The BEANO, November 1, 1958.
Laugh to your Heart's Content
THE BEANO
No. 850. Nov. 1st, 1958.
2D
EVERY THURSDAY
BIFFO THE BEAR
I'VE SPENT ALL MY MONEY ON FIREWORKS ~ AND FORGOTTEN TO BUY MATCHES!
FIREWORKS
AH! I'LL GET A LIGHT HERE!
NOW WATCH THIS!
GULP!
JUST MY LUCK! HE'S A FIRE-EATER!
FIREWORKS
10 MINUTES LATER
NOW'S MY CHANCE. THAT GENT'S GOING TO LIGHT A CIGARETTE.
GOT A LIGHT, MATE?
I WAS JUST GOING TO ASK YOU THAT!
½ AN HOUR LATER
AH! I'LL LIGHT MY FIREWORKS FROM THAT STREET LAMP!
BAH! IT'S GONE OUT!
FIREWORKS
FLICKER!
PLOP!
JUST MY LUCK!
DRINK, HORSEY, DRINK!
DRINK, HORSEY, DRINK!
SOMEONE'S FALLEN IN THE HORSE TROUGH! BRING A LIGHT!
A FAT LOT OF GOOD ALL YOUR LIGHTS ARE NOW!
YOUR FIREWORKS ARE SODDEN, BIFFO!

At first glance, the cover of the issue of November 1, 1958, hasn't changed much from that four years earlier. Look again. The style of lettering on the main title is different and 'Dennis' has replaced 'Big Eggo', probably demonstrating how important his character had become to the comic.

The prose stories have disappeared although there are four adventure picture strips in this issue. But look at that line-up of comic stars. 'Dennis', 'Minnie', 'Plum' and 'Roger' are joined by 'The Bash Street Kids' and 'Jonah'.

Pages 2 and 3 of The Beano *for November 1, 1958, with an amazing 'Little Plum' strip, which is taken over by bears, and 'The Hogan Boy', a Western tale illustrated by John Nichol. The 'Little Plum' is classic Baxendale. Just how many bears are there in that opening frame?*

LITTLE PLUM
UM PESKY BEARS HAVE HEARD THAT I'VE GOT A WHOLE PAGE TO MYSELF, AND NOW THEY ALL WANT TO GET IN THE PICTURE!
THERE ARE UM HEAP TOO MANY BEARS IN THIS STRIP. THEY GOTTA GO! BUT WHERE?
TO THE MOON! THAT'S THE PLACE FOR THEM!
NEWSAGEN
DAILY NEWS
ROCKET TO THE MOON SOON?
SO—
ROLL UP! ROLL UP! SPEND YOUR HOLIDAY ON THE MOON!
PLUM'S ROCKET TO THE MOON. BEARS TRAVEL FREE!
WE'LL BE THE FIRST BEARS ON THE MOON. VERY NICE OF PLUM TO LET US TRAVEL FREE!
WHAT ABOUT YOU, PLUM?
SLAM
I AIN'T COMIN'!
TI-TUM-TI-TEE!
WOOSH
TOO BAD PLUM FORGOT TO PUT UM FLOOR IN UM ROCKET!
WOOSH
HO! HO! ME GOT RID OF UM STUPID BEARS TO UM MOON!
ME NEXT!
ME NEXT!
BAM! BAM! BAM!
THE BEARS DECIDED THERE WAS ONE LITTLE PLUM TOO MANY IN THIS STRIP!
LET ME IN! THIS IS MY STRIP!

The HOGAN BOY
Young Jeff Hogan has vowed to capture Hank Millard, a crook who shot his father, Murray Hogan, during a bank robbery in Battle City. Jeff's Dad is paralysed and only a long and costly operation will enable him to walk again. There is a 10,000 dollars reward on Hank Millard's head, and Jeff means to get it to pay for the operation. In Battle City, Jeff gets into a fight and the Sheriff puts him in jail to prevent the boy getting into more trouble.
Jeff sat in the cell reading the list of Millard's crimes. Late that night, the sound of horses' hoofs took him to the cell window.
WANTED
Through the iron bars, Jeff could dimly make out the forms of three men.
The riders dismounted, and, drawing their guns, rushed to break in the doors of the bank. As one of the men looked round, Jeff recognised Hank Millard!
BANK
"Sheriff!" shouted Jeff. "Millard and his gang are robbing the State Bank!" Quickly, the Sheriff seized his guns and raced for the door.
As soon as the Sheriff appeared in the light from the open doorway, Millard's colts roared.
SHERIFF
SADDLER
HANK'S
Mortally wounded, the Sheriff staggered back into his office.
Suddenly, he pitched forward on his face, and lay still, his six-shooter clattering on the floor.
Reaching between the iron bars, Jeff could just grasp the gun.
With one shot he shattered the lock on the cell door.
A quick look at the Sheriff showed Jeff he could do nothing for him. Now Millard had one more murder to answer for!
Jeff grabbed his own gunbelt which the Sheriff had taken away from him and swiftly buckled it on before dousing the light.
In the darkness, Jeff wormed his way outside to where his horse was tethered. By the time he reached it, the Millard gang were on their way out of town.
NEXT WEEK:—Jeff gets an ally in his chase after Millard!

Pages 4 and 5 of The Beano *for November 1, 1958, featuring the second week of an adventure strip about feuding Vikings, drawn by Vitor Peon.*

THE BLINDING SHIELD
A DEADLY FEUD EXISTS BETWEEN THREE BRAVE VIKING BROTHERS, VAL, ALEK AND SIGURD, AND THE VILLAINOUS FAMILY OF THE VOLDAGS. THE VOLDAGS, HUMILIATED BY A RECENT DEFEAT AT THE HANDS OF THE BROTHERS, PERSUADE WOLFRAM, A SORCERER, TO MAKE THEM A BLINDING SHIELD. WITH THIS WEAPON THEY INTEND TO EXACT TERRIBLE VENGEANCE.
FROM THE RAMPARTS OF THE BROTHERS' CASTLE, YOUNG VAL WATCHED ONE OF THE VOLDAGS APPROACH ON HORSEBACK AT A GALLOP
TO VAL'S SURPRISE, THE MAN HURLED OVER THE RAMPART WHAT APPEARED TO BE A BIG SHIELD, WRAPPED IN A SKIN COVER. "A PRESENT FOR YOUR BROTHERS!" HE ROARED AS HE SWUNG AWAY.
LOOK, BROTHERS, A STRANGE PRESENT FROM THE VOLDAGS!
UNWRAP IT THEN AND LET'S HAVE A LOOK AT IT!
MY EYES!
FIERCE BLINDING RAYS OF LIGHT BLAZED FROM THE SHIELD AS VAL UNWRAPPED IT, CAUSING HIS BROTHERS TO CLAP THEIR HANDS TO THEIR EYES IN AGONY
THE LIGHT FROM THE SHIELD HAS BLINDED US, VAL!
VAL WAS HORRIFIED AND HASTILY SUMMONED MARLIN, THE CASTLE PHYSICIAN AND WISE-MAN.
I CANNOT CURE YOUR BROTHERS' BLINDNESS, BUT I SUSPECT THAT WOLFRAM, THE SORCERER, MAY HAVE MADE THE SHIELD. IF SO, ONLY HE CAN CURE THEM!

WHAT HOPE HAVE MY BLINDED BROTHERS IF THE VOLDAGS ATTACK NOW?
THAT SAME DAY, THE EVIL VOLDAGS AND THEIR SOLDIERS APPEARED OUTSIDE THE CASTLE. THEY HAD COME TO COMPLETE THEIR VENGEANCE, THINKING THAT ALL THREE BROTHERS HAD BEEN BLINDED.
WITHOUT THE FIGHTING STRENGTH OF THE BROTHERS ALEK AND SIGURD, THE CAPTAIN OF THE CASTLE GUARD WAS NOT HOPEFUL OF REPELLING THE VOLDAGS WHEN THEY ATTACKED. AT THAT, VAL MADE HIS DECISION TO TAKE HIS BROTHERS AT ONCE TO THE SORCERER, WOLFRAM.
AT FULL SPEED, VAL DROVE HIS BROTHERS FROM THE CASTLE ON A HORSE-DRAWN SLED. HE TOOK WITH HIM THE BLINDING SHIELD.
THE BREAK-OUT WAS QUICKLY SPOTTED BY THE VOLDAGS WHO SWOOPED TO THE ATTACK.
IN DESPERATION, VAL TURNED THE BLINDING SHIELD ON THE FAST APPROACHING WARRIORS.
THE VOLDAGS HURRIEDLY REINED IN THEIR HORSES AT THE SIGHT OF THE MENACING SHIELD. THE WEAPON THEY HAD SENT TO CRIPPLE THE BROTHERS WAS NOW BEING TURNED AGAINST THEM.
VAL DROVE LIKE THE WIND, WHILE THE VOLDAGS FOLLOWED AT A DISTANCE, NOT DARING TO APPROACH WITHIN RANGE OF THE SHIELD'S BLINDING RAYS.
YOU WILL NOT ESCAPE OUR VENGEANCE FOR LONG!
Next week—The grim pursuit across the ravine!

Pages 6 and 7 of The Beano *for November 1, 1958, with one page devoted to 'Minnie the Minx' and the other containing a reprint of 'The Shipwrecked Circus' and two small short-lived strips.*

Minnie the Minx
I'M OFF TO POST THE INVITATIONS TO YOUR BIRTHDAY PARTY, MINNIE.
THERE'LL BE LOTS OF GRUB AT MY PARTY. I WISH I COULD HAVE IT ALL TO MYSELF.
AND SO—AS THE FIRST INVITATION IS BEING DELIVERED.
MUST BE POTTY.
I'M JUST MEASURING THE PATH, POSTMAN.
SPLAT!
WHAT'S SHE UP TO NOW?
MEAT PASTE
HERE'S A NICE LITTLE SNACK FOR YOU, DOGGIE.
ANOTHER INVITATION IS BEING DELIVERED.
THANKS VERY MU-
ANOTHER ONE LESS FOR MINNIE'S PARTY.
HAVE A SWEET, CHARLIE. IT'S A GOOD ONE. I KNOW, 'COS I'VE BEEN SUCKING IT.
?
LETTER FOR YOU, M'BOY.
PLOP
HEH, HEH, HE'S TEARING THE INVITATION UP TRYING TO FREE IT FROM THAT STICKY SWEET I GAVE HIM.
GOOD. THAT'S THE LAST OF THE INVITATIONS DEALT WITH.
SNIP SNIP SNIP
WHOOPEE! ALL THAT GRUB TO MYSELF.
SICKENING THUD
TOO BAD YOU'RE UNABLE TO EAT ANYTHING JUST NOW, MINNIE. I'LL HAVE TO DIG INTO IT ON MY OWN.

Samson the Strongman is looking for Gloopy, the little circus clown. Gloopy is missing along with a fortune in jewels the chums of the Shipwrecked Circus found on the island on which they have been castaways.
THE SHIPWRECKED CIRCUS
Helping Samson in the hunt for Gloopy is Pegleg, a shipwrecked sailor, recently arrived on the island. Pegleg has actually stolen the jewels and got rid of Gloopy by pushing him into a deep ravine—the same one in which he intends to get rid of the Strongman!
Pegleg led the unsuspecting Strongman to the ravine edge. "There he is!" he cried, pointing downwards, and as Samson moved forward the treacherous sailor pushed him over the edge.
The Strongman's falling body disappeared into the darkness of the chasm far below. Pegleg could not see the bottom of the ravine but he thought he was well rid of Samson.
By good fortune, Samson escaped death. Like Gloopy, who was there in the ravine, he fell into thick moss which saved his life. Anxiously, Gloopy tended the Strongman.
Fully recovered, Samson swung Gloopy on to his back, and started the hazardous climb back up the cliff face.
On the cliff edge Gloopy showed Samson the spot where he had seen Pegleg bury the treasure. The treasure had been removed.
With all speed, Samson and Gloopy returned to camp.
Back at base, they found Pegleg threatening the other circus chums with a whip and making them wait on him hand and foot.
Quickly, Samson made a plan. Silently, he climbed on the ship, dropped a noose over Pegleg and pulled it tight.
Pegleg was hoisted into the air and dangled there, helpless. Samson did not free him until he told him where the treasure was hidden.
That day the chums provisioned a raft and set Pegleg adrift on it, glad to be rid of such a scoundrel.
Next Week:—Samson attacks the chums!
BETTY'S GRANDAD
GRANDAD, HEARING BETTY'S SHOUT—RUNS TO PUT THE FIRE OUT!
FIRE! FIRE!
BETTER GET SOME WATER, QUICK!
FIRE! GO ON, FIRE!
COOKIE
COOKIE MAKES A SLIGHT MISTAKE—AND HAS TO BAKE ANOTHER CAKE!
I'M PRETTY GOOD AT ICING CAKES AND THINGS!
YESSIR!
UM!
?
NEVER MIND, THOUGH!
A FEW MORE STIRS AND IT'LL BE O.K.!
I'M A CLEVER LITTLE COOK—I AM!

Pages 8 and 9 of The Beano *for November 1, 1958, containing two comic strips, with 'Roger the Dodger' and 'Pansy Potter', now no longer on the back cover, and an adventure from the eleventh series of 'Red Rory', illustrated by Andy Hutton.*

ROGER THE DODGER
I'M JUST ON MY WAY TO SPIFLICATE ROGER AS HE LEAVES FOR SCHOOL! THE TWISTER RUBBED HIS OWN NAME OFF THE LIST FOR THE SCHOOL CROSS-COUNTRY RUN TEAM AND PUT MY NAME DOWN INSTEAD.
BUT, AT ROGER'S HOUSE—
I'M GOING YOUR WAY, ROGER—
BAH! HIS DAD'S WITH HIM.
—BUT ONLY AS FAR AS THE BUS STOP! 'BYE, SON.
'BYE, DAD.
NOW'S MY CHANCE.
ROUND THE CORNER—
'MORNING TEACHER! CAN I WALK TO SCHOOL WITH YOU?
CERTAINLY, M'BOY.
FOILED AGAIN.
IN CLASS—
HEH, HEH! I KNEW BASHER BRIGGS WAS AFTER ME. THAT'S WHY I WORKED THOSE DODGES.
AFTER LESSONS—
I WANT ALL CROSS-COUNTRY RUNNERS TO STAY BEHIND FOR HALF AN HOUR'S TRAINING.
GR-R-R!
SO LONG, BASHER.
LATER—
THAT'S A FEW MORE FIREWORKS TOWARDS THE GREAT NIGHT.
FIREWORKS
HELLO, PERCY. I'VE JUST GOT TO TELL YOU ABOUT A FAST ONE I'VE PULLED ON BASHER—BLAH—BLAH—
HALF AN HOUR LATER—
AND NOW HE'LL BE STAGGERIN' ACROSS MUDDY FIELDS, AND JUMPING FENCES. HAH-HAH-HAH—
ULP!
EEK!
I'VE JUST FINISHED MY HALF-HOUR'S TRAINING, ROGER.
—AND I FEEL TOUGHER THAN EVER NOW!
SPLAT
HAVE ANOTHER.
BIFF
AWLK!
FIZZ-Z-Z
MY FIREWORKS!
SHWOOSH
YOWLK!
MY! WHAT AGILITY.
BANG
BANG
BANG
BANG
I'M SO IMPRESSED BY YOUR DEMONSTRATION THAT I'VE PERSUADED BRIGGS TO LET YOU TAKE HIS PLACE IN THE CROSS-COUNTRY TEAM!
GASP! GURGLE!
ROGER PLAYS SOME EXTRA-SPECIAL DODGES IN THIS YEAR'S SUPER BEANO BOOK
THE BEANO BOOK
GET YOUR COPY NOW!
PANSY POTTER—The Strongman's Daughter
I MUST REMEMBER THAT.
THIS IS BE-CHUMS WEEK
BE HELPFUL AND FRIENDLY TO ONE AND ALL.
I'LL MAKE FRIENDS WITH THIS LITTLE CHAP.
PAT
LOOK WHAT YOU'VE DONE TO MY SYDNEY, YOU BRUTE!
I DIDN'T MEAN TO PAT SO HARD.
?
LATER
IT'S STARTING TO RAIN AND THAT GENT CAN'T GET HIS BROLLY UP.
ALLOW ME!
PEST!
LATER
MMM! THAT POOR CHAP'S HAVING A TOUGH TIME PUSHING THAT CRATE UP THE STEPS.
ALLOW ME!
THERE YOU ARE!
DOLT! I WAS TRYING TO GET IT DOWN!
GR-R!
I KNOW WHERE I'M GOING!
WHY HAVE YOU LOCKED YOURSELF IN, PANSY?
IT'S THE ONLY WAY I CAN STOP BE-CHUMS WEEK BECOMING BE-GLUM WEEK, MUM!

RED RORY OF THE EAGLES
It is the Summer of 1746, following the defeat of Prince Charlie's army at Culloden. Red Rory of the Eagles and Black Duncan are escorting Lady Fiona Stewart and her children to join their father, Lord Donald Stewart, who is a fugitive in France. Pursued by Redcoat soldiers, the party take refuge in a cave behind a waterfall. There Flora, Lady Fiona's daughter, drops her doll, which is carried away by the rushing water and swept into the river.
The doll was seen by Redcoat soldiers searching downriver. Luckily, the officer in charge of the patrol jumped to the wrong conclusion.
The officer led his men farther up river, thinking that the doll had come from there.
At last, Rory emerged from behind the waterfall to spy out the land.
When Rory gave the all-clear, Black Duncan led the fugitives from the cave.
With all possible speed, the little band of friends forded the river and made for the hills. Black Duncan looked anxiously for signs of pursuit as he brought up the rear.
Suddenly, the horse which the children were riding stumbled, and little Flora fell heavily, twisting her ankle.
Despite the danger, Lady Fiona insisted that Flora be given every attention, and pointed to a distant croft where she suggested Flora be taken.
Rory, wary of an ambush, started on ahead to make sure that the croft was safe.
The Highland woman in the croft was willing to help. Happily, Rory signalled to his friends on the hill, not noticing a man hidden in a nearby pile of straw.
As the fugitives entered the croft, the man emerged from the straw. With many a backward glance, he set off in a direction that would take him to the searching Redcoats.
Next Week.—Red Rory's prisoner.

SPLOOSH!

Pages 10 and 11 of The Beano *for November 1, 1958, with a classic partnering of Bash Street and Dennis, along with the 'Krazy Corner', which includes tricks with cigarettes – one instruction starts: 'A cigarette will furnish a lot of fun if you slip a piece of metal between the paper and the tobacco near the end.' Another requires 'Dad' to provide cigarette smoke to make smoke rings.*

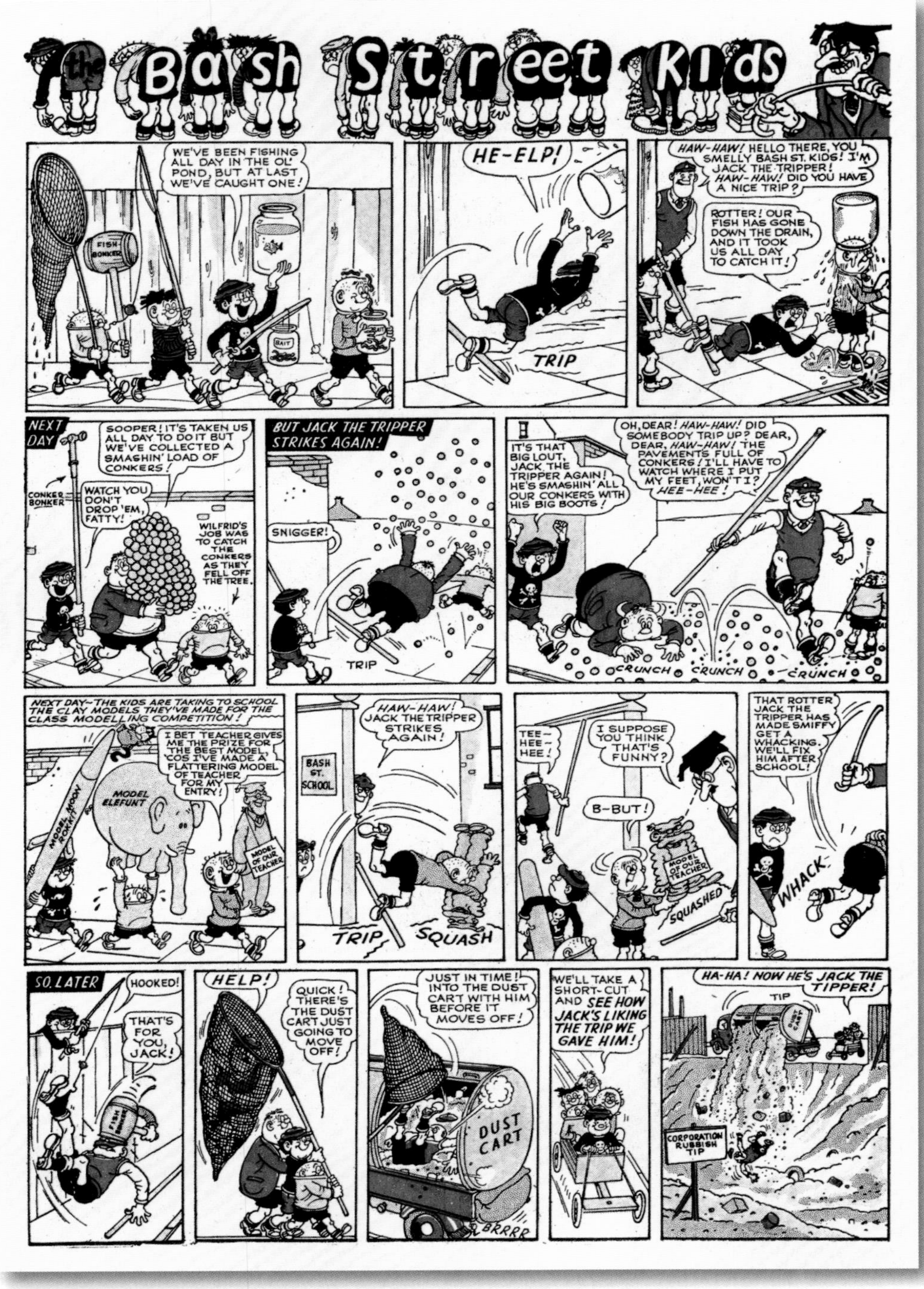
the Bash Street Kids
WE'VE BEEN FISHING ALL DAY IN THE OL' POND, BUT AT LAST WE'VE CAUGHT ONE!
FISH-BONKER
BAIT
HE-ELP!
TRIP
HAW-HAW! HELLO THERE, YOU SMELLY BASH ST. KIDS! I'M JACK THE TRIPPER! HAW-HAW! DID YOU HAVE A NICE TRIP?
ROTTER! OUR FISH HAS GONE DOWN THE DRAIN, AND IT TOOK US ALL DAY TO CATCH IT!
NEXT DAY
SOOPER! IT'S TAKEN US ALL DAY TO DO IT BUT WE'VE COLLECTED A SMASHIN' LOAD OF CONKERS!
CONKER-BONKER
WATCH YOU DON'T DROP 'EM, FATTY!
WILFRID'S JOB WAS TO CATCH THE CONKERS AS THEY FELL OFF THE TREE.
BUT JACK THE TRIPPER STRIKES AGAIN!
SNIGGER!
TRIP
IT'S THAT BIG LOUT, JACK THE TRIPPER AGAIN! HE'S SMASHIN' ALL OUR CONKERS WITH HIS BIG BOOTS!
OH, DEAR! HAW-HAW! DID SOMEBODY TRIP UP? DEAR, DEAR, HAW-HAW! THE PAVEMENT'S FULL OF CONKERS! I'LL HAVE TO WATCH WHERE I PUT MY FEET, WON'T I? HEE-HEE!
CRUNCH
CRUNCH
CRUNCH
NEXT DAY—THE KIDS ARE TAKING TO SCHOOL THE CLAY MODELS THEY'VE MADE FOR THE CLASS MODELLING COMPETITION!
I BET TEACHER GIVES ME THE PRIZE FOR THE BEST MODEL, 'COS I'VE MADE A FLATTERING MODEL OF TEACHER FOR MY ENTRY!
MODEL ELEFUNT
MODEL OF OUR TEACHER
BASH ST. SCHOOL
HAW-HAW! JACK THE TRIPPER STRIKES AGAIN!
TRIP
SQUASH
TEE-HEE-HEE!
I SUPPOSE YOU THINK THAT'S FUNNY?
B-BUT!
SQUASHED
THAT ROTTER JACK THE TRIPPER HAS MADE SMIFFY GET A WHACKING. WE'LL FIX HIM AFTER SCHOOL!
WHACK
SO, LATER
HOOKED!
THAT'S FOR YOU, JACK!
HELP!
QUICK! THERE'S THE DUST CART JUST GOING TO MOVE OFF!
JUST IN TIME! INTO THE DUST CART WITH HIM BEFORE IT MOVES OFF!
DUST CART
BRRRR
WE'LL TAKE A SHORT-CUT AND SEE HOW JACK'S LIKING THE TRIP WE GAVE HIM!
HA-HA! NOW HE'S JACK THE TIPPER!
TIP
CORPORATION RUBBISH TIP

DENNIS THE MENACE
WALTER'S GOT A TUCK HAMPER! YUMMY-YUM!
WALTER'S HUT
HE'S LOCKED THE DOOR—BUT I'LL GET IN FOR SOME OF THAT TUCK—NEVER FEAR!
HEAVE
RIGHT, CURLY—CHARGE!
THUMP
TOO BAD YOU CAN'T STOP!
GOODBYE!
WOOSH
SPLOOSH!
WE'LL GET IN YET, CURLY!
WE'LL SMOKE 'EM OUT!
WALTER'S HUT
BAH! THE WIND'S CHANGED!
COUGH
SPLUTTER
COUGH
A FEW CREEPY-CRAWLY, STINGIN' ANTS WILL SOON SHIFT THEM!
YEOW! OW!
OUCH! YEOW!
WE'RE IN! TUCK, HERE WE COME!
I CAN HARDLY WAIT!
GOLLY! WE'VE BLUNDERED. WALTER'S GOT HIMSELF A DOG CALLED "TUCK"!
GRRR-OWL
LET'S GET OUT OF HERE! THIS ISN'T THE TUCK WE WERE AFTER!
GRRR
KRAZY KORNER
FUN FOR ALL AND ALL FOR FUN
Each of the designs around the circle stands for the letter with it. Try to read the code message below.
A DANCING COIN
Dip a coin in water and place it over the mouth of a bottle. Grip the bottle, as shown, and hold it for a minute or so. The heat from your hands will expand the air in the empty bottle, thus causing the coin to dance.
Here is a clever and simple trick to mystify your friends. Lay a match on a table and balance another across it, as shown. Move a coin across in front of the balanced match without touching it and the match will move. The secret is simple—blow lightly on the match as you move the coin.
SMOKE RINGS
ASK DAD TO DO THIS
Cut a small hole in the centre of an envelope and seal it. Blow smoke into the hole to fill it.
You can then produce a series of smoke rings by making light taps on the envelope.
A cigarette will furnish a lot of fun if you slip a piece of metal between the paper and the tobacco near the end, as shown. You can astonish a crowd by performing "impossible" feats of balance with them.
TRY THESE STUNTS
PIECE OF METAL
ANSWER

Every Thursday
THE BEANO
November 1, 1958.
JONAH
ONE WEEK HAS PASSED SINCE WE LEFT JONAH DRIFTING ON A PLANK—AFTER A MIRACULOUS ESCAPE FROM CHINESE PIRATES.
THEN—
QUEER LOOKIN' OBJECT ON PORT-BOW, MISTER MATE!
RIGHT, CRUMP. HAUL IT ABOARD!
CRUMP DOES—
AGH-H!
GLURK!
AND TEN SECONDS LATER—
CAP'N! CAP'N! WE'VE JUST FISHED THAT NAUTICAL GOON OUT OF THE SEA! WE'RE FINISHED!
I TAKE IT YOU MEAN JONAH!
WELL, DON'T PANIC, PENTERGHAST. I'VE AWAITED THIS OPPORTUNITY FOR SOME YEARS. AS YOU KNOW, DURING THE WAR I WAS IN COMMAND OF A HOSPITAL SHIP—
PSYCHIATRY
—AND THERE I LEARNED QUITE A BIT ABOUT PSYCHIATRY! NOW, IT'S MY BELIEF THAT, WITH THE RIGHT TREATMENT, THIS JONAH COULD BECOME AS NORMAL AS YOU ARE, PENTERGHAST!—
—OR, RATHER, AS NORMAL AS YOU WERE BEFORE YOU FISHED HIM OUT OF THE SEA!
SO—
NOW, SON! WE DON'T WANT TO SINK OUR NICE BIG COASTER, DO WE-M-M-M?
I SHOULDN'T RECKON SO!
'COURSE WE DON'T!! WE JUST WANT IT TO GO S-A-I-L-I-N-G ON ACROSS THE SPLISHY-SPLASHY OCEAN, UNTIL IT REACHES ITS SNUG, SAFE HARBOUR—DON'T WE?
THAT'S RIGHT!
THEN LET US SAY OVER AND OVER AGAIN, NICE AND SLOWLY,—"THIS SHIP SHALL REACH SAFE HARBOUR!"
THIS SHIP SHALL REACH SAFE HARBOUR! THIS SHIP SHALL REACH—
HALF AN HOUR LATER—
CAPTAIN
—SAFE HARBOUR! THIS SHIP SHALL REACH SAFE HARBOUR—
—THIS SHIP SHALL REACH SAFE HARBOUR— OOPS!!?! THIS SHIP SHALL REACH SAFE HARBOUR!
TRIP
—THIS SHIP SHALL REACH SAFE HARBOUR!
TUG!
RUMBLE
SNAP!
SNAP!
COO! I'M SURE THAT SHOULDN'T BE RUNNING AROUND LOOSE!
CLANK
I'D BETTER PUT THE BRAKE ON!—IF I CAN FIND IT!
RUMBLE
ON THE BRIDGE—
WELL, PENTERGHAST, IT WORKED! JONAH'S ONE OBSESSION NOW, IS TO SEE THAT THIS SHIP REACHES SAFE HARBOUR—
RUMBLE
AND— AWLK!
CRASH
THE BRAKE! WHERE'S THE BRAKE?
CRUNCH
I CAN'T FIND THE— ERK!
DOING!
THIS SHIP SHALL REACH—
—SAFE HARBOUR
CRASH
THIS SHIP SHALL—
PENTERGHAST! HE'S COMING BACK!
—REACH SAFE HARBOUR.
CRASH
S.O.S!
TWO HOURS LATER—
THIS SHIP SHALL REACH—
ABANDON SHIP!
EVERY MAN FOR HIMSELF!
—SAFE HARBOUR!
CRASH
THIS SHIP SHALL REACH SAFE HARBOUR— GLOOP!
THIS SHIP SHALL GLUG! SAFE HARBOUR.
GLUG!
CRUNCH
THIS GLOOP! SHALL HIC! SAFE HARBOUR!
CRUNCH
ULK!
THIS SHIP SHALL BOILK! SAFE HARBOUR.
GLUB!
CRUMP
AWLK!
SQUELCH
THIS SHIP SHALL— CRIKEY!! WHERE IS IT?
?
!
NEXT WEEK—BOY ON A BELL-BUOY.
© D. C. THOMSON & CO., LTD., 1958.
Printed and Published in Great Britain by D. C. THOMSON & Co., Ltd., and JOHN LENG & Co., Ltd., 12 Fetter Lane, Fleet Street, London, E.C.4. Registered for transmission by Canadian Magazine Post.

And 'Jonah' on the back page is Ken Reid at his riotous best. There are 31 pictures packed onto this page, each one guaranteed to have the reader laughing out loud.

In 1959 George Moonie was appointed Editor of the new girls' paper *Judy* and Harry Cramond took over as Editor of *The Beano* with Walter Fearn as his chief sub. It had been a decade of extraordinary change but two things remained the same. The page count was still twelve and *The Beano* still cost only 2d.

Beano

PART 4

The Swinging Sixties

1960-1969

BLUES BREAKERS
JOHN MAYALL
DECCA
WITH ERIC CLAPTON

The 1960s started on a huge high for *The Beano*. With the new Editor, Harry Cramond, settling in at the helm, the comic was dominating the market. On sales it was Number 1 in the children's comic charts. It went into the new decade outselling its closest rival and stablemate, *The Dandy*, by 100,000 copies – by the end of that year the gap would become 200,000. *The Beano* was the comic to be seen with. In October 1960, *The Beano* had its first-ever price increase. For 22 years it had been 2d and now it moved up to 3d. With the price rise came extra pages, growing from 12 to 16 pages, and the first freebies since a war-torn 1940. Week one had a Flying Snorter Balloon, with Biffo showing readers how to use it in his cover story and week two was a Dennis the Menace Clickitty Clicker, two noisy gifts that must have driven parents and teachers nuts.

The Beano
SUPER FREE GIFT INSIDE!
EVERY THURSDAY
No. 953—OCTOBER 22nd, 1960
3D
BIFFO THE BEAR
THERE'S A
THERE'S A SMASHING
THERE'S A SMASHING FREE GIFT
THERE'S A SMASHING FREE GIFT FOR YOU INSIDE
BRRR
SO HAVE FUN WITH THE FLYING SNORTER!

FREE TO EVERY BOY and GIRL
CLICK! CLICK! CLICK!
CLICK! CLICK!
CLICKITTY CLICK!
The BEANO CLICKITTY CLICKER
THE SUPER, SOUND-EFFECTS TOY IN THE BEANO
The Famous Comic Paper – 16 Pages! 3d
— OUT NEXT WEEK —

This elevated status was justified, and the scripting and art teams were all at their peak. There were laughs galore in all the classic strips, and even the title logos were funny, Leo Baxendale drawing a comical happening for each one.

"The BEANO" SUITS EVERYBODY!
THE BEANO
No. 930—May 14th, 1960.
2D
EVERY THURSDAY

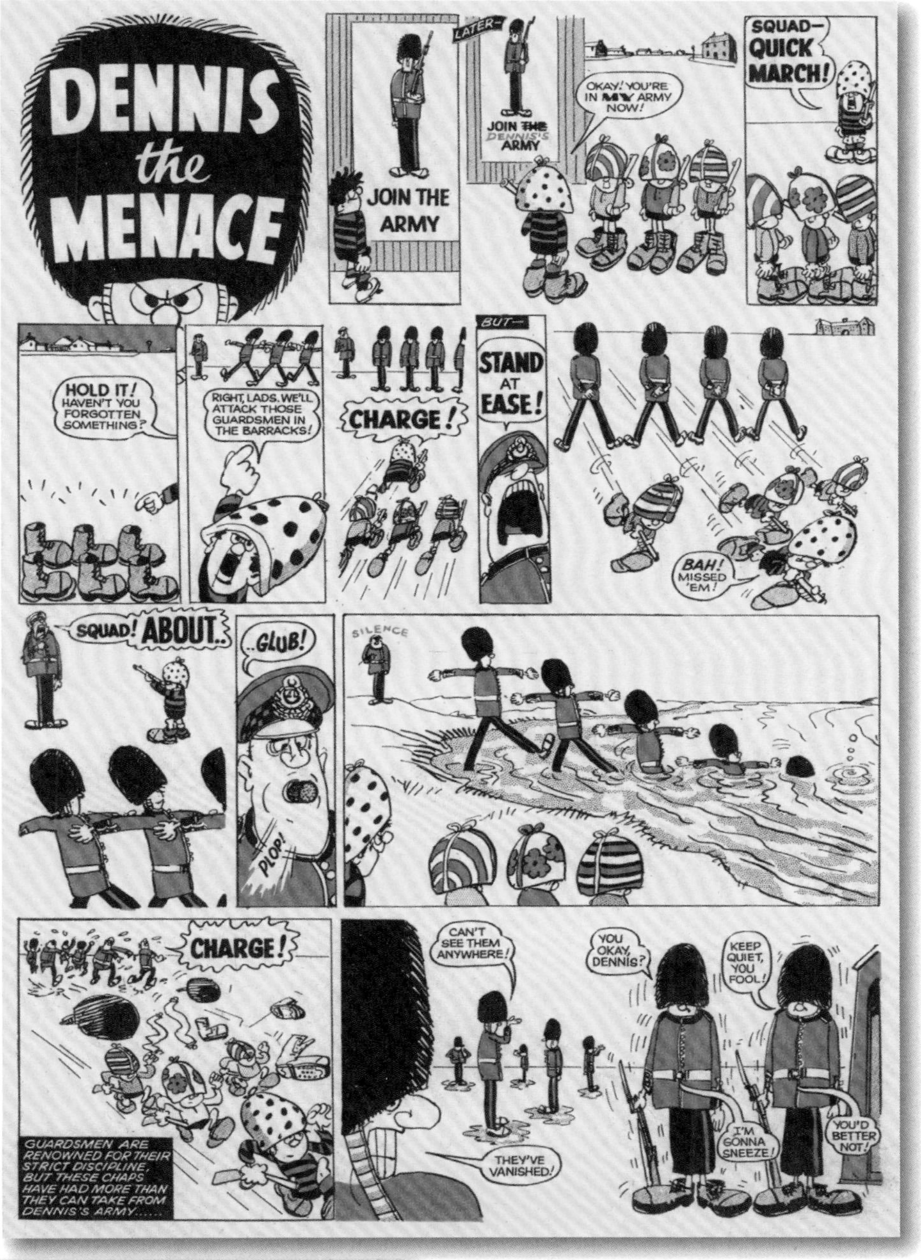
DENNIS the MENACE
JOIN THE ARMY
LATER—
JOIN ~~THE~~ DENNIS'S ARMY
OKAY! YOU'RE IN MY ARMY NOW!
SQUAD—QUICK MARCH!
HOLD IT! HAVEN'T YOU FORGOTTEN SOMETHING?
RIGHT, LADS, WE'LL ATTACK THOSE GUARDSMEN IN THE BARRACKS!
CHARGE!
BUT—
STAND AT EASE!
BAH! MISSED 'EM!
SQUAD! ABOUT...
..GLUB!
PLOP!
SILENCE
CHARGE!
GUARDSMEN ARE RENOWNED FOR THEIR STRICT DISCIPLINE. BUT THESE CHAPS HAVE HAD MORE THAN THEY CAN TAKE FROM DENNIS'S ARMY......
CAN'T SEE THEM ANYWHERE!
THEY'VE VANISHED!
YOU OKAY, DENNIS?
KEEP QUIET, YOU FOOL!
I'M GONNA SNEEZE!
YOU'D BETTER NOT!

KEEP AN EYE ON "THE BEANO" EVERY THURSDAY
THE BEANO
No. 931—May 21st, 1960.
2D
EVERY THURSDAY

THE WINNER!-EVERY WEEK!
THE BEANO
No. 919—Feb. 27th, 1960.
2D
EVERY THURSDAY

HATS OFF TO A GREAT PAPER!
THE BEANO
No. 920—Mar. 5th, 1960.
2D
EVERY THURSDAY

BE GOOD TO YOURSELF - BE A "BEANO" READER!
THE BEANO
No. 918—Feb. 20th, 1960.
2D
POP
EVERY THURSDAY

NEVER BE WITHOUT A 'BEANO'!
THE BEANO
No. 924—Apr. 2nd, 1960.
2D
ZONK!
EVERY THURSDAY

KEEP TUNED IN TO "THE BEANO"!
THE BEANO
No. 923—Mar. 26th, 1960.
2D
EVERY THURSDAY

"The BEANO" Is Good For You!
THE BEANO
No. 925—Apr. 9th, 1960.
2D
EVERY THURSDAY

TOPS for HIGH JINKS!
THE BEANO
No. 916—Feb. 6th, 1960.
2D
EVERY THURSDAY

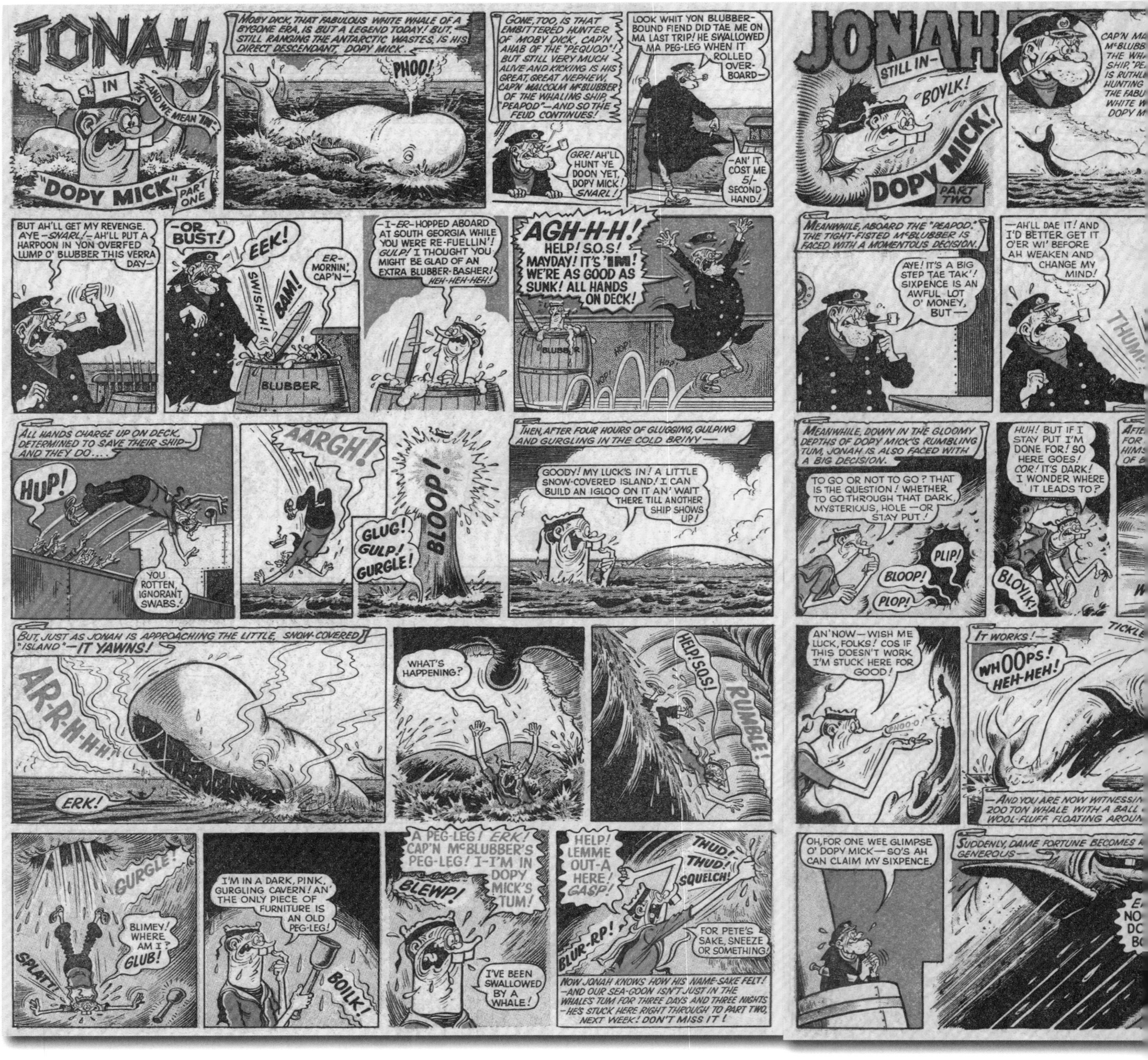
JONAH
IN
AND WE MEAN "IN"
"DOPY MICK" PART ONE
MOBY DICK, THAT FABULOUS WHITE WHALE OF A BYGONE ERA, IS BUT A LEGEND TODAY! BUT, STILL RANGING THE ANTARCTIC WASTES, IS HIS DIRECT DESCENDANT, DOPY MICK.
PHOO!
GONE, TOO, IS THAT EMBITTERED HUNTER OF MOBY DICK, CAP'N AHAB OF THE "PEQUOD"! BUT STILL VERY MUCH ALIVE AND KICKING IS HIS GREAT, GREAT NEPHEW, CAP'N MALCOLM McBLUBBER OF THE WHALING SHIP, "PEAPOD"—AND SO THE FEUD CONTINUES!
GRR! AH'LL HUNT YE DOON YET, DOPY MICK! SNARL!
LOOK WHIT YON BLUBBER-BOUND FIEND DID TAE ME ON MA LAST TRIP! HE SWALLOWED MA PEG-LEG WHEN IT ROLLED OVER-BOARD—
—AN' IT COST ME 5/- SECOND-HAND!
BUT AH'LL GET MY REVENGE. AYE—SNARL!—AH'LL PUT A HARPOON IN YON OVERFED LUMP O' BLUBBER THIS VERRA DAY—
—OR BUST!
EEK!
SWISH-H!
BAM!
ER-MORNIN', CAP'N—
BLUBBER
—I—ER—HOPPED ABOARD AT SOUTH GEORGIA WHILE YOU WERE RE-FUELLIN'! GULP! I THOUGHT YOU MIGHT BE GLAD OF AN EXTRA BLUBBER-BASHER! HEH-HEH-HEH!
AGH-H-H! HELP! S.O.S.! MAYDAY! IT'S 'IM'! WE'RE AS GOOD AS SUNK! ALL HANDS ON DECK!
BLUBBER
ALL HANDS CHARGE UP ON DECK, DETERMINED TO SAVE THEIR SHIP—AND THEY DO....
HUP!
YOU ROTTEN, IGNORANT SWABS.
AARGH!
GLUG! GULP! GURGLE!
BLOOP!
THEN, AFTER FOUR HOURS OF GLUGGING, GULPING AND GURGLING IN THE COLD BRINY—
GOODY! MY LUCK'S IN! A LITTLE SNOW-COVERED ISLAND! I CAN BUILD AN IGLOO ON IT AN' WAIT THERE TILL ANOTHER SHIP SHOWS UP!
BUT, JUST AS JONAH IS APPROACHING THE LITTLE, SNOW-COVERED "ISLAND"—IT YAWNS!
AR-R-H-H-H!
ERK!
WHAT'S HAPPENING?
HELP! S.O.S!
RUMBLE!
GURGLE!
BLIMEY! WHERE AM I? GLUB!
SPLATT!
I'M IN A DARK, PINK, GURGLING CAVERN! AN' THE ONLY PIECE OF FURNITURE IS AN OLD PEG-LEG!
BOILK!
A PEG-LEG! ERK! CAP'N McBLUBBER'S PEG-LEG! I-I'M IN DOPY MICK'S TUM!
BLEWP!
I'VE BEEN SWALLOWED BY A WHALE!
HELP! LEMME OUT-A HERE! GASP!
THUD! THUD! SQUELCH!
BLUR-RP!
FOR PETE'S SAKE, SNEEZE OR SOMETHING!
NOW JONAH KNOWS HOW HIS NAME-SAKE FELT! —AND OUR SEA-GOON ISN'T JUST IN THE WHALE'S TUM FOR THREE DAYS AND THREE NIGHTS —HE'S STUCK HERE RIGHT THROUGH TO PART TWO, NEXT WEEK! DON'T MISS IT!
JONAH
STILL IN—
BOYLK!
DOPY MICK! PART TWO
MEANWHILE, ABOARD THE "PEAPOD," THE TIGHT-FISTED McBLUBBER IS FACED WITH A MOMENTOUS DECISION.
AYE! IT'S A BIG STEP TAE TAK'! SIXPENCE IS AN AWFUL LOT O' MONEY, BUT—
—AH'LL DAE IT! AND I'D BETTER GET IT O'ER WI' BEFORE AH WEAKEN AND CHANGE MY MIND!
MEANWHILE, DOWN IN THE GLOOMY DEPTHS OF DOPY MICK'S RUMBLING TUM, JONAH IS ALSO FACED WITH A BIG DECISION.
TO GO OR NOT TO GO? THAT IS THE QUESTION! WHETHER TO GO THROUGH THAT DARK, MYSTERIOUS, HOLE—OR STAY PUT!
PLIP!
BLOOP!
PLOP!
HUH! BUT IF I STAY PUT I'M DONE FOR! SO HERE GOES! COR! IT'S DARK! I WONDER WHERE IT LEADS TO?
BLOYLK!
AN' NOW—WISH ME LUCK, FOLKS! COS IF THIS DOESN'T WORK I'M STUCK HERE FOR GOOD!
IT WORKS!—
WHOOPS! HEH-HEH!
OH, FOR ONE WEE GLIMPSE O' DOPY MICK—SO'S AH CAN CLAIM MY SIXPENCE.

This series of three 'Jonah' stories is regarded by many as Ken Reid's most inspired creations.

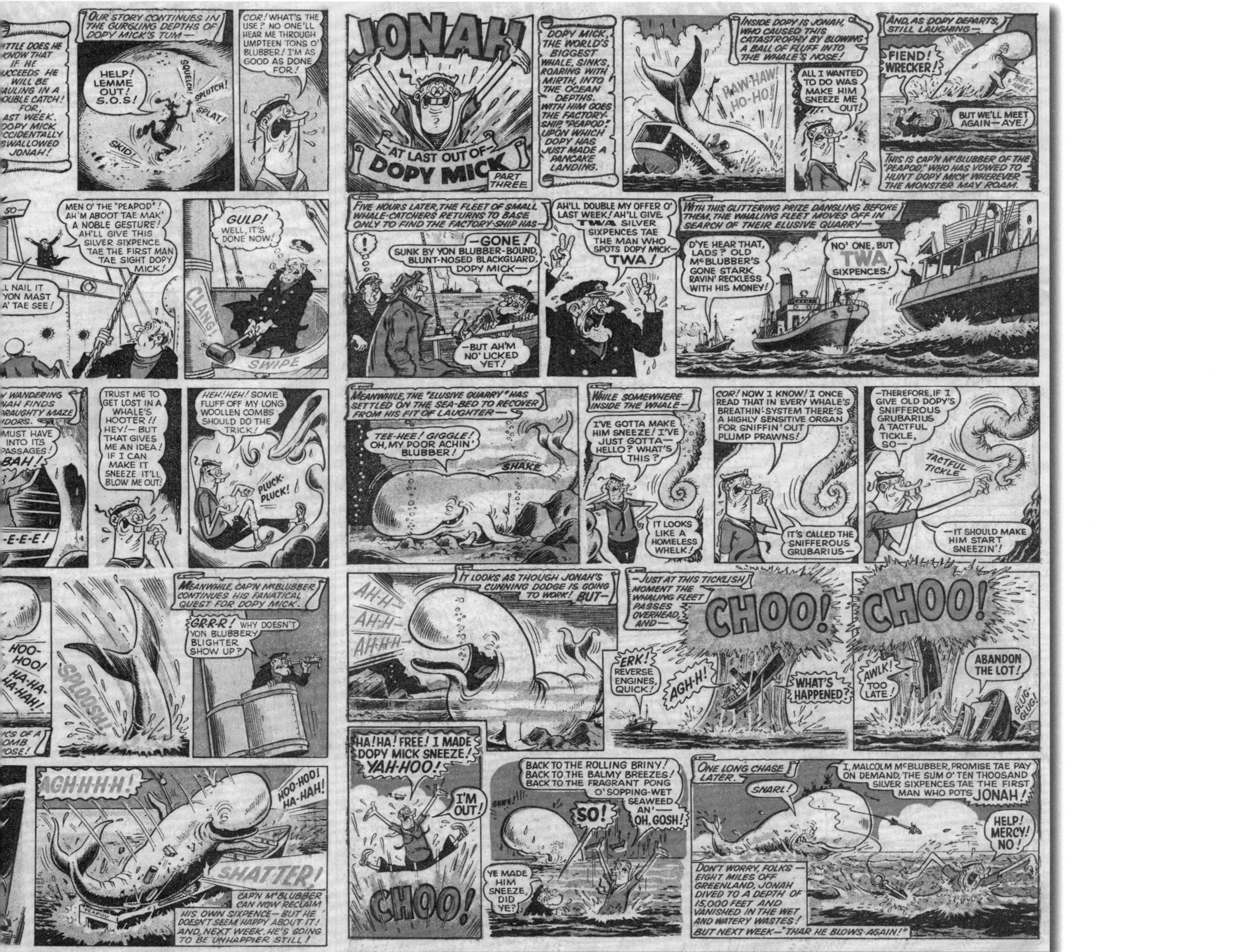
ITTLE DOES HE KNOW THAT IF HE UCCEEDS HE WILL BE HAULING IN A DOUBLE CATCH! FOR, AST WEEK, DOPY MICK CCIDENTALLY SWALLOWED JONAH!
OUR STORY CONTINUES IN THE GURGLING DEPTHS OF DOPY MICK'S TUM—
HELP! LEMME OUT! S.O.S!
SQUELCH!
SPLUTCH!
SPLAT!
SKID!
COR! WHAT'S THE USE? NO ONE'LL HEAR ME THROUGH UMPTEEN TONS O' BLUBBER! I'M AS GOOD AS DONE FOR!
JONAH
AT LAST OUT OF
DOPY MICK
PART THREE
DOPY MICK, THE WORLD'S BIGGEST WHALE, SINKS, ROARING WITH MIRTH, INTO THE OCEAN DEPTHS. WITH HIM GOES THE FACTORY-SHIP "PEAPOD," UPON WHICH DOPY HAS JUST MADE A PANCAKE LANDING.
HAW-HAW! HO-HO!
INSIDE DOPY IS JONAH, WHO CAUSED THIS CATASTROPHY BY BLOWING A BALL OF FLUFF INTO THE WHALE'S NOSE!
ALL I WANTED TO DO WAS MAKE HIM SNEEZE ME OUT!
AND, AS DOPY DEPARTS, STILL LAUGHING—
HA HA!
FIEND! WRECKER!
HEE! HEE!
BUT WE'LL MEET AGAIN—AYE!
THIS IS CAP'N McBLUBBER OF THE "PEAPOD," WHO HAS VOWED TO HUNT DOPY MICK WHEREVER THE MONSTER MAY ROAM.
SO
MEN O' THE "PEAPOD"! AH'M ABOOT TAE MAK' A NOBLE GESTURE! AH'LL GIVE THIS SILVER SIXPENCE TAE THE FIRST MAN TAE SIGHT DOPY MICK!
LL NAIL IT YON MAST A' TAE SEE!
GULP! WELL, IT'S DONE NOW!
CLANG!
SWIPE
FIVE HOURS LATER, THE FLEET OF SMALL WHALE-CATCHERS RETURNS TO BASE ONLY TO FIND THE FACTORY-SHIP HAS—
—GONE! SUNK BY YON BLUBBER-BOUND, BLUNT-NOSED BLACKGUARD, DOPY MICK—
—BUT AH'M NO' LICKED YET!
AH'LL DOUBLE MY OFFER O' LAST WEEK! AH'LL GIVE TWA SILVER SIXPENCES TAE THE MAN WHO SPOTS DOPY MICK—TWA!
WITH THIS GLITTERING PRIZE DANGLING BEFORE THEM, THE WHALING FLEET MOVES OFF IN SEARCH OF THEIR ELUSIVE QUARRY—
D'YE HEAR THAT, LADS? OLD McBLUBBER'S GONE STARK RAVIN' RECKLESS WITH HIS MONEY!
NO' ONE, BUT TWA SIXPENCES!
Y WANDERING NAH FINDS RAUGHTY MAZE DORS.
MUST HAVE INTO ITS PASSAGES! BAH!
E-E-E!
TRUST ME TO GET LOST IN A WHALE'S HOOTER!! HEY!—BUT THAT GIVES ME AN IDEA! IF I CAN MAKE IT SNEEZE IT'LL BLOW ME OUT!
HEH! HEH! SOME FLUFF OFF MY LONG WOOLLEN COMBS SHOULD DO THE TRICK!
PLUCK-PLUCK!
MEANWHILE, THE "ELUSIVE QUARRY" HAS SETTLED ON THE SEA-BED TO RECOVER FROM HIS FIT OF LAUGHTER—
TEE-HEE! GIGGLE! OH, MY POOR ACHIN' BLUBBER!
SHAKE
WHILE SOMEWHERE INSIDE THE WHALE—
I'VE GOTTA MAKE HIM SNEEZE! I'VE JUST GOTTA—HELLO? WHAT'S THIS?
IT LOOKS LIKE A HOMELESS WHELK!
COR! NOW I KNOW! I ONCE READ THAT IN EVERY WHALE'S BREATHIN'-SYSTEM THERE'S A HIGHLY SENSITIVE ORGAN FOR SNIFFIN' OUT PLUMP PRAWNS!
IT'S CALLED THE SNIFFEROUS GRUBARIUS—
—THEREFORE, IF I GIVE OLD DOPY'S SNIFFEROUS GRUBARIUS A TACTFUL TICKLE, SO—
TACTFUL TICKLE
—IT SHOULD MAKE HIM START SNEEZIN'!
HOO-HOO! HA-HA-HA-HAH!
SPLOOSH!
MEANWHILE, CAP'N McBLUBBER CONTINUES HIS FANATICAL QUEST FOR DOPY MICK.
GR-R-R! WHY DOESN'T YON BLUBBERY BLIGHTER SHOW UP?
IT LOOKS AS THOUGH JONAH'S CUNNING DODGE IS GOING TO WORK! BUT—
AH-H— AH-H— AH-H-H—
—JUST AT THIS TICKLISH MOMENT THE WHALING FLEET PASSES OVERHEAD, AND—
CHOO! CHOO!
ERK! REVERSE ENGINES, QUICK!
AGH-H!
WHAT'S HAPPENED?
AWLK! TOO LATE!
ABANDON THE LOT!
GLUG-GLUG!
AGH-H-H-H!
HOO-HOO! HA-HAH!
SHATTER!
CAP'N McBLUBBER CAN NOW RECLAIM HIS OWN SIXPENCE—BUT HE DOESN'T SEEM HAPPY ABOUT IT! AND, NEXT WEEK, HE'S GOING TO BE UNHAPPIER STILL!
HA! HA! FREE! I MADE DOPY MICK SNEEZE! YAH-HOO!
I'M OUT!
CHOO!
BACK TO THE ROLLING BRINY! BACK TO THE BALMY BREEZES! BACK TO THE FRAGRANT PONG O' SOPPING-WET SEAWEED AN'—
SO!
OH, GOSH!
YE MADE HIM SNEEZE, DID YE?
ONE LONG CHASE LATER.
SNARL!
I, MALCOLM McBLUBBER, PROMISE TAE PAY ON DEMAND, THE SUM O' TEN THOOSAND SILVER SIXPENCES TAE THE FIRST MAN WHO POTS JONAH!
HELP! MERCY! NO!
DON'T WORRY, FOLKS—EIGHT MILES OFF GREENLAND, JONAH DIVED TO A DEPTH OF 15,000 FEET AND VANISHED IN THE WET AND WATERY WASTES! BUT NEXT WEEK—"THAR HE BLOWS AGAIN!"

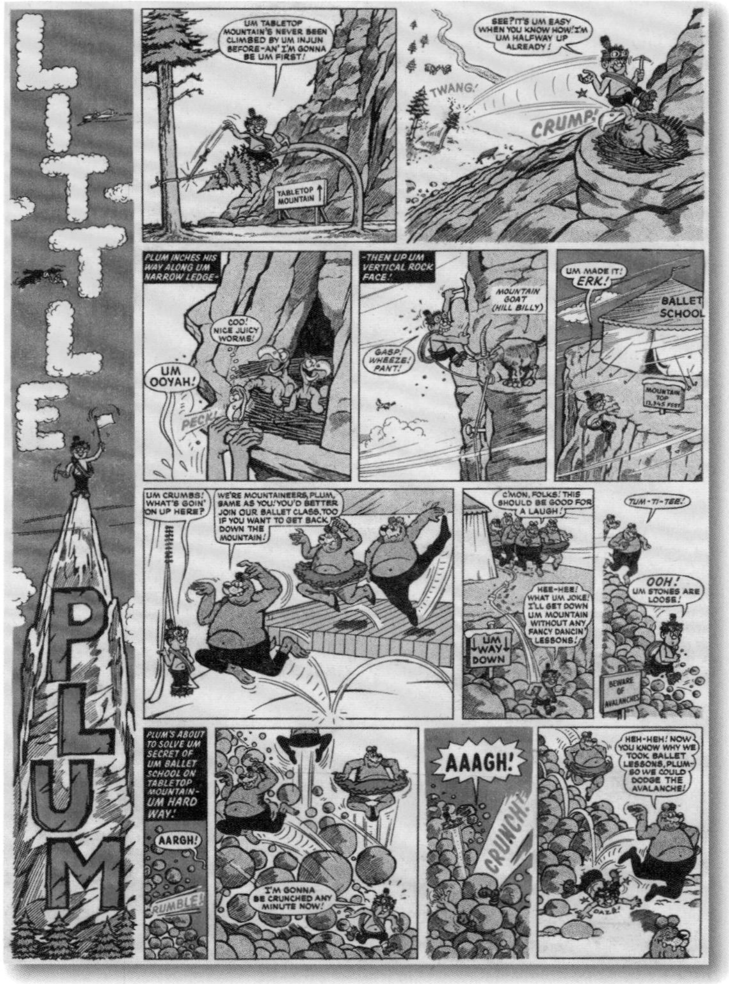
LITTLE PLUM
UM TABLETOP MOUNTAIN'S NEVER BEEN CLIMBED BY UM INJUN BEFORE–AN' I'M GONNA BE UM FIRST!
TABLETOP MOUNTAIN
SEE? IT'S UM EASY WHEN YOU KNOW HOW! I'M UM HALFWAY UP ALREADY!
TWANG!
CRUMP!
PLUM INCHES HIS WAY ALONG UM NARROW LEDGE–
COO! NICE JUICY WORMS!
UM OOYAH!
PECK!
–THEN UP UM VERTICAL ROCK FACE!
MOUNTAIN GOAT (HILL BILLY)
GASP! WHEEZE! PANT!
UM MADE IT! ERK!
BALLET SCHOOL
UM CRUMBS! WHAT'S GOIN' ON UP HERE?
WE'RE MOUNTAINEERS, PLUM, SAME AS YOU! YOU'D BETTER JOIN OUR BALLET CLASS, TOO IF YOU WANT TO GET BACK DOWN THE MOUNTAIN!
C'MON, FOLKS! THIS SHOULD BE GOOD FOR A LAUGH!
HEE-HEE! WHAT UM JOKE! I'LL GET DOWN UM MOUNTAIN WITHOUT ANY FANCY DANCIN' LESSONS!
UM WAY DOWN
TUM-TI-TEE!
OOH! UM STONES ARE LOOSE!
BEWARE OF AVALANCHES
PLUM'S ABOUT TO SOLVE UM SECRET OF UM BALLET SCHOOL ON TABLETOP MOUNTAIN–UM HARD WAY!
AARGH!
RUMBLE!
I'M GONNA BE CRUNCHED ANY MINUTE NOW!
AAAGH!
CRUNCH!
HEH-HEH! NOW YOU KNOW WHY WE TOOK BALLET LESSONS, PLUM–SO WE COULD DODGE THE AVALANCHE!

MINNIE the MINX

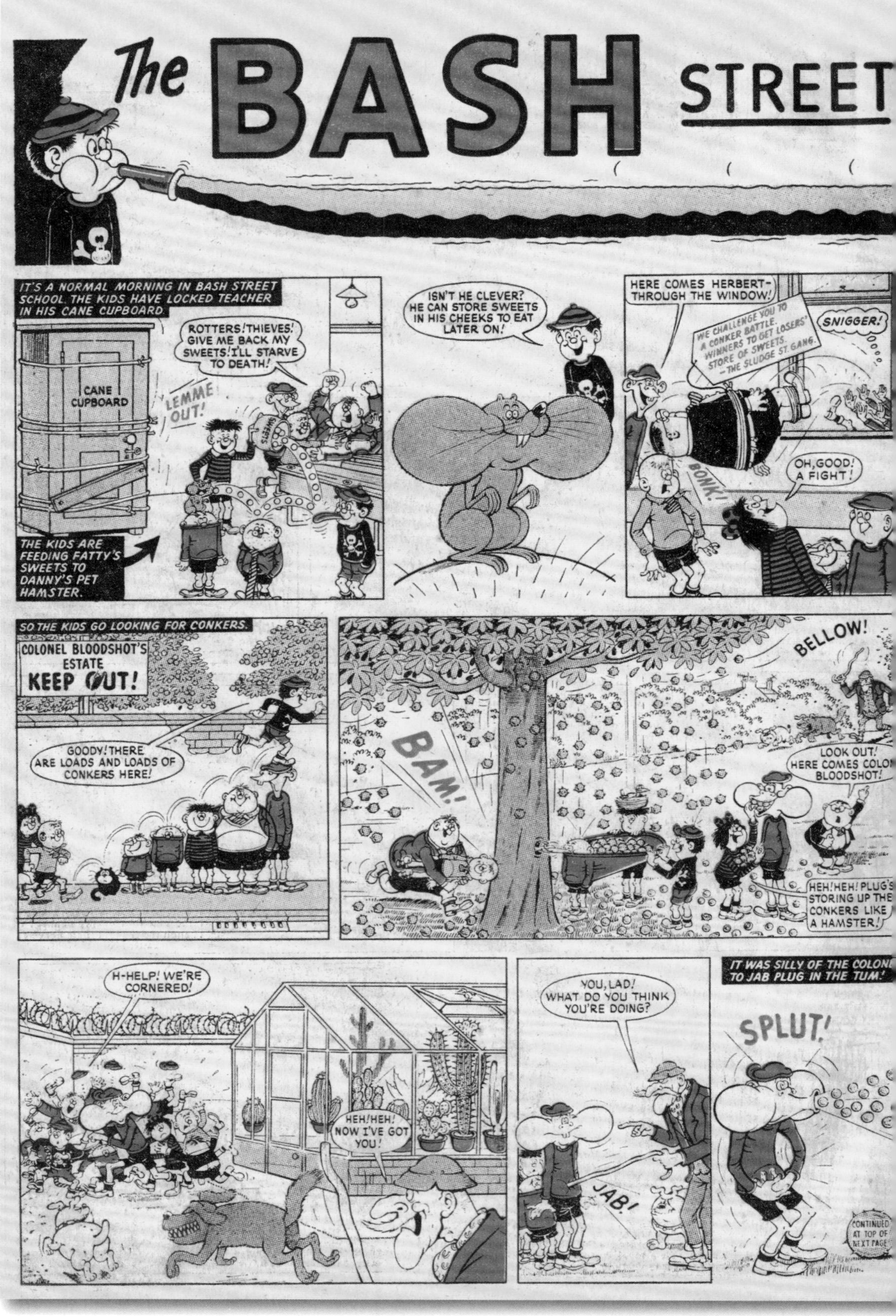
The BASH STREET
IT'S A NORMAL MORNING IN BASH STREET SCHOOL. THE KIDS HAVE LOCKED TEACHER IN HIS CANE CUPBOARD.
CANE CUPBOARD
LEMME OUT!
ROTTERS! THIEVES! GIVE ME BACK MY SWEETS! I'LL STARVE TO DEATH!
THE KIDS ARE FEEDING FATTY'S SWEETS TO DANNY'S PET HAMSTER.
ISN'T HE CLEVER? HE CAN STORE SWEETS IN HIS CHEEKS TO EAT LATER ON!
HERE COMES HERBERT–THROUGH THE WINDOW!
WE CHALLENGE YOU TO A CONKER BATTLE. WINNERS TO GET LOSERS' STORE OF SWEETS. –THE SLUDGE ST GANG.
SNIGGER!
BONK!
OH, GOOD! A FIGHT!
SO THE KIDS GO LOOKING FOR CONKERS.
COLONEL BLOODSHOT'S ESTATE KEEP OUT!
GOODY! THERE ARE LOADS AND LOADS OF CONKERS HERE!
BAM!
BELLOW!
LOOK OUT! HERE COMES COLON BLOODSHOT!
HEH! HEH! PLUG'S STORING UP THE CONKERS LIKE A HAMSTER!
H-HELP! WE'RE CORNERED!
HEH! HEH! NOW I'VE GOT YOU!
YOU, LAD! WHAT DO YOU THINK YOU'RE DOING?
JAB!
IT WAS SILLY OF THE COLONE TO JAB PLUG IN THE TUM!
SPLUT!
CONTINUED AT TOP OF NEXT PAGE

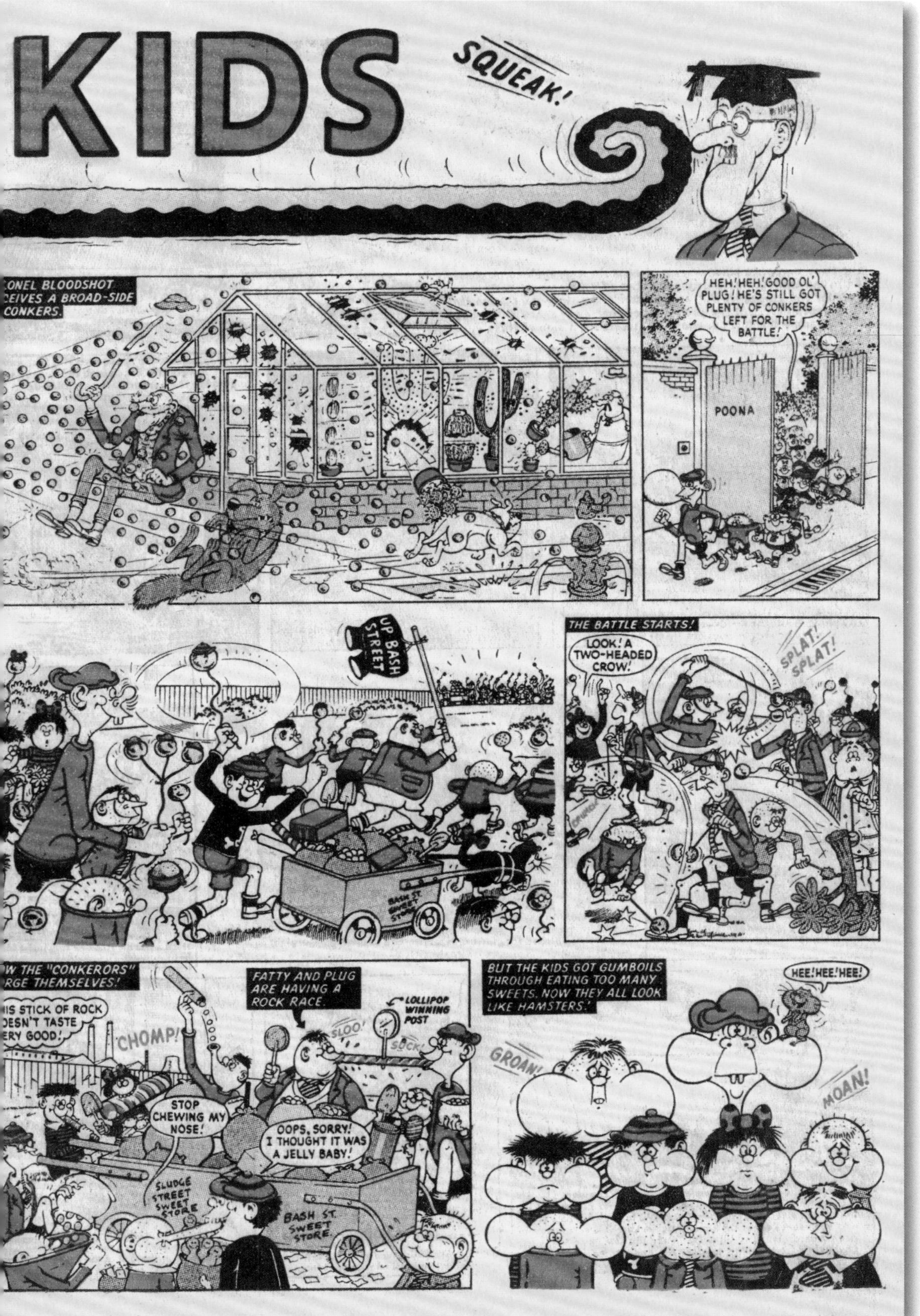
KIDS
SQUEAK!
ONEL BLOODSHOT CEIVES A BROAD-SIDE CONKERS.
HEH! HEH! GOOD OL' PLUG! HE'S STILL GOT PLENTY OF CONKERS LEFT FOR THE BATTLE!
POONA
UP BASH STREET
THE BATTLE STARTS!
LOOK! A TWO-HEADED CROW!
SPLAT! SPLAT!
BASH ST. SWEET STORE
W THE "CONKERORS" RGE THEMSELVES!
HIS STICK OF ROCK DESN'T TASTE ERY GOOD!
CHOMP!
FATTY AND PLUG ARE HAVING A ROCK RACE.
LOLLIPOP WINNING POST
SLOO!
STOP CHEWING MY NOSE!
OOPS, SORRY! I THOUGHT IT WAS A JELLY BABY!
SLUDGE STREET SWEET STORE
BASH ST. SWEET STORE
BUT THE KIDS GOT GUMBOILS THROUGH EATING TOO MANY SWEETS. NOW THEY ALL LOOK LIKE HAMSTERS.
HEE! HEE! HEE!
GROAN!
MOAN!

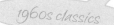

a selection of classic early 1960s strips. Leo Baxendale was always keen to give 'The Bash Street Kids' more space and drew them as a double-page spread.

MINNIE THE MINX
PAY ATTENTION, YOU LOT! WE'RE GOING TO PLAY AT SCHOOLS – AN' I'M THE TEACHER!
OH, NO!
RHUBARB
RHUBARB PATCH
I'LL USE THIS SHEET AS A GOWN!
BUT, MINNIE, TEACHERS' GOWNS ARE BLACK!
I KNOW. JUST WATCH THIS!
HOW'S THAT?
RIGHT! WE'LL START WITH SOME SUMS. NOW WHAT ARE TWO AN' TWO?
TEACHER'S DESK
SO YOU DON'T KNOW, EH? TAKE THAT!
WHACK!
WE'LL TRY AGAIN. IF A SAUSAGE AND A HALF COSTS ONE AND SIXPENCE, HOW MANY SAUSAGES WOULD YOU GET FOR FIVE SHILLINGS?
TEACHER'S DESK
YOU CAN'T ANSWER THAT EITHER! WHAT A LOT OF SILLY NITS YOU ARE!
HELP!
RHUBARB WEEVIL
AH! THE BASH ST. KIDS. MAYBE THEY'LL HELP US!
SIT QUIETLY WHILE I WRITE A FEW SUMS ON THE BLACKBOARD!
TEACHER'S DESK
1+1 1×1
WHISPER! WHISPER....
SILENCE IN CLASS!
SCUFFLE! SCUFFLE! SCUFFLE!
1+1 1×1
AARGH! I-I-I'VE GOT A NEW CLASS – THE BASH ST. KIDS!
NOW I KNOW HOW THAT POOR TEACHER OF THEIRS SUFFERS, OH, MOTHER! I'LL NEVER PLAY AT SCHOOLS AGAIN!
CORNER!

THE THREE BEARS

HARRY

Baxendale aslo started to produce a page strip of the crafty bears that had become such a fun part of the 'Little Plum' strips, constantly outwitting Plum, Chiefy and the Smellyfoot tribe. A family group was selected, Pa, Ma and little Teddy – 'The Three Bears'. Their way-out wild west stories was signature *Beano* humour. Leo Baxendale called the buffalo 'Harry' after *The Beano* Editor, Harry Cramond.

CHOMP
TEDDY
the Three Bears
PA
MA
MA'S MENU SOSS AND MASH
THAT'S THE LAST OF THE SOUP. WE'LL HAVE TO GO AND HUNT BUFFALO!
ULK!
BEARS' CAVE
TEDDY
PA
MA
HMMM! MOVIN' MOLEHILLS, EH? THERE'S SOMETHIN' FISHY GOIN' ON HERE! I'LL INVESTIGATE.
KEEP DOWN FLAT—
—FLATTER!
—FLATTER!
FLATTEST!
STOMP
STOMP
STOMP
HARRY
RUMBLE
ARGH!
WE'LL HAVE TO THINK OF SOMETHIN' ELSE.
HARRY
SO THEY TRY FISHIN'— NO LUCK!
SNIP
TA, THAT WORM WAS DELICIOUS
BETTER LUCK NEXT TIME
AFTER MUCH THOUGHT—
YEP, WE'LL GET SOME GRUB YET! TEDDY, ISSUE A CHALLENGE TO OLD HARRY THE BUFFALO.
BEARS' CAVE
THE CHALLENGE IS ACCEPTED, AND PA PREPARES FOR BATTLE!
BEARS' CAVE
OLAY!
PA'S RED FLANNEL PYJAMAS
HEE! HEE! I'VE GOT HIM ON THE RUN.
HARRY
SNORT! SNORT!
TO RIVER
SNORT
GRUNT
HERE COMES THE BIG LUMP. YOU KNOW WHAT TO DO NOW, TEDDY!
RIGHT, PA!
THUNDER OF HOOVES
OLAY!
HARRY
OIL
HOP
YUM! YUM! WHAT A CATCH!
SKID
DINNER'S READY!
MA'S MENU SMOKED SALMON

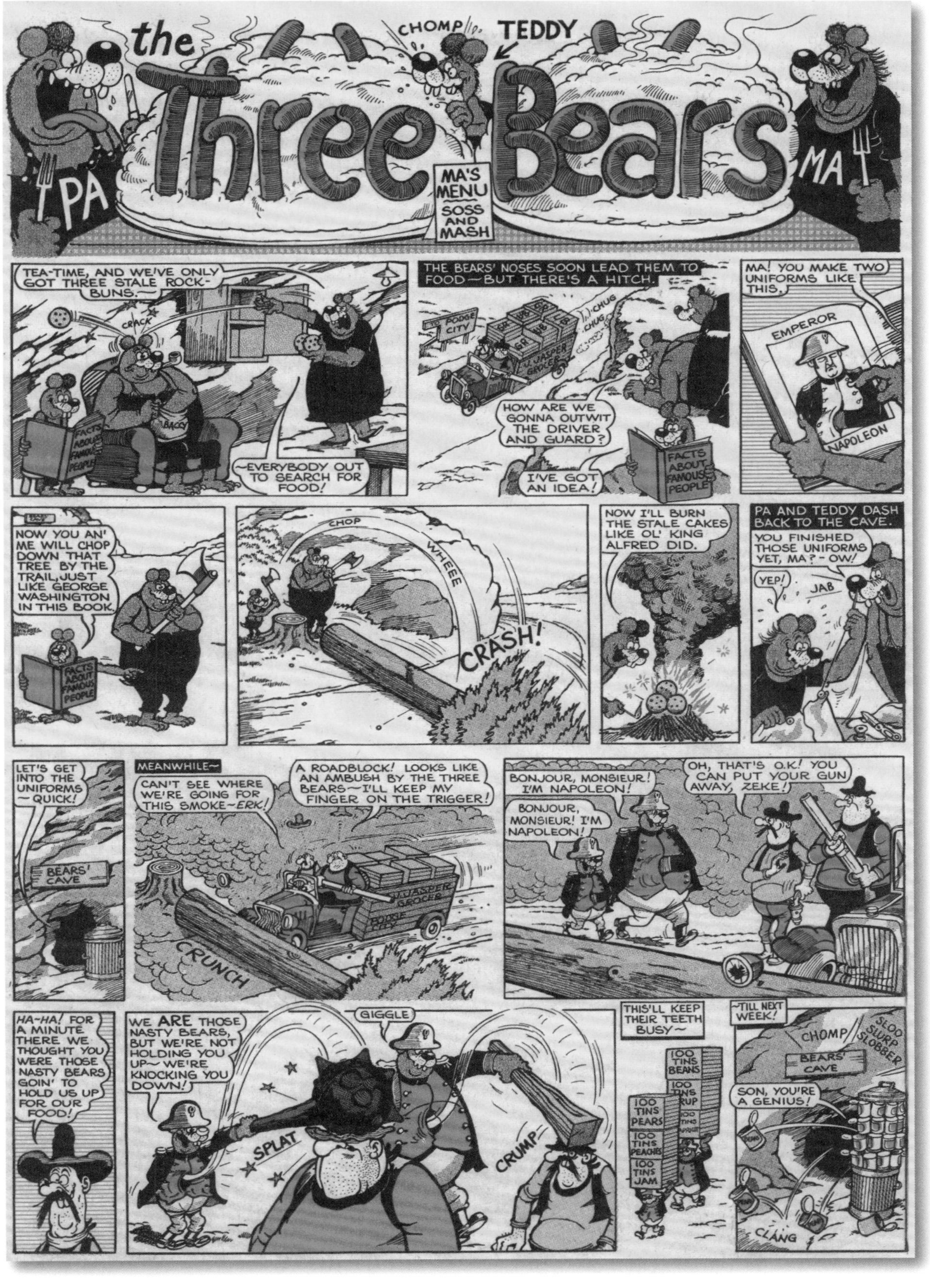
the Three Bears
CHOMP
TEDDY
PA
MA
MA'S MENU
SOSS AND MASH
TEA-TIME, AND WE'VE ONLY GOT THREE STALE ROCK-BUNS.
CRACK
FACTS ABOUT FAMOUS PEOPLE
BACCY
—EVERYBODY OUT TO SEARCH FOR FOOD!
THE BEARS' NOSES SOON LEAD THEM TO FOOD—BUT THERE'S A HITCH.
DODGE CITY
CHUG
CHUG
HOW ARE WE GONNA OUTWIT THE DRIVER AND GUARD?
I'VE GOT AN IDEA!
FACTS ABOUT FAMOUS PEOPLE
MA! YOU MAKE TWO UNIFORMS LIKE THIS.
EMPEROR
NAPOLEON
NOW YOU AN' ME WILL CHOP DOWN THAT TREE BY THE TRAIL, JUST LIKE GEORGE WASHINGTON IN THIS BOOK.
FACTS ABOUT FAMOUS PEOPLE
CHOP
WHEEE
CRASH!
NOW I'LL BURN THE STALE CAKES LIKE OL' KING ALFRED DID.
PA AND TEDDY DASH BACK TO THE CAVE.
YOU FINISHED THOSE UNIFORMS YET, MA?—OW!
YEP!
JAB
LET'S GET INTO THE UNIFORMS —QUICK!
BEARS' CAVE
MEANWHILE—
CAN'T SEE WHERE WE'RE GOING FOR THIS SMOKE—ERK!
A ROADBLOCK! LOOKS LIKE AN AMBUSH BY THE THREE BEARS—I'LL KEEP MY FINGER ON THE TRIGGER!
CRUNCH
BONJOUR, MONSIEUR! I'M NAPOLEON!
BONJOUR, MONSIEUR! I'M NAPOLEON!
OH, THAT'S O.K! YOU CAN PUT YOUR GUN AWAY, ZEKE!
HA-HA! FOR A MINUTE THERE WE THOUGHT YOU WERE THOSE NASTY BEARS GOIN' TO HOLD US UP FOR OUR FOOD!
WE ARE THOSE NASTY BEARS, BUT WE'RE NOT HOLDING YOU UP—WE'RE KNOCKING YOU DOWN!
GIGGLE
SPLAT
CRUMP
THIS'LL KEEP THEIR TEETH BUSY—
100 TINS BEANS
100 TINS PEARS
100 TINS PEACHES
100 TINS JAM
—TILL NEXT WEEK!
CHOMP
SLOO SLURP SLOBBER
BEARS' CAVE
SON, YOU'RE A GENIUS!
CLANG

The year before a four-week tryout had been published and reader reaction had been very positive. 'The Three Bears' had first appeared naked but in week two they were cleverly given the clothes that would become their uniform and further humanise them.

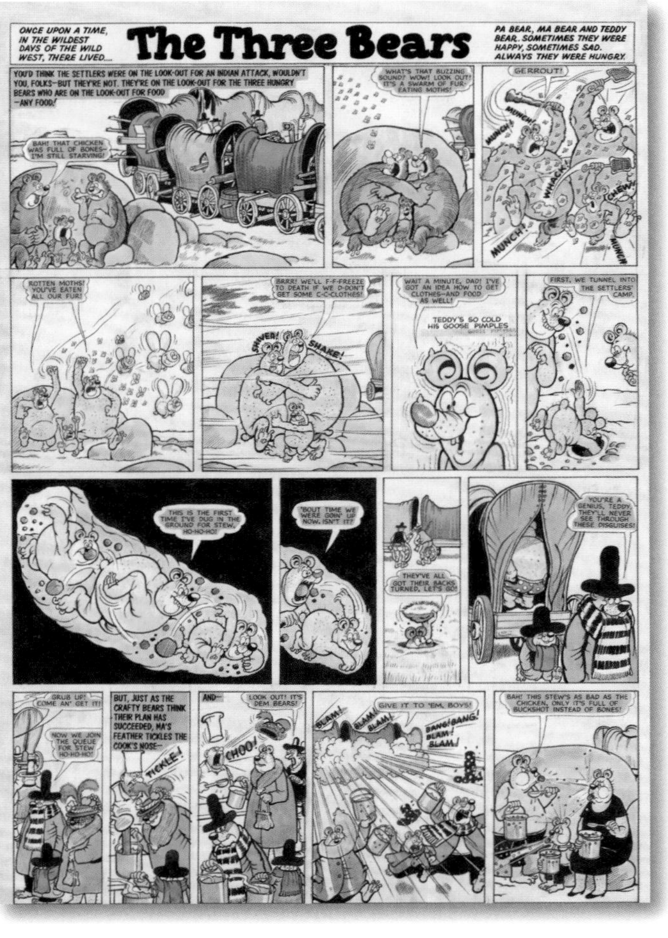
ONCE UPON A TIME, IN THE WILDEST DAYS OF THE WILD WEST, THERE LIVED...
The Three Bears
PA BEAR, MA BEAR AND TEDDY BEAR. SOMETIMES THEY WERE HAPPY, SOMETIMES SAD. ALWAYS THEY WERE HUNGRY.
YOU'D THINK THE SETTLERS WERE ON THE LOOK-OUT FOR AN INDIAN ATTACK, WOULDN'T YOU, FOLKS—BUT THEY'RE NOT. THEY'RE ON THE LOOK-OUT FOR THE THREE HUNGRY BEARS WHO ARE ON THE LOOK-OUT FOR FOOD —ANY FOOD!
BAH! THAT CHICKEN WAS FULL OF BONES— I'M STILL STARVING!
WHAT'S THAT BUZZING SOUND? WOW! LOOK OUT! IT'S A SWARM OF FUR-EATING MOTHS!
GERROUT!
MUNCH!
WHACK!
CHEW!
ROTTEN MOTHS! YOU'VE EATEN ALL OUR FUR!
BRRR! WE'LL F-F-FREEZE TO DEATH IF WE D-DON'T GET SOME C-C-CLOTHES!
SHIVER!
SHAKE!
WAIT A MINUTE, DAD! I'VE GOT AN IDEA HOW TO GET CLOTHES—AND FOOD AS WELL!
TEDDY'S SO COLD HIS GOOSE PIMPLES
FIRST, WE TUNNEL INTO THE SETTLERS' CAMP.
THIS IS THE FIRST TIME I'VE DUG IN THE GROUND FOR STEW, HO-HO-HO!
'BOUT TIME WE WERE GOIN' UP NOW, ISN'T IT?
THEY'VE ALL GOT THEIR BACKS TURNED, LET'S GO!
YOU'RE A GENIUS, TEDDY. THEY'LL NEVER SEE THROUGH THESE DISGUISES!
GRUB UP! COME AN' GET IT!
NOW WE JOIN THE QUEUE FOR STEW HO-HO-HO!
BUT, JUST AS THE CRAFTY BEARS THINK THEIR PLAN HAS SUCCEEDED, MA'S FEATHER TICKLES THE COOK'S NOSE—
TICKLE!
AND—
LOOK OUT! IT'S DEM BEARS!
CHOO!
GIVE IT TO 'EM, BOYS!
BLAM!
BLAM!
BLAM!
BANG! BANG!
BLAM!
BLAM!
BAH! THIS STEW'S AS BAD AS THE CHICKEN, ONLY IT'S FULL OF BUCKSHOT INSTEAD OF BONES!

CRACKPOT'S CIRCUS

Colonel Crackpot's Circus started in 1960. It was the first *Beano* work for artist Mal Judge. Mal had been trying since the 1940s to get accepted by *The Beano* and perhaps the change of editor was the key that unlocked the door for him.

COLONEL
CRACKPOTS
CIRCUS
WHAT ARE YOU DOING HERE, CAP'N RINGO?
COLONEL CRACKPOT'S CIRCUS SEE LANKY LARRY THE WORLD'S TALLEST MAN 9 FEET 4 INCHES IN HEIGHT
YOU CAN SCRAP THAT POSTER! MY CIRCUS HAS THE WORLD'S TALLEST MAN—NINE FEET SIX INCHES! HEH! HEH!
I DON'T BELIEVE IT!
HO! HO! COME OVER TO MY CIRCUS AND SEE FOR YOURSELF!
I'VE MEASURED HIM. HE'S NINE FEET SIX INCHES ALL RIGHT—AND HE'S NO FAKE! THAT'S A GENUINE HAIRY LEG! GRRR!
HA! HA! HA!
NEXT DAY
THERE! OKAY, CHARLIE....
...STRETCH HIM!
GRUNT!
EEEK!
BAH! STILL ONLY NINE FEET FOUR!
LISTEN, LARRY! FROM NOW ON I WANT YOU TO DO STRETCHING EXERCISES! YOU'VE GOT TO GROW THREE MORE INCHES! UNDERSTAND?
YES, COLONEL!
LATER
BONK!
BLAM!
WHEN I SAID STRETCH, I DIDN'T MEAN STRETCH OUT ON THE GROUND!
HMM! THAT LOOKS INTERESTIN'
THIS BUMP'S EXACTLY THREE INCHES TALL!
GRRRRR!
COLONEL CRACKPOT'S CIRCUS SEE LANKY LARRY THE WORLD'S TALLEST MAN 9 FEET 7 INCHES IN HEIGHT
HO! HO! HO!
HA! HA!

COLONEL
CRACKPOT'S CIRCUS
BOY, WHAT A CIRCUS I'VE GOT—BIG-TOP, HELTER-SKELTER, ROUNDABOUTS, SCENIC RAILWAY, SIDE-SHOWS — THE LOT!
CIRCUS
NOT QUITE, COLONEL. YOUR CIRCUS HASN'T GOT A DIVING TOWER WITH A MAN PLUNGING INTO A BLAZING TANK!
GOSH! YOU'RE RIGHT, CYNTHIA! I'LL HAVE TO GET ONE.
ONE WEEK LATER-
NOW, I'VE GOT EVERYTHING!
NOT QUITE, COLONEL! YOU HAVEN'T GOT A DIVER.
FOR THE FIRST TIME IN ANY CIRCUS, I WILL PROUDLY PRESENT A FAT LADY'S DEATH-DEFYING DIVE OF 100 FEET INTO A BLAZING TANK!
OH, NO!
NEXT DAY-
I-I'LL N-N-NEVER F-FORGIVE THE C-C-COLONEL F-FOR THIS!
OKAY, CYNTHIA! GET ON WITH THE REHEARSAL! DIVE!
SPUL-ASH!
LOOK OUT! SHE'S SPLASHED THE FLAMES ALL OVER THE CIRCUS!
AND NOW YOU HAVE A DIVING TOWER, BUT NO BIG-TOP, NO HELTER-SKELTER, NO ROUNDABOUTS, NO SCENIC RAILWAY, NO SIDE-SHOWS! HA! HA! HA! HA!
HE! HE! HA! HA! HAW!
HAW! HAW!

BILLY WHIZZ

In 1964 Mal and his seemingly simple art style would introduce us to 'Billy Whizz'. Editorial thought they might get a year out of the world's fastest boy before the storylines became laboured. Inspired by the characters Mal drew, the scriptwriters found different and Billy is still whizzing today.

BILLY WHIZZ
PUMP! PUMP! PUMP!
ONE OF THESE DAYS I'LL PLAY FOR THE ROVERS!
BIFF!
THUD!
SALE
SALE
THUD!
OOF!
WHIZZ!
GRR! WHIZZING ABOUT THE STREET AS USUAL, EH? THE PARK'S THE PLACE FOR FOOTBALL. GET GOING!
HUH! HE WON'T SPEAK TO ME LIKE THAT WHEN I PLAY FOR THE ROVERS.
IN THE PARK—
A QUICK BODY SWERVE ROUND THIS BUSH, AND...
THUD!
C-CORKS! I'VE BUMPED INTO JOCK KEEN, THE ROVERS' MANAGER!
YOU'RE JUST THE BOY I WANT FOR THE ROVERS. REPORT TO ME BEFORE SATURDAY'S GAME.
COO!
ON SATURDAY—
BAH! HE JUST WANTED ME FOR A BALL BOY!
AFTER THE GAME—
THEY SAID I WAS THE FASTEST BALL BOY THEY'D EVER HAD! AND I GOT A CLOSE VIEW OF THE GAME, TOO! AND THE ROVERS WON—YAHOO!

BILLY WHIZZ
DAD'S ARRIVING HOME FROM THE OFFICE—
WHAT HAS HE SEEN?
BILLY, OF COURSE!
HELLO, DAD!
WHIZZ!
THAT BOY'S MAKING ME A BAG OF NERVES! HOW MUCH LONGER CAN THIS GO ON?
STILL, ONE DAY IT MAY BE WORTH IT—BILLY MIGHT BRING HONOUR TO HIS OLD DAD BY WINNING A GOLD MEDAL AT THE OLYMPICS!
NEXT MORNING—
A LETTER FOR YOU—
—BILLY.
SNATCH
GOSH! THE INTERNATIONAL TEAM SELECTORS HAVE HEARD ABOUT ME AND THEY WANT ME TO RUN IN A BIG RACE!
WHIZZ!
THE NIGHT BEFORE THE RACE—
NO NEED TO BE NERVOUS, DAD. I'M NOT!
NOW TO PUT SOME MORE SCRAPS IN MY SCRAP BOOK.
BUMP!
GLUE
NEXT DAY—
THAT'S MY SON. HE'S AS FAST AS A JET! HE'S BOUND TO WIN!
PROUD!
SHOW THEM, BILLY!
YES, MY SON WILL RUN IN THE OLYMPICS ONE DAY!
ON YOUR MARKS!
CRACK!
ULP! WHAT'S HAPPENED? I'M STUCK!
THE RACE IS OVER AND YOU HAVEN'T LEFT THE STARTING BLOCKS YET!
YOU'VE BEEN RUNNING LIKE A WHIRLWIND FOR YEARS, AND JUST WHEN IT MATTERS MOST YOU CAN'T RUN!
I WONDER HOW THIS GLUE GOT ON BILLY'S RUNNING SHOE?

THE LAUGHING PIRATE

Away from the funnies, the Portuguese artist Vitor Peon started a real swashbuckler of a story, 'The Laughing Pirate', which would run for an exciting 22 weeks. Like thousands of schoolboys, the story caught the imagination of Dennis the Menace.

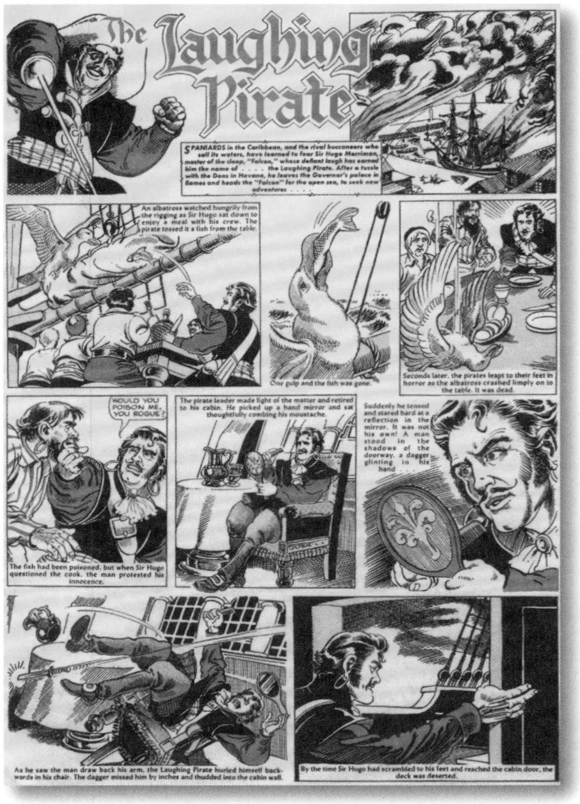
The Laughing Pirate

DENNIS THE LAUGHING MENACE
SMASHIN' STORY THIS "LAUGHING PIRATE"!
LAUGHING PIRATE
SLASH
HO! HO! HO! MEET THE LAUGHING MENACE!
ON GUARD —GUARD!
CHOP
CHOP
CHOP
CHOP
CHOP
LATER—
HO! HO! HO! HO!
AH! I SEE. A DOG OF A SPANIARD!
WOT? NO LAUGH, DENNIS?
The SPANISH RESTAURANT
YOUR DAYS ARE NUMBERED!
GRRR!
CRUNCH!
WUFF!
CRUNCH!
SNARL!
CRUNCH!
GROWL!
CRUNCH!
HEH! HEH!
WOT? STILL NO LAUGH, DENNIS?
LATER—
SHIVER ME TIMBERS! A SPANISH GALLEON!
I'LL BLOW THAT GALLEON CLEAN OUT OF THE WATER!
BOOM
WHEE-E-E-E-E
SPLOOSH
HO! HO! HO! HO! HO! HO!
THE EDITOR THOUGHT YOU'D RATHER SEE THE REAL LAUGHING PIRATE — COS WHAT'S HAPPENING TO DENNIS RIGHT NOW IS NO LAUGHING MATTER!

THE BEANO BOOKS

THE
BEANO
BOOK
PRINTED AND PUBLISHED BY
D.C.THOMSON & CO., LTD., AND JOHN LENG & CO., LTD.
LONDON — GLASGOW — MANCHESTER — DUNDEE

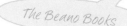

The early 1960s *Beano Books* sold in excess of 400,000 copies each Christmas. They reflected the hilarious quality of the weekly comic. To give a flavour of what was included, the pages that follow reproduce the original artwork for a selection of pages from *The Beano Book* for 1961. You will see that the cover below has no date on it, for it was not until the 1966 annual that a date appeared, 26 years after the appearance of the first *Beano Book*.

THE
BEANO
BOOK

These two pages show the original artwork for a four-page story by Leo Baxendale.

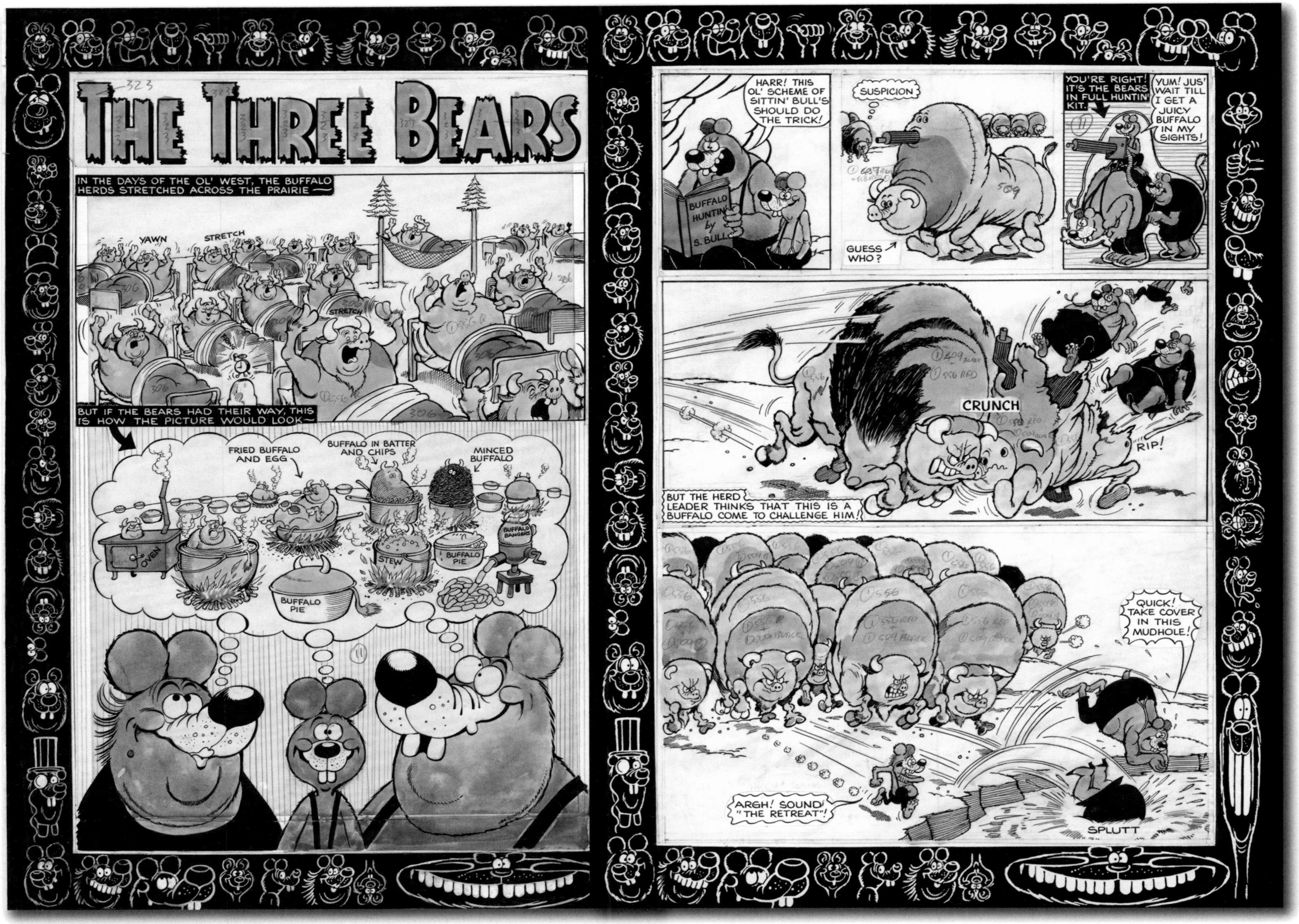
THE THREE BEARS
IN THE DAYS OF THE OL' WEST, THE BUFFALO HERDS STRETCHED ACROSS THE PRAIRIE—
YAWN
STRETCH
STRETCH
BUT IF THE BEARS HAD THEIR WAY, THIS IS HOW THE PICTURE WOULD LOOK—
FRIED BUFFALO AND EGG
BUFFALO IN BATTER AND CHIPS
MINCED BUFFALO
OVEN
STEW
BUFFALO PIE
BUFFALO BANGERS
BUFFALO PIE
HARR! THIS OL' SCHEME OF SITTIN' BULL'S SHOULD DO THE TRICK!
BUFFALO HUNTIN' by S. BULL
SUSPICION
GUESS WHO?
YOU'RE RIGHT! IT'S THE BEARS IN FULL HUNTIN' KIT.
YUM! JUS' WAIT TILL I GET A JUICY BUFFALO IN MY SIGHTS!
CRUNCH
RIP!
BUT THE HERD LEADER THINKS THAT THIS IS A BUFFALO COME TO CHALLENGE HIM!
QUICK! TAKE COVER IN THIS MUDHOLE!
ARGH! SOUND "THE RETREAT"!
SPLUTT

BUT ALAS, OL' GRANPAW BUFFALO HAPPENED TO BE WALLOWING IN THE MUD!
AHEM! THE THREE BEARS, I PRESUME?
ARGH!
GETTOUT OF MY BATH!
THUD
THEN THE BUFFALO FOOTBALL TEAM GET IN SOME HEADING PRACTICE AND—
CRUMP!
CRACK
GROAN!
ZOOM
TRAINER
HEH! HEH! HEH! HEH!
IT SAYS HERE, "IT IS SAFER TO HUNT THE STRAGGLERS OF THE HERD."
BUFFALO HUNTIN' S. BULL
WELL NOW, HERE'S A STRAGGLER IF EVER I SAW ONE!
LIMP
SHUFFLE
SPEAK UP, YOUNG FELLER!
WE'VE COME TO TAKE YOU TO THE OLD BUFFALOES HOME.
YOUR VOICE IS FAMILIAR—SO IS YOUR FACE. IT'S THOSE BEARS AGAIN!
TRAMPLE ALL OVER THEM, GRANPAW!
HE-E-LP!
NOW IT'S THE THREE BEARS WHO ARE STRETCHING ACROSS THE PRAIRIE.
PA BEAR CAN'T SEE WHERE HE'S GOIN' 'COS OF THE MASK.
KEEP RUNNIN' AND WE'LL BE OK!
15,000 FT.
AAAGH!
WHEEEEEEEEE
ZIPPPPPPP
WHIZZZZZNN
ONE THING ABOUT THE BEARS— THEY SURE CAN MAKE THE BEST OF A BAD JOB.
MENU
BUFFALO STEW
CACTUS SOUP

Another four-page story, this time with original artwork from Davey Law.

YIPPEE-E-E-E-E-E-E!
DENNIS the MENACE
SCHOOL BUS
HUH! THE OL' BUS HAS BROKEN DOWN AGAIN!
RECKON I CAN GET THE BOYS TO THE DOGGONE SCHOOL IN TIME... YES, SIRREE!
AND SO—
GOTTA GET ME SOME HOSSES. YOU'LL DO FOR ONE, SILVER—
—AN' YOU, DAISY—
—YOU'RE NEEDED, BILLY BOY—
—AN' YOU, CURLY.
MUSEUM
ALL THIS WEEK SPECIAL EXHIBITION OF WILD-WEST RELICS
MUSEUM
WELLS FARGO
GIDDUP! WE GOTTA PICK UP A LOAD O' KIDS!

YAAA!
WELLS FARGO

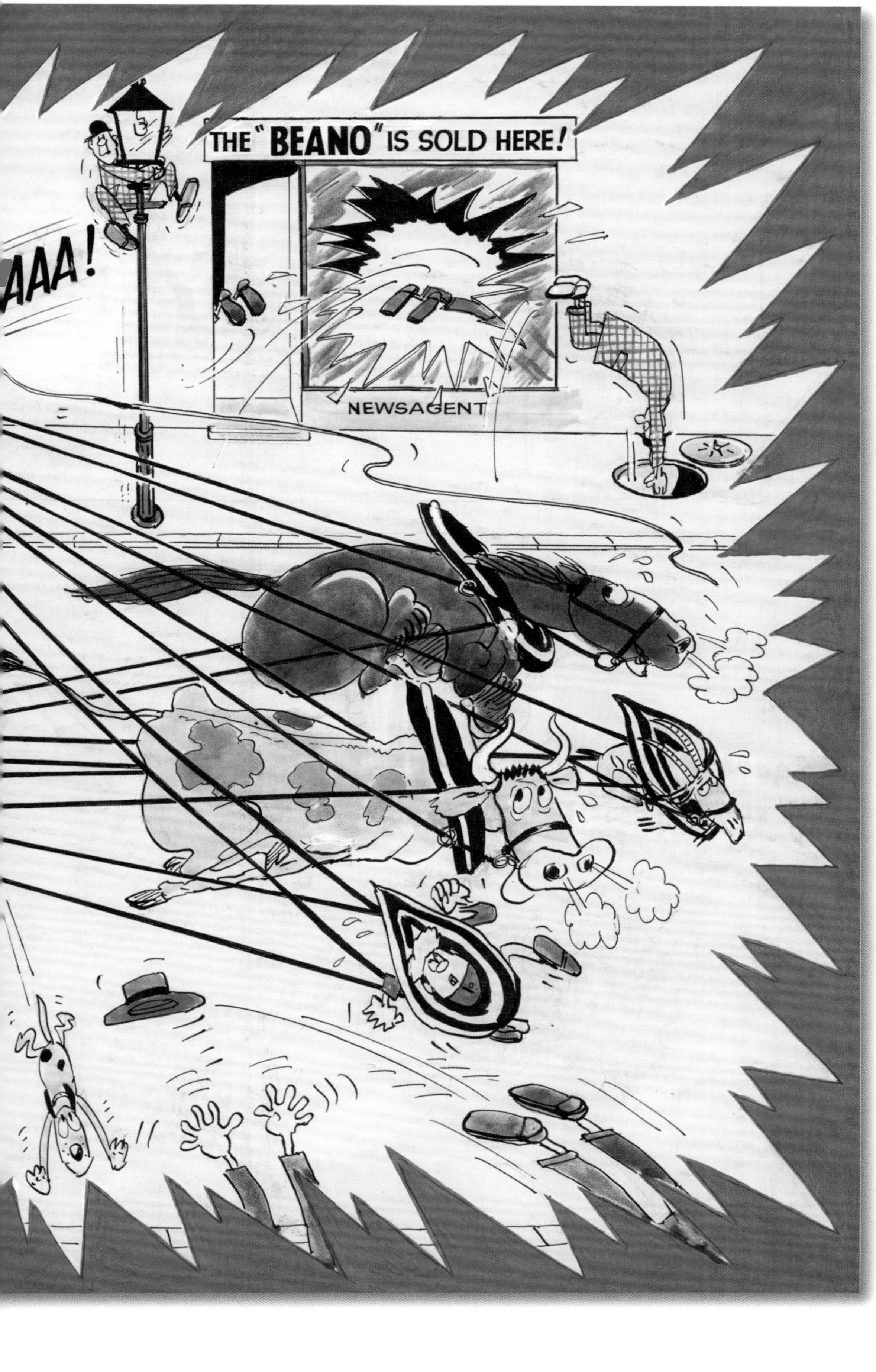
AAA!
THE "BEANO" IS SOLD HERE!
NEWSAGENT

BUT THE OL' STAGECOACH CAN'T STAND THE STRAIN!
WELLS FARGO
H'M! DENNIS IS AT THE BOTTOM OF THIS, I'M SURE!
SO TEACHER FERRIES THE BOYS—AND THE WRECKAGE OF THE STAGECOACH—TO SCHOOL.
WELLS FARGO
IN THE WOODWORK CLASS.
TODAY, BOYS, WE'RE GOING TO ASSEMBLE A STAGECOACH...
LATER—
WELL DONE, CLASS. NOW YOU CAN ALL RIDE HOME IN IT—
WELLS
—ALL EXCEPT YOU, DENNIS!
WELLS FARGO
YAAA! YAAA!

A two-page story from Bash Street, with the original artwork of Leo Baxendale.

INK
The BASH STREET KIDS
MONDAY MORNING IN SCHOOL.
ZZZZ!
HOT WATER BOTTLE
SNORE!—URK!—SNORE!
SUDDENLY—
ZIP!
THUNK!
EEEEEEEK!
PRANG!
GLUG! GASP!
POP!
ZIP!
WAKEY, WAKEY, YOU DOZY LOT! YOU'RE GOING TO WRITE AN ESSAY THIS MORNING. THE SUBJECT IS "MY PET DOG." HERE ARE YOUR PENS.
SCHOOL PENS
BOO! WE'D RATHER WRITE ABOUT OUR HERO, CHARLIE GLOBE, COLONEL CRACKPOT'S STRONGMAN. HE TEARS TELEPHONE DIRECTORIES IN HALF!
YOU'LL DO AS I SAY! WRITE ABOUT YOUR PET DOG!

Teacher, take a bow — you're a hero now!
AND WHEN TEACHER CORRECTS THE ESSAYS.
BAH! WHAT UTTER RUBBISH!
GASP! THIS CHILD'S A NIT!
UGH! I FEEL ILL!
GRR! NOW I'M GETTING REALLY ANGRY!
GRR! GNASH! GRIND! SPLUTTER!
SPEECHLESS WITH RAGE.
THEN.
THERE!—THAT'S WHAT I THINK OF YOUR HORRIBLE ESSAYS!
COO!
RIP!
TEACHER'S STRONGER THAN CHARLIE GLOBE!
MY HERO
KISS!
FLUTTER
SWOON
LET ME FEEL YOUR MUSCLES, TEACHER.
SIMPER
PLONK!
WASTE PAPER
NOW THE KIDS ARE WRITING ANOTHER ESSAY —THIS TIME ABOUT THEIR NEW HERO— "OUR TEACHER."
INK
SMUG SMILE

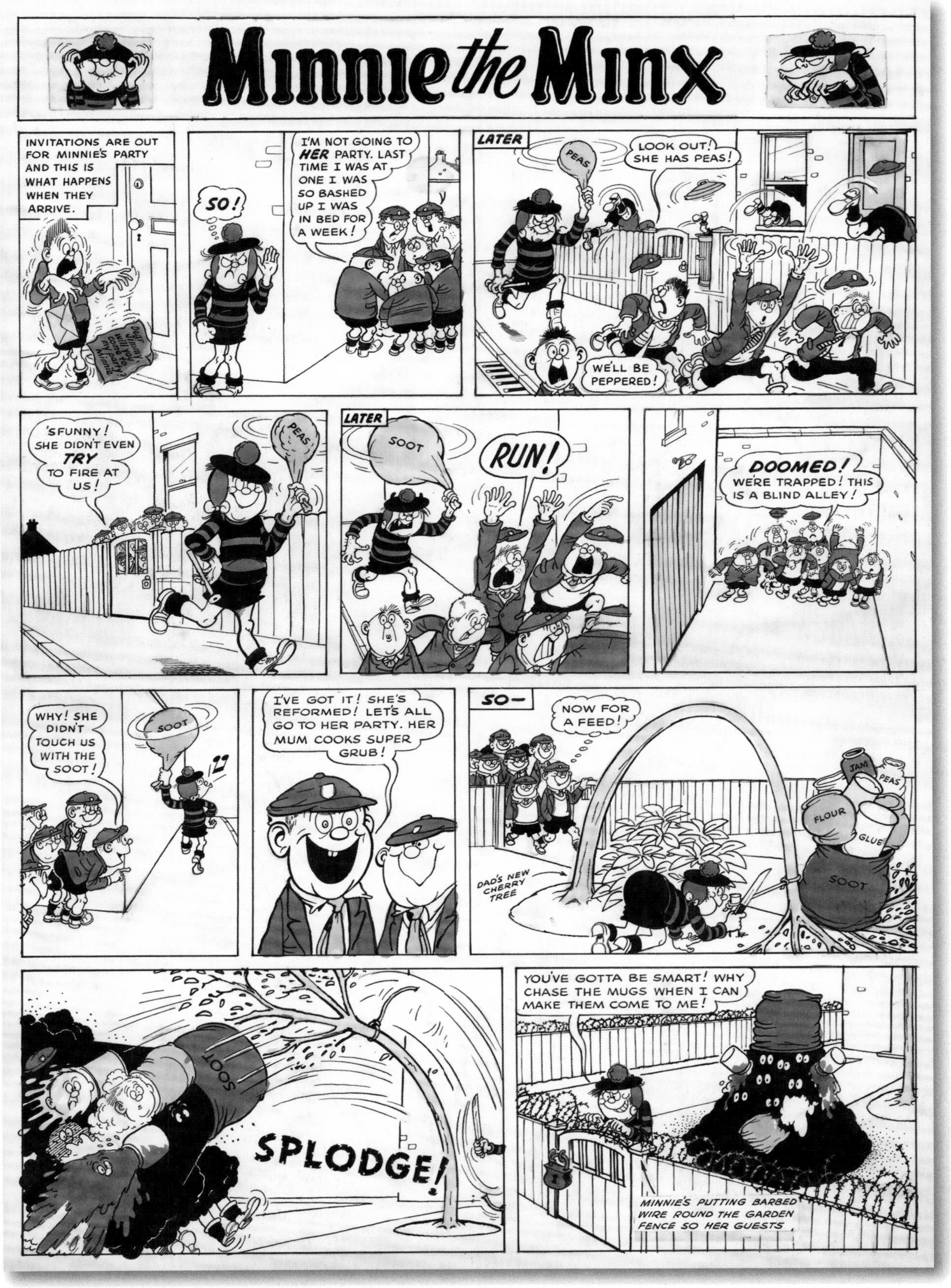

Minnie the Minx
INVITATIONS ARE OUT FOR MINNIE'S PARTY AND THIS IS WHAT HAPPENS WHEN THEY ARRIVE.
Dear Jimmy, will you come to my party? Minnie
SO!
I'M NOT GOING TO HER PARTY. LAST TIME I WAS AT ONE I WAS SO BASHED UP I WAS IN BED FOR A WEEK!
LATER
PEAS
LOOK OUT! SHE HAS PEAS!
WE'LL BE PEPPERED!
'SFUNNY! SHE DIDN'T EVEN TRY TO FIRE AT US!
PEAS
LATER
SOOT
RUN!
DOOMED! WE'RE TRAPPED! THIS IS A BLIND ALLEY!
WHY! SHE DIDN'T TOUCH US WITH THE SOOT!
SOOT
I'VE GOT IT! SHE'S REFORMED! LET'S ALL GO TO HER PARTY. HER MUM COOKS SUPER GRUB!
SO—
NOW FOR A FEED!
JAM
PEAS
FLOUR
GLUE
SOOT
DAD'S NEW CHERRY TREE
SOOT
SPLODGE!
YOU'VE GOTTA BE SMART! WHY CHASE THE MUGS WHEN I CAN MAKE THEM COME TO ME!
MINNIE'S PUTTING BARBED WIRE ROUND THE GARDEN FENCE SO HER GUESTS

A single-page Minnie story, again from Leo Baxendale, and an amazing back cover image of Jonah drawn and coloured by Ken Reid, from the 1962 Beano Book

NEW TALENT ARRIVES

With his usual good foresight, Editor Harry Cramond was picking up some new young artists. Local talents Gordon Bell (below) and Bob McGrath (right) were working 'ghosting' the regular strips. Often young artists would start this way, developing their skills by copying popular characters. Bob McGrath was a natural talent who had had minimal formal training and had done a variety of jobs prior to sending samples into D. C. Thomson. He was given his own short strip 'Wonder Boy' during 1960.

KNOCK! KNOCK!
COME IN!
BEANO OFFICE
IN
SOMEONE TO SEE YOU, MR EDITOR. HERE'S HIS VISITING CARD!
ROGER the DODGER
HELLO, ROGER! WHAT ARE YOU DOING HERE?
MY FANS WANTED ME BACK IN "THE BEANO"-SO HERE I AM!
HO! HO! I DIDN'T THINK YOU'D FALL FOR AN OLD DODGE LIKE THAT!
M'M! WELL NOW THAT YOU'RE HERE, YOU'D BETTER HAVE A LOOK ROUND THE "BEANO" WORKS.
THE OFFICE-BOY SHOWS ROGER ROUND.
THIS IS A SPECIAL MACHINE FOR FOLDING UP LARGE-SIZE EXHIBITION "BEANOS."
FOLDING MACHINE
H'MM! MUST BE A DODGE HERE!
HEH! HEH! HANDY THINGS, SCREWDRIVERS! DODGE Nº I COMING UP!
BUT PAPER AEROPLANES DON'T ALWAYS FLY WHERE YOU WANT 'EM TO!
EEK! NO!
AAARGH!
THAT'S THE MACHINE FIXED!
FIVE SECONDS LATER
HELP!
HO! HO! ROGER THE DODGER'S BACK IN "THE BEANO" ALL RIGHT, FOLKS!

RIP!

THE GREAT FLOOD OF LONDON
NEXT WEEK
STORM OVER LONDON

Bob McGrath's Wonder Boy

WONDER BOY
I wonder what it'd be like t'be...
...a lumberjack?
I'd take part in a tree-felling competition...
CHOP! CHOP! CHOP! CHOP! CHOP!
...an' before the other trees hit th' ground...
TIMBER!
...I'd have mine chopped up into firewood!
FIREWOOD!
I'd be the fastest log-roller on the river, too...
...'cos I'd chop propeller shapes at each end...
...and fairly whizz along like a torpedo!
Then I'd have a go at tree-climbing with the leg-irons...
BUT, HOLDEVERYTHIN'!
Suppos'n I went up th' tree so fast that my climbin' rope...
...frayed right through...
...an' I fell down an' landed on a...
PORCUPI-I-I-I-INE!
DON'T WANNA BE A LUMBERJACK!
NEXT WEEK HE'S WONDERIN' ABOUT... BIG-GAME FISHIN'!

Another new artist to arrive was David Sutherland and what a find this man would turn out to be. Dave, who was working in a Glasgow art studio, was persuaded to enter one of the talent-seeking D. C. Thomson drawing competitions. D. C. Thomson, on seeing Dave's entry, which came fourth and won him a princely £10, despatched R. D. Low, George Moonie and Harry Cramond to Glasgow to interview Dave and sign him up for work. To that point his studio work had been a variety of advertising drawings – Dave remembers drawing gooseberries for fruit jar labels. Sometimes the agency would be contracted to alter the whole foyer of a cinema to advertise the launch of a special big film. This would entail drawing promotional figures of film stars like Marilyn Monroe and Jane Russell, some of the drawings being eight feet in height. During one such commission Dave was doodling a Disneyesque little dog on the foyer wall, when the cinema owner spotted it. He adopted the dog as mascot of his cinema group and it appeared on screen as Davy's Dug, advertising coming attractions and other treats available in the cinemas. As a boy reading ***The Beano***, young Sutherland had been a great admirer of Paddy Brennan's artwork, so it was no surprise that his first ***Beano*** strip, 'Danny on a Dolphin', was Brennan-like in its look. Dave used a similar style for 'The Great Flood of London', 'Cannonball Crackshots' and 'Lester's Little Circus', which he drew between 1960 and 1962.

BEANO MILESTONES

On September 10, 1961, *The Beano* celebrated 1000 editions with this special cover (shown on the right). By the time that 'Biffo' led the partying for *The Beano*'s 25th anniversary on July 27, 1963 (see cover below), there were changes under way, for Leo Baxendale had left *The Beano* in 1962 and Ken Reid's work for *The Beano* would stop within the year. As they were producing six very popular strips per week, these new artists had to be brought on quickly.

WHOOPEE! "BEANO" NUMBER 1,000!
The Beano
EVERY THURSDAY
No. 1000—SEPTEMBER 16th, 1961
3D
THE "BEANO" CELEBRATION CAKE—CHOCK-FULL OF FUN!
NOW'S MY CHANCE TO GIVE BIFFO A GOOD LICKING!
I'VE HOOKED IT, HEADMASTER - A NICE LITTLE SLICE WE CAN SHARE BETWEEN US!
DON'T FORGET TO THROW SOME DOWN TO US, COLONEL!
1,000 BEANOS
THIS'LL BE QUICKER THAN CUTTING IT!
DYNAMITE
MMM! THAT WAS SMASHING!
STAND ASIDE! I'M COMING FOR MY SHARE!
TO LITTLE PLUM

The Beano
SUPER BIRTHDAY NUMBER!
EVERY THURSDAY
No. 1097—JULY 27th, 1963
3D
WE'LL HAVE A HISTORY LESSON TODAY. WHEN WAS THE BATTLE OF HASTINGS?
1066, TEACHER!
BIFFO the BEAR
GOOD! WHEN WAS THE GREAT FIRE OF LONDON?
1666, MISS!
GOOD! WHEN DID THE FIRST "BEANO" COME OUT?
GLOOMY SILENCE
YOU DON'T KNOW, EH? BIFFO! GO TO THE CANE CUPBOARD!
WHAT'S THIS? A WHACKING GREAT BIRTHDAY CAKE!
"THE BEANO" 25 YEARS OLD THIS WEEK
YES! "THE BEANO" Nº 1 CAME OUT ON TUESDAY, 26TH JULY, 1938.
AND SO—
HAPPY BIRTHDAY, DEAR "BEANO," HAPPY BIRTHDAY TO YO-OO-OU!
"THE BEANO" 25 YEARS OLD THIS WEEK

STARTS TODAY
Jinx
BEANO
HI, READERTH! MY NAME'TH JINX!
I'M ON MY WAY TO THEE THE "BEANO" EDITOR.
IN THE EDITOR'S OFFICE—
HELLO, JINX! I'M THINKING OF GIVING YOU A PAGE OF YOUR OWN IN "THE BEANO" THE ARTIST, HERE, IS GOING TO MAKE A FEW SKETCHES OF YOU.
JUST ACT NATURAL AND I'LL START.
OK!
EDITOR
AT TEA BREAK—
HERE'TH THE TEA, GENTTH! JUTHT THIT COMFORTABLY AND I'LL POUR.
CARRY ON!
OOPTH! I'VE TRIPPED OVER MY LOOTHE SHOE LATHE!
BOY! I MUST MAKE A QUICK SKETCH OF THIS!
OOO! OOO! THAT TEA'TH HOT!
HO! HO! IF THIS IS HER NORMAL BEHAVIOUR, SHE'LL MAKE A SMASHING SUBJECT FOR A COMIC PAGE.
HA! HA!
LATER—
NOW WHAT'S SHE UP TO?
HEY! THAT'TH MY DEAR BROTHERTH PORTRAIT UP THERE! HUH! THE CHEEK! LETTING IT GET ALL DUTHTY AND NEGLECTED LIKE THAT!
I'LL CLIMB UP AND DUTHT IT.
START SKETCHING—SHE MIGHT FALL!
OK!
WHOOPTH! THITH BOOK CATHE ITH A BIT WOBBLY!
EEEH! IT'TH TIPPING OVER!
ERK! NO!
CRASH!
OO!—ER!—TH-THORRY, MITHTER EDITOR........ MITHTER ARTITHT!—ER—A-ARE YOU ALL RIGHT?
DOH-H-H! WAIL! MOAN! GASP! GROAN!
G-GOSH! I THINK I'VE JUTHT ATHKED A THILLY QUETHTION!
I-I'D BETTER CALL THE HOTHPITAL!
THE NEXT DAY—
HELLO AGAIN, READERTH—
GENERAL HOSPITAL
—I'M JUTHT GOING TO VITHIT THE EDITOR AND MY ARTITHT!
ER-H-HELLO! DID I GET A PAGE IN "THE BEANO"?
GRA-APH!—RAH-GH! BLA-BLA-BLA!—SNARL! GR-R-R! OUGH-H! BLUB!
ER!—I THINK HE THAID "YETH"!
WAY OUT
THEE YOU NEXT WEEK, FOLKTH!

Ken Reid's last work for ***The Beano*** was a strip about Jonah's sister, a schoolgirl with a lisp called 'Jinx'. Added to this, the top scriptwriter, Walter Fearn, had been moved away from ***The Beano*** to edit a new pre-school title called ***Bimbo.***

THE ART OF DODGING BY ROGER VOL. I
DODGES GALORE

GOLLY! WHAT'S THIS—ROGER CHASING DAD? IT CAN'T BE!
NO, IT ISN'T! DAD'S CHASING ROGER ROUND AND ROUND THE HOUSE—AND ROGER'S GOING SO FAST HE'S ALMOST LAPPED DAD!
LATER—GOODNESS! WHAT'S WRONG WITH ROGER? HE SEEMS "NETTLED" ABOUT SOMETHING!
GR-R-R! ALL RIGHT, LAUGH! BUT I STILL SAY I'M A BETTER DODGER THAN DAD. IT'S JUST THAT HE HAS ALL THE PESKY LUCK!

THE NEXT GENERATION

On taking over 'The Bash Street Kids' permanently, Dave Sutherland was given the luxury of two pages and full colour as the centre spread.

THE BASH STREET KIDS
THAT'S ALL THE BUILDINGS SCRUBBED CLEAN, YOUR WORSHIP!
VERY GOOD, SNUGGS. NOW PUT OUT THAT FOUL PIPE! THIS IS A SMOKELESS ZONE!
I'M SLIPPING! I MEANT TO HIT HIS EAR!
HOTEL POSH
NIFF
DUST BIN
REFUSE
SAM SNUGGS HEAD STREET ORDERLY
THEN THE KIDS SPOT SILAS SUDDS, THE WEALTHY LAUNDRY OWNER
SUDDS' LAUNDRY
SOLID GOLD
HEY, KIDS–THERE'S MONEY TO BE MADE IN THE LAUNDRY BUSINESS!
SO–
B-BUT MY CLOTHES DON'T N-NEED WASHING!
QUIET, NIT!
ZONK!
TRAMPLE
HORSE TROUGH
DANNY'S LAUNDRY
AGH! RUN FOR IT! IT'S A MAD HORSE!
SOAPY SUDS
HELP! IT'S FOAMING AT THE MOUTH!
THEN ANOTHER CUSTOMER APPEARS
CAN I HAVE MY TROUSERS CLEANED AND PRESSED, PLEASE?
DANNY'S LAUNDRY WE'LL TACKLE ANYTHING!
HE HAD A DIRTY FACE
CERTAINLY, TEACHER. PLUG WILL ATTEND TO YOU.
CORKS! THIS SHIRT HAS SHRUNK!
MANGLE
WASH TUB
YOU NIT, PLUG. TAKE TEACHER OUT OF THE TROUSERS FIRST!
HEH! HEH! I'VE ALWAYS WANTED TO DO THIS.
ARGH! MERCY!
DANNY'S LAUNDRY WE'LL TACKLE ANYTHING
STAGGER
BIG-TOP
I SEE BY YOUR SIGN THAT YOU'LL TACKLE ANYTHING! I'LL GIVE YOU FIVE BOB IF YOU'LL WASH MY BIG-TOP.
DANNY'S MUM'S WASHING MACHINE
OK!
I DON'T LIKE THIS PROGRAMME. I'LL CHANGE TO THE OTHER CHANNEL!
GOSH! THE COLONEL'S LEFT HALF THE MENAGERIE IN THE TENT!
YUM! YUM! I LOVE A TURNIP, I DO.
WE'LL HAVE TO GET A BIGGER WASH-TUB FOR THIS TENT!
TURNIP?
COR! WHAT A HORRIBLE FACE!
SO THE KIDS INVADE THE BOILER HOUSE AT THE LOCAL SWIMMING POOL
POOL
BOILER HOUSE
CRACK!
I'LL ADJUST THE HEAT REGULATOR. WE WANT THE WATER TO BE REALLY HOT!
WE CAPTURED SOME OF THOSE BLOB ST. SAPS TO ACT AS SLAVES. GET SHOVELLING, YOU DOGS!
FIVE MINUTES LATER THE WATER IN THE POOL'S BOILING
HIGH DIVING BOARD
A HIGH DIVER – THAT WAS
YEOW!
AARGH!
BOIL
EEK!
BOYLK
OOYAH!
SKID
CIRCUS
MORE SOAP, WILFRID. WE'LL GIVE THE BIG TOP A SUPER SHAMPOO
BACK IN THE DUNGEON– ER–BOILER HOUSE.
SHOVEL FASTER, YOU SLAVES!
AND OUTSIDE
LOOK, FRED. WE'LL BE ABLE TO DO SOME NIGHT-FLYING PRACTICE IN THAT SMOKE.
THIS IS A SMOKELESS ZONE
PUBLIC BATHS
LATER
AAAIEEE!
NICE COLONEL–ER–GENERAL CRACKPOT! HERE'S YOUR BIG TOP. IT'S SHRUNK A LITTLE–BUT YOU MUST ADMIT IT'S CLEAN!
NEVER MIND, COLONEL! NOW YOU CAN SAY YOU'VE GOT THE SMALLEST BIG TOP IN THE WORLD! HAW! HAW!
HEE! HEE!
30FT DEEP
AND OUTSIDE THE BATHS, THERE'S MORE TROUBLE
YOU YOUNG NITS! THE SMOKE FROM THAT BOILER-HOUSE HAS BLACKENED ALL OUR LOVELY WHITE BUILDINGS–SO GRAB A SCRUBBING BRUSH EACH AND START CLEANING THEM AGAIN!
BONK!
MR MAYOR
OFFICIAL BARROW
THOSE YOUNG BOUNDAHS SHOULD BE HORSE-WHIPPED!
I ONCE WAS A BLACKBIRD LIKE YOU, CLAUDE–BUT THOSE KIDS HAVE SCRUBBED ME WHITE!
I CAN HARDLY SEE IN THIS FOG.
CRUMBS! THE COAL'S WHITE!
I'M SURE I LEFT A BLACK HORSE HERE!
I ALWAYS HATED SOAP AN' WATER–NOW I LOATHE 'EM!
SCRUB
BAH! NO MORE CLEANING FOR US! WE'RE SICK OF SCRUBBING!
A WHITE LETTER BOX?
MORE FUN NEXT WEEK!

the
TEDDY
Three Bears
PA
MA
NO, FOLKS, THIS AIN'T SHERLOCK HOLMES! IT'S PA BEAR ON THE TRAIL OF.... GRUB!!
HEH! HEH! I GOT THIS BLOODHOUND CHEAP. HE'LL SOON PICK UP THE SCENT.
SNUFFLE
WA-A-A-H! THE SIGHT OF BLOOD MAKES ME FEEL FAINT!
HUH! NO WONDER I GOT HIM CHEAP. HE CAN'T STAND THE SIGHT OF BLOOD. BUT IS IT BLOOD?
SWOON!
NOPE! IT'S KETCHUP!
FOOD EXHIBITION
TOMATO KETCHUP FOR FOOD EXHIBITION
PA FIRES THE SIGNAL ARROW.
PLOP
MA AND TED FOLLOW THE STRING.
10 MILES LATER.
WE'LL DISGUISE OURSELVES AS CHEFS AND SNEAK IN.
FOOD EXH
CHEF OUTFITS
FRED'S GIANT HOT DOGS
FREE SAMPLES
YAHOO! WE'LL HAVE SOME FREE SAMPLES.
THE ORIGINAL SLOBBER-CHOP PIES
O'FLAHERTY'S FAMOUS IRISH STOO
WHERE'S THE EXHIBITION?
FRED'S GIANT HOT DOGS
GULP! THE BEARS HAVE EATEN IT!
TA!
EMPTY
SO THE EXHIBITORS TAKE THE BEARS TO HOSPITAL AND GET THEM X-RAYED.
BURP!
BURP!
BURP!
—AND LATER, THE EXHIBITION CONTINUES WITH X-RAY PICTURES OF THE BEARS' TUMS!
THE ORIGINAL SLOBBER-CHOP PIES.
A MOST SUMPTUOUS STEW!
O'FLAHERTY'S FAMOUS IRISH STOO
FRED'S GIANT HOT DOGS
PA'S TUM
TED'S TUM
MA'S TUM
DROOL!
A WEEK LATER.
ANOTHER WEEK OF GRUEL SHOULD SEE YOU FIT ONCE MORE!
AARGH! THIS GRUEL'S CRUEL! GLUG!
MERCY! GIVE US FOOD!

One of Bob McGrath's early 'Three Bears' strips.

This is where Harry Cramond's pool of new talent came into their own and the strong ***Beano*** stories were divided up between them. Dave Sutherland was given 'The Bash Street Kids', which had been stepped up to a double page, full-colour centre spread. Dave also drew the amazing 'Super Teacher' below. Bob McGrath was the new 'Three Bears' artist and between them Gordon Bell and Bob McGrath were doing 'Roger the Dodger'.

Young art teacher Jim Petrie was given 'Minnie the Minx', and his first strip is shown here. He continued to draw Minnie for 2,000 episodes, which means he must have drawn tens of thousands of individual Minnie drawings. One of these, with Dennis, is shown opposite. Dave Sutherland drew Mrs Teacher, in Bash Street, with a moustache just like Teacher (see below).

MINNIE THE MINX
MINNIE! WHY CAN'T YOU SIT DOWN AND READ A BOOK LIKE NORMAL GIRLS?
PYONNG!
NOW AIN'T THAT INTERESTIN'! THERE'S AN INDIAN GIRL IN THIS BOOK CALLED MINNEHAHA! I'LL BET SHE WAS AN ANCESTOR OF MINE. I MUST SEE HOW I LOOK IN AN INDIAN OUTFIT.
HIAWATHA
BOOK WORM
MUM'S FEATHER DUSTER BEFORE MINNIE READ ABOUT MINNEHAHA —
BUT AFTER MIN'S SCALPING KNIFE'S BEEN IN ACTION IT LOOKS LIKE THIS —
NOW THE MODERN MINNEHAHA GOES ON THE WARPATH.
MIN'S SECRET SPY-HOLE
BEEZER
BEANO
BAIT
HUP, YOU LOT! HUP!
MIN'S CAPTIVES MAKE A FINE TOTEM POLE
WOOO-WALLAH-WOOO! I'M READY TO DO SOME SCALPIN' NOW! WOOO!
DAD HASN'T GOT ENOUGH HAIR TO MAKE IT WORTH WHILE SCALPING HIM, SO I'LL TAKE HIS FACE FUNGUS INSTEAD.
SNORE! ZZZZZ
IT'S NOT MUCH OF A SCALP, BUT IT'S A START.
LATER.
SNIP SNIP
HEH! HEH! I'VE JUST SWIPED A SCALP FROM BIG CHIEF SLEEPING BULL.
BUT THE SLEEPING BULL AWAKES.
HA! HA! I SEE YOU'RE HAVING TROUBLE WITH BIG CHIEF SITTING BULL! WELL.....
... ONE OF MY ANCESTORS WAS A CHIEF OF THE BIG FEET TRIBE AND THIS IS ONE OF HIS MOCCASINS!
LOOK AT MINNIE-HO! HO!
YOU MEAN MINNIE-HA! HA! OUCH! GRRR!

MEANWHILE, ON THE PIER—
I'LL JUST POP ALONG AND SEE HOW TEACHER AND THE CHILDREN ARE GETTING ALONG.
NEW HAT
TEACHER'S WIFE
SHRIEK!
SKID

Ron Spencer took on 'Little Plum'.

LITTLE PLUM
I ORDERED UM BOX OF EGGS AT UM STORE IN CACTUSVILLE. FETCH THEM FOR ME, PLUM — AND BE CAREFUL!
OK, CHIEFY.
EGGS
CHEESE
SO—
HERE ARE THE EGGS CHIEFY ORDERED, PLUM.
FRESH EGGS
ASSORTED EGGS
ON UM WAY BACK TO UM VILLAGE—
GULP!—UM COUGAR—AND I DON'T LIKE UM WAY HE'S LOOKING AT UM EGGS!
I JUST LOVE EGGS!
GROWL!
EEK! OH, NO! I'VE DROPPED UM EGGS!
I MUST SAVE THEM!
PHEW! JUST IN TIME!
ZOOM!
RUMBLE!
WHEEZE!
PUFF!
GASP!
EGGS
EEK! UM AVALANCHE!
EEK! OUCH! OOYAH!
THUD!
AH, WELL, AT LEAST I'VE SAVED UM EGGS!
HERE ARE UM EGGS, CHIEFY— GASP!— SAFE AND SOUND.
EGGS
CHORTLE! IT WAS ALL UM JOKE, PLUM! UM EGGS ARE MADE OF RUBBER!
EH?
LOOK—YOU CAN THROW THEM AGAINST UM ROCKS AND THEY WON'T BREAK!
BUT THEY REBOUND, CHIEFY!
EEK! OUCH! OOYAH!
TEE-HEE-HEE!

Only 'Jonah' ceased, the nautical nutcase stopping in June 1963. The full-colour back cover slot was given over to 'Dennis the Menace', now wilder than ever with a new writer, Ian Gray, providing Davey Law with the stories. Within a remarkably short time, through diligent work by the artists and concentrated editorial back up, the established strips continued to flourish.

Jim Petrie's Minnie and Dennis.

Every Thursday ★ ★ ★ ★ THE BEANO ◆ ◆ ◆ ◆ April 17, 1965
Dennis The Menace
TUT-TUT! WE'LL HAVE TO GET THIS ROOM DECORATED.
WHISPER! IT'S ALL HIS FAULT! HE MADE THOSE MARKS!
THEN—
I WANT YOU ALL TO SKETCH A DESIGN FOR DECORATING THE CLASSROOM WALLS.
SO—
MINE WILL BE BEST!
SPLASH!
THESE ARE BOTH LOVELY, BOYS!
YOU HAVEN'T LOOKED AT MINE YET, TEACHER!
UGH! I WON'T BOTHER. IT'S SURE TO BE AWFUL!
AND NOW I'LL FETCH THE HEADMASTER TO DECIDE WHICH IS THE PRETTIEST PATTERN.
TEE-HEE! I KNOW MINE WILL BE BEST!
I STILL SAY MY PATTERN'S BEST— AND I'LL MAKE SURE THE HEAD SEES IT WHEN HE ARRIVES!
LATER—
THEY'RE ALL LOVELY PATTERNS, HEADMASTER!
I'M SURE THEY ARE!
SPLAT!
THIS IS A SMASHING PATTERN FOR A CLASSROOM WALL!
ERK!
GRRR! I'LL MAKE SURE THAT BOY SCRUBS THOSE WALLS!
LATER—
—AND NOW YOU CAN DECORATE THE BLACKBOARD WITH FIVE HUNDRED LINES!
TEE-HEE! TITTER!
I MUST NOT BE A NAUGHTY PUPIL. I MUST NOT BE A NAUGHTY PUPIL. I M
Printed and Published in Great Britain by D. C. THOMSON & Co., Ltd., and JOHN LENG & Co., Ltd., 12 Fetter Lane, Fleet Street, London, E.C.4.
© D. C. THOMSON & CO., LTD., 1965.

THE DANDY - BEANO SUMMER SPECIAL

A very unusual landmark comic was created in spring 1963. For the first time the two heavyweights of the British comic world, *The Dandy* and *The Beano*, got together to produce a large format 32-page, gravure printed publication, *The Dandy–Beano* Summer Special. It was a selection of reprinted strips from both comics laid out to make a bright, summer holiday read. This format was never repeated for the special was so successful that both comics would produce

Dandy-Beano
SUMMER SPECIAL
1/6
COW PIE
(TINY)
What happens? See the back page!

HO! HO! HO! LISTEN TO THIS HOWLER! "PEOPLE IN VENICE TRAVEL ON GORGONZOLAS!"
WHAT'S SO FUNNY?
DANNY'S ESSAY

COW PIE

BIFFO THE BEAR
ANYONE FOR TENNIS ?
I'LL MAKE THIS ROUND STONE LOOK LIKE A TENNIS BALL.
HIT THIS ONE, BIFFO!
FISH AND CHIPS
CHIPS LATER TONIGHT— CHIP-CUTTER BROKEN DOWN. ALL CHIPS CUT BY HAND, Toni
IDEA
I'LL THREAD THIS THIN WIRE THROUGH MY TENNIS RACKET.
READY!
POTATOES
I PAY YOU WELL FOR THIS, BIFFO!
SMACK
POTATOES
THIS IS BETTER THAN A CHIP-CUTTING MACHINE!
?
CHIPS
CHIPS

their own *Summer Special* every year thereafter – a summer treat that comic fans looked forward to almost as much as the Christmas *Annual*. The writers enjoyed working on the holiday stories as they could take their chosen characters to summer holiday destinations. Print schedules were such that these summer strips were written and drawn in the middle of winter. The large pages gave great scope for a real splash of colour. The first joint cover and subsequent early *Beano Summer Special* covers were drawn by Dudley Watkins; the front cover scene was a happening that would have a conclusion on the back cover.

ANCHOR'S AWAY, SIR!
OH, NO!
MINNIE FORGOT TO TIE THE ROPE TO THE ANCHOR!

WE'RE OUT AT SEA NOW, THANKS TO YOU, PEST—AND THERE'S NO WIND AT ALL! I'LL HAVE TO ROW US BACK—HAND ME THE OARS!

DENNIS the MENACE
STOP MOONING AROUND, THINKING UP MISCHIEF TO DO. GO AND SELL FLAGS IN AID OF THE DOGS' HOME LIKE THE OTHER LITTLE BOYS!
BAH! DAD'S ALWAYS INTERFERIN'!
WHERE ARE YOU GOING WITH THAT?
I'VE CHANGED MY MIND, I'M GONNA SELL FLAGS.
DENNIS! STOP THAT AT ONCE!
WHY DOESN'T DAD MAKE UP HIS MIND? I WAS GOING TO CHOP DOWN THIS FLAG AND SELL IT!
LATER
THE SOONER I GET THESE FLAGS SOLD THE SOONER I CAN DO SOMETHIN' USEFUL!
FLAG, MISTER!
I DON'T MIND HELPING THE DOGS' HOME!
HOI! YOU HAVEN'T GIVEN ME A FLAG!
OW!
HE'S FOUND HIS FLAG!
THIS FAN WILL HELP!
BUS STOP
FIVE FLAGS, MISTER! THAT'LL BE ONE AND THREE-PENCE!
WE'D BETTER PAY—THAT'S THE MENACE!
THERE'S A MAN GOIN' UP IN A BALLOON—MUST SELL HIM A FLAG BEFORE HE GOES!
BUY A FLAG!
I'VE GOT HIS MONEY. NOW I'LL GIVE HIM HIS FLAG!
HOI!
BANG
HERE'S THE MONEY FOR THE DOGS' HOME!
DOGS HOME
LOOK WHAT YOU'VE COST US, I GOT THE BILL IN FOR THE DAMAGE YOU DID—AND THE BANG YOU MADE SCARED ALL THE DOGS OUT OF TOWN!
BILL
HULLO, DENNIS—THEY SENT FOR ME! I HAVE A JOB TO DO!
AN' IF THEY EVER BUILD A DOGS' HOME I'M GOING TO GET THEM TO KEEP YOU IN IT!
I'VE PUT THE FLAGS AT HALF-MAST!

General JUMBO
"THE Army exercises are about to begin!" chuckled young Jumbo Johnson. "Very good, General Jumbo, sir," returned the plump, cheery-faced man beside Jumbo, and he began to strap a strange gadget to Jumbo's left arm. The man was Professor Carter, and that gadget was a wonderful device by which Jumbo controlled an army —an army of model soldiers, tanks and planes.
The models were the marvellous invention of the Professor, and the brilliant inventor had put Jumbo in charge of them. Now Jumbo was going to have full-scale manoeuvres in Dinchester Park. As the Professor went off to open his van, Jumbo heard a boy's startled shout from the other side of a hedge. Some children were having a picnic—and a bullying tramp was trying to steal their food.
"Clear off, you kids," growled the man, giving one of the boys a push that sent him rolling on the ground. "I'll have that grub." Jumbo's eyes glinted. "This is a job for the Army," he muttered, and ran over to the van, the back of which the Professor was busy opening. Quickly Jumbo told the Professor about the thieving tramp.
From the other side of the hedge came a yell. Jumbo gave a quick glance into the open back of the van. On the shelves inside were rows and rows of small model soldiers, tanks, vehicles and planes. Jumbo began to twiddle the knobs and buttons on the control gadget, and immediately tanks and soldiers started to move down ramps.
Left-right! Left-right! The tiny soldiers marched in step and the tanks rumbled along in a long column. Jumbo took his models to the end of the hedge and peered round. The children were huddled beside the hedge, and now the tramp had the picnic to himself. Jumbo pressed two buttons on the controls. Two of the tanks began to roll forward and two soldiers charged with fixed bayonets.
The tramp was licking his lips as he cut himself a thick slice of bread. "I'll start with a sandwich," he muttered. "Then half a dozen o' them tarts, then—OW!" The tramp leaped to his feet with a startled yelp of pain. Jumbo's leading soldier had jabbed the ruffian in the seat of his ragged pants. "OW!" The tramp yelled again as the second soldier's bayonet pricked his leg.
The tramp whipped round and saw his midget attackers. He just gaped. Then the two soldiers charged again. With a frightened howl the ruffian began to run. But Jumbo had brought two tanks round to cut off the tramp's escape. Now the boy brought the whole squadron into action. The tiny turret guns swivelled round and—Pop! Pop! Pop! —volleys of hard peas peppered the tramp's face.
The startled tramp jumped a foot in the air, and the rascal's legs fairly twinkled as he scuttled across the park! But Jumbo wasn't finished. He had launched a flight of miniature jet fighters, and now they went screaming after the tramp. The rascal was pelting along past the children's paddling pool when the planes overtook him, and their lightning swoops drove him into the water.
Wheeeee! The high-pitched whining of the jets drowned the tramp's yells of fear. Wet from head to foot, the ruffian hared out of the Park entrance which a workman was busy painting. With a chuckle, Jumbo made one of his planes swoop towards a paint pot. The plane's wing knocked over the pot and bright red paint landed on the tramp's head.
Down the street staggered the tramp, scuttling about like a frightened hen. And after him went Jumbo and his planes. As he passed the painter, Jumbo apologised for using the paint-pot as a bomb. But now the tramp had given up trying to escape. He was clinging desperately to a lamp-post with the planes buzzing briskly round him.
"Call 'em off!" whined the tramp, as General Jumbo came up to him, followed by nearly every boy and girl in the neighbourhood. Word had spread quickly about Jumbo's miniature army going into action against a tramp, and scores of children had come to see the fun. Jumbo looked stern. "You are my prisoner!" he said in the gruffest voice he could muster. "On your feet!" The tramp shakily obeyed, and gave an extra big shudder as the Professor brought up the tanks and soldiers. Jumbo arranged them on either side of the tramp as an escort. "Prisoner and escort—atten-shun!" he rapped. "To the police station—quick MARCH!" Off went the marching column and soon the tramp was being dealt with by the Law, while the children held their picnic after all—with General Jumbo as the guest of honour!

WHAT A SQUEAKING MY NEW BOOTS ARE MAKING!
YOU SHOULD PUT THEM IN OIL MISTER DAN!
GARAGE
PETROL
THAT'S THE VERY THING. HERE'S A POOL OF IT OUTSIDE THIS GARAGE.
GARAGE
PETROL
I'LL RUB MY BOOTS INTO IT HARD~GEE! I'M GOING SO FAST THE OIL'S HEATING UP!
~WELL, IF IT HASN'T CAUGHT FIRE!
QUICK, PUT IT OUT~YOU'LL SET THE GARAGE ON FIRE!
PETROL
PETROL
HERE'S A HOSE FULL OF WATER~THERE~SQUIRT OUT THE FLAMES!
YOU MUTT! THAT'S NOT WATER. IT'S PETROL!
SO IT IS! THE FLAMES ARE WORSE THAN EVER!
WATCH THIS~I'LL BLOW THEM OUT~BLOW~OH! I'VE BLOWN THEM INTO A FIREBALL!
LOVELY COLD ICES TO COOL YOU DOWN. ICES!
ICES

Readers of the *Summer Special* were treated to a colour two-page General Jumbo story. 'Desperate Dan' (see left) was among *The Dandy* characters who appeared.

PUNCH AND JIMMY

Canadian artist Dave Jenner brought two rough and tumble characters to *The Beano*. 'Punch and Jimmy' arrived in 1962 and ran until 1967. He worked in a quite different American strip style, not unlike that of newspaper cartoonist artist Dik Browne.

If we keep out of each others way we won't be able to fight.
Good idea!

PUNCH
AND
JIMMY
THE TERRIER TWINS
THE TWINS ARE PLAYING THEIR FAVOURITE GAME—FIGHTING!
I'm a better fighter than you are, Punch!
Oh, no you're not, Jimmy!
Tut! Tut!
BOOF!
POW!
BIFF!
THEN MUM STEPS IN—
There's to be no more fighting in this house. You can both join a boxing club and fight there!
BLOB STREET BOXING CLUB
You'll join separate clubs. Then you won't be able to fight with one another!
I wish Jimmy was coming.
Jimmy, you can join this club!
NOGGINHILL BOXING CLUB
Huh! It's no fun without ol' Punch to fight with!
Hee! Hee! What a clever ol' Mum I am. Now I'll have peace in the house!
BUT NOT FOR LONG—
CRASH!
Eek! They're at it again!
THUMP!
THUMP!
UPSTAIRS
What are you up to, Jimmy?
THUMP!
I'm training for a boxing match at the club tomorrow night.
THUMP!
SUDDENLY—
POW!
SMACK!
BIFF!
BIFF!
BANG!
CRACK!
Take that! —an' that!
I've had enough of this!
But, Mum, I'm only doin' some trainin'— Oooh! Leggo!
NEXT EVENING, MUM GOES ALONG TO SEE JIMMY BOX.
In the red corner—Jimmy Terrier of the Nogginhill Club!
Hooray for Jimmy! You can win, boy.
... and in the green corner—Punch Terrier of the Blob Street Club! This is the final of the Town Boys' Championship!
Erk! After all my trouble trying to keep them apart, this has to happen!
BOOF!
POW!
MIDNIGHT— AFTER EVERYBODY HAS GONE HOME ——
I'm a better fighter than you!
BIFF!
POW!
Oh, no, you're not!
EXIT
More Next Week.

BILLY THE CAT

BILLY the CAT
THE amazing story of William Grange, the Burnham schoolboy who is also the famous Billy the Cat, an amazing athletic crime-fighter.
GOOD GRIEF!
One very rainy day, Billy was patrolling Burnham in his own special way—from the rooftops—when . . .
Carlton Dam, weakened by pressure caused by the heavy rain, had given way—and Burnham was directly in the path of the flood-waters!
EVERYONE OFF THE STREETS! THE DAM'S BURST! THE WATER WILL BE HERE IN SECONDS!
Four-year-old Mickey Swanson tripped and fell. He was right in the path of the flood.
Billy quickly unwound the rope from his waist.
Billy launched himself from the roof as the water roared towards Mickey.
2 : 12 : 67

Dave Sutherland found time to draw up a new *Beano* creation in 1967, 'Billy the Cat'. Schoolboy William Grange, also known as the leather-clad avenging acrobat Billy the Cat, was a popular character but, overall, the adventure series were no longer as popular as the cartoon strips. So Billy, though he ran for many years, became the last new adventure hero *The Beano* designed and used.

Next day, William Grange—alias Billy the Cat—smiled as he read the newspaper.
BURNHAM NEWS
BILLY THE CAT
-FLOOD HERO
2 : 12 : 67

ROGER AND SNOOTY

Bob Nixon's 'Roger', from the 1965 *Beano Summer Special*.

ROGER THE DODGER
NO, DAD! PLEASE, DAD — ANYTHING BUT THAT!
YOU'RE GOING TO DANCING LESSONS AND THAT'S FINAL!
AT THE OUTFITTERS —
AH! DOESN'T HE LOOK SWEET?
NEXT — THE DANCING SCHOOL —
YOU CAN HAVE JUNE FOR A PARTNER, ROGER.
I FEEL A DODGE COMING ON!
HEH-HEH! WATCH ME STAMP ON HER TOOTSIES! THEY'LL CHUCK ME OUT OF THE CLASS FOR THAT!
NEXT SECOND —
MISSED — AARGH!
OOPS! HOW CLUMSY OF ME!
MISSED
CRUNCH!
FANCY BEING OUT-DODGERED BY A GIRL! I'LL HAVE TO DO SOMETHING ABOUT HER!
THROB!
I'LL GIVE HER A DOSE OF THIS, THEN SHE'LL FORGET ABOUT DANCING FOR A BIT! HEH-HEH!
ITCHING POWDER
THAT'LL FIX HIM! TRA-LA!
WHAT'S HAPPENED?
KICK
THUD!
OH, NO!
STOP! STOP!
EEK! AGH! HELP!
ITCH
SCRATCH
ITCH
ROGER DIDN'T KNOW HE COULD DANCE SO WELL!
CRASH!
YOUR SON IS WRECKING MY CLASS!
EEK!
BANG!
OO-YAH!
EEK! DODGERED TWICE BY A GIRL! OOYAH!
AGH!

Middlesbrough-born artist Bob Nixon, known better as R. T. Nixon, took over illustrating 'Roger the Dodger' in the mid 1960s. After a start lacking in confidence, Bob really warmed to the character and 'Roger' grew with him. His distinctive, charming style gave 'Roger' terrific reader appeal and for a time, illustrating the scripts of *Beano* writer Al Bernard, 'Roger' was more popular than 'Dennis the Menace'.

ITCHING POWDER

LORD SNOOTY
HA! HA! READING "THE BEANO" IS MUCH BETTER THAN DOING HOMEWORK!
WHO'S YOUR FAVOURITE "BEANO" CHARACTER, SCRAPPER?
DENNIS THE MENACE, BECAUSE HE'S TOUGH!
JOE LIKES THE THREE BEARS BEST, BECAUSE THEY EAT SO MUCH!
MY FAVOURITE "BEANO" CHUM IS ROGER, BECAUSE HE'S A QUICK-THINKER LIKE ME!
WE LIKE THE BASH ST. KIDS. WE WANT TO BE LIKE THEM WHEN WE GROW UP!
WHO'S YOUR FAVOURITE, SNOOTY?
LITTLE PLUM, OF COURSE!
DENNIS IS BEST!
RUBBISH!
IT'S ROGER!
THE BASH ST. KIDS ARE BEST!
THE THREE BEARS!
ROG—AH!
OUCH!
LITTLE PLUM!
OOH!
DENNIS!
BASH ST. KIDS!
STOP! STOP! LET'S SETTLE THIS IN A CIVILISED WAY.
WE'LL LET THE NEXT PERSON WHO COMES IN DECIDE WHO'S BEST—I THINK I CAN HEAR SOMEONE COMING NOW.
WHO'S YOUR FAVOURITE "BEANO" CHARACTER, LIZ?
ME, OF COURSE!
THAT'S NO GOOD! HERE'S AUNT MAT—WE'LL LET HER DECIDE. WHO'S YOUR FAVOURITE IN "THE BEANO", AUNT MAT?
I HAVE FOUR—TEACHER IN THE BASH ST. KIDS, AND DENNIS'S, MINNIE'S, AND ROGER'S DADS. AND IF YOU DON'T GET ON WITH YOUR HOMEWORK, INSTEAD OF MAKING ALL THIS NOISE, I'LL TAKE A LEAF OUT OF THEIR BOOK!
THERE'S ONE THING CERTAIN—NONE OF THEM LIKE HOMEWORK!
SILENCE
29.6.68

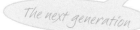

The scriptwriters found R. T. Nixon superb to work with, always able to lift a less-than-inspired storyline by adding a quite stunning picture in his beautiful clean, clear ink line. He was professional, prolific and punctual, something hard worked subs really appreciated when meeting the demanding weekly schedule.

Bob took over 'Lord Snooty' from Dudley Watkins in 1967 and it is a huge compliment to his artistry to say that the story lost nothing and, if anything, took on that special Nixon appeal.

DENNIS MEETS GNASHER

August 31, 1968, was the major red-and-black letter day in the life of 'Dennis the Menace'. He meets and adopts a scruffy stray mutt, deciding to call him 'Gnasher'. The pair would become friends for life. This perfectly suited duo struck dread into adult authority who were already struggling to keep suburbia peaceful against the single menace.

Every Thursday ★ ★ THE BEANO August 31, 1968
Dennis the MENACE
IT SAYS HERE THAT PEOPLE ALWAYS OWN DOGS THAT LOOK LIKE THEMSELVES.
WHAT A LOT OF ROT!
BUT OUTSIDE—
MAYBE DAD WAS RIGHT AFTER ALL!
HEH-HEH!
WHAT'S GOING ON, WALTER?
THERE'S A DOG SHOW AT THE TOWN HALL. TIDDLUMS HERE IS SURE TO WIN.
THEN—
AH! THERE'S A LIKELY LOOKING SHOW SPECIMEN!
GNASH!
GRAND DOG SHOW
COME ON, GNASHER!
GNASH!
HEH-HEH! GNASHER'S SWIPED THAT PAMPERED POOCH'S BONE!
GNASH!
A DOG FIGHT BEGINS—
YAP!
SHRIEK!
SNARL!
GET THAT UGLY BRUTE UNDER CONTROL!
THAT BOY'S FATHER SHALL HEAR OF THIS!
GNASH! GNASH!
THEN—
OOPS! HERE'S DAD! LET'S GO, GNASHER!
GNASH!
BUT DAD BROUGHT A RETRIEVER WITH HIM—
SNIGGER! GOT YOU!
AS FOR YOU! YOU'D BETTER GO AND JOIN "PUP PARADE"!
OK! I'LL BE THERE NEXT WEEK!
GNASH!
Printed and Published in Great Britain by D. C. THOMSON & Co., Ltd., 12 Fetter Lane, Fleet Street, London, E.C.4.
© D C THOMSON & Co. Ltd., 1968.

Every Thursday
THE BEANO
December 28, 1968
DENNIS THE MENACE
THAT ANIMAL IS A DISOBEDIENT DISGRACE, AND SO ARE YOU, DENNIS!
DENNIS'S DOG, GNASHER
DOG OBEDIENCE CLASS
SORRY, GNASHER, OLD PAL, BUT DAD INSISTS.
THE FIRST COMMAND IS "SIT"
INSTRUCTOR
SIT, GNASHER! HEH-HEH! HOW'S THAT?
THE NEXT ORDER IS "HEEL".
HMPH!
WALKING AT HEEL
HEEL, GNASHER!
YAROO! MY HEEL!
GNASH!
NEXT—
NOW PRINCE WILL FETCH THE STICK.
Every Thursday
THE BEANO
August 31, 1968
GNASHER FETCHES A STICK—WITH WALTER'S TOFFEE APPLE ON IT—
HEH-HEH! GOOD DOG, GNASHER!
I'LL HAVE TO PUT A STOP TO THIS!
SO—
THEY'RE BOTH EXPELLED!
INDEED?
THEN—
FETCH MY SLIPPER, GNASHER!
HEH-HEH! HE WON'T DO IT—GULP!
ZIP!
BAH! LET DOWN BY MY FAITHFUL HOUND!
HEE-HEE! GNASHER MUST HAVE LEARNED SOMETHING AFTER ALL! FETCH IT HERE, BOY!
PANT!
PANT!
GASP! THE BRUTE HAS CHEWED MY SLIPPER TO SHREDS!
WELL DONE, GNASHER! YOU'RE NOT AS STUPID AS YOU LOOK!
PAT
Printed and Published in Great Britain by D. C. THOMSON & Co., Ltd., 12 Fetter Lane, Fleet Street, London, E.C.4.
© D C THOMSON & Co. Ltd., 1968.

When Dennis artist Davey Law, was struggling for a design for Gnasher, scriptwriter Ian Gray gave him the following instructions –'Draw Dennis the Menace's hair, put a leg at each corner and eyes, nose and teeth at the front.' It worked out perfectly. Dennis thought Gnasher was a mongrel but in fact he was a rare comic breed, the Abyssinian Wire-Haired Tripe Hound.

In real life Ian Gray was a dog breeder and sheepdog handler of some renown, and always found fun in crazy Gnasher stories.

GNASHER AND I ARE INSEPARABLE!
GNESH!

BIFFO'S FAMILY TREE

During the spring of 1969 *The Beano* ran a great series of 'Biffo' covers, where the first bear in hotpants looked back and imagined stories from his family tree. Once again the stories came from the imaginative Ian Gray and artist Dudley Watkins was able to indulge in his love for costumed figures, much needed in these historical hoots.

BIFFO
STILL READING HIS FAMILY TREE—
AHA! SIR BIFFO RALEIGH, THE COURTEOUS COURTIER!
Biffo's Family Tree
BACK TO THE DAYS OF COURTLY SIR BIFFO—
GOOD MORROW, MA'AM!
GREETINGS, KIND SIR!
CEASE, SOOTY ONE!
THEN GOOD QUEEN BESS ARRIVES—
OH, DEAR! WHAT A NASTY, MUDDY PUDDLE!
ALLOW ME, YOUR MAJESTY!
PLOP!
BUT—
SHRIEK! TO THE DUNGEON WITH HIM!
GLURK!
OOPS! IT'S DEEPER THAN I THOUGHT!
BAH! NOW MY GOOD NAME IS MUD!

The Beano
4d
EVERY THURSDAY
No. 1396—April 19th, 1969.
Biffo THE BEAR
HELLO, SNOOTY! HOW'S IT GOING?
FINE, BIFFO! I'M MAKING A STUDY OF MY FAMILY TREE.
OH! YOU MUST COME AND SEE MY FAMILY TREE!
MY GRANDAD PLANTED IT!
OH! NO, NO, BIFFO—
A FAMILY TREE IS A LIST OF YOUR ANCESTORS!
LOOK—HERE'S MINE.
MOST INTERESTING! I WOULDN'T MIND FINDING OUT ABOUT MY ANCESTORS. I'LL BET THERE WERE SOME FAMOUS ONES.
LATER—
HEY, BIFFO! I'VE MANAGED TO UNEARTH THE BIFFO FAMILY TREE FROM THE MUSEUM!
SPLENDID!
I SHOULD HAVE SOME GOOD FUN TRACING BACK ALL MY NOBLE ANCESTORS!
THE BIFFO FAMILY TREE
READERS! YOU'LL HAVE FUN, TOO, IF YOU JOIN BIFFO IN HIS RESEARCH NEXT WEEK!

BIFFO
STILL READING HIS FAMILY TREE—
AH! CAPTAIN BIFFO OF THE KING'S OWN HUSSARS WHO CARRIED THE NEWS OF VICTORY AT WATERLOO.
Biffo's Family Tree
CAPTAIN BIFFO SETS OUT ON HIS MISSION—
ONWARD, MY TRUSTY STEED.
BUT—
CORKS! NEDDY'S OUT OF PUFF.
BUT CAPTAIN BIFFO PRESSES ON—
THROUGH TREACHEROUS SWAMPS—
O'ER HILL AND DALE—
MESSAGE FROM THE DUKE OF WELLINGTON, SIRE. WE ARE VICTORIOUS.
THANK YOU, CAPTAIN BIFFO! PLEASE ACCEPT A SPARE PAIR OF BOOTS. THEY BELONG TO THE DUKE OF WELLINGTON.
THROB
LIKE MY "WELLINGTON" -BOOTS, FOLKS?

BIFFO
THE BEAR
COO! KING BIFFEAU THE CONQUERER! WONDER WHAT HE WAS LIKE?
Biffo's Family Tree
1066—THE NORMANS LANDED AT HASTINGS—
YE SAXON DONKEY RIDES 6D
COME, LADS! LET'S GET ON WITH YE BUSINESS OF CONQUERING ENGLAND!
SO THE BATTLE OF HASTINGS BEGAN—
ROAR!
CLASH!
Hastings F.C.
BOYS' GATE
FULL
Normans v English
KICK OFF 2 p.m.
YE HEREWARD THE BUSTER.
NOW WE MUST MAKE OUT A LIST OF OUR NEW POSSESSIONS—FETCH ME MY EDITOR!
GRR! YE NORMANS ARE VICTORIOUS!
WRITE YE, O EDITOR—
YE QUEEN MATILDA (ANCESTOR OF LORD SNOOTY'S AUNT MAT) SEWING YE BIFFEAU TAPESTRY.
WELL, BIFFEAU THE CONQUERER NOT ONLY CONQUERED ENGLAND, HE ALSO INVENTED THE FIRST "BEANO BOOK" AND THE FIRST COMIC STORY!
YE DOMESDAY BEANO BOOK
NO 1 DEC. 1066
BIFFEAU, 1ST DUKE OF NORMANDY CROWNED BIFFO 1ST OF ENGLAND.
Biffo's
YE BIFFEAU TAPESTRY
KING HAROLD LOSING HIS CROWN
WHISTLE!
YE SCOTS REFEREE
YE NORMAN KING BIFFEAU KICKETH CENTRE FORWARD, KING HAROLD, AND YE BALL RIGHT INTO YE GOAL TO WIN YE BATTLE OF HASTINGS.
HE'S ONLY KIDDING, READERS!

BIFFO THE BEAR
BIFFO IS STILL STUDYING HIS FAMILY TREE—
The Biffo family Tree
HM! ODIN BIFFOSEN, THE DREADED VIKING! I WONDER WHAT HE WAS LIKE?
BACK TO THE DAYS OF THE VIKINGS—
YAHAA! NOW TO CONQUER ANGLELAND AND PILLAGE THE VILLAGE!
ODIN BIFFOSEN
CHARGE!
AHA! ANOTHER BULL WANTING A FIGHT, EH?
CLANG!
DIZZY
ER—WE'LL LEAVE ANGLELAND FOR A WHILE! WE'LL MAYBE COME BACK AND CONQUER IT NEXT YEAR—MAYBE!

These 'Biffo' drawings by Dudley Watkins, some of the last he drew, provide wonderfully entertaining glimpses of British history – and, of course, the Bayeux (well, Biffeau) Tapestry was the first comic story!

BEANO PUPPETS

An unexpected feature appeared in *The Beano* centre spread in autumn 1967 and ran through most of 1968 – cut-out *Beano* character puppets, 48 in all! How many were ever actually cut out and made to work we will never know, but *Beano* readers are notoriously reluctant about taking scissors to their beloved *Beanos.*

OP
CRISPS
HERE'S A SPANKING PUPPET FOR YOU, READERS! HEH-HEH!
25.5.68
1. STICK PICTURE ON FIRM CARDBOARD.
2. NEATLY CUT OUT THE PARTS WITH A PAIR OF SCISSORS (CAREFULLY NOW!).
3. BORE HOLES IN PLACES MARKED.
4. LOOP SHORT THREADS THROUGH THE DOUBLE HOLES AND TIE PARTS TOGETHER (NOT TOO TIGHTLY!).
5. FIT LONG CONTROLLING THREADS TO THE OTHER HOLES IN THE ELBOWS AND TOES -AND WATCH THIS PUPPET DANCE AND KICK!

MUMBLE!
20-6-68.
1. STICK PICTURE ON FIRM CARDBOARD.
2. NEATLY CUT OUT THE PARTS WITH A PAIR OF SCISSORS (CAREFULLY NOW!)
3. BORE HOLES IN PLACES MARKED.
4. LOOP SHORT THREADS THROUGH THE DOUBLE HOLES AND TIE PARTS TOGETHER (NOT TOO TIGHTLY!)
5. FIT LONG CONTROLLING THREADS TO THE OTHER HOLES IN THE ELBOWS AND TOES -AND WATCH THIS PUPPET DANCE AND KICK!

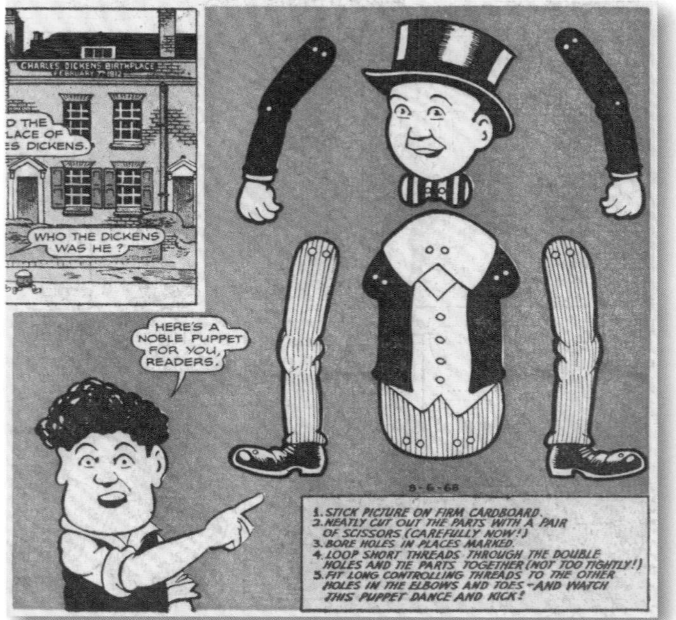
CHARLES DICKENS BIRTHPLACE FEBRUARY 7th 1812
WHO THE DICKENS WAS HE?
HERE'S A NOBLE PUPPET FOR YOU, READERS.
8-6-68
1. STICK PICTURE ON FIRM CARDBOARD.
2. NEATLY CUT OUT THE PARTS WITH A PAIR OF SCISSORS (CAREFULLY NOW!)
3. BORE HOLES IN PLACES MARKED.
4. LOOP SHORT THREADS THROUGH THE DOUBLE HOLES AND TIE PARTS TOGETHER (NOT TOO TIGHTLY!)
5. FIT LONG CONTROLLING THREADS TO THE OTHER HOLES IN THE ELBOWS AND TOES -AND WATCH THIS PUPPET DANCE AND KICK!

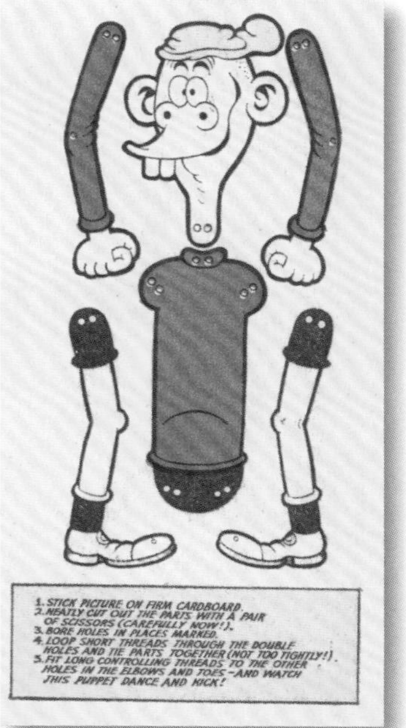
1. STICK PICTURE ON FIRM CARDBOARD.
2. NEATLY CUT OUT THE PARTS WITH A PAIR OF SCISSORS (CAREFULLY NOW!).
3. BORE HOLES IN PLACES MARKED.
4. LOOP SHORT THREADS THROUGH THE DOUBLE HOLES AND TIE PARTS TOGETHER (NOT TOO TIGHTLY!).
5. FIT LONG CONTROLLING THREADS TO THE OTHER HOLES IN THE ELBOWS AND TOES -AND WATCH THIS PUPPET DANCE AND KICK!

DUDLEY WATKINS

The Beano
4D
EVERY THURSDAY
No. 1423—October 25th, 1969.
BIFFO THE BEAR
HELLO, BUSTER! HA-HA! IT'S AN AWFUL DAY! TEE-HEE!
WHAT'S HE SO HAPPY ABOUT?
HERE'S MY BUTCHER'S BILL—HO-HO!—MY MILKMAN'S BILL—HAW-HAW!
TEE-HEE! THE LIGHT'S FUSED! HO-HO!
PHUT!
CLICK!
HA-HA-HA!
CACKLE!
SNIGGER!
THIS—HA-HA!—NEW HAIRY CARPET OF MINE—TEE-HEE!—ISN'T HALF TICKLY! HAW-HAW!
CHUCKLE!
GUFFAW!
CHORTLE!
HE'S POTTY!
BIFFO
I'D BETTER FIND OUT WHAT'S GOING ON!
BIFFO
TICKLE
TICKLE

If the 1960s had started on a high, it certainly ended in a very great low. On August 20, 1969, Dudley Watkins suffered a fatal heart attack. He died very suddenly at his drawing board with a 'Biffo' about to be inked. Until that moment he had been the firm's top artist. Of their five comics he drew the covers for three of them and contributed to them all, as well as producing, weekly, the iconic characters 'Oor Wullie' and 'The Broons' for the top selling ***Sunday Post*** newspaper.

Once again Harry Cramond turned to the versatile Dave Sutherland for help. Dave took on 'Biffo' immediately, inking Dudley's last pencilled page, and the cover story shown here is that combination of the last Dudley Watkins and the first Dave Sutherland 'Biffo'. He took the new character in his stride and was now producing magnificent sets in the different styles of Paddy Brennan, Leo Baxendale and Dudley Watkins.

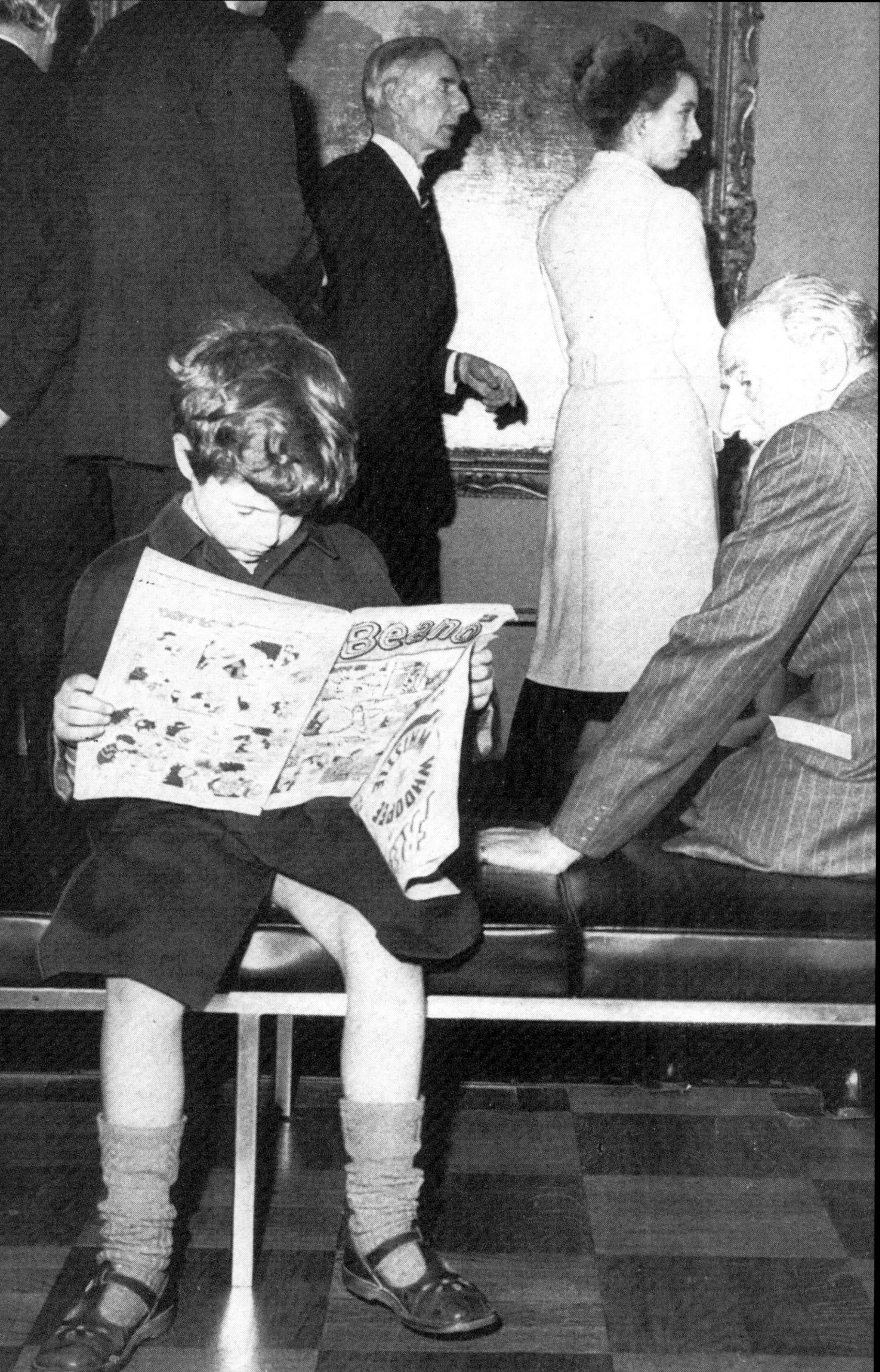
Beano

PART 5

Dennis Comes of Age

1970–1979

The 1970s were a memorable decade for Britain's favourite spiky-haired scamp. In July 1970, after drawing 'Dennis the Menace' since his first appearance back in March 1951, Davey Law hung up his pen and handed 'Dennis' on to another artist. The new hand behind 'Dennis' was to be Dave Sutherland, who was already drawing 'The Bash Street Kids' and 'Biffo the Bear' for *The Beano*.

'I got a call from Harry [Harry Cramond, the Editor] saying to come into the office', remembers Dave. 'He told me that Davey Law wasn't well and couldn't draw his *Annual* pages. He said, "You can draw that." And that was it. I was drawing Dennis for the *Annual*. Davey Law really wasn't well and Harry told me I was taking over Dennis for the weekly. He didn't ask me. He told me. He said, "You can do it. Go home and draw some ideas." I did and that was that. I was referring to Davey Law's original pages for six months or a year for things like characters' movements. He had such a good style to draw in. It's so relaxed and loose.'

Every Thursday ★ ★ ★ ★ THE BEANO July 25, 1970
DENNIS THE MENACE AND GNASHER
GASP! THAT DOG HAS RUINED THE LINO!
GNASH!
LATER—
YOU TWO ARE GOING TO HELP ME LAY THIS NEW LINO.
HUMPH!
SO—
YOU HOLD IT DOWN AT THAT END, GNASHER.
HUH! THIS ISN'T MUCH FUN!
BANG!
BANG!
BANG!
AHA! A NAUGHTY THOUGHT HAS JUST OCCURRED TO ME!
I'M GOING FOR A DRINK OF WATER.
SLURP! ME TOO!
BEND
ZIP!
WHERE'S THAT BOY GOT TO?
BANG! BANG!
HOWL! SPLUTTER! WAIT TILL I GET MY SLIPPER!
BAH! HE'S TACKED THEM TO THE FLOOR!
GRR! IT TAKES MORE THAN A COUPLE OF TACKS TO FOIL AN ANGRY DAD!
AGH! RUN FOR IT, GNASHER! DAD'S GOT A WOODEN-SOLED SLIPPER!
Printed and Published in Great Britain by D. C. THOMSON & Co., Ltd., 12 Fetter Lane, Fleet Street, London, E.C.4.
© D. C. THOMSON & CO., LTD., 1970.

Davey Law's last original 'Dennis the Menace' strip appeared in *The Beano* on July 25, 1970. Gordon Bell filled in for a week and then Dave Sutherland took over as the regular 'Dennis' artist from the August 8 issue.

Every Thursday
THE BEANO
August 1, 1970
DENNIS the MENACE AND GNASHER
ON THE WAY HOME FROM SCHOOL—
AH! IT'S GREAT TO BE FREE AGAIN!
AAAA—
AAA! STOP SNIFFLING, WALTER!
POLITE CHOO!
COO! WHAT AN UNHEALTHY WEED!
POOR LITTLE WATTIE! INTO BED WITH YOU, DIDDUMS.
AND A MUMMY'S BOY, TOO!
SHUDDER
COUGH! COUGH!
SNIFF! SNIFF!
NASTY TASTE
I'M A TOUGH GUY, WALTER! YOU'LL NEVER CATCH ME SNIFFLING AND SNEEZING!
SEVERAL DAYS LATER—
FETCH ME THE PAPER, PLEASE, DENNIS.
OK, DAD.
FETCH THE PAPER, GNASHER!
BUT THEN—
NO, NO, YOU HAIRY DIMWIT! I SAID 'PAPER'—NOT PEPPER!
AW-SH!
PUFF!
DROP
AAAH-
CHOO!
CHOO!
CHOO!
HO-HO! LOOK AT THE TOUGH GUY WHO NEVER SNEEZES!
SPLUTTER!
GNASHOO!
GNASHOO!
Printed and Published in Great Britain by D. C. THOMSON & Co., Ltd., 12 Fetter Lane, Fleet Street, London, E.C.4.
© D. C. THOMSON & CO., LTD., 1970

Every Thursday
THE BEANO
August 8, 1970
DENNIS THE MENACE and GNASHER
AT THE CIRCUS—
COOOO!
FEARLESS THE LION TAMER
LATER—
BET I COULD DO THAT!
THAT'LL BE THE DAY!
BACK AT THE CIRCUS—
CAN I BORROW RAJAH FOR A WHILE, FEARLESS?
RAJAH
SORRY! IT'S HIS BATH NIGHT.
HMM!
SUSPICION
THAT SHOULD DO IT.
B-Z-Z-Z
BROWN
COME AND SEE THE FEARLESS DENNIS PUT HIS HEAD IN THE LION'S MOUTH! ADMISSION 3d
THIS SHOULD BE GOOD!
CRACK!
OPEN WIDE, RAJAH!
OOH! IT'S TICKLY!
IT'S THAT HORRIBLE DOG! WE WANT OUR MONEY BACK!
GNASH! GIGGLE!
TWITCH
NOW I KNOW WHY LION TAMERS ALWAYS HAVE SHORT HAIR!
Printed and Published in Great Britain by D. C. THOMSON & Co., Ltd., 12 Fetter Lane, Fleet Street, London, E.C.4.
© D. C. THOMSON & CO., LTD., 1970.

The change in artist did nothing to halt the growing popularity of 'Dennis' with *Beano* readers and the nation as a whole. And so it was inevitable that 'Dennis' would menace his way on to the front cover of *The Beano*, shoving aside 'Biffo the Bear', who had held court on the cover since January 1948. In the September 14, 1974, issue of *The Beano*, 'Dennis' became *the Beano's* cover star, with his story now occupying the front and back covers.

Dennis and Gnasher celebrating their arrival on the front cover in 1974 while (below) Dennis appears within a 'Biffo' story two years earlier, wondering when his time might come.

DENNIS THE MENACE AND GNASHER
COO! MUST GET THIS!
GNASH!
LAST WEEK'S BEANO
BIFFO THE BEAR
HELLO, READERS! I'VE ALWAYS FANCIED BEING ON THE FRONT PAGE!
BUT FIRST I'LL HAVE TO SCARE BIFFO OFF!
BONK!
BET YOU LIKE ME BETTER ON THE COVER, READERS!
WHAT'S GOING ON HERE?

THUNDER!
ZOOM

The age of the menace was truly here. 'Dennis' and his faithful hound, Gnasher, still occupy *The Beano's* front cover at the time of writing in 2008.

In 1972 there was a taste of what was to come a few years later when Dennis made an appearance in a 'Biffo the Bear' story on the front cover. Some of the dialogue concerning Dennis' wish to be on the cover was to prove prophetic.

GNASHER'S TALE

STARTING TODAY!
GNASHER'S TALE
Many years ago, young Dennis, Pie-Face and Curly were collecting creepy-crawlies—
HI, PALS—WANT TO KNOW HOW DENNIS AND I MET?
COO! LOVELY CREEPIES!
SLOOP!
THEY TICKLE!
RUN! IT'S THOSE AWFUL MENACES!
YAH!
HERE'S CREEPY-CRAWLIES!
Later—
OOH! WHAT A SUPER HAIRY CATER-ER — CATER-ER — CRAWLY!
Back home—
HERE'S A NICE LETTUCE, LITTLE CRAWLY—HEY! THAT'S DAD'S DINNER!
CHOMP!
YOU—YOU THING! YOU'VE SCOFFED MY SAUSAGES!
PROD
BURP!
OOYAH! GET RID OF THIS BRUTE, DENNIS!
CRUNCH!
BNO. 21.5.77
Soon—
GOOD! NO SIGN OF THAT HORRID CREEPY CRAWLY.
HEH! HEH! I'M NOT GIVING UP MY PET FOR ANYONE!
GNASH!

Every boy loves his pet dog – even the World's Wildest Boy, 'Dennis the Menace'. Dennis' popularity reached new heights when he was joined by his faithful Abyssinian Wire-Haired Tripe Hound, Gnasher. Gnasher became a star in his own strip, 'Gnasher's Tale', in May, 1977, drawn by Dave Sutherland. By the time Gnasher became a star in his own right, his appearance had undergone an evolution from his early days. Sutherland remembers, 'When Davey Law drew Gnasher he was this wonderful jaggy black shape with eyes, but it was Harry who asked me to give him a face. Harry wanted Gnasher to have scope for expressions.'

The strip was later retitled 'Gnasher And Gnipper', as Gnasher was joined in his adventures by his fang-toothed son, Gnipper. The story remains a popular part of *The Beano* 30 years on, with art duties now handled by Barry Glennard.

BONES?
HMM! GNASHER DOESN'T KNOW WHAT BONES ARE.
BNO. 9.9.78
Later—
GAAH! MY GARDEN! WHAT HAS DENNIS BEEN TEACHING THAT CREATURE TO DO? HE'S NOT GOING TO GET AWAY WITH THIS!
SCRAPE! SCRAPE!
GASP! WHERE HAVE ALL MY SLIPPERS GONE?
SLIPPER CUPBOARD
THAT'S RIGHT, GNASHER—ONLY ONE MORE "BONE" TO GO NOW! HEH! HEH!
Bone

BILLY'S LAST PROWL

BILLY THE CAT AND KATIE
THE amazing story of Burham Town's mysterious young crime-fighters.
One day, cousins William and Kathleen Grange, two seemingly quiet Burnham schoolchildren, were visiting a local fair.
See FIREBRAND FOWLER at 3PM
LET'S TAKE A LOOK AT THE DIVER, KATHLEEN.
GOSH! HE DOESN'T LOOK AT ALL CONFIDENT!
WE'LL GET CHANGED—JUST IN CASE ANYTHING GOES WRONG!
Hidden in a nearby clump of bushes the cousins swiftly donned black leather cat-suits — the uniforms of Billy the Cat and Katie.
Yes, the Granges and the Cats were one and the same.
The Cats bounded back into the fairground
LOOK! THE DIVER'S SLIPPED!
Instantly, they sprang into action . . . .
IT'S OK—WE'VE GOT YOU, CHUM!
Billy, Katie and the diver landed softly on a tent roof.
WHAT WENT WRONG, FIREBRAND?
I'VE LOST MY NERVE—I'LL NEVER DIVE AGAIN!
BNO 7.9.74
POOR CHAP! PITY THERE ISN'T SOME WAY WE CAN HELP HIM.
MORE OVER THE PAGE.

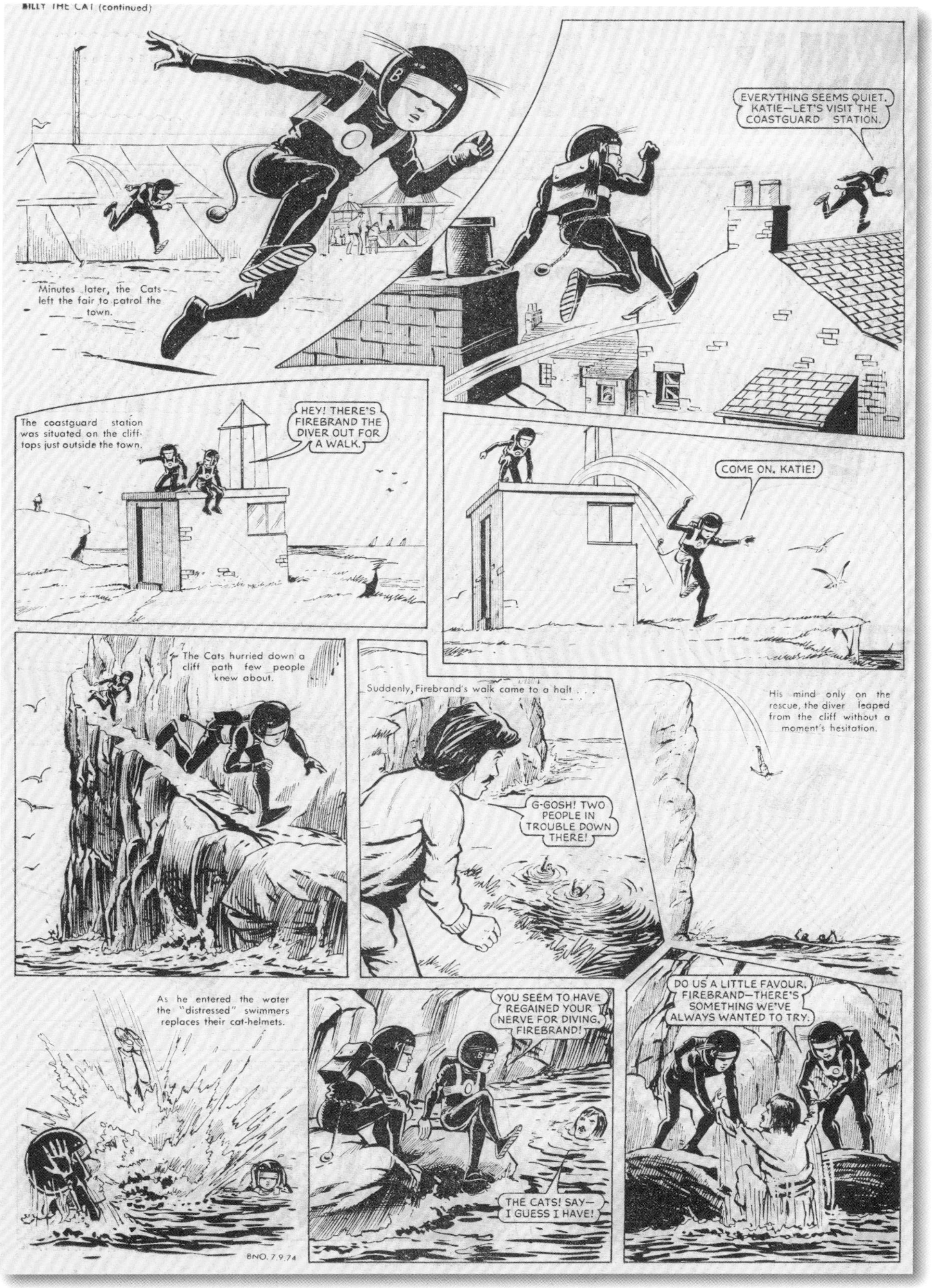
BILLY THE CAT (continued)
Minutes later, the Cats left the fair to patrol the town.
EVERYTHING SEEMS QUIET, KATIE—LET'S VISIT THE COASTGUARD STATION.
The coastguard station was situated on the cliff-tops just outside the town.
HEY! THERE'S FIREBRAND THE DIVER OUT FOR A WALK.
COME ON, KATIE!
The Cats hurried down a cliff path few people knew about.
Suddenly, Firebrand's walk came to a halt . . .
G-GOSH! TWO PEOPLE IN TROUBLE DOWN THERE!
His mind only on the rescue, the diver leaped from the cliff without a moment's hesitation.
As he entered the water the "distressed" swimmers replaces their cat-helmets.
YOU SEEM TO HAVE REGAINED YOUR NERVE FOR DIVING, FIREBRAND!
THE CATS! SAY—I GUESS I HAVE!
DO US A LITTLE FAVOUR, FIREBRAND—THERE'S SOMETHING WE'VE ALWAYS WANTED TO TRY.
BNO. 7.9.74

Dave Sutherland is one of the few artists to have successfully drawn both comedy strips and adventure stories. 'I drew picture stories – "The Great Flood of London", the "Cannonball Crackshots", "Billy the Cat" and things like that – but picture stories weren't doing so well in the polls. Great artists, like Dudley Watkins and Paddy Brennan, saw their stories sliding down the polls too. Harry said "Things are changing. Kids don't want to read all that text. You want to change as well, Dave." That's why I started doing the funnies. I spent hours, working late in the night, so that the style felt free-er to me.'

In 1974 'Billy the Cat' reached the end of its run, bringing to an end Dave's work on adventure stories.

That evening at the fair—
YAHOO! GOOD FOR BILLY AND KATIE!
THAT'S ALL FOR NOW, READERS! BE SEEING YOU!
BNO 7.9.74

A FAN CLUB FOR DENNIS

The popularity of 'Dennis the Menace' was further enhanced in 1976, with the creation of the Dennis the Menace Fan Club. For just 30p, a reader could get a membership card, a club wallet, club secrets, a metal Dennis badge and, best of all, a hairy Gnasher badge. The club's membership ultimately reached over 1.5 million before it was replaced by *The Beano* Club in the late 1990s. Dennis' Fan Club even had celebrities among its number. Olympic Gold Medallist Linford Christie, ex-Manchester United striker Mark Hughes, Radio 1 DJ Mike Read and TV Presenter Timmy Mallett all became members and the Fan Club's Force was strong enough to attract Luke Skywalker himself (actor Mark Hamill) to the red and black side in 1979. Two weeks later a letter appeared from a lad named Reeson Shearsmith, who would later find fame as actor Reese Shearsmith, one of the famous League of Gentlemen. Proving Dennis ruled the waves as well as the comics, the crew of the HMS Ark Royal wrote to the fan club.

DENNIS the MENACE
FAN CLUB

DO YOU WANT A "DENNIS THE MENACE" JERSEY? ONE OF THESE WILL BE AWARDED TO THE SENDER OF THE WEEK'S STAR LETTER!

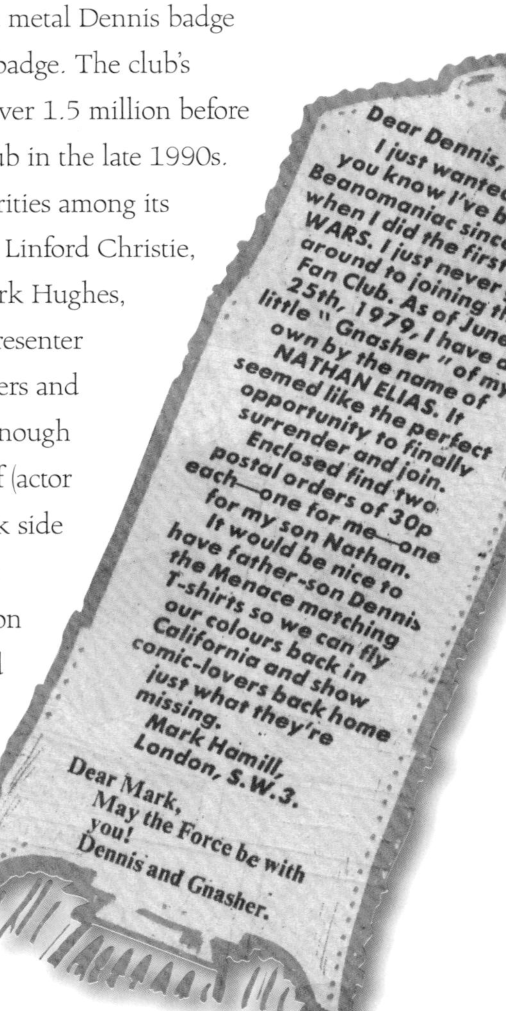
Dear Dennis,
I just wanted to let you know I've been a Beanomaniac since 1976 when I did the first STAR WARS. I just never got around to joining the Fan Club. As of June 25th, 1979, I have a little "Gnasher" of my own by the name of NATHAN ELIAS. It seemed like the perfect opportunity to finally surrender and join. Enclosed find two postal orders of 30p each—one for me—one for my son Nathan. It would be nice to have father-son Dennis the Menace matching T-shirts so we can fly our colours back in California and show comic-lovers back home just what they're missing.
Mark Hamill,
London, S.W.3.

Dear Mark,
May the Force be with you!
Dennis and Gnasher.

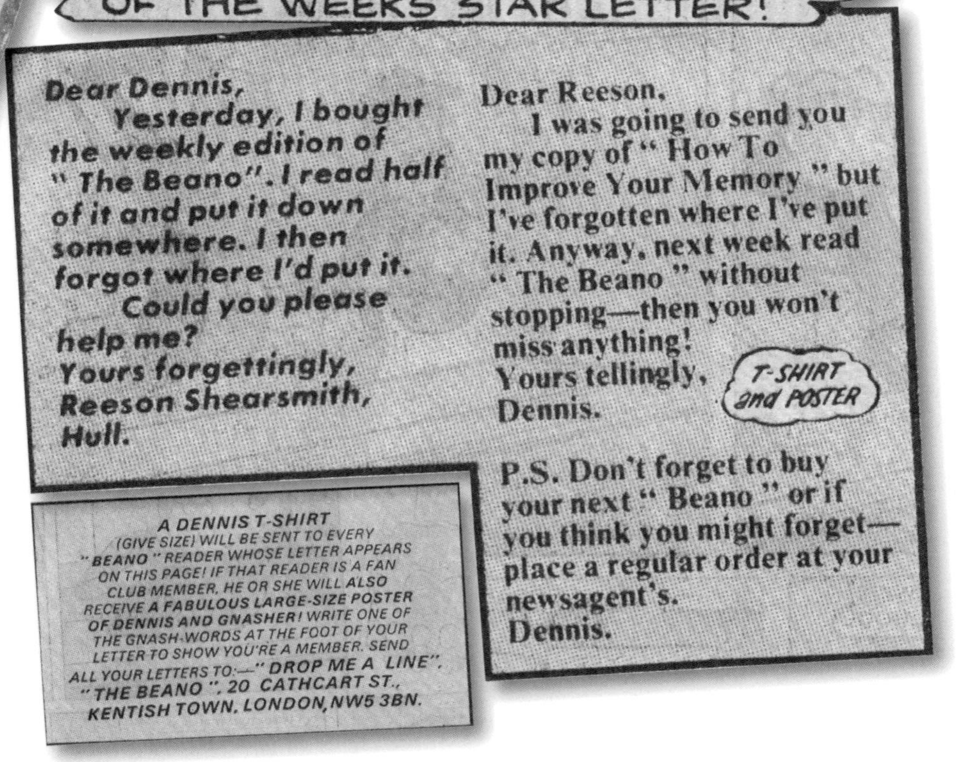
Dear Dennis,
Yesterday, I bought the weekly edition of "The Beano". I read half of it and put it down somewhere. I then forgot where I'd put it.
Could you please help me?
Yours forgettingly,
Reeson Shearsmith,
Hull.

Dear Reeson,
I was going to send you my copy of "How To Improve Your Memory" but I've forgotten where I've put it. Anyway, next week read "The Beano" without stopping—then you won't miss anything!
Yours tellingly,
Dennis.

T-SHIRT and POSTER

P.S. Don't forget to buy your next "Beano" or if you think you might forget—place a regular order at your newsagent's.
Dennis.

A DENNIS T-SHIRT (GIVE SIZE) WILL BE SENT TO EVERY "BEANO" READER WHOSE LETTER APPEARS ON THIS PAGE! IF THAT READER IS A FAN CLUB MEMBER, HE OR SHE WILL ALSO RECEIVE A FABULOUS LARGE-SIZE POSTER OF DENNIS AND GNASHER! WRITE ONE OF THE GNASH-WORDS AT THE FOOT OF YOUR LETTER TO SHOW YOU'RE A MEMBER. SEND ALL YOUR LETTERS TO:—" DROP ME A LINE", "THE BEANO", 20 CATHCART ST., KENTISH TOWN, LONDON, NW5 3BN.

When a new 'Dennis the Menace' T-shirt became the prize for appearing on the Club Page in 1978, it needed not one but two comic icons to promote the fact in a 'Dennis the Menace' strip.

THE BEANO
WIN A DENNIS JERSEY
SEE PAGE NINE!
No. 1894—NOV. 4th, 1978
EVERY THURSDAY
6D
DENNIS THE MENACE AND GNASHER
I SEND A SUPER JERSEY LIKE THIS TO A LUCKY READER EVERY WEEK. YOU CAN READ ALL ABOUT IT ON PAGE NINE!
GNICE, EH?
ALL THE BEST PEOPLE ARE WEARING "DENNIS" JERSEYS!
THERE'S ME!
SEE WHAT I MEAN?
HI, DENNIS!
MENACES! FLEE, FRIENDS!
THE SOFTIES
HEY! WHY ARE YOU SOFTIES WEARING "MINNIE" JERSEYS?
MINNIE THE MINX
EH?
THEY'RE "DENNIS" JERSEYS!
THEY'RE "MINNIE" JERSEYS!
WHUMP!
RRIP!
CRUNCH!
THUMP!
WHACK!
MORE ON BACK PAGE

Every Thursday ★ ★ ★ ★ THE BEANO NOV. 4th, 1978
DENNIS the MENACE AND GNASHER
CONTINUED FROM FRONT PAGE
DENNIS! I'M SURPRISED AT YOU! HITTING A LADY!
EDITOR'S ARM
YES, BOYS SHOULDN'T HIT LADIES.
DUST
A LADY? HAW! HAW!
CHEEK! SNARL!
WHUMP!
CRUNCH!
WHACK!
I GIVE UP!
EDITOR'S VOICE
SOON—
GASP!
TRUCE! SHAKE ON IT! GREAT FIGHT, PAL!
HMM! LOOK AT MY JERSEY! MUST GET THIS SORTED!
BACK HOME—
THAT'S THE ONLY JERSEY YOU HAVE! YOU'LL HAVE TO WEAR IT AS IT IS! IT'S YOUR OWN FAULT FOR FIGHTING!
WHAT? I CAN'T GO ABOUT LOOKING LIKE THIS!
GNASH!
ER...OK, GNASHER, I UNDERSTAND. I'M NOT GETTING YOUR JERSEY! RIGHT?
SOON—
I'LL WEAR THIS INSTEAD! EVERYBODY WHO GETS A LETTER PRINTED IN MY FAN CLUB PAGE GETS ONE OF THESE T-SHIRTS!
GNICE!
I'LL WRITE MYSELF A LETTER NOW AND MAYBE GET A "DENNIS" JERSEY FOR NEXT WEEK!
Printed and Published in Great Britain by D.C. THOMSON & CO., LTD., 185 Fleet Street, London, EC4A 2HS.
© D.C. THOMSON & CO., LTD., 1978.

Appearing on the Dennis the Menace Club Pages became a great honour. The current *Beano* staff regularly receive requests from former readers, asking for prints of their appearances on the Club pages.

THE END OF ADVENTURE

JUMBO JOHNSON, from Dinchester, is the young commander of an amazing army of radio-controlled models. One day, at a large mansion house near Dinchester—
General Jumbo
I'M KEEPING AN EYE ON COLONEL RADCLIFFE'S HOUSE WHILE HE'S AWAY ON HOLIDAY.
I SEE THE GARDENER'S HARD AT WORK.
Jumbo made a routine check round the house and its grounds.
EVERYTHING SEEMS TO BE OK, SO I'LL HAVE SOME ARMY MANOEUVRES IN THE GROUNDS.
Soon, with the help of his radio-controller, Jumbo was staging a fast and furious battle.
Suddenly a hard rubber bazooka shell scored a direct hit on a tank's turret.
Thrown out of control, the tank thudded into the gardener's wheel-barrow.
The wheelbarrow tipped over—a large gold cup had been hidden beneath the leaves.
THAT'S ONE OF COLONEL RADCLIFFE'S SHOOTING TROPHIES!
OUT OF MY WAY, KID—THIS TROPHY'S WORTH A LOT OF MONEY TO ME!
Jumbo had recognised the crook as James Lee, a known thief from the Dinchester area.
I'LL GET AFTER LEE—HE CAN'T HAVE GOT FAR, CARRYING THAT HEAVY CUP!
BNO 11.10.75
MORE ON NEXT PAGE.
GENERAL JUMBO (contd.)
Jumbo mounted a full-scale search round the grounds of the house, and at an ornamental pond—
THERE'S THE CUP! I BET OUR THIEF'S DUMPED IT THERE AND PLANS TO COME BACK FOR IT LATER!
In response to Jumbo's radio control gadget, two frogmen dived out of a helicopter.
I'LL PREPARE A LITTLE SURPRISE FOR FRIEND LEE!
Later, as Jumbo was hiding in the summer-house near the pond—
AH! HERE'S LEE NOW!
As Lee waded into the water to collect the cup, Jumbo jabbed certain buttons on his controller.
Below the surface of the pond—
The models had soon pushed the cup to the surface.
GASP! THE CUP'S RISING BY ITSELF!
At Jumbo's signal, the frogmen hurled the cup after Lee . . .
I'M GETTING OUT OF HERE—THE PLACE IS HAUNTED!
Jumbo had earlier alerted the police, who were waiting at the mansion gates.
GET ME AWAY FROM HERE!
BNO 11.10.75
POLICE
BETTER GUARD THIS CUP CAREFULLY, OFFICER—IT MAY "FLOAT" AWAY!
HEH! HEH! GOOD WORK, JUMBO!
POLICE
The End
STARTING NEXT WEEK—2 new fun-stories for you—TOM DICK AND SALLY and BALL BOY (he's football daft)!

This 'General Jumbo' strip, from October 11, 1975, was the last regular adventure story to appear in the weekly Beano.

At its birth in 1938, ***The Beano*** was a mixture of funny comic strips and adventure stories. Over the years, the balance shifted in favour of the comic strips. In 1974, the eighth and final series of 'General Jumbo' began. This was to be the last regular adventure story to appear in the pages of the weekly ***Beano*** comic, although they have continued to be a part of many ***Beano*** annuals since.

There have been several attempts at adventure stories for ***The Beano*** since the last 'General Jumbo' series, though none have made it to the pages of the comic itself and this is the first time these illustrations have seen print. These versions of 'General Jumbo' are from the late 1990s.

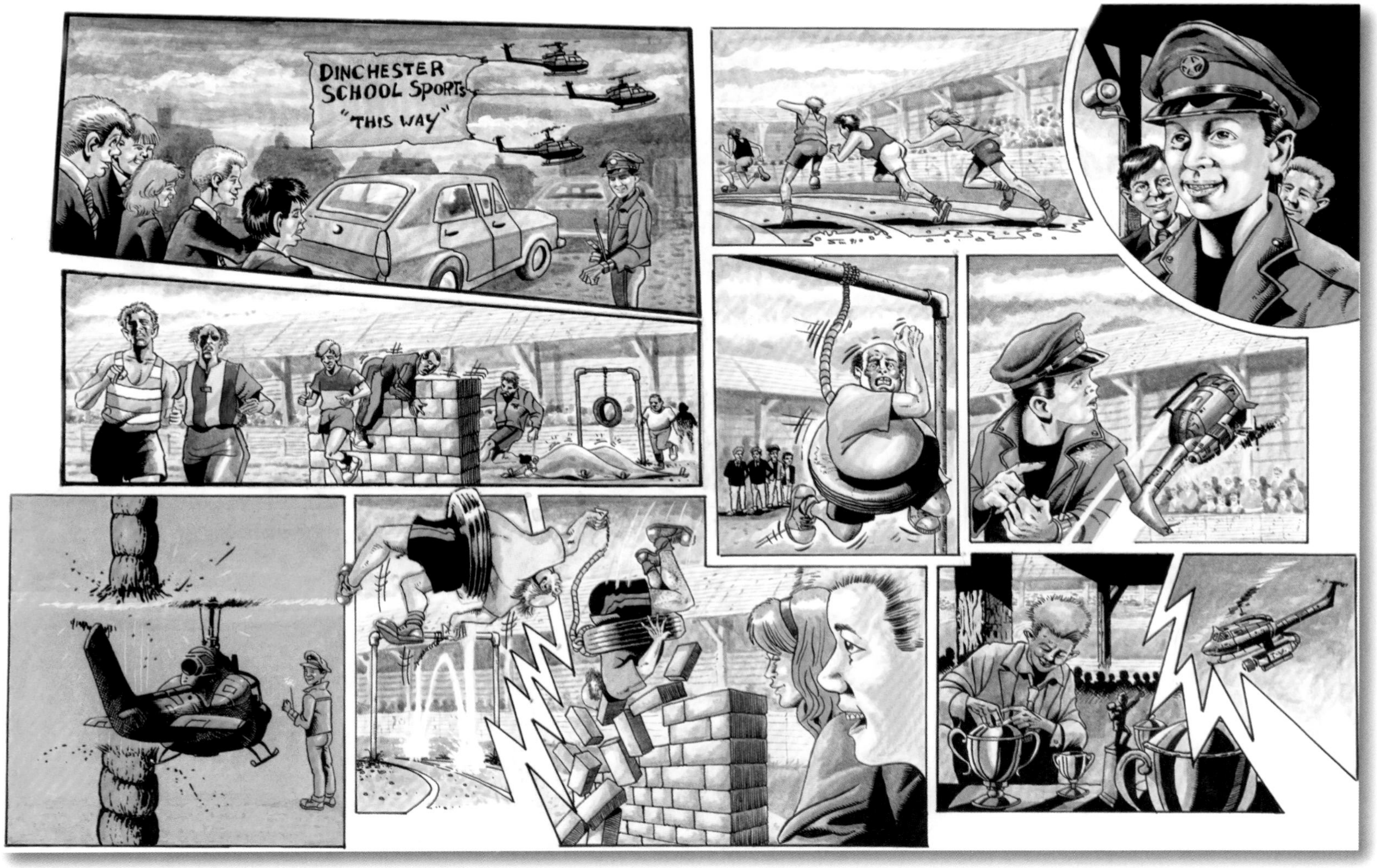
DINCHESTER SCHOOL SPORTS
"THIS WAY"

THE GREAT FLOOD OF LONDON
RIVER SECURITY

A few years later, Keith Robson drew this two-page test for an updated version of the classic serial, 'The Great Flood of London'.

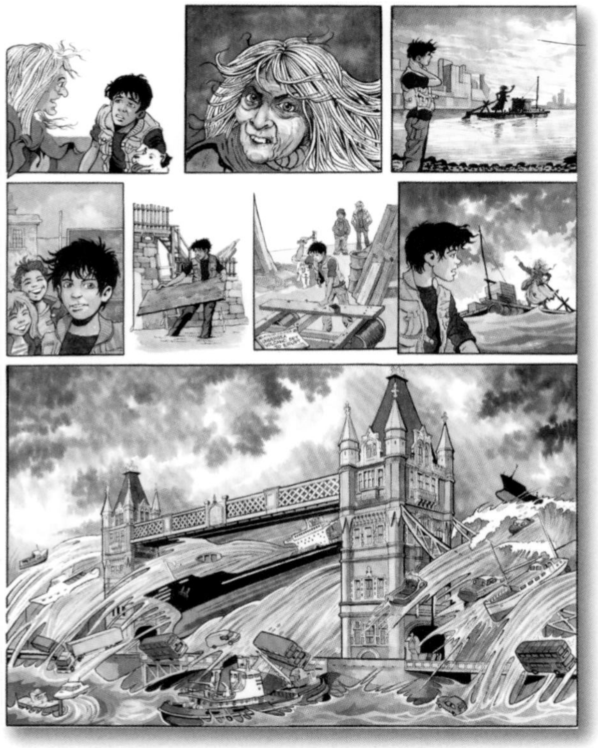

BALL BOY

NEW!
BALL BOY
DAD SENT ME TO PICK UP HIS NEWSPAPER—I'D FAR RATHER BE PLAYING FOOTBALL!
SWERVE
I'VE JUST HAD A THOUGHT—A CRUMPLED-UP NEWSPAPER MAKES A . . .
. . . SUPER FOOTBALL!
SNORT! HERE COMES THAT FOOTBALL DAFT PEST!
BOK!
BALL-BOY PICKS UP A HEAD-FLICK FROM THE CENTRE-BACK . . .
. . . THEN A DELICATE CHIP SHOT OVER A DEFENDER . . .
. . . HE ROUNDS THE POOR FOOL AND SHOOTS . .
THUMP!
. . . THE BALL HITS THE POST . . .
THUD!
. . . BUT IT'S A PENALTY! A FULL-BACK'S HANDLED THE BALL!
?
Meanwhile—
WHERE HAS MY SON GOT TO? HE'S BEEN AGES GETTING MY PAPER!
BALL-BOY RUNS UP TO TAKE THE PENALTY . . .
. . . BUT DAD SAVES IT!
GRR! LOOK AT THE STATE OF MY NEWSPAPER!
WHUMP!
EEK! I WISH SOMEONE WOULD SAVE ME NOW!

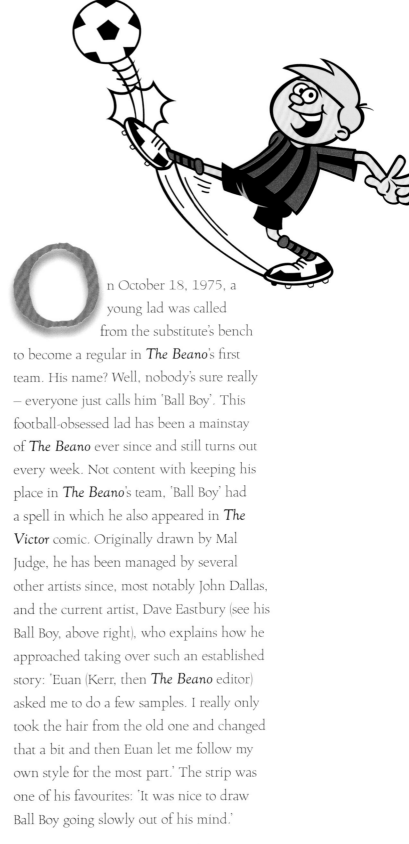

On October 18, 1975, a young lad was called from the substitute's bench to become a regular in *The Beano*'s first team. His name? Well, nobody's sure really – everyone just calls him 'Ball Boy'. This football-obsessed lad has been a mainstay of *The Beano* ever since and still turns out every week. Not content with keeping his place in *The Beano*'s team, 'Ball Boy' had a spell in which he also appeared in *The Victor* comic. Originally drawn by Mal Judge, he has been managed by several other artists since, most notably John Dallas, and the current artist, Dave Eastbury (see his Ball Boy, above right), who explains how he approached taking over such an established story: 'Euan (Kerr, then *The Beano* editor) asked me to do a few samples. I really only took the hair from the old one and changed that a bit and then Euan let me follow my own style for the most part.' The strip was one of his favourites: 'It was nice to draw Ball Boy going slowly out of his mind.'

PLUG

Dennis the Menace wasn't the only ***Beano*** star enjoying increased popularity in the 1970s. In 1977, ***Plug,*** the resident hunk in 'The Bash Street Kids' was the star of his own comic called, surprisingly enough, ***Plug***. It was edited by the former ***Beano*** chief-sub and self-professed comic icon, Ian Gray, a larger than life figure who could easily have stepped out of a comic strip. ***Plug*** ran for 75 issues from September 24, 1977, until February 24, 1979, when it amalgamated with ***The Beezer.***

The cover of the first issue (right) features an athletic Plug. Just like the first Beano, there is a free gift! Below is the team line up for Antchester United; the start of 'D' ye Ken John Squeal and His Hopeless Hounds' is below right.

No1
No. 1—Sept. 24th, 1977. Every Saturday.
FREE INSIDE-Noisy Goon Balloon
PLUG
introducing
PERCIVAL PROUDFOOT
PLUGSLEY KNOWN AS PLUG
WORLD CHAMPION SPORTING SUPERGOON
9p
FREE INSIDE
THE SCREAMIN' DEMON
YEEEEEEE IT'S A SCREAM!
GET "PLUG" AND BE ONE JUMP AHEAD
IT'S FUN! IT'S POP!
IT'S SPORT! IT'S TREND!
IT'S TODAY'S COMIC
PLUG'S PET MONKEY 'CHUNKEE'
LEAP OVER TO PAGE 20→

ANTCHESTER UNITED
THE INSECT FOOTBALL TEAM WITH ALL THE TALENT AND ALL THE LEGS —
DAVID LARVAE
BRIAN GREENFLY
GNAT LOFTHOUSE
MANTIS BUCHAN
CRAWLIN' TODD
STIRLING MOTH
FRANCIS FLEA
SPIDER WEBB
GEORGE BEASTIE
ANTY GRAY
MIKE SUMMERBEE
KEVIN BEATLE

D'YE KEN
JOHN SQUEAL and his HOPELESS HOUNDS
FLASH
HMM!
'QUICK-BROWN' THE FOX
AAAH. WHAT NICE DAY!
ULP! WHASSAT?

PLUG
No. 63 – Dec. 2nd., 1978.
Every Saturday.
9p
O.K. BIG JOHN PAIN! IT'S TIME WE SETTLED ONCE AND FER ALL WHO'S THE TOUGHEST GUNSLINGER IN THE WILD WEST!
KACHUNG!
BLAM!
PISTOL PACKIN PLUG
BLAM!
CONSARN IT! THE FIRST TIME I COME ON THE COVER OF THIS HERE COMIC AND SOME GOON'S PICKIN' A FIGHT ALREADY!
HAVE YA JOINED THE PLUG CLUB?

No 75.– Feb. 24th, 1979. Every Saturday.
PLUG
9P
IN A SPINE-CHILLING ENCOUNTER WITH A VAMPIRE
HORROR OF HORRORS! MAD BRAVE PLUG IS BOUND FOR COUNT DRACULA'S CASTLE. SEE THE BACK PAGE... IF YOU DARE!
IT'S REALLY TOMATO SAUCE, FOLKS!

PLUG
CONTINUED IN BEEZER AND PLUG NEXT WEEK

The front cover featuring John Wayne, and the front and back cover of the last edition in 1979. The announcement (above) tells of the merger with The Beezer.

IMPORTANT ANNOUNCEMENT
EEBAGOOM and UNCLE ALBERT
I've got news for you!
FIRST Ada
Dear Plug fans,
NEXT WEEK your PLUG comic teams up with the BEEZER to make a super comic— "BEEZER and PLUG".
I'll be inside it and so will EEBAGOOM, FIRST ADA, ANTCHESTER UNITED and HUGH'S ZOO.
On sale every Wednesday.
See you!
Percival Proudfoot Plugsley
ANTCHESTER UNITED
Hugh's Zoo
ORDER Beezer and PLUG NOW!
ON SALE EVERY WEDNESDAY. PRICE 8p.

Joining our handsome hero in the pages were some delightfully oddball stories, such as 'Hugh's Zoo', 'Violent Elizabeth', 'Eebagoom' and the wonderfully titled 'D' Ye Ken John Squeal And His Hopeless Hounds', drawn by David Mostyn. John Geering's 'Antchester United' featured a team of footballing bugs. Where other than in a comic would you see players like Gnat Lofthouse, Anty Gray and George Beastie?

Plug was the first comic to make use of the gravure printing, which made for crisper images with much brighter and more vibrant colours, very much in keeping with the content. ***Plug***'s covers were often clearly influenced by the style of **Mad Magazine** and featured caricatures of celebrities. When a number of these celebrities unfortunately died just before or after their appearances in the comic, 'The Curse of the ***Plug***' was born.

THE BASH STREET KIDS

The science fiction craze of the late 1970s found its way onto the pages of 'The Bash Street Kids' in this story from 1978. Luke Skywalker never had to face anything as horrid as Plug.

Spurred on by the success of 'Plug' in having a comic of his own, 'The Bash Street Kids' made a bid for Christmas domination in Autumn 1979 with the launch of their first annual to go alongside their appearances in The *Beano Book* and the *Beano Summer Special.* A mixture of reprinted classic strips and new stories, *The Bash Street Kids Book* was an instant success and continues to be a Christmas favourite.

THE BASH STREET KIDS
MOST INTERESTING!
CEREAL
UNIDENTIFIED FLYING OBJECTS SEEN ALL OVER THE COUNTRY
FIERY CROSS IN THE SKY
AT SCHOOL –
BLAH! BLAH! FLYING OBJECTS! BLAH! OUTER SPACE!
THAT EVENING AT TEACHER'S HOUSE –
PROCEED TO YOUR LOOK-OUT POSTS AND SCAN THE SKIES FOR FLYING OBJECTS
CORKS! A FLYING OBJECT! CATCH IT WITH YOUR NET, FATTY!
LOOK, TEACHER– A LIGHT IN THE SKY.
DOLTS! THAT'S A MINER ON THE NIGHT SHIFT! SORRY, SIR!
AT BASH ST. PARK –
NOW TO CONQUER EARTH!
HULLO, PALS! I'M PLUG
PANT! FLYING SAUCER! GASP! LITTLE GREEN MEN! WHEEZE!
FLYING SAUCER? LITTLE GREEN MEN? THERE, THERE, PLUG–YOU'RE SUFFERING FROM STRAIN. GO HOME AND REST!
BNO. 12.8.78

AFTER SHAVE LOTION

HIS IS WHAT WE THINK THE MEN
ROM MARS MAY LOOK LIKE
THAT'S A DRAWING OF MY GRANNY.
YOU WILL DO NO HOMEWORK THIS EVENING....
PAT PAT
POLISH
NICE TEACHER!
DUST
COMB
AFTER SHAVE LOTION
YOU WILL INSTEAD REPORT TO MY HOUSE FOR FLYING OBJECT SPOTTING!
SNIP
AW!
SHAVING CREAM
THAT'S AN OWL, IDIOT! RELEASE IT AT ONCE!
IS THIS A FLYING SAUCER, TEACHER?
NO! IT'S A FLYING DUSTBIN LID!
INTO THE SAUCER QUICKLY!
NOW I WONDER—?
BASH STREET BUGLE
PROFESSOR FUZZBONCE SEES FLYING SAUCER OVER BASH ST. PARK LAST NIGHT
THE Beano SUMMER SPECIAL 22p
IT'S OUT OF THIS WORLD!
ON SALE EVERYWHERE!
32 BIG PAGES

FROM "THE BEANO"
The BASH STREET KIDS
1980

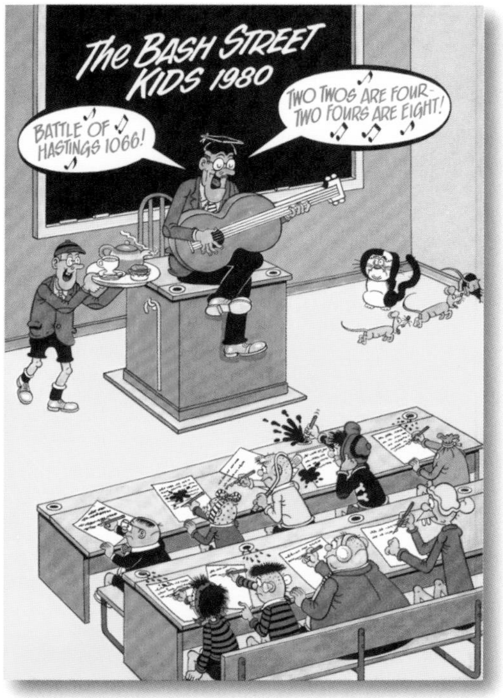
The BASH STREET KIDS 1980
BATTLE OF HASTINGS 1066!
TWO TWOS ARE FOUR- TWO FOURS ARE EIGHT!

The first Bash Street Kids Book, *produced for Christmas 1979, with the front and back telling very different stories.*

PETS' PICTURE GALLERY

One of the most unlikely *Beano* successes during the 1970s was the 'Pets' Picture Gallery', which encouraged readers to send in drawings of their pets. Morris Heggie, a sub-editor on the comic at the time, recalls, 'The notion for Pets' Picture Gallery was Ian Gray's – he was chief sub on *The Beano* and it reeks of his thinking. The mailbag of little drawings of pets was several thousand per week – the first few months it was tens of thousand per week – and the popularity lasted and lasted. The pets were selected at random from the masses of entries and some had been drawn perhaps months before they surfaced.'

But sadly, not all the pets saw their 15 minutes of fame. Morris continues, 'As a lot of pictures were of creatures like tadpoles or caterpillars, by the time the picture got to press the beastie would have gone through its life cycle and be long gone.'

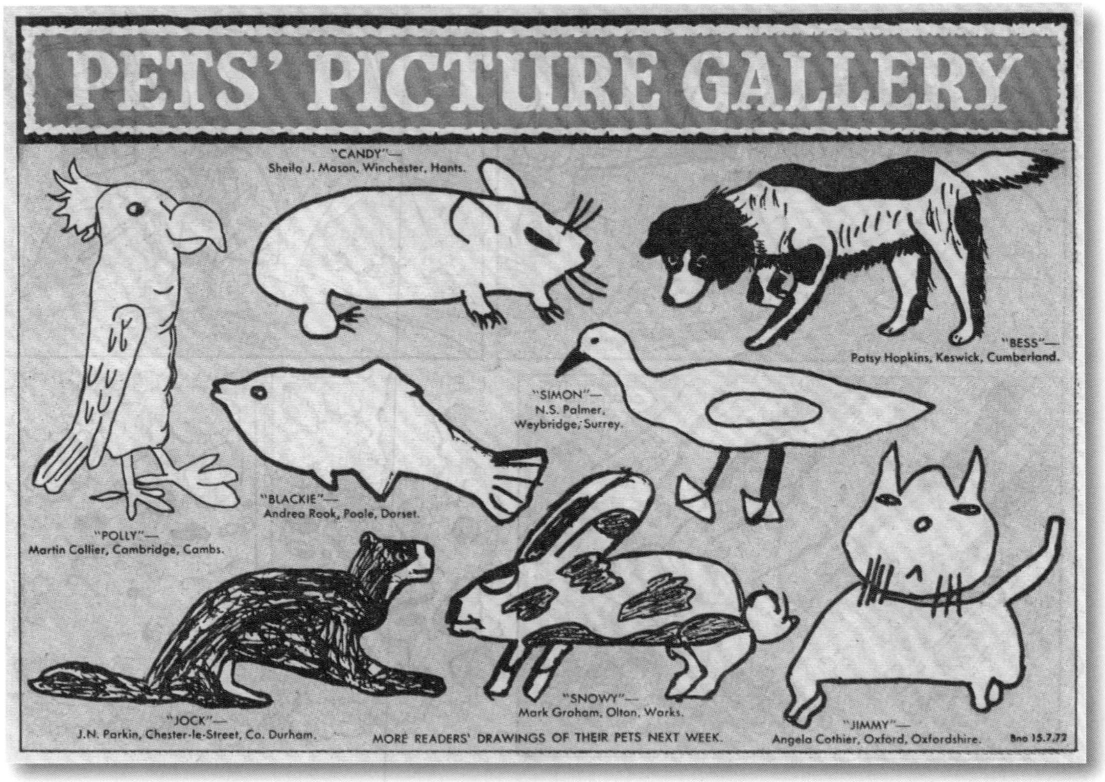
PETS' PICTURE GALLERY
"CANDY"—
Sheila J. Mason, Winchester, Hants.
"BESS"—
Patsy Hopkins, Keswick, Cumberland.
"SIMON"—
N.S. Palmer,
Weybridge, Surrey.
"BLACKIE"—
Andrea Rook, Poole, Dorset.
"POLLY"—
Martin Collier, Cambridge, Cambs.
"JOCK"—
J.N. Parkin, Chester-le-Street, Co. Durham.
"SNOWY"—
Mark Graham, Olton, Works.
"JIMMY"—
Angela Cothier, Oxford, Oxfordshire.
MORE READERS' DRAWINGS OF THEIR PETS NEXT WEEK.
Bno 15.7.72

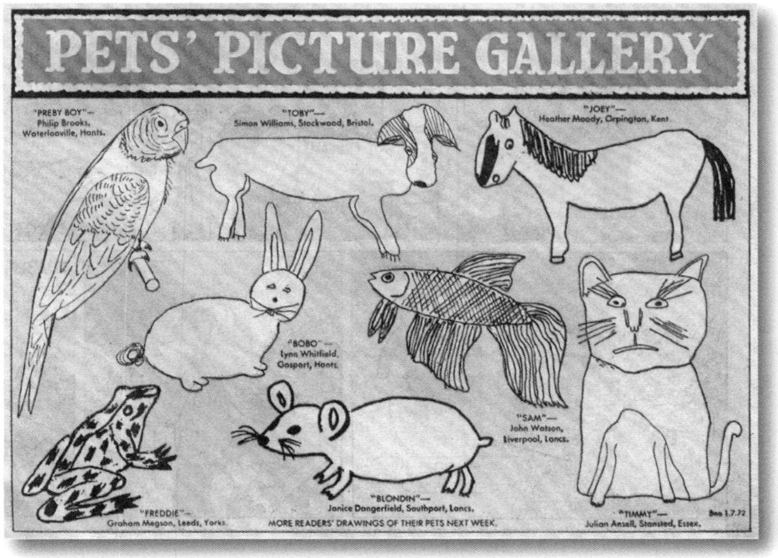
PETS' PICTURE GALLERY
"PREBY BOY"—
Philip Brooks,
Waterlooville, Hants.
"TOBY"—
Simon Williams, Stockwood, Bristol.
"JOEY"—
Heather Moody, Orpington, Kent
"BOBO"—
Lynn Whitfield,
Gosport, Hants.
"SAM"—
John Watson,
Liverpool, Lancs.
"FREDDIE"—
Graham Megson, Leeds, Yorks.
"BLONDIN"—
Janice Dangerfield, Southport, Lancs.
MORE READERS' DRAWINGS OF THEIR PETS NEXT WEEK.
"TIMMY"—
Julian Ansell, Stansted, Essex.
Bno 1.7.72

PETS' PICTURE GALLERY
"SQUAK"—
Paul Smith,
Middlesborough, Yorks.
"JONKIE"—
Mary Locke, London.
"TIDDLES"—
Sharon Sullivan,
Crowborough, Sussex.
"SYLVESTER"—
Lydia Ward, Newark, Notts.
"TINA"—
Anne Bateson,
Wingate, Co. Durham.
"DIXIE"—
Rosalynd Atkinson,
Newcastle, Co. Durham.
"SPRING"—
Tony Pulham, London.
"TAMSEY"—
Frances Stellitano,
St Neots, Hunts.
Bno 30.9.72
MORE READERS' DRAWINGS OF THEIR PETS NEXT WEEK.

THE BEANO AT 40

THE BEANO
40 YEARS OF FUN
FIRST BEANO JULY 30th 1938
No. 1880 JULY 29th, 1978
EVERY THURSDAY
5p
DENNIS THE MENACE AND GNASHER
WAHEY! IT'S MY BIRTHDAY!
GNEEK!
WONDER WHAT'S IN MY PARCELS?
TO DENNIS
A WATER-PISTOL FROM CURLY, A PEA-SHOOTER FROM PIE-FACE, AND A COWBOY SUIT FROM GRANNY!
PEAS
AND WHERE DO YOU THINK YOU'RE GOING?
OUT, DAD— TO PLAY WITH THESE!
BUT—
YOU'RE GOING NOWHERE UNTIL YOU'VE WRITTEN YOUR "THANK-YOU" LETTERS!
OH, ALL RIGHT!
GNO FUN!
MORE ON BACK PAGE.

The Beano's 40th anniversary in July 1978 was celebrated in a low-key manner, with the only reference to the landmark appearing on the front cover. The 'Dennis the Menace' story for that week had Dennis celebrating his birthday, showing that Dennis and *The Beano* share a birthday. Fancy that!

Every Thursday
THE BEANO
JULY 29th, 1978
DENNIS the MENACE AND GNASHER
CONTINUED FROM FRONT PAGE
MY MASTER GNEEDS HELP!
LATER—
STOP! LEAVE ME ALONE, YOU HORRID CREATURE!
GNASH!
WALTER THE SOFTY
KEEP MOVING!
HO! HO! GOOD THINKING, GNASHER! WRITING LETTERS IS SOFTY WORK!
THIS IS SLAVERY!
GRR!
SCRIBBLE! SCRIBBLE!
LATER—
FINISHED!
THANKS, WALTER! YOU'RE A PAL! NOW TO DELIVER THEM...
HI-HO, GNASHER! AWAY!
CLIP! CLOP!
LETTER FOR YOU, GRAN!
DENNIS'S GRANNY
ZONK!
TO GRANNY
HEY, YOU TWO!
SCOOSH!
PING!
PUFF!
HERE, TAKE THESE THANK-YOU" LETTERS!
SO, FEELING A BIT MISCHIEVOUS ON YOUR BIRTHDAY, EH?
CURLY
PIE-FACE
WOO! WOO!
HEY! CAREFUL, PALS!
HAPPY BIRTHDAY!
ZONK!
SPLOSH!
GNEEK!
LATER—
WHAT HAPPENED TO YOU? DID YOU SEND THOSE "THANK-YOU" LETTERS?
YES, THE MAIL GOT THROUGH — WITH A STRUGGLE!
Printed and Published in Great Britain by D. C. THOMSON & CO., LTD., 185 Fleet Street, London, EC4A 2HS.
© D. C. THOMSON & CO., LTD., 1978.

FREE GIFTS AGAIN!

It's common for comics and magazines to carry free gifts these days, but back in the 1970s they were a special event and big news in a comic, as this full page advert in the October 14 issue of *The Beano* shows. Because the gifts were such a rarity, they were often incorporated into the stories of those issues.

Free!
WHEE-OWWW-WHEE-OWWW!
The HAPPY HOWLER
SIREN
Yes, it's FREE in your "BEANO"
NEXT WEEK!
ISSUE DATE SEPT. 14th
Also Inside
NEW FUN!
RICHARD The LION
BOSS ANIMAL IN A COMICAL SAFARI PARK!
NEW THRILLS!
GENERAL JUMBO
WHO HAS AN ARMY AND AIR FORCE OF HIS VERY OWN!
NEW FUN!
1 TON
WEE BEN NEVIS
THE STRONGEST HIGHLAND LADDIE EVER!
And there's another FREE GIFT in "THE BEANO" the week after!

Every Thursday ★ ★ ★ THE BEANO Sept. 14, 1974.
DENNIS the MENACE AND GNASHER
CONTINUED FROM FRONT PAGE
EEK! A MAD DOG!
SNIGGER! THAT'S GOT RID OF THE QUEUE!
TRY SOME OF THIS, GNASHER.
NEWSAGENT
GNASH! SPLUTTER! GNASH!
IN THE SHOP–
ONE "BEANO," PLEASE! THERE'S A SUPER FREE GIFT THIS WEEK!
READ THE BEANO
BACK HOME, DAD'S READING A GHOST STORY–
THE EERIE WAILING OF THE HOUND COULD BE HEARD IN THE MARSHES...
HOUND OF THE BASKET BALLS
WHEEOWOOOOW!
IT'S THE HOUND OF THE BASKETBALLS!
SHUDDER
HOW DO YOU LIKE MY HAPPY HOWLER, DAD?
GRR! NO MORE NONSENSE, BOY!
AT THE OPERA HOUSE–
AND NOW THE WONDERFUL SOPRANO, MARIA POULTICE, WILL HIT HER FAMOUS HIGH NOTE!
WAILWEEOO!
OH, HORRORS!
GO AWAY SOMEWHERE ELSE! I SHALL INFORM YOUR FATHER OF THIS!
STAGE DOOR
ALL THIS WEEK THE WONDERFUL MARIA POULTICE
LATER–
LOOK, DENNIS! THE OPERA HOUSE MANAGER GAVE ME A FREE GIFT! WHAT DO YOU THINK OF IT?
GROAN! IT'S A SLIPPER!
WOOYAH!
YOWOOW!
LISTEN, READERS! THAT'S AN UNHAPPY HOWLER!
Printed and Published in Great Britain by D. C. THOMSON & CO., LTD., 12 Fetter Lane, Fleet Street, London, EC4A 1BL.
© D. C. THOMSON & CO., LTD., 1974.

This glove puppet of Dennis was very popular when it was given away in the issue of October 28, 1978.

THE BEANO
FREE inside A "DENNIS the MENACE" GLOVE PUPPET
DENNIS the MENACE FAN CLUB
No. 1893—OCT. 28th, 1978
EVERY THURSDAY
6p
DENNIS THE MENACE AND GNASHER
WE'RE DENNIS...
THE MENACE...
PUPPETS!
I HOPE YOU LIKE YOUR PUPPET, READER!
SOON—
STAND BY, FOLKS, FOR THE GREATEST PUPPET SHOW ON EARTH!
HELLO, WALTER! WOULD YOU LIKE SOME SEASIDE ROCK?
SQUEAKY VOICE
OH, YES PLEASE!
SPECIAL "SOFTY PUPPET" UNSUITABLE FOR "BEANO" READERS.
GRUNT! HERE'S A NICE BIT OF ROCK!
SQUEAL!
WAHEY!
GREAT SHOW!
CLAP! CLAP!
CRUMP!
I LIKE IT!
MORE ON BACK PAGE.

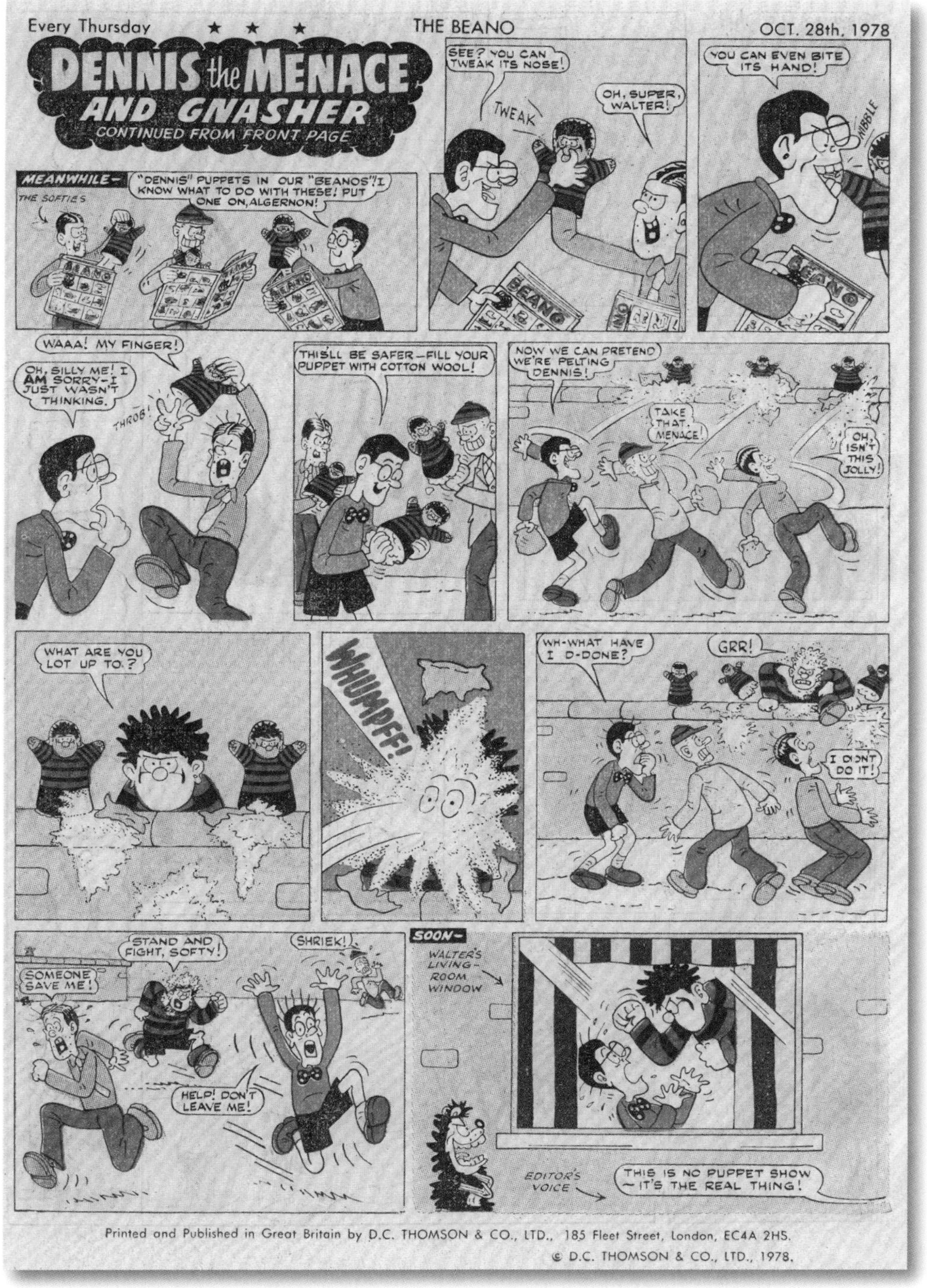
Every Thursday ★ ★ ★ THE BEANO OCT. 28th, 1978
DENNIS the MENACE AND GNASHER
CONTINUED FROM FRONT PAGE
MEANWHILE—
THE SOFTIES
"DENNIS" PUPPETS IN OUR "BEANOS"! I KNOW WHAT TO DO WITH THESE! PUT ONE ON, ALGERNON!
SEE? YOU CAN TWEAK ITS NOSE!
TWEAK
OH, SUPER, WALTER!
YOU CAN EVEN BITE ITS HAND!
NIBBLE
WAAA! MY FINGER!
OH, SILLY ME! I AM SORRY—I JUST WASN'T THINKING.
THROB!
THIS'LL BE SAFER—FILL YOUR PUPPET WITH COTTON WOOL!
NOW WE CAN PRETEND WE'RE PELTING DENNIS!
TAKE THAT, MENACE!
OH, ISN'T THIS JOLLY!
WHAT ARE YOU LOT UP TO?
WHUMPF!
WH-WHAT HAVE I D-DONE?
GRR!
I DIDN'T DO IT!
STAND AND FIGHT, SOFTY!
SHRIEK!
SOMEONE SAVE ME!
HELP! DON'T LEAVE ME!
SOON—
WALTER'S LIVING-ROOM WINDOW
EDITOR'S VOICE
THIS IS NO PUPPET SHOW—IT'S THE REAL THING!
Printed and Published in Great Britain by D.C. THOMSON & CO., LTD., 185 Fleet Street, London, EC4A 2HS.
© D.C. THOMSON & CO., LTD., 1978.

SPECIALS

With more pages, more colour, and printed on glossy paper, the *Beano Summer Specials* became a regular part of the summer holidays. What better way was there to pass a wet summer's day than with a bright and colourful *Beano Summer Special*?

BALL BOY
OH, BOY! I LOVE PLAYING BEACH FOOTBALL!
YOU DON'T HURT YOURSELF WHEN YOU FALL . . .
FLUMP
. . . AND A BEACH BALL IS LOVELY AND SOFT FOR HEADERS!
IT'S EASY TO CATCH WHEN YOU'RE IN GOAL, TOO!
SAND'S NICE AND SOFT ON YOUR FEET—NO HEAVY, MUDDY BOOTS NEEDED!
THE HALF-TIME REFRESHMENTS ARE UNBEATABLE!
SLURP!
ICES
CANDY FLOSS
Second half—
ANOTHER THING I DON'T MISS . . .
. . . IS GRUMPY OLD PARK-KEEPERS WHO BURST THE BALL WITH THEIR SHARP STICKS!
DONKEY RIDES
BANG!
DONKEY RIDES
NEEIGH!
STAMPEDE!
YOW!
BAH! THIS WOULDN'T HAPPEN ON A GOOD OLD REAL FOOTBALL PITCH!

BILLY WHIZZ

PUP PARADE
HELP!
EEK!
GULP! IS THERE A SHARK BEHIND US? . . . NO!
PERHAPS IT'S PUG'S FACE THAT FRIGHTENS THEM, MANFRID!
IT CAN'T BE—I'M WEARING GOGGLES!
MAYBE IT'S BECAUSE I'M SO TOUGH AND FEROCIOUS!
SCREAM! A MONSTER!
NO—I DON'T THINK IT'S BECAUSE YOU'RE TOUGH AND FEROCIOUS, SNIFFY!
HI!
IT COULD BE BECAUSE 'ENRY'S COVERED IN SEAWEED AND THE KIDS THINK HE'S A SEA-MONSTER!
OR BECAUSE THEY'RE SCARED TUBBY PINCHES THEIR PICNICS!
NO, PUPS, IT'S NONE OF THOSE THINGS . . .
. . . IT'S BECAUSE WE'RE SCARED OF GETTING SOAKED WHEN YOU SHAKE YOURSELVES! HAR-HAR!

THE
Beano
SUMMER SPECIAL
10P
CANDY FLOSS
SOLD OUT
DENNIS WON'T HAVE THAT CANDY FLOSS FOR LONG!
SEE BACK PAGE!

CANDY FLOSS
SOLD OUT
SLURP!
SLURP!

R. D. Low on the golf course.

In 1971, decimalisation brought a change to *The Beano's* price, switching from 4d to 2p. By the end of the decade, *The Beano's* price had rocketed to 7p. During this time, *The Beano* increased from 16 to 20 pages, giving more laughs for those pocket-money pennies. There were changes behind the scenes, too. Harry Cramond remained *Beano* editor throughout the 1970s, but in 1974, the much-loved R. D. Low, who had overseen the birth of *The Beano* in 1938, retired, aged 78. He was replaced as head of Juvenile Publications by George Moonie, *The Beano's* original editor.

PART 6

DENNIS AND THE GIANT *BEANO*

1980-1989

2000TH BEANO

No 2000
with FREE COMPETITION INSIDE
The BEANO
OVER 2000 PRIZES!
No. 2000—NOV. 15th, 1980
EVERY THURSDAY
8p
HERE'S THE 2000th "BEANO," GNASHER!
AND I'LL SHOW YOU A PICTURE OF THE COVER OF THE VERY FIRST "BEANO" ON THE BACK PAGE, READERS!

Every Thursday ★ ★ THE BEANO NOV. 15th, 1980
AH! THE GOOD OLD DAYS!
THE BEANO COMIC
No 1 · JULY 30 · 1938 EVERY TUESDAY
2D
SOMEONE'S TAKEN MY EGG AGAIN
DID YOU TAKE MY EGGS?
NO! BUT I SAW ONE BY THE RIVER!
BIG EGGO
HE'S GOT MY EGG!
?
FREE INSIDE
WHOOPEE MASK
I WAS IN IT!
Printed and Published in Great Britain by D.C. THOMSON & CO., LTD., 185 Fleet Street, London, EC4A 2HS. © D.C. THOMSON & CO., LTD., 1980.

The low-key celebration of the 2000th issue of *The Beano* on November 15, 1980 was a model of how the comic operated under Harry Cramond. Nothing flamboyant, with everything quietly concentrated on putting out a quality comic that held onto its readers with a TV-soap-like loyalty. You had to have every *Beano* to see what Dennis and the gang were doing – he was one of your best pals after all.

MORGYN THE MIGHTY—1938

BALL BOY
HARD GAME TODAY—WE'RE PLAYING THE BEST TEAM IN OUR LEAGUE!
PLAYING FIELDS
DRESSING ROOM 1
So—
LOOKING FORWARD TO THE MATCH, BOYS?
DRESSING ROOM 1
The BEANO 2000
1938-1980
NO ANSWERS
NO COMMENTS
NOT A WORD
NO REPLIES
HEH! BIG EGGO WAS REALLY FUNNY!
HMM! THEY'RE TOO INTERESTED IN "THE BEANO" 2000 TO WORRY ABOUT OUR MATCH!
HEH! THE THREE BEARS!
COME ON—GET READY!
BOOTS ON!
ZOOM! THERE GOES BILLY WHIZZ!
I'LL TRY SOMETHING ELSE!
I SEE FROM THE RECORD BOOK, THAT WE'VE SCORED 1,999 GOALS IN THE PAST!
EH?
COME ON! LET'S SCORE GOAL NUMBER 2000!
WE'RE PLAYING WELL! EVERYONE'S DETERMINED TO SCORE!
CHIP
And—
WHAT A GOAL!
BOOT!
WE'VE BEATEN THE LEAGUE LEADERS 1-0!
TIME UP!
ACTUALLY, WE'VE ONLY SCORED 130 GOALS BETWEEN US, NOTHING LIKE 2000! BUT DON'T TELL THEM THAT!
BNO. 15.11.80

The response to the competition which ran in the 2000th issue, in conjunction with Ariel balloons, showed how active this readership was. A massive 100,000 readers sent in entries. The prize was a handsome £100, and the winner was invited to *Beano* headquarters in Dundee to receive the prize from former World Cup referee Bob Valentine, who just happened to have been a compositor in Thomson's printing department, before his retiral the previous year.

JACK FLASH—1949

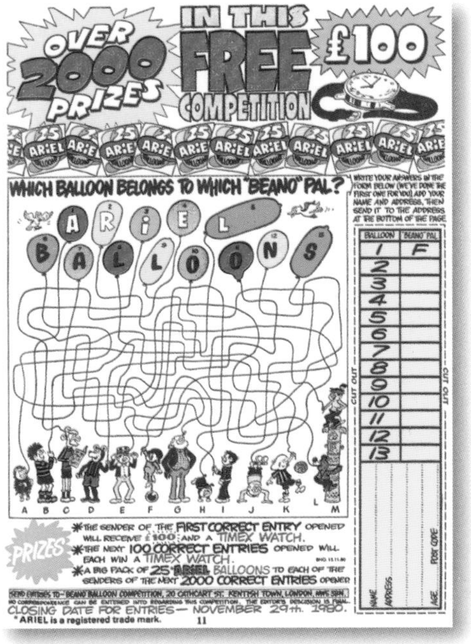
OVER 2000 PRIZES
IN THIS FREE COMPETITION
£100
WHICH BALLOON BELONGS TO WHICH "BEANO" PAL?
WRITE YOUR ANSWERS IN THE FORM BELOW (WE'VE DONE THE FIRST ONE FOR YOU) ADD YOUR NAME AND ADDRESS, THEN SEND IT TO THE ADDRESS AT THE BOTTOM OF THE PAGE.
ARIEL BALLOONS
BALLOON "BEANO" PAL
1 F
2
3
4
5
6
7
8
9
10
11
12
13
A B C D E F G H I J K L M
CUT OUT
NAME
ADDRESS
AGE
POST CODE
PRIZES
THE SENDER OF THE FIRST CORRECT ENTRY OPENED WILL RECEIVE £100 AND A TIMEX WATCH.
THE NEXT 100 CORRECT ENTRIES OPENED WILL EACH WIN A TIMEX WATCH.
A BIG PACK OF 25 ARIEL BALLOONS TO EACH OF THE SENDERS OF THE NEXT 2000 CORRECT ENTRIES OPENED
SEND ENTRIES TO— BEANO BALLOON COMPETITION, 20 CATHCART ST. KENTISH TOWN, LONDON, NW5 3BN.
NO CORRESPONDENCE CAN BE ENTERED INTO REGARDING THIS COMPETITION. THE EDITOR'S DECISION IS FINAL.
CLOSING DATE FOR ENTRIES— NOVEMBER 29th. 1980.
*ARIEL is a registered trade mark.
11

THE BEANO ON TV

Most comic watchers were surprised the following year by a change in *The Beano*'s softly-softly approach to publicity. In April 1981 TV cameras were allowed in to the cramped cloisters of *The Beano* office. A Thames TV unit featured *The Beano* and D. C. Thomson in a programme for its 'Middle English' educational series for schools and colleges. Editorial staff and artists, including George Moonie, the managing editor, editors Harry Cramond of *The Beano* and Albert Barnes of *The Dandy*, along with artist Dave Sutherland were interviewed and filmed working and they talked freely about the problems of their work.

George Moonie, The Beano's *first Editor, being briefed by a 'Middle English' presenter.*

THE BEANO
IT'S FAN-TASTIC!
WHAT IS? SEE PAGE NINE
No. 2020—APRIL 4th, 1981
EVERY THURSDAY
9p
DENNIS THE MENACE AND GNASHER
I'M FROM THE LOCAL TELEVISION COMPANY. WE'D LIKE GNASHER TO ADVERTISE THE LATEST DOG FOOD!
I THINK HE'D LIKE TO TRY IT OUT FIRST!
GNASHO GNOSH
DOES HE LIKE IT?
NO— I DON'T THINK SO! PERHAPS IF YOU ADDED SOME OF THE THINGS GNASHER LIKES TO CHEW BEST...
SLURP! GUZZLE!
PET PIG
GNASHER'S SWILL TROUGH
Soon—
THIS MAN WOULD LIKE TO BUY SOMETHING FROM YOU...
EXPENSES
GREAT! TWO POUNDS!
RIGHT! THAT'S THE FIRST INGREDIENT...
...POSTIE'S TROUSER LEGS— GNASHER'S FAVOURITE!
WHIRR!
SWITCH TO THE BACK PAGE

Every Thursday ★ ★ THE BEANO APRIL 4th, 1981
DENNIS the MENACE
AND GNASHER
CONTINUED FROM FRONT PAGE
GNASHER SHOULD LIKE THIS, TOO!
POWDERED BONES
I'LL MIX IT IN WITH THE REST OF THE STUFF!
POWDERED BONES
GNASHER
GNARGH!
GNASHER
ERK!
GNASTY!
NOW I SEE! YOU'VE BEEN FEEDING GNASHER CAT FOOD!
GULP!
POWDERED FISH BONES
JUST A MINUTE! I'LL BE ABLE TO MAKE AN ADVERT AFTER ALL!
Soon—
"GNASHO-GNOSH" PLANT FOOD WILL MAKE YOUR GARDEN GROW!
WHIRR!
GNASHO GNOSH
GNESH!
THAT DOG FOOD'S DONE WONDERS FOR THE DAFFODILS!
Printed and Published in Great Britain by D. C. THOMSON & CO., LTD., 185 Fleet Street, London EC4A 2HS.
© D. C. THOMSON & CO., LTD., 1981.

George Moonie and Albert Barnes, Editor of The Dandy, *watch the cameras being set up.*

Dave had drawn a 'Dennis the Menace' front and back cover story (shown here) about the visit of producer Peter Tabern and his crew, which went on sale the week the programme was screened. This was a real departure from the usual anonymity of ***The Beano*** team and enough to get some of the older subs checking to see if the ravens had left Thomson Towers.

The same change of attitude was evident when Dennis and Gnasher were signed up by Nestlé for a 'Smarties' advertising campaign. Billboard posters saw giant-sized Dennis, Gnasher and Walter appear all over the country. The Dennis scenes were drawn by Dave Sutherland, making use of his earlier advertising experience with cinema posters.

BEANO COMIC LIBRARIES

The cover of King Dennis the Menace, the first Comic Library title, and a double –page spread from within. The series was created by Ian Gray, seen in the photograph below.

BEANO
COMIC LIBRARY
No. 1
20p
KING
Dennis
the
Menace
PRINCE GNASHER

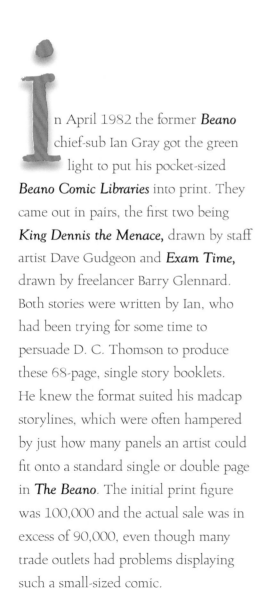

In April 1982 the former *Beano* chief-sub Ian Gray got the green light to put his pocket-sized *Beano Comic Libraries* into print. They came out in pairs, the first two being *King Dennis the Menace,* drawn by staff artist Dave Gudgeon and *Exam Time,* drawn by freelancer Barry Glennard. Both stories were written by Ian, who had been trying for some time to persuade D. C. Thomson to produce these 68-page, single story booklets. He knew the format suited his madcap storylines, which were often hampered by just how many panels an artist could fit onto a standard single or double page in *The Beano*. The initial print figure was 100,000 and the actual sale was in excess of 90,000, even though many trade outlets had problems displaying such a small-sized comic.

Later—
THIS IS MY MUD-HOLE WHERE I MAKE MUD-BOMBS!
WALLOW
AND THIS IS MY MUD-CANNON AND THAT'S WALTER OVER THERE!
SPLATCH!
WHIZZ!
BOING!
6
THIS CANNON ALSO MAKES A SUPER PEA-SHOOTER!
MUSHY PEAS
PEAS
I'LL SEND A BROAD-SIDE INTO SOFTIE TERRITORY!
WOOOSH!
PYONG!
7

BEANO BOOKS

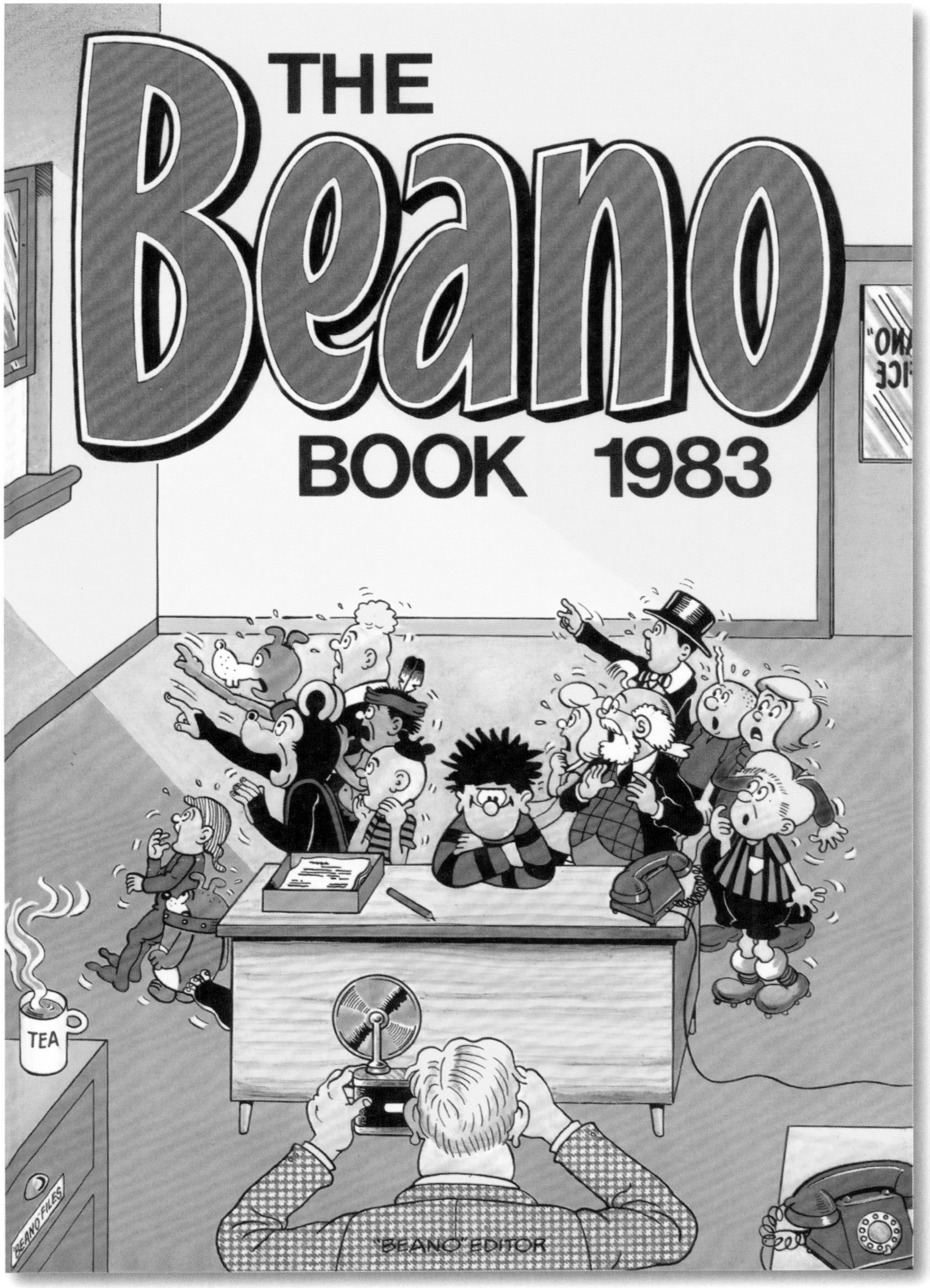
THE
Beano
BOOK 1983
TEA
BEANO FILES
"BEANO" EDITOR

For all British comics the 1980s were seen as the graveyard shift as far as sales were concerned. Increasing competition from children's new media entertainments meant that many weekly titles stumbled to a halt. The annuals reversed this trend as far as ***The Beano*** was concerned. The 1983 dated *Beano Book* became the highest selling annual to date. Christmas shoppers picked up 554,000 copies.

The front cover (above) and back cover (right) for the best-selling Beano Book.

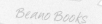

THE
Beano
BOOK 1983
"BEANO" OFFICE
TEA
"BEANO" EDITOR

SMUDGE

Very few new characters were introduced into the weekly at this time. In fact just one made an appearance between 1980 and 1984. This new face was 'Smudge' a boy who loved mess and would never keep himself tidy. He brought with him another new face to ***The Beano***, that of his artist John K. Geering (with his friend, Ken Dodd, above). This talented Lancashire humorist was well known and liked by ***The Beano*** staff but Harry Cramond puzzlingly felt that John was not a 'finished artist', and he had never used him. It took persuasion from his chief-sub Euan Kerr, who admired John's work on 'Bananaman' for the ***Nutty*** comic and the legendary 'Puss 'n' Boots' strip for ***The Sparky,*** before Harry agreed to try out 'Smudge'. John, like fellow Lancastrian Ken Reid, lived for humour and was full of good story ideas.

The staff enjoyed John's visit to the offices which invariably led to a laugh and some drinks in the local pub. John had been brought up in the same area as comedian Ken Dodd and they were friends who shared a similar sense of humour. He had designed the characters and costumes for Ken's troup of 'Diddymen' which were a big part of his stage act.

Dennis's Fan Club is on page 9-
Smudge
ERK! I'VE LOST MY WEDDING RING! DAD'LL BE FURIOUS!
PERHAPS YOU SUCKED IT UP IN THE VACUUM-CLEANER!
NO—NOT HERE!
COULD HAVE FALLEN INTO THE DUSTBIN WHEN I WAS EMPTYING RUBBISH.
I'LL LOOK!
NO SIGN!
COULD IT HAVE BEEN THROWN INTO THE COMPOST HEAP WITH THE POTATO PEELINGS?
But—
CAN'T FIND IT!
Then—
HERE COMES THE BRIDE . . .
SMUDGE'S LITTLE SISTER
WHAT'S THAT SHINING?
URSULA! GIVE ME MY RING AT ONCE!
AW! I ONLY BORROWED IT!
WAH! NOW WE CAN'T PLAY OUR GAME! WAIL!
NEVER MIND!
I DISOWN HIM!
HERE'S A CAN OF JUICE FOR HELPING ME GET DIRTY!
ICES
DRINKS
CRISPS
BNO 4.4.81
AND YOU CAN USE THE RING-PULL FOR YOUR WEDDING RING!
SUPER!
14

CHANGING EDITOR

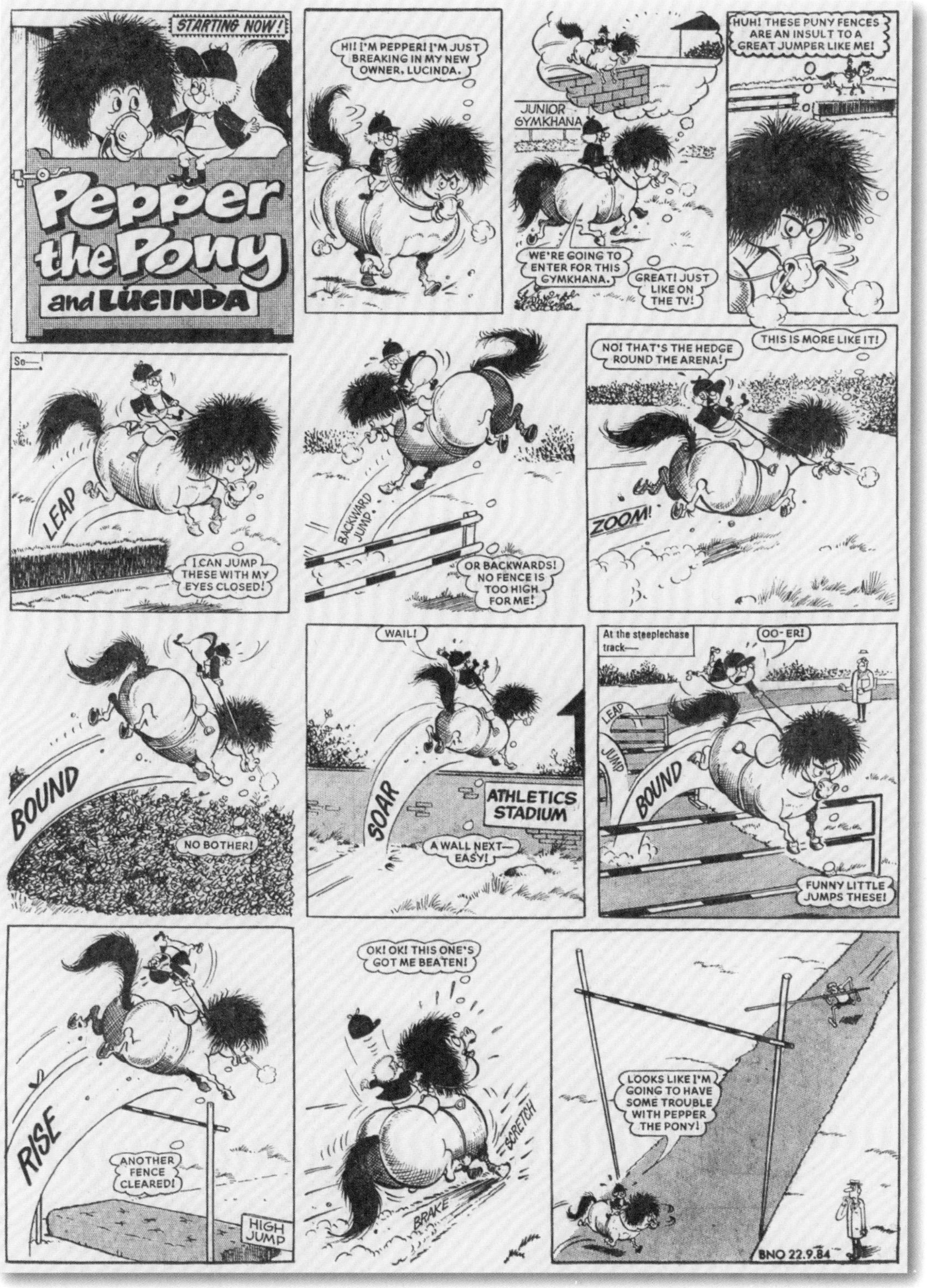
STARTING NOW!
Pepper the Pony and LUCINDA
HI! I'M PEPPER! I'M JUST BREAKING IN MY NEW OWNER, LUCINDA.
JUNIOR GYMKHANA
WE'RE GOING TO ENTER FOR THIS GYMKHANA.
GREAT! JUST LIKE ON THE TV!
HUH! THESE PUNY FENCES ARE AN INSULT TO A GREAT JUMPER LIKE ME!
So—
LEAP
I CAN JUMP THESE WITH MY EYES CLOSED!
BACKWARD JUMP.
OR BACKWARDS! NO FENCE IS TOO HIGH FOR ME!
NO! THAT'S THE HEDGE ROUND THE ARENA!
THIS IS MORE LIKE IT!
ZOOM!
BOUND
NO BOTHER!
WAIL!
SOAR
ATHLETICS STADIUM
A WALL NEXT— EASY!
At the steeplechase track—
OO-ER!
LEAP
JUMP
BOUND
FUNNY LITTLE JUMPS THESE!
RISE
ANOTHER FENCE CLEARED!
HIGH JUMP
OK! OK! THIS ONE'S GOT ME BEATEN!
SCRETCH
BRAKE
LOOKS LIKE I'M GOING TO HAVE SOME TROUBLE WITH PEPPER THE PONY!
BNO 22.9.84

The influence of chief-sub Euan and senior writer Alan Digby was becoming more apparent in the day-to-day running of *The Beano* as Harry Cramond prepared for retirement. His last major change as Editor was to bring in a new character, 'Pepper the Pony and Lucinda', a strip drawn by Ron Spencer. The first 'Pepper' strip is shown on the left. Among the first acts Euan was to do when he became Editor was to put Pepper and Lucinda out to pasture. Harry also gave Rasher, Dennis' pet pig, his own strip, drawn by Dave Sutherland. The first strip is shown on the next page.

In October, 1984, Harry passed over the red and black reins to Euan permanently. Harry had joined D. C. Thomson in 1937 and worked on *Adventure, The Beezer* and *The Beano*, where he had been Editor for 25 years. He guided the comic through its 1000th and 2000th landmark editions and would sadly pass away the week his former charge reached its 3000th edition in January 2000.

The new staff of *The Beano* were Editor Euan Kerr, chief-sub Alan Digby, and subs John Kemp, Alan Matheson and Roddie Watt. Years later Euan reflected on the time he took up the editorship: 'I had been left a wonderful legacy of great comic characters and I was maybe slightly concerned that the buck now stopped with me regarding the comic's future. However, I realised very early on that there were certain characters I just couldn't meddle with. They were of course "Dennis the Menace", "Minnie the Minx", "The Bash

'Rasher', drawn by Dave Sutherland, was one of the last new strips introduced by retiring Beano Editor Harry Cramond. The first strip, shown here, dates from September 1984. 'Simply Smiffy', drawn by Jerry Swaffield, was one of the first new strips from Euan Kerr as he settled into the Editor's chair. The first strip, shown here, appeared in September 1985.

RASHER
STARTING NOW!
A LOT OF READERS HAVE SAID THEY WANT TO SEE MORE OF MY PET PIG, RASHER . . .
HOI!
THAT'S NOT WHAT THEY MEANT—THEY WANT YOU TO HAVE YOUR OWN PAGE!
I'M GLAD TO SEE THE BACK OF THAT MENACE PIG!
RASHER WILL TELL YOU ALL ABOUT THE MENACING HE GOT UP TO ON WURZLE FARM BEFORE HE CAME TO LIVE WITH ME.
PIG STY
I'LL INTRODUCE YOU TO SOME OF MY FAMILY . . .
. . . SUCH AS MY SISTER, VIRGINIA HAM—SHE THINKS SHE'S BEAUTIFUL!
WHAT A PRETTY FACE!
WE DON'T THINK SO—GO AWAY!
MY BROTHER, HAMLET, WANTS TO GO ON THE STAGE!
" TWO BEES OR NOT TWO BEES, THAT IS THE QUESTION."
WE'RE WASPS ACTUALLY—THAT'S THE ANSWER!
BNO 22.9.84
THEN THERE IS UNCLE CRACKLING—HE'S A VERY OLD BOAR . . .
AH! WHEN I WAS A PIGLET . . .
. . . OR SHOULD I SAY BORE!
. . . BLAH . . . SNORT . . . DRONE . . .
SNZZZ!
I'LL SHOW YOU LITTLE PIGLET—IF I CAN FIND HIM!
GULP! SLURP! GOBBLE!
HEH-HEH! WHAT A CRAFTY WAY OF GETTING FIRST FEED!
SNOINK!

SIMPLY SMIFFY
STARTING NOW!
YOU COULD DO WITH REDECORATING THE HOUSE, SMIFFY!
NORMAL NORMAN
YOU'RE RIGHT, BROTHER NORMAN!
I KNOW—PAINT A MURAL!
GREAT IDEA!
So—
NEARLY FINISHED!
THERE! MURIEL HIGGENBOTTOM!
I SAID MURAL—NOT MURIEL!
Then—
TRY PUTTING WOOD PANELLING UP!
HMM, NOT TOO SURE HOW TO GO ABOUT THIS! I'D BETTER START IN A SMALL WAY!
LUCKY I HAD THIS SCREWDRIVER TO HAMMER IN THE NAILS!
SCREWDRIVER
GOOD, EH? I THINK I'VE GOT THE HANG OF IT!
GASP! NOW I'LL MISS "BROOKSIDE".
SEEMS TO BE DOING THE SENSIBLE THING NOW!
EDITOR'S VOICE
AARGH! YOU WERE SUPPOSED TO PAPER THE INSIDE WALLS!
DON'T WORRY, NORMAN—I'LL SOON SOLVE THAT PROBLEM!
THERE! CLEVER, EH?
I DON'T KNOW, I JUST DON'T KNOW! GROAN!

Street Kids" and "Roger the Dodger". This gang of rebels still forms the core of the comic today, of course, and back then I was sure I'd be okay so long as I didn't muck around with them too much. Basically, the naughtier and wilder a character is, the more the kids will love them – hence the reason why "Ivy the Terrible" joined that list of untouchable characters when she proved similarly popular with the readers.' Singling out Smiffy from 'The Bash Street Kids' and giving him his own page was one early change. A new artist, the young Jerry Swaffield, was selected to do the illustrations.

IVY THE TERRIBLE

Another early improvement Euan made was to persuade the artist Bob Nixon, who had been working solely for the opposition, namely the IPC comic titles, to return to work for *The Beano.* The first new story that they did was 'Ivy the Terrible'. Alan Digby was the man behind the idea and based Ivy's bunched hair design on his own toddler daughter. For that reason Bob always rated 'Ivy' to be his personal favourite out of his many D. C. Thomson stories. His return to *The Beano* as an artist was seamless and he was given a staff job, though he continued to work from his Guisborough home in North Yorkshire.

IVY'S FAVOURITE NIGHTMARES
YEAH-YEAH! SHAKE YOUR TAIL TO THE BEAT, SAMMY!
RATTLE!
RATTLE!
BONG!
BONG!

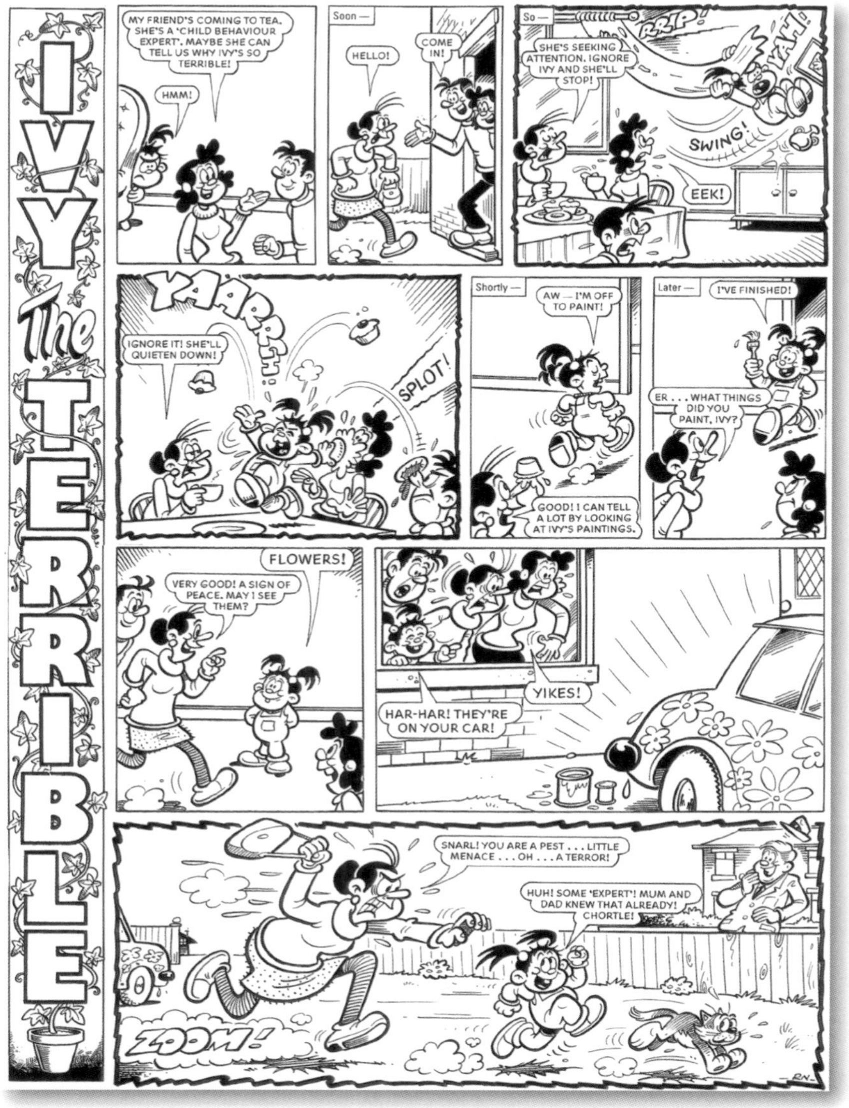
IVY The TERRIBLE
MY FRIEND'S COMING TO TEA. SHE'S A 'CHILD BEHAVIOUR EXPERT'. MAYBE SHE CAN TELL US WHY IVY'S SO TERRIBLE!
HMM!
Soon —
HELLO!
COME IN!
So —
SHE'S SEEKING ATTENTION. IGNORE IVY AND SHE'LL STOP!
RRIP!
YAH!
SWING!
EEK!
YAARRGH!
IGNORE IT! SHE'LL QUIETEN DOWN!
SPLOT!
Shortly —
AW — I'M OFF TO PAINT!
GOOD! I CAN TELL A LOT BY LOOKING AT IVY'S PAINTINGS.
Later —
I'VE FINISHED!
ER . . . WHAT THINGS DID YOU PAINT, IVY?
FLOWERS!
VERY GOOD! A SIGN OF PEACE. MAY I SEE THEM?
YIKES!
HAR-HAR! THEY'RE ON YOUR CAR!
SNARL! YOU ARE A PEST . . . LITTLE MENACE . . . OH . . . A TERROR!
HUH! SOME 'EXPERT'! MUM AND DAD KNEW THAT ALREADY! CHORTLE!
ZOOM!

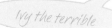

CALAMITY JAMES

For some time Euan and his *Beano* boys had been working on an idea about an unlucky character. Several artists, including John Geering and Henry Davies, had done preliminary sets but nothing had really pleased them, until the arrival of Tom Paterson. This talented cartoonist, though he lived not far from Dundee, was an IPC illustrator. A chance meeting between Tom and *Dandy* editor Morris Heggie resulted in Tom being willing to develop characters for D. C. Thomson. Between *The Beano* office and Tom, they designed 'Calamity James, the World's Unluckiest Boy'. James lives under a permanent cloud and has a pet lemming, Alexander. *The Beano* staff and the artist liked the story, especially the quirky asides Tom added when inking the drawings. *The Beano* readers, however, were split into two camps – some loved the story and thought it the best

LUCKY WHITE HEATHER GET YOUR LUCKY WHITE HEATHER HERE!
I'LL BUY THE LOT!
LUCKY WHITE HEATHER
YERK! LIGHTNING!
BLACK HEATHER! GET YOUR LUCKY BLACK HEATHER HERE!
BAH! THAT CLOUD DOESN'T WANT MY LUCK TO CHANGE!
Then-
WOW! A FOUR-LEAFED CLOVER!
GULP! A SUDDEN BLIZZARD!
HMPH, CAN'T FIND THE CLOVER NOW.
WHEN WILL MY LUCK TURN?
A BLACK CAT CROSSING MY PATH – THAT'S... THAT'S LUCKY!
OH HAPPY DAY! MY LUCK'S CHANGED!
EH?
RUMBLE!
GROAN! IT WAS A WHITE CAT COVERED IN SOOT!

Sample drawings by Henry Davies produced in the process of creating 'Calamity James'.

CALAMITY JAMES
THE WORLD'S UNLUCKIEST BOY!
THE TROUBLE WITH BEING UNLUCKY IS . . .
FARCICAL CUP-TIE
NAMPHERTON CASUALS
V
THRIPTON STRINGWORKS
PIMPLY HERBERTS' GATE
ADMIT ME
JAMES'S PET, ALEXANDER LEMMING
CLEAR OFF!
CHIP!
NOD!
DON'T SUPPORT US — WE'LL NEVER WIN!
. . . NOBODY WANTS YOU!
HOOF!
COME AND SEE ROUND THE GLASS FACTORY
I'LL HAVE A LOOK IN HERE!
GET OUT! WITH YOUR LUCK, EVERYTHING WILL GET SHATTERED!
KNEAD! SQUELCH! WOBBLE!
MASSAGE IN A BOTTLE.
BOOT!
THIS IS BAD ENOUGH . . .
GO AWAY, JAMES!
JAMES OUT!
RASSP!
NO ENTRY TO CALAMITY JAMES
PUSH OFF, JAMES
CALAMITY JAMES IS A BORING, LITTLE [CENSORED!]
JAMES'S MUM
JAMES MUST GO!
REVOLTING RASPBERRY!
. . . BUT IT'S AT MY OWN HOUSE!
EMIGRATION PAPERS TO OUTER MONGOLIA SIGN HERE
HEART-BREAKING, ISN'T IT?
Soon —
CAN I PLAY?
OH, ALL RIGHT. YOU BE A COWBOY.
PATHETIC PLEADING POSE!
SNIFF! THEY DIDN'T REALLY WANT ME TO PLAY WITH THEM! THEY'VE JUST TIED ME UP AND LEFT ME!
SO YOU WANT TO HURL YOURSELF OFF VERY TALL BUILDINGS
NOBODY WANTS ME! NOBODY WANTS ME!
JAMES'S UNFRIENDLY CLOUD
BLUB SOB WAIL!
DOLEFUL SCREECHES AND SAD STRAINS.
Suddenly —
FLASH!
WOW! THANKS, CLOUD!
RUMBLE!
AT LEAST YOU WANT ME, CLOUD!
LASH! TEEM!
BATTER!
SPLISH!
HO-HUM!
I STILL DON'T KNOW WHY!

thing in the comic – and others could not stand it at any price. There appeared to be no middle ground with Calamity. This was the same reaction another brilliant madcap strip had prompted years previously, 'Jonah'.

In February 1984, D. C. Thomson brought out a new title called **Champ,** with a mix of adventure and comic strips. 'Dennis the Menace' hosted his own fan section, and one of the stories Dennis introduced was 'Puss 'n Boots', reprints of the classic strips John Geering drew for Ian Chisholm in ***The Sparky*** comic.

GNASHER GOES MISSING

THE BEANO
2 SUPER BADGES for EVERY MEMBER!
see page 8
No. 2279 MARCH 22nd, 1986.
EVERY THURSDAY
16p
I.R. 28p (inc. VAT)
DENNIS the MENACE and GNASHER
THERE'S NO ANIMAL QUITE LIKE GNASHER!
NEW, EXTRA TOUGH LEAD
WHO'S THIS CHAP?
PURSE
I'LL GIVE YOU A MILLION POUNDS FOR GNASHER!
COO!
HE'S MINE! ALL MINE!
GREAT SWOP!
GNEH?
GRRWHAT?
I WAS WAITING FOR THAT!
ONLY JOKING. GNASHER'S WORTH FAR MORE THAN A MILLION POUNDS TO ME!
THROW
GNPHEW!
IMAGINE! TURNING DOWN A MILLION!
HUG
YOU GET SOME GREAT PARTNERSHIPS — LIKE FISH AND CHIPS, LAUREL AND HARDY, DENNIS AND GNASHER — WE'RE ALWAYS TOGETHER!
MORE ON BACK PAGE

Every Thursday ★ ★ ★ ★ THE BEANO MARCH 22nd, 1986.
DENNIS the MENACE AND GNASHER
CONTINUED FROM FRONT PAGE
BONE LORRY
EEK!
YEOWP!
GNASH!
ZOOM!
SCREECH!
WAIT FOR IT!
Later—
FOR ME? HOW LOVELY!
WHAT A PERFECT SET-UP FOR SOME GREAT GNASHING!
But—
GASP! GNASHER'S MISSED HIS CHANCE—HE CAN'T BE FEELING WELL!
GNASHER
HIS BEDDING'S STILL WARM—AND HIS BONE IS ONLY HALF GNASHED!
ODD—GNASHER USUALLY LETS ME KNOW IF HE'S GOING OFF TO DO SOME MENACING!
SCRATCH
I ONLY USE THIS IN CASE OF EMERGENCIES!
SPECIAL GNASHER WHISTLE
TINKLE!
EEK!
PHEEP!
But, much later—
GNASHER'S NEVER BEEN GONE THIS LONG BEFORE—I'VE GOT A FEELING SOMETHING'S WRONG.
BED-TIME, DENNIS!
JUST IN CASE HE COMES BACK LATE.
ARE YOU READERS GOING TO HELP ME FIND GNASHER?
All over the country—
YOU BET! WE WANT HIM BACK TOO, DENNIS! WE WON'T LET YOU DOWN!
DON'T MISS GNEXT WEEK'S "BEANO" AS THE GREAT GNATIONAL GNASHER SEARCH BEGINS!
Printed and Published in Great Britain by D. C. Thomson & Co. Ltd., 185 Fleet Street, London EC4A 2HS.
© D. C. Thomson & Co. Ltd., 1986.

An Alan Digby storyline kicked off on the cover of *The Beano* on March 22, 1986 – GNASHER GOES MISSING. Such was the popularity of Dennis and Gnasher that the story was taken up by the national media, and reports about the missing dog were broadcast on radio and television. Updates were constantly in the press, while reader response into *The Beano* office was overwhelming – GNASHER MUST BE FOUND!! There was even a 'Who's Gnicked Gnasher?' campaign started and to make matters worse, his solo spot in the comic, 'Gnasher's Tale', had been replaced by a strip featuring Walter the Softie's poodle entitled, 'Foo Foo's Fairy Story'.

Brian Leveson from Birmingham was so distraught that he felt compelled to write to *The Times*, *'Sir, although I am aware that at any one time there is too much happening in the world for it all to be included in this or any newspaper, I believe that it is vitally important that room should be made to publicise the disappearance of Gnasher from the pages of The Beano. He has not been seen for over a week and Dennis (The Menace) is very concerned about his safety.'*

He was missing for seven weeks and when he returned he was the proud father of six pups: Gnatasha, Gnancy, Gnaomi, Gnanette, Gnorah and one son, Gnipper. Gnipper would join his father in the comic in a strip titled 'Gnasher and Gnipper'. Many observers liked this ending, commenting that it was not a typical *Beano* finish.

Of course, in no time at all normality had returned, but not before many a column inch had been dedicated to what was going on at *The Beano*. The media heralded Gnasher's return as a victory for common sense, but of course it was never Euan's intention to banish him for good anyway.

THE BEANO
HAVE YOU SEEN THIS DOG?
No. 2280 MARCH 29th, 1986.
EVERY THURSDAY
16p
I.R. 26p (inc. VAT)
DENNIS the MENACE and
Last week Gnasher went missing. Loyal "Beano" fans are on the march—
WE BEG YOU TO COME BACK, GNASHER
"The Beano" NEEDS
We want Gnasher
GNASHER COME HOME
IT'S OK FOR YOU LOT —I HAD TO PUT UP WITH THE LITTLE BRUTE BEFORE HE WENT MISSING!
FOR ONCE I DON'T HAVE TO CHASE THE HAIRY HORROR OFF MY SEAT!
HUH!
BRR! IT'S NOT NICE AND WARM LIKE IT USED TO BE WHEN GNASHER HAD BEEN ON IT!
HEH! HEH!
Later—
THIS DUMPLING LOOKS HEAVY—I'LL GIVE IT TO GNASHER AND MUM'LL NEVER KNOW.
HE'LL POUNCE ON IT BEFORE IT HITS THE GROUND!
FLIP
GNASHER'S NOT HERE TO EAT WHAT YOU DON'T WANT, DAD.
ERK! FOUND OUT!
CRASH!
MORE ON BACK PAGE

THE BEANO
JOIN THE GNATIONAL GNASHER SEARCH!
No. 2281 APRIL 5th, 1986.
EVERY THURSDAY
16p
I.R. 26p (inc. VAT)
DENNIS the MENACE and
GNO GNASHER GNO MORE?
I CAN'T SPELL "NASHIR"!
I HOPE YOU'RE OK WHEREVER YOU ARE
We miss you, Gnasher
BRING BACK GNASHER
OI! WHERE'S GNASHER?
WE'RE MARCHING TO ASK A GREAT MAN TO HELP US FIND THE MISSING GNASHER!
"BEANO" OFFICE
AAARGH! IT'S DENNIS!
ZOOM!
YIKES!
EDITOR
...AND THIS IS HIM!
M-M-ME?
SCREECH TO HALT!
READERS—TAPE THESE TO YOUR "DENNIS THE MENACE FAN CLUB" BADGES IF YOU WANT TO HELP IN THE SEARCH FOR GNASHER!
WHO'S GNICKED GNASHER?
COME HOME GNASHER
I'M A 'BEANO' GNASHER SPOTTER
MORE ON BACK PAGE

FOO-FOO'S
FAIRY STORY

THE BEANO
GNASHER'S BACK!
No. 2286 MAY 10th, 1986
EVERY THURSDAY
16p
I.R. 26p (inc. VAT)
DENNIS the MENACE and GNASHER
Dennis's famous dog, Gnasher, has been missing. Now a pram has appeared at Dennis's door—
WH-WHAT'S IN TH-THERE, DENNIS?
TUG
SOFT WALTER
IT'S A LITTLE GIRL PUPPY!
YIP! YIP!
AAW!
HER NAME'S GNATASHA, AS IT HAPPENS!
YAHOO! IT'S GNASHER!
GNASHER, YOU'RE A DAD NOW!
MEET GNANCY, GNANETTE, GNAOMI AND LITTLE GNORAH!
BLUSH
YIP! YAP!
YAP! YAP!
YIP!
WHAT'S THIS?
DAD
YAP! YAP!
YIPPITY YAP!
GNIP! GNAP!
PUPS—MEET YOUR GRANDAD!
GNESH!
LICK
HEE-HEE! SHUCKS!
NIBBLE
MORE ON BACK PAGE

Every Thursday ★ THE BEANO MAY 10th, 1986
DENNIS the MENACE AND GNASHER
CONTINUED FROM FRONT PAGE
NO BOYS, GNASHER?
PHEEP!
GNYAP!
BOUNCE
BOUNCE
OOW! THAT HURT!
ZOOM
GNIP
MEET GNIPPER— THAT'S MY BOY!
YAHOO!
GNIP! GNIP!
WHY DIDN'T YOU COME HOME, GNASHER?
HELP!
HEH! HEH! YOU'VE BEEN BABY SITTING FULL-TIME FOR THE PAST EIGHT WEEKS!
RIGHT BUNCH OF LITTLE MENACES, THIS LOT!
STAMP
STAMP
STAMP
STAMP
NOW I KNOW WHERE YOU'VE BEEN STAYING—THE READERS AND I NEVER DREAMED OF LOOKING THERE!
MATERNITY HOME
GO!
HUMPH!
GUARD DOG
SO—
VISIT US AGAIN SOMETIME.
THANK GOODNESS THEY'VE GONE!
YOWL!
HEH! HEH! ONE HASN'T LEFT YET!
GNIP
Then—
SO THAT'S THE GNASHER MYSTERY SOLVED! THE NEXT MYSTERY IS— HOW ARE WE GOING TO FIND HOMES FOR THAT LOT?
ZOOM!
DON'T MISS NEXT WEEK'S "BEANO," WHEN GNASHER DEFINITELY WON'T GO MISSING AGAIN!
Printed and Published in Great Britain by D. C. Thomson & Co. Ltd., 185 Fleet Street, London EC4A 2HS.
© D. C. Thomson & Co. Ltd., 1986.

THE BEANO VS THE DANDY

Morris Heggie (top), The Dandy *Editor, with a familiar friend; Euan Kerr (bottom left) at the Editor's desk in* The Beano *office; Alan Digby (bottom right), then chief-sub on* The Beano; *and the Churchill Toby jug.*

Some changes at ***The Dandy*** had an impact on both the Editor and chief-sub of ***The Beano***. Morris Heggie was made Editor of ***The Dandy*** in early 1986. He and Euan had started work with D. C. Thomson in the same week in 1969 and together with Alan Digby had all worked under Harry Cramond on ***The Beano***. With their friend now in the opposing camp, rivalry between the two comics was upped a gear or two. They vied for sales, though ***The Beano*** outsold ***The Dandy*** 2 : 1. They fought for the best artists and staff writers who produced the most promising storylines. Away from the office there were Beano versus Dandy football games, bowling matches, quizzes, 'Call My Bluff' contests and even a curling match on ice. The prize was a cracked 'Winston Churchill' Toby jug which gave great honour to whichever office held it. Invariably the winner in these bizarre meetings was the Dundee licensed trade and late-night taxi drivers. The following year Alan Digby left ***The Beano*** in July to take over as editor of ***The Beezer***. Al Bernard then moved from ***The Dandy*** to return to ***The Beano*** for a second time, now as chief-sub.

KARATE SID AND LITTLE MONKEY

Two new characters were introduced in May 1987. 'Karate Sid', drawn by former *Beano* editorial staff member, now freelance artist, Steve Bright, who, for this character, adopts a Davey Law like style and 'Little Monkey', a Bob Nixon set. Both stories had short runs of exactly one year.

LITTLE MONKEY
YAHOO! I'VE BEEN GIVEN MY OWN PAGE IN "THE BEANO". LET ME SHOW YOU HOW I GET AROUND THE HOUSE.
I'VE GROWN MY OWN VINES.
DINNER!
AHA!
HERE I COME!
ERK! WRONG LANDING!
SPLUELCH!
TIME I WAS AWAY!
SHLOOP!
SWING
COME HERE!
SWING!
SWING!
LUCKY I'VE GOT MY VINES!
ERK! THEY'VE RUN OUT!
WAH!
SPLOOSH!
MONKEY'S HAD ENOUGH OF VINES!
BUT I'VE GOT A USE FOR THEM!
THERE! YOUR CLOTHES WILL SOON BE DRY!
HMPH!
BNO 16.5.87

STARTS TODAY
KARATE SID
Meet Sid and his Mum who's just made a very silly move.
ERK! SORRY, MUM— BUT YOU SHOULDN'T APPROACH ME LIKE THAT.
THUD!
YOU NEED SHOES! YOU CAN'T WALK ABOUT WITH BARE FEET!
AW, BUT, MUM . . .
DRAG
Soon—
SHOES
BE POLITE, SIDNEY. GET THE DOOR FOR ME.
ANYTHING YOU SAY, MUM!
CRASH!
Inside—
TEE-HEE-HEE! THAT TICKLES!
MAKES MY FEET TWITCH. OOPS!
WHAP!
OOFYAH!
T-TRY THESE ON!
HMM! TOO LOOSE!
WHEEE!
MUMF!
Soon—
I'VE CHANGED MY MIND ABOUT BUYING SID SHOES . . .
. . . HIS KARATE TRAINING HAS MADE HIS FEET QUITE TOUGH ENOUGH NOT TO NEED THEM!
SKIP
SKIP
CRACK!
CRACK!
CRACK!
CRACK!
CRACK!

THE COMIC WITH IVY THE TERRIBLE
THE BEANO
No. 2396 JUNE 18th, 1988
EVERY THURSDAY
20p
I.R. 29p (inc. VAT)
WHERE'S DENNIS?
NOT PLAYING FOOTBALL
NOT DOING HOMEWORK
NOT FIGHTING MINNIE
NOT PICKING PANSIES
NOT RACING BILLY WHIZZ
NOT SHARING RASHER'S SWILL
HERE HE IS!
SCARBOROUGH FESTIVAL
SEE THIS PAGE AS A GIANT SAND MODEL IN THE SCARBOROUGH FESTIVAL ... BEING BUILT ON JUNE 16TH

The Beano helped the Crescent Art Society from Scarborough create the World's Biggest Comic Strip by drawing a huge version of *The Beano*'s June 18, 1988 cover on the sands of Scarborough beach. Euan and Al had a jolly day out at the seaside lending a hand with their bucket and spades. Speed was important as the Yorkshire tide will not wait and the sea covered the record-breaking drawing minutes after it was completed.

BEANO AT 50

A celebration edition of *The Beano* was produced to mark its 50 years in print. The copy was dated July 30, 1988 – 50 years to the day since issue No. 1. With it came big design changes. It was on glossier paper, was printed on a gravure press, the pages were 25mm wider and there were now 10 pages in full colour. Two new strips were included, 'Danny's Nanny' illustrated by David Mostyn and 'Gordon Gnome' drawn by Eric Wilkinson. *The Beano* had stayed at the top of the British

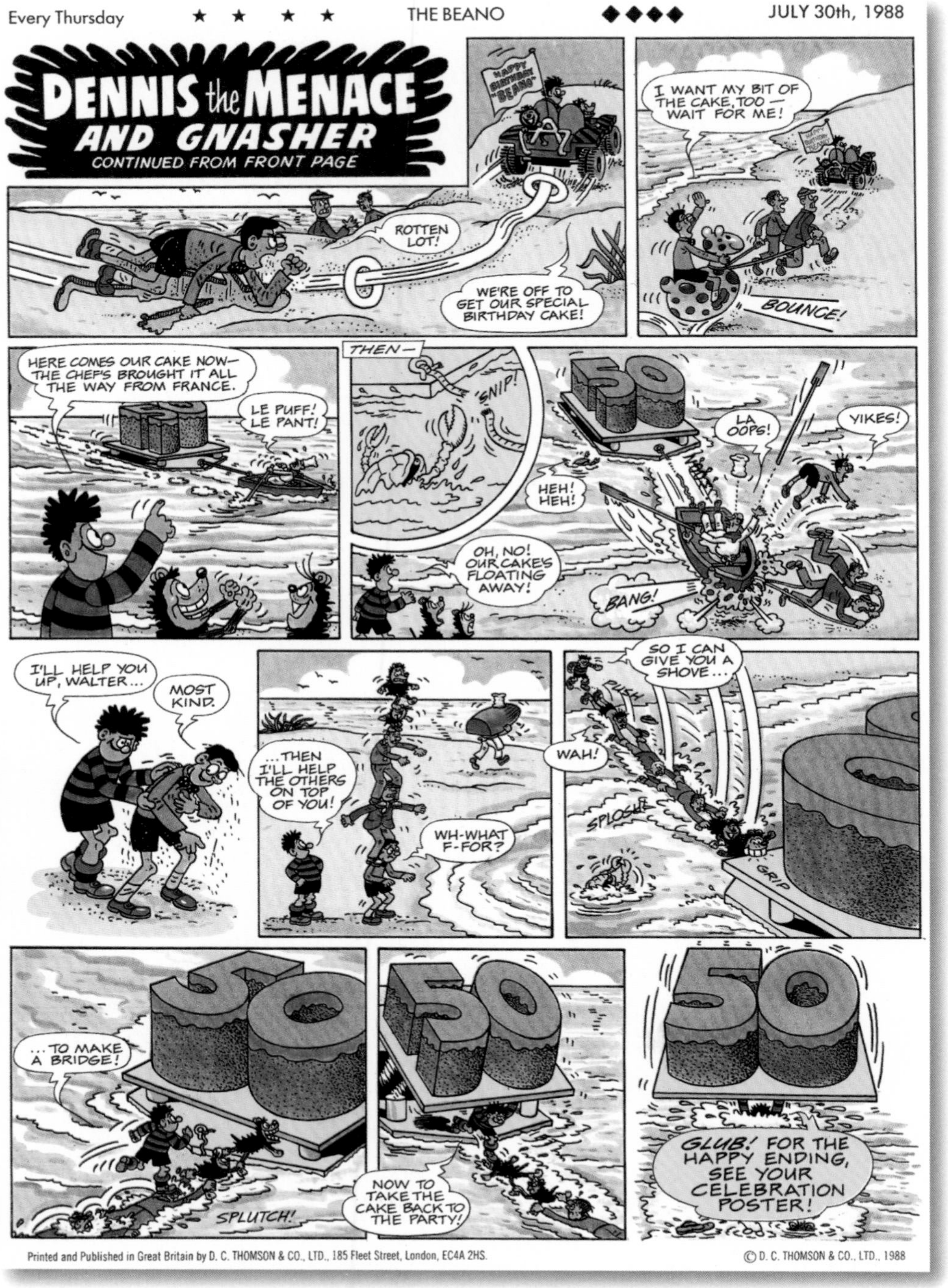
Every Thursday
THE BEANO
JULY 30th, 1988
DENNIS the MENACE
AND GNASHER
CONTINUED FROM FRONT PAGE
HAPPY BIRTHDAY "BEANO"
I WANT MY BIT OF THE CAKE, TOO — WAIT FOR ME!
ROTTEN LOT!
WE'RE OFF TO GET OUR SPECIAL BIRTHDAY CAKE!
BOUNCE!
HERE COMES OUR CAKE NOW— THE CHEF'S BROUGHT IT ALL THE WAY FROM FRANCE.
LE PUFF! LE PANT!
THEN—
SNIP!
HEH! HEH!
OH, NO! OUR CAKE'S FLOATING AWAY!
LA OOPS!
YIKES!
BANG!
I'LL HELP YOU UP, WALTER...
MOST KIND.
...THEN I'LL HELP THE OTHERS ON TOP OF YOU!
WH-WHAT F-FOR?
SO I CAN GIVE YOU A SHOVE...
PUSH
WAH!
SPLOSH
GRIP
...TO MAKE A BRIDGE!
SPLUTCH!
NOW TO TAKE THE CAKE BACK TO THE PARTY!
GLUB! FOR THE HAPPY ENDING, SEE YOUR CELEBRATION POSTER!
Printed and Published in Great Britain by D. C. THOMSON & CO., LTD., 185 Fleet Street, London, EC4A 2HS.
© D. C. THOMSON & CO., LTD., 1988

THE BEANO
SPECIAL 50TH BIRTHDAY ISSUE
No. 2402 JULY 30th, 1988
EVERY THURSDAY
20p
I.R. 29p (inc VAT)
HAPPY BIRTHDAY "BEANO"
50
FREE CELEBRATION POSTER INSIDE

STARTS TODAY . . . STARTS TODAY . . . STARTS TODAY . . .
DANNY'S NANNY
DON'T LIKE THAT BABY-FOOD RUBBISH.
PRUNE AND PILCHARD PUD
LITTLE DANIEL IS A BIT HIGH-SPIRITED.
PPURT!!
PERHAPS I COULD FIND A NANNY TO LOOK AFTER HIM.
THAT BABY-FOOD WAS HANDY FOR WRITING AN ADVERT IN.
NANNY WANTED
Presently—
I'LL SOON LICK HIM INTO SHAPE.
NAUGHTY NOISE
SIT UP STRAIGHT! DON'T FIDGET! BE QUIET!
HAVE A TEDDY, LADY!
DANNY'S VOICE
ZONK!
SOON GOT RID OF HER, EH?
SILENT SCREAM!
I'M OFF!
Just then—
WONDER IF THERE ARE ANY SCRAPS IN THIS GARDEN?
YAHOO! RIDE HIM, HORSIE.
HO-HUM!
TRUNDLE!
GIDDY-UP!
SO, I'M A HORSE, AM I?
CASUAL THROW
WELL, THIS HORSE HASN'T BEEN "BROKEN" YET!
YOURS, I BELIEVE!
WOW! SOMEONE WHO CAN CONTROL DANNY!
WHEEE!
THUD!
BE DANNY'S NANNY AND YOU CAN HAVE EVERYTHING YOU'VE EVER WANTED.
WE'LL SEE! WE'LL SEE!
NIFF!
BNO 30.7.88

NUMBER 13
FIENDISH
BORIS DAD FRANKIE MUM GRAN TIDDLES
I'M GOING TO MAKE A FIFTIETH ANNIVERSARY CAKE.
So—
WING OF PLANE . . .
. . . AND HAIR OF CAT . . .
. . . LOADS OF GUNGE AND RANCID FAT . . .
GROO!
. . . ADD SOME LOVELY STINGING NETTLES . . .
. . . THEN SOUR MILK FROM RUSTY KETTLES . . .
. . . STIR IT BRISKLY WITH A STICK . . .
. . . STOP IT, GRAN, I'M FEELING SICK!
NO-ONE WOULD EAT THAT TO CELEBRATE THE BEANO'S FIFTIETH.
OVEN
IT'S NOT FOR THE BEANO'S FIFTIETH . . .
WHOOSH!
IT'S THE FIFTIETH ANNIVERSARY OF OLD WITCH MANDRAKE PINCHING MY FIRST EDITION OF THE COMIC.
SPLAT!
SO, TAKE THAT, YOU OLD HAG!

comics tree for an amazing half a century and everyone connected with it was delighted. Festivities on a scale not usually associated with British comics got into gear. Daily newspapers, radio and television news all carried birthday wishes. Prime Minister Margaret Thatcher sent her congratulations. Euan and a 'Dennis the Menace' costume character were invited onto BBC's prime-time 'Wogan' show. While in London they did a photo shoot on Tower Bridge and made a guest appearance on Chris Tarrant's radio show.

Panini launched a ***Dandy Beano Celebration Sticker Album*** and sticker collection. D. C. Thomson took ***The Dandy*** chief-sub John Methven away from his weekly work to produce a book, ***Fifty Golden Years of The Dandy and Beano,*** and demand for his excellent book was so great that the initial print run was sold out immediately and by Christmas it had been reprinted three times. This series is now a regular annual on the Christmas market and in its third decade as ***Seventy Years of Beano and Dandy.***

The highly regarded BBC 2 arts programme 'Arena' moved to Dundee to take an in-depth look at the 50 year history of ***The Dandy*** and ***The Beano***. They filmed in the editorial offices, art department and print works. The whole of their 50-minute programme was devoted to the two comics. The producer Helen Gallagher camped in the editorial base for weeks and became a familiar face, so much so that she and the crew were invited to ***The Dandy***'s 50th birthday party (but not their cameras, for Dandy parties could be on the wild side).

10 DOWNING STREET

THE PRIME MINISTER

Congratulations on the 50th Anniversary of "The Dandy" and "The Beano".

These must be among the world's most famous and most loved comics.

Over the years they have given enjoyment to countless numbers of children and the characters in their pages - such as "Desperate Dan" and "Minnie the Minx" - have become household names.

I very much hope that both comics will continue to delight boys and girls for another 50 years.

Margaret Thatcher

STARTS TODAY
GORDON GNOME
WE'LL PUT THIS UGLY GNOME BESIDE THE GOLDFISH POND, KEVIN.
WHO ARE YOU CALLING UGLY, WARTHOG FACE?
HOW AM I SUPPOSED TO CATCH A FISH WITH THIS PUNY ROD?
I'M GOING TO GIVE YOU A MOUTH FULL OF FINS, GNOME.
OUCH!
SKLAPP!
THAT DOES IT! A GNOME'S GOT TO DO WHAT A GNOME'S GOT TO DO!
HEE-HEE!
I'LL NEED THIS STRAWBERRY NET.
NOW TO CATCH THAT NASTY GOLDFISH.
SO YOU THINK YOU CAN SMACK GORDON GNOME AND GET AWAY WITH IT.
C'MERE, BUSTER!
OO-ER!
Soon—
MY BELOVED STRAWBERRIES! WHERE'S THE NET GONE?
GASP! THAT'S NOT THE ONLY STRANGE THING THAT'S HAPPENED, DAD. LOOK IN THE POND.
GASP!
HOW DID OUR GOLDFISH GET A BLACK EYE?
LET'S KEEP IT OUR SECRET, EH, READERS? CHORTLE!

Minnie THE Minx
SINCE IT'S "THE BEANO'S" 50TH BIRTHDAY, THE EDITOR HAS ASKED ME TO PRETEND TO BE PANSY POTTER — ONE OF OUR OLD CHARACTERS.
SHE HAD A REALLY DAFT HAIRCUT . . .
MIAOW!
. . . AND I'M NOT TOO KEEN ON THE DRESS.
SHE WAS REALLY STRONG, THOUGH.
THAT'S BECAUSE HER DAD WAS A STRONGMAN.
MINE CERTAINLY ISN'T.
I'LL SORT THAT, THOUGH.
HE'S PRETTY STRONG LOOKING NOW.
WOW! PANSY USED TO SINK ENEMY SUBMARINES DURING THE WAR.
Ye Olde BEANO
MUST TRY IT.
SUBMARINE BASE
NO SPIES ALLOWED
WATCH OUT, SUB.
OOF!
CLUNK!
THAT DIDN'T WORK.
THROB
THEY MUST MAKE THEM TOUGHER THESE DAYS.
BANG!
CLUNK!
BANG!
WHO'S JUMPING ON OUR SUB?
STOP IT! WE CAN'T STAND THE RACKET.
AW, GET LOST!
YOU'RE TOO TOUGH FOR US — WE'LL LET YOUR STRONG LOOKING DAD PUNISH YOU.
YOU'RE FOR IT, MINX.
NO, I'M NOT!
BANG!
BANG!
FORGET WHAT I SAID EARLIER ABOUT THIS DAFT HAIRCUT — IT'S GREAT!
BNO 30.7.88

COMIC GREETINGS
HAPPY 50th BIRTHDAY, BEANO FROM ALL AT The BEEZER!
HAVE A "TOPPER" OF A 50th BIRTHDAY, BEANO!
NOTHING FISHY ABOUT THIS MESSAGE—HAPPY 50th BIRTHDAY, BEANO!
WE'RE DESPERATE TO WISH ALL AT The BEANO A HAPPY 50th BIRTHDAY! FROM ALL YOUR DANDY PALS!
BNO 30.7.88

Six months later and *The Beano* hold their seriously grand bash aboard the historic ship *Unicorn*, berthed at Dundee dock – The Beanoversary Ball. Staff, artists and writers past and present travelled from all over the British Isles to be there. 'Jonah' writer Walter Fearn was one of the guests but the good ship *Unicorn* managed to stay afloat. What a terrific night – a proper BEANO!

The *Beano Summer Special* for the summer of 1988 was the 25th in the series and included a spread marking that fact. It also included a funny feature on The Beano's 50-year history – '*The Beano* Rest Home' – Lord Snooty showed us the occupants, all old *Beano* characters from the past.

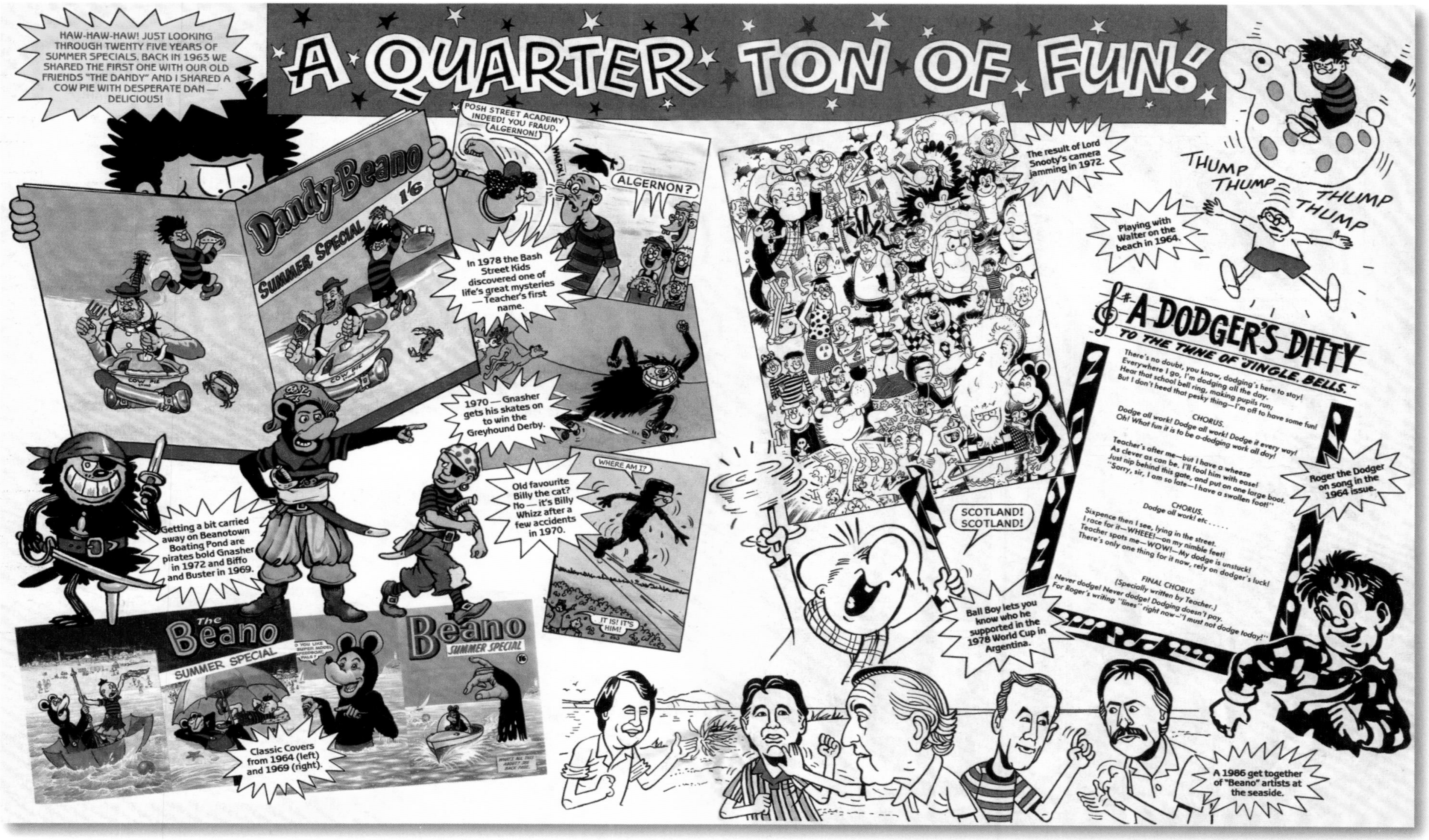
HAW-HAW-HAW! JUST LOOKING THROUGH TWENTY FIVE YEARS OF SUMMER SPECIALS. BACK IN 1963 WE SHARED THE FIRST ONE WITH OUR OLD FRIENDS "THE DANDY" AND I SHARED A COW PIE WITH DESPERATE DAN — DELICIOUS!
A QUARTER TON OF FUN!
Dandy-Beano
SUMMER SPECIAL
1/6
POSH STREET ACADEMY INDEED! YOU FRAUD, ALGERNON!
WHACK!
ALGERNON?
In 1978 the Bash Street Kids discovered one of life's great mysteries — Teacher's first name.
1970 — Gnasher gets his skates on to win the Greyhound Derby.
The result of Lord Snooty's camera jamming in 1972.
THUMP THUMP
THUMP THUMP
Playing with Walter on the beach in 1964.
A DODGER'S DITTY
TO THE TUNE OF "JINGLE BELLS."
There's no doubt, you know, dodging's here to stay!
Everywhere I go, I'm dodging all the day.
Hear that school bell ring, making pupils run;
But I don't heed that pesky thing—I'm off to have some fun!
CHORUS.
Dodge all work! Dodge all work! Dodge it every way!
Oh! What fun it is to be a-dodging work all day!
Teacher's after me—but I have a wheeze
As clever as can be. I'll fool him with ease!
Just nip behind this gate, and put on one large boot.
"Sorry, sir, I am so late—I have a swollen foot!"
CHORUS.
Dodge all work! etc . . . . .
Sixpence then I see, lying in the street.
I race for it—WHEEE!—on my nimble feet!
Teacher spots me—WOW!—My dodge is unstuck!
There's only one thing for it now, rely on dodger's luck!
FINAL CHORUS
(Specially written by Teacher.)
Never dodge! Never dodge! Dodging doesn't pay.
For Roger's writing "lines" right now—"I must not dodge today!"
Roger the Dodger on song in the 1964 issue.
Getting a bit carried away on Beanotown Boating Pond are pirates bold Gnasher in 1972 and Biffo and Buster in 1969.
Old favourite Billy the cat? No — it's Billy Whizz after a few accidents in 1970.
WHERE AM I?
IT IS! IT'S HIM!
SCOTLAND! SCOTLAND!
Ball Boy lets you know who he supported in the 1978 World Cup in Argentina.
The Beano
SUMMER SPECIAL
Beano
SUMMER SPECIAL
Classic Covers from 1964 (left) and 1969 (right).
A 1986 get together of "Beano" artists at the seaside.

AS IT'S THE "BEANO'S" FIFTIETH BIRTHDAY ON JULY 30TH, I THOUGHT I'D VISIT SOME OF MY OLD FRIENDS WHO'VE APPEARED WITH ME IN THE COMIC OVER THE YEARS. THEY ALL STAY AT . . .
Big Eggo — star of the first "Beano".
THE BEANO REST HOME
THE BEANO EDITOR BUILT THIS LOVELY PLACE, SPECIALLY FOR OLD "BEANO" STARS.
HOI! DON'T TELL ME DENNIS THE MENACE HAS TAKEN EARLY RETIREMENT.
PING! PING!
AH! IT'S GENERAL JUMBO AND HIS RADIO-CONTROLLED ARMY.
HEH-HEH! HI, SNOOTY!
WONDER WHO ELSE I'LL MEET?
Suddenly—
WOW! THE IRON FISH!
HERE, DUCKIES!
ROCK CAKES
OH-OH! HERE'S THAT DANGER TO SHIPPING, JONAH!
Then—
SMASH!
OOPS!
GULP! SORRY!
GLUB!
SINK!
GLUB!
HASN'T LOST HIS TOUCH, I SEE!
Turn to inside back cover.
Printed and Published in Great Britain by D. C. THOMSON & CO., LTD., 185 Fleet Street, London EC4A 2HS. © D. C. THOMSON & CO., LTD., 1988.
Continued from page 2.
COME AND JOIN US, SNOOTY!
Little Plum.
Punch and Jimmy.
Biffo.
RUSKS
Pansy Potter.
"Baby-Face"—
ERK! THE NIBBLERS!
GRAB THE GRUB!
WHISKERS HERE CAN'T CONTROL THESE PESTS.
BUT WE HAVE ANOTHER CAT WHO CAN — BILLY THE CAT!
GOT YOU!
ZOOM!
SOME OF MY OLD FRIENDS ARE MISSING.
Suddenly—
EH?
WHOOSH!
HERE THEY ARE — THOSE GREEDY THREE BEARS!
Then—
MUST BE QUITE A JOB KEEPING THIS LOT UNDER CONTROL.
Then—
BEHAVE!
Y-YES, SIR!
HAR-HAR! MORGYN THE MIGHTY CAN KEEP THEM IN CHECK!
31

It was 1988 before ***The Beano*** started to carry paid-for advertising, for until then the only ads carried were for D. C. Thomson's own products. Pages in ***The Dandy*** and ***The Beano*** were sold as a package and advertising revenue became increasingly important. This all helped keep ***The Beano*** a pocket-money buy, something Chairman Brian Thomson was adamant about. Even then, because of inflation, ***The Beano*** that had started the 1980s costing 7p ended it priced 24p.

SAVE BASH STREET SKO
BEANO

PART 7

The Best Comic Ever

1990–1999

CHOPPED CHARACTERS

The 1990s saw the axe fall on several *Beano* characters, as Editor Euan Kerr explained, 'Characters were generally dropped for one of two reasons – either the character was too old-fashioned and had little or no relevance to modern readers or the strip just wasn't performing well in the regular readers' polls we conducted through the comic.' He was by no means shy when it came to dropping characters whose best days were behind them. Three notable examples were such previously cherished stalwarts as 'Lord Snooty', the one remaining character from the very first *Beano* in July 1938, 'Pansy Potter, The Strongman's Daughter', who made her debut in December 1938, and 'Biffo the Bear', who originally featured in January 1948.

Lord Snooty
AND HIS PALS
HAVING A PET STAG LIKE ANGUS HAS MANY ADVANTAGES.
NO-ONE COMES NEAR ANGUS'S SHARP ANTLERS WHEN I PLAY POLO.
YEEK!
COCKTAIL SNACKS ARE SO PUNY AT PARTIES . . .
. . . BUT ANGUS LETS YOU HAVE A BIG FEED!
HE MAKES A BRILLIANT SNOW-PLOUGH IN WINTER . . .
. . . AND YOU CAN PLAY HOOPLA WITH HIM IN THE SUMMER.
BUT THE BEST PART OF HAVING A STAG AS A PET IS . . .
. . . WHEN YOU HAVE AN ITCH IN THE MIDDLE OF YOUR BACK . . . AAAH!

The last 'Lord Snooty' strip, drawn by Ken Harrison.

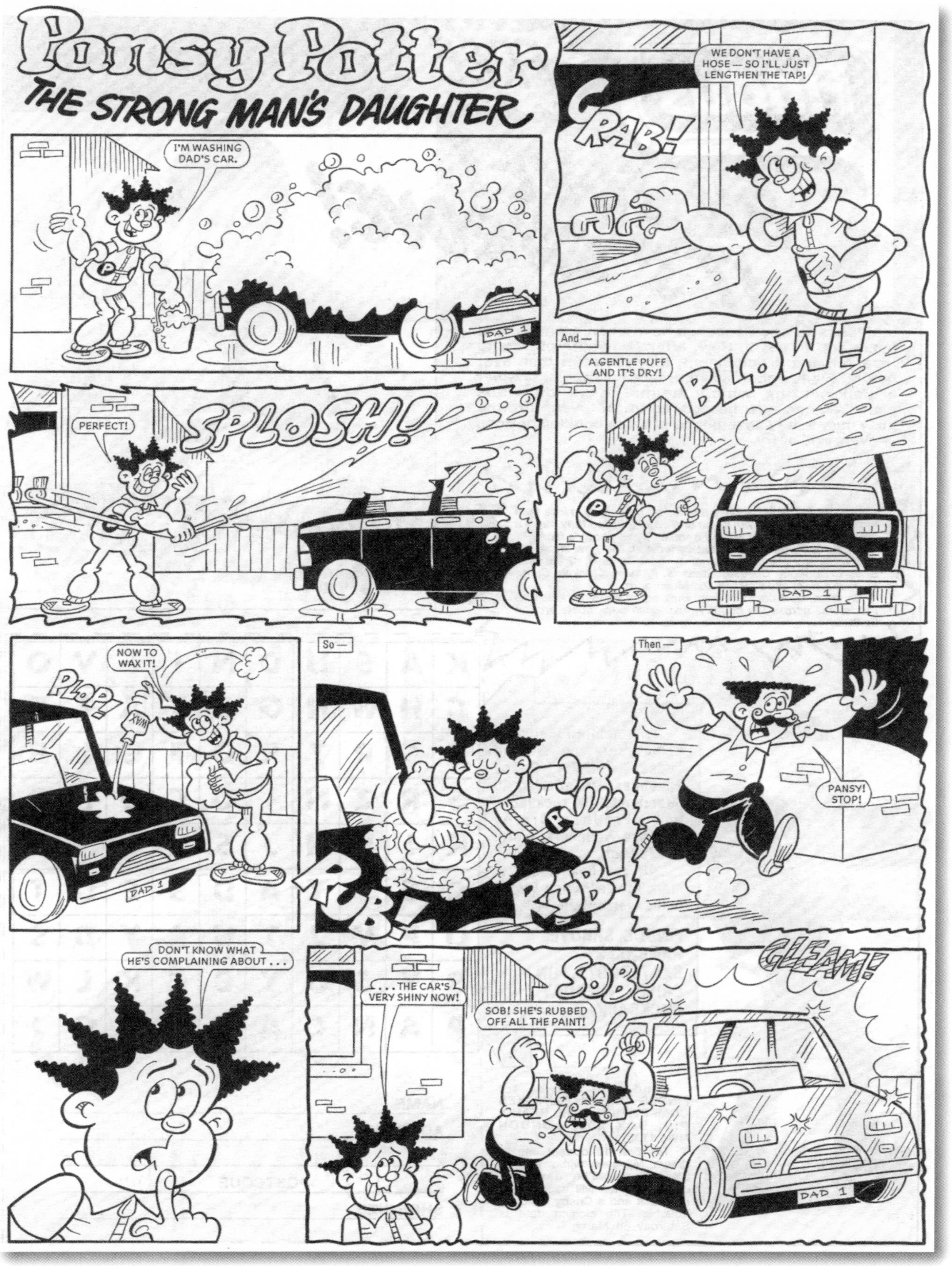
Pansy Potter
THE STRONG MAN'S DAUGHTER
I'M WASHING DAD'S CAR.
DAD 1
WE DON'T HAVE A HOSE — SO I'LL JUST LENGTHEN THE TAP!
GRAB!
PERFECT!
SPLOSH!
And—
A GENTLE PUFF AND IT'S DRY!
BLOW!
DAD 1
NOW TO WAX IT!
PLOP!
WAX
DAD 1
So—
RUB!
RUB!
Then—
PANSY! STOP!
DON'T KNOW WHAT HE'S COMPLAINING ABOUT . . .
. . . THE CAR'S VERY SHINY NOW!
SOB! SHE'S RUBBED OFF ALL THE PAINT!
SOB!
GLEAM!
DAD 1

The last 'Pansy Potter' strip (left), drawn by Barry Glennard.
A detail (below) from The Fatty Fudge World Championships, drawn by Jim Petrie.

Euan Kerr admitted that 'Lord Snooty' was his least favourite character to write for and commented that 'I never liked "Lord Snooty" at all and I suppose I was the cause of his demise in the end. He was completely outdated by the time I sat in the Editor's chair, though, and I could see absolutely no way of updating him. Although there were some great "Lord Snooty" strips in the 1940s, he was becoming increasingly difficult to write for in the modern era and the readers just couldn't relate to him anymore.'

The last 'Danny's Nanny' strip (right), drawn by David Mostyn. The last 'Biffo' strip, drawn by Sid Burgon (below).

Biffo
WUNDA GROW PLANT FOOD
LATER
BIFFO

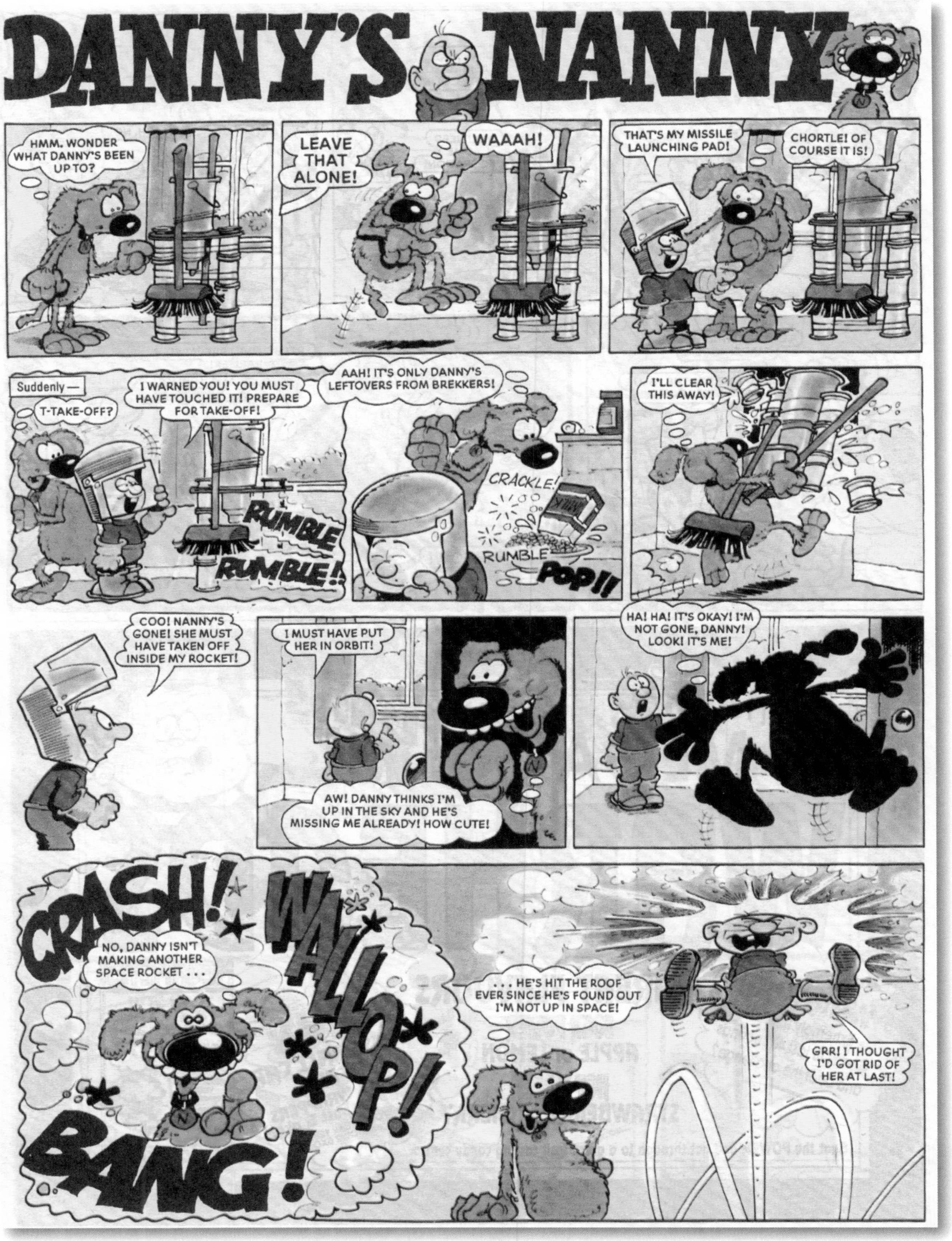
DANNY'S NANNY
HMM. WONDER WHAT DANNY'S BEEN UP TO?
LEAVE THAT ALONE!
WAAAH!
THAT'S MY MISSILE LAUNCHING PAD!
CHORTLE! OF COURSE IT IS!
Suddenly —
T-TAKE-OFF?
I WARNED YOU! YOU MUST HAVE TOUCHED IT! PREPARE FOR TAKE-OFF!
RUMBLE
RUMBLE!!
AAH! IT'S ONLY DANNY'S LEFTOVERS FROM BREKKERS!
CRACKLE!
RUMBLE
POP!!
I'LL CLEAR THIS AWAY!
COO! NANNY'S GONE! SHE MUST HAVE TAKEN OFF INSIDE MY ROCKET!
I MUST HAVE PUT HER IN ORBIT!
AW! DANNY THINKS I'M UP IN THE SKY AND HE'S MISSING ME ALREADY! HOW CUTE!
HA! HA! IT'S OKAY! I'M NOT GONE, DANNY! LOOK! IT'S ME!
CRASH!
WALLOP!
BANG!
NO, DANNY ISN'T MAKING ANOTHER SPACE ROCKET . . .
. . . HE'S HIT THE ROOF EVER SINCE HE'S FOUND OUT I'M NOT UP IN SPACE!
GRR! I THOUGHT I'D GOT RID OF HER AT LAST!

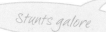

STUNTS GALORE

Prior to the 1990s, D.C. Thomson had never been too concerned with advertising its comics, let alone approaching the national press for promotional column inches. However, the increasing range of news media coupled with a dip in readership for *The Beano* meant that attitudes within the company started to change. Euan and his editorial team started to wonder if extravagant publicity stunts might gain the comic some coverage in the national press. Where did the idea originally come from, however? Euan explains, 'It all came about when there was a "Coronation Street" storyline on TV where Deirdre Barlow was possibly going to leave her husband Ken and go off with Mike Baldwin. And we saw in the papers that it was actually flashed up on the screen at a Manchester United game, "Deirdre's Staying With Ken!", and the whole crowd began to cheer! It struck us as amazing how fiction could suddenly become newsworthy, so we started coming up with ideas for various stunts and we knew that the more outrageous they were the better.' The first of these stunts was when Gnasher disappeared from the pages of *The Beano* in 1986 (see page 238). D.C. Thomson saw the positive effect these kinds of press stories could have and Euan Kerr was convinced that further publicity gimmicks could cause the same commotion. He was adamant, however, that further manipulations of the media must be done sparingly or they would no doubt lose their effect.

WHO'S
GNICKED
GNASHER?

COME HOME
GNASHER

I'M A
'BEANO'
GNASHER SPOTTER

DENNIS TURNS TRENDY

STEREO

With this in mind, the nation had to wait five years before Euan attempted his next major publicity stunt. The year was 1991 and the occasion was the 40th anniversary of 'Dennis the Menace' in ***The Beano***. Having bounced ideas around on how to mark such a momentous event, Euan and his team settled on the idea of turning Dennis into a trendy teenager. This involved replacing his knobbly knees, tackety boots and famous red and black striped jumper with designer sunglasses, a trendy tracksuit and top-of-the-range trainers. Plus Dennis would also ditch his catapult in favour of a personal stereo.

Euan Kerr was quoted in the press at the time explaining that ***The Beano***'s writers felt that their cover star badly needed some 'street cred' and that an Italian designer was brought in especially for the job. Then anticipating the public furore that he hoped would soon ensue, Euan commented, 'It may well go down badly – we'll just have to wait and see.'

And predictably, of course, the idea did go down badly. In much the same way as with Gnasher's disappearance, readers' letters pages across the land were filled with bemused ***Beano*** fans making their opinions on the proposed changes known. For instance, J Chamberlain of Camberley in Surrey wrote in to one national newspaper screaming:

I don't think the Italian designer who has revamped children's comic favourite 'Dennis the Menace' knows what he has done!

This character isn't supposed to be a designer-labelled, street-wise, Walkman-equipped Sloane Ranger.

He is an untidy, lovable rascal who gets into scrapes of his own making and thousands of children can identify with him.

While the front cover featured Dennis in his new tracksuit, the back page (below) brings him back to normal.

EVERY THURSDAY
THE BEANO
MARCH 23rd, 1991
DENNIS and GNASHER
GNASH! GNASH!
WAA! STOP! IT'S ME, GNASHER! STOP!
GNASH!
RIP!
GNASH! THOUGHT YOU WERE A POSTIE WHEN I SAW BLUE TROUSERS!
AT LEAST I HAVE ONE WHOLE LEG LEFT IN THESE NEW TROUSERS!
BUT—
HUH! KNEES TOO BIG FOR LONG TROUSERS!
RRRIP!
WELL THIS JACKET'S GREAT...
BLOW
BUS STOP
PING!
PING!
...FOR KEEPING PEASHOOTER AMMO!
HOLD IT, MENACE!
ULP! DAD!
HOI! STOP! WHAT ARE YOU DOING?
SNARL! NOW I KNOW WHY I NEVER WEAR A JACKET! GRR!
CHORTLE! A COATHANGER FIXED HIM!
THEN—
HAR-HAR! A NEW LOOKS OKAY— BUT A TRUE MENACE NEVER CHANGES!
OW!
SPLUT! SPLAT!
BLOW
ZOOM!
DON'T MISS NEXT WEEK'S "CRACKING" ISSUE—WHEN THE CIRCUS COMES TO BEANOTOWN!
CRACK!
Printed and Published in Great Britain by D. C. THOMSON & CO., LTD., 185 Fleet Street, London, EC4A 2HS.
© D. C. THOMSON & CO., LTD., 1991

Let's hope that Dennis will wisely tear a hole in his new tracksuit and go back to his more wild pursuits in that black and red striped jumper he has worn so successfully for the last 40 years!

When Dennis' new image was eventually introduced on March 23, 1991 (with Dennis exclaiming 'Yeah! Cool! How do you like my new look? Pretty rad, eh?' on the front cover), it only lasted until the end of that week's ***Beano*** – when on the last page Dennis suddenly remembered why he'd stuck to the same trusty, old outfit for so long. . . .

ED IN THE CLOUDS

Comics
BEST
COMIC
EVER

Euan Kerr became editor of ***The Beano*** in 1984, stepping down in 2006, only to return to comic editing with the launch of ***The BeanoMax*** in 2007. Here he shares some of his thoughts . . .

MY FAVOURITE CHARACTER TO WRITE FOR

'I'd probably say "The Bash Street Kids". They were certainly much easier to write for than "Dennis the Menace". The problem with Dennis was that despite his menacing persona, you still had to make him very likeable to the reader. One of the golden rules that Harry Cramond drilled into me was to always make sure you have the characters as people the readers would want to have as friends. So Dennis could never be a complete hooligan and I always found it quite difficult to strike that balance. I always enjoyed writing for "Baby-Face Finlayson" and "Calamity James" too – probably because I had a hand in their creation and therefore felt a connection to them. I can't stress enough, though, how important it is to write what the kids want to read and not be guided solely by what you think is funny. The comic has always been very reader-led.'

MY PROUDEST MOMENTS AS *BEANO* EDITOR

'One of the things I'm most proud of is our annuals. I spent a lot of time on these and while the sales of the weekly comic have dipped, the annuals have consistently sold well and have gone up, in fact. Although the comic was selling around the two million mark in 1950 and is selling much less today, on the positive side we're now selling loads more annuals than we did back then because of the huge nostalgia market that has developed. A lot of people who don't necessarily read the comic look forward to these and I think it's imperative to get the best strips of the year in there. I regularly kept back particularly excellent strips from being printed in the weekly, so we could include them in the

annual. So yes, I'm very proud of the annuals.

'Being named Best Comic Ever was a very pleasing moment too!' This happened in 1997. The result was decided in a telephone poll and the award was presented in London, at the end of National Comics week. The result angered many readers of *Eagle*. 'The people who read the *Eagle* are more serious-minded than our readers. *The Beano* is the comic of the people. The result seemed to back this up as *The Beano* claimed over 70 per cent of the votes cast.'

THE BEANO AND REAL LIFE

'I definitely felt a sense of responsibility in making sure the characters did nothing that was easily imitable. We generally tried to keep their antics so outrageous that the readers were not in any real danger of trying them at home. The evidence is that the kids understand a comic is a comic and that it isn't anything like real life. The relationship between Dennis and Walter was always one that worried me, though. We decided the best way to approach it was to make sure that even though he and Dennis didn't get along, Walter was completely happy about who he was and a confident, likeable character in his own right. Walter might be a wimp and a show-off – but he loves who he is!

I must admit, I used to love writing about Walter because he was such a funny character.'

THE BEANO IN THE AGE OF POLITICAL CORRECTNESS

'The comic has certainly changed in some ways over the years to come in line with political correctness. For example, every strip used to end with the rogue of the story being punished in some way – usually a smack across the head or a slipper across the bottom. This sort of corporal punishment obviously became outdated and eventually it was phased out by *The Beano* – and rightly so. However, the success of *The Beano* has always stemmed from the fact that it was anti-establishment and anti-authority. This was one of the ways in which it differed from *The Dandy*, which veered towards fantasy characters, while *The Beano* became mainly about naughty kids getting one over on grown-ups. So as much as some aspects of the comic have had to succumb to the politically correct world, I think it's important not to forget the comic's roots. Luckily for us, I think there's a real resistance to the overt political correctness creeping into British life and *The Beano* can hopefully continue to use this to its advantage.'

SHOWING THEIR TRUE COLOURS

THE BEANO
FREE A GLOW-IN-THE DARK STICKER
IN THE NEW ALL-COLOUR BEANO
No. 2674 OCTOBER 16th 1993
EVERY THURSDAY 35p
DENNIS the MENACE and GNASHER
HEH-HEH! HERE THEY COME!
GOT YOU!
SWOOOSH!
HEY, WE'RE ALL IN COLOUR!
YEP! AND THAT'S THE WAY YOU'RE GOING TO STAY IN THE NEW ALL-COLOUR BEANO!
BLOW
GNEEK!
FOLLOW THE ACTION OVER THE PAGE.

In a bid to find out ways to improve *The Beano* still further, D.C. Thomson hired a market research company to conduct a major survey of the comic's readers in 1993. There was one question in particular to which the answer was completely unanimous. The survey asked – 'Would you prefer *The Beano* to be full-colour, from front to back?' and the collective answer was a resounding 'Yes, please!'

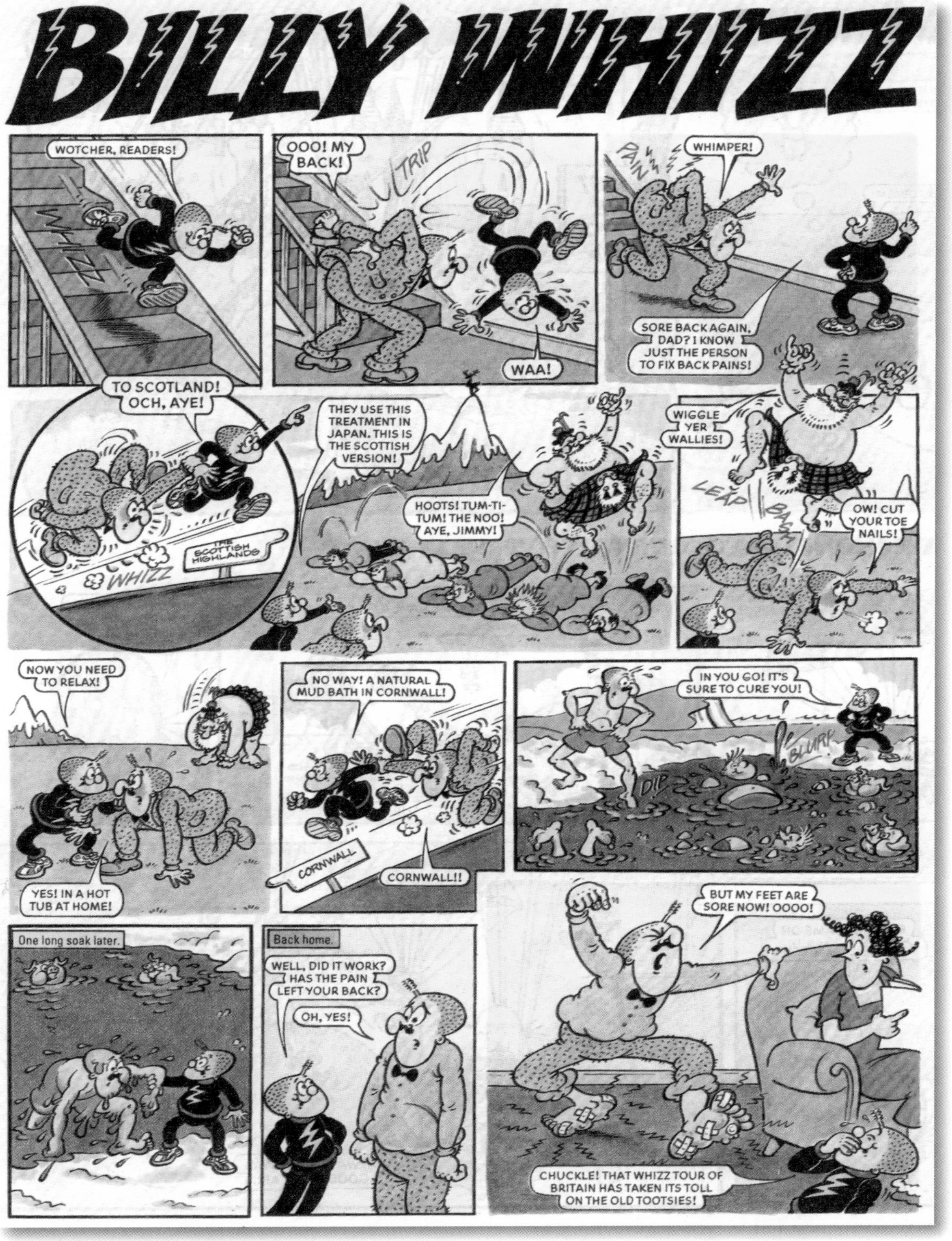
BILLY WHIZZ
WOTCHER, READERS!
WHIZZ
OOO! MY BACK!
TRIP
WAA!
WHIMPER!
SORE BACK AGAIN, DAD? I KNOW JUST THE PERSON TO FIX BACK PAINS!
TO SCOTLAND! OCH, AYE!
THE SCOTTISH HIGHLANDS
WHIZZ
THEY USE THIS TREATMENT IN JAPAN. THIS IS THE SCOTTISH VERSION!
HOOTS! TUM-TI-TUM! THE NOO! AYE, JIMMY!
WIGGLE YER WALLIES!
LEAP
OW! CUT YOUR TOE NAILS!
NOW YOU NEED TO RELAX!
YES! IN A HOT TUB AT HOME!
NO WAY! A NATURAL MUD BATH IN CORNWALL!
CORNWALL
CORNWALL!!
IN YOU GO! IT'S SURE TO CURE YOU!
BLURK
DIP
One long soak later.
Back home.
WELL, DID IT WORK? HAS THE PAIN LEFT YOUR BACK?
OH, YES!
BUT MY FEET ARE SORE NOW! OOOO!
CHUCKLE! THAT WHIZZ TOUR OF BRITAIN HAS TAKEN ITS TOLL ON THE OLD TOOTSIES!

AT OLD TRAFFORD FOOTBALL CLUB.
CHANGING THINGS' COLOURS CAN BE GREAT MENACING FUN!
NOW FOR SOME MENACING!
YAHOO! THE GAME'S ABOUT TO START!
SQUEEZE
GASP! MARK HUGHES AND RYAN GIGGS HAVE JOINED CITY!
EH? LOOK AT YOU!
EEK!
AT THE STRETFORD END.
FAINT
FAINT
ONLY JOKING, UNITED FANS. GREAT MENACING THOUGH!

In previous rounds of market research, the fact that *The Beano* still printed many of its strips in black and white had never really been flagged up as an issue.

D.C. Thomson set about making changes to its printing processes, and later that year, on October 16, 1993, the first full-colour issue of *The Beano* dropped through the letterboxes of its loyal subscribers. It has remained full-colour ever since. On the cover, the historic change was heralded by Dennis blasting his fellow *Beanotown*-ers into the colourful new era with his paint gun. . . . Dennis then went on to menace Manchester United footballers by changing their colours to that of their local rivals, Manchester City, while Billy Whizz rushed through his first colour adventure.

MERCHANDISING MANIA

the MENACE and
SCREAM!
Licensed by Copyright Promotions Ltd.
Made in Britain.
JAMES

It was in the late 1980s that D.C. Thomson first realised the huge potential of using ***The Beano***'s characters in a way that they had never been used before – in merchandising. By this time, it was common practice for most new movies and TV shows to be involved in massive merchandising campaigns and it was hoped that comics, and ***The Beano*** brand in particular, could have some success in this area as well.

The first ever official ***Beano*** product was a lamp, featuring none other than Dennis and Gnasher terrorising Walter and his cat on its shade. The lamp hit the shelves in early 1990 and proved to be an unmitigated success. Since those lamps first graced the bedside tables of many a ***Beano*** reader, there have been literally thousands of ***Beano***-related products thought-up, designed, manufactured and sold. In fact, every year D.C. Thomson is inundated with countless requests from companies who wish to acquire licenses to use the likes of

275g ℮
6 ADDED VITAMINS & IRON
DENNIS the MENACE
DENNIS the MENACE
Digital Watch
OFFER
Chocolate SCOFFERS
Chocolate flavour Dennis and Gnasher shaped rice and oat cereal
DENNIS the MENACE Chocolate Scoffers
NUTRITION INFORMATION

Cute... yeah, right!
FABRIC FLAVOURS

'Dennis the Menace', 'Minnie the Minx' and 'Roger the Dodger' on their products, but the majority are never approved.

One area of merchandising that excited adult collectors in the mid-1990s was when Robert Harrop Designs coaxed the characters of ***The Beano*** and ***The Dandy*** off the pages of the comics and brought them to life as quality china figurines. '***The Beano*** and ***The Dandy*** Collection' proved immediately popular.

Here is a selection of genuine ***Beano*** merchandise created through the years.

Minnie feet
Minnie feet

GLOVE PUPPET
HARMLESS TOY
THE Beano BOOK 1973

DENNIS the MENACE and GNASHER
THE BOARD GAME
OFFICIAL BEANO PRODUCT
BEING GOOD IS NOT AN OPTION!
2-6 PLAYERS. AGED 6+

THE BASH STREET KIDS GO PC

PLUG
SMIFFY
SIDNEY
TOOTS
Fatty
SPOTTY
CUTHBERT CRINGEWORTHY
WILFRID
DANNY
'ERBERT
WINSTON
ACADEMY

What a rotter! The way they were (left) and as they will be at the Academy — without buck-teeth, sticking out ears and spcts. From left to right Wilfrid, Plug, Smiffy, Spotty, Danny, Sidney, Toots, 'Erbert and Fatty

Beano unveils new kids on the Bash Street block

THE BEANO has enthralled children for 55 years, writes *Hugh Muir*. But it has never claimed to be at the cutting edge — until yesterday when DC Thomson announced changes to the Bash Street Kids in an attempt to make it more relevant to the 90's.

The publishers say this means the death of Bash Street School, to be replaced by the Bash Street Academy. And in a clear out, Teacher, Headmaster, Janitor and Winston the janitor's cat, are being pensioned off. Plug will lose his buck-teeth and sticking-out-ears, Fatty is being weaned off pork pies and on to muesli, pea-brained Smiffy will become intelligent and Spotty will become, well, less spotty.

The changes will take effect in the next three issues, but it remains to be seen to what extent computer playing children will notice. It will also be interesting to see how long the changes endure. After a wave of publicity, the last attempt at modernisation, changing Dennis The Menace's boots for training shoes and updating his clothes, was scrapped between the front and back page of one edition.

Mr Euan Kerr, editor of the Beano, said: "It could all go wrong and no doubt many adult readers will be upset. I've grown up with The Bash Street Kids too, and I like them as they are.

"But it is very difficult because it is a children's comic and you have got to think from the kids' point of view. The comic has always evolved and with The Bash Street Kids we just felt it was time to bring them into the Nineties.

"It is the only strip in the comic that hasn't changed since the Fifties and things like teachers wearing mortar boards are alien to modern children."

The Beano was launched in 1938 and quickly became an instrument of wartime propaganda. One of the early characters, Musso the Wop ("He's a bigga da flop") was modelled on Benito Mussolini. Other stories concluded with lines such as "Hitler is a rotter".

The comic was produced fortnightly throughout the war, because it was believed to be good for morale on the home front. After Dennis, the menace to the Beano these days is a circulation hampered by the advent of computer games and reluctance of children to spend their leisure time reading printed material.

The Beano sells around 250,000 copies. But sales have been in decline since the 1950's when they peaked at two million

In the quest for sales, the comic has not been afraid to plunder territory previously annexed by VIZ magazine, the adult comic of lavatorial humour.

The next major milestone for *The Beano* came in 1994 when 'The Bash Street Kids' celebrated their 40th anniversary. Hoping to emulate previous publicity stunts, this time Euan and his staff came up with the idea to completely update 'The Bash Street Kids', making it look like the comic was kowtowing to political correctness in the process. He drew up a press release that detailed just what the much-loved comic strip was going to look like henceforth.

BEANO

News of the proposed changes at Bash Street became a major news story (above). Here is a report from The Times.
Stanwix School in Carlisle (below) campaigns to save Bash Street School.

WITH A FREE BASH STREET KIDS BADGE!
THE BASH STREET KIDS
THE BEANO
No. 2692 FEBRUARY 19th 1994
EVERY THURSDAY 35p
DENNIS the MENACE AND GNASHER
SNIFF! SNIFF! THE BASH STREET KIDS HAVE CHANGED THEIR LOOK AND SCHOOL AFTER FORTY YEARS! SNIFF! THIS IS HOW THEY USED TO LOOK! I WONDER IF WE'LL EVER SEE THEM LIKE THIS AGAIN?
SNIFF! OINK!
SNACK
TURN THE PAGE FOR A SPECIAL FOUR PAGE 40th ANNIVERSARY ADVENTURE WITH THE NEW LOOK BASH STREET KIDS!

This included closing Bash Street School to be replaced by the newly built, glass-walled Bash Street Academy – sacking Teacher, Headmaster, Olive the dinner lady, Janitor and Winston, the janitor's cat, along the way. Instead, the naughty bunch's education would now be in the hands of a robot teacher. Moreover, all the kids were going to get a long-overdue make-over – Plug was going to lose his buckteeth and sticky-out ears by having cosmetic surgery, class idiot Smiffy was going to become intelligent, Spotty was going to say goodbye to his acne by way of some wonderful beauty regime, 'Erbert was going to ditch his glasses in favour of contact lenses, Fatty was going to be put on a crash diet in a bid to make him more aesthetically appealing and the collective group's behaviour was going to be toned down in all future editions of the strip.

As was expected, though, the kids (and many adults too!) disagreed with *The Beano* Editor's apparent sentiments. One girl at Stanwix Primary School in Cumbria was so upset that she set about organising a petition to have Euan's plans halted. Sarah Gudgeon, 11 years old at the time, spent her lunch hours collecting 407 signatures from her teachers and fellow pupils, before sending off her petition to *The Beano*'s offices.

The BASH STREET KIDS
SCHOOL
CONDEMNED
I, HECTOR THE INSPECTOR, HAVE CLOSED BASH STREET SCHOOL, SACKED THE STAFF AND REMODELLED THE KIDS FOR THE NEW BASH STREET ACADEMY WHERE THEY'LL BE TAUGHT BY THE FINEST ROBOT TEACHER TECHNOLOGY COULD MAKE!
RIGHT, CHILDREN — TIME FOR LESSONS!
BASH STREET ACADEMY
PYOING
SACK
WHIZZ
EH?
Soon —
COULD WE HAVE MORE HOMEWORK, PLEASE?
COMPUTER BAR
MY OLD MATES! WHAT'S HAPPENED TO THEM?
GET THEM BACK TO NORMAL, YOU FIEND!
TIME YOU WERE EXPELLED, LAD!
GRAB
WHIRR
SCOOP
Soon —
I MISS THE OLD SCHOOL, I WONDER IF THERE'S ANYTHING WE CAN DO!
DING DONG!
SCHOOL
So —
MY UNCLE'S LETTING US RECORD A SONG TO REMIND THE KIDS WHO THEY REALLY ARE.
RECORDING STUDIO
HMM!
AAIEEE — OOOOOO — OWW!
PHEW!
TWANG
BOOM-BA-BOOM
CLANG-A-CLANG

REMODELLING WORK HAS BEEN A HUGE UCCESS BUT I THINK UG'S MAGNIFICENT ASTIC SURGERY HAS EEN MY GREATEST ACHIEVEMENT!
AW, SHUCKS!
BLUSH
WHAT A PERFECT PROFILE, THE FINEST OF FEATURES. HE IS TRULY WONDERFUL!
OH, OH! PLUG'S OVERHEATING WITH EMBARRASSMENT!
OOH . . . ER! HIS PLASTIC SURGERY'S MELTING!
MELT
MELT
YAHOO!
PYOING
OH, NO! ONE OF MY WORKS OF ART — GONE!
BURST OUT
WASTE DISPOSAL
THROW
'BYE, PLUG!
ZOOOM
WAH!
SOME ADVANCED NUCLEAR PHYSICS NOW, I THINK!
CHANGE OVER
CLICK
HMM! SO THAT'S HOW THAT ROBOT TEACHER WORKS — A COMPACT DISC, EH!
NOW FOR THE NEXT PART OF MY PLAN!
X = RT IF B IS . . .
NOW FOR A QUICK CHANGE!
MATHS DISC OFF — OUR DISC ON!
LIFT
WAIT TILL MY PALS HEAR THIS. IT'LL REMIND THEM ALL WHO THEY ARE!

Delighted with the uproar this latest stunt had caused, upon receipt of the petition from Cumbria, Euan Kerr commented to the press, 'I've had 2,500 protest letters and no-one who wrote to us was in favour of the new look. It's absolutely amazing – we even got death threats! However, the Stanwix children summed up better than any others the depth of opposition – and Sarah showed Bash Street devotion beyond the call of duty. It was her petition that convinced me to change the kids back again.'

FOUND OUT?!

Not everyone was fooled by Euan's stunts. Robert Hanks of **The Independent** wrote just after news broke that 'The Bash Street Kids' were to be updated:

Fatty on a crash diet? 'Erbert put into contact lenses? It'll never happen! Announcements that The Beano is to be updated are publicity gimmicks – a clever strip tease. The whole thing was a clever piece of promotion designed to draw attention to the strip's 40th anniversary. The fact that the truth failed to come out should not, perhaps, be a surprise; as the media doesn't ever give you the good news.

NOW READ — OR SING ON!
THEY'RE THE KIDS FROM THE BASH STREET SCHOOL, NEVER BEHAVE — BREAK EVERY RULE!
EH?
COO!
DANNY'S SO COOL, SMIFFY'S A FOOL, PLUG'S FACE'S SCAR SIDNEY'S ALL HAIRY
Suddenly —
POP
RIP
SHRED
RUB
HAIR RESTORER
PING
PING
STOP THIS! STOP IT! OBEY YOUR TEACHER!
YAH! THIS IS WHAT WE THINK OF HIM!
SQUIRT
SWOOSH
SPLASH
EH?
SHATTER
TINKLE
SHATTER
BASH STREET ACADEMY
CHORTLE! NOW LET'S GET BACK TO GOOD OLD BASH STREET SCHOOL! YAHOO!
OOPS!
SNIFF! IT'S GOOD TO BE BACK!
SCHOO
OLIVE'S HOME MADE SWEETS

TOOT'S SURE IS NAUGHTY, PIMPLY WEE SPOTTY, FATTY'S WELL . . . FAT! 'ERB'S BLIND AS A BAT. WILFRID'S SO SHY, LET'S HEAR YOU ALL CRY . . .
. . . WE'RE THE KIDS FROM BASH STREET SCH NEVER BEHAVE — BREAK EVERY RULE! WE'RE THE KIDS FROM BASH STREET SCHOOL NEVER BEHAVE — BREAK EVERY RULE!
H-HEH! THAT'S US!
FIZZZ
BANG
'S GOT RID OF HIM! ET'S GET OUT OF THIS PLACE!
ACADEMY
ZOOM
HOLD ON A MINUTE!
MY GOODNESS! I LOOK EVEN MORE HANDSOME THAN EVER!
IT'LL NEVER STAND IT!
U SAVED THE SCHOOL, PLUG. S A MARK OF APPRECIATION, WE'VE PUT TWO STATUES UP OF YOU!
COO — SHUCKS!
THEY SHOULD MAKE ABSOLUTELY CERTAIN SCHOOL INSPECTORS NEVER COME NEAR BASH STREET SCHOOL AGAIN!
WAH!
EEK!
I'VE MADE A SPECIAL CELEBRATION CAKE!
NOT NICE
FISHY
PONG
GREAT TO BE BACK . . . OR IS IT?

In any case, it would have meant admitting being fooled twice: exactly the same thing happened three years ago, when it was announced that 'Dennis the Menace' would be swapping the familiar stripy jersey and shorts for tracksuit, trainers and Walkman, to appeal to modern youth. In this case, Dennis turned up on the front cover in the promised new get-up, only to rip it all off on the back page!

RUDE READERS

Throughout the 1990s, readers of *The Beano* corresponded more than ever with the comic, hundreds of letters arriving at *The Beano* office every single week. There were always a few that would send the staff into fits of giggles. In fact, with *The Beano* mailbag constantly bulging with hilarious bits and pieces addressed to Dennis, Roger, Minnie, Joe King and the gang, it was not long before two whole pages in the comic were eventually given over to readers' letters, photos, jokes and drawings! Here are some of the most memorable entries, selected by Euan Kerr.

LLANDENNIS
Funny Places
Is this where Welsh Menaces live? Thanks to
Sam Hogg BNO111156
from Cardiff for spotting this funny place.
SILVER MEMBER

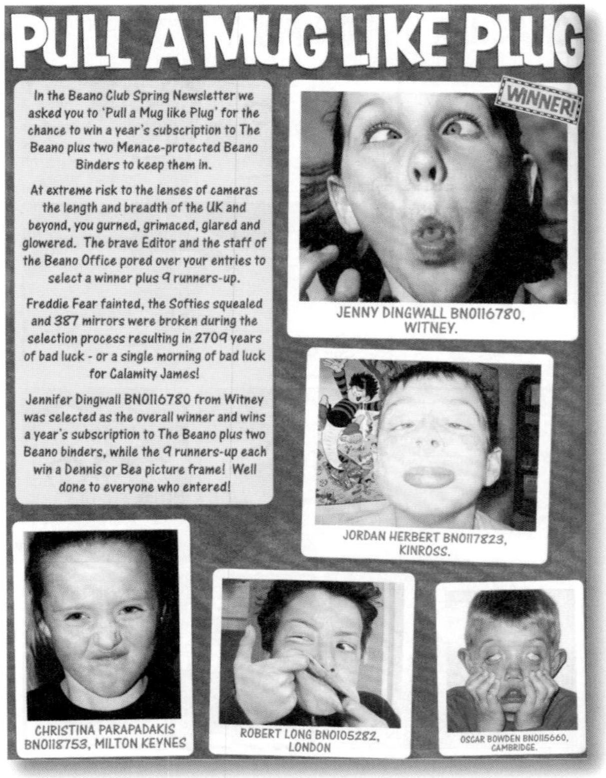
PULL A MUG LIKE PLUG

In the Beano Club Spring Newsletter we asked you to 'Pull a Mug like Plug' for the chance to win a year's subscription to The Beano plus two Menace-protected Beano Binders to keep them in.

At extreme risk to the lenses of cameras the length and breadth of the UK and beyond, you gurned, grimaced, glared and glowered. The brave Editor and the staff of the Beano Office pored over your entries to select a winner plus 9 runners-up.

Freddie Fear fainted, the Softies squealed and 387 mirrors were broken during the selection process resulting in 2709 years of bad luck - or a single morning of bad luck for Calamity James!

Jennifer Dingwall BNO116780 from Witney was selected as the overall winner and wins a year's subscription to The Beano plus two Beano binders, while the 9 runners-up each win a Dennis or Bea picture frame! Well done to everyone who entered!

WINNER!

JENNY DINGWALL BNO116780, WITNEY.

JORDAN HERBERT BNO117823, KINROSS.

CHRISTINA PARAPADAKIS BNO118753, MILTON KEYNES

ROBERT LONG BNO105282, LONDON

OSCAR BOWDEN BNO115660, CAMBRIDGE.

BRONZE MEMBER

Hello Beano Club
This is a picture of all my Beanos on the stairs! Dad was a bit unsure because he thought it was too slippery!
Sebastian Johns@Aylesbury
BNO114674

SILVER MEMBER

Dear Beano Club
Your comic is so fab even my chicken reads it…
Arran Pedder@Charmouth

OOOHH! Yeah!
SILVER MEMBER

Joshua Facer BNO108531 from Coventry casts Dennis and Gnasher as 'The Menace Brothers' in this drawing. You'll not be blue with your Comic Maker Kit, Joshua!

Dear Dennis
My mum said I have not to buy any more Beano's so could You Please send me a Beano. The reason She is not letting me buy the beano is because she is saving up for the polltax and I am also not alowd to buy Dandy and beano stikers because of the same reason.
P.S
I hope Mrs. Thatcher changes her mind about the polltax as I enjoy reading the beano.

Dear Wilfred,
In this world you are not the only person with no neck. The English cricketer Gladstone Small is also neck-less. ~~Do you kn~~ Is he related or a friend of yours, or do you know anyone else with no neck.

DENNIS I have good news and bad news. The good news is I once had a dog called Scamp he would run off with my dads slippers and did not give them back. The bad news is he ran under a car and got squashed.

21-4-87
Dear Smudge,
The other day my dad ordered 1½ tons of manure, and I had to move it all and I slipped over and my head got covered with it. After we had finished my mum made me have two baths and it was dreadful.

Dear Dennis,
I took my nanna's greedy dog for awalk. It is so greedy it eats anything that doesn't move quickly enough. In the fields we came upon some big, green, smelly mushy cowpats, covered whith flies and she gobbled them all up. I bet even Gnasher isnt as gross as this.

Dear Dennis
My Dad was born on July 30th 1938, the same time the first Beano came out. Why is it that Lord snooty is still at school and my Dad left years ago?

Hi Beano Club
This Beano looks really tasty! Eye-eye!
Isaac Parsons@Salisbury
BNO108481

WISH LIST
Your Wish Is Granted
THE BEANO
SILVER MEMBER

Dear Roger,
Please could you send a dodge so that I won't have to change my brothers nappy when it's at its smelliest.

THE BEANO AT 60

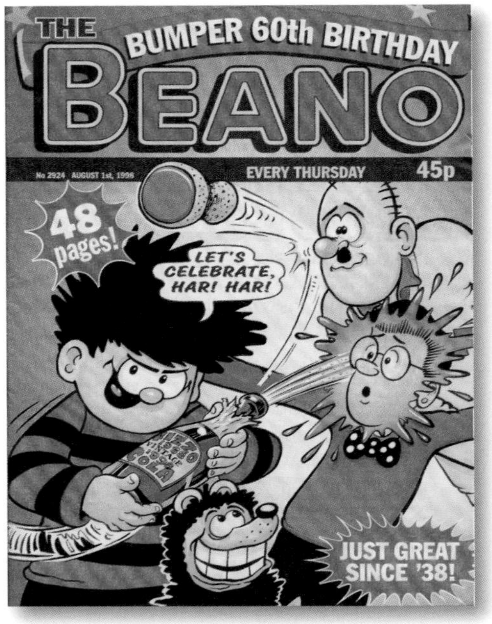
THE BEANO
BUMPER 60th BIRTHDAY
EVERY THURSDAY
45p
48 pages!
LET'S CELEBRATE, HAR! HAR!
JUST GREAT SINCE '38!

The Beano passed another milestone on August 1, 1998 when it celebrated its 60th anniversary. A cause for huge celebration, this momentous landmark was marked with a 'Double-Sized, Double-The-Fun, 48-Page Bumper 60th Birthday Beano' – the cover of which proudly announced, 'JUST GREAT SINCE '38!' This issue was packed with special birthday editions of all the usual strips.

60th BEANO PARTY
60th BEANO PARTY

BEANO TOWER
TIME FOR A SPOT OF POSTMAN'S KNOCK.
KNOCK!
KNOCK!
WAHEY! LOOK WHO'S HERE.
YANK!
ZOOM!
HI, MR EDITOR, SIR.
YOU DIDN'T THINK I'D DODGE THE BEANO'S SIXTIETH BIRTHDAY PARTY, DID YOU?
THUD!
BOOM!
THUD-BOOM!

Be Another Beano reader –
HAPPY 60TH ANNIVERSARY
ROGER THE DODGER

GNASHER AND GNIPPER
HOI! WAKEN UP OR YOU'LL MISS ME!
GNEH?
The postie!
GNICE OF HIM TO TELL US!
So —
WAA!
GNASH!
GNIP!
ZONK!
GOT 'IM!
THUD!
OOF!
But —
HELLO!
MUM!
GNEH?
HOI! CHASE ME SOME MORE!
GNO! WE'VE SEEN SOMETHING BETTER!
A HUGE CAT! GNASH!
GNIP!
ZOOM!
Then —
GNASH!
But —
RRRRIP!
GNEEK!
HELLO, EVERYONE!
DAD?
COO . . . EE!
HUMPH! THE LENGTHS SOME PEOPLE WILL GO TO APPEAR IN THIS SPECIAL BIRTHDAY BEANO!

LES PRETEND
THE LITTLE KID WITH THE BIG IMAGINATION!
One very important morning —
CONGRATULATIONS TO THE BEANO. IT'S SIXTY YEARS OLD TODAY.
WHAT A COINCIDENCE. SO AM I!
WITH NOT A TOOTH LEFT IN MY OLD HEAD.
BOOT POLISH
SIGH! I'M AS WRINKLED AS A DRIED-UP PRUNE.
LES! WHAT HAVE YOU DONE TO THAT MIRROR?
SORRY, GIRLIE, BUT I'M DEAF AS A DOORPOST.
Sixty minutes later —
TIME I WAS OFF FOR MY DAILY HOBBLE.
FUME! WITH MY GOLF PUTTER.
YOUNG MAN! GET UP AND GIVE ME A SEAT. I FOUGHT IN TWO WORLD CUPS FOR THE LIKES OF YOU.
Y'WOT?
ALL I'LL GIVE YER IS A KICK IN THE SEAT.
OOYAH! YOUNGSTERS NOWADAYS HAVE NO RESPECT.
WOOPS!
THE WORST THING ABOUT BEING SIXTY IS LOSING YOUR HAIR.
SIGH! I'LL CHEER MYSELF UP BY GOING TO A FANCY NIGHTCLUB.
REMOVAL SERVICE
BOOGIE NITES DISCO
WAHEY! THEY SAID I'M TOO YOUNG TO GET IN. BEING SIXTY'S OKAY — I'M JUST A BOY.
PENSIONERS CLUB
I BLAME THE PARENTS.
DAFT LITTLE WHAPPERSNIPPER.
BEANO'S 60 OK! Just great...since '38!

JOIN THE CLUB

THE 2 CLUB BADGES
METAL BADGE IN BRIGHT COLOURS
DENNIS the MENACE FAN CLUB
HAIRY BADGE WITH MOVING EYES
Only U.K. and Eire readers can apply.
No stamps accepted as payment.
To join the "Dennis the Menace Fan Club" (including "Gnasher's Fang Club") fill in the coupon opposite and send it with a 55p P.O. or Cheque to DENNIS THE MENACE FAN CLUB, P.O. Box 66, DUNDEE, DD1 9LN.

In 1998 the decision was taken to scrap the long-running Dennis the Menace Fan Club (incorporating 'Gnasher's Fang Club!'), which had been running since 1976 and by the time of its disbandment boasted well over a million members (see above). However, come 1998 the Dennis the Menace Fan Club's legions of members were forced to retire their hairy Gnasher membership badges (with moving eyes), as *The Beano* looked to the future. The launch of the new *Beano* Club coincided with a revamp of the comic (including a change to its long-standing logo). In the first four months, 28,000 applications for membership were received. The Club now receives around 8,000 applications a year from around the world.

THE BEANO CLUB

© D.C. Thomson & Co. Ltd, 1998.

THE BEANO CLUB No.1

● NEWSLETTER ● NEWSLETTER ● NEWSLETTER ●

Hi There, all you Beano Clubbers.

Welcome to the first-ever Beano Club Newsletter! There's bags of stuff to do and lots to giggle at. A word of warning, though, Menace-mates.

The Editor tells me that this club is s-o-o-o cool that even Softies are trying to join! Yes, Walter, Bertie and Spotty all sent in application forms. Their Fan Club Welcome Packs were sent out to them but don't worry — those wimps couldn't even rip through the wrapping!!!

Here's some exclusive news for fans of my dear little sister, Bea — the December 5th issue of The Beano is an extra-special edition, where me and Gnasher take the superbabe to meet all the other Beano characters in the comic. You'll love it!

There's lot more about Bea on the Beano Web Site. Look for it at www.beano.co.uk — check it out! Dennis

Just look at these famous club members

From: The Office of HRH The Prince of Wales

2nd October, 1998

Prince William and Prince Harry have asked me to thank you for making them Honorary Members of The Beano Club and for sending them the Beano t-shirts.

The two Princes were pleased to hear about the Club and have asked me to pass on their best wishes for its success as The Beano celebrates its 60th Birthday.

Miss Henrietta Rolston

Virgin Radio boss and TFI Friday presenter Chris Evans is Member No. 1215.

"Thank you very much for making me an Honorary Member of the brand new Beano Club. One of only thirty people — Wow!"

● Chris is honoured.

● Prince William, Member No. 16 and Prince Harry, Member No. 12.

Johnny Vaughan of Channel 4's "The Big Breakfast" is Member No. 4.

"It is very exciting to be an honorary member of the all-new Beano Club, although I think I'm a member of the all-old Dennis The Menace Fan Club — in fact, I was a weekly Beano reader until the age of 17."

● Heeeeere's No. 4

TV and radio presenter Chris Tarrant is Member No. 958.

"Just a quick note while a particularly boring record is going round to say thank you very much for the membership to The Beano Club. I am indeed honoured — in fact this is definitely the highpoint of my life so far!

Thanks again . . . and Happy 60th Birthday!"

HUNT THE WHIZZ!

There are loads of Billy Whizzes just like this one hidden all over your newsletter. How many can you find? Answer on page 4.

THE BEANO
©D.C.Thomson&Co.,Ltd.,2006

Among those granted the status of lifelong membership at the very beginning were radio and TV presenters Johnny Vaughan, Chris Evans and Chris Tarrant. A royal seal of approval for the new club was also given by Princes William and Harry who passed on their best wishes, after receiving their complimentary membership packs.

Further down the line, *The Beano* Club's members were asked to nominate the person they would most like to see become an honorary member and the vote concluded that pop singer, Robbie Williams, should be inducted. His membership number was BNO2000, in reference to his hit song, Millennium. Post-millennium, other lifelong inductees have included Kaiser Chiefs, Frank Skinner, Jonathan Ross, McFly, Chris Moyles, Mike Read, The Proclaimers, Andy Nicol and The Chuckle Brothers.

BEANO
CLUB

Anyone who joins *The Beano* Club is given the status of 'bronze' member. They are issued with a membership pack – including a T-shirt, bag, membership card, blow-up chair, wallet, key ring, poster and an assortment of random goodies – while newsletters are also sent out on a regular basis. Depending upon the time spent as a member, the ranking system then allows members to progress to being 'silver' then 'gold' members. After that, extreme loyalty to the club is rewarded by being upgraded to an 'Ultim8' member – a new level that was created in 2007 to reward the club's most avid fans!

DINMAKERS UNVEIL A NEW BAND MEMBER!
THE BEANO
80p

BEA ARRIVES IN BEANOTOWN

THE
FREE
Chewits
BEANO
No. 2925 AUGUST 8th 1998
EVERY THURSDAY 45p
DENNIS and GNASHER
READ ON FOR A BIG SURPRISE!

. . . MUM'S GOING TO HAVE A BABY!

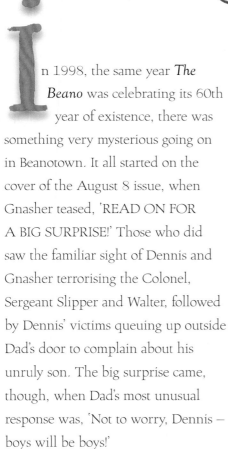

In 1998, the same year *The Beano* was celebrating its 60th year of existence, there was something very mysterious going on in Beanotown. It all started on the cover of the August 8 issue, when Gnasher teased, 'READ ON FOR A BIG SURPRISE!' Those who did saw the familiar sight of Dennis and Gnasher terrorising the Colonel, Sergeant Slipper and Walter, followed by Dennis' victims queuing up outside Dad's door to complain about his unruly son. The big surprise came, though, when Dad's most unusual response was, 'Not to worry, Dennis – boys will be boys!'

THE
MENACE MYSTERY SOLVED-INSIDE!
BEANO
No. 2930 SEPTEMBER 12th 1998
EVERY THURSDAY 45p
DENNIS the MENACE and GNASHER
HEH-HEH! WE'VE ALWAYS WANTED TO DO THIS!
HAW-HAW!
DOH!
DENNIS FAINTED LAST WEEK WHEN MUM AND DAD LET HIM IN ON THEIR BIG SECRET!

Meet Dennis's new sister in a BIGGER, BRIGHTER
THE BEANO
No. 2931 September 19th, 1998
Every Thursday 50p
IT'S A GIRL!
WITH A FREE BEANO BANGER
WIN a Legoland Holiday
Join the fantastic new Beano Club INSIDE

DENNIS the MENACE and GNASHER
CONTINUED...
A BABY, GNASHER — THINK WHAT THIS MEANS...
HUMPH!
...IT'LL BE LIKE A MONSOON IN THE HALL WITH ALL OF THE WET NAPPIES!
WE'LL HAVE TO WEAR GAS-MASKS WITH THE CLOUDS OF PERFUMED TALC AT BATH TIME!
WAAAAA
WE WON'T BE ABLE TO HEAR THE TELLY FOR ALL THE HOWLING!
SIGH!
HAW-HAW!
GASP! DOLLIES AND SOFT TOYS WILL TURN UP EVERYWHERE!
BEING A GIRL, IT'LL BE WORSE — THINK OF THE TIME GIRLS SPEND IN THE BATHROOM!
BATHROOM
HURRY UP, SIS! YOU'VE BEEN IN THERE FOR THREE HOURS!
I DON'T KNOW WHY YOU'RE LAUGHING, GNASHER...
GNEE-HEE!
...THINK OF ALL OF THE 'DRESSING-UP' GAMES LITTLE GIRLS LIKE TO PLAY!
GNEEK!
THEN —
I SIMPLY MUST TAKE A FAMILY PHOTO WITH THE NEW ARRIVAL.
MATERNITY
WALTER — PRINCE OF SOFTIES.
SO —
LOVELY, GORGEOUS! NICE AND CLOSE... SMILE, DENNIS AND GNASHER!
FLASH!
TURN THE PAGE TO SEE DENNIS'S SISTER FOR THE FIRST TIME!

THAT'S MY SISTER, THAT IS!

Eventually, on the cover of the September 12 issue, the words every anxious *Beano* reader wanted to read were scrawled above the masthead 'MENACE MYSTERY SOLVED – INSIDE!' It turned out to be that Mum was pregnant and that Dennis was going to have a baby brother or sister – the first human addition to the Menace family since 1951. That particular strip, which ended with Mum going into labour and being rushed to hospital, sparked another journey into the mainstream media for *The Beano*'s characters. Says Euan Kerr, 'We once again made national news and I think that was down to the fact it was the first pregnancy ever in a children's comic. I suppose it did seem like a strange subject for *The Beano* to cover.'

It was being reported up and down the country that Dennis was not going to be an only child any longer, and one particularly memorable news story concerned a bookmaker, who was taking bets on what the name of *Beanotown*'s new baby would be! When the following Thursday arrived and the September 19 issue hit the shelves, there was a sharp increase in sales as people clamoured to meet Dennis' baby sister, who was eventually named Bea. Euan Kerr said, 'Of all the publicity stunts we attempted, Bea was definitely the best. It was just a great story and really captured everyone's interest.'

PART 8

Into a New Century

2000-2008

THE MILLENNIUM

Forget the expensive flop that was the Millennium Dome, even if it did not all go as planned. This inspired strip was drawn by Dave Sutherland. Dennis had a far better idea for the menacing new millennium.

The first menacing of the new Millennium!
WELCOME TO THE MENACE DOME!
ENTRANCE 50p
No Refunds
THIS WAY TO THE FIRST ZONE — THE LIGHT SHOW!
Inside —
COO!
VERY NICE!

THE BEANO
2000
web site address www..beano.co.uk
No. 2998 January 1st, 2000. Every Thursday 52p
THE BEANO
A NEW MILLENNIUM DAWNS

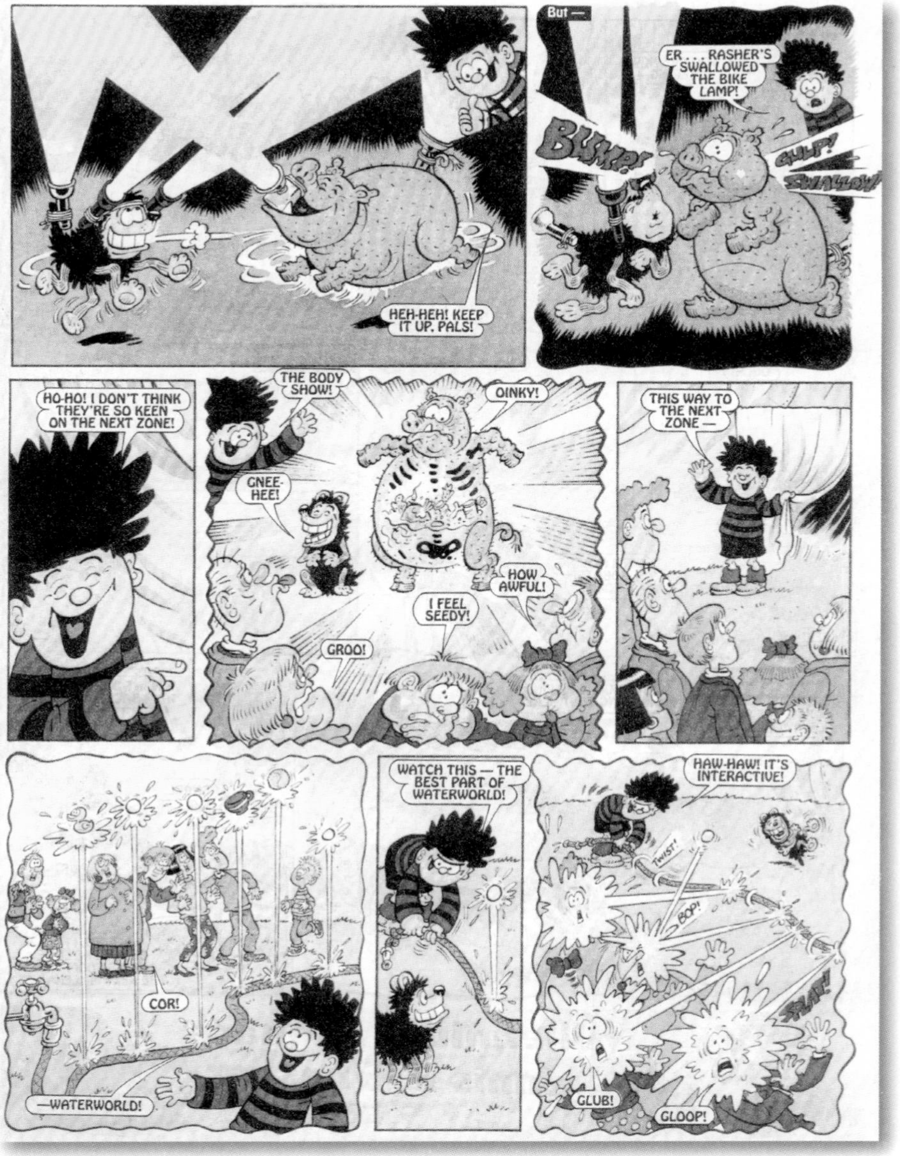
HEH-HEH! KEEP IT UP, PALS!
But —
ER . . . RASHER'S SWALLOWED THE BIKE LAMP!
GULP!
SWALLOW!
HO-HO! I DON'T THINK THEY'RE SO KEEN ON THE NEXT ZONE!
THE BODY SHOW!
OINKY!
GNEE-HEE!
HOW AWFUL!
I FEEL SEEDY!
GROO!
THIS WAY TO THE NEXT ZONE —
COR!
—WATERWORLD!
WATCH THIS — THE BEST PART OF WATERWORLD!
HAW-HAW! IT'S INTERACTIVE!
GLUB!
GLOOP!

Next —
YOU ARE NOW ENTERING —
— THE FUTURE ZONE!
OUCH!
OW!
BOOT!
TUG!
WITH MOVING ROBOTS! HO-HO!
EEK!
Wow! Two more Domes!
No — It's Dad and the Colonel's bald heads!
LOOK AT THE STATE OF MY GARDEN!
GRR! THOUGHT I'D FIND MY MISSING TENT HERE!
TRAMPLE!
WE WANT OUR CASH BACK!
SNARL!
'ULP!
WAIT TILL I FIND DENNIS! HE'LL BE IN HIS ROOM TILL THE NEXT MILLENNIUM!

BEANO 3000

Two weeks into the new millennium another *Beano* landmark was reached. The 3000th issue was given the superb cover it deserved, while the issue linked celebrities with the comic's own renowned characters. *Beano* readers voted in their thousands through the *Beano* website for the celebrities who most resembled the characters. Clues were given on the inside front page on a 'Guess the Guests' page.

No.3000 JANUARY 15, 2000. Every Thursday. 52p
THE BEANO

BEANO 3000
GUESS the GUESTS
Through the BEANO WEB SITE www.beano.co.uk we asked you to vote for the personalities who you thought were most like BEANO stars. You voted in your thousands and Dennis would like to say that he is sending Gnasher round to deal with the person who suggested that he is most like Julian Clary.
Look out for the guest stars chosen popping up throughout this celebration issue of The BEANO.
The pictures below might give you a clue who to look out for...
CHOCOLATE TEAPOTS
Pst!
Look out for a few other personalitities. Guess who me's pretending to be.
THANKS TO EVERYONE WHO VOTED. HERE'S TO THE NEXT 3000!

BILLY WHIZZ
SPORTS MEETING
I'LL ENTER FOR EVERY EVENT — AS USUAL!
So —
PHEEP!
FIRST RACE!
I CAN'T LAUGH — OR I'LL DROP MY EGG! NNN-HEE!
SPLAT!
WHOOSH!
ZOOM
YEUCH!
HOI!
Y—ES!
Next race —
BANG!
JUMP
WHIZZ
OOPS!
WAA!
HAR-HAR!
THUD
THUD
THUD
HUH!
THE WINNER!
THUD
THUMP!
BILLY WON'T BE ABLE TO TAKE PART IN THE NEXT RACE!
SET!
BILLY DOESN'T HAVE A PARTNER!
SNIGGER!
ZOOM
HOLD ON!
Seconds later —
SNAP!
SNAP!
WOW!
OH, NO!
WHOOSH!
SUPER WHIZZ
YOU LOT SHOULDN'T HAVE BEEN SO SURE — MY MATE, LINFORD CHRISTIE'S FAST ENOUGH TO BE MY PARTNER! HO-HO!

BEANO

PLUG
PSST! PLUG. HAVE ALL THE GIRLS GONE?
A TALKING BIN — VERY ODD!
CLICK! CLICK!
OO! IT'S RONAN KEATING FROM BOYZONE.
BEING A POP STAR HAS ITS PROBLEMS.
MY EARS GET SORE WITH MY FANS' SCREAMS.
SCREAM!
OH-OH! BETTER HIDE.
LOVE ME FOR A REASON . . .
SCREAM! HOWL!
MY POOR EARS! I SEE WHAT RONAN MEANS.
GRAB
SOMETIMES THEY TRY TO TAKE MY CLOTHES AS SOUVENIRS.
ME TOO!
GIMME THIS . . .
TUG!
. . . SO I CAN COVER YOUR FACE.
PYOING
HOI!
DONK!
CAN'T SEE! OOF!
OOO . . . MY HEAD!
TUG!
THANKS, PLUG — AFTER SEEING WHAT YOU HAVE TO GO THROUGH, I REALISE HOW LUCKY I AM.
HAPPY TO HELP A FELLOW HEART-THROB!
ACHE
SHAKE

For those unable to guess, the celebrities chosen were: Chris Evans with 'Dennis the Menace'; Spice Girl Geri Halliwell in 'Minnie the Minx'; Ken Dodd appears in 'Gnasher and Gnipper'; Ronan Keating in 'Plug'; Michael Owen and Alan Shearer in 'Ball Boy'; Mr Bean in 'Calamity James'; Linford Christie is likened to 'Billy Whizz'; Brooklyn Beckham appears with Dennis' infant sister, Bea and Del Boy Trotter stars in 'Roger the Dodger'.

BEANOLAND

In 2000, the mayhem and mischief of 'Dennis the Menace' and his friends was brought to life in the *Beanoland* theme park. Featuring all the best-loved characters from *The Beano*, the rides and general design theme of *Beanoland* were created by a design team following D. C. Thomson artwork reference guides. Once the final concepts had been through an approvals process, D.C. Thomson gave the go-ahead for the opening of the *Beanoland* theme park at Chessington World of Adventures in Surrey. Despite *The Beano*'s base being in Dundee, the higher population and greater number of potential customers meant that the multi-million pound attraction opened in the south of England. Euan Kerr was present at the launch to ensure everything ran smoothly but may have regretted his trip after receiving a custard pie in the face from Dennis on arrival! Featured rides and activities include Billy's Whizzer (a flying chair ride), Roger the Dodger's Dodgems, The Bash Street Bus and Dennis' Madhouse, which is a no-go area for softies! Chessington World of Adventures has grown in recent years to become one of Britain's top theme parks attracting millions of visitors each year and *Beanoland* continues to be a very popular attraction.

ROGER
the
DODGERS
DODGEMS

BEANOLAND

ONLY

DODGE 1

NON-STOPPING

BEANOTOWN.COM

MARKET ST.
CINEMA
WIZZY'S WIGS
BEANO
NEWS
Les can take you to the Costume Shop

BEANOTOWN
BEANOTOWN
BEANO HISTORY
BEANO CLUB
SUBSCRIBE/SHOP
BEANOTOWN HELP
CONTACT US

Above: An early pre-Beanotown game from 1999
Below: The Homepage in 2002

Replacing the *Beano* website, *Beanotown.com* was launched in July 2000. The launch was cleverly unveiled to the readers when they opened the comic to find that all the characters except Dennis the Menace and Gnasher had gone. Dennis started to search for his missing pals only to discover them sitting in an internet café logged onto the new website, described by Euan Kerr as 'bright and cheery, slightly chaotic and very *Beano*'.

The original homepage, within the town square, led the reader through to high street shops, a museum and the Bash Street School. To become a resident of Beanotown, the user had to pay an annual £5 fee. They could then move into their own virtual house and decorate and furnish it how they wished, so giving children the opportunity of participating and not just watching.

One *Beanotown.com* story that attracted a fair amount of interest came about in the lead-up to Desperate Dan's 65th birthday. The website was about to play host to the embassy of its nearest neighbour, *The Dandy*. Their ambassador to *Beanotown* was, of course, to be Dan himself. *The Dandy* Editor, Morris Heggie said, 'Only Desperate Dan could take on a job of this stature. He's also the only man brave enough – and dim enough – to take the job.' While the embassy had no existence in the comic, the fact that it was on the website was enough for Dennis to say, 'What? Dan? From *The Dandy*? In *Beanotown*? We'll see about that!' Several attempts were made by many of *The Beano*'s citizens to overrun the embassy but without success!

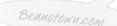

Some dodge requests

- My dad/brother are always leaving unpleasant smells in the bathroom. WHAT SHOULD I DO?!
- I need a way to be able to listen to music in class.
- I need a dodge to help me stop eating peas. YUCK!
- My sister snores just as bad as my dad and I share a room with her! What should I do?!

The original concept and subsequent games and plots, such as *The Dandy* embassy, were popular, but, as more people came online, users started to look for some sound and animation. Regardless of how popular the website became the company was all too aware that the comic had to come first. In order for the website to run alongside the comic, its content had to become more manageable and editorial time, already at a premium, could not become more stretched. New click-and-point games continued to be added to the site every two months as opposed to every two weeks at the outset. The company also attempted to put comic strips online, where people could download versions that could be put on to their PSPs. Positive feedback was received from this and further developments are planned. In 2006 a new content management system allowed *The Beano* staff to update the site themselves. This has enabled comic deadlines to be met while allowing the website to be updated every week.

The most popular topic of e-mails (well, B-mails) is dodge requests. Answering these requests falls to Claire Bartlett: 'I really do have to be careful about how I answer them as kids are so literal. For example, if a reader wanted to dodge eating broccoli, I couldn't say "shove it up your nose to hide it" because they probably would! I also avoid dodging school requests like the plague! You just can't tell a kid how to avoid school. Could you imagine the parents' and teachers' reactions?'

www.beanotown.com
Press UP to jump!
Press DOWN to crouch!
LIVES: 3
SCORE:0
CRISPS

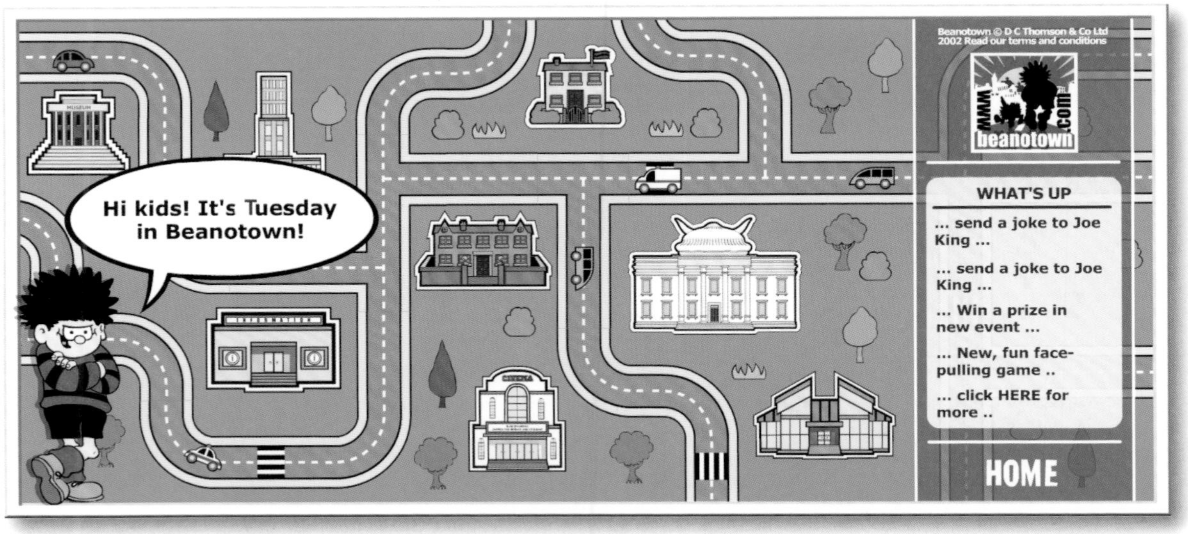
Hi kids! It's Tuesday in Beanotown!
Beanotown © D C Thomson & Co Ltd 2002 Read our terms and conditions
www.beanotown.com
WHAT'S UP
... send a joke to Joe King ...
... send a joke to Joe King ...
... Win a prize in new event ...
... New, fun face-pulling game ..
... click HERE for more ..
HOME

Above: A game from 2003.
Below: The Beanotown map.

BEANOTOWN
FOR FUN AND LAUGHTER ALL DAY LONG!
BUY 15 ISSUES OF BEANO ...AND GET 3 FREE
ADVERT
Welcome
Our Stuff
Fun Stuff
Toon Stuff
Other Stuff
contact us
beano club
subscribe
shop
legal stuff
OUR STUFF
We talk to you and you talk to us!
READ
GO
FUN STUFF
Things to play make and do!
PLAY
GO
TOON STUFF
Beano stars in cartoon capers!
SEE
GO
Urgh! No, thanks! I hate tests!
Oh, goody, good! I love tests!
I've already done the test. What's new round here?
Hello. Hey! Hello? Hi? Howdy? 'Ello? Yoo-hoo! Hello-ooo! HOI! You! Look here! Yes, you! The one at the computer! Yeah, you! I'm talking to you! Not the great, big, smelly, fang-faced spidery thing that's crawlin' up your leg.
Tell me more...
START OVER
STRIPZ
SEE HOW YOU LIKE IT!
A friend in need is a pain in the neck!
© D.C.THOMSON & Co Ltd 2008. Use of this website constitutes agreement to our terms and conditions.
ADVERTISEMENT
BEANO CLUB ROCKS

BACK
NEXT
CLEAR
PRINT
HELP
PANEL
CLOSE
BIGGER
SMALLER
FLIP
STAGE
RIGHT
LEFT
CHARACTERS
BALLOONS
EFFECTS
WORDS
MORE

Another popular aspect of the website is the reader polls. These give the reader a say in how their comic is put together and some recent poll questions have been:

- Dennis the Menace is everyone's fave, but what about our other characters? Click an' tell!
- We've smartened up our cover. What do you think?
- Which character from The Beano would you like to have as your best mate?
- What's your fave page in this week's Beano?

In 2008 the site generated around 35–40,000 unique visitors per month, and with animation and further multi-media projects planned, more and more web hits are sure to be had.

Above: The Homepage in 2008.
Below: The 2005 'Create a comic' game.

50 NOT OUT!

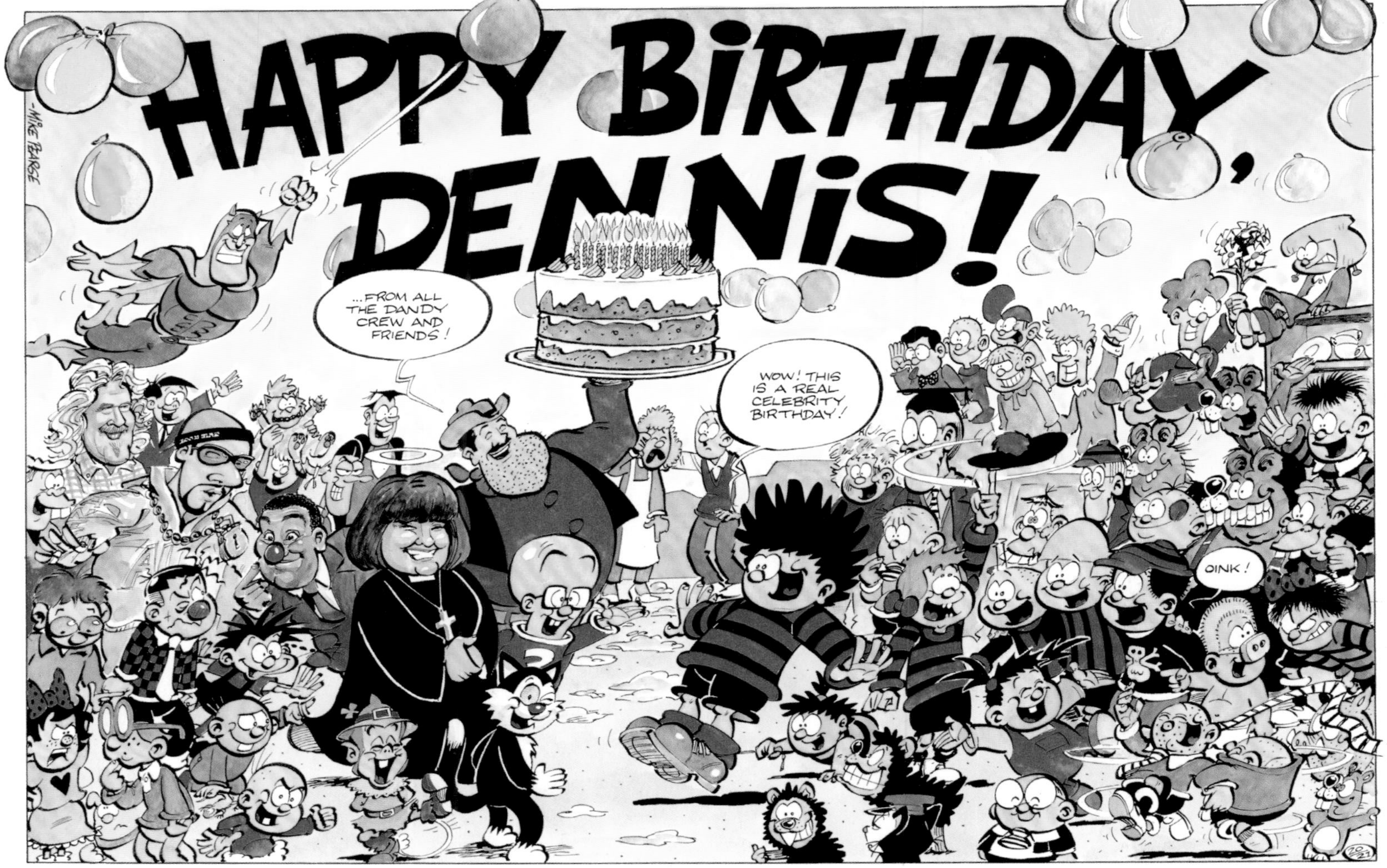
HAPPY BIRTHDAY, DENNIS!
...FROM ALL THE DANDY CREW AND FRIENDS!
WOW! THIS IS A REAL CELEBRITY BIRTHDAY!
OINK!

In 2001, Britain's longest surviving comic villain, 'Dennis the Menace', celebrated his 50th birthday. Boasting a fan club of over 1.5 million members, Dennis continued to lead the popularity stakes among *Beano* characters with not the slightest sign that his manners were improving.

First drawn in 1951 by Davey Law, Dennis became an overnight success, quashing fears he may have a bad influence on children and lead them astray. Euan Kerr said, 'Until Dennis arrived there had never been a comic character like him. You could call him the world's first anti-hero.'

FREE DENNIS ALBUM
Plus STICKERS
THE BEANO
web site address www.beanotown.com
No.3061 March 17th. 2001. Every Thursday 55p Canada $2.50
IT'S MY BIG BIRTHDAY SO...
...LET'S PARTY!

DENNIS THE MENACE
A LITTLE SCAMP IN A VERY DULL SHIRT SMASHED MY CAR WINDOW WITH HIS BALL.
LOVE A DUCK! MUST THINK HE'S THAT YOUNG STANLEY MATTHEWS.
COULD BE HIM WITH THE LAD IN THE VERY STRIKING HOOPED JERSEY.
HUMPH! THEY'RE RIGHT - IT IS A VERY DULL SHIRT. TIME FOR A MENACING SCHEME.
WONDER WHEN ANYONE WILL SET FOOT ON THE MOON?
JULY 20th. 1969 WOULD BE MY GUESS. LET'S SEE IF WE CAN BEAT THAT.
CAREFUL WITH THAT POP, DENNIS.
?
GRANNY'S POP SURE IS POWERFUL STUFF.
READY TO MAKE HISTORY, TUFTY?
SHAKE!
THAT SHOULD DO THE TRICK.
-3-2-1-
FISS!
-LIFT OFF!
WHOOSH!
POP!
POP!
POP!
HAR-HAR! TUFTY WON'T NEED THIS ON THE MOON-I'LL HAVE IT.
FEELS RIGHT, SOMEHOW!

To help with publicity around the time of his 50th birthday, this spoof strip, telling the origin of the striped jumper, was created. Drawn by David Parkins in the style of Davey Law, it was never published in the comic or annual.

It was another 17 years before his canine-sidekick, Gnasher appeared to enliven proceedings, and he has remained a constant companion of Dennis ever since. As a simple dumb animal he could get away with many things that even Dennis could not. Dennis has also ventured outside the comic to become a national TV celebrity with his own animated series on BBC. Not content with this, Dennis has become the star of *Beanoland* and the *Beanotown* website, as well as featuring on masses of merchandise and collectibles for fans.

In the issue to celebrate his milestone, he is seen in a number of money-raising activities in aid of Comic Relief, including a food fight with comedians Ali G and Billy Connolly.

But in a concession to the age of political correctness, Dennis at 50 no longer got whacked with a slipper every week or bullied Walter the Softy, while even his catapult, deemed a dangerous weapon, had mysteriously disappeared. However, some things never change. Fashion trends have been ignored (apart from his trendy stunt in 1996, see page 256) as his attire remained constant and there has never been a let up in his menacing behaviour!

A NEW EDITOR

Fiction
DENNIS THE MENACE & GNASHER
Annual 2007

In early 2006 after 22 years at the helm of *The Beano*, Euan Kerr handed over to Alan Digby, who became only the fourth Editor in 70 years. Having previously worked as chief-sub when Euan first became Editor, it was a chance to return that surprised even Alan. Here are some of his thoughts.

ON DIFFERENCES BETWEEN *THE BEANO* THIS DECADE AND IN THE 1990s

'Working practices haven't really changed in the last decade. Computer effects have come on quite a bit and layouts are more sophisticated but I don't think *The Beano*, even of the 1950s, is wildly different to today's version. I think of all the company's publications, *The Beano* has probably changed the least. It is readership driven and if we make any drastic changes there'd be immediate resistance to it. However, we also know the perils of staying in the past too long and it's about striking up the right balance.'

'I would also say it's been very difficult to get top-class new artists. A lot of our artists have been around for a while. It may have something to do with design or other courses, but it seems to me that the school of self-taught cartooning has dried up. We still get the brown envelopes sent in and you always hope "let this be the new Baxendale, Ken Reid, Bob Nixon".'

ON A FAVOURITE CHARACTER

'My favourite is "Ivy the Terrible" because she was loosely based on my younger daughter's appearance. It's not often you think of an idea that hasn't been done before and that was the case at the time. It was an idea I had sat on for a while. The late Bob Nixon was a great artist and his style was a crossover between Disney and our style and so he gave it instant appeal. He was working in London but when I became aware he might be available for a bit extra work I went straight to Euan and said I'd like to go ahead with the character. She went right up the charts to number six just outside the big characters. She got close to toppling Minnie and Bob Nixon must get credit for breathing a lot of life into the character.'

ON LEAST FAVOURITE CHARACTERS

'I'd probably say "Lord Snooty". I would also say "Calamity James". Some people loved him but I never quite got into it and he was always consistently near the bottom of the poll. I don't think it was badly written or drawn but I don't think

No. 2275 FEBRUARY 22nd, 1986.
EVERY THURSDAY
16p
I.R. 26p (inc. VAT)
DENNIS the MENACE and GNASHER
AT 4P.M.
JUMP
SNIFFLE! I HAD TO STAY OFF SCHOOL TODAY—I HAD A WHOLE SNEEZE LAST NIGHT!
HMMM...
HI, GNASHER—SCHOOL HASN'T BEEN TOO AWFUL TODAY—WALTER THE SOFTY WAS OFF!
WOW! THEN YOU WON'T KNOW WHAT SPECIAL THING WE'RE DOING AT SCHOOL TOMORROW!
MAKING THIS UP
GOSH, NO! HARD SUMS? LONG ESSAYS? WHAT?
NONE OF THAT BORING STUFF. WE'RE HAVING A ROLF HARRIS PARTY!
OH, THAT AUSTRALIAN CHAPPIE ON CHILDREN'S TV!
WE'D BETTER GET YOU READY—EVERYONE ELSE WILL BE DRESSED LIKE ROLF TOMORROW...
TUG
OH, DEAR!
THERE!
DAB DAB
PAINT
HMM. NOT MUCH CHANCE OF YOU GROWING A BEARD IN TIME...
OOER!
RUB
MORE ON BACK PAGE

Every Thursday ★ ★ ★ THE BEANO FEBRUARY 22nd, 1986.
DENNIS the MENACE AND GNASHER
CONTINUED FROM FRONT PAGE
...SO I'D BETTER MAKE YOU ONE!
SNIP!
CAREFUL!
YOU'RE STARTING TO LOOK LIKE THE GREAT MAN, WALTER!
SO—
DAD'S OLD WHITE FLAG TO SURRENDER...OH, HERE WE ARE!
DAD'S ARMY KIT-BAG
A DEAD RINGER FOR ROLF!
DAD'S DESERT GEAR
WOBBLE THIS, AND IT MAKES ROLFISH NOISES!
WOOGA!
YOU'D EVEN FOOL A KANGAROO!
EEK!
LICK
BOING! BOING!
Next day—
SCHOOL
WOBBLE
GASP! CAN'T MOVE TOO FAST IN THESE BOOTS—HOPE I'M NOT LATE!
In class—
MY STAR PUPIL, WALTER. SURELY CAN'T BE FEELING BETTER, YET!
TIE MY KANGAROO UP, SPORT!
GASP!
BUT NO-ONE ELSE IS DRESSED LIKE MR HARRIS!
GASP!
HOO! HOO! HE BELIEVED ME!
THERE, THERE, DEAR BOY, PERHAPS A FEW MORE DAYS IN BED AND YOU'LL FEEL BETTER!
HEH! HEH! MORE DAYS WITHOUT THAT SOFTY! GOOD OLD ROLF!
Printed and Published in Great Britain by D. C. Thomson & Co. Ltd., 185 Fleet Street, London EC4A 2HS.
© D. C. Thomson & Co. Ltd., 1986.

it deserved its cult status. There's also "Freddie Fear" who isn't a huge favourite of mine but what it does give you is the opportunity for storylines because he lives in a castle and, within reason, anything can happen.'

ON FUTURE CHARACTERS TO RIVAL DENNIS

'I often thought it would be ideal if Dennis became the least popular character as it would give others a chance to become the most popular. Euan didn't think this would be healthy and I can see his point. Dennis is so engrained in the public psyche I think he'd be difficult to shift. If something did come along I think it would be unplanned. One we are working on is "The Ultras". They are loosely based on "The X Men" and have limited superpowers that they haven't learned how to harness and, while I can't see them toppling "Dennis", I can see them fitting in. We will have to wait and see.'

ON A FAVOURITE STRIP OF ALL TIME

'Some friends of mine had a party where you had to go dressed as Rolf Harris. Around that time I was writing a script about Walter being off school (which never happened!). Dennis had to take home his homework and soon spied a chance for menace. He then said there was no homework and instead everyone had to go dressed as Rolf Harris to school the next day. You can never be sure how a script's going to turn out but I think that one worked and that'd be my favourite.'

CHARACTERS NO MORE

COMIC
IDOL

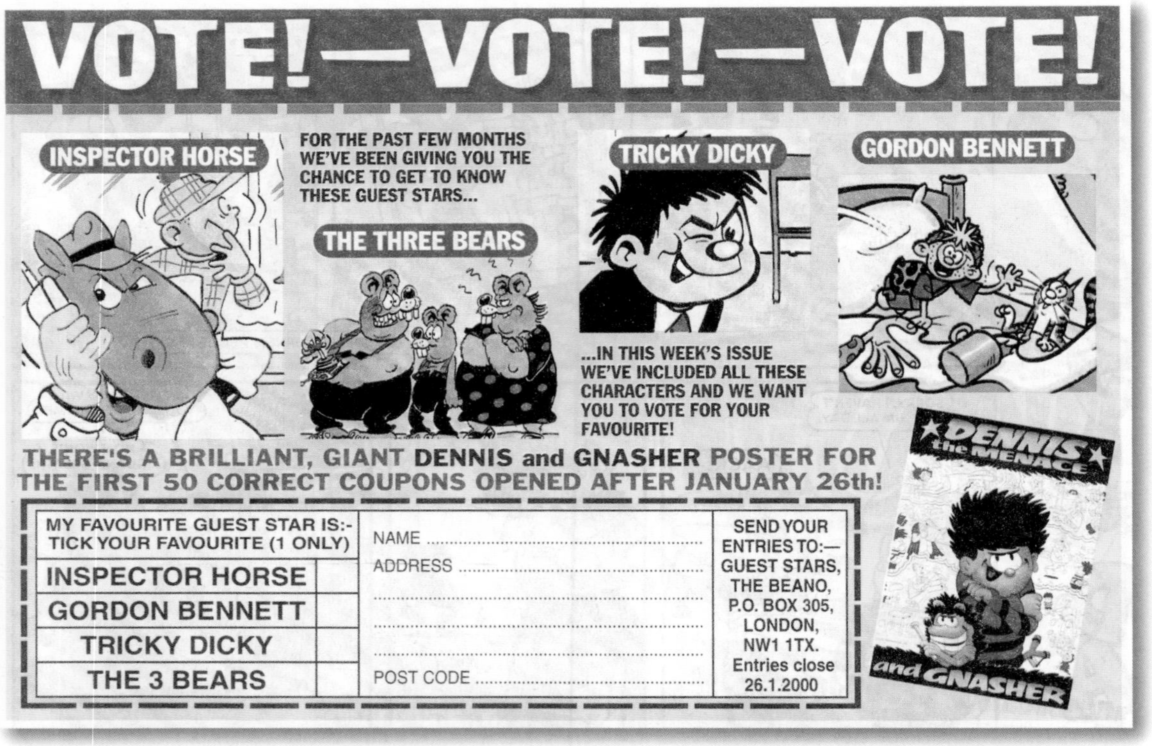
VOTE!—VOTE!—VOTE!
INSPECTOR HORSE
FOR THE PAST FEW MONTHS WE'VE BEEN GIVING YOU THE CHANCE TO GET TO KNOW THESE GUEST STARS...
THE THREE BEARS
TRICKY DICKY
GORDON BENNETT
...IN THIS WEEK'S ISSUE WE'VE INCLUDED ALL THESE CHARACTERS AND WE WANT YOU TO VOTE FOR YOUR FAVOURITE!
THERE'S A BRILLIANT, GIANT DENNIS and GNASHER POSTER FOR THE FIRST 50 CORRECT COUPONS OPENED AFTER JANUARY 26th!
DENNIS the MENACE and GNASHER
MY FAVOURITE GUEST STAR IS:- TICK YOUR FAVOURITE (1 ONLY)
INSPECTOR HORSE
GORDON BENNETT
TRICKY DICKY
THE 3 BEARS
NAME
ADDRESS
POST CODE
SEND YOUR ENTRIES TO:— GUEST STARS, THE BEANO, P.O. BOX 305, LONDON, NW1 1TX.
Entries close 26.1.2000

As *The Beano* moved in to the 21st century, reader opinions were easier to obtain than ever. Internet polls allowed readers to let staff know what characters they rated and hated and, if they weren't proving popular, they would soon end up on the comic scrapheap. As Alan Digby said, 'Some of the long-term characters, who had never been that popular and who'd been retained for loyalty reasons, have been axed. In the days of reader polls and websites there's been a gradual sharpening up and characters haven't been retained for sentimental reasons.'

In 2000 there was a reader vote to decide on who to keep from 'Inspector Horse', 'Tricky Dicky', 'Gordon Bennett' and 'The Three Bears', with the latter winning. Constant reader polls were then set up through the new ***Beanotown*** website and did not always throw up results that staff expected as Euan Kerr remembers, 'The one failure I was surprised about was 'Splodge the Goblin' who had been a very popular ***Topper*** character. It was drawn by the excellent Ken Harrison but absolutely bombed in the poll. Reader voting competitions were also successful. With Comic Idol, four new characters were tried over a four-week period and readers voted by phone for the one new character they'd like to keep as a regular in the comic.

Some characters, such as 'Little Plum' and 'The Three Bears', peaked in popularity in the 1960s during the heyday of westerns on TV. Others such as 'Les Pretend' had to be dropped after the artist, John Sherwood, died suddenly. Editor Alan said, 'We just couldn't find anyone suitable to replace him, but I'd imagine Les will return eventually.' Among some of the characters to stop in this decade are 'Baby-Face Finlayson' (1990–2005); 'Little Plum' (1953–2007); 'The Three Bears' (1959–2007); 'Calamity James' (1990–2007); 'Crazy for Daisy' (1997–2007); and 'Les Pretend' (1990–2007).

CALAMITY JAMES
JAMES, COME OVER HERE AND TRY ON YOUR NEW OUTFIT.
VERY RARE PARAGUAYAN PANT-PINCHING PINK PARROT.
MUM
OOH. NEW CLOTHES.
COAL
ER... IT FEELS A BIT LIKE CLAY, MUM.
DIRTY BIG BAG OF CLAY
THAT'S BECAUSE IT REALLY IS CLAY!
THAT'S... DIFFERENT.
HARDEN CRACK
HOT BLAST
MEMO: BUY NEW KNICKER ELASTIC
I CAN'T MOVE, MUM.
I KNOW. I'M TAKING YOU TO AN AUCTION TODAY.
HARD CONCRETE
AH, I UNDERSTAND. YOU'RE SCARED I MIGHT MOVE AND BID FOR SOMETHING EXPENSIVE BY MISTAKE.
NOPE! I'M ACTUALLY PUTTING YOU UP FOR SALE.
AUCTION HOUSE
PLONK
LOT 51
LOT 13
LOT 62
LOT 274
MEDIEVAL KNIGHT'S KNICKERS
Soon...
LET'S START WITH THIS MODERN ART LAMP. WE'LL START THE BIDDING AT £50.
CACKLE. THIS WAY I GET SHOT OF JAMES AND I MAKE SOME CASH TOO – RE-SULT!
LOT 49
LOT 13
AUCTIONEER
SOB. HOW TERRIBLY CRUEL AND NASTY.
Alexander Lemming – James' sometimes faithful pet.
HOW COULD ANYONE BE NASTY ENOUGH TO LEAVE ME OUT OF THE STORY UNTIL PICTURE 9?
ANY MORE BIDS?
ABANDON LEMMING, CHAPS! HIS FUR'S FLOODING! MAKE FOR THE ODD-LOOKING OLDER WOMAN!
Fleas.
EH? AAAAAAAAAAAH!
£1,000 – SOLD TO THE NOISY LADY AT THE BACK!
BITE!
SCRITCH CLAW SCRATCH
A GRAND! I HAD A GRAND UNTIL YOUR PERISHING PET... I'LL JUST GET YOU OUT OF THAT CLAY, JAMES...
I DO SO LIKE A HAPPY ENDING.

The last 'Calamity James' strip and details from the last 'Three Bears' and 'Little Plum' strips.

The last 'Crazy For Daisy' strip and details from the last 'Baby-Face Finlayson' and 'Les Pretend' strips.

CRAZY FOR DAISY
PUFF! PANT!
POOR DAISY LOOKS POOPED. NOW COULD BE JUST THE CHANCE I'VE BEEN WAITING FOR.
SHOP
YEEK! DON'T DO THAT!
DON'T BE LIKE THAT, DAISY - YOU'LL BE GLAD I'M HERE SOON.
LEAP!
YOU LOOK PUFFED, M'DEAR - MAY I CARRY SOMETHING?
GASP! PUFF! CARRY? THAT'S DIFFERENT. HERE - HAVE THESE.
BOW!!!
NOT WHAT I HAD IN MIND FOR CARRYING.
CRUNCH!
M-M-MY TOOTSIES!
YOU ARE WHAT I HAD IN MIND FOR CARRYING!
UNHAND ME, YOU LOUT! PUT ME DOWN!
WHAT'S THE MAGIC WORD? HMMMM?
NICK BRENNAN
NOW!
THUMP!
WHUMP!
Y-YOU KNOW, S-SOMETIMES YOU C-C-CARRY THINGS T-T-TOO FAR, DAISY!
YUK-YUK!
STAGGER!

BABY-FACE FINLAYSON
THE CUTEST BANDIT PEST! IN THE WEST.
SIP

Laura Howell

LAURA HOWELL

In July 2006, Laura Howell finished a seven-year career in children's publishing to become a full-time comic artist and illustrator. By November she had won her first comic prize and was soon counting *The Beano* among her client list. She was the first woman to regularly draw for *The Beano*. She reflects on this.

'Historically women have only ever made up a small percentage of comic artists. There are more of us these days, although the vast majority of younger women artists these days go for Manga – the percentage doing funny comics is still small. Maybe girls more readily accept the idea that they should dismiss childish things when they reach a certain age, so only a few carry their childhood love of comics into adulthood. If I am working on a strip I have never done before, I'll send Alan the pencilled page so he can see how I'm approaching it before I go to inks, but otherwise he e-mails a script and I e-mail a finished page and that seems to work fine. It can seem tricky sometimes to fit 11 or 12 frames into a page. But then again, you go back and look at Ken Reid in the 1950s and 1960s getting in well over 20, and every one of them gorgeous, and you instantly feel like a namby-pamby whinger. My regular strip is "Johnny Bean from Happy Bunny Green".'

TALES OF Johnny Bean FROM
HAPPY BUNNY GREEN
In Happy Bunny Green, Mr Garden is in his garden watering his flowers —
HELLO, DAISIES.
Mrs Garden is calling him in for tea. They'll have buns and biscuits.
CLONG
But what's this? Little Johnny Bean's come to visit the garden.
Oh, no, readers. Johnny's stealing Mr Garden's flowers and we all know it's bad to steal.
QUICK, BEFORE OLD GREEDY GUTS FINISHES STUFFING HIS FAT FACE.
OH, NO, MR MOLE!
OH, YES, MR WORM.
Oh, oh! Sounds like Mr Garden's finished stuffing his fat face.
JOHNNY BEAN! YOU THIEVING LITTLE... YOU'RE AS BAD AS YOUR COUSIN!
Mr Garden is very upset.
PUT THOSE FLOWERS BACK OR I'LL GIVE YOU A TASTE OF MY PITCH FORK!
Oh, dear. Now it's Johnny who's upset.
BUT... THEY'RE FOR WHISTLING JIM, MY GUINEA PIG, WHO DIED YESTERDAY.
R.I.P.
Now Mr Garden feels ashamed.
I'M ASHAMED, I AM.
Now he feels frightened. Johnny's cousin "Mean Dean" is out for a day from the bad boys' school. He loved that guinea pig, too.
ULP!
R.I.P.
Do you think he loves Mr Garden?
Now Mr Garden's in his garden again. He does look funny. And Johnny's cousin's banged up at the bad boys' school for another three months.
MUMFLE!

MAX POWER

As *The Beano* approached its 70th birthday, D. C. Thomson decided it was time to launch its first comic since *Hoot* in 1985. Billed as a big brother to the weekly *Beano*, *BeanoMax* was to be aimed at nine to 13-year-olds, an older audience than *The Beano*'s normal readership. The first issue went on sale in February 2007 and was a Comic Relief Special. The special edition not only helped to raise funds for Comic Relief but it also gained the new comic maximum exposure in the media.

The Comic Relief theme meant it burst into life with a celebrity bang and it included Dr Who and the Daleks having a troublesome encounter with 'The Bash Street Kids'. Jamie Oliver also took over the school canteen, while 'Dennis the Menace' met Jonathan Ross and top football stars Frank Lampard and Steven Gerrard appeared in the 'Ball Boy' strip of the debut issue.

While the original *Beano* still continues to keep a core readership entertained with its unique brand of humour, *BeanoMax*'s immediate aims were not to rely on comic strips but instead give readers more stories, puzzles, competitions, features,

NEW!
3 FREE GIFTS!!
IN SUPPORT OF COMIC RELIEF
BEANOMAX
ISSUE 1, MARCH 2007
Price £2.48
NEW ZEALAND $8.70 (inc. GST)
No.1
CRACKING POSTER!
TOP CELEBS
DALEKS INVADE BASH STREET
MONTHLY MEGA MAG

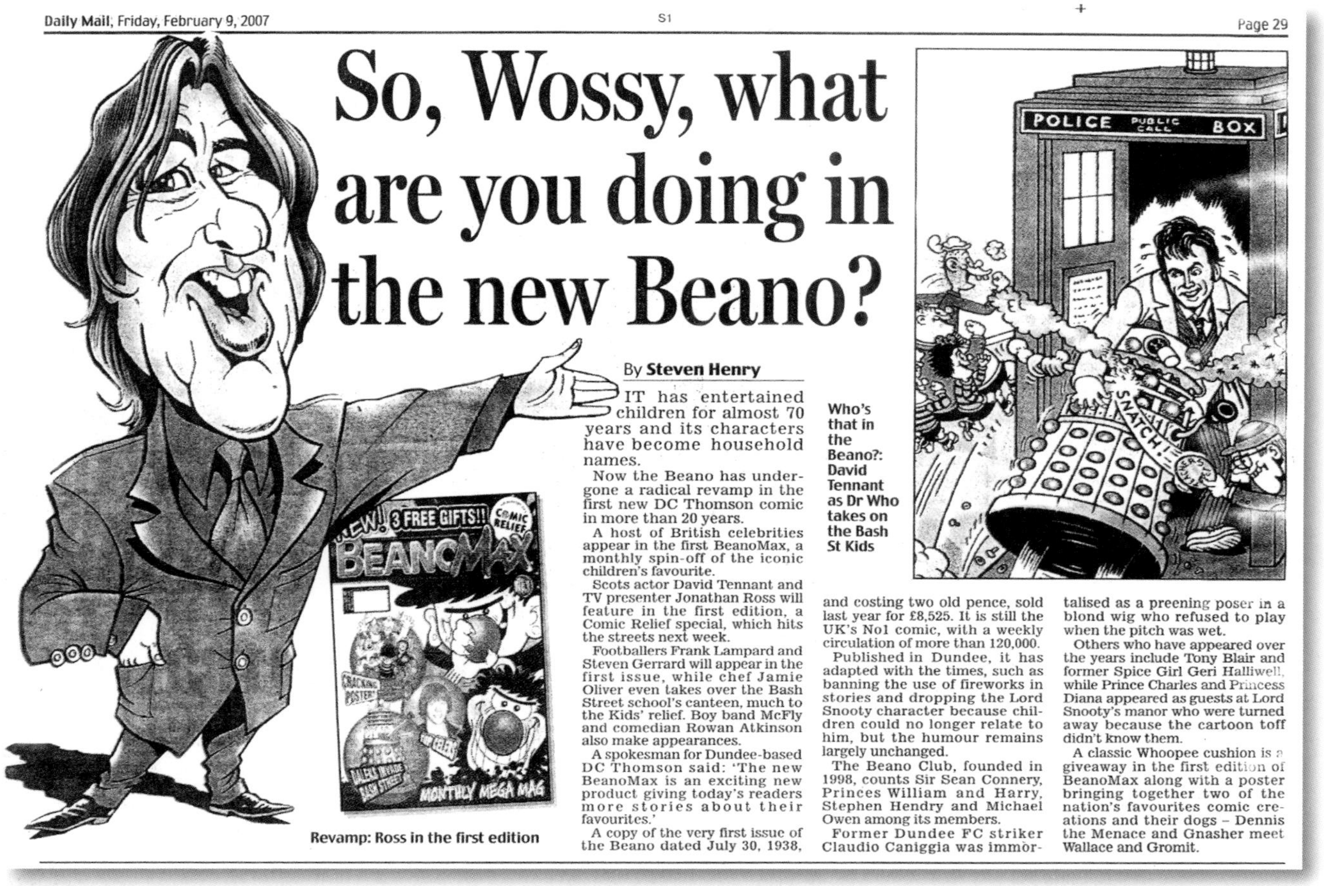

Daily Mail, Friday, February 9, 2007 S1 Page 29

So, Wossy, what are you doing in the new Beano?

By Steven Henry

IT has entertained children for almost 70 years and its characters have become household names.

Now the Beano has undergone a radical revamp in the first new DC Thomson comic in more than 20 years.

A host of British celebrities appear in the first BeanoMax, a monthly spin-off of the iconic children's favourite.

Scots actor David Tennant and TV presenter Jonathan Ross will feature in the first edition, a Comic Relief special, which hits the streets next week.

Footballers Frank Lampard and Steven Gerrard will appear in the first issue, while chef Jamie Oliver even takes over the Bash Street school's canteen, much to the Kids' relief. Boy band McFly and comedian Rowan Atkinson also make appearances.

A spokesman for Dundee-based DC Thomson said: 'The new BeanoMax is an exciting new product giving today's readers more stories about their favourites.'

A copy of the very first issue of the Beano dated July 30, 1938, and costing two old pence, sold last year for £8,525. It is still the UK's No1 comic, with a weekly circulation of more than 120,000.

Published in Dundee, it has adapted with the times, such as banning the use of fireworks in stories and dropping the Lord Snooty character because children could no longer relate to him, but the humour remains largely unchanged.

The Beano Club, founded in 1998, counts Sir Sean Connery, Princes William and Harry, Stephen Hendry and Michael Owen among its members.

Former Dundee FC striker Claudio Caniggia was immortalised as a preening poser in a blond wig who refused to play when the pitch was wet.

Others who have appeared over the years include Tony Blair and former Spice Girl Geri Halliwell, while Prince Charles and Princess Diana appeared as guests at Lord Snooty's manor who were turned away because the cartoon toff didn't know them.

A classic Whoopee cushion is a giveaway in the first edition of BeanoMax along with a poster bringing together two of the nation's favourites comic creations and their dogs – Dennis the Menace and Gnasher meet Wallace and Gromit.

Revamp: Ross in the first edition

Who's that in the Beano?: David Tennant as Dr Who takes on the Bash St Kids

NEW!
3 FREE GIFTS!!
COMIC RELIEF
BEANOMAX
MONTHLY MEGA MAG
POLICE PUBLIC CALL BOX
SNATCH!

How the Daily Mail *of February 9, 2007, reported the arrival of* BeanoMax.

reviews and celebrity interviews. There was also to be an emphasis placed on quality free gifts. However, at a time when overall sales of comics continued to fall, the risks of such a launch were apparent to all at D. C. Thomson. Other factors were also considered, for instance, would it detract from the original ***Beano*** or eat into its readership? However, eagerly anticipated sales figures for July – December 2007, showed ***The Beano*** had outsold its big brother with an average sale of 74,419 to a still impressive 51,431 for the ***BeanoMax***.

Former ***Beano*** editor Euan Kerr, back in the editor's seat on the ***BeanoMax***, gives some background on a new character to replace Dennis on the cover. 'The feedback we were getting was that readers wanted the covers of ***The Beano*** and ***The Max*** to be separated more. So we really needed to get Dennis off ***The Max***'s cover. What we came up with was a character called "Max". We're lucky to have an artist (Jimmy Dewar) who has a more grown-up, realistic drawing style and it seems to be going down well with readers at market research. We used to try out characters for six weeks in the comic and see how they'd get on, but this is different from the norm because we have to do lots of research and make sure he's absolutely right before he goes in. The reaction in schools has been good. Max is more modern than Dennis and we think there's more scope for him to be developed for animation and transfer to other mediums. We've got to think that way now. With slightly older readers comes a slightly older style.'

TOPICAL TIMES

HOWL!
WIDDLING WALLABIES! CUT! CUT!
BTV
TEST KIT
TOXIC WASTE BIN
BAM!

Even after 70 years *The Beano* remains as topical as ever. Where once it dealt with wartime propaganda and punk rock, it now deals with today's celebrity-obsessed society. Celebrity lives are scrutinised more than ever while reality shows and soaps have become the staple diet of family viewing.

Surveys and news of the day have continued to influence strips as well. One report said that children in Britain were becoming lazier, soon highlighted in a 'Les Pretend' strip in 2002. Another said that people were not getting enough hugs anymore. That story became an immediate 'Minnie the Minx' strip. She straightaway went out and hugged a football team, a guy dressed up as bear outside a shop and her dad, who then couldn't get to work.

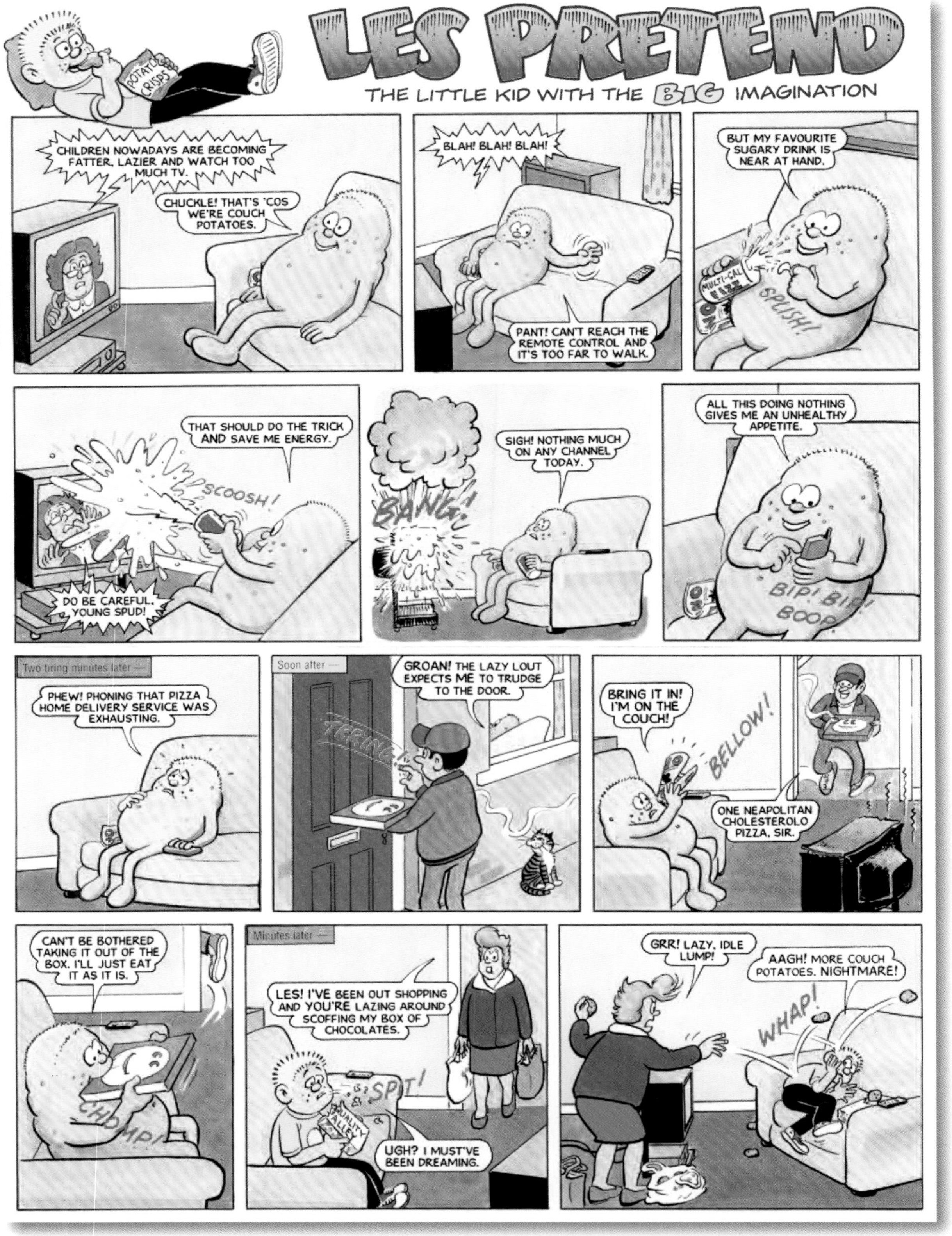
LES PRETEND
THE LITTLE KID WITH THE BIG IMAGINATION
POTATO CRISPS
CHILDREN NOWADAYS ARE BECOMING FATTER, LAZIER AND WATCH TOO MUCH TV.
CHUCKLE! THAT'S 'COS WE'RE COUCH POTATOES.
BLAH! BLAH! BLAH!
PANT! CAN'T REACH THE REMOTE CONTROL AND IT'S TOO FAR TO WALK.
BUT MY FAVOURITE SUGARY DRINK IS NEAR AT HAND.
SPLISH!
THAT SHOULD DO THE TRICK AND SAVE ME ENERGY.
SCOOSH!
DO BE CAREFUL, YOUNG SPUD!
SIGH! NOTHING MUCH ON ANY CHANNEL TODAY.
BANG!
ALL THIS DOING NOTHING GIVES ME AN UNHEALTHY APPETITE.
BIP! BIP! BOOP!
Two tiring minutes later —
PHEW! PHONING THAT PIZZA HOME DELIVERY SERVICE WAS EXHAUSTING.
Soon after —
GROAN! THE LAZY LOUT EXPECTS ME TO TRUDGE TO THE DOOR.
BRING IT IN! I'M ON THE COUCH!
BELLOW!
ONE NEAPOLITAN CHOLESTEROLO PIZZA, SIR.
CAN'T BE BOTHERED TAKING IT OUT OF THE BOX. I'LL JUST EAT IT AS IT IS.
CHOMP!
Minutes later —
LES! I'VE BEEN OUT SHOPPING AND YOU'RE LAZING AROUND SCOFFING MY BOX OF CHOCOLATES.
SPIT!
UGH? I MUST'VE BEEN DREAMING.
GRR! LAZY, IDLE LUMP!
AAGH! MORE COUCH POTATOES. NIGHTMARE!
WHAP!

What opera is all about hamburgers?
Ivy The Terrible
What's with the hat, Ivy?
It's not cold today.
TA-DAAA!
SWOON!
ERK!
Well, what do you think?
My sweet little girl . . . my baby . . .
Come on! Do you like it or not? Be honest!
SPEECHLESS!
Keep yer hair on, it's only a skull-cap. Tee-hee!
SNAP!
PHEW!
That's a relief!
You might be wondering why I'm wearing this?
There's a new Megabucks coffee shop opening today and one of my heroes is opening it!
SHOPPING CENTRE
STEVE McFADDEN, alias PHIL MITCHELL! He's so tough and he just doesn't care! The ultimate COOL!
TODAY
PHIL MITCHELL
But —
Gosh! I'll never meet him if I don't get to the front!
MEGABUCKS COFFEE SHOP
GERRAHTAMYWAY! I WANNA SPEAK WIV MY BRUVVER, PHIL! YOU GORRA PROBLEM WIV 'AT?
N-no! On you go, Mr Mitchell, sir!

The Barbecue of Seville!
It's his little brother!
Wouldn't mess with him, if I was you!
Hardest of them all, they say!
OPENING TODAY BY PHIL MITCHELL
There he is!
CHARGE!
PHOOO!
What did you do that for? You've hurt him!
He's hard as nails! He can take it.
You CAN take it, can't you?
Wheeze! No!
I'm sorry! I'm your biggest fan. I thought you'd be hard, just like on the telly!
Hang on — you're Ivy, from The Beano!
I'm YOUR biggest fan! And you ARE hard in real-life!
Wow!
So —
YEAH! Two Ivy's are better than one!
SQUIRT!
My customers!!!
He's still my hero — even if he is softer than on the telly!
THUD!

Indeed some soap storylines have helped to influence some of the storylines in *The Beano*. In 2001, we had 'Ivy the Terrible' donning a skull-cap and going to Megabucks to meet one of her heroes, EastEnders' hardman Phil Mitchell. Together they caused mayhem and Phil ended up dressing up as 'Ivy the Terrible'! Other TV shows have been integrated into storylines such as 'Animal Hospital', when 'Robbie Rebel' took his dog Defido to the filming. Chaos ensued, of course, as the strip ended with Robbie cutting off Rolf Harris' beard!

BEST OF 2005
THE BEANO
Jan 7th. 2006 No. 3311. www.beanotown.com
80p
WANT ME TO WAKE YOU UP, BOYS? YOU'VE GOT A COMIC TO GUEST EDIT!
MMM! GREEN STUFF!
THE PICK OF THE PAST YEAR!
DICK & DOM APPEAR BY KIND PERMISSION OF THE BBC

Dick and Dom, the stars of hit Saturday morning TV kids show 'In Da Bungalow', acted as guest editors at the start of 2006. They picked the best strips of 2005 and each had a comment to make on their chosen strips. Sporting contests have also been covered, whether it be the World Cup, 'Minnie the Minx' riding a dog home to win the Chilltenham Gold Cup or Bea playing in her own version of Wimbledon! In July 2006 the Scottish music festival, T in the Park, was replaced in ***The Beano*** by Din in the Park as Dennis and Gnasher cranked up noise levels, scaring all the residents.

WHAT A STINKING MESS ROGER'S IN AT THE END OF THIS STORY. REMINDS ME A LOT OF HOW OUR GUESTS END UP ON OUR SHOW!
ROGER the DODGER
INSECT
GOOD DODGERS CAN LEARN A LOT FROM NATURE, READERS.
THINGS AREN'T ALWAYS WHAT THEY SEEM TO BE - THAT TWIG'S NOT A REAL TWIG - IT'S AN INSECT.
STICK INSECT
FOR EXAMPLE - CRUNCHER, HERE, SEEMS TO BE PRETTY THICK...
I HEARD THAT! THE TOOTH FAIRY'S GONNA BE MAKIN' YOU RICH!
...BUT HE ISN'T...
PAT!
THAT'S BETTER - NICE OF YOU TO SAY SO.
...HE'S NOT PRETTY AT ALL AND HE'S VERY, VERY THICK!
OOO, YOU'LL PAY FOR THAT CHEAP JOKE, ROGER!
I'M CATCHING HIM! I'M CATCHING HIM!
ZOOM!
AND N-NOW I'M S-STOPPING!
SKID!
POLICE
GRR! HOW CAN I GET EVEN WITH ROGER WHEN HE SEEMS TO BE SO PALLY WITH THE POLICE?
HEY! HE ISN'T! I'VE BEEN DODGERED!
VRUM!
THAT'S RIGHT, CRUNCHER THINGS AREN'T ALWAYS WHAT THEY SEEM, BUT I SEEM TO BE GOING - 'BYE!
WATCH THIS, READERS - CRUNCHER'S GOING TO FOLLOW, BECAUSE I SEEM TO BE VAULTING RIGHT OVER THIS WALL...
...BUT I'M NOT, BECAUSE I KNOW THERE'S A BIG HEAP OF VERY SMELLY STUFF ON THIS SIDE! SNIGGER!
CACKLE! SO DO I! THIS LITTLE PIGGY WENT TO MARKET! THIS LITTLE...
NO! MERCY!
YOU'RE RIGHT, ROGER - NO MERCY! SOMETIMES THINGS ARE WHAT THEY SEEM...
...FOR EXAMPLE - YOU REALLY ARE A ROTTEN STINKER THIS WEEK, ROGER! POOOOOOOH!
DANGER!
SMELLY COMPOST! KEEP AWAY!
OUT-DODGERED BY CRUNCHER - OOH, THE SHAME - IT'LL TAKE AGES TO LIVE THIS DOWN - AND LONGER TO GET RID OF THIS HORRID SMELL!
THANKS FOR LETTING US BE GUEST EDITORS OF THE BEANO. WE HOPE THAT YOU AGREE WITH OUR SELECTION.
IF NOT, COMPLAIN TO THE REAL BEANO EDITOR, COS OUR JOB'S OVER! SEE YOU!
Printed and published in Great Britain by D.C. THOMSON & CO LTD 185 Fleet Street, LONDON, EC4A 2HS
D C THOMSON & CO LTD 2006

In December 2007, the hit TV show 'Strictly Come Dancing' was featured in a 'Robbie Rebel' strip. The strip included Len Goodman and his fellow judges as well as featuring the host Bruce Forsyth. When *Beano* fan, Bruce Forsyth celebrated his 80th birthday two months later, he was presented with the issue by Len Goodman, much to his delight!

ROBBIE REBEL
NOBODY TELLS HIM WHAT TO DO!
OOH, LOOK. SHE HAD BOTH HER FEET OFF THE GROUND. THAT'S AGAINST THE RULES.
EVERY TIME THEY WATCH STRICTLY DANCING THINGY IT'S THE SAME... RULES, RULES, RULES!
YEP. BREAKS THE RULES.
TOO MANY HEEL LEADS, HAD A LIFT IN THERE, ALL AGAINST THE RULES.
SEE?
NOD! NOD!
RULES... RULES... RULES...
FUME!
FIZZZ!
SLAM!
RULES SCHMULES!
WELL, HE DID THE QUICKSTEP OUT THE DOOR.
OH, LOOK. HERE'S ROBBIE.
STOMP!
KYLIE. YOU WANT TO DANCE? YEAH? GOOD. COME ON.
ER, GOING DANCING. SEE YOU LATER.
STRICTLY COME DANCING STUDIO
HURRY IT UP, WOMAN!
NICE TO SEE YOU, TO SEE YOU, NICE! AND WE'VE GOT A CHANGE THIS WEEK...
...OUR NEXT COUPLE ARE BEANO STAR, ROBBIE REBEL AND HIS FRIEND, KYLIE.
FRIEND? I TOLD HIM TO SAY GIRLFRIEND.
LESS TALK, THINK ABOUT DANCING AND...
BRUCIE
AGOG!
GALUMPH!
...BOOGIE! CUT LOOSE! GO WILD! WOOT!
SPIN!
GYRATE!
TA-DA! WHADDYA THINK? GIVE US A TEN, LEN!
SCREECH!
DANCEFLOOR DISASTER.
REBEL WITHOUT A CLUE. NO POINTS.
BROKE ALL THE RULES, DOUGHNUT.
MAGNIFICENTLY APPALLING.
SEETHE!
SHEEP! YOU'RE ALL SHEEP! BREAK THE RULES!
SNATCH!
GIVE ME THOSE.
THAT'S IT. REJECT RULES. REBEL AGAINST THE JUDGES.
UM... KYLIE, DON'T DO ANYTHING I'LL REGRET.
SLAP!
BLATTER!
CLOUT!
OW! OW! OOYAH! THAT'S NOT IN THE RULES!
10's FOR KYLIE – SHE'S GETTING SOME GOOD MARKS – ON ROBBIE.
I WAS ON TV. I WAS GOING TO BE GLAMOROUS! A STAR! I WANTED TO DANCE! YOU ROTTER!
KEN H. HARRISON

THE BEANO AT 70

And so, with Issue No. 3443, on August 2, 2008, *The Beano* reached another landmark, celebrating 70 years since the first issue was published. Never one to be shy, the celebrations have been wide-ranging, from Gnashional Menace Day (a fund-raising day of menacing) to a warm welcome from that bastion of establishment BBC Radio 4's 'Today' programme, everyone recognises the achievement of the comic that has played a part in the childhood of the majority of people in the country. For its 70th birthday edition, Nick Park, creator of 'Wallace and Gromit', agreed to be the guest editor, and he wrote with great feeling about the part *The Beano* played in his childhood, views many of us will recognise.

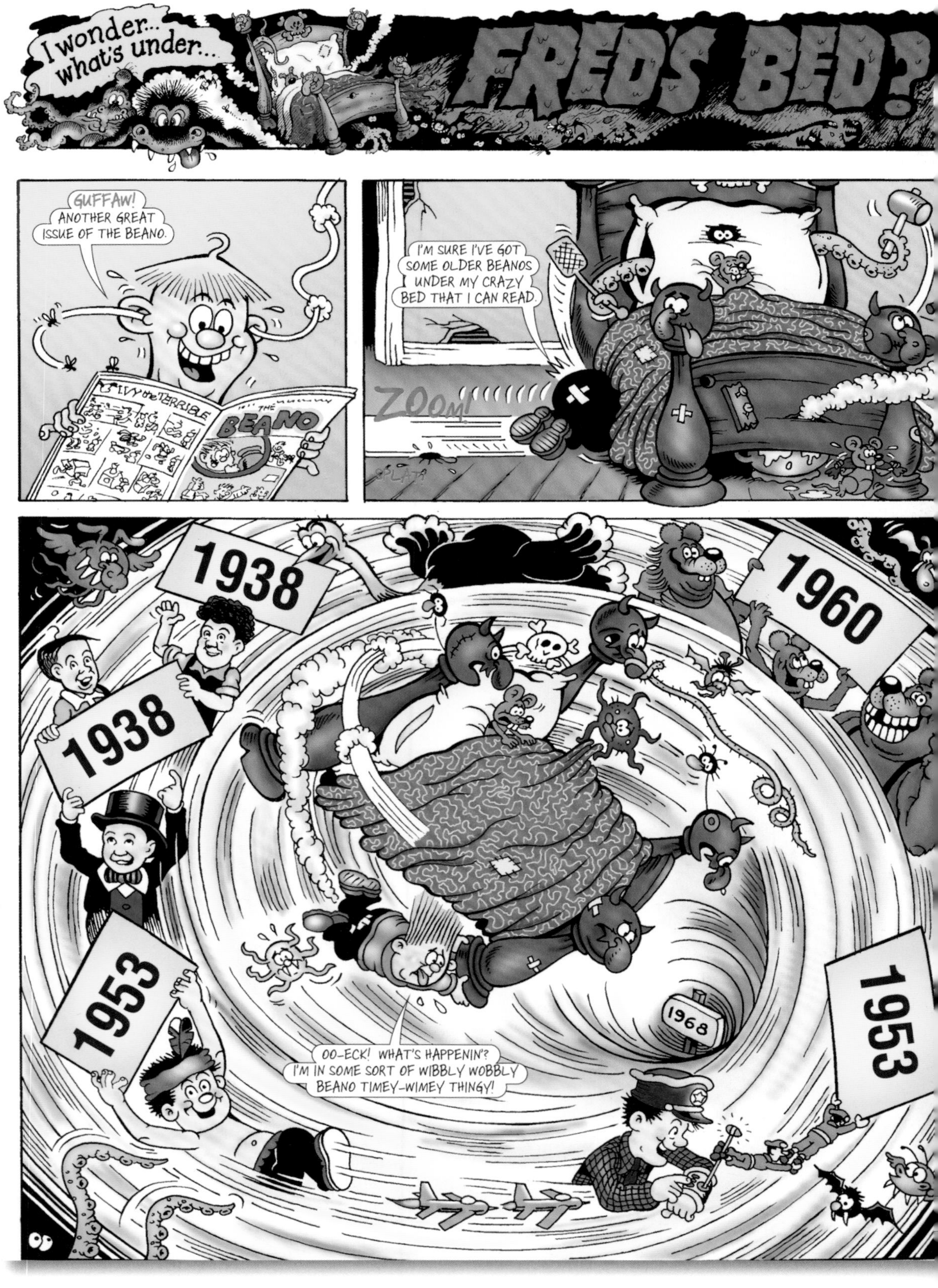
I wonder... what's under...
FRED'S BED?
GUFFAW! ANOTHER GREAT ISSUE OF THE BEANO.
I'M SURE I'VE GOT SOME OLDER BEANOS UNDER MY CRAZY BED THAT I CAN READ.
ZOOM!
1938
1960
1938
1953
1968
1953
OO-ECK! WHAT'S HAPPENIN'? I'M IN SOME SORT OF WIBBLY WOBBLY BEANO TIMEY-WIMEY THINGY!

HAPPY BIRTHDAY
THE BEAN
8 EXTRA PAGES!
AUG 2nd
EVERY WEDNESDAY
BE A STAR! YOUR CHANCE TO BE A CARTOON CHARACTER!
WHAT'S IN STORE FOR THE KIDS?
HAPPY BIRTHDAY
FRED MEETS A FAMOUS BEANO READER!

WHEE!
HUD!
BLOIK! I FEEL A BIT TIME-TRAVEL SICK. WHO ARE YOU, MATE, AN' WHERE AM I?
SCRAPE
I'M NICK PARK AND YOU'RE IN PRESTON.
SKETCH PAD
I'M FRED...I THINK. COR! AN OLD BEANO - WANNA SWAP?
YEAH! I LOVE THE BEANO!
AAARGH! WHAT'S GOING ON?
1960
ZOOM
SUCK
DON'T WORRY, NICK. THIS HAPPENS TO ME ALL THE TIME. IT MUST BE SOMETHIN' TO DO WITH BEANO'S BIRTHDAY. OOH LOOK, 1960 - GROOVY!
IT'S ONE OF THE THREE BEARS FROM THE BEANO.
DROP
WOO-HOO! CHEESE HERE WE COME!
KNICKER ELASTIC
INALLY BACKGROUND CHARACTERS IN E LITTLE PLUM STRIP, THE 3 BEARS GIVEN THEIR OWN STORY IN JUNE 1959.
THIS IS SO NOT A GOOD IDEA!
STRETCH!
UIET, TED. EVERYONE KNOWS E MOON IS MADE OF CHEESE. 'LL BE THERE IN NO TIME.
MMM....CHEESE....HOPE IT'S WENSLEYDALE.
WAAAAAAARGH! I DON'T WANNA GO TO THE MOOOOOOOON!
TWANG
ONE SMALL STEP FOR BEAR, ONE GIANT SLAP IN THE FACE FOR FRED-KIND!
CHUCKLE
HO-HO!
LITTLE PLUM WAS A PROUD MEMBER OF THE SMELLYFEET TRIBE - THEIR ARCH ENEMIES WERE THE PUTTYFEET!
WE REBOUNDED UNDER MY BED.
1953
LOOK, WE'RE HEADING FOR 1953.
HOI! GETTOFF ME!
WHEEE
CHEW
THUD
HO-HO! LOOKS LIKE YOU'RE WEARING THE WRONG TROUSERS TODAY, FRED!
BAAA!
COO. IT'S LITTLE PLUM. MUST GET SKETCHING!
STOP ALL UM WAILING. YOU'LL FRIGHTEN UM SHEEP.
CHEW
WHATCHA GOT SHEEP FOR?

The Beano was my world when I was younger and has been a huge influence on my career since. It was bought for me by my gran when I visited her every weekend and I read it from cover to cover . . . then I read it again. My older brother and I were always thinking up ideas for inventions and we got lots of ideas from stories in The Beano.

At school, I was a real daydreamer, particularly during the boring subjects! I enjoyed English because I loved writing stories. One day my homework was to write a story about life as a caveman. In it, I had a pet Brontosaurus, named 'Arrgh'. I got the idea for the character's name from The Beano *as I loved all the crazy sound effects! The story was really ridiculous, but while my teacher was reading it out to the class, she started to cry with laughter. That was the first time I realised I was able to make people laugh through my work.*

My dream job was always to work on The Beano *and it's such an honour for me to be Guest Editor for* The Beano's *70th birthday issue. It's shown me just how much thought goes into every detail of the comic. It's also amazing to appear in the 'Fred's Bed' story – it's the ultimate honour I can think of!*

THE BEANO INDEX

This index provides much information on *The Beano* and is divided into two sections. The first section is organised chronologically. For each year there is a summary of key events and then a listing of the characters that first appeared in that year. This listing also provides information on how long the strip ran, the artist involved, and, in most cases, a brief synopsis. After each strip there is a symbol which identifies the type of strip:

- (C) Comic strip
- (A) Adventure strip
- (S) Prose story
- (CA) Comic adventure strip

The second section is an index of artists, listing, for each artist, the strips worked on.

The material up to the end of 1989 has been taken from *The Beano Diaries*, written by Ray Moore and published as a limited edition by British Comic World in 1991. The information after 1989 has been provided by Ray Moore and by the staff of D. C. Thomson. We are most grateful to Ray Moore for his permission to reproduce his work and offer our sincere thanks.

1938

Thirty-five weeks after they published the first *Dandy* comic, D. C. Thomson of Dundee publish the first issue of *The Beano* on July 26 (dated for July 30). The original talents involved were:

Editorial

Editor – George Moonie; Chief Sub-Editor – Ron Fraser; Sub-Editors – Ian Chisholm, Freddie Simpson; Junior Sub-Editor – Stanley M. Stamper. Managing Editor of D. C. Thomson's Juvenile Publications was R. D. 'Bert' Low.

Artistic

D. C. Thomson staff artists: Dudley Watkins, George 'Dod' Anderson, Richard 'Toby' Baines, Jack Glass and Charles 'Chic' Gordon. Title logo artist was James Crighton.

Freelance artists: Reg Carter, Hugh McNeill, Roland Davies, James Jewell, Charles Holt, Basil Blackaller, S. K. Perkins, Eric Roberts and Allan Morley.

Important first issue character appearances: Big Eggo, Lord Snooty and His Pals, Morgyn the Mighty, Tom Thumb, Hairy Dan, Rip Van Wink, Wild Boy of the Woods and Tin-Can Tommy.

November

First appearance of a popular early *Beano* adventure character – Prince Dermod of Runa ('The Prince on the Flying Horse') – which also featured the first *Beano* artwork of Thomson staff artist James 'Peem' Walker. (His artwork on the feature 'Lost Among the Silver Dwarves' debuts at the same time).

December

The 'Little Magic Man' begins featuring the first *Beano* artwork from Thomson staff artist George Ramsbottom.

'Frosty McNab' begins featuring the first *Beano* artwork from artist Sam Fair.

First appearance of 'Pansy Potter' and 'Good King Coke'.

The Dandy Christmas issue (No. 56) features the first instance of a *Dandy–Beano* crossover strip when 'Our Gang' and 'Lord Snooty and His Pals' share a Christmas Party.

Year Information

Issues for year: Nos. 1–23; original page size 8.5 inches by 12 inches; price 2d; page count 28; published every Tuesday.

Free gifts: No. 1 (30.07.38) Whoopee Mask

No. 2 (06.08.38) 8 Sugar Buttons

No. 15 (05.11.38) Jelly Baby Sweets

No. 21 (17.12.38) Merry Christmas Mask

Big Eggo (C)

No. 1 (30.07.38) – No. 358 (02.04.49)

Art: Reg Carter (later one-line strips drawn by George Drysdale).

Covers: Last front cover appearance No. 326 (10.01.48)

Ping the Elastic Man (C)

No. 1 (30.07.38) – No. 126 (21.12.40)

Art: Hugh McNeill

Brave Captain Kipper (C)

No. 1 (30.07.38) – No. 57 (26.08.39)

Art: An Italian reprint supplied by the Milan-based Torelli Bros. Art Agency.

Lord Snooty and His Pals (C)

No. 1 (30.07.38) – No. 367 (30.07.49) First Series

Art: Dudley Watkins

Notes: For further 'Snooty' series see 1950 and 1959.

Morgyn the Mighty (A)

No. 1 (30.07.38) – No. 14 (29.10.38)

Synopsis: Adventures with the world's strongest man on the isolated Black Island where, after being shipwrecked on the schooner *Hebrides*, he has remained a castaway for 13 years.

Art: George 'Dod' Anderson

Notes: 'Morgyn' also appeared in his own storybook in September 1951, priced 4/–. It contained 214 pages and had 14 illustrations and a pictorial dustjacket drawn by Dudley Watkins.

The Adventures of Tom Thumb (S)

No. 1 (30.07.38) – No. 115 (5.10.40) First Series

Synopsis: Exploits of the woodcutter's son, who is only six inches high, made famous in the Charles Perrault fairytale.

Notes: For further 'Tom Thumb' series see 1940, titled 'Jungle Leader of the Little Lost Ones'; 1941; 1948, titled 'Sir Tom Thumb'; 1949; 1950, titled 'Tom Thumb's Schooldays'; 1957.

'Tom Thumb' also appeared throughout the 1960s in the nursery comic *Bimbo* in a strip drawn by Dudley Watkins beginning in No. 1 (18.03.61), and subsequently appeared in the other nursery comic *Little Star* in the years 1973–75.

Black Flash the Beaver (S)

No. 1 (30.07.38) – No. 20 (10.12.38)

Synopsis: A young beaver learns to survive the dangers of life in the forest.

Art: Richard 'Toby' Baines

Whoopee Hank – The Slap-dash Sheriff (C)

No. 1 (30.07.38) – No. 53 (29.07.39)

Art: Roland Davies

Cracker Jack – The Wonder Whip Man (A)

No. 1 (30.07.38) – No. 35 (25.03.39)

Synopsis: Modern-day cowboy Cracker Jack Silver uses his 30-foot lash to fight crime.
Art: Jack Glass

Hooky's Magic Bowler Hat (CA)

No. 1 (30.07.38) – No. 108 (17.08.40)
Synopsis: After being kind to an old Indian carpet seller, young Hooky Higgs is given a magic bowler hat which, when rubbed, will grant any wish.
Art: Charles 'Chic' Gordon

The Wangles of Granny Green (S)

No. 1 (30.07.38) – No. 26 (21.01.39) First Series
Synopsis: Motherless 11-year-old Jimmy Green impersonates his own granny, a ruse which allows him to live alone while his father is away for a time working in a distant town.
Art: Charles 'Chic' Gordon
Notes: For a reprint of this serial see 'Artful Granny Green' (1945). For second series see 1951.
The Topper comic strip 'Al Change' drawn by Tom Bannister (1980–86) bore more than a passing resemblance to this story.

Wee Peem (He's a Proper Scream) (C)

No. 1 (30.07.38) – No. 89 (6.04.40) First Series
Art: James Jewell
Notes: Reprinted in Thomson's magazine-cum-newspaper *The People's Journal* followed by new *People's Journal* strips drawn by James Malcolm.
For further series see 1951 (Titled 'Wee Peem's Magic Pills') and 1956.
Peem is Scots nickname for anyone called James, e.g., Thomson staff artist James 'Peem' Walker.

Little Dead-Eye Dick (C)

No. 1 (30.07.38) – No. 20 (10.12.38) First Series
Art: Charles Holt
Notes: For second and third series see 1949.

Hairy Dan (C)

No. 1 (30.07.38) – No. 297 (16.11.46), latterly not every week
Art: Basil Blackaller (later George Drysdale)
Notes: 'Hairy Dan' reappeared in *Sparky* No. 1 (23.01.65) and continued to appear sporadically throughout the first year of *Sparky's* run.

Contrary Mary (the Moke) (C)

No. 1 (30.07.38) – No. 97 (01.06.40)
Art: Roland Davies
Notes: Reprinted in D. C. Thomson's magazine-cum-newspaper *The People's Journal* (from 16.06.45) under the title 'Neddy the Cuddy'.
Mary was revived in *The Beano* in 1950 when she became a new animal member of Lord Snooty's gang.

Smiler the Sweeper (S)

No. 1 (30.07.38) – No. 20 (10.12.38)
Art: Steve Perkins

Helpful Henry (C)

No. 1 (30.07.38) – No. 35 (25.03.39)
Art: Eric Roberts.

The Wishing Tree (S)

No. 1 (30.07.38) – No. 35 (25.03.39)
Synopsis: An old oak tree grants people's wishes.
Art: Jack Glass
Notes: For instantaneous sequel to this story see 'Acorns from the Wishing Tree' (1939).

Big Fat Joe (C)

No. 1 (30.07.38) – No. 35 (25.03.39)
Art: Allan Morley
Notes: In 1950 Big Fat Joe returned to *The Beano* as one of Lord Snooty's new pals.

The Shipwrecked Kidds (S)

No. 1 (30.07.38) – No. 17 (19.11.38)
Synopsis: When the splendid steam yacht *Swallow* is wrecked, Cyril and Ethel Kidd, the children of the yacht's owner, and two of the crew (Mickey Swift the assistant cook and Big Bill Thomson) become castaways.
Art: Jack Glass

Rip Van Wink (C)

No. 1 (30.07.38) – No. 336 (29.5.48), latterly not every week (First Series)
Art: Eric Roberts (1938–41); James Crighton (1941–48).
Notes: For further series of new and reprint strips see 1958.

My Dog Sandy (S)

No. 1 (30.07.38) – No. 14 (29.10.38)
Synopsis: The adventures of Sandy, a pure-bred Border collie, when he runs away from his cruel master.
Art: Jack Glass

The Ape's Secret (S)

No. 1 (30.07.38) – No. 14 (29.10.38)
Synopsis: How young Jimmy Samson tries to gain rightful control of his uncle's circus after Algy, the intelligent chimp, steals and hides the old man's will.
Art: Richard 'Toby' Baines
Notes: For a picture strip with the same storyline see 'The Kangaroo Kid' in 1959.

Wild Boy of the Woods (A)

No. 1 (30.07.38) – No. 175 (14.03.42) First Series
Synopsis: A young lad called Derek is brought up by an old hermit to live like a young Tarzan in a great wood.
Art: Richard 'Toby' Baines
Notes: For further series see 1947, 1949 and 1958.

Uncle Windbag (He Tells Tall Tales) (C)

No. 1 (30.07.38) – No. 20 (10.12.38) First Series
Art: Charles Holt
Notes: For further series see 1953 and 1956.

Monkey Tricks (C)

No. 1 (30.07.38) – No. 20 (10.12.38)
Art: Reg Carter

Little Peanut's Page of Fun

No. 1 (30.07.38) – No. 112 (14.09.40)
Synposis: Jolly jokes and tricky riddles from the small black boy who adorns *The Beano's* front page title heading.
Art: Charles 'Chic' Gordon
Notes: On the front page title heading 'Peanut' is drawn by James Crighton.

Tin-Can Tommy (The Clockwork Boy) (C)

No. 1 (30.07.38) – No. 303 (08.02.47)
Art: Italian reprint from the Milan-based Torelli Bros. Art Agency, until No. 69 (18.11.39), then new strips drawn by Sam Fair and latterly George Drysdale and Charles 'Chic' Gordon.

Jimmy's Pet – The Kangaroo (S)

No. 15 (05.11.38) – No. 35 (25.03.39)

Synopsis: Fun when Jimmy Jones is sent a kangaroo as a birthday present from his uncle in Australia.
Art: Richard 'Toby' Baines

The Prince on the Flying Horse (S)
No. 15 (05.11.38) – No. 35 (25.03.39) First Series
Synopsis: In the land of Runa young prince Dermod, with the help of his flying horse Silverwing, tries to regain the throne of the kingdom which is rightfully his from the wicked usurper King Jarl.
Art: James 'Peem' Walker
Notes: For the immediate sequel, again in prose form, see 'The King on the Flying Horse' (1939) and for the third series, this time in picture story format, see 1940. See also semi-sequel to all these, the story 'Wildfire – The Magic Horse' in 1952.

Lost Among the Silver Dwarves (A)
No. 15 (05.11.39) – No. 89 (06.04.40)
Title changed to 'In the Land of the Silver Dwarves' from No. 36 (01.04.39)
Synopsis: In a lost world under the North Pole explorer Captain Steele, his children Tim and Betty, and their eskimo friend Blubby, have many adventures in the caverns which hold the strange city of the troglodyte Silver Dwarves and their ruler King Zak.
Art: James 'Peem' Walker
Notes: For strip with a similar theme see 'Kilty MacTaggart' in 1957 and also see prose story 'Willie in the Lost World' in 1951.

Hicky the Hare (C)
No. 15 (05.11.38) – No. 62 (30.09.39)
Art: Italian reprint supplied by the Torelli Bros. Art Agency in Milan.

Little Master of the Mighty Chang (S)
No. 18 (26.11.38) – No. 35 (25.03.39)
Synopsis: The adventures of Taba the Indian boy and his elephant Chang in the teak forests of Burma.
Art: Jack Glass
Notes: For a slightly altered picture strip version of this story see 'Teeko' in 1959.

The Little Magic Man (S)
No. 21 (17.12.38) – No. 35 (25.03.39)
Synopsis: The story of Ted Robins and Helpful, the marvellous magical gnome built by Ted's inventor father.
Art: George Ramsbottom

Good King Coke (He's Stony Broke) (C)
No. 21 (17.12.38) – No. 177 (11.04.42) First Series
Art: Eric Roberts
Notes: For second series see 1945.

Frosty McNab (The Freezy Wheeze Man) (C)
No. 21 (17.12.38) – No. 130 (18.01.41)
Art: Sam Fair

Pansy Potter (The Strongman's Daughter) (C)
No. 21 (17.12.38) – No. 325 (27.12.47)
Art: Hugh McNeill (1938–40); Basil Blackaller (1940–44); Sam Fair (1944–47).
Notes: For second series titled 'Pansy Potter in Wonderland' see 1949, for third series see 1958 and for fourth series see 1989.
Pansy Potter was originally, but for a late editorial change of mind, to have been called 'Biff Bang Bella'.

1939

April
'Acorns from the Wishing Well' begins featuring the first *Beano* work from Thomson staff artist Jack Prout.

July
First appearance of D. C. Thomson's short-lived comic *The Magic* on July 22.

September
The first *Beano Book* is published.

October
The first page count reduction as a result of the wartime paper shortages, from 28 to 24 pages, is introduced.

November
First appearance of *Beano's* sharp-witted bird 'Cocky Dick'.
'Follow the Secret Hand' begins, the first story featuring the early *Beano* adventure favourite Prince Ivor of Arkania.

Undateable Wartime information
Beano Editor George Moonie joins the Royal Marines and the Editorship passes to *Adventure* boys paper Editor Stuart Gilchrist.
Beano Chief Sub-Editor Ron Fraser joins the RAF. He is subsequently shot down in action and spends several years in prisoner-of-war camp.
Beano Sub-Editor Freddie Simpson, due to ill-health, has to leave Thomsons.

Year Information
Issues for year: Nos. 24–75; price 2d; page count 28 to No. 62 (30.09.39), then 24 from No. 63 (07.10.39) onwards.
Free gifts: No. 36 (01.04.39) Big Bang Fun Gun
No. 47 (17.06.39) Licorice Bow
No. 69 (18.11.39) Licorice Pipe

King of Thunder Mountain (S)
No. 27 (28.01.39) – No. 46 (10.06.39)
Synopsis: The adventures of a Rocky Mountain Bighorn deer.
Art: Richard 'Toby' Baines

Boney the Brave (He Lives in a Cave) (C)
No. 36 (01.04.39) – No. 46 (10.06.39)
Art: Roland Davies

Puffing Billy (C)
No. 36 (01.04.39) – No. 81 (10.02.40)
Art: Hugh McNeill

Young Strongarm the Axeman (A)
No. 36 (01.04.39) – No. 81 (10.02.40)
Synopsis: The thrilling escapades of young Strongarm, a Viking marksman at axe throwing.
Art: Jack Glass
Notes: For further series see 1949 and 1957

Acorns from the Wishing Tree (S)
No. 36 (01.04.39) – No. 62 (30.09.39)
Synopsis: In this direct sequel to 'The Wishing Tree' (see 1938), magic acorns from the tree grant wishes to people in trouble.

(C) Comic Strip (A) Adventure Strip (S) Prose Story (CA) Comic Adventure Strip

Art: Jack Prout
Notes: This story had no proper ending because it was dropped suddenly when the page count was reduced with No. 63 (07.10.39).

The Singing Giant (S)

No. 36 (01.04.39) – No. 59 (09.09.39)
Synopsis: A mysterious 13-year-old boy with a penchant for singing causes a town's authorities trouble mainly because he also happens to be 10 feet tall.
Art: Richard 'Toby' Baines

Twelve Happy Horners (S)

No. 36 (01.04.39) – No. 68 (11.11.39)
Synopsis: A family live in a giant mobile shoe and travel the country performing certain tasks in order to obtain an inheritance left them in a will.
Art: George Ramsbottom

The King on the Flying Horse (S)

No. 36 (01.04.39) – No. 52 (22.07.39) Second Series
Synopsis: In this direct sequel to 'The Prince on the Flying Horse', Dermod and his flying horse Silverwing find they still have many exciting adventures, even after Dermod regains the throne of Runa.
Art: James 'Peem' Walker

Tricky Dicky Ant (C)

No. 38 (15.04.39) – No. 62 (30.9.39)
Art: Italian reprint supplied by the Torelli Bros. Art Agency in Milan.
Notes: For second series see 1949.

The Pranks of Peanut (C)

No. 41 (06.05.39) – one-off, then No. 52 (22.07.39) – No. 67 (04.11.39)
Art: Charles 'Chic' Gordon
Notes: Strip featuring *The Beano's* front page title star.

Deep Down Daddy Neptune (C)

No. 47 (17.06.39) – No. 124 (07.12.40)
Art: Basil Blackaller

Wily Willie Winkie (C)

No. 47 (17.06.39) – No. 100 (22.06.40).
Art: Unknown

The Bulldog Trail (S)

No. 47 (17.06.39) – No. 62 (30.09.39)
Synopsis: 'Grip' the bulldog on the trail of a wolverine that has killed his pal, 'Baldy' the eagle.
Art: Jack Glass
Notes: This story had no proper ending when the page count was reduced with No. 63 (07.10.39). Another dog called 'Grip' (this time an alsatian) appeared in a *Beano* picture story in 1952.

The Little Joker in the Land of Nod (S)

No. 53 (29.07.39) – No. 89 (06.04.40)
Synopsis: Sammy B. Smart, the most unruly boy at Ramshaw Orphanage, is taken by Baron Wurz to the Land of Nod, the laziest country in the world, to liven up the inhabitants.
Art: James 'Peem' Walker
Notes: For a partial reprint of this series see 'Sammy B. Smart in the Land of Nod' in 1948.

Laddie Longlegs (C)

No. 54 (05.08.39) – No. 64 (14.10.39)
Art: Unknown

Hands Off the Talking Lamb (S)

No. 60 (16.09.39) – No. 66 (28.10.39)
Synopsis: In the Wild West a little girl called Mary seeks her missing brother with the help of a talking lamb.
Art: James 'Peem' Walker

Jack Sprat's Battle Cat (S)

No. 67 (04.11.39) – No. 78 (20.01.40) First Series
Synopsis: Jack Sprat, the kitchen boy and his bewitched giant cat Whiskers, have to catch 5000 rats a week for 10 weeks in order to earn 10,000 crowns from the miserly King Kasper of Robania or be executed if they fail.
Art: James 'Peem' Walker
Notes: For sequel see 'When will the Golden Peacock Speak?' in 1940.

Cocky Dick (He's Smart and Slick) (C)

No. 69 (18.11.39) – No. 325 (27.12.47)
Art: Allan Morley

Follow the Secret Hand (S)

No. 69 (18.11.39) – No. 81 (10.02.40) First Series (Prince Ivor)
Synopsis: When Greatheart, the King of Arkania, went missing during a fierce storm, the country fell into the hands of the tyrant Rudolph, and, on the same night as the king disappeared, the right hand of the statue of Varna, the goddess of freedom, vanished too. Prince Ivor, Greatheart's son, is told that while the hand is missing the kingdom will never be free of tyranny and so he therefore sets out to find it.
Art: Dudley Watkins
Notes: For the complex sequels to this story see 'The Whistling Scythe' (1940), 'The Whistling Scythe' (1942), 'Keeper of The Magic Sword' (1949) and finally 'The Boy with the Wonder Horse' (1950). The last two were also part sequels to the 1940 story 'The Black Witch is Waiting'. Finally also see 'The Vengeance of the Last Crusader' (1959).

1940

January

First 'Lord Snooty' strip with a war theme published in No. 76 (06.01.40).

April

'Doubting Thomas' begins, the first *Beano* strip from Thomson staff artist James Crighton.

June

Page count reduced to 22 and then 20.

November

Page count reduced to 18.

December

Mussolini, the Italian Fascist leader, is given short shrift in the new comic strip 'Musso the Wop'.

Year Information

Issues for year: Nos. 76–127; price 2d; page count 24 from Nos. 76–97; 22 pages from Nos. 98–100; 20 pages from Nos. 101–119; and then 18 pages from Nos. 120–127.
Free gift: No. 90 (13.04.40) 2 Licorice Black Eyes. This was the last free gift to be given away in *The Beano* for over twenty years!

When will the Golden Peacock Speak? (S)

No. 97 (27.01.40) – No. 89 (06.04.40) Second Series
Synopsis: In this sequel to 'Jack Sprat's Battle Cat' Jack and Whiskers go in search of the golden feathers of the Golden Peacock, feathers which, when returned to the golden bird, will allow it to tell the whereabouts of the kidnapped prince of Khar whose homeland, in the meantime, suffers under the tyranny of an evil sultan.
Art: James 'Peem' Walker

Winken and Blinken (The Little Dutch Kids) (C)

No. 82 (17.02.40) – No. 129 (11.01.41)
Art: Sam Fair

Prince on the Flying Horse (S)

No. 82 (17.02.40) – No. 126 (21.12.40) Third Series
Synopsis: Early sci-fi and a return to princely status for Dermod as he and his flying horse Silverwing try to prevent a spacecraft full of flying aliens taking over control of the Earth.
Art: Jack Glass

The Boy with the Magic Masks (S)

No. 82 (17.02.40) – No. 100 (22.06.40)
Synopsis: Adventures at Hornbridge school in England of the Indian boy Kip who has access to the 'Hall of a Thousand Faces' where there are masks which, when worn, change a person's personality.
Art: Dudley Watkins
Notes: For reprint series see 1948.

Doubting Thomas (C)

No. 90 (13.04.40) – No. 174 (28. 02.42)
Art: James Crighton
Notes: Doubting Thomas returned to *The Beano* in 1950 as one of Lord Snooty's new pals.

Tiger Trail to Kandabar (A)

No. 90 (13.04.40) – No. 126 (21.12.40)
Synopsis: In the eastern city of Nampur Tarka the Tiger Boy takes the dangerous trail to Kandabar to find the keys which will release six honest officials from the iron masks in which they have been imprisoned by an evil rajah.
Art: James 'Peem' Walker

Keeper of the Crooked Cross (S)

No. 90 (13.04.40) – No. 110 (31.08.40)
Synopsis: The warring clans in a Scottish glen set great store by what a mysterious voice emanating from a stone cairn embellished with a wooden cross says to them, little knowing that the voice is that of young Kenneth McDonnel, who transmits his voice up through the cairn from a secret cave below it.
Art: George Ramsbottom

The King's Got a Tail (S)

No. 90 (13.04.40) – No. 112 (14.09.40)
Synopsis: Until he proves his generosity to his people the miserly King Humbert is changed into a monkey by Fortuno the magician.
Art: Dudley Watkins

Down with Lord Haw-Haw (S)

No. 101 (29.06.40) – No. 114 (28.09.40)
Synopsis: The boys of Northtown try to get the better of the Honourable Augustus Snobley and his thuggish bodyguards, nicknaming Snobley 'Lord Haw-Haw' because he sounds just like the Nazi propagandist from Hamburg and tells just as many lies.
Art: Jack Glass

Cinderella and the Ugly Sisters (C)

No. 109 (24.08.40) – No. 151 (14.06.41)
Art: Basil Blackaller

A Wonderful Bird is Bill Pelican (S)

No. 111 (07.09.40) – No.126 (21.12.40)
Synopsis: The amazing jungle adventures of the world's biggest pelican and his little black pal.
Art: Richard 'Toby' Baines

The White Mouse will Get You (If You Don't Watch Out) (S)

No. 113 (21.09.40) – No. 137 (08.03.41) First Series
Synopsis: Thanks to a magic spell the local village bobby Sergeant Mulligan becomes a large white mouse called Nibbler from time to time.
Art: Dudley Watkins
Notes: For second series see 1941.

Little Noah's Ark (S)

No. 115 (05.10.40) – No. 128 (04.01.41)
Synopsis: Noah Carter, an orphan in the Wild West uses an old cabin that floats to rescue animals during a flood.
Art: Richard 'Toby' Baines
Notes: For picture strip version of this story see 1949, and for a further series in the prose format see 1952.

Jungle Leader of the Little Lost Ones (S)

No. 116 (12.10.40) – No. 129 (11.01.41) Second Series
Synopsis: Tom Thumb leads the Minns, a tribe of six-inch tall min-men, across Africa to find them a new homeland after their island home is destroyed in an earthquake.
Art: Dudley Watkins

Big Heep (C)

No. 125 (14.12.40) – No. 177 (11.04.42)
Art: Basil Blackaller
Notes: *The Beano's* first redskin chum 13 years before the arrival of 'Little Plum'.

Musso The Wop (C)

No. 127 (28.12.40) – No. 203 (10.04.43)
Art: Sam Fair

The Whistling Scythe (A)

No. 127 (28.12.40) – No. 130 (18.01.41) Second Series
Synopsis: In this spin-off from the 1939 story 'Follow the Secret Hand' Prince Ivor proves that, with a scythe fashioned from his father Greatheart's sword, he is Arkania's greatest warrior.
Art: Jack Glass
Notes: For third series under this title see 1942.

The Black Witch is Waiting (S)

No. 127 (28.12.40) – No. 147 (17.05.41)
Synopsis: King Dermane of the ancient land of Ish is cursed by a wicked witch and his son, Ronald, is turned into a statue of solid gold, leaving the land to be taken over by the wicked Prince Jago. To release the kingdom from Jago's tyranny Eldric, the minstrel boy with his magic talking harp, sets forth to track down the seven dwarves who each must make an apple of gold to break the spell on Dermane and his son.
Art: George Ramsbottom

(C) Comic Strip (A) Adventure Strip (S) Prose Story (CA) Comic Adventure Strip

Notes: For semi-sequels see 1949 ('Keeper of the Magic Sword') and 1950 ('The Boy with the Wonder Horse').

1941

January

Page count reduced to 16.
First adventure strip drawn by Dudley Watkins anywhere appears as he draws the early episodes of the new 'Tom Thumb' picture strip.
'The March of the Wooden Soldiers' begins, featuring the first *Beano* artwork from Thomson staff artist Fred Sturrock.
Publication of *The Magic Comic* ceases with issue No. 80 (25.01.41), an undoubted victim of the wartime paper shortage.

February

Publication of the Thomson boys' paper *Skipper* ceases with issue No. 543 (01.02.41).

August

Due to the wartime paper shortages, fortnightly publication schedules are introduced.

Year Information

Issues for year: Nos. 128–169; price 2d; page count 18 to No.128, then 16 pages from Nos. 129–169. *Beano* published fortnightly from No. 161 (30.08.41) onwards.

Tom Thumb (CA)

No. 131 (25.01.41) – No. 315 (09.08.47) Third Series
Synopsis: Tom's adventures continue but now in the picture strip format.
Art: Dudley Watkins/James 'Peem' Walker

The March of the Wooden Soldiers (S)

No. 131 (25.01.41) – No. 146 (10.05.41)
Synopsis: Danger for Rondel the Barefoot Boy and the little country of Tronia when Mad King Karl of Hamsburg sends an army of 50 feet high wooden soldiers to invade the country.
Art: Fred Sturrock

The Boy who Bossed the Man in the Moon (S)

No. 138 (15.03.41) – No. 151 (14.06.41)
Synopsis: Sammy Dawson, the first Earth boy on the Moon, is given the job by the Moon people, the Moonkins, of making sure that the lazy 'Man in the Moon' does his job of polishing up the Moon reflectors, the devices which ensure that we on Earth always get enough moonlight.
Art: James Crighton

The Invisible Giant (S)

No. 147 (17.05.41) – No. 170 (03.01.42)
Synopsis: Cedric the orphan helps the giant Calibar, made invisible by Nejdi the wicked wizard, to find Zaid the Mysterious, the only one who can break the spell and allow Calibar to return to Giant-land.
Art: Jack Glass
Notes: For further series with the same title but different storylines see 1949 and 1957.

Waifs of the Wild West (S)

No. 148 (24.05.41) – No. 160 (23.08.41)
Synopsis: Mountie Bill Drummond helps two British youngsters, Jack and Kitty Wilson, to take control of a western ranch they have inherited.
Art: George Ramsbottom

The Magic Lollipops (Suck 'Em And See) (C)

No. 152 (21.06.41) – No. 306 (05.04.47) First Series
Art: Allan Morley
Notes: For second series see 1948.

Blacksmith Bob Eats Hay at Night (S)

No. 152 (21.06.41) – No. 168 (06.12.41)
Synopsis: Because of a spell put on him by a wizard, Black Bob, the blacksmith of Bumbleswick, turns into a horse every night at six o' clock.
Art: James Crighton

Plucky Little Nell (S)

No. 161 (30.08.41) – No.176 (28.03.42)
Synopsis: After her father is lost at Dunkirk, little Nell Dawson looks after her invalid mother and uses Horace, one of her father's old ventriloquist dummies, to foil the criminal activities of her evil uncle Ned.
Art: Jack Prout
Notes: For a reworking of this story see 1952.

The White Mouse will Get You (If You Don't Watch Out) (S)

No. 169 (20.12.41) – No. 182 (20.06.42) Second Series
Synopsis: More adventures of the police sergeant who is sometimes a mouse.
Art: James Crighton

1942

January

Page count reduced to 14.

March

'Handy Sandy' begins, the first regular *Beano* strip from artist Arthur Jackson.

April

Page count reduced to 12.

September

First combined *Magic–Beano Book* published.

November

'Jimmy's Mother Wouldn't Run Away' begins featuring the first *Beano* artwork from Thomson staff artist Jack Gordon, elder brother of Charles 'Chic' Gordon.

Year Information

Issues for year: Nos. 170–195; price 2d; page count 16 to No. 170, 14 pages from Nos. 171–177 and then 12 pages from Nos. 178–195; published fortnightly.

Handy Sandy (C)

No. 175 (14.03.42) – No. 199 (13.02.43) First Series
Art: Arthur Jackson
Notes: For second series see 1944.

The Whistling Scythe (A)

No. 176 (28.03.42) – No. 187 (29.08.42) Third Series
Synopsis: More adventures with Prince Ivor of Arkania.
Art: Jack Glass

Nobody Wanted Nancy (S)

No. 177 (11.04.42) – No. 191 (24.10.42)
Synopsis: Young and motherless Nancy Robertson, tired of being looked down upon by the snobbish relatives with whom she lives, tries to discover what has happened to her father, Vox the clown.
Art: Jack Prout

Jack in the Bottle (S)

No. 183 (04.07.42) – No. 197 (16.01.43)

Synopsis: After being apprenticed to the Wizard of the Woods a young lad is able to move himself into and out of a small bottle.
Art: James Crighton

Lone Wolf (A)

No. 188 (12.09.42) – No. 199 (13.02.43)
Synopsis: The adventures of a masked lawman in the Wild West.
Art: Dudley Watkins

Jimmy's Mother Wouldn't Run Away (S)

No. 192 (07.11.42) – No. 208 (19.06.43)
Synopsis: Jimmy Allen (a 12-year-old British boy) and his mother are evacuated to a small town in the USA only to find that it is under the control of the widow of a Chicago gangster, a woman who takes an instant dislike to the Allens and swears to run them out of town.
Art: Jack Gordon

1943

February

First appearance of *The Beano* adventure strip favourite 'The Shipwrecked Circus'.

Year Information

Issues for year: Nos. 196–221; price 2d; page count 12; published fortnightly.

The Goat with the Magic Wand (S)

No. 198 (30.01.43) – No. 215 (25.09.43)
Synopsis: The wizard Zomba is accidentally turned into a goat for six months by his young assistant Simple Simon.
Art: James Crighton

The Shipwrecked Circus (A)

No. 200 (27.02.43) – No. 221 (18.12.43) First Series
Synopsis: When the cargo ship *Margo* sinks in the South Seas, the Samson travelling circus (consisting of Samson the Strongman, his young assistant Danny, Gloopy the clown, Trixie the girl acrobat and Horace the educated chimp) find themselves castaway on Crusoe Island.
Art: Dudley Watkins (Nos. 200–212)
Jack Prout (Nos. 213–221)
Notes: For further series see 1946,1951, 1955, 1957 and 1958, the last being a reprint.

The Girl with the Golden Voice (S)

No. 209 (03.07.43) – No. 221 (18.12.43)
Synopsis: In the Wild West a young girl called Betty, with a beautiful singing voice, is entrusted into the hands of a crooked horse doctor and his wife when she is separated from her parents during an Indian raid.
Art: Jack Prout
Notes: For a reprint of this story see 'In the Clutches of the Wicked Wilsons' in 1952.

Kitty with the Coat of Many Colours (S)

No. 216 (09.10.43) – No. 226 (26.02.44)
Synopsis: Little Kitty, a young girl with a magic colour-changing camouflage cloak, tries to track down the Golden Stag with a secret message hidden in its antlers. This message can be used to usurp the wicked King Conras as it tells how he came to the throne by having his brother's son cast into the forest to die.
Art: James Crighton
Notes: A story with a similar theme had appeared in the 1942 *Beano Book* under the title 'Red Riding Hood's Rainbow Cloak'.

1944

January

First appearance of *The Beano* adventure strip favourite 'Jimmy and His Magic Patch'.

Year Information

Issues for year: Nos. 222–248; price 2d; page count 12; published fortnightly.

Jimmy and His Magic Patch (A)

No. 222 (01.01.44) – No. 239 (26.08.44) First Series
Synopsis: On his way to school one day, young Jimmy Watson saves an old gypsy's cat from the jaws of a bull terrier, tearing his pants in the process. Suitably grateful, the gypsy fixes his pants with a piece cut from a magic carpet, henceforward giving Jimmy the ability to travel back into history just by thinking about it.
Art: Dudley Watkins
Notes: For further series see 1945, 1947, 1950, 1955, 1956, 1957 and 1959.

King Kong Charlie (S)

No. 222 (01.01.44) – No. 235 (01.07.44)
Synopsis: Johnny Russell, a young boy on the run from the welfare authorities in New York, meets and befriends a showman called Whitey and his ape, King Kong Charlie.
Art: Jack Gordon

Wun Tun Joe (S)

No. 227 (11.03.44) – No. 241 (23.09.44)
Synopsis: Adventures of a plump little Chinese boy at Greytowers public school.
Art: James Crighton

The Wicked Uncle and the Terrible Twins (S)

No. 236 (15.07.44) – No. 253 (10.03.45)
Synopsis: When their father is lost on an expedition, Peter and Pam Fraser have to try and stop their South American ranch from falling into the hands of their wicked uncle Ezra.
Art: Jack Prout

Strang the Terrible (A)

No. 240 (09.09.44) – No. 235 (10.03.45)
Synopsis: Adventures in South America with the strongest man in the world as he searches for the lost city of Goz.
Art: Dudley Watkins

Handy Sandy (C)

No. 242 (07.10.44) – No. 255 (10.02.45) Second Series
Art: Arthur Jackson

Whitefang Guards the Secret Gold (S)

No. 242 (07.10.44) – No. 255 (07.04.45)
Synopsis: In the forest one day young Bart saves a golden retriever from a trap and is repaid for his kindness by having the dog bring him gold and jewels from a secret horde.
Art: James Crighton

(C) Comic Strip (A) Adventure Strip (S) Prose Story (CA) Comic Adventure Strip

1945

April

'Artful Grannie Green' begins featuring the last *Beano* work from Thomson staff artist Charles 'Chic' Gordon.

Year Information

Issues for year: Nos. 249–274; price 2d; page count 12; published fortnightly.

Six Brands for Bonnie Prince Charlie (A)

No. 254 (24.03.45) – No. 264 (11.08.45)
Synopsis: During the days of the Spanish Armada a Spanish galleon loaded with treasure sank in Tobermory Bay, and years later the MacLean of Calgary near the isle of Mull found the treasure and tattoed its whereabouts on the backs of his six sons. It is therefore the task of Red Fergie and young Coll MacDonald to track down the six MacLean sons in order to find the treasure and use it to help finance the cause of Bonnie Prince Charlie, a cause to which the MacLeans are vehemently opposed.
Art: Dudley Watkins

The Boy that Nobody Wanted (S)

No. 254 (24.03.45) – No. 267 (22.09.45)
Synopsis: Because his father is a notorious rustler and gunman, young Bob Steele has to cope with the prejudice of the townspeople of the western town of Red Gulch.
Art: Richard 'Toby' Baines

Smart Alec (C)

No. 256 (21.04.45) – No. 264 (11.08.45)
Art: Basil Blackaller

Good King Coke (C)

No. 256 (21.04.45) – No. 300 (28.12.46) Second Series
Art: Eric Roberts

Artful Grannie Green (S)

No. 256 (21.04.45) – No. 281 (06.04.46)
Art: Charles 'Chic' Gordon
Notes: This is a reprint of the 1938 series.

Jimmy and His Magic Patch (A)

No. 265 (25.08.45) – No. 299 (14.12.46) Second Series
Synopsis: More adventures in the past with Jimmy Watson.
Art: Dudley Watkins

Tick-Tock Timothy (S)

No. 268 (06.10.45) – No. 281 (06.04.46)
Synopsis: Toymaker's daughter Peggy, with the help of her father's life-size clockwork soldier creation called Timothy, sets out to rescue her father from the clutches of wicked King Bluster of Algonia.
Art: Jack Prout
Notes: For picture strip version of this story see 1956.

1946

June

'Polly Wolly Doodle' begins featuring the first *Beano* work from Thomson staff artist George Drysdale.

September

Dudley Watkins begins to sign his work with 'Lord Snooty' in No. 292 (07.09.46) and 'Jimmy and His Magic Patch' and 'Tom Thumb' in No. 293 (21.09.46).

Undateable 1946 information

George Moonie returns as Editor, replacing stand-in Stuart Gilchrist.

Year Information

Issues for year: Nos. 275–300; price 2d; page count 12; published fortnightly.

The Witch's Spell on Poor King Kell! (S)

No. 282 (20.04.46) – No. 293 (21.09.46)
Synopsis: King Kell of Mercia's dog kills the cat of Zora the witch and as a punishment the witch puts a spell on the King which makes him turn into all sorts of animals.
Art: Jack Prout

The Wishing Tree (S)

No. 282 (20.04.46) – No. 292 (07.09.46)
Art: Jack Glass
Notes: Reprints from the 1938 series.

Polly Wolly Doodle (and Her Great Big Poodle) (C)

No. 286 (15.06.46) – No. 306 (05.04.47)
Art: George Drysdale
Notes: In 1950 Polly and her 'poodle' Pongo returned as members of Lord Snooty's new gang.

Sammy Shrinko (C)

No. 287 (29.06.46) – No. 335 (15.05.48)
Art: Allan Morley

Sooty Solomon (S)

No. 293 (21.09.46) – No. 314 (26.07.47)
Synopsis: Adventures of a big black cat and his young friends from the Muffin Alley School after he inherits a shop in the will of old Betty Goodheart.
Art: Jack Prout

Ben o' the Beanstalk (S)

No. 294 (05.10.46) – No. 302 (25.01.47)
Synopsis: When young Ben Fearless is given some beanstalk-producing beans by Jack of the Beanstalk, he tries to sell them so that his father and friends can buy provisions and weapons to help in their fight with the evil Baron Hugo.
Art: Jack Prout

The Shipwrecked Circus (A)

No. 300 (28.12.46) – No. 322 (15.11.47) Second Series
Synopsis: More adventures on Crusoe Island.
Art: Dudley Watkins

Sticky Willie (C)

No. 300 (28.12.46) – No. 303 (08.02.47)
Art: Unknown

1947

January

Kent-based freelance artist Allan Morley signs his work with his initials for the first time with No. 301 (11.01.47)

February

First appearance of 'Alf Wit the Ancient Brit' featuring the first *Beano* work from the artist Bill Holroyd.

March

A month elapses between issues 305 and 306 as the scheduled issue for 22nd is not published due to production and distribution problems.

(C) Comic Strip (A) Adventure Strip (S) Prose Story (CA) Comic Adventure Strip

April

Page count reduced to 10 (the final reduction of pages due to the paper shortage).

June

No. 311 (14.06.47) is the first issue to give co-publishing credit for *The Beano* to John Leng. (The John Leng in question having been Sir John Leng (1828–1906) who started publishing in Dundee in 1852 and who had once been notable as the first publisher to attempt illustrations in a daily newspaper).

December

Last Peanut front page title logo appears.

Year Information

for year: Nos. 301–325; price 2d; page count 12 from Nos. 301–306, then 10 pages from Nos. 307–325; published fortnightly.

Wavy Davy and His Navy (C)

No. 301 (11.01.47) – No. 316 (23.08.47)
Art: Dudley Watkins/Basil Blackaller

The King on the Flying Horse (S)

No. 303 (08.02.47) – No. 314 (26.07.47)
Art: Jack Prout
Notes: Edited reprint of the 1939 series.

Alf Wit the Ancient Brit (C)

No. 304 (22.02.47) – No. 306 (05.04.47)
Art: Bill Holroyd
Notes: Devised under the working title 'Og the Caveman'.

Freddy Flipperfeet (C)

No. 315 (09.08.47) – No. 331 (20.03.48)
Art: Reg Carter

The Runaway Russells (S)

No. 315 (09.08.47) – No. 326 (10.01.48)
Synopsis: In the Old West orphans Peter and Patsy Russell run away from the house of their wicked aunt and go to live in the backwoods with their grandfather Reuben.
Art: Fred Sturrock

Jimmy and His Magic Patch (A)

No. 316 (23.08.47) – No. 354 (05.02.49)
Third Series
Art: Dudley Watkins
Notes: Last series of this strip drawn by Dudley Watkins.

Maxy's Taxi (C)

No. 317 (06.09.47) – No. 482 (13.10.51)
Art: George Drysdale

The Magic Penny (S)

No. 317 (06.09.47) – No. 326 (10.01.48)
Synopsis: In an old wishing well in Tuckleberry Wood a magic penny is found which grants anyone who holds it anything they desire.
Art: Jack Prout

Wild Boy of the Woods (A)

No. 323 (29.11.47) – No. 356 (05.03.49)
Second Series
Synopsis: More Adventures of the boy from the woods when he comes to stay in Portford, a harbour town in the South of England.
Art: Richard 'Toby' Baines

1948

January

Publication of last 'Big Eggo' cover strip.
'Winnie the Witch' begins featuring *The Beano's* first artwork from Thomson staff artist James Clark
'Peter the Penguin' begins featuring the last *Beano* artwork from freelance artist Reg Carter.
Due to the paper shortage, the page size of *The Beano* is reduced from its original 8.5 inches by 12 inches to 7 inches by 11.75 inches.
First appearance of new *Beano* cover star 'Biffo the Bear'.

October

Page count returned to 12 but only on alternate fortnights.

December

'Lucky Streak' published, featuring the last *Beano* work from artist Sam Fair.

Year Information

Issues for year: Nos. 326–351; price 2d; page count 10 from Nos. 326–344 then 12 pages in alternate issues (i.e. 12 pages in Nos. 345, 347, 349, 351, and 10 pages in Nos. 346, 348, 350); published fortnightly.

Winnie the Witch (C)

No. 326 (10.01.48) – No. 343 (04.09.48)
Art: James Clark

Peter Penguin (C)

No. 326 (10.01.48) – No. 361 (14.05.49)
Art: Reg Carter

Biffo the Bear (C)

No. 327 (24.01.48) – No. 2310 (25.10.86), then No. 2445 (27.05.89) – No. 2954 (27.02.99)
Art: Dudley Watkins, Nos. 327–1422, then Dave Sutherland and latterly Jimmy Glen. Biffo's reappearance in 1989–99 drawn by Sid Burgon.
Covers: Last front cover appearance No. 1677 (07.09.74)
Notes: After his appearance in No. 2310, Biffo did appear in three more new strips drawn by Jimmy Glen in Nos. 2315, 2322, 2337 in the 'Readers Request' feature and in one reprint strip by Dudley Watkins in the 'Old Masters' feature in No. 2399.
Biffo reappeared for a second series in *The Beano* on a regular weekly basis from No. 2445 (27.05.89) to No. 2954 (27.02.99).
Biffo's long-time chum Buster first appeared in *Beano* No. 575 (25.07.53).
Biffo appeared in two pocket-sized nursery-style *Twinkle* books in the early 1980s titled 'Biffo the Bear' and 'Biffo the Carpenter'; both were drawn by Bill Ritchie.
Biffo occasionally appeared in the nursery strip featuring his two nephews 'Cuddly and Dudley' in the revived *Magic Comic* in the years 1976–79, drawn by the Glaswegian artist Turnbull.

Sammy B. Smart in the Land of Nod (S)

No. 327 (24.01.48) – No. 335 (15.05.48)
Art: Fred Sturrock
Notes: Partial reprint of the 1939 story 'The Little Joker in the Land of Nod'.

(C) Comic Strip (A) Adventure Strip (S) Prose Story (CA) Comic Adventure Strip

Cocky Jock (C)
No. 332 (03.04.48) – No. 353 (22.01.49)
Art: George Drysdale

Swanky Lanky Liz (C)
No. 336 (29.05.48) – No. 368 (06.08.49)
Art: Charles Holt
Notes: Liz returned as a member of Lord Snooty's new gang in 1950.

The Boy with the Magic Masks (S)
No. 336 (29.05.48) – No. 342 (21.08.48)
Art: Fred Sturrock
Notes: Partial reprint of 1940 story.

Smarty Smokum (and His Pipe of Peace) (C)
No. 337 (12.06.48) – No. 385 (03.12.49)
Art: Allan Morley

Sir Tom Thumb (A)
No. 343 (04.09.48) – No. 356 (05.03.49) Fourth Series
Synopsis: Tom Thumb is given certain tasks to perform to prove himself worthy of being dubbed an English knight by the king.
Art: James Crighton

The Hungry Goodwins (S)
No. 343 (04.09.48) – No. 352 (08.01.49)
Synopsis: Two children Jeff and Nell Goodwin, in search of their father, are helped by Dick Turpin the legendary highwayman.
Art: Fred Sturrock
Notes: For picture strip reprint of the above see 1951. A similar story in strip form entitled 'Runaways with Turpin' appeared in 1955. Dick Turpin returned again in picture strip form as a special investigator in 1959.

Hairy Hugh and His Cockatoo (C)
No. 343 (04.09.48) – No. 361 (14.05.49)
Art: Basil Blackaller

The Magic Lollipops (C)
No. 344 (18.09.48) – No. 475 (25.08.51)
Second Series
Art: Allan Morley

Big Bill – The Mascot Nobody Wanted (S)
No. 345 (02.10.48); one-off feature
Synopsis: This, the first of a series of one-off lucky mascot stories, tells of Simba, a young cabin boy on a pearl fishing boat in the Indian Ocean who adopts a pelican as a pet, much to the annoyance of the rest of the crew.
Art: Fred Sturrock

Jumping Jenny (S)
No. 347 (30.10.48); one-off feature
Synopsis: Another mascot story, this time in which a kangaroo and a koala bear become the mascots of some Australian gold miners.
Art: Jack Gordon

Can Guy Fox You?
No. 347 (30.10.48); one-off feature
Synopsis: Guy Fawkes Puzzles.

High Guy the Mascot with a Lucky Tail (S)
No. 349 (27.11.48); one-off feature
Synopsis: How a plucky little squirrel saves the lives of two steeple-jacks.
Art: Fred Sturrock

Lucky Streak (S)
No. 351 (25.12.48); one-off feature
Synopsis: On board the whaling ship *Barga* a stowaway cat has trouble with the cat-hating captain.
Art: Sam Fair

1949

February
First appearance of popular *Beano* adventure strip character 'Jack Flash – the Flying Boy' featuring the last new *Beano* adventure strip art from Dudley Watkins.

March
After five months of alternating 10 and 12 page issues, the page count stabilises at 12.
'The Taylors' Goose' appears, featuring the last *Beano* artwork from Thomson staff artist Jack Prout.

April
'Sam Spitfire' appears, featuring the last *Beano* artwork from Thomson staff artist Jack Gordon.
'Big Eggo' artist Reg Carter dies on April 24, aged 62.

July
Weekly publication of *The Beano* recommences, each issue being available every Friday instead of Tuesday as had previously been the case.
With issue No. 367 (30.07.49), exactly 11 years after its debut, the first *Beano* era draws to a close when the first 'Lord Snooty' series ends, leaving no original first issue item within the comic. (After a similar number of issues *The Dandy* still contained five of its original features: Korky the Cat, Desperate Dan, Keyhole Kate, Hungry Horace and Freddy the Fearless Fly.)
First appearance of 'Deep-Sea Danny's Iron Fish' whose adventures would eventually run to fifteen series, a record for *The Beano*.

August
Full colour comes to *The Beano* back page to celebrate the commencement of Pansy Potter's second series in which she becomes a temporary resident of Wonderland.

September
Last combined *Magic–Beano Book* published.
After being available every Friday for two months, *The Beano* changes its publication day to Thursday, which it has remained to the present day.
The third series of 'Little Dead-Eye Dick' begins, featuring the last *Beano* artwork from artist Charles Holt.

November
First appearance of popular 1950s *Beano* adventure strip character 'Tick-Tock Tony – the Clockwork Horse' in 'The Horse that Jack Built'.

Year Information
Issues for year: Nos. 352–389; price 2d; page count 10 for Nos. 352, 354, 356 and 12 pages for Nos. 353, 355, 357–389. Published fortnightly to No. 366 (23.07.49), then published every Friday to No. 375 (24.09.49), after which *The Beano* was published every Thursday.
First *Beano* full-colour back page, No. 369 (13.08.49).

Keeper of the Magic Sword (S)
No. 353 (22.01.49) – No. 363 (11.06.49)
Fourth Series
Synopsis: In a semi-sequel to the 1939 story 'Follow the Secret Hand' Eldric the Blacksmith's boy holds the sword of the dead King Greatheart in safe keeping while waiting for the exiled Prince Ivor to return to wrest the throne of Marania from the clutches of evil King Otto.
Art: Fred Sturrock

Black Flash the Beaver (S)
No. 353 (22.01.49); one-off
Synopsis: In Newfoundland, the adventures of the mascot with the best set of teeth in the world.
Art: Jack Gordon

Have-A-Go Joe (C)
No. 354 (05.02.49) – No. 458 (28.04.51) First Series
Art: Bill Holroyd
Notes: For further series see 'The Beano Cinema' (1951)

Jack Flash – The Flying Boy (A)
No. 355 (19.02.49) – No. 388 (24.12.49) First Series
Synopsis: The town of Colbay in Cornwall is visited by Jack Flash, the flying boy from Mercury with wings on his feet.
Art: Dudley Watkins: Nos. 355–366 Fred Sturrock: Nos. 367–388
Notes: For further series see 1950–51 and 1955–58

Buster – The World's Mightiest Mascot (S)
No. 355 (19.02.49); one-off
Synopsis: In the Sahara Desert the men of the Foreign Legion fort of Aziba have to cope with their stubborn mascot, Buster the mule.
Art: Jack Prout

The Invisible Giant (CA)
No. 357 (19.03.49) – No. 362 (28.05.49) First Series
Synopsis: In the land of Caronia, Hector the cobbler's lad makes the 30-foot high giant Presto, who is always getting into trouble, a pair of magic boots which render him invisible.
Art: James Clark
Notes: For further series see December 1949 and 1957. The1941 story with the same title not part of this series.

The Taylor's Goose (S)
No. 357 (19.03.49); one-off
Synopsis: Set in 1868 in the American Rockies, this is the incredible story of a goose that saves nine lives.
Art: Jack Prout

Tricky Dicky Ant (C)
No. 358 (02.04.49) – No. 374 (17.09.49) Second Series
Art: James Clark/Allan Morley

Sam Spitfire (S)
No. 358 (02.04.49); one-off
Synopsis: The story of three mounties in British Columbia who have a wolverine as a lucky mascot.
Art: Jack Gordon

Skinny Flint – The Meanest Uncle in the World (S)
No. 359 (16.04.49) – No. 366 (23.07.49)
Synopsis: When orphan Mickey Dixon comes to live with his miserly uncle Silas, he uses his ability as a ventriloquist to try and get the old man to change his ways.
Art: James 'Peem' Walker
Notes: A comic strip titled 'Skinny Flint' appeared in *The Beano* in 1951.

Wandering Willie (C)
No. 362 (28.05.49) – No. 368 (06.08.49)
Art: Bill Holroyd
Notes: 'Wandering Willie' appeared as 'See the World Sam' in the boys' paper *Wizard* in 1954, again drawn by Bill Holroyd.

Little Dead-Eye Dick (C)
No. 362 (28.05.49) – No. 368 (06.08.49) Second Series
Art: Charles Holt

Wild Boy (A)
No. 363 (11.06.49) – No. 366 (23.07.49) Third Series
Synopsis: Adventures with the wild boy in Africa as he tracks down 12 hoopoe birds for Melson's Circus.
Art: Richard 'Toby' Baines

Young Strongarm the Axe Man (C)
No. 364 (25.06.49) – No. 370 (20.08.49) Second Series
Synopsis: Strongarm helps a group of Saxon children to escape from their Norman captors and reach the safety of the Isle of Ely.
Art: Fred Sturrock

Little Noah's Ark (A)
No. 367 (30.07.49) – No. 376 (01.10.49)
Synopsis: Picture strip version of the 1940 story with the same name.
Art: James Clark

Deep-Sea Danny's Iron Fish (S)
No. 367 (30.07.49) – No. 382 (12.11.49) First Series
Synopsis: In the Coral Sea professor Jim Gray builds a mechanical swordfish which is piloted by his 12-year-old son Danny.
Art: Jack Glass
Notes: For further series see 1950 (2 series, both prose stories), then henceforth all adventure strips: 1951–57, 1958 (series), and 1964–66

Ding-Dong Belle (C)
No. 368 (06.08.49) – No. 465 (16.06.51)
Art: Bill Holroyd

Pansy Potter in Wonderland (C)
No. 369 (13.08.49) – No. 652 (15.01.55) Second Series
Synopsis: Pansy finds a set of steps inside an old wishing well which lead her to Wonderland.
Art: James Clark
Notes: Pansy remained in Wonderland until issue No. 590 (07.11.53), when she returned home and the words 'in Wonderland' were dropped from the title.
Pansy's last full-colour back page strip appeared in issue No. 603 (06.02.54), after which she continued her adventures in a two-colour two-line strip within the comic until the end of the series.

The Adventures of Tom Thumb (S)
No. 371 (27.08.49) – No. 384 (26.11.49) Fifth Series
Synopsis: When Eldred the blind boy overhears a plot to kill Richard the Lionheart on his return from the Crusades, Tom Thumb leads Eldred to warn the King.
Art: Fred Sturrock

Little Dead-Eye Dick (C)
No. 375 (24.09.49) – No. 410 (27.05.50) Third Series
Art: Charles Holt

Chingo the Fearless (CA)
No. 377 (08.10.49) – No. 381 (05.11.49)
Synopsis: When Jess and Jim Walker arrive at

their father's trading post at Lothi in Africa, they befriend Chingo the chimpanzee, who keeps them safe from the dangers of the jungle.
Art: James Clark

The Horse that Jack Built (CA)

No. 382 (12.11.49) – No. 399 (11.03.50) First Series
Synopsis: In Merrie England, to escape the evil tax collector Baron Grimface, Cedric the Toymaker and his wife flee from the town of Carlton with the help of their young son Jack and his self-made clockwork horse, Tick-Tock Tony.
Art: Bill Holroyd
Notes: For further series see 1950 (titled 'Tick-Tock Tony – the Clockwork Horse') 1954–55, 1956 (titled 'Stop That Horse'), and 1957

Sandy's Magic Bagpipes (S)

No. 383 (19.11.49) – No. 390 (07.01.50)
Synopsis: Sandy MacPherson is given a set of old bagpipes by his grandad and one day, while practising on them in the hills, his music awakens a group of Highlanders, led by Sandy's ancestor Rory Macpherson, who have been asleep in a cave since 1745 thanks to a witch's spell.
Art: Jack Glass

The Invisible Giant (S)

No. 385 (03.12.49) – No. 391 (14.01.50)
Second Series
Synopsis: Presto helps a bewitched prince who has been turned into a mouse.
Art: Fred Sturrock

Danger! Len at Work (C)

No. 386 (10.12.49) – No. 410 (27.05.50)
Art: Bill Holroyd

The Runaway Robinsons (A)

No. 389 (03.12.49) – No. 409 (20.05.50)
Synopsis: Separated from their father after a shipwreck, two twins *Judy* (a cripple) and Jim Robinson, are rescued by lifeboat but soon find themselves on the run from the police when they are accused of theft.
Art: Fred Sturrock

1950

March

'Sinbad the Sailor' begins featuring the first artwork for the weekly *Beano* from Irish artist Paddy Brennan.

June

'Sammy's Super Rubber' begins, the last new comic strip for *The Beano* from artist Allan Morley.
The page size of *The Beano* returns to 8.5 inches by 12 inches.
The word Comic is dropped from *The Beano* title.

September

The first non-amalgamated *The Beano Book* since 1942 is published. It is also the first which credits John Leng as co-publisher.

December

'Lord Snooty' returns for a second series with a few new pals.

Year Information

Issues for year: Nos. 390–441; Price 2d; page count 12; published every Thursday. Page size returns to 8.5 inches by 12 inches with No. 411 (03.06.50). With No. 412 (10.06.50) the word Comic is dropped from the front page *Beano* title.

The Ticklish Tasks of Billy Barrel (S)

No. 391 (14.01.50) – No. 403 (08.04.50)
Synopsis: In the country of Campania, Billy Barrel, the local window cleaner, becomes the royal tax gatherer and on his first assignment is given a wild man from Borneo in exchange for payment.
Art: George Drysdale

Bob in the Bottle (S)

No. 392 (21.01.50) – No. 402 (01.04.50)
Art: Fred Sturrock
Notes: Reprint of the 1942 story 'Jack in the Bottle'. For new series of adventures see 1951.

Sinbad the Sailor (A)

No. 400 (18.03.50) – No. 415 (01.07.50) First Series
Synopsis: The adventures of the world's most famous young sailor with his pal Peg Leg and monkey *Bimbo*.
Art: Paddy Brennan
Notes: For second series in the prose format see 1951, and for the third series in the adventure strip format see 1958.

Deep-Sea Danny's Iron Fish (S)

No. 402 (01.04.50) – No. 408 (13.05.50)
Second Series
Synopsis: Danny investigates the case of the monster of Loch Linn.
Art: Jack Glass

The Boy with the Wonder Horse (S)

No. 404 (15.04.50) – No. 411 (03.06.50) Fifth Series
Synopsis: In this final sequel to the 1939 story 'Follow the Secret Hand', Edric the blacksmith's boy, riding a horse shod with magic shoes, tries to track down King Ivor's magic sword, which has been stolen by the wicked magician Merla.
Art: Fred Sturrock

Ting-A-Ling Bill (S)

No. 409 (20.05.50) – No. 423 (26.08.50)
Synopsis: The most peculiar story of a big ape from Pepp's Circus who roams the wild west with his favourite toy, a prison door with a bell on it!
Art: Jack Glass

Jack Flash – The Flying Boy (A)

No. 410 (27.05.50) – No. 429 (07.10.50)
Second Series
Synopsis: Fun when Jack takes on the job of looking after four children while their parents are away tending a sick relative.
Art: Fred Sturrock

Sammy's Super Rubber (C)

No. 411 (03.06.50) – No. 451 (10.03.51)
Art: Allan Morley

The Wily Ways of Simple Simon (S)

No. 412 (10.06.50) – No. 421 (12.08.50)
Synopsis: Simon Simkin, a farmer's boy, finds a mysterious old bottle while ploughing, the contents of which when sniffed by an animal make the animal invisible.
Art: George Drysdale
Notes: For second series, this time in strip form, see 1951.

Jimmy and His Magic Patch (A)

No. 416 (08.07.50) – No. 452 (17.03.51)
Fourth Series
Synopsis: More adventures in the past with Jimmy Watson.
Art: Paddy Brennan

Deep-Sea Danny's Iron Fish (S)

No. 422 (19.08.50) – No. 435 (18.11.50) Third Series
Synopsis: In the southern Pacific Danny is forced by the native chief Zago to collect rare underwater speciments for his aquarium.
Art: Jack Glass

Tom Thumb's Schooldays (S)

No. 424 (02.09.50) – No. 441 (30.12.50)
Sixth Series
Synopsis: Tom and his cat Peterkin help to keep an outlawed school going when the evil Baron Dubold outlaws education for the local villagers.
Art: George Drysdale

Tick-Tock Tony – The Clockwork Horse (A)

No. 430 (14.10.50) – No. 447 (10.02.51)
Second Series
Synopsis: In this sequel to 'The Horse that Jack Built' Jack's mechanical horse built in 1250 ends up 700 years later in the Eastdale Museum where, after seven centuries, young Mickey Mills brings it back to life.
Art: Bill Holroyd

The Bird Boy (S)

No. 436 (25.11.50) – No. 448 (17.02.51) First Series
Synopsis: The story of a wild boy who roams the Antarctic wastes with his giant albatross pet.
Art: Jack Glass
Notes: For further series, all in the adventure strip format, see 1952, 1954 and 1956.

Lord Snooty and His Pals (C)

No. 440 (23.12.50) – No. 811 (01.02.58)
Second Series
Art: Nos. 440 – 690: Dudley Watkins
Nos. 691 – 718: Leo Baxendale
Nos. 719 – 811: reprints

1951

March

'The Quick Tricks of Granny Green' begins featuring the final weekly artwork for *The Beano* from Thomson staff artist George Ramsbottom. 'Dennis the Menace', probably the most popular of all *Beano* comic characters, makes his first appearance. The art, by Thomson staff artist Davey Law, was his first for *The Beano*.

May

'Skinny Flint' begins, featuring the last weekly *Beano* artwork from artist Basil Blackaller.

August

First appearance of popular *Beano* adventure character 'Red Rory of the Eagles'.

November

'Wee Peem's Magic Pills' begins featuring the first *Beano* artwork from artist Charles Grigg.

Year Information

Issues for year: Nos. 442–493; price 2d; page count 12; published every Thursday.

Bob in the Bottle (S)

No. 442 (06.01.51) – No. 451 (10.03.51)
Synopsis: New adventures of the boy who can magic himself into and out of a bottle by incanting a wizard's spell.
Art: Fred Sturrock

The Hungry Little Goodwins (A)

No. 448 (17.02.51) – No. 455 (07.04.51)
Synopsis: Picture story adaption of the 1948 prose story 'The Hungry Goodwins'.
Art: Fred Sturrock

Tommy's Clockwork Town (S)

No. 449 (24.02.51) – No. 466 (23.06.51) First Series
Synopsis: Fun with the son of a New York bus driver when he discovers the robot inhabited clockwork town built by the inventor Professor Corker.
Art: Bill Holroyd
Notes: For further series see 'Tommy's Clockwork Brother' (1952).

The Quick Tricks of Granny Green (S)

No. 452 (17.03.51) – No. 460 (12.05.51) Second Series
Synopsis: Further adventures of Jimmy Green, the boy who impersonates his own grandmother.
Art: George Ramsbottom

Dennis the Menace (C)

No. 452 (17.03.51) – present
Art: Nos. 452–1462: Davey Law
Notes: Dennis also appeared in a half page strip in Thomson's tabloid magazine cum-newspaper *The Weekly News* from issue No. 5134 (07.11.53) – No. 5331 (17.08.57), as well as being given his own fun section in the whole 87 issue run of the boys' comic *Champ* in 1984–85. The fun section also featured reprints of 'Send for Kelly' (*Topper*) by George Martin, 'Puss 'n' Boots' (*Sparky*) by John Geering, and new 'I-Spy' strips drawn by Brian Walker.

Jack Flash and the Terrible Twins (A)

No. 453 (24.03.51) – No. 484 (27.10.51) Third Series
Synopsis: Jack's parents, Pa and Ma Flash, come to Earth from Mercury and bring Jack's small twin brother and sister, Jet and Jane, with them to visit their big brother.
Art: Paddy Brennan

The Wily Ways of Simple Simon (CA)

No. 456 (14.04.51) – No. 463 (02.06.51) Second Series
Synopsis: Picture strip continuation of the 1950 prose story.
Art: George Drysdale

Skinny Flint (C)

No. 459 (05.05.51) – No. 475 (25.08.51)
Art: Basil Blackaller

Jack of Clubs (S)

No. 461 (19.05.51) – No. 472 (04.08.51) First Series
Synopsis: Jack Osmand, a young lad brought up by a band of gypsies, is a marksman with wooden throwing clubs, a skill which he uses to try and regain his rightful title as the local lord of the manor from the evil Black Bart.
Art: Jack Glass
Notes: For second series in strip form see 1955.

(C) Comic Strip (A) Adventure Strip (S) Prose Story (CA) Comic Adventure Strip

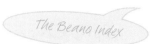

Bucktooth – The Boy Who Lives in a Barrel (C)
No. 464 (09.06.51) – No. 487 (17.11.51) First Series
Synopsis: The adventures of a lad in the Old West who carries his home around with him.
Art: Bill Holroyd
Notes: For Second Series see 1952.

The Iron Fish (A)
No. 467 (30.06.51) – No. 476 (01.09.51) Fourth Series
Synopsis: The first 'Iron Fish' series in the adventures strip format sees Danny Gray and five other young pilots setting out to deliver six Iron Fish, built by Danny's father, to the British Government, all the while being tracked by the evil Captain Sun who seeks to waylay the mechanical fish and sell them to a hostile foreign government.
Art: Bill Holroyd

The Beano Cinema (C)
No. 468 (07.07.51) – No. 485 (03.11.51) Second Series
Art: Bill Holroyd
Notes: This contains two separate serials, the first ten-parter titled 'Secret Agent' and the second eight-parter titled 'Bodyguard'.

Smarty Smokey (S)
No. 473 (11.08.51) – No. 484 (27.10.51) First Series
Synopsis: Smarty Smokey, an apprentice genie, is sent by his master, the genie Mysto, to attend school at the Holly Academy for boys in Britain.
Art: James Clark
Notes: For further series see 1952 (titled 'Smarty Smokey's Classmates'), January 1954 (titled 'Smarty Smokey the Genie in the six Gun') and July 1954 (titled 'Shorty's Magic Six Gun').

Red Rory of the Eagles (S)
No. 477 (08.09.51) – No. 485 (03.11.51) First Series
Synopsis: In 1747, two years after the Great Rebellion. young Rory Macpherson from Black Mountain in Inverness-shire uses his two eagle pets Flame and Fury to fight his own war against the English redcoats.
Art: Jack Glass
Notes: For further series, all in the adventure strip format, see 1952–54, 1955 (2 series), 1956–57, 1958 (2 series), 1959, 1962.

Willie's Wonder Gun (C)
No. 483 (20.10.51) – No. 499 (09.02.52)
Art: James Clark

The Shipwrecked Circus (A)
No. 485 (03.11.51) – No. 5050 (22.03.52)
Third Series
Synopsis: More adventures with the Robinson Crusoesque members of Samson's Circus.
Art: Paddy Brennan

Willie in the Lost World (S)
No. 485 (03.11.51) – No. 490 (08.12.51)
Synopsis: Shades of the 1938 picture strip 'In the Land of the Silver Dwarves' when young Willie Brown and his sheepdog Rex get lost in a cavern and stumble on an ancient subterranean world of dwarves and strange creatures.
Art: James Clark

Wee Peem's Magic Pills (C)
No. 486 (10.11.51) – No. 507 (05.04.52)
Second Series
Synopsis: Wee Peem has fun with a bottle of strange pills which fall from Dr. Quack's medicine truck.
Art: Charles Grigg

Goggo – The Wizard in the Goldfish Bowl (S)
No. 486 (10.11.51) – No. 501 (23.02.52)
Synopsis: Laughs when young Jimmy Wilson buys a goldfish from a Hindu salesman which has the power to hypnotise.
Art: Davey Law

Hawkeye – Bravest of the Braves (A)
No. 488 (24.11.51) – No. 493 (29.12.51)
Synopsis: The old Red Indian keeper of the Forbidden Forest dies and entrusts Hawkeye, a young Indian brave, with the mystical hunting horn, an instrument with which he can control all the forest animals.
Art: Richard 'Toby' Baines

Sinbad on the Island of Fear (S)
No. 491 (15.12.51) – No. 496 (19.01.52) Second Series
Synopsis: On the island of Moluk Sinbad helps a race of centaurs escape the power of Gringa the Giant.
Art: Paddy Brennan

1952

March
'Multy the Millionaire' begins, featuring the first weekly *Beano* artwork from artist Richard Cox.

April
'The Stick-em-up Picture Competition' appears as the first *Beano* competition.

May
London-born Thomson staff artist Charles 'Chic' Gordon, whose *Beano* credits included 'Hooky's Magic Bowler Hat' dies on May 9.
'Wee Davie and the Great Big Giant' begins, featuring the first weekly *Beano* artwork from artist Ken Hunter.
'The Whatizzit? Competition' features the last *Beano* artwork from Thomson staff artist Fred Sturrock.

June
Due to industrial action *The Beano* has distribution problems between No. 517 (14.06.52) and No. 528 (30.08.52).
'Little Noah's Ark' begins, featuring the last weekly *Beano* artwork from Thomson staff artist Richard 'Toby' Baines.

November
'The Nippers' begins featuring the last weekly *Beano* comic strip work from artist Richard Cox.

Year Information
Issues for year: Nos. 494–545; price 2d; page count 12; published every Thursday.

Runaway Jack (A)
No. 494 (05.01.52) – No. 502 (01.03.52)
Synopsis: A young lad named Jack Kidd runs away to sea and accidentally becomes a cabin boy on the pirate ship *Sea Vulture*.
Art: Bill Holroyd

Rolling Jones (S)
No. 497 (26.01.52) – No. 504 (15.03.52)
Synopsis: Giant Welshman Stalky Jones pushes a giant hand-roller from his village in Wales to his Uncle's house in London.
Art: James Clark

Multy the Millionaire (C)
No. 500 (16.02.52) – No. 559 (04.04.53)
Art: Richard Cox

Mickey's Magic Bone (S)
No. 502 (01.03.52) – No. 517 (14.06.52) First Series
Synopsis: Mickey Watson fishes a telephone receiver-shaped bone out of a stream and finds that with it he can talk to any dog.
Art: Davey Law
Notes: For second series see 1953. See also 'Slave to the Talking Horse' (1954).

Bucktooth – The Boy Who Lives in a Barrel (C)
No. 503 (08.03.52) – No. 512 (10.05.52) Second Series
Art: Bill Holroyd

Grip (A)
No. 503 (08.03.52) – No. 512 (10.05.52)
Synopsis: In the wilds of Canada an alsatian dog named Grip is entrusted with delivering the secret map of his sick master's gold strike to his brother.
Art: Richard 'Toby' Baines

Young Robin Hood (S)
No. 505 (22.03.52) – No. 510 (26.04.52)
Synopsis: The early exploits of the hero of Sherwood, in this instance helped in his conflict with the Sheriff of Nottingham by a dwarf who has strange power over the wild forest animals.
Art: Jack Glass

The Iron Fish (A)
No. 506 (29.03.52) – No. 515 (31.05.52) Fifth Series
Synopsis: When Danny Gray and his father discover The Magical Blinding Shield in a chest on the seabed they run into trouble with the evil witch doctor Kala the cruel.
Art: Bill Holroyd

The Stick-em-up Picture Competition
No. 509 (19.04.52) – No. 512 (10.05.52) Feature
Art: Fred Sturrock
Notes: A competition with prizes of cowboy and cowgirl outfits and cowboy guns, etc.

Tommy's Clockwork Brother (S)
No. 511 (03.05.52) – No. 519 (28.06.52) Second Series
Synopsis: Tommy Tucker and Professor Corker come to England and Tommy attends Cockle College with one of the Professor's clockwork people acting as his 'big brother'.
Art: Bill Holroyd

Wee Davie and the Great Big Giant (CA)
No. 513 (17.05.52) – No. 518 (21.06.52) First Series
Synopsis: In the country of Pomegrania Wee Davie is given the job of Royal Giant Tamer by King Willie.
Art: Ken Hunter
Notes: For further series see 1953, 1954 (2 series), 1955 (2 series) and 1957.

The Whatizzit? Competition
No. 514 (24.05.52) – No. 517 (14.06.52) Feature
Art: Fred Sturrock/James Crighton
Notes: Prizes of Revojet planes and nurses outfits.

Red Rory of the Eagles (A)
No. 516 (07.06.52) – No. 523 (26.07.52) Second Series
Synopsis: In 1746 Rory leads three of his Jacobite kinsmen to Tobermory Bay in the hope that they can escape to the safety of France.
Art: Paddy Brennan

Little Noah's Ark (S)
No. 518 (21.06.52) – No. 523 (26.07.52)
Synopsis: More adventures with Noah Carter, the boy who lives in the wilds of Canada with his floating 'ark' of wild animals.,
Art: Richard 'Toby' Baines

Wildfire – The Magic Horse (A)
No. 519 (28.06.52) – No. 522 (19.07.52)
Synopsis: In this sequel to the 1938 story 'Prince on the Flying Horse', Cedric, the son of a blacksmith in the country of Morania, is given a magic sword which gives his horse Wildfire the ability to fly, and it is Cedric's mission to return the throne of Morania to its rightful ruler Prince Dermod and overthrow the evil King Karl. (Note: Some names have been changed).
Art: Ken Hunter

Smarty Smokey's Classmates (S)
No. 520 (05.07.52) – No. 527 (23.08.52) Second Series
Synopsis: Mr Brown, Smokey's teacher at Holly Academy, does such a good job at teaching him that Mysto sends all his other apprentice genies to be taught at the school.
Art: James Clark

Ali Ha Ha and the Potty Thieves (CA)
No. 523 (26.07.52) – No. 534 (11.10.52)
Synopsis: The young bazaar owner Ali Ha Ha continually foils the criminal ploys of Sidi El Bong and his Potty Thieves.
Art: Ken Hunter

Waifs of the Wild West (A)
No. 524 (02.08.52) – No. 531 (20.09.52)
Synopsis: The same title as a 1941 story but with a different script. In this tale young Dick and Nora Brady travel through the Wild West to deliver supplies of seeds to farmers on the frontier.
Art: Bill Holroyd

TV Stevie – The Boy on Hookey's Wrist (S)
No. 524 (02.08.52) – No. 535 (18.10.52)
Synopsis: Hookey Walker retrieves a wristwatch from an alien spacecraft which has crashed on Earth, and finds that it puts him in visual and verbal contact with the distant futuristic Planet TV.
Art: George Drysdale

Kat and Kanary (C)
No. 526 (16.08.52) – No. 713 (17.03.56) First Series
Art: Charles Grigg/Leo Baxendale
Notes: For further series see 1957–58, and also see the 1957 Puzzle feature 'Kat's Krazy Korner'.

Plucky Little Nellie Kelly (S)
No. 528 (30.08.52) – No. 541 (29.11.52)
Synopsis: Reworking of the 1941 prose story 'Plucky Little Nell'.
Art: James Clark

The Bird Boy (A)
No. 532 (27.09.52) – No. 536 (25.10.52) Second Series
Synopsis: More adventures with Kelvin Wayne, the son of a dead explorer, who lives in the Antarctic wastes with his pet albatross Harrk.
Art: Paddy Brennan

Nobby – The Enchanted Bobby (CA)
No. 535 (18.10.52) – No. 563 (02.05.53) First Series
Synopsis: Laughs when, unknown to him, PC

(C) Comic Strip (A) Adventure Strip (S) Prose Story (CA) Comic Adventure Strip

Nobby Clark has the toe cap of his boot replaced with a piece of metal from a magic lamp which grants him every wish, both good and bad, that he innocently utters.
Art: Bill Holroyd
Notes: For second series see 1953

Catapult Jack (S)
No. 536 (25.10.52) – No. 544 (20.12.52)
Synopsis: Young Jack Shaw, the son of a Canadian trapper, sets out to stop a tribe of Red Indians from going on the warpath.
Art: Jack Glass

The Nippers (C)
No. 537 (01.11.52) – No. 550 (31.01.53)
Art: Richard Cox

Big Bazooka (CA)
No. 537 (01.11.52) – No. 552 (14.02.53)
Synopsis: The adventures on a South African ostrich farm of Sammy Parker and his huge ostrich pet, Big Bazooka.
Art: Charles Grigg

The Boy on the Flying Trapeze (S)
No. 542 (06.12.52) – No. 549 (24.01.53)
Synopsis: The Wild West adventures of young Tommy Simson, the brilliant trapeze artist of Boffin's Mammoth Circus and Menagerie.
Art: James Clark

In the Clutches of the Wicked Wilsons (S)
No. 545 (27.12.52) – No. 556 (14.03.53)
Synopsis: Reprint of the 1943 story 'The Girl with the Golden Voice'.
Art: James 'Peem' Walker

1953

January
'Percy from the Pole Star' begins featuring the last weekly *Beano* artwork from Thomson staff artist James Crighton.

February
Ex-*Beano* chief Sub-Editor Ron Fraser is made Editor of the new Thomson tabloid comic *The Topper*. The first issue appears on February 7.

April
Beano favourite 'Roger the Dodger' makes his debut, featuring the first *Beano* artwork from artist Ken Reid.

September
First appearance of *Beano* comic favourite 'Little Plum', featuring the first *Beano* artwork from artist Leo Baxendale.

December
First appearance of *The Beano's* female menace 'Minnie the Minx'.
The number of weekly prose stories in *The Beano* reduced from two to one with issue No. 597 (26.12.53).

Undateable 1950s information
By 1953 the editorial staff of *The Beano* comprised Editor George Moonie, Chief Sub-Editor Ken Walmsley (who had worked on *The Dandy* in its early days), Harold Cramond in charge of adventure strips, and Walter Fearn. Other *Beano* staff members who would come along in the 1950s included Derek Reid (who left in 1959), Jimmy 'Jasper' Thomson and Ian Gray.

Year Information
Issues for year: Nos. 546–597; price 2d; page count 12; published every Thursday.

Percy From the Pole Star (S)
No. 550 (31.01.53) – No. 563 (02.05.53)
Synopsis: Young Buster Brown teams up with the alien Percy, who has come to Earth to study its people and their habits.
Art: James Crighton

Red Rory of the Eagles (A)
No. 553 (21.02.53) – No. 567 (30.05.53)
Third Series
Synopsis: To aid the cause of Bonnie Prince Charlie, Rory sets out to track down the various objects which will reveal the hiding place of the treasure of the clan chief Callum More.
Art: Paddy Brennan

Cast-Iron Stan – Circus Superman (S)
No. 557 (21.03.53) – No. 566 (25.05.53)
Synopsis: The story of 'Cast-Iron' Bar, the roughest, toughest circus boss in the world.
Art: Bill Holroyd

Roger the Dodger (C)
No. 561 (18.04.53) – No. 928 (30.04.60)
Art: 1953–59: Ken Reid
1959–60: Gordon Bell
Notes: For second series see 1961. Roger also had his own 'Dodge Clinic' feature in *The Beano* from 1986–88, then sporadically in 1989. A one-off feature titled 'Roger the Toddler, drawn by Robert Nixon, also appeared in *The Beano* in 1989.

Mickey's Magic Bone (S)
No. 564 (09.05.53) – No. 573 (11.07.53)
Second Series
Synopsis: More adventures with the lad who can understand the language of dogs.
Art: George Drysdale

Desperate Days for Deep-Sea Danny (A)
No. 564 (09.05.53) – No. 571 (27.06.53) Sixth Series
Synopsis: Danny and a pilot he has saved during a storm at sea are washed ashore on an island inhabited by strange web-footed Fish Men.
Art: Jack Glass

'Pick the Tricky Triplets' Coronation Competition
No. 564 (09.05.53) – No. 565 (16.05.53) Feature
Art: Dudley Watkins/Charles Grigg
Notes: Prizes of Coronation 5/– pieces and sets of Coronation coins.

Nutty – The Coal Imp (S)
No. 567 (30.05.53) – No. 598 (02.01.54)
Synopsis: Ten year-old Peter Wilson finds Nutty, a tiny magical coal imp who has been imprisoned in a lump of coal by the Coal Wizard for stealing his magic spells.
Art: Bill Holroyd
Notes: For second series see 1954.
The title of this series was changed to 'Nutty the Wizard up our Chimney' with No. 587 (17.10.53).

Wee Davie – Big Game Hunter (CA)

No. 568 (06.06.53) – No. 583 (19.09.53) Second Series
Synopsis: Wee Davie the Pomegranian Giant Tamer is sent by King Willie to find unusual animal with which to restock the Pomegranian Zoo.
Art: Ken Hunter

Big Hugh – and You (The Comic With You in it!) (C)

No. 572 (04.07.53) – No. 585 (03.10.53)
Synopsis: The comic exploits of Big Hugh the hick who talks to *Beano* readers throughout his adventures.
Art: Bill Holroyd

The Magic Bottle (S)

No. 574 (18.07.53) – No. 581 (05.09.53)
Synopsis: Danny Dixon is the owner of a strange bottle with a hinged mirrored lid, and any creature looking into the mirror becomes small and disappears into the bottle.
Art: James 'Peem' Walker

Uncle Windbag (That Story Teller Feller) (C)

No. 579 (22.08.53) – No. 596 (19.12.53) Second Series
Art: Charles Grigg

Runaways with Grandad (S)

No. 582 (12.09.53) – No. 596 (19.12.53)
Synopsis: Two young orphans, Jim and Jane Richmond, start a new life on their grandad's lonely ranch in the Wild West and stumble across a strange and terrifying mystery.
Art: James 'Peem' Walker

General Jumbo (A)

No. 584 (19.09.53) – No. 599 (09.01.54) First Series
Synopsis: Young Alfie 'Jumbo' Johnson is given a miniature mechanical Army, Navy and Air Force by Professor Carter whose life he has saved.
Art: Paddy Brennan
Notes: For further *Beano* series see 1956, 1963–65, 1969, 1971 (titled 'Admiral Jumbo') and 1974.

Matt Hatter (C)

No. 586 (10.10.53) – No. 657 (19.02.55)
Art: George Drysdale

Little Plum (Your Redskin Chum) (C)

No. 586 (10.10.53) – No. 2310 (18.10.86), and No. 2436 (25.03.89) and No. 2470 (18.11.89)
Art: 1953–62: Leo Baxendale
1962–86: Ron Spencer
Notes: After his last weekly appearance in October 1986, Plum did appear occasionally in *The Beano's* 'Reader's Request' feature in 1987 and turned up in 1988 in the comic's 'Old Masters feature'. He also made two one-off appearance in 1989.
'Little Plum' was devised under the working title 'Booster'. See also 2002 for a further appearance of 'Little Plum'.

Minnie the Minx (C)

No. 596 (19.12.53) – present
Art: 1953–62: Leo Baxendale
1962–present: Jim Petrie/Tom Paterson/ Ken Harrison
Notes: Minnie had her own reprint sections in both the 1977 and 1981 *Beryl the Peril Books*.
Minnie also had a special 'Agony Column' in No. 2469 (11.11.89).

Nobby – The Enchanted Bobby (CA)

No. 597 (26.12.53) – No. 604 (13.02.54) Second Series
Synopsis: More adventures with the copper who can unknowingly make his wishes come true.
Art: Bill Holroyd

1954

February

First appearance of *Beano* favourites 'The Bash Street Kids' in the strip 'When The Bell Rings'.
First full-colour back page 'Dennis the Menace' strip in No. 604 (13.02.54).

July

'Shorty's Magic Six-Gun' begins featuring the last new weekly *Beano* artwork from Thomson staff artist James Clark.

November

First appearance of *Beano* adventure strip favourite 'Longlegs – the Desert Wild Boy'.

December

'Jenny Penny' begins featuring the first weekly *Beano* artwork from artist Jimmy Thompson.

Year Information

Issues for year: Nos. 598–649; price 2d; page count 12; published every Thursday.

Smarty Smokey – The Genie in the Six-Gun (S)

No. 599 (09.01.54) – No. 608 (13.03.54) Third Series
Synopsis: Fun in the Wild West when Smarty's magic lamp is melted down to make a six-gun for Sheriff Hawkeye Hankey.
Art: George Drysdale

Get Rid of the Runaway Twins (A)

No. 600 (16.01.54) – No. 606 (27.02.54)
Synopsis: When the ship on which they are travelling is mined, two twins, Tom and Trixie Kidd, are marooned on an island with the evil ship's officer Karl Jason who the twins know to be a thief and a murderer.
Art: James 'Peem' Walker

When the Bell Rings (C)

The Bash Street Kids
No. 604 (13.02.54) – present
Art: 1954–62: Leo Baxendale
1962–present: Dave Sutherland
Notes: 'The Bash Street Kids' also had their own reprint section in the 1977 *Beryl the Peril Book*.
For further *Beano* spin-off items of Bash Street see 'Pup Parade' (1967) and 'Simply Smiffy' (1985).
The title of the strip 'When the Bell Rings' was changed to 'The Bash Street Kids' with *Beano* No. 748 (17.11.56).
'The Bash Street Kids' also appeared in a prose story with heading illustrations by Leo Baxendale in issue No. 1522 (16.04.55) – 1554 (26.11.55) of the boys story paper *Wizard*, and *Wizard* No. 1536 (23.07.55) and No. 1547 (08.10.55) also sported a 'Bash Street Kids' cover strip drawn by Leo Baxendale.

The Horse that Jack Built (CA)

No. 605 (20.02.54) – No. 614 (24.04.54) Third Series
Synopsis: Back in Merrie England Jack and his

Clockwork Horse help a knight who has lost his memory and is being tracked by the mysterious Hooded Archer.
Art: Ken Hunter

The Bird Boy (A)

No. 607 (06.03.54) – No. 610 (27.03.54) Third Series
Synopsis: Kelvin Wayne and Harrk come to the rescue of a ship's cat.
Art: Bill Holroyd

My Pal Nutty (S)

No. 609 (20.03.54) – No. 629 (07.08.54) Second Series
Synopsis: When Peter Wilson becomes the unwitting owner of the Coal Wizard's wand, he develops magical powers, powers which spell trouble for him and his coal imp friend Nutty.
Art: Bill Holroyd
Notes: With issue No. 620 (05.06.54) the title changes to 'In the power of the Coal Wizard'.

Red Rory of the Eagles (A)

No. 611 (03.04.54) – No. 631 (21.08.54) Fourth Series
Synopsis: Rory and his eagle pets help some outlaw Highlanders to escape the clutches of the English Redcoats.
Art: Bill Holroyd

Wee Davie and the Great Big Baby (CA)

No. 615 (01.05.54) – No. 616 (08.05.54) Third Series
Synopsis: Davie is asked to look after Chunk, the baby of Hunk the giant.
Art: Ken Hunter

The Iron Fish (A)

No. 617 (15.05.54) – No. 618 (22.05.54)
Seventh Series
Synopsis: Danny helps to catch a frogman bank crook.
Art: Bill Holroyd

Nothing's Too Big for Wee Davie (CA)

No. 619 (29.05.54) – No. 625 (10.07.54) Fourth Series
Synopsis: King Willie makes Davie a knight so that he can fight the giant bully Baron Thug, with the victor's prize being the throne of Pomegrania.
Art: Ken Hunter

Shorty's Magic Six-Gun (CA)

No. 626 (17.07.54) – No. 629 (07.08.54)
Fourth Series
Synopsis: Sheriff Hawkeye Hankey leaves Rattler Gulch to look for gold and leaves his magic six-gun with his lawman successor Shorty Brown.
Art: James Clark

Danger for Deep-Sea Danny (A)

No. 630 (14.08.54) – No. 641 (30.10.54) Eighth Series
Synopsis: On Kuwpal Island Danny finds a curved sword with a dragon-shaped hilt which holds a mysterious secret.
Art: Jack Glass

Slave to the Talking Horse (S)

No. 630 (14.08.54) – No. 646 (04.12.54)
Synopsis: In this sequel to The Magic Bone stories, Mickey saves a horse from being destroyed and, since he can talk to it, finds it knows the whereabouts of a great treasure.
Art: James 'Peem' Walker

Hookey's Bust'em Book (CA)

No. 632 (28.08.54) – No. 651 (08.01.55) First Series
Synopsis: Hookey Hutton rescues an old book from a garden fire and finds it once belonged to Merlin the Magician. From its pages historical characters can come to life.
Art: Charles Grigg
Notes: For further series see 1955 and 1958.

Longlegs – The Desert Wild Boy (A)

No. 642 (06.11.54) – No. 654 (29.01.55) First Series
Synopsis: While Sheriff Bill Barclay is looking for outlaw Pedro Gomez in the Hungry Desert of Arizona, he comes across an amazing wild boy with a pet bob cat.
Art: Paddy Brennan
Notes: For further *Beano* series see 1955 and 1957– 1959.

Jenny Penny (C)

No. 646 (04.12.54) – No. 694 (05.11.55)
Art: Jimmy Thompson

The Spell of Geordie's Whistle (S)

No. 647 (11.12.54) – No. 652 (15.01.55)
Synopsis: Wee Geordie Wilson is given a whistle by an Indian pedlar and finds that when it is blown it reverses situations, for example a dog walks a man instead of a man walking a dog.
Art: James 'Peem' Walker

1955

January

'Ace from Space' begins, the last prose story to be featured in the weekly *Beano*.
'Clumsy Claude' begins, featuring the first comic art for *The Beano* from Thomson staff artist Bill Ritchie.

March

First all-picture strip issue of *The Beano* appears – No. 659 (05.03.55).

July

'Scrapper' begins, featuring the first comic art for *The Beano* from artist Albert Holroyd, brother of Bill.
First appearance of *Beano* comic favourite 'Grandpa'.

September

First *Dennis The Menace Book*, for 1956, is published.

November

'Jack of Clubs' begins, featuring the first artwork for *The Beano* from artist Michael Darling.

December

'Runaways with Turpin' begins, featuring the first artwork for *The Beano* from artist John Nichol.

Year Information

Issues for year: Nos. 650–702; price 2d; page count 12; published every Thursday.

Dick on the Draw (C)

No. 650 (01.01.55) – No. 658 (26.02.55)
Art: Jimmy Thompson

The Horse that Jack Built (A)

No. 652 (15.01.55) – No. 663 (02.04.55) Fourth Series
Synopsis: Jack is forced to build a monster-sized clockwork soldier to lead the army of the Black Baron in his evil quest to conquer the country of Marania.
Art: Jack Glass

Ace From Space (S)

No. 653 (22.01.55) – No. 658 (26.02.55)
Synopsis: An alien lad called Ace arrives on Earth

from Mars with his parents, and causes havoc with his Multi-Ray gun.
Art: Leo Baxendale

Clumsy Claude – The Blunder Boy (C)
No. 653 (22.01.55) – No. 696 (19.11.55)
Art: Bill Ritchie

Red Rory Of The Eagles (A)
No. 655 (05.02.55) – No. 666 (23.04.55) Fifth Series
Synopsis: Rory does battle with the hooded traitor of the clans.
Art: Bill Holroyd

Wee Davie and the Great Big Spell (CA)
No. 659 (05.03.55) – No. 667 (30.04.55) Fourth Series
Synopsis: Davie and King Willie have a spell put on them by Ali Bong, the wizard from Baghdad.
Art: Ken Hunter

Longlegs – The Desert Wild Boy (A)
No. 664 (09.04.55) – No. 676 (02.07.55) Second Series
Synopsis: When his blind grandfather Josh Slade accidentally kills an Indian chief, Longlegs has to protect him from the revenging tribe who come to hunt him down.
Art: Paddy Brennan

All the Best People go to School (C)
No. 667 (30.6.55); one – off feature
Art: Leo Baxendale

Hooky's Bust'em Book (CA)
No. 668 (07.05.55) – No. 679 (23.07.55) Second Series
Synopsis: More fun with the magic history book.
Art: Bill Holroyd

The Shipwrecked Circus (A)
No. 668 (07.05.55) – No. 683 (20.08.55) Fourth Series
Synopsis: Jim Silver, an old sailor, is washed ashore half-dead on Coral Island, the home of the Shipwrecked Circus. With him he has a chart showing the whereabouts of some fabulous pearl beds.
Art: Paddy Brennan

Thunderflash (A)
No. 677 (09.07.55) – No. 681 (06.08.55)
Synopsis: The adventures of a ram in the Rocky Mountains.
Art: Ken Hunter

Prince Whoopee – Your Pal from the Palace (C)
No. 680 (30.07.55) – No. 759 (02.02.57) First Series
Art: Charles Grigg
Notes: For second *Beano* series see 1957.

Wee Davie and King Willie (C)
No. 680 (30.07.55) – No. 712 (10.03.56) Fifth Series
Art: Ken Hunter

Scrapper (C)
No. 680 (30.07.55) – No. 769 (13.04.57) First Series
Synopsis: Lord Snooty's pal Scrapper Smith in his own comic strip.
Art: George Drysdale/Albert Holroyd
Notes: For second series see 1959.

Grandpa (C)
No. 680 (30.07.55) – No. 798 (02.11.57) First Series
Art: Ken Reid
Notes: For second series see 1971.

Jimmy and His Magic Patch (A)
No. 682 (13.08.55) – No. 694 (05.11.55) Fifth Series
Art: Dudley Watkins
Notes: Reprints from the 1944 and 1945 series.

Red Rory of the Eagles (A)
No. 684 (27.08.55) – No. 695 (12.11.55) Sixth Series
Synopsis: To stop some of Bonnie Prince Charlie's gold from falling into the hands of the Redcoats, Rory has the gold made into horse shoes and placed on the hooves of Ruath, the magnificent white horse of Kilroy.
Art: Bill Holyord

Jack of Clubs (A)
No. 695 (12.11.55) – No. 700 (17.12.55) Second Series
Synopsis: Young Jack Osmond falls foul of the pirate, Captain Hawk, when he discovers the secret of six belts which lead to a buried treasure.
Art: Michael Darling

On the Heels of the Hated Hooknose (A)
No. 696 (19.11.55) – No. 700 (17.12.55)
Synopsis: When young Kitty Foster is kidnapped by Shawnee chief Hooknose, her brother Roddy and their mother set out to track them down.
Art: Bill Holroyd

Jack Flash (A)
No. 701 (24.12.55) – No. 719 (28.04.56) Fourth Series
Synopsis: Thrills in darkest Africa when a class from Helmsford School is marooned there after Jack Flash's space ship crash lands during a special geography lesson.
Art: Paddy Brennan

Runaways with Turpin (A)
No. 701 (24.12.55) – No. 703 (07.01.56)
Synopsis: Dick Turpin the legendary highwayman helps two children, Jeremy and Gwen Hamilton on the run from their cruel guardians, to catch a ship to America to join their parents.
Art: James 'Peem' Walker/John Nichol

1956

January
On January 15 Dennis the Menace becomes a TV star during 'Children's Hour', when he appears in an advert to promote the new Thomson comic *The Beezer*.
Original *Beano* Sub-Editor Iain Chisholm becomes Editor of the new Thomson tabloid comic *The Beezer*. The first issue debuts on January 21.

March
'Wee Peem' begins, featuring the first art for *The Beano* from artist Hugh Morren.

September
The fourth series of 'The Bird Boy' begins, featuring the first *Beano* artwork from artist Andy Hutton.

Year Information
Issues for year: Nos. 703–754; price 2d; page count 12; published every Thursday.

Our Ned (C)
No. 703 (07.01.56) – No. 816 (08.03.58)
Art: Albert Holroyd

The Iron Fish (A)
No. 704 (14.01.56) – No. 712 (10.03.56) Ninth Series
Synopsis: After finding a message for help in a bottle, Danny comes into conflict with the evil Birdman.
Art: John Nichol

(C) Comic Strip (A) Adventure Strip (S) Prose Story (CA) Comic Adventure Strip

Stop that Horse! (A)
No. 712 (10.03.56) – No. 717 (14.04.56) Fifth Series
Synopsis: When the king is besieged in a castle by Vikings, Jack sends the Clockwork Horse for help.
Art: Bill Holroyd

Daniel the Spaniel (C)
No. 713 (17.03.56) – No. 736 (25.08.56)
Art: Ken Hunter

Johnny on the Hop (He Brings the Beano from the Shop) (C)
No. 713 (17.03.56) – No. 736 (25.08.56)
Art: George Drysdale

Wee Peem (C)
No. 714 (24.03.56) – No. 765 (16.03.57) Third Series
Art: Hugh Morren
Note: 'Wee Peem' looks distinctly different in this series compared with the previous two (1938 and 1951).

Young Davy Crockett (A)
No. 718 (21.04.56) – No. 723 (26.05.56) First Series
Synopsis: Wild West adventures of the wagon train trail with the great grandson of the famous frontiersman.
Art: Paddy Brennan
Notes: For second series see October 1956.

Nik o' Lightning (A)
No. 720 (05.05.56) – No. 726 (16.06.56)
Synopsis: The story of a boy who, after a plane crash, has been brought up alone in the wild bush country of Africa and has developed a strange power over zebras.
Art: Michael Darling

Red Rory of the Eagles (A)
No. 724 (02.06.56) – No. 731 (21.07.56) Seventh Series
Synopsis: Rory on the trail of a travelling fiddler who is betraying outlawed Highlanders to the Redcoats.
Art: Bill Holroyd

Jimmy and His Magic Patch (A)
No. 727 (23.06.56) – No. 743 (13.10.56) Sixth Series
Art: Dudley Watkins
Notes: More reprints from the 1940s.

General Jumbo (A)
No. 732 (28.07.56) – No. 739 (15.09.56) Second Series
Synopsis: A series of single issue adventures with Jumbo and his miniature army.
Art: John Nichol

The Bird Boy (A)
No. 737 (01.09.56) – No. 743 (13.10.56) Fourth Series
Synopsis: Kelvin Wayne helps the crew of the whaling ship Berga after it is sunk by a sea monster in the Antarctic.
Art: Andy Hutton

The Happy-Go-Luckies (A)
No. 740 (22.09.56) – No. 749 (24.11.56) Fifth Series
Synopsis: Jack Flash helps the Luckie family from Kent move to their new home in Africa.
Art: Paddy Brennan

Young Davy Crockett (A)
No. 744 (20.10.56) – No. 749 (24.11.56) Second Series
Synopsis: The great grandson of the famous frontiersman in a script adapted from the 'Little Noah's Ark' story from 1940.
Art: Andy Hutton

Uncle Windbag (That Story Teller Feller) (C)
No. 744 (20.10.56) – No. 763 (02.03.57) Third Series
Art: Bill Ritchie

The Wooden Horse (A)
No. 750 (01.12.56) – No. 757 (19.01.57)
Synopsis: Shades of the legend of ancient Troy when, in the Wild West, the six Oakley children escape the clutches of a band of warriors by hiding the two youngest children inside a home-built wooden horse.
Art: Paddy Brennan

Tick-Tock Timothy (A)
No. 750 (01.12.56) – No. 759 (02.02.57)
Art: John Nichol
Notes: Revised picture strip version of the 1940s prose story with the same title.

1957

June
'The Invisible Giant' begins, featuring the last weekly *Beano* artwork from artist Bill Holroyd.

October
Beginning of *The Beano's* first regular puzzle feature, 'Kat's Krazy Korner'. It also features the first regular *Beano* artwork from artist Frank MacDiarmid.

November
The second series of 'Prince Whoopee' begins, featuring the last *Beano* artwork from Thomson staff artist George Drysdale.
'Fusspot Annie' begins, featuring the last *Beano* artwork from artist Jimmy Thompson.
'Bringing Up Dennis' begins, featuring the first weekly *Beano* artwork from artist Ken Wilkins.

December
The seventh and final series of *Beano* adventure favourite 'Tom Thumb' begins.

Year Information
Issues for year: Nos. 755–806; price 2d; page count 12; published every Thursday.

Longlegs – the Desert Wild Boy (A)
No. 758 (26.01.57) – No. 762 (23.02.57) Third Series
Synopsis: Longlegs helps to get a shipment of money to safety when the plane on which it was being transported crashes in the Hungry Desert.
Art: Paddy Brennan

Wee Davie and King Willie (A)
No. 760 (09.02.57) – No. 798 (02.11.57) Sixth Series
Synopsis: Fun when hard-up King Willie enters a crossword competition to win a television set.
Art: Ken Hunter

The Horse that Jack Built (A)
No. 760 (09.02.57) – No. 772 (04.05.57) Sixth Series
Synopsis: Jack travels with some Vikings on a mission to Rome.
Art: Michael Darling

The Shipwrecked Circus (A)
No. 763 (02.03.57) – No. 768 (06.04.57) Fifth Series
Synopsis: Samson and Co.come to the aid of a US submarine which is trapped on the seabed.
Art: Paddy Brennan

Red Rory of the Eagles (A)
No. 764 (09.03.57) – No. 772 (04.05.57) Eighth Series

Synopsis: Adventures with Rory and young Cripple Jamie.
Art: Andy Hutton

Pooch (C)

No. 767 (30.03.57) – No. 799 (09.11.57)
Art: Bill Ritchie

Parachute Reg (C)

No. 767 (30.03.57) – No. 779 (22.06.57)
Art: Albert Holroyd

The Vengeance of One-Eye (A)

No. 769 (13.04.57) – No. 777 (08.06.57)
Synopsis: Trouble in the far north of Canada when young Jim Nelson does battle with One-Eye, a savage wolverine.
Art: Andy Hutton

The Iron Fish (A)

No. 769 (13.04.57) – No. 776 (01.06.57) Tenth Series
Synopsis: After being caught up in a water spout, Danny and the Iron Fish are cast ashore on an island inhabited by pygmies who are being terrorised by a mysterious giant.
Art: John Nichol

Kat and Kanary (C)

No. 770 (20.04.57) – No. 794 (05.10.57) Second Series
Art: Albert Holroyd

Kilty Mactaggart (A)

No. 773 (11.05.57) – No. 778 (15.06.57)
Synopsis: In an adventure strip similar to the 1951 story 'Willie in the Lost World', a young Scots lad finds the entrance to a lost world inhabited by troglodyte dwarves in a cavern on the Yorkshire Moors.
Art: Andy Hutton

Wizards at War (CA)

No. 773 (11.05.57) – No. 790 (07.09.57)
Synopsis: The comical battles of the two wizards Ding and Dong.
Art: Charles Grigg

Brannigan's Boy (A)

No. 777 (08.06.57) – No. 783 (20.07.57)
Synopsis: Sheriff's son Billy Brannigan tries to bring justice to the Kelly Boys, a gang of outlaws who have wounded his father.
Art: John Nichol

The Invisible Giant (CA)

No. 778 (15.06.57) – No. 788 (24.08.57) Third Series
Synopsis: Presto, the invisible giant with the magic boots, helps a prince who is turned into a mouse by the evil Wizard Zorra.
Art: Bill Holroyd

Thrill-a-Day Jill (A)

No. 779 (22.06.57) – No. 783 (20.07.57)
Synopsis: The adventures of Jill Jarvis, a clever young ventriloquist, and her puppet Charlie as stars of Benson's Circus.
Art: John Nichol

Dippy the Diver (C)

No. 780 (29.06.57) – No. 788 (24.08.57)
Art: Hugh Morren

Jimmy and His Magic Patch (A)

No. 784 (27.07.57) – No. 794 (05.10.57)
Seventh Series
Synopsis:Another reprint series but this time with the first episode being a redrawn retelling of the very first Magic Patch adventure from 1944.
Art: Dudley Watkins (with redrawn first episode by artist Andy Hutton)

Jack's the Boy (A)

No. 789 (31.08.57) – No. 801 (23.11.57) Sixth Series
Synopsis: Jack Flash helps a football team from Moorfield school to win £10,000 for their school funds.
Art: Paddy Brennan

Red Rory of the Eagles (A)

No. 791 (14.09.57) – No. 802 (30.11.57) Ninth Series
Synopsis: If Rory fails to find a lost Redcoat patrol in the Highlands, three of his clansmen will die.
Art: Andy Hutton

Runaways with Thunderbird (A)

No. 795 (12.10.57) – No. 803 (07.12.57)
Synopsis: At a cavalry fort in the West, young Jerry and Meg Foster help the Chief Thunderbird to escape from custody. In return he shows them the whereabouts of their missing Indian scout father.
Art: John Nichol

Kat's Krazy Korner

No. 795 (12.10.57) – No. 927 (23.04.60) Feature
Synopsis: Puzzles with Kat, of Kat and Kanary fame.
Art: Frank MacDiarmid
Notes: With No. 817 (15.03.58) the title reduced to simply 'Krazy Korner'.

Rummy Rhymes

No. 795 (12.10.57) – No. 831 (21.06.58) Feature
Synopsis: Loopy limericks!
Art: Frank MacDiarmid

Prince Whoopee (C)

No. 799 (09.11.57) – No. 841 (30.08.58) Second Series
Art: George Drysdale

Fusspot Annie (C)

No. 801 (23.11.57) – No. 816 (08.03.58)
Art: Jimmy Thompson

Bringing up Dennis (C)

No. 801 (23.11.57) – No. 808 (11.01.58)
Synopsis: The adventures of Dennis the Menace as a tiny tot.
Art: Ken Wilkins

Strongarm the Axeman (A)

No. 802 (30.11.57) – No. 813 (15.02.58) Third Series
Synopsis: Young Strongarm sets out to repay the debts owed to people by the blind warrior Hal o' the Axe.
Art: Albert Holroyd

Tom Thumb – The Brave Little One (A)

No. 803 (07.12.57) – No. 811 (01.02.58)
Seventh Series
Synopsis: Tom is kidnapped and taken to sea by a piratical knight.
Art: John Nichol

Quick an' Slick (C)

No. 803 (07.12.57) – No. 829 (07.06.58)
Art: Frank MacDiarmid

Tough Duff (A)

No. 804 (14.12.57) – No. 808 (11.01.58)
Synopsis: The adventures of a circus boss whose circus flies the world.
Art: Andy Hutton

1958

February

The third series of *Beano* favourite 'Pansy Potter' begins, featuring the last weekly *Beano* artwork from artist Charles Grigg.
The fourth and final series of *Beano* adventure strip favourite 'Wild Boy' begins.

March

The six-week run of the comic strip 'A Funny Thing Happened the Other Day' draws to a close, thus ending the second series of 'Lord Snooty and his Pals', to which it had been a coda.
'Pom-Pom' begins, featuring the first *Beano* artwork from artist Gordon Bell.
First appearance of *The Beano's* seafaring goon 'Jonah'.

May

Seventh and final series of *Beano* adventure strip favourite 'Jack Flash'.

June

'Bristol Billy' begins featuring the first *Beano* artwork from Portuguese artist Vitor Peon.

August

Sixth and final series of 'The Shipwrecked Circus' begins.
'Cookie' begins, featuring the last weekly *Beano* artwork from artist Ken Wilkins.

December

The twelfth series of 'The Iron Fish' begins, featuring the final weekly *Beano* artwork from Thomson staff artist Jack Glass.

Year Information

Issues for year: Nos. 807–858; price 2d; page count 12; published every Thursday.

Rory and the Pirates (A)

No. 809 (18.01.58) – No. 820 (05.04.58) Tenth Series
Synopsis: Rory and Bonnie Prince Charlie fall foul of pirate captain Black Ketch and his band of buccaneers when their ship is wrecked off the Scottish coast.
Art: Andy Hutton

A Funny Thing Happened the Other Day (C)

No. 812 (08.02.58) – No. 818 (22.03.58)
Synopsis: A minor coda to the second Lord Snooty series.
Art: Albert Holroyd

Pansy Potter – The Strongman's Daughter (C)

No. 812 (08.02.58) – No. 854 (29.11.58) Third Series
Art: Charles Grigg/Gordon Bell

Wild Boy (A)

No. 812 (08.02.58) – No. 823 (26.04.58) Fourth Series
Synopsis: When the Foster family return to the family home in the isolated Birchdale woods after 15 years in South Africa they find an animal-skin-clad wild boy in residence.
Art: Andy Hutton

Johnny Go Back! (A)

No. 814 (22.02.58) – No. 827 (24.05.58)
Synopsis: During the Dunkirk evacuation a young English boy, Johnny Desmond, stows away on a boat to France to find his sister.
Art: Albert Holroyd

Pom-Pom (The Boy who Brightens Darkest Africa) (C)

No. 817 (15.03.58) – No. 848 (18.10.58)
Art: Gordon Bell

Jonah (C)

No. 817 (15.03.58) – No. 1090 (08.06.63)
Art: Ken Reid
Notes: See also the 'Jinx' strip (1963) featuring Jonah's schoolgirl sister.

Kat and Kanary (C)

No. 819 (29.03.58) – No. 841 (30.08.58) Third Series
Art: Gordon Bell

The Iron Fish (A)

No. 821 (12.04.58) – No. 828 (31.05.58)
Eleventh Series
Synopsis: Danny sets out to find a young girl who has been kidnapped.
Art: John Nichol

Jack Flash (A)

No. 824 (03.05.58) – No. 835 (19.07.58) Seventh Series
Synopsis: Jack helps to capture an escaped circus lion.
Art: Andy Hutton

Bristol Billy (A)

No. 829 (07.06.58) – No. 841 (30.08.58)
Synopsis: Shades of the 1945 picture strip 'Six Brands for Bonnie Prince Charlie', as 'Bristol Billy' Dalton and Long John Daring track down five pirates, each of whom have part of a treasure map tattoed on their arms.
Art: Vitor Peon

Rattlesnake Ranch (A)

No. 829 (07.06.58) – No. 840 (23.08.58)
Synopsis: Two young British children, Sandy and Sue Bartley, set off to live with their grandfather on his ranch in Arizona.
Art: John Nichol

Hookey's Bust'em Book (C)

No. 836 (26.07.58) – No. 846 (04.10.58) Third Series
Synopsis: More adventures with the book that brings history to life.
Art: Albert Holroyd

The Shipwrecked Circus (A)

No. 841 (30.08.58) – No. 856 (13.12.58) Sixth Series
Art: Dudley Watkins/Paddy Brennan
Notes: Reduced size series of reprints.

Cookie (C)

No. 841 (30.08.58) – No. 856 (13.12.58)
Art: Ken Wilkins

Betty's Grandad (C)

No. 841 (30.08.58) – No. 856 (13.12.58)
Art: Hugh Morren

Longlegs – The Desert Wild Boy (A)

No. 842 (06.09.58) – No. 848 (18.10.58)
Fourth Series
Synopsis: Prehistoric monsters terrify the townsfolk of Cactus Gulch in the Hungry Desert.
Art: Paddy Brennan

Red Rory of the Eagles (A)

No. 842 (06.09.58) – No. 854 (29.11.58)
Eleventh Series

Synopsis: Rory helps Lord Donald Stewart to rescue his wife and children from the Redcoats.
Art: Andy Hutton

The Hogan Boy (A)
No. 847 (11.10.58) – No. 857 (20.12.58)
Synopsis: After his father is shot and paralysed by the bandit Hank Millard, young Jeff Hogan sets out to track Millard down for the $10,000 reward on his head. Jeff intends to use this money to get treatment for his father to make him well again.
Art: John Nichol

The Blinding Shield (A)
No. 849 (25.10.58) – No. 856 (13.12.58)
Synopsis: With the help of the mysterious 'Blinding Shield' made by Wolfram the Sorceror, the evil Valdags swear to wreak vengeance on Val the Viking and his brothers.
Art: Vitor Peon
Notes: Quite a different 'Blinding Shield' appeared in a 1952 Iron Fish story.

Sparky's Space Helmet (CA)
No. 855 (06.12.58) – No. 863 (31.01.59)
Synopsis: A spaceship crash lands on Earth and *Sparky* Spencer finds in the wreckage not only a miraculous helmet but also three small chubby aliens called Eeky, Beeky and Squeaky.
Art: Albert Holroyd

Dashalong Dot (She Raises Laughs Chasing Autographs) (C)
No. 855 (06.12.58) – No. 870 (21.03.59)
Art: Gordon Bell

The Iron Fish (A)
No. 857 (20.12.58) – No. 867 (28.02.59) Twelfth Series
Synopsis: Danny does battle with a swarm of gigantic hornets led by the strange Insect Man.
Art: Jack Glass

Sinbad the Sailor (A)
No. 857 (20.12.58) – No. 867 (28.02.59) Third Series
Synopsis: A magic bottle with a genie inside is washed aboard Sinbad's boat.
Art: Michael Darling

Rip Van Wink (C)
No. 857 (20.12.58) – No. 866 (21.02.59) Second Series
Synopsis: A series of new and reprinted strips
Art: Gordon Bell (new)/Eric Roberts (reprints)

Fox on the Run (A)
No. 858 (27.12.58) – No. 869 (14.03.59)
Synopsis: In 1941 Donald Fox, a cabin boy, is on board a ship that is wrecked by dive bombers and is given information by a passenger, mortally wounded in the attack, that a fellow passenger is a Nazi spy. It becomes Donald's task to get the information identifying the spy to the proper authorities.
Art: Albert Holroyd

1959

January
Last 'Biffo the Bear' strip signed by Dudley Watkins appears in No. 860 (10.01.59).

April
Final series of 'Longlegs – the Desert Wild Boy' begins.

June
First appearance of *Beano* favourites 'The Three Bears'.

July
'Bob on the Beat' begins featuring the last weekly *Beano* artwork from artist John Nichol.

August
Final series of 'Jimmy and his Magic Patch' begins.

September
Last *Beano Book* with a James Crighton cover is published. It is also the last *Beano Book* to contain 128 pages.

November
The third series of 'Lord Snooty' begins.

Undateable 1959 information
In the summer of 1959 George Moonie, the original *Beano* Editor, leaves the post to set up publication of the proposed new Thomson girls comic *Judy*, which debuted in January 1960. Harold Cramond becomes the new Editor of *The Beano*.

Year Information
Issues for year: Nos. 859–910; price 2d; page count 12; published every Thursday.

Red Rory of the Eagles (A)
No. 864 (07.02.59) – No. 884 (27.06.59) Twelth Series
Synopsis: In September 1745 Rory tries to track down a would-be assassin of Bonnie Prince Charlie.
Art: Andy Hutton

Black Star (A)
No. 867 (28.02.59) – No. 875 (25.04.59)
Synopsis: Young ranchhand Neil Harvey tries to save the life of a big white stallion with a black star on its forehead, when it throws and injures the wealthy ranch owner Luke Slade, who then decides to kill it.
Art: John Nichol

The Vengeance of the Lost Crusader (A)
No. 868 (07.03.59) – No. 875 (25.04.59)
Synopsis: On his way home by ship from the Crusades, young Sir Ivor Greatheart is thrown overboard by the henchmen of his wicked uncle Sir Boris Blakely. Sir Boris knows that with Ivor's death he will inherit his nephew's lands, but Ivor survives and, from the desert island on which he is washed ashore, the young knight swears vengeance.
Art: Vitor Peon

Joe for Champ (C)
No. 870 (21.03.59) – No. 879 (23.05.59)
Art: Hugh Morren

Longlegs – The Desert Wild Boy (A)
No. 872 (04.04.59) – No. 880 (30.05.59) Fifth Series
Synopsis: In the Hungry Desert Longlegs helps Marshall Matt Slade to track down a band of outlaws, the Kelly Brothers.
Art: Andy Hutton

Dick Turpin – Special Investigator (A)
No. 876 (02.05.59) – No. 889 (01.08.59)
Synopsis: Dick Turpin the highwayman leads a double life as the respectable squire Tremaine, and sets out to stop two children being murdered by their evil uncle who is after their inheritance.
Art: John Nichol

Smarty Smokey – The Wee Black Dragon (CA)
No. 877 (09.05.59) – No. 886 (11.07.59)
Synopsis: Young Edric, on his way to pay his family's taxes at the king's court, comes across a

(C) Comic Strip (A) Adventure Strip (S) Prose Story (CA) Comic Adventure Strip

small dragon in a cave with a thorn in its foot. The dragon becomes his friend when, like Androcles, Edric removes the thorn.
Art: Vitor Peon
Notes: This series is nothing at all to do with *The Beano* genie of the early 1950s with the same name.

Scrapper (C)
No. 880 (30.05.59) – No. 890 (08.08.59) Second Series
Art: Albert Holroyd

The Three Bears (C)
No. 881 (06.06.59) – No. 884 (27.06.59) First Series
Art: Leo Baxendale
Notes: This short series was seemingly an editorial tryout for the strip as, after the four weeks were up, readers were asked to write in if they wanted to see the Bears again. Then in No. 900 (17.10.59), an advert appeared saying that the Bears would return when space allowed.
For second series see 1960, and for the third series see 1988.

The Danger Man (A)
No. 886 (11.07.59) – No. 932 (28.05.60) First Series
Synopsis: At the age of five, an Earthboy is taken from his home on the Yorkshire Moors by Martians and is given special training on Mars so that, as an adult, he can return to Earth as a superman to be the world's champion when danger threatens.
Art: Michael Darling
Notes: For further series see 1960 and 1961 (titled 'The Danger Twins' in 1961).

Bob on the Beat (A)
No. 887 (18.07.59) – No. 903 (07.11.59)
Synopsis: The adventures of Bob Bennet, a smart, hardworking policeman whose beat is in the industrial town of Dolton.
Art: John Nichol

The Kangaroo Kid (A)
No. 890 (08.08.59) – No. 904 (14.11.59)
Synopsis: A strip which owes its storyline to the 1938 prose tale, 'The Ape's Secret'.
Art: Andy Hutton

Jimmy and his Magic Patch (A)
No. 891 (15.08.59) – No. 903 (07.11.59) Eighth Series
Synopsis: Jimmy travels back into history for the final time in *The Beano*.
Art: Paddy Brennan

Mountain Boy (A)
No. 904 (14.11.59) – No. 912 (09.01.60)
Synopsis: The story of the young Sherpa boy Dawa who, along with his snow leopard Spitfire, has a job as guide to mountaineers in the Himalayas.
Art: Vitor Peon

Lord Snooty (C)
No. 904 (14.11.59) – No. 2565 (07.09.91) (except Nos. 2436, 2455, 2462 and 2463)
Art: 1959–68: Dudley Watkins
(reprints during 1959–64)
1968–73: Bob Nixon
1973–88: Jimmy Glen
1988–91: Ken Harrison

Pete of the Spitfires (A)
No. 904 (14.11.59) – No. 932 (28.05.60)
Synopsis: In 1940, on an island off the British coast, a wild boy called Pete helps a Spitfire pilot who has crash-landed.
Art: Michael Darling
Notes: This is a picture story version of a prose story which appeared in *The Magic* comic in 1940.

Teeko (A)
No. 905 (21.11.59) – No. 912 (09.01.60)
Synopsis: The adventures of the Burmese boy Chang and his elephant Teeko in the teak forests of Burma.
Art: Andy Hutton
Notes: This is a picture strip version of the 1938 *Beano* prose story 'Little Master of the Mighty Chang'.

1960

January
'The Laughing Pirate' begins, featuring the last weekly *Beano* artwork from Portuguese artist Vitor Peon.

May
'Wonder Boy' begins, featuring the first weekly *Beano* artwork from artist Bob McGrath.

June
'Danny on a Dolphin' begins, featuring the first *Beano* artwork from artist Dave Sutherland.
'The Queen's Highway' begins, featuring the first *Beano* artwork from artist Terry Patrick.

September
First all-picture 144–page shiny-covered *Beano Book* is published.
Veteran D. C. Thomson and *Beano* freelance artist Allan Morley dies in Kent on September 5, aged 65.

October
The first sixteen-page *Beano* with full-colour centrespread is published, and *The Beano's* price increases to 3d.
The 'Flying Snorter Balloon' is given away, the first *Beano* free gift since 1940.
'Colonel Crackpot's Circus' begins, featuring the first *Beano* artwork from artist Mal Judge.

Year Information
Issues for year: Nos. 911–963; price 2d to No. 951 (08.10.60), then 3d from No. 952 (15.10.60) onwards. Page count also changes in the same issues from 12 to 16 pages.
Free gifts: No. 953 (22.10.60) Flying Snorter Balloon
No. 954 (29.10.60) *Beano* Clickitty Clicker.

The Laughing Pirate (A)
No. 913 (16.01.60) – No. 935 (18.06.60)
Synopsis: The adventures of Sir Hugo Merriman the 'Falcon', who, as a privateer on the Spanish Main, literally laughs at danger.
Art: Vitor Peon

Lazy Jones (C)
No. 920 (05.05.60) – No. 945 (27.08.60)
Art: Hugh Morren

Wonder Boy (C)
No. 930 (14.05.60) – No. 979 (22.04.61)
Art: Bob McGrath

Teaser Time
No. 930 (14.05.60) – No. 1677 (07.09.74) Feature
Art: Frank McDiarmid
Notes: 10/– prizes were offered to readers for each puzzle published.

Danny on a Dolphin (A)
No. 933 (04.06.60) – No. 951 (08.10.60) First Series

Synopsis: Young Danny Weston and his friends, the dolphins, try to track down Danny's parents when, during the Second World War they are taken prisoner by the Japanese and removed from their island home of Viam in the Pacific.
Art: Dave Sutherland
Notes: For second series see 1962.

THE QUEEN'S HIGHWAY (A)

No. 936 (25.06.60) – No. 951 (08.10.60)
Synopsis: Big Jim Queen, accompanied by his twin sons, Rip and Rick, and his daughter Mary, is the leader of a team of engineers building a highway across Africa.
Art: Terry Patrick

THE THREE BEARS (C)

No. 952 (15.10.60) – No. 2253 (21.09.85) Second Series
Art: 1960–61: Leo Baxendale
1961–85: Bob McGrath
Notes: 'The Three Bears' also featured in the 'Readers Request' and 'Old Masters' features in *The Beano* in 1987 and 1988.
The two main adversaries of 'The Three Bears', Grizzly Gus and Hank Huckleberry, appeared for the first time in No. 966 (21.01.61) and No. 991 (15.07.61) respectively.

THE TING-A-LING TAYLORS (A)

No. 952 (15.10.60) – No. 982 (13.05.61)
Synopsis: Fun and thrills when the Taylor family, wardens of an African game reserve, are sent a fire engine by mistake.
Art: Terry Patrick

THE GREAT FLOOD OF LONDON (A)

No. 952 (15.10.60) – No. 1015 (30.12.61)
Synopsis: A fireball from outer space passes over the Arctic and melts some of the polar ice cap, causing flooding in much of Europe including London, leading to many adventures for Londoners like Harry and Mabel Foster and their children Ted, Trixie and Tiny Tim.
Art: Dave Sutherland
Note: This was *The Beano's* first centrespread strip in full colour.

THE DANGER MAN (A)

No. 952 (15.10.60) – No. 983 (20.05.61) Second Series
Synopsis: The Danger Man on board his flying craft, the zoomer rescues two young twins, Jet and Jane Hardwick, from a shipwreck and trains them to be his young associates, the Danger Minors.
Art: Michael Darling

COLONEL CRACKPOT'S CIRCUS (C)

No. 952 (15.10.60) – No. 1107 (05.10.63)
Art: Mal Judge

1961

MARCH

Walter Fearn leaves the editorial staff of *The Beano* to become Editor of the new nursery comic *Bimbo*, which has its debut on March 18.

SEPTEMBER

Beano No. 1000 (16.09.61) is published.

NOVEMBER

'The Danger Twins' begins, featuring the last weekly *Beano* artwork from artist Michael Darling.

YEAR INFORMATION

Issues for year: Nos. 964–1015; price 3d; page count 16; published every Thursday.

ROGER THE DODGER (C)

No. 980 (29.04.61) – present Second Series
Art: 1961–62: Bob McGrath
1962–64: Ken Reid
1964–73: Robert Nixon
1973–74: Tom Lavery
1974–86: Frank MacDiarmid
1986–present: Robert Nixon/Brian Appleby
Notes: See also 'Roger the Dodger's Dodge Clinic' (1986)

THE CANNONBALL CRACKSHOTS (A)

No. 983 (20.05.61) – No. 1007 (04.11.61)
Synopsis: The story of master gunner Ezra Applegate and his companions, Jack Armstrong and young Billy Ready, who between them man the six-pounder cannon 'Vulcan' during the Napoleonic Wars.
Art: Dave Sutherland

THE ADVENTURES OF JOHNNY LEOPARD (A)

No. 984 (27.05.61) – No. 1001 (23.09.61)
Synopsis: The tale of a friendship between a 12-year-old boy named Johnny Morris and a savage leopard, as they both become hunted outlaws.
Art: Michael Darling

PADDY'S PRIVATE ARMY (A)

No. 1002 (30.09.61) – No. 1024 (03.03.62) First Series
Synopsis: Separated from his mother in Singapore in 1942, young Paddy Watson collects all the pets left behind by his friends and creates a private army to fight the invading Japanese.
Art: James 'Peem' Walker

THE DANGER TWINS (A)

No. 1008 (11.11.61) – No. 1035 (19.05.62) Third Series
Synopsis: More adventures with the superman from Mars and his helpers Jet and Jane the Danger Twins, as they fight crime on Earth.
Art: Michael Darling

1962

JANUARY

'G for Giant' begins, featuring the last weekly *Beano* artwork from artist Ken Hunter.

FEBRUARY

Veteran *Beano* and *Dandy* artist James Crighton, who had drawn 'Korky the Cat' on the cover of *The Dandy* for nearly 25 years, dies on February 14, aged 70.

MAY

Beginning of the last series featuring *The Beano's* young Jacobite hero, 'Red Rory of the Eagles'.

AUGUST

'Punch and Jimmy' begins, featuring the first weekly *Beano* artwork from artist Dave Jenner.
First double-page full-colour centrespread 'Bash Street' strip published in No. 1046 (04.08.62).
Note: 1962 also saw the last weekly work for *The Beano* from artist Leo Baxendale as he drew 'Little Plum', 'Minnie the Minx' and 'The Bash Street Kids' for the last time. The three strips were taken over by artists Ron Spencer, Jim Petrie and Dave Sutherland respectively.

YEAR INFORMATION

Issues for year: Nos. 1016–1067; price 3d; page count 16; published every Thursday.

'G' for Giant (A)

No. 1016 (06.01.62) – No. 1045 (28.07.62)
Synopsis: When there is an explosion at the Hawley Chemical Works, some of Professor Dawson's super-grow plant mixture 'G' escapes into the atmosphere, causing all sorts of animals and insects to grow to giant size.
Art: Ken Hunter
Notes: This was the second and final full-colour centre-spread adventure strip in *The Beano*.

Danny on a Dolphin (A)

No. 1025 (10.03.62) – No. 1055 (06.10.62)
Second Series
Synopsis: Danny helps defeat Captain Bruno and his submarine 'The Red Shark' which is pirating ships in the Pacific.
Art: Dave Sutherland

Red Rory of the Eagles (A)

No. 1036 (26.05.62) – No. 1067 (29.12.62)
Synopsis: Rory is given the task of driving a small herd of cattle through the Highland into the safe hands of Sir Donald Stuart. For some mysterious reason, Bonnie Prince Charlie's life is at risk if the cattle are not safely delivered.
Art: Andy Hutton

Punch and Jimmy (The Terror Twins) (C)

No. 1046 (04.08.62) – No. 1073 (09.02.63)
First Series
Art: Dave Jenner
Notes: For second series see 1963.

Lester's Little Circus (A)

No. 1056 (13.10.62) – No. 1071 (26.01.63)
Synopsis: The exciting adventures of two circus orphans, Tom and Mary Lester, and their trained elephant in the Old West.
Art: Dave Sutherland

1963

February

First appearance of *Beano* adventure strip favourites 'The Q Bikes'.
'The Country Cuzzins' begins, featuring the last *Beano* artwork from artist Hugh Morren.

June

Beano No. 1090 (08.06.63) features 'The Bash Street Kids Colouring Competition', with prizes including cowboy and cowgirl outfits.
The Dandy–Beano Summer Special comprising all reprints, is published as D. C. Thomson's first Summer Special.
'The Danger Bus' begins, featuring the last weekly *Beano* artwork from artist Terry Patrick.

July

No. 1097 (27.07.63) is *The Beano's* 25th anniversary Issue.

October

'Jinx' begins, featuring the last weekly *Beano* artwork from artist Ken Reid.

Year Information

Issues for year: Nos. 1068–1119; price 3d; page count 16; published every Thursday.

General Jumbo (A)

No. 1072 (02.02.63) – No. 1094 (06.07.63) Third Series
Synopsis: The comic strip revival of the boy with a miniature mechanical task-force in his control.
Art: Nos. 1068–1073: Paddy Brennan
Nos. 1074–1094: Dave Sutherland

The Q Bikes (A)

No. 1072 (02.02.63) – No. 1120 (04.01.64)
Synopsis: Britain's youngest flying squad: (Q1) Johnny Master, (Q2) Billy Brown, (Q3) Alfie Thomas, (Q4) Tom Steptoe and (Q5) *Judy* Baxter, all fine expert young cyclists out to fight crime and help people in distress.
Art: Andy Hutton
Notes: For further series see 1964, 1966–67, 1969 (titled 'The Q Karts') and 1971.

The Country Cuzzins (C)

No. 1075 (23.02.63) – No. 1138 (09.05.64)
Art: Hugh Morren

Punch and Jimmy (The Terror Twins) (C)

No. 1091 (15.06.63) – No. 1325 (09.12.67) Second Series
Art: Dave Jenner

The Danger Bus (A)

No. 1095 (13.07.63) – No. 1125 (08.02.64)
Synopsis: In 1940, on a ferry trip to the cinema, a bus load of school children and their teacher are washed off course in a storm and end up in German-occupied France.
Art: Terry Patrick

Jinx (C)

No. 1108 (12.10.63) – No. 1137 (02.05.64)
Synopsis: Misadventures with Jonah's lisping schoolgirl sister.
Art: Ken Reid

1964

January

The thirteenth series of 'The Iron Fish' begins, featuring the last weekly *Beano* artwork from artist Albert Holroyd.

May

First appearance of speedy *Beano* favourite 'Billy Whizz'.

June

First *Beano Summer Special* is published.

August

Last 'Roger the Dodger' strip drawn by Ken Reid is published in No. 1152 (15.08.64).

September

Last undated *Beano Book* published.

Year Information

Issues for year: Nos. 1120–1171; price 3d; page count 16; published every Thursday.

The Iron Fish (A)

No. 1121 (11.01.64) – No. 1151 (08.08.64)
Thirteenth Series
Synopsis: In this 1960s revival of the 1950s favourite, Danny Gray and his sister Penny pilot an Iron Fish built by their uncle Jim, an improved model of that built by their father, who is away on an expedition in the Arctic.
Art: Albert Holroyd

General Jumbo (A)

No. 1126 (15.02.64) – No. 1175 (23.01.65) Fourth Series
Synopsis: Jumbo and Professor Carter take the

miniature mechanical army on a world tour.
Art: Dave Sutherland

Billy Whizz (C)
No. 1139 (16.05.64) – present
Art: 1964–89: Mal Judge. 1989–present: Steven Horrocks/David Parkins/Vic Neill/ Graeme Hill/Trevor Metcalfe

The Q Bikes (A)
No. 1152 (15.08.64) – No. 1204 (14.08.65) Second Series
Synopsis: More adventures with the bicycling five.
Art: Andy Hutton

1965

January
The second and last series of 'Paddy's Private Army' begins, featuring the last weekly *Beano* artwork from Thomson staff artist James 'Peem' Walker'.

April
Beano No. 1185 (03.04.65) is the last issue giving co-publication credit to John Leng.

August
The 14th series of 'The Iron Fish' begins, featuring the first weekly *Beano* artwork from artist Sandy Calder.

September
First dated *Beano Book* is published.

December
Occasional *Beano* illustrator, Thomson staff artist Jack Gordon, dies on December 8.

Year Information
Issues for year: Nos. 1171–1223; price 3d; page count 16; published every Thursday.

Paddy's Private Army (A)
No. 1176 (30.01.65) – No. 1200 (17.07.65) Second Series
Synopsis: More adventures with Paddy Watson in Japanese-held Singapore in 1942, this time with an army of other children – Abu the Malay boy, Crackshot Annie from Texas and Terry the faithful terrier, his doggy chum.
Art: James 'Peem' Walker

General Jumbo (A)
No. 1201 (24.07.65) – No. 1271 (26.11.66) Fifth Series
Synopsis: Jumbo and his miniature army become an attraction at Big Bill Bronco's Circus.
Art: Dave Sutherland

The Iron Fish (A)
No. 1025 (21.08.65) – No. 1247 (11.06.66)
Fourteenth Series
Synopsis: Penny and Danny Gray's inventor father presents them with a single-seater Iron Fish each.
Art: Sandy Calder

1966

April
The 'General Jumbo Colouring Competition', with prizes including tents, typewriters and James Bond Thunderballs, is featured in *Beano* No. 1238 (09.04.66).

September
Publication of the *Beano Book* giving co-publication credit to John Leng.

December
The fifteenth and final series of the *Beano* adventure favourite 'The Iron Fish' begins.

Year Information
Issues for year: Nos. 1224–1276; price 3d; page count 16; published every Thursday.

The Q Bikes (A)
No. 1248 (18.06.66) – No. 1288 (25.03.67) Third Series
Synopsis: The five go on a countrywide tour to give Road Safety lectures.
Art: Andy Hutton

The Iron Fish (A)
No. 1272 (03.12.66) – No. 1309 (19.08.67)
Fifteenth Series
Synopsis: Danny and Penny Gray's father gives them a new jet-powered Iron Fish with the ability to fly.
Art: Sandy Calder

1967

April
The first appearance of *The Beano*'s last great adventure strip character, 'Billy the Cat'.

August
'Biffo the Bear' and his pal Buster become the first in a series of cut-out puppets of *Beano* characters. The puppets feature weekly from November to September 1968, with a final puppet, of 'Billy the Cat', in April 1969.
Veteran *Beano* illustrator, Thomson staff artist George Drysdale, dies on August 12, aged 52.

December
First appearance of the canine Bash Street spin-off, 'Pup Parade'.
Veteran *Beano* illustrator,Thomson staff artist Richard 'Toby' Baines, dies on December 28, aged 72.

Year Information
Issues for year: Nos. 1277–1328; price 3d; page count 16; published every Thursday.

Billy the Cat (A)
No. 1289 (01.04.67) – No.1332 (27.01.68)
Synopsis: The story of bespectacled schoolboy William Grange who secretly fights crime as Billy the Cat.
Art: Dave Sutherland
Notes: For further series see 1968, 1970, 1971 (titled 'Billy the Cat and Katie') and 1973.

The Q Bikes (A)
No. 1310 (26.08.67) – No. 1344 (20.04.68) Fourth Series
Synopsis: More adventures with the Junior Flying Squad
Art: Andy Hutton

Pup Parade (C)
No. 1326 (16.12.67) – No. 2401 (23.07.88)
Synopsis: The comic adventures of the canine pets of the Bash Street Kids. Names are as follows, with the owner's name after each dog: Bones (Danny), Sniffy (Smiffy), Pug (*Plug*), Manfred (Wilfred), Peeps (Toots), Blotty (Spotty), Tubby (Fatty), 'Enry ('Erbert) and Wiggy (Sid).
Art: Gordon Bell

1968

March
The price of *The Beano* rises to 4d.

April
Last new Dudley Watkins 'Lord Snooty' strip published in *Beano* No. 1342 (06.04.68).

August
Debut of Gnasher in the 'Dennis the Menace' strip in *Beano* No. 1362 (31.08.68)

Year Information
Issues for year: Nos. 1329–1380; price 3d to No. 1339 (16.03.68), then 4d from No. 1340 (23.03.68) onwards; page count 16; published every Thursday.

Danny on a Dolphin (A)
No. 1333 (03.02.68) – No. 1377 (07.12.68) Third Series
Synopsis: Danny Watson helps his doctor father rebuild his island hospital in the Pacific after the island is hit by a tidal wave.
Art: Sandy Calder

The King Street Cowboys (A)
No. 1345 (27.04.68) – No. 1372 (02.11.68)
Synopsis: The story of four children, Jane, Jeff, John and Jimmy Jardine, who look after the seaside donkeys on Southborough beach whilst their owner is taken ill.
Art: Sandy Calder

Billy the Cat (A)
No. 1373 (09.11.68) – No. 1412 (09.08.69) Second Series
Synopsis: More adventures with the Burnham town orphan and super hero who lives with his Aunt Mabel.
Art: Dave Sutherland

Send for the Hovertank (A)
No. 1378 (14.12.68) – No.1408 (12.07.69)
Synopsis: Inventor Mr Knight builds a hovertank and, along with his twin sons Kevin and Kenneth, uses the strange vehicle to fight crime and to aid people in distress.
Art: Sandy Calder

1969

August
The great Dudley Watkins dies on August 20 aged 62.

October
Dudley Watkins' last new *Beano* strip of all, his 'Biffo the Bear' cover strip for *Beano* No. 1423 (25.10.69), is published.

Year Information
Issues for year: Nos. 1381–1432; price 4d; page count 16; published every Thursday.

General Jumbo (A)
No. 1409 (19.07.69) – No. 1455 (06.06.70) Sixth Series
Synopsis: Professor Carter builds Jumbo a new army of giant models.
Art: Sandy Calder

The Q Karts (A)
No. 1413 (16.08.69) – No. 1455 (06.06.70) Fifth Series
Synopsis: The Q Bikes lose their bikes in an airport mix-up over crates and inherit, for a time, the use of some motorized go-karts.
Art: Andy Hutton

1970

June
'The Nibblers' begins, featuring the first weekly *Beano* art from artist John Sherwood.

July
The last new 'Dennis the Menace' strip drawn by Davey Law appears in *Beano* No. 1462 (25.07.70).

Year Information
Issues for year: Nos. 1433–1484; price 4d; page count 16; published every Thursday.

Billy the Cat (A)
No. 1456 (13.06.70) – No. 1494 (06.03.71) Third Series
Synopsis: More thrills with the Burnham town super hero.
Art: Sandy Calder

The Nibblers (C)
No. 1456 (13.06.70) – No. 1677 (07.09.74)
Synopsis: Porky and his cat Whiskers are constantly outwitted by the band of mice known as the 'Nibblers', which consists of His Nibs, Chiseller, Sniffler, Cheddar George, Gordonzola, Enormouse, Scritch and Scratch.
Art: John Sherwood/Ron Spencer
Notes: For second series see 1977. There were also two one-off appearances in 1989 as part of the 'Readers Request' feature.

1971

February
Price of *The Beano* is decimalised.

March
Extra pages and a new front page title logo for *The Beano*.

April
The superb Thomson staff artist Davey Law, artistic creator of 'Dennis the Menace', dies on April 6, aged 63.

September
'The McTickles' begins, featuring the first weekly *Beano* artwork from artist Vic Neill.
Undateable 1971 information
Original *Beano* artist on the 'Wee Peem' strip, James Jewell, dies.

Year Information
Issues for year: Nos. 1485–1536; price 4d to No. 1491 (13.02.71), then 2p from No. 1492 (20.02.71) onwards. Page count 16 to No. 1494 (06.03.71), then 20 pages from No. 1495 (13.07.71) onwards. Published every Thursday.
Free gifts: No. 1522 (18.09.71) The Flying Fizzer
No. 1523 (25.09.71) The Humming Birdie

Admiral Jumbo (A)
No. 1495 (13.03.71) – No. 1521 (11.09.71)
Seventh Series
Synopsis: Professor Carter builds Jumbo a whole new navy including a two-seater aircraft carrier.
Art: Sandy Calder

The Belles of St. Lemons (C)
No. 1495 (13.03.71) – No. 1552 (15.04.72)
Synopsis: The comic adventures of public schoolgirls Curli, Piggi, Kooki, Poni, Swotti, Dizzi, Dozi, Dumpling, Mini and their leader Prune.
Art: Gordon Bell

The Q Bikes (A)
No. 1495 (13.03.71) – No. 1521 (11.09.71)
Sixth Series
Synopsis: The Q Bikes get new bicycles and a new member, Q6 Buzz Taylor. This is the last 'Q Bikes' series in *The Beano*.
Art: Andy Hutton

Grandpa (C)
No. 1522 (18.09.71) – No. 2200 (15.09.84)
Second Series
Art: Robert Nixon/Jimmy Glenn

The McTickles (C)
No. 1522 (18.09.71) – No. 1676 (31.08.74)
Art: Vic Neill

Says Smiffy (C)
No. 1522 (18.09.71) – No. 1550 (01.04.72)
Synopsis: Silly ideas for inventions, etc., sent in by *Beano* readers are tried out by Smiffy, the Bash Street boy who always does things wrong.
Art: Jim Petrie
Notes: For the other Bash Street spin-off strip featuring Smiffy see 'Simply Smiffy' (1985).

Billy the Cat and Katie (A)
No. 1522 (18.09.71) – No. 1608 (12.05.73)
Fourth Series
Synopsis: Billy's cousin Katie comes to stay in Burnham while her parents are away in America. She becomes Billy's crimefighting companion Katie the Cat.
Art: Sandy Calder

1972

April
First appearance of *Beano* comic favourite 'Baby-Face Finlayson'.

Year Information
Issues for year: Nos. 1537–1589; price 2p; page count 20; published every Thursday.

Pets Picture Gallery
No. 1538 (08.01.72) – No. 1677 (07.09.74)
Synopsis: *Beano* readers send in drawings of their pets.
Notes: This feature appeared sporadically in 1971.

Baby-Face Finlayson (C)
No. 1553 (22.04.72) – No. 1817 (14.05.77)
Art: Ron Spencer
Notes: See also 1980 and 1989.

1973

January
Last 'Lord Snooty strip drawn by Robert Nixon published in *Beano* No. 1593 (27.01.73)

February
First 'Lord Snooty' strip drawn by Thomson staff artist Jimmy Glen in *Beano* No. 1594 (03.02.73), which was his first regular work for *The Beano*.
Ron Fraser, the original Chief Sub-Editor on *The Beano* and latterly *Topper* Editor, dies on February 27, aged 55.

May
'Johnny Hawke' begins, featuring the last weekly *Beano* artwork from artist Andy Hutton.
Undateable 1973 information
Veteran Thomson staff artist and one-time *Beano* illustrator Jack Glass dies in retirement in Bournemouth.

Year Information
Issues for year: Nos. 1590–1641; price 2p; page count 20; published every Thursday.

Johnny Hawke (A)
No. 1609 (19.05.73) – No. 1636 (24.11.73)
Synopsis: The story of a young lad who has a host of birds of prey, from golden eagles to kestrels, as pets.
Art: Andy Hutton

Billy the Cat and Katie (A)
No. 1637 (01.12.73) – No. 1677 (07.09.74)
Fifth Series
Synopsis: A final series of adventures for the two superheroes as they go (as their alter-egos) on an educational cruise with the other children from Burnham school.
Art: Sandy Calder

1974

May
Head of D. C. Thomson juvenile papers department for over 40 years and overseer of *The Beano's* launch in 1938, R. D. Low, retires aged 78 on May 31.

June
Original *Beano* Editor George Moonie is made Head of the D. C. Thomson juvenile papers department.

July
Price of *The Beano* rises to 3p.

September
Beano No. 1677 (07.09.74) is the last to feature a 'Biffo the Bear' strip on the front cover.
Beano No. 1678 (14.09.74) is the first to feature a 'Dennis the Menace' strip on the front cover.
'Richard the Lion' begins, featuring the first weekly *Beano* artwork from artist David Gudgeon.
The eighth and final series of 'General Jumbo' begins, it being *The Beano's* final adventure strip and also the final *Beano* strip drawn by artist Sandy Calder.

Year Information
Issues for year: Nos. 1642–1693; price 2p to No. 1667 (29.06.74), then 3p from No. 1668 (06.07.74) onwards. Page count 20; published every Thursday.
Free gifts: No. 1678 (14.09.74) The Happy Howler Siren
No. 1679 (21.09.74) The Super Zoomer Balloon

Wee Ben Nevis (C)
No. 1678 (14.09.74) – No. 1816 (07.05.77)
Art: Vic Neill

Richard the Lion (C)
No. 1678 (14.09.74) – No. 1765 (15.05.76)
Art: David Gudgeon

General Jumbo (A)
No. 1678 (14.09.74) – No. 1734 (11.10.75)
Eighth Series
Synopsis: The final *Beano* adventures of Jumbo and his miniature army in *The Beano's* last weekly adventure strip.
Art: Sandy Calder

(C) Comic Strip (A) Adventure Strip (S) Prose Story (CA) Comic Adventure Strip

Dear Dennis (Letters)

No. 1679 (21.09.74) – No. 1767 (29.05.76)
Synopsis: Win £1 if Dennis or one of the other *Beano* characters answers your questions.
Notes: With No. 1687 (16.11.74) the title of this feature changed to 'Drop us a Line!'.

1975

June

Price of *The Beano* rises to 4p.

October

First appearance of *The Beano's* football-mad favourite, 'Ball Boy'.
'Tom, Dick and Sally' begins, featuring the first *Beano* artwork from artist Keith Reynolds, and the last from artist Dave Jenner.
Beano No. 1735 (18.10.75) was the first entirely comic strip issue.

Year Information

Issues for year: No. 1694–1745; price 3p to No. 1717 (14.06.75), then 4p from No. 1718 (21.06.75) onwards. Page count 20; published every Thursday.

Ball Boy (C)

No. 1735 (18.10.75) – present
Art: 1975–89: Mal Judge
1989–present: John Dallas/Dave Eastbury

Tom, Dick and Sally (C)

No. 1735 (18.10.75) – No. 2305 (20.09.86)
Art: Dave Jenner/Keith Reynolds

1976

June

Formation of the Dennis the Menace Fan Club.
'Jacky Daw' begins, featuring the last weekly *Beano* artwork from artist David Gudgeon.

Year Information

Issues for year: Nos. 1746–1797; price 4p; page count 20; published every Thursday.

Dress the Menace Competition

No. 1766 (22.05.76) – No. 1767 (29.05.76)
Notes: 250 Dennis T-shirts to be won.

Jacky Daw with Maw and Paw (C)

No. 1768 (05.06.76) – No. 1891(14.10.78)
Art: David Gudgeon

1977

May

Beano price increased to 5p.
Gnasher gets his own comic strip in *The Beano*.

July

Veteran Thomson staff artist and *Beano* illustrator James Clark dies on July 10, aged 82.

September

The gravure comic *Plug*, featuring the Bash Street star is published for the first time on 24 September, edited by long-time *Beano* Sub-Editor Ian Gray.

Year Information

Issues for year: Nos. 1798–1850; price 4p to No. 1817 (14.05.77), then 5p from No. 1818 (21.05.77) onwards. Page count 20; published every Thursday.
Free gifts: No. 1818 (21.05.77) Pop Pistol
No. 1819 (28.05.77) Super Skimmer
No. 1820 (04.06.77) Dennis and Gnasher Chewy Toffee Bar

Two-Gun Tony – The King Street Cowboy (C)

No. 1818 (21.5.77) – No. 1891 (14.10.78)
Art: Bill Ritchie

The Nibblers (C)

No. 1818 (21.05.77) – No. 2199 (08.09.84)
Second Series
Art: John Sherwood/Ron Spencer

Gnasher's Tale (Doggy Deeds from the Past) (C)

No. 1818 (21.05.77) – present
Art: Dave Sutherland
Notes: With issue No. 2311 (01.11.86) the title changes to 'Gnasher and Gnipper'.

1978

July

No. 1880 (29.07.78) was *The Beano's* 40th anniversary issue.

September

Veteran Thomson staff artist and *Beano* illustrator Jack Prout, who was most famous for drawing the adventures of Black Bob in *The Dandy*, dies in retirement on September 27, aged 75.

October

The price of the *The Beano* rises to 6p.
'Sweet Sue' begins, featuring the last weekly *Beano* artwork from Thomson staff artist Bill Ritchie.

Year Information

Issues for year: Nos. 1851–1902; price 5p to No. 1891 (14.10.78), then 6p from No. 1892 (21.10.78) onwards. Page count 20; published every Thursday.
Free gifts: No. 1892 (21.10.78) Super Fruity Lollipop
No. 1893 (28.10.78) Dennis the Menace Glove Puppet

The Fix-It Twins (C)

No. 1892 (21.10.78) – No. 1968 (05.04.80)
Art: Ron Spencer

Sweet Sue (C)

No. 1892 (21.10.78) – No. 1969 (12.04.80)
Art: Bill Ritchie

1979

February

Plug comic featuring Bash Street's handsomest pupil is combined with *The Beezer* after 75 issues, the last dated February 24.

May

Dennis' pet pig Rasher makes his first appearance in *Beano* No. 1920 (05.05.79).

September

First edition of *The Bash Street Kids Book* is published.

October

Price of *The Beano* rises to 7p.

November

First issue *Beano* artist and original 'Pansy Potter' illustrator Hugh McNeill dies on November 22, aged 68.

Year Information

Issues for year: Nos. 1903–1954; price 6p to No. 1941 (29.09.79), then 7p from No. 1942 (06.10.79) onwards. Page count 20; published every Thursday. No new characters appeared in *The Beano* in 1979.

1980

April

'Smudge' begins, featuring the first weekly *Beano* artwork from artist John Geering.

July

The price of *The Beano* rises to 8p.

November

Beano No. 2000 (15.11.80) is published.

December

Managing Editor of the Thomson Juvenile Publications for many years and supervisor of *The Beano*'s launch in 1938, R. D. Low, dies in retirement aged 85.

Year Information

Issues for year: Nos. 1955–2006; price 7p to No. 1982 (12.07.80), then 8p from No. 1983 (19.07.80) onwards. Page count 20; published every Thursday.
Free gifts: No. 1970 (19.4.80) The Gnasher Snapper
No. 1971 (26.4.80) The Gnasher Glove Puppet

Baby-Face Finlayson (C)

No. 1970 (19.04.80) – No. 2338 (09.05.87) Second Series
Art: Ron Spencer
Notes: See 1989 for third series.

Smudge (C)

No. 1970 (19.04.80) – No. 2288 (24.05.86), followed by one-offs; last appearance No. 2949 (23.01.99)
Notes: Appeared in the following years: 1989 (1), 1990 (1), 1991 (5), 1992 (10), 1993 (13), 1994 (5), 1996 (1), 1999 (1).
Art: John K.Geering

Hall of Fame

No. 2000 (15.11.80) (Special Feature)
Synopsis: Portraits of famous *Beano* stars from the past: Morgyn the Mighty 1938, Jonah 1958, The Iron Fish 1949, Maxy's Taxi 1947, Tin-Can Tommy 1938, Billy the Cat 1967, The McTickles 1971, Jack Flash 1949, Pansy Potter 1938, Red Rory of the Eagles 1954 (sic. It should have been 1951), Ding Dong Belle 1949, Nobby the Enchanted Bobby 1952, Jimmy and his Magic Patch 1945 (sic.it should have been 1944), General Jumbo 1953, Hooky's Magic Bowler 1938, Tom Thumb 1938, Bucktooth 1951, and the Shipwrecked Circus 1951 (sic. it should have been 1943).
Art: David Gudgeon
Notes: *Beano* No. 2000 also reprinted the front page 'Big Eggo' strip from *Beano* No. 1.

1981

March

The price of *The Beano* rises to 9p.
Original *Beano* Sub-Editor Ian Chisholm, who had subsequently been the first Editor of *The Beezer* and later the Editor of *Sparky* and *Mandy*, dies on March 16, aged 58.

April

Television cameras enter *The Beano* office to record a 15-minute schools programme for Independent Television's 'Middle English' series titled 'Dennis and Friends', featuring original *Beano* Editor George Moonie, the then current Editor Harold Cramond, as well as the then *Beano* Chief Sub-Editor (later Editor) Euan Kerr. 'Dennis the Menace' artist Dave Sutherland also draws a special Dennis strip to commemorate the event, which is published in *Beano* No. 2020 (04.04.81).

Year Information

Issues for year: Nos. 2007–2058; price 8p to No. 2015 (28.02.81), then 9p from No. 2016 (07.03.81) onwards. Page count 20; published every Thursday. No new characters appeared in *The Beano* is 1981.

1982

March

The price of *The Beano* rises to 10p.

April

The first two issues of the procket *Beano Comic Libraries* are published under the Editorship of former *Beano* Sub-Editor and *Plug* Editor Ian Gray.

Year Information

Issues for year: Nos. 2059–2110; price 9p to No. 2070 (20.03.82), then 10p from No. 2071 (27.03.82) onwards. Page count 20; published every Thursday. No new characters appeared in *The Beano* in 1982.

1983

August

The price of *The Beano* rises to 12p.

November

Original *Beano* Editor George Moonie retires as Head of D. C. Thomson Juvenile Publications, to be succeeded by Bill Mann.
Undateable 1983 information
Early *Beano* and longtime *Dandy* artist Eric Roberts dies in London aged 70.

Year Information

Issues for year: Nos. 2111–2163; price 10p to No. 2141 (30.07.83), then 12p from No. 2141 (06.08.83) onwards. Page count 20; published every Thursday. No new characters appeared in *The Beano* in 1983.

1984

September

The price of *The Beano* rises to 14p.
Rasher, Dennis' pet pig, gets his own strip.

October

Veteran Thomson staff artist and occasional *Beano* illustrator James 'Peem' Walker dies on October 28 aged 81.
Harold Cramond retires after 25 years as *Beano* Editor and is replaced by *Beano* Chief Sub-Editor Euan Kerr.

Year Information

Issues for year: Nos. 2164–2215; price 12p to No. 2200 (15.09.84), then 14p from No. 2201 (22.09.84) onwards. Page count 20; published every Thursday.
Free gifts: No. 2201 (22.09.84) The Gnasher Snapper
No. 2202 (29.09.84) Dennis/Gnasher Stickers
No. 2203 (6.10.84) Leaf Strawberry Bubble Gum

Rasher Ⓒ

No. 2201 (22.09.84) – No. 2744 (18.02.95)
Art: Dave Sutherland

Pepper the Pony and Lucinda Ⓒ

No. 2201 (22.09.84) – No. 2232 (27.04.85)
Art: Ron Spencer

1985

May

'Ivy the Terrible' begins, featuring a return to *The Beano* for artist Robert Nixon.

September

The price of *The Beano* rises to 16p.
'Simply Smiffy' begins, featuring the first weekly *Beano* artwork from artist Jerry Swaffield.
The first *Beano Calendar* (for 1986) is published.
Undateable 1985 information
Early *Beano* artist Sam Fair dies.

Year Information

Issues for year: Nos. 2216–2267; price 14p to No. 2252 (14.09.85), then 16p from No. 2253 (21.09.85) onwards. Page count 20; published every Thursday.
Free gifts: No. 2254 (28.09.85) Dennis/Gnasher Glove Puppet
No. 2255 (05.10.85) 3 Super Stickers Dennis (2), Plug (1)

Ivy the Terrible Ⓒ

No. 2253 (04.05.85) – present
Art: Robert Nixon/Nigel Parkinson

Simply Smiffy Ⓒ

No. 2254 (28.09.85) – No. 2338 (09.05.87)
Synopsis: Solo adventures with Bash Street's prize dunce.
Art: Jerry Swaffield

1986

June

The *Beano Summer Special* features many *Beano* artists and two *Beano* Editors in a special holiday comic strip.

September

The price of *The Beano* rises to 18p.

October

Last regular weekly 'Biffo the Bear' strip appears in *Beano* No. 2310 (25.10.86)

November

'Calamity James' begins, featuring the first weekly *Beano* artwork from artist Tom Paterson.

Year Information

Issues for year: Nos. 2268–2319; price 16p to No. 2305 (20.09.86), then 18p from No. 2306 (27.09.86) onwards. Page count 20; published every Thursday.
Free gifts: No. 2306 (27.09.86) Hot Cinnamon Flavour Blasting Powder Popping Candy
No. 2311 (01.11.86) Twirly Copter

Foo Foo's Fairy Story Ⓒ

No. 2279 (22.03.86) – No. 2286 (10.05.86)
Art: Dave Sutherland
Notes: When Gnasher went missing (see page 238) and 'Gnasher's Tale' was suspended for six weeks, Walter the Softy's pet poodle Foo Foo filled the gap.

Roger the Dodger's Dodge Clinic Ⓒ

No. 2290 (07.06.86) – No. 2405 (20.08.88)
Synopsis: Roger answers readers' dodge problems.
Art: Robert Nixon
Notes: 'Roger's Dodge Clinic' also appeared sporadically from 1989 to 1992. Last appearance in No. 2629 (05.12.92)

Calamity James (The World's Unluckiest Boy) Ⓒ

No. 2311 (1.11.86) – No. 3375 (7.4.07)
Art: Tom Paterson

1987

February

The excellent one-time *Beano* artist Ken Reid dies on February 2, aged 67.

May

'Karate Sid' begins, featuring the first weekly *Beano* artwork from artist Steve Bright.

July

First issue of the pocketsized *Beano Puzzle Book* is published, edited by Graham Noble.

August

First *Beano Special* is published, edited by David Donaldson.

September

To celebrate *The Dandy* and *The Beano's* coming 50th birthdays, the celebration volume *The Dandy* and *The Beano – Fifty Golden Years* is published, edited by John Methven.

October

The price of *The Beano* rises to 20p.

December

On December 4 *The Beano's* sister paper *The Dandy* celebrates its 50th birthday.

Year Information

Issues for year: Nos. 2320–2371; price 18p to No. 2359 (03.10.87), then 20p from No. 2360 (10.10.87), onwards. Page count 20; published every Thursday.
Free gifts: No. 2360 (10.10.87) Bar of Highland Toffee
No. 2361 (17.10.87) *Beano* Button Badge

Karate Sid Ⓒ

No. 2339 (16.05.87) – No. 2390 (07.05.88)
Art: Steve Bright
Notes: Karate Sid has appeared on a few one-off occasions since No. 2390.

Little Monkey Ⓒ

No. 2339 (16.05.87) – No. 2390 (07.05.88)
Art: Robert Nixon
Notes: 'Little Monkey' had appeared before this in six strips in the 'Reader's Request' feature.

Number 13 Ⓒ

No. 2346 (04.07.87) – No. 3152 (14.12.02)
Synopsis: Ghoulish fun with Boris, Dad, Mum, Frankie, Gran, Tiddles and Fiendish.
Art: John Geering
Notes: 'Number 13' had appeared before this in two

strips in the 'Reader's Request' feature.
Only three strips appeared after 1997.

The Germs (C)

No. 2361 (17.10.87) – one-off
Synopsis: A preview appearance for the 1988 comic strip featuring Ill Will and his germs.
Art: Dave Sutherland.

1988

January

On January 15 the BBC2 arts programme 'Arena' devotes a whole 50-minute show to the celebration of *The Dandy* and *The Beano's* combined 50th birthdays. The programme is complemented by an article by original *Beano* Editor George Moonie in *The Radio Times*.

February

The final member of the original *Beano* Editorial team still working at Thomsons, Stan Stamper, retires on February 5, having spent the last 26 years as editor of the girls' comic *Judy*.
Panini issue a 50th anniversary *Dandy* and *Beano* Celebration Sticker Album.
In No. 2379 (20.02.88) Ken Harrison takes over the artwork on the 'Lord Snooty' strip, this being his first weekly artwork for *The Beano*.

May

The third series of 'The Three Bears' begins, featuring the first weekly *Beano* artwork from artist Bob Dewar.

July

D. C. Thomson's women's magazine *Celebrity*, dated July 21–27, contains a special *Dandy–Beano* Bumper 8-Page Anniversary Pull-Out.
On the eve of *The Beano's* fiftieth birthday the Editor, Euan Kerr, and Dennis the Menace make an appearance on BBC1's 'Wogan' show.
The 50th anniversary issue of *The Beano*, No. 2402 (30.07.88), is published with a new weekly format featuring glossy paper, a new page size, and ten pages in full colour plus staple binding for the first time.
'Gordon Gnome' begins, featuring the first weekly *Beano* artwork from artist Eric Wilkinson.
'Danny's Nanny' begins featuring the first weekly *Beano* artwork from artist David Mostyn.

August

The 50th edition of *The Beano Book* is published, featuring, for the first time, 90 pages in full colour.

September

Beano No. 2407 (03.09.88) is the first to feature non-Thomson advertising (in this first instance the advertisement is for the 'Tesco Olympic challenge').
The price of *The Beano* increases to 22p.
The *Beano* page count is increased to 24 pages, 12 in full colour.

Year Information

Issues for year: Nos. 2372–2424; price 20p to No. 2408 (10.09.88), then 22p from No. 2409 (17.09.88) onwards. Page count increases from 20 to 24 pages with the same issues. Page size 8.5 inches by 12 inches to No. 2401 (23.07.88), then 9 inches by 12 inches from No. 2402 (30.07.88) onwards. Published every Thursday.
Free gifts: No. 2379 (20.02.88) *Dandy–Beano* Celebration Sticker Album and six stickers
No. 2380 (05.03.88) six free stickers
No. 2381 (04.06.88) six free stickers
No. 2394 (04.06.88) McCowan Tangy Lemon and Lime Bar
No. 2402 (30.07.88) *Beano* 50th Anniversary Celebration Poster
No. 2415 (29.10.88) Rainbow Fruit Flavour Nerds

The Germs (C)

No. 2374 (16.1.88) – No. 3247 (02.10.04)
Art: Dave Sutherland/Vic Neill

The Three Bears (C)

No. 2391 (14.05.88) – No. 2768 (05.08.95) Third Series
Art: Bob Dewar/David Parkins/Mike Pearse
Notes: The strip returns in 1999, finishing in 2007.

Karate Syd (C)

No. 2401 (23.07.88) – one-off (Also Nos. 2403 and 2414)
Art: Steve Bright

Gordon Gnome (C)

No. 2402 (30.07.88) – No. 2444 (20.05.89)
Art: Eric Wilkinson

Danny's Nanny (C)

No. 2402 (30.07.88) – No. 2696 (19.3.94)
Art: David Mostyn

Little Plum (C)

No. 2405 (20.08.88) – one-off
Art: Ron Spencer

Proctor Doolittle (The Boy who can Talk to Animals) (C)

No. 2409 (17.09.88) – No. 2444 (20.05.89)
Art: Ron Spencer

We Do Like to be Beside the Seaside (Photos)

No. 2409 (17.09.88) – one-off
Notes: Fun on Scarborough beach.

Alligator Dundee (C)

No. 2410 (24.09.88) – one-off
Art: Jerry Swaffield

The Ugly Plugling (Poem)

No. 2411 (01.10.88) – one-off
Art: Dave Sutherland

The McTickles (C)

No. 2414 (22.10.88) – one-off
Art: Doug Jensen
Note: One further one-off in No. 2484 (24.02.90).

Fact File – Alexander Falstaff Lemming (C)

No. 2415 (29.10.88) – one-off
Art: Tom Paterson

Fatty Fudge in 'Fishfinger' (C)

No. 2417 (12.11.88) – one-off
Art: Jim Petrie
Notes: For further appearances of 'Fatty Fudge' see 1989.

Billy Whizz's 'Photo-Laughs' (Photos)

No. 2418 (19.11.88) – one-off
Art: Jimmy Glen

Getting to Know You (Beano Character File) (C)

No. 2419 (26.11.88) – one-off

Art: Jerry Swaffield
Notes: This strip featured Spotty from the Bash Street Kids.

JONAH (THE BOY WHO SANK 1000 SHIPS) (C)
No. 2420 (03.12.88) – one-off
Art: Jerry Swaffield

ROBIN HOOD AND HIS RUBBER BAND (C)
No. 2422 (17.12.88) – one-off
Art: Jerry Swaffield

PLEASANT PRESENTS
No. 2423 (24.12.88) – one-off feature
Art: Jerry Swaffield
Notes: A Christmas poem.

MONSTER SOFTIES (C)
No. 2424 (31.12.88) – one-off
Art: Robert Nixon

1989

JANUARY
One of *The Beano's* longest-serving freelance artists Mal Judge dies on January 17, aged 70.

MARCH
Cadburys produce a range of chocolate *Beano* Easter Eggs featuring Minnie the Minx, Roger the Dodger and the Bash Street Kids, highlighting the trend towards the merchandising of *Beano* characters.

MAY
Retired Thomson staff artist George Ramsbottom, who had first drawn for *The Beano* in December 1938, dies on May 4, aged 85.
'Biffo the Bear' returns to *The Beano* featuring the first *Beano* artwork from freelance artist Sid Burgon.

AUGUST
For the first time since 1976 an adventure strip, in this instance 'General Jumbo', appears in the yearly *Beano Book*.

SEPTEMBER
Current *Beano* editorial staff consists of Euan Kerr (Editor), Al Bernard (Chief Sub-Editor), and John Kemp, George Cobb and Craig Ferguson (Sub-Editors).

YEAR INFORMATION

Issues for year: Nos. 2425–2476; price 22p to No. 2464 (07.10.89), then 24p from No. 2465 (14.10.89) onwards. Page count 24 (except Nos. 2425, 2426, 2429, 2432 and 2434, which had 20 pages). Published every Thursday.
Free gifts: No. 2445 (27.05.89) McCowans Dennis the Menace Blackcurrant and Raspberry Flavour Chew Bar
No. 2460 (09.09.89) Fizzers Sweets
No. 2465 (14.10.89) 'The Magic of *The Beano*' Sticker album
No. 2466 (21.10.89) Pack of five free stickers

FATTY FUDGE (C)
No. 2425 (07.01.89) – No. 2562 (24.08.91)
Art: Jim Petrie

THE NIBBLERS (C)
No. 2430 (11.02.89) and No. 2437 (01.04.89)
Art: Ron Spencer
Note: *The Beano* mice return as a readers' request (also appearing in No. 2437)

GETTING TO KNOW YOU (DENNIS' PAL PIE FACE) (C)
No. 2430 (11.02.89) – one-off
Art: Unknown

ROGER THE TODDLER (C)
No. 2430 (11.02.89) – one-off
Art: Robert Nixon

PLUG BLUNDER, DOWN UNDER (C)
No. 2431 (18.02.89) – one-off
Art: Jerry Swaffield

LITTLE MONKEY (C)
No. 2433 (04.03.89) – one-off
Art: Barrie Appleby

THE MINI MINX (C)
No. 2435 (18.03.89) – one-off
Art: Jim Petrie

LITTLE PLUM (C)
No. 2436 (25.3.89) and No. 2470 (18.11.89)
Art: Ron Spencer

A DAY IN DODGE CITY (C)
No. 2438 (08.04.89) – one-off
Art: Robert Nixon

IT'LL NEVER HAPPEN (C)
No. 2439 (15.04.89) – henceforth sporadically
Art: Eric Wilkinson
Notes: Sporadic strip featuring various *Beano* characters in unlikely situations.

BIFFO THE BEAR (C)
No. 2445 (27.05.89) – No. 2954 (27.05.99)
Second Series
Art: Sid Burgon
Notes: Return of the old *Beano* favourite, first run in 1948.

EMLYN THE GREMLIN (A FIEND INDEED) (C)
No. 2445 (27.05.89) – No. 2506 (28.07.90)
Art: Bob Dewar

BABY-FACE FINLAYSON (C)
No. 2455 (05.08.89) – No. 3304 (12.11.05) Third Series
Art: Ron Spencer/Emilios Hatjoulis
Notes: The strip appeared regularly until 1992, with only eight strips from 1993 to 2005.

LITTLE LARRY (THE RUDEST YOUTH IN BEANOTOWN!) (C)
No. 2462 (23.09.89), No. 2468 (04.11.89), No. 2472 (02.12.89), then No. 2475 (23.12.89) – No. 2582 (11.01.92)
Art: Tom Paterson

MINNIE'S AGONY COLUMN (C)
No. 2469 (11.11.89) – one-off
Art: Eric Wilkinson

PANSY POTTER (C)
No. 2474 (16.12.89) – No. 2640 (20.02.93)
Fourth Series
Art: Barry Glennard

1990

YEAR INFORMATION

Issues for year: Nos. 2477–2528; price 24p to No. 2512 (08.09.90), then 26p from No. 2513 (15.09.90) onwards. Page count 24.

Les Pretend (C)
No. 2493 (28.04.90) – No. 3402 (13.10.07)
Synopsis: The boy with the *big* imagination. Les takes dressing up and role playing to a new level.
Art: John Sherwood

Lee's Fleas (C)
No. 2521 (10.11.90) – No. 2558 (27.07.91)
Art: Bob Dewar

1991

March
'Dennis the Menace' celebrates his 40th birthday. New look Dennis appears on front of No. 2538 (23.03.91), only to return to his familiar style on the back page.

October
The last 'Lord Snooty' appears in No. 2566 (14.09.91), drawn by Ken Harrison. 'Snooty' first appeared in No. 1 (30.07.38).

Year information
Issues for year: Nos. 2529–2580; price 24p to No. 2568 (05.10.91), then 28p from No. 2569 (12.10.91) onwards. Page count 24.
No new characters appeared in *The Beano* in 1991.

1992

Year information
Issues for the year: Nos. 2581–2632; price 28p to No. 2619 (26.09.91) then 30p from No. 2620 (03.10.91) onwards. Page count 24.

Henry Burrows (C)
No. 2587 (15.02.92) – No. 2594 (04.04.92)
Art: Trevor Metcalfe

Merboy (C)
No. 2587 (15.02.92) – No. 2590 (07.03.92)
Art: Emilios Hatjoulis

Son of Jonah (C)
No. 2606 (27.06.92) – No. 2657 (19.06.93)
Art: Jerry Swaffield

Zig's Gags (C)
No. 2607 (04.07.92) – one-off
Art: Jerry Swaffield

The Great Geraldoes (C)
No. 2609 (18.07.92) – No. 2639 (24.04.93)
Art: Terry Bave

The Beano Birds (C)
No. 2610 (25.07.92) – No. 2634 (09.01.93)
Art: Barry Glennard

Go, Granny, Go (C)
No. 2611 (01.08.92) – No. 2905 (21.03.98)
Synopsis: The colourful adventures of Dennis the Menace's wild, motorbike-riding grandmother.
Art: Brian Walker

Oscar Knight – Child Actor (C)
No. 2622 (10.10.92) – No. 2654 (29.05.93)
Art: Dave Sutherland

1993

February
'Pansy Potter' makes her last appearance in No. 2640 (20.02.93). She first appeared in December 1938.

April
'Roger the Dodger' celebrates his 40th anniversary.

October
The Beano moves to full colour for every page in No. 2674 (16.10.93).

Year information
Issues for year: Nos. 2633–2684: price 30p to No. 2673 (09.10.93), then 35p from No. 2674 (16.10.93) onwards. Page count 24. The first *Beano Video* is released.

The Yeti with Betty (C)
No. 2633 (02.01.93) – No. 2698 (02.04.94)
Synopsis: The Yeti has left the Himalayas and jetted to England. There he meets schoolgirl Betty who befriends him, keeping the huge but gentle Yeti out of trouble.
Art: Robert Nixon

Ruff and Freddy (C)
No. 2667 (28.08.93) – one-off
Art: Bob Dewar

The Numskulls (C)
No. 2674 (16.10.93) – present
Art: Tom Paterson/Barry Glennard
Notes: Originally appeared in *The Beezer*.

1994

February
The 40th anniversary of 'The Bash Street Kids'. The strip, initially called 'When the Bell Rings', first appeared in No. 604 (13.02.54).

Year information
Issues for year: Nos. 2685–2737; price 35p to No. 2724 (01.10.94), then 38p from No. 2725 (16.10.94) onwards. Page count 24. *The Beano Video 2* released.

Jenny Orange (C)
No. 2737 (31.12.94) – one-off
Art: Bob Dewar

1995

Year information
Issues for year: Nos. 2738–2789; price 38p to No. 2777 (07.10.95), then 40p from No. 2778 (13.10.95) onwards. Page count 24. The Robert Harrop *Beano* figurines launched.

Minder Bird (C)
No. 2739 (14.01.95) – No. 2751 (01.04.95)
Art: Terry Willers

Sort Out Squad (C)
No. 2742 (04.02.95) – No. 2751 (01.04.95)
Art: Robert Nixon

Chip – the Stone Age Boy (C)
No. 2745 (25.02.95) – No. 2751 (01.04.95)
Art: John Dallas

Vic Volcano (C)
No. 2748 (18.03.95) – No. 2836 (23.11.96)
Art: Trevor Metcalfe

(C) Comic Strip (A) Adventure Strip (S) Prose Story (CA) Comic Adventure Strip

THE WORLD'S WORST (C)
No. 2753 (22.04.95) – No. 2929 (05.09.98)
Art: Bob Dewar
Notes: Only one strip appeared after 1996.

TECHNO – THE HANDY ANDROID (C)
No. 2764 (08.07.95)
Art: Kirk Houston

WHAT TO DO WITH A SLEEPING DAD (C)
No. 2781 (04.11.95) – No. 2863 (31.05.97)
Art: Jim Petrie

JOE KING (C)
No. 2783 (18.11.95) – No. 3058 (28.02.01)
Synopsis: The master joker. Wearing his Joke Power jersey, Joe tells jokes non-stop. He has a wisecrack for every occasion.
Art: Bob Dewar

1996

APRIL
Dennis appears on the BBC.

YEAR INFORMATION
Issues for year: Nos. 2790–2841; price 40p to No. 2825 (07.09.96), then 42p from No. 2826 (14.09.96) onwards. Page count 24.
No new characters appeared in *The Beano* in 1996.

1997

FEBRUARY
The Beano selected as 'The Best British Comic Ever' in a telephone poll organised by the National Comics Awards.

YEAR INFORMATION
Issues for year: Nos. 2842–2894; price 42p to No. 2879 (20.09.97), then 45p from No. 2880 (27.09.97) onwards. Page count 24.

WILL (C)
No. 2847 (08.02.97) – one-off
Art: Bob Dewar

HAVE-A-GO JOE (C)
No. 2856 (12.04.97) – No. 2875 (23.08.97)
Art: David Mostyn

CAMP COSMOS (C)
No. 2859 (03.05.97) – No. 2878 (13.09.97)
Art: John Geering

TIM TRAVELLER (C)
No. 2864 (07.06.97) – No. 3228 (29.05.04)
Synopsis: Tim finds a very special bicycle; it is a time machine! It can take him forwards into the future or back into the past.
Art: Vic Neill

CRAZY FOR DAISY (C)
No. 2865 (14.06.97) – No. 3400 (29.09.07)
Synopsis: There is only one girl in the world for hopeless romantic Ernest Valentine – Daisy, prettiest girl in *Beanotown*. This is not a match made in heaven.
Art: Nick Brennan

SYDD (SNEAKY, YUKKY, DUMP DWELLER) (C)
No. 2868 (05.07.97) – No. 2874 (16.08.97)
Art: John Geering

TRASH CAN ALLEY (C)
No. 2871 (26.07.97) – No. 2879 (20.09.97)
Art: Bob Dewar

1998

First 'Dennis' strip drawn by David Parkins.

AUGUST
The 60th anniversary edition of *The Beano* (No. 2924) published on 1 August.
Beano Club formed, to replace the Dennis the Menace Fan Club.

SEPTEMBER
Bea, the first human addition to Dennis's family arrives in No. 2931 (19.09.98).

YEAR INFORMATION
Issues for year: Nos. 2894–2945; price 45p to No. 2930 (12.09.98), then 50p from No. 2931 (19.09.98) onwards. Page count 24 (except for No. 2924 (01.08.98), which had 48 pages).

THE LEGEND OF LITTLE PLUM (C)
No. 2917 (13.06.98) – No. 2923 (25.07.98)
Art: Tom Paterson

GENERAL JUMBO (A)
No. 2924 (01.08.98) – one-off
Art: Keith Robson

EVEN STEVEN – HE'S OUT FOR REVENGE (C)
No. 2931 (19.09.98) – No. 3013 (15.04.00)
Art: Mark Morgan

BEAGINNINGS (C)
No. 2935 (17.10.98) – present
Synopsis: Dennis the Menace's little sister Bea stars in her own strip. Title cut to Bea – the Mini Menace later in the year.
Art: Nigel Parkinson

MR APE (C)
No. 2937 (31.10.98) – No. 2945 (26.12.98)
Art: John Eastwood
Note: A Dick King-Smith story

1999

FEBRUARY
The last appearance of Biffo the Bear. He first featured in January 1948.

YEAR INFORMATION
Issues for year: Nos. 2946–2997; price 50p to No. 2984 (25.09.99), then 52p from No. 2985 (02.10.99) onwards. Page count 24.

DEAN'S DINO (C)
No. 2946 (02.01.99) – No. 3211 (31.01.04)
Art: John Geering
Notes: The strip appeared 37 times in 1999 and then just a further five times in 2004.

DOG'S BREAKFAST TV (C)
No. 2956 (13.03.99) – No. 2969 (12.06.99)
Art: Steven Baskerville

INSPECTOR HORSE AND JOCKY (C)
No. 2971 (26.06.99) – No. 3001 (22.01.00)
Art: Terry Bave

Tricky Dicky (C)
No. 2972 (03.07.99) – No. 3088 (22.09.01)
Art: John Dallas
Notes: Originally appeared in *Topper*.

Gordon Bennett (C)
No. 2973 (27.11.99) – No. 3293 (27.08.05)
Art: Jim Hansen
Notes: Nine strips appeared in 1999–2000 and then 12 in 2005.

The Three Bears (C)
No. 2974 (04.12.99) – No. 3365 (27.01.07)
Fourth series
Art: David Parkins

2000

January
The Beano's 3000th edition published on 15 January.

July
The *Beanotown.com* website launched.
Beanoland at Chessington World of Adventure opened.

Year information
Issues for year: Nos. 2998–3050; price 52p to No. 3041 (28.10.00), then 55p from No. 3042 (04.11.00) onwards. Page count 24.

Splodge (C)
No. 3028 (29.07.00) – No. 3085 (01.09.01)
Art: Ken Harrison
Notes: This strip originally appeared in *Topper*.

Come to Beanotown (C)
No. 3028 (29.07.00) – No. 3107 (02.02.02)
Art: John Rushby

2001

January
Jim Petrie draws his 2000th and last 'Minnie the Minx' strip in No. 3052 (13.01.01).

March
Dennis celebrates his 50th anniversary.

Year information
Issues for year: Nos. 3051–3102; price 55p to No. 3093 (27.10.01), then 60p from No. 3094 (03.11.01). Page count 24.

Dasher (C)
No. 3051 (06.01.01) – No. 3062 (24.03.01)
Art: Gary Whitlock

2002

The Beano topped a nationwide poll as the greatest children's comic of all time.

Year information
Issues for year: Nos. 3103–3154; price 60p to No. 3144 (19.10.02), then 65p from No. 3145 (26.10.02) onwards. Page count 24.

Freddie Fear – Son of a Witch (C)
No. 3103 (05.01.02) – present
Synopsis: Freddie has a big problem, he just wants a normal life but his mother is a witch.

Space Kidette (C)
No. 3103 (05.01.02) – one-off
Art: Robert Nixon

Phone a Fiend (C)
No. 3103 (05.01.02) – one-off
Art: Wayne Thomson

Robbie Rebel – Nobody Tells Him What to Do (C)
No. 3104 (12.01.02) – present
Synopsis: The boy with 'attitude'! Nobody tells HIM what to do – especially grown-ups.
Art: Ken Harrison

Hot Foot (C)
No. 3120 (04.05.02) – No. 3129 (06.07.02)
Art: From an agency

Thunderpants (C)
No. 3123 (25.05.02) – one-off
Art: Ken Harrison
Notes: Based on the film of the same name.

Doctor Beastly's Tales of the Slightly Unpleasant (C)
No. 3142 (05.10.02) – No. 3145 (26.10.02)
Art: Brian Walker

Little Plum (C)
No. 3154 (28.12.02) – No. 3364 (20.01.07)
New Series
Art: Hunt Emerson

2003

February
'The Bash Street Kids' celebrate their 50th anniversary.

Year information
Issues for year: Nos. 3155–3207; price 65p to No. 3198 (01.11.03), then 70p from No. 3199 (08.11.03) onwards. Page count 24.

Pup Parade (C)
No. 3162 (22.02.03) – No. 3204 (13.12.03)
Art: Gordon Bell

Ricky Grainger – He Laughs at Danger (C)
No. 3177 (07.06.03) – No. 3204 (13.12.03)
Art: Tom Plant

Billy the Cat (CA)
No. 3195 (11.10.03) – No. 3200 (15.11.03)
Art: Wayne Thomson

2004

Year information
Issues for year: Nos. 3207–3259; price 70p to No. 3243 (11.09.04), then 75p from No. 3244 (18.09.04) onwards. Page count 24.

Joe Jitsu (C)
No. 3207 (03.01.04) – No. 3337 (08.07.06)
Synopsis: Joe is a budding martial arts expert who tries to teach his smart little sister, Jade, as he learns himself.
Art: Wayne Thomson

(C) Comic Strip (A) Adventure Strip (S) Prose Story (CA) Comic Adventure Strip

Colin the Vet (C)
No. 3207 (03.01.04) – No. 3350 (07.10.06)
Synopsis: Most of Colin's animal patients do the funniest things when Colin tends to them.
Art: Duncan Scott

Derek the Sheep (C)
No. 3214 (21.02.04) – present
Synopsis: The grass is always greener on the other side for Derek, so life in the field is never dull when he's around.
Art: Gary Northfield

Bash Street – Singled Out (C)
No. 3226 (15.05.04) – present
Synopsis: As the title suggests, these are tales about the individuals that make up the world of Bash Street School.
Art: Mike Pearse/Tom Paterson

2005

Year information
Issues for year: Nos. 3259–3310; price 75p to No. 3295 (10.09.05), then 80p from No. 3296 (17.09.05) onwards. Page count 24.

Christmas Carole (C)
No. 3259 (01.01.05) – No. 3263 (29.01.05)
Art: Keith Page

Hugh Dunnit (C)
No. 3259 (01.01.05) – No. 3263 (29.01.05)
Art: David Mostyn

Zap Zodiac (C)
No. 3259 (01.01.05) – No. 3280 (28.05.05)
Art: Steve Horrocks

Billy the Cat (CA)
No. 3301 (22.10.05) – No. 3308 (10.12.05)
Art: Nigel Dobbyn

The Neds (C)
No. 3309 (17.12.05) – No. 3382 (26.07.07)
Art: Duncan Scott
Notes: In total only 10 strips appeared.

2006

January
Dick and Dom are guest editors for the first issue of the year.
Alan Digby takes over from Euan Kerr as *The Beano's* fourth Editor.

Year information
Issues for year: Nos. 3311–3362; price 80p to No. 3336 (01.07.06), then 85p from No. 3337 (08.07.06) onwards. Page count 24.

Mia Starr (C)
No. 3312 (14.01.06) – No. 3315 (04.02.06)
Art: Duncan Scott

Nicky Nut Job (C)
No. 3312 (14.01.06) – No. 3386 (23.06.07)
Art: Kelly Dyson/Wayne Thomson

Scammin' Sam (C)
No. 3312 (14.01.06) – No. 3315 (04.02.06)
Art: Steve Horrocks

Big Brad Wolf (C)
No. 3323 (01.04.06) – No. 3340 (29.07.06)
Art: Ken Harrison

Ratz (C)
No. 3343 (19.08.06) – present
Art: Hunt Emerson

Pirates of the Caribeano (C)
No. 3348 (23.09.06) – present
Synopsis: The crew of the pirate ship, *The Floating Disgrace*, are the terrors of the old Caribbean. Oh, and the captain's a dinosaur!
Art: Barrie Appleby

2007

February
BeanoMAX launched.

October
Laura Howell becomes the first woman to draw regularly for *The Beano* with the strip 'Johnny Bean from Happy Bunny Green'.
The year sees the last appearances of 'Little Plum', 'The Three Bears' and 'Calamity James'.

Year information
Issues for year: 3362–3412; price 80p to No. 3403 (20.10.07), then 99p from No. 3404 (27.10.07) onwards. Page count 24.

Fred's Bed (C)
No. 3375 (07.04.07) – present
Art: David Parkins
Notes: Previously appeared in *The Beezer* and *The Topper*.

The Riot Squad (C)
No. 3375 (07.04.07) – present
Art: Ken Harrison
Notes: Originally appeared in *Hoot*, as 'The Hoot Squad'.

Tales of Johnny Bean (from Happy Bunny Green) (C)
No. 3404 (27.10.07) – to present
Synopsis: Johnny lives in Happy Bunny Green, a village that looks like it belongs in a nursery rhyme – but with Johnny around, things aren't what they seem in Happy Bunny Green.
Art: Laura Howell

London B4 12 (C)
No. 3404 (27.10.07) – present
Art: Barrie Appleby

2008

August
The Beano's 70th anniversary issue, No. 3443 (02.08.08), with Nick Park as guest editor.

Year information
Issues for year (to August 2): Nos. 3413–3443; price 99p. Page count 24.

Olaf the Madlander (C)
No. 3441 (19.07.08) – present
Art: Sid Burgon
Notes: Previously appeared in *The Beezer* and *Beezer and Topper* as 'Adrian the Barbarian'.

BEANO ARTISTS

This is an alphabetical index of artists and their work for *The Beano*. Under each artist's name is a list of his work that has been published in the weekly comic, annual or summer special.
Note: Artists whose weekly comic character appeared in annuals or summer specials under a different title are not included (e.g. Jack Glass' annual appearance of 'King on the Flying Horse' (1950) is not given due to the artist having drawn 'Prince on the Flying Horse' in weekly format in 1940). Appearances in the weekly comic therefore take precedence over appearances in the annual or summer special.
(a) = feature appeared in annual (s) only.
(ss) = feature appeared in summer special (s) only.

GEORGE 'DOD' ANDERSON

Invisible Giant, The (a); Morgyn the Mighty; Terrible Joe Jenner (a); Tom Thumb (a); White Mouse Will Get You, The (a); Young Buffalo Bill (a).

BARRY APPLEBY

Little Monkey (a/ss); London B4 12; Pirates of the Caribeano; Roger the Dodger.

RICHARD 'TOBY' BAINES

Ape's Secret, The; Black Flash the Beaver; Boy that Nobody Wanted, The; Detective Marjorie (a); Grip; Hawkeye – Bravest of the Braves; Jimmy's Pet – The Kangaroo; Keeper of the Magic Sword, The (a); King of Thunder Mountain; Little Noah's Ark; Orphan Jim and Jacko (a); Singing Giant, The; Wild Boy; Wild Boy of the Woods; Wonderful Bird is Bill Pelican, A.

TERRY BAVE

Great Geraldoes, The; Inspector Horse and Jocky.

MICHAEL BARRATT

Once Upon a Time (a); Sorcerer's Apprentice, The (a).

STEVEN BASKERVILLE

Dog's Breakfast TV.

LEO BAXENDALE

Ace from Space; All The Best People Go To School!; Biffo the Bear (a); Charlie Choo (a); Daring Deeds of Cabbage Muncher, The (a); General Jumbo (a); Kat and Kanary; Little Plum; Lord Snooty and his Pals; Minne the Minx; Three Bears, The; Watch That Hand! (a); When the Bell Rings (The Bash Street Kids); Who Dun It? (a); You Can Catch Crooks at Cricket: (a).

GORDON BELL

Bash Street Cats, The (a); Bash Street Dogs, The (a); Bash Street Kids, The (a/ss); Belles of St. Lemons, The; Biffo the Bear (a/ss); Dashalong Dot (She Raises Laughs Chasing Autographs); Dennis the Menace (a/ss); Kat and Kanary; Little Plum (a); Lord Snooty (a); Minnie the Minx (a); Pansy Potter – the Strongman's Daughter; Pom-Pom (The Boy Who Brightens Darkest Africa); Pup Parade; Rip Van Wink; Roger the Dodger.

BASIL BLACKALLER

Big Heap; Cinderella and the Ugly Sisters; Deep Down Daddy Neptune; Dick Turpentine (a); Hairy Dan; Hairy Hugh and his Cockatoo; Misery Dick (a); Pansy Potter (The Strongman's Daughter); Playful Pete (a); Roland Ham and his Magic Dough (a); Skinny Flint; Smart Alec; Smokey Joe (a); Wavy Davy and his Navy.

NICK BRENNAN

Crazy for Daisy.

PADDY BRENNAN

Bird Boy, The; General Jumbo; Happy-Go-Luckies, The; Jack Flash; Jack Flash and the Terrible Twins; Jack's the Boy; Jimmy and his Magic Patch; Longlegs – the Desert Wild Boy; Moving Island, The (a); Red Rory of the Eagles; Shipwrecked Circus, The; Sinbad on the Island of Fear; Sinbad the Sailor; Strongarm the Axeman (a); Wooden Horse, The; Young Davy Crockett.

STEVE BRIGHT

Animal Antics (a); Girls, Girls, Girls (Minnie, Toots and Ivy) (a); Karate Sid; Let's Have a Party (*Beano* Office Staff Party) (a); Roger's Dodge Clinic (a).

SID BURGON

Biffo the Bear.

SANDY CALDER

Admiral Jumbo; Biffo the Bear (a/ss); Billy the Cat; Billy the Cat and Katie; Danny on a Dolphin; General Jumbo; Hovertank, The (a/ss); Iron Fish, The; King Street Cowboys, The; Roger the Dodger (ss); Send for the Hovertank.

REG CARTER

Big Eggo; Freddy Flipperfeet; Inky, Binky and Fluff (a); Monkey Tricks; Peter the Penguin.

JAMES CLARK

Ball that Baffled Billy Bunbridge, The (a); Biffo the Bear (a); Boy on the Flying Trapeze, The; Boy with the Magic Masks, The (a); Chingo the Fearless; Here Comes Nellie Kelly (a); How Boxer Pulled Them Through (a); Invisible Giant, The; Jack in the Bottle (a); Johnny's Magic Touch (a); King and the Key, The (a), King Kong Charlie (a); Kipper Feet (a); Little Joker in the Forty Winks, The (a); Little Joker in the Lank of Nod, The (a); Little Noah's Ark; Mr.Minton's 'Mint' Toffee (a); Pansy Potter in Wonderland; Plucky Little Nellie Kelly; Red Riding Hood's Rainbow Cloak (a); Rogue Hero, The (a); Rolling Jones; Shorty's Magic Six-Gun; Smarty Smokey; Smarty Smokey's Classmates; Sooty Solomon (a); Sooty Solomon and Santa Claus (a); Teddy's Good Deeds (a); Three Bears, The (a); Tick-Tock Tony (a); Tommy Tipper and the Five Dwarves (a); Tom Thumb (a); Tom Thumb and the Blind Knight (a); Tricky Dicky Ant; Wakko, the Absent Minded Wizard (a); When Simon Showed Up at the Dog Show (a); Willie in the Lost World; Winnie the Witch; Willie's Wonder Gun.

RICHARD COX

Multy the Millionaire; Nippers, The.

JAMES CRIGHTON

Big Eggo and Koto the Pup (a); Blacksmith Bob Eats Hay at Night; Boy who Bossed the Man in the Moon, The; Doubting Thomas; Goat with the Magic Wand, The; Jack in the Bottle; Kitty with the Coat of Many Colours; Koko the Pup (a);

Korky the Cat (ss); Pansy Potter (a); Percy from the Pole Star; Rip Van Wink; Sir Tom Thumb; Whitefang Guards the Secret Gold; White Mouse Will Get You (If You Don't Watch Out), The; Wun Tun Joe.

John Dallas

Ball Boy; Chip – the Stone Age Baby; Tricky Dicky.

Michael Darling

Adventures of Johnny Leopard, The; Cannonball Crackshots. The (a); Danger Man, The; Danger Twins, The; Horse that Jack Built, The; Jack of Clubs; My Uncle Tex (a); Nik o' Lightning; Paul Strike of the Flying Squad (a); Pete of the Spitfires; Red Rory of the Eagles (a); Sinbad the Sailor.

Roland Davies

Boney the Brave (He Lives in a Cave); Contrary Mary (The Moke); Tough Nellie Duff (a); Whoopee Hank.

Bob Dewar

Emlyn the Gremlin (A Fiend Indeed); Jenny Orange; Joe King; Lee's Fleas; Ruff and Freddy; Three Bears, The; Trash Can Alley; Will; World's Worst, The.

Nigel Dobbyn

Billy the Cat.

George Drysdale

Basil is Boss (a); Benny Blowhard (Oompah Pete) (a); Big Eggo; Big Eggo and Koko (a); Cocky Jock; Hairy Dan; Johnny on the Hop (He Brings *The Beano* from the Shop); Koko the Pup (a); Little Plum (a); Matt Hatter; Maxy's Taxi; Mickey's Magic Bone; Minne the Minx (a); Peter Pud and Sammy Snake (a); Polly Wolly Doodle (and her Great Big Poodle); Prince Whoopee; Quick-Stick Dick (a); Roger Ye Dodger (a); Scrapper; Smarty Smokey – The Genie in the Six-Gun; Ticklish Tasks of Billy Barrell, The; Tin-Can Tommy (The Clockwork Boy); Tom Thumbs's Schooldays; TV Stevie – The Boy on Hookey's Wrist; Wee Jake and Sam Snake (a); Wily Ways of Simple Simon, The.

Kelly Dyson

Nicky Nut Job.

Dave Eastbury

Ball Boy; Freddie Fear.

John Eastwood

Mr Ape.

Hunt Emerson

Little Plum; Ratz.

Sam Fair

Bobby's Record Run (a); Frosty McNab (The Freezy Wheeze Man); Gulliver (a); How Toby Made Good (a); Johnny's Magic Rocking Horse (a); King with the Magic Touch, The (a); Lucky Streak; Musso the Wop; Mystery of the Seaside Donkey, The (a); Pansy Potter (The Strongman's Daughter); Tin-Can Tommy (The Clockwork Boy); Winken and Blinken (The Little Dutch Kids).

John K. Geering

Camp Cosmos; Dean's Dino; Number 13; Smudge; Sydd (Sneaky Yukky Dump Dweller).

Jack Glass

Bird Boy, The; Black Mask (a); Bulldog Trail, The; Catapult Jack; Cracker Jack; Danger for Deep-Sea Danny; Deep-sea Danny's Iron Fish; Desperate Days for Deep-Sea Danny, Down with Lord Haw-Haw; Horse That Jack Built, The; Invisible Giant, The; Iron Fish, The; Jack of Clubs; Little Master of the Mighty Chang; My Dog Sandy; Prince on the Flying Horse; Red Rory of the Eagles; Sandy's Magic Bagpipes; Shipwrecked Kidds, The; Ting-a-Ling Bill; Whistling Scythe, The; Wishing Tree, The; Young Robin Hood; Young Strongarm the Axeman.

Jimmy Glen

Biffo the Bear; Grandpa; Lord Snooty.

Barry Glennard

Pansy Potter; Numskulls, The.

Charles 'Chic' Gordon

Artful Grannie Green; Hooky's Magic Bowler Hat; Pranks of Peanut, The; Tin-Can Tommy (The Clockwork Boy); Wangles of Granny Green, The.

Jack Gordon

Black Flash the Beaver; Jimmy's Mother Wouldn't Run Away; Jumping Jenny; King Kong Charlie; Sam Spitfire; Young Buffalo Bill (a).

Charles Grigg

Biffo the Bear (a); Big Bazooka; Charlie the Chimp (ss); Cracker Jack (a); Hookey's Bust'em Book; Kat and Kanary; King with the Cauliflower Conk, The (a); Pansy Potter – the Strongman's Daughter; Prince Whoopee – Your Pal from the Palace; Softy's Centaur (a); Taffy's Centaurs (a); Tom Thumb (a); Uncle Windbag (That Story Teller Feller); Wee Peem's Magic Pills; Wizards at War; Young Robin Hood (a).

David Gudgeon

Ball Boy (ss); Hall of Fame; Jack Daw with Maw and Paw; Richard the Lion.

Jim Hansen

Gordon Bennett.

Ken Harrison

Beano Rest Home, The (ss); Big Brad Wolf; Lord Snooty; Riot Squad, The; Robbie Rebel; Splodge; Thunderpants; The.

Emilios Hatjoulis

Baby-Face Finlayson; Merboy.

Graeme Hill

Billy Whizz.

Albert Holroyd

Big Bazooka (a); Bob in the Bottle (a); Fox on the Run; Funny Thing Happened the Other Day, A; Geordie's Magic Whistle (a); Hickory's Talking Frog (a); Hookey's Bust'em Book; Iron Fish, The; Jack of Clubs (a); Johnny Go Back!; Kat and Kanary; Our Ned; Parachute Reg; Scrapper; Sparky's Space Helmet; Stongarm the Axeman.

Bill Holroyd

Alf Wit the Ancient Brit; *Beano* Cinema, The; Big Hugh – And You (The Comic With You In It!); Bird Boy, The; Boy on the Flying Trapeze, The (a); Bucktooth – The Boy who lives in a Barrel; Cast Iron Stan – Circus Superman; Danger! Len At Work; Ding-Dong Belle; Have-a-go Joe; Hookey's Bust'em Book; Horse That Jack Built, The; Invisible Giant, The; Iron Fish, The; My Pal Nutty; Nobby – the Enchanted Bobby; Nutty – the Coal Imp; On the Heels of the Hated Hooknose; Red Rory of the Eagles; Runaway Jack; Skinny Flint (a);

Stop that Horse! (The Clockwork Horse); Tick-Tock Tony – The Clockwork Horse; Tommy's Clockwork Brother; Tommy's Clockwork Town; Waifs of the Wild West; Wandering Willie; What Made Toni Do It? (a).

Charles Holt
Cock Sparrer (a); Little Dead-Eye Dick; Swanky Lanky Liz; Uncle Windbag (He Tells Tall Tales).

Steve Horrocks
Billy Whizz; Scammin' Sam; Zap Zodiac.

Kirk Houston
Techno – the Handy Android.

Laura Howell
Tales of Johnny Bean.

Ken Hunter
Ali Ha-Ha and the Potty Thieves; Daniel the Spaniel; Doctor Dopey (a); Doctor Dopey's Farm (a); 'G' for Giant; Horse that Jack Built, The; Jack the Giant Killer (a); Nothing's Too Big for Wee Davie; Thunderflash; Wee Davie – Big Game Hunter; Wee Davie and King Willie; Wee Davie and the Great Big Baby; Wee Davie and the Great Big Giant; Wee Davie and the Great Big Spell; Wildfire – the Magic Horse.

Andy Hutton
Bird Boy, The; Cat That Saved Nine Lives, The (a); General Jumbo (a); Iron Fish, The (a); Jack Flash; Jimmy and his Magic Patch; Johnny Hawke; Kangaroo Kid, The; Kilty MacTaggart; Longlegs – The Desert Wild Boy; Nik o' Lightning (a); Q Bikes, The; Q Karts, The; Rory and the Pirates; Red Rory of the Eagles; Sandy (a); Teeko; Thunderflash (a); Tough Duff; Vengeance of One-Eye, The; Wild Boy; Young Davy Crockett.

Arthur Jackson
Busybody Bessie (a); Handy Sandy; Postie Hastie (a).

Dave Jenner
Punch and Jimmy (The Terror Twins); Punch and Rosie (a); Tom, Dick and Sally.

Doug Jenson
McTickles, The; Wee Ben Nevis.

James Jewell
Wee Peem.

Mal Judge
Ball Boy; Ball Boy and the Nibblers (a); Big Laughs There! (a); Billy the Kidd the King Street Cowboy (a); Billy Whizz; Colonel Crackpot's Circus; Little Alfie (Billy Whizz) (a).

Tom Lavery
Roger the Dodger.

Davey Law
Corporal Clott (ss); Dennis the Menace; Ginger's Magic Ear (a); Gnasher (ss); Goggo – The Wizard in the Goldfish Bowl; Lord Dennis (a); Mickey's Magic Bone.

Joseph Lee
Jungle Jim (a).

Frank Macdiarmid
Bash Street Kids, The (a/ss); Bash Street Kids Mini-Book, The (a); Johnny on the Hop (a); Jonah ye Ancient Mariner (a); Pancho (a); Quick an' Slick; Roger the Dodger; Ye Bashe Streete Kyddes (a).

Robert Macgillivray
Sooty Snowball (a); Tickler Twins, The (a).

Ian Mackay
Cripple Charlie (a); Man on the Moon, A (a).

George Martin
Wily Smiley – The Jungle Joker (ss).

John R.Mason
Tootsy McTurk (a).

Bob McGrath
Bash Street Bears, The (a); Roger the Dodger; Three Bears, The; Three Bears/Biffo the Bear, The (ss); Wonder Boy.

Hugh McNeill
Pansy Potter (the Strongman's Daughter); Ping the Elastic Man; Puffing Billy; Stanley Sting the Wasp (a).

Trevor Metcalfe
Billy Whizz; Henry Burrows; Vic Volcano.

Phil Millar
Ho Lummy (Wee Hi Lo) (a); Wee Hi-Lo (a).

Mark Morgan
Even Steven.

Allan Morley
Baby Bustem the 7 HP Kid (a); Big Fat Joe; Cocky Dick (He's Smart and Slick); Cocky Jock (a); Dolly Dimple (a); Larry Less and Less (The Shrinking Boy) (a); Little Nell and Peter Pell; Magic Lollipops, The; Tricky Dicky Ant; Sammy Shrinko; Sammy's Super Rubber; Sly Guy Fox (a); Smarty Smokum (And his Pipe of Peace); Softy Sam (a).

Hugh Morren
Betty's Grandad; Country Cuzzins, The; Dippy the Diver; Get Your Hair Cut (a); Joe for Champ; Lazy Jones; Smasher, The (ss); Tough Tot (a/ss); Wee Peem.

Robert Mortimer
Wily Willie Winkie (a).

David Mostyn
Danny's Nanny; Have-a-go-Joe; Hugh Dunnit.

Vic Neill
Billy Whizz; Germs, The; McTickles, The; Tim Traveller.

John Nichol
Black Star; Bob on the Beat; Brannigan's Boy; Cool Kit Kelly (a); Dick Turpin – Special Investigator; General Jumbo; Hogan Boy, The; Horse That Jack Flash (a); Nik o' Lightning (a); Rattlesnake Ranch; Runaways with Thunderbird; Runaways with Turpin; Thrill-a-day Jill; Tick-Tock Timothy; Tom Thumb – The Brave Little One.

Robert T. Nixon
Day in Dodge City, A; Grandpa; Ivy the Terrible; Little Monkey; Lord Snooty; Monster Softies; Roger the Dodger; Roger the Dodger and Ivy the Terrible (ss); Roger the Dodger's Dodge Clinic; Roger the Minx (a); Roger the Toddler; Sort Out Squad; Space Kidette; Tom, Dick and Sally (ss). Yeti with Betty, The; Sort Out Squad; Space Kidette.

Gary Northfield
Derek the Sheep.

Keith Page
Christmas Carole.

David Parkins
Billy Whizz; Fred's Bed; Three Bears, The.

Nigel Parkinson
Beaginnings; Ivy the Terrible.

Tom Paterson
Bash Street – Singled Out; Calamity James (The World's Unluckiest Boy); Fact File – Alexander Falstaff Lemming; Little Larry (The Rudest Youth in *Beanotown*!); Minnie the Minx; Numskulls, The.

Terry Partick
Danger Bus, The; Hoverclass; The (a/ss); Queen's Highway, The; Ting-a-Ling Taylors, The.

Mike Pearse
Bash Street – Singled out; Three Bears, The.

Vitor Peon
Blinding Shield, The; Bristol Billy; Laughing Pirate, The; Mountain Boy; Smarty Smokey – The Wee Black Dragon; Stage Coach Mystery, The (a); Strongarm the Axeman (a); Thrill-a-day Jill (a); Vengeance of the Lost Crusader, The.

Steve Perkins
Smiler the Sweeper.

Jim Petrie
Fatty Fudge; Mini Minx, The; Minnie the Minx; Minnie Whizz (a); Says Smiffy; What to Do With a Sleeping Dad?

Tom Plant
Ricky Grainger.

Jack Prout
Acorns from the Wishing Tree; Ben o' the Beanstalk; Black Bob (ss); Buster – The World's Mightiest Mascot; Girl with the Golden Voice, The; King on the Flying Horse, The; Magic Penny, The; Nemo the Nameless (a); Nobody Wanted Nancy; Plucky Little Nell; Shipwrecked Circus, The; Sooty Solomon; Taylor's Goose, The; Tick-Tock Timothy; Witch's Spell on Poor King Kell!, The; Wicked Uncle and the Terrible Twins, The; Young Buffalo Bill (a).

George Ramsbottom
Black Witch is Waiting, The; Keeper of the Crooked Cross; Little Magic Man, The; Quick Tricks of Granny Green, The; Sooty Solomon (a); Twelve Happy Horners; Waifs of the Wild West.

Ken Reid
Dog That wouldn't Talk, The (a); Grandpa; Hal o' the Axe (a); Jinx; Jonah; Little Angel Face (ss); Roger the Dodger.

Keith Reynolds
Tom, Dick and Sally.

Bill Ritchie
Boy Who Made Faces, The (a); Clumsy Claude – The Blunder Boy; Geordie's Magic Whistle (a); Pooch; Sweet Sue; Two-Gun Tony – The King Street Cowboy; Uncle Windbag (That Story Teller Feller).

Eric Roberts
Good King Coke (He's Stony Broke); Helpful Henry; Podge (a); Rip Van Wink

Keith Robson
General Jumbo.

John Rushby
Come to *Beanotown*.

Duncan Scott
Colin the Vet; Mia Starr, Neds, The.

John Sherwood
Billy Whizz (ss); Les Pretend; Lost Resort, The (ss); Nibblers, The.

Ron Smith
Goggo (a); Goggo the Goldfish (a); Mickey's Magic Bone (a); Walkie Talkie Tree, The (a).

Ron Spencer
Baby-Face Finlayson; Fix-It Twins, The; Little Plum; Little Plum and Baby-Face (a); Nibblers, The; Pepper the Pony and Lucinda; Proctor Doolittle (The Boy who can Talk to Animals); Three Plums, The (a).

Fred Sturrock
Adventures of Tom Thumb, The; Big Bill the Mascot Nobody Wanted; Bob in the Bottle; Boy with the Magic Masks, The; Boy with the Wonder Horse, The; Danger in the Dark Street (a); Happy Andy (a); High Guy the Mascot with a Lucky Tail; Hungry Goodwins, The; Hungry Little Goodwins, The; Invisible Giant, The; Jack Flash – The Flying Boy; Keeper of the Crooked Cross (a); Keeper of the Magic Sword; March of the Wooden Soldiers, The; Runaway Robinsons, The; Runaway Russells, The; Sammy B. Smart in the Land of Nod; Tick-Tock Timothy (a); Wangles of Granny Green, The (a); Win Tin's Weights and Means (a); Wishing Tree, The (a); Young Strongarm the Axeman.

Dave Sutherland
Baby-Face Finlayson (a); Bash Street Dogs; The (a); Bash Street Kids, The; Bash Street Kids/Sandy Hints, The (ss); Biffo the Bear; Billy the Cat; Cannonball Crackshots, The; Danny on a Dolphin; Dennis the Menace; Dennis and Pieface (a); Foo Foo's Fairy Story; General Jumbo; Germs, The; Gnasher and Gnipper; Gnasher's Tale; Great Flood of London, The; Lester's Little Circus; Little Plum (ss); Oscar Knight – Child Actor; Rasher; Shaping Up (*Beano* artists) (ss); Soft Spot (a); Ugly Pluging, The.

Jerry Swaffield
Alligator Dundee; Bash Street Kids, The (ss), Getting to Know You (*Beano* Character File); Jonah (The Boy who Sank 1000 ships); Plug Blunder, Down Under; Robin Hood and his Rubber Band; Simply Smiffy; Son of Jonah; Zig's Gags.

Jimmy Thompson
Dick on the Draw; Fusspot Annie; Jenny Penny.

Wayne Thomson
Billy the Cat; Joe Jitsu; Nicky Nut Job; Phone a Fiend.

Brian Walker
Doctor Beastly's Tales of the Slightly Unpleasant; Go Granny Go.

James 'Peem' Walker

Black Flash the Beaver (a); Finest Ears in Texas, The (a); Georgie's Magic Whistle (a); Get Rid of the Runaway Twins; Hands off the Talking Lamb; In the Clutches of the Wicked Wilsons; Jack Sprat's Battle Cat; King Kong Charlie (a); King on the Flying Horse, The; Little Joker in the Land of Nod, The; Lost Among the Silver Dwarves; Magic Bottle, The; Paddy's Private Army; Poobah the Elephant (a); Prince on the Flying Horse, The; Robin Hood (a); Runaways with Grandad; Runaways with Turpin; Skinny Flint – The Meanest Uncle in the World; Slave to the Talking Horse; Spell of Geordie's Whistle, The; Tiger Trail to Kandabar; Tom Thumb; When Will the Golden Peacock Speak; You Can't Keep a Coal Horse Down (a).

Dudley Watkins

Adventures of Tom Thumb, The; Biffo the Bear; Biffo the Menance (a); Boy with the Magic Masks, The; Desperate Dan (ss); Follow the Secret Hand; Gulliver (a); Jack Flash – The Flying Boy; Jimmy and his Magic Patch; Jungle Leader of the Little Lost Ones; King's Got a Tail, The; Lone Wolf; Lord Snooty and His Pals; Peter Piper (a); Shipwrecked Circus, The; Six Brands for Bonnie Prince Charlie; Strang the Terrible; Tom Thumb; Wavy Davy and His Navy; White Mouse Will Get You (If You Don't Watch Out), The.

Gary Whitlock

Dasher.

Terry Willers

Minder Bird.

INDEX

Notes

1. For ease of use the definite article has been dropped from names of publications and the names of the strips that appear in *The Beano*.
2. These index entries refer the reader both to the main text of the book and to the information in the reference section at the back of the book. Any page reference above 303 will refer you to the reference section.
3. When a page number appears in bold against the name of a strip, this indicates that there is an illustration of the strip on that page.
4. For information on a year-by-year basis (important events, issue numbers, price and extent, etc.), please refer directly to the relevant year on pages 304–41.

ARGH!
BOOF! POW!
THUD!
BANG!
CRASH!
OUCH!
WALLOP!
CLANG
BANG!
CRASH!
POW
BIFF